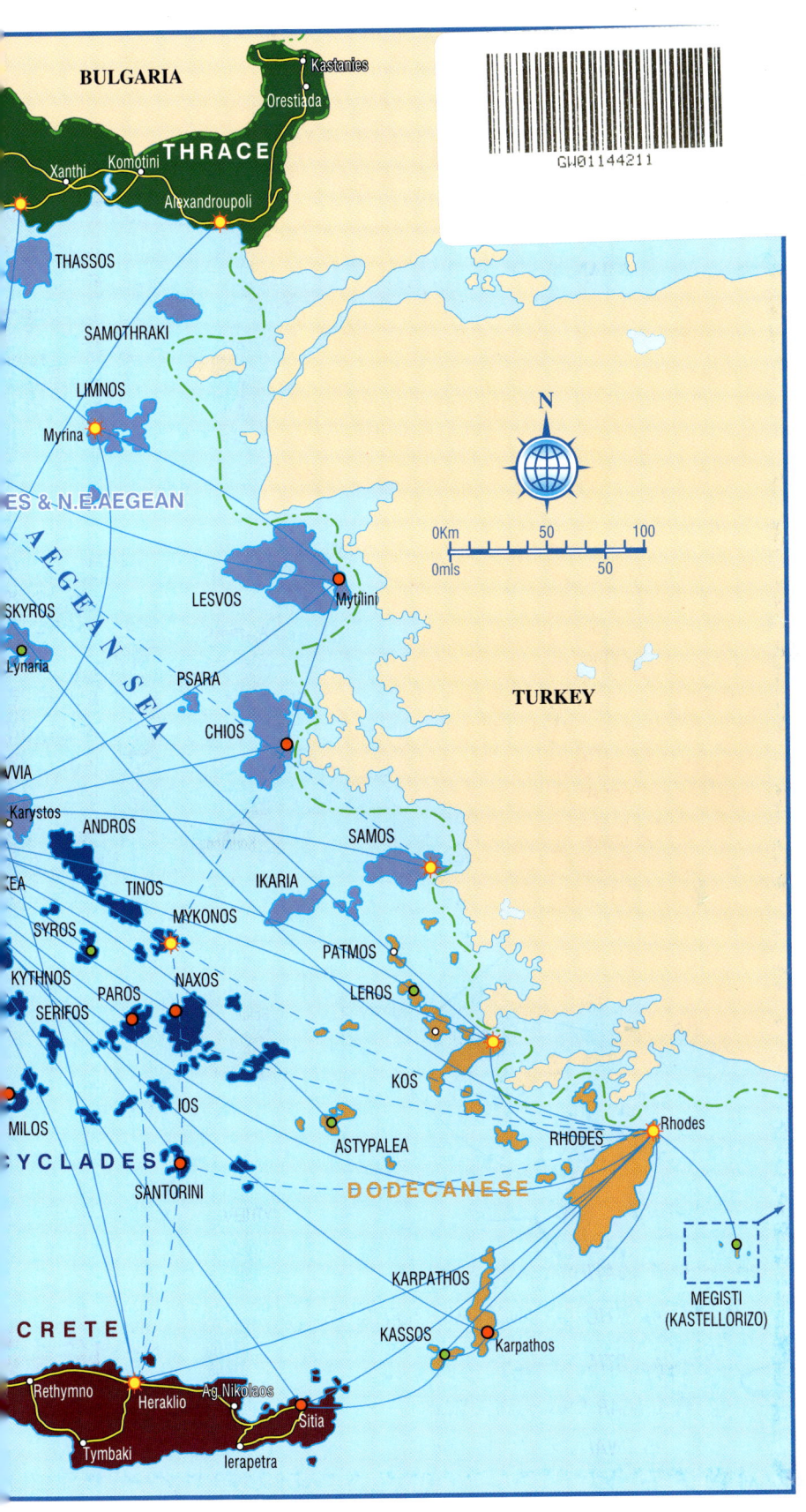

Only the BEST

ONLY THE BEST: CREDITS

Publisher & Editor in Chief	Alexander Kyrtsis
Editor	Veti Nikolopoulou
Travel Research	Alexander Kyrtsis
	Veti Nikolopoulou
	Julia Klimi
Editorials & Historical Research	Maria Kyriaki
	Nikos Faroupos
Photographer	Tolis Zacharakis
	Julia Klimi
	Alexis Rodopoulos
Translators	Doolie Sloman
	Diana Loui
	Angelika Timms
Editing	Androniki Potamianou
	Marian Theodorouli
	Graziella Seferiadi
Research	Faye Nikolopoulou
Communication	Effie Loupakou
Secretariat	Athena Serlis
Public Relations	Vicky Magoulioti
Art Advisor	Anthony Psychas
Logistics	Dimitris Athanasopoulos
Art Work & Production	EPIPHANIA S.A.
Maps	EMVELIA

Second Edition, June 2000
COPYRIGHT © 2000, AXON PUBLICATIONS S.A.
52 Aigialias Street, 151 25 Maroussi, Greece, tel. (01) 6856093, fax. 6856095
e - mail: axon @ hol.gr
I.S.B.N.: 960-377-023-X

Any reproduction, electronic storage, republication, copying or retransmition of part or of the whole book with any electronic, photocopying, registration or other means without the previous approval of the editor is prohibited.

SPECIAL THANKS TO:

Nicholas Gage for accepting to endorse the first edition "ONLY THE BEST". *Efi Kanellopoulou* for her assistance with maps and slides. *George Zorbas* for his contribution toward a successful production. *Phil Dopoulos* for editing the English version. *Liza Evert* for providing slides from her personal collection. *George Zaphiropoulos* for his slides on Mount Athos and elsewhere. *Niki Tsiligiroglou* for providing slides for Lake Tavropos. *E.P.Kouros* for his exceptional write - ups on Athens restaurants.

WARM THANKS TO OUR AREA CONSULTANTS

Basilis Ardamis on Monemvassia. *Anna Assimakopoulou* on Metsovo, Ioannina and Zagoria. *Giannis Averoff* on Metsovo, *Maria Christina Averoff* on Metsovo. *Constantine Boutaris* on Hydra. *Vasilis Brovas* and his daughters Loukia & Sophia on Thessaloniki. *Olga Fotinaki* on Kythera. *Nicos Frantzeskakis* on Vamos. *Giannis Giannakis* on Sifnos. *Niki Giannakis* on Sifnos. *Manolis Kaklamanos* on Rethymnon. *Nicos Karelas* on Rhodes. *Michalis Kefalogiannis* on Heraklio. *Haris Kerasiotis* on Rhodes. *Irena Kyrtsis* on Corfu. *Christos Lambrakos* on Spetses. *Harry & Katerina Mylonas* on Thessaloniki. *Christina Nevrou* on Hydra. *Nicos Nicolopoulos* on Ahaia. *Artemis Papadaki* on Vamos. *Mirella Papaeconomou* on Kythera and Spetses. *Makis Papoulias* on Arcadia and Lake Tavropos. *Lia Raka* on Patmos and Marathi. *Giannis Vassilakos* on Lake Tavropos and Agrafa. *Nicos Velianitis* on Corfu. *Trekking Hellas* for their contribution on walks and mountain sports.

ALSO THANKS TO

Niki Akrioti, Alexandra Drakou, Christos Georgalas, Ileana Kirkili, Katia Lembessi, Achilleas Paparsenos, Giannis Petritsis and Mary Politis

NOBODY'S PERFECT!

The publisher and the authors, cannot accept any responsibility for any loss, inconvenience or injury resulting from information or advice contained in this guide.

They have made every effort to ensure that the information contained in this guide book is correct at the time of writing. They were, however, obliged to make some very difficult choices as objectively as possible in their evaluations and star - ratings.

If readers or third parties identify mistakes or oversight in this book, the publisher would be delighted to receive written comments or suggestions which would lead to an even more accurate and succesful second edition. Significant contributions will be rewarded with a free copy of the next edition!

WHY YET ANOTHER TRAVEL BOOK?

Very simply because Alexander Kyrtsis, the publisher and conceptualizer of ONLY THE BEST didn't like the existing ones!

For 35 years after his return from the U.S. and Canada where he grew up and was educated, Alexander Kyrtsis visited every corner of Greece and collected experiences and photographs.

The guide books he used for his travels were invariably lacking. Most of them had few if any photographs and placed all their emphasis on historical sites with hardly a mention of the extraordinary beaches and variation of scenery which are packed into such a small country as Greece. But most important, none, we repeat none, of the books made an effort to evaluate the historical sites, the areas of natural beauty, the hotels, the beaches and restaurants with a star system which would assist the traveller in making his choices.

Given the time restrictions imposed on most travellers, the star-rating system created by the Publisher and used in ONLY THE BEST, makes it easy for the reader to prepare his program before beginning his holidays. He simply apportions his time according to the number and importance of the sights in each area and makes his hotels reservations accordingly (hotels are also star-rated, described, priced and evaluated for value for money).

Star - rating evaluations of hotels and restaurants are a particularly difficult process. If, for example, the island of Myconos has 60 hotels and 50 restaurants and tavernas, the easy solution is simply to list them from the existing catalogues. What is difficult is to visit all of them, make a short list, evaluate them and star - rate them. This was the most difficult job undertaken by ONLY THE BEST.

Furthermore, none of the travel guides included maps in sufficient scale for each area, with all the recommended sights and beaches highlighted and color-coded according to their importance, so that the reader could decide on his itinerary at a glance.

In order to gain space for in depth descriptions and insider tips in each specific area, a star-rated choice of the best 43 destinations was made by the publisher with criteria which cover all ages, interests and cost levels. The reader can make a quick choice of his next destination by turning to the table on pages 8 and 9 titled "Select your Excursion" where all 43 destinations are evaluated against each of the 22 criteria.

All this and much more are included in ONLY THE BEST.

WOULD YOU LIKE TO CONTRIBUTE PROFESSIONALLY?

If you would like to contribute professionally toward making the existing book even more successful or toward future editions, please contact us.

Future editions will include sections of Greece such as Crete and Rhodes treated separately, area by area, as well as other popular country destinations such as Spain, U.K., Italy and France.

We are always interested in travel authors on third countries as well as Greece. Book distributors, translators for French, German, Russian and Italian editions, salespersons specializing on books, specialists in book promotion, or artwork.

You are all welcome to apply by submitting your C.V.'s.

TABLE OF CONTENTS

INTRODUCTION .... Why yet another travel guide? 3
HOW TO USE "*BEST*" .... The travel information system 6
SELECT YOUR EXCURSION ..... Table of the 43 excursions with 22 selection criteria 8
HISTORY & CULTURE .... History, Myth, Architecture, Art and Philosophy 11

PART I

ATHENS & ENVIRONS 23

🌀🌀🌀 HISTORICAL AREA OF ATHENS .... 🌀🌀🌀 Acropolis, 🌀🌀 Plaka, 🌀🌀 Ancient Agora 25
🌀🌀🌀 CONTEMPORARY ATHENS .... 🌀🌀🌀 Museums, 🌀 Parliament, 🌀 Neo-Classical Buildings 35
🌀🌀 ATHENS ENVIRONS .... 🌀🌀 Sounion, 🌀🌀 Daphni, 🌀 Piraeus, Beaches 45
ATHENS HOTELS, etc .... Hotels, Restaurants, Entertainment, Information 51

PART II

PELOPONNESE 75

Excursion 1: 🌀🌀🌀 NAFPLIO AREA .... 🌀🌀🌀 Mycenae, 🌀🌀🌀 Epidaurus, 🌀🌀 Nafplio,
                                                🌀🌀 Ancient Corinth 77
Excursion 2: 🌀🌀 KASTANIA .... 🌀🌀 Kastania, 🌀🌀 Lake Doxis, 🌀 Lake Stymphalia 95
Excursion 3: 🌀 ZAROUCHLA .... 🌀 Zarouchla, 🌀 Lake Tsivlou 99
Excursion 4: 🌀🌀 KALAVRYTA .... 🌀🌀🌀 Cog-wheel Railway, 🌀🌀 Kalavryta 103
Excursion 5: 🌀🌀 ARCADIAN HIGHLANDS .... 🌀🌀 Stemnitsa, 🌀🌀 Loussios river, 🌀🌀 Dimitsana,
                                                🌀🌀 Karytena, 🌀 Vytina, 🌀 Andritsena 109
Excursion 6: 🌀🌀🌀 ANCIENT OLYMPIA 117
Excursion 7: 🌀 ANCIENT MESSENE 125
Excursion 8: 🌀🌀 PYLOS .... 🌀🌀 Methoni, 🌀 Pylos, 🌀 Koroni 131
Excursion 9: 🌀🌀 MANI 139
Excursion 10: 🌀🌀🌀 MYSTRAS 149
Excursion 11: 🌀🌀🌀 MONEMVASSIA 155

PART III: THE GREEK ISLANDS

ARGOSARONIC GULF & KYTHERA 165

Excursion 12: 🌀🌀 KYTHERA .... 🌀🌀 Kythera, 🌀 Elafonissos 167
Excursion 13: 🌀🌀 SPETSES .... 🌀🌀 Spetses, 🌀 Porto Heli 177
Excursion 14: 🌀🌀🌀 HYDRA 185

CYCLADES 193

Excursion 15: 🌀🌀🌀 MYKONOS-DELOS 199
Excursion 16: 🌀🌀 PAROS .... 🌀🌀 Paros, 🌀 Antiparos 215
Excursion 17: 🌀🌀 SIFNOS 225
Excursion 18: 🌀🌀 FOLEGANDROS 235
Excursion 19: 🌀🌀🌀 SANTORINI 241

TABLE OF CONTENTS

CRETE 253

- Excursion 20: ✿✿✿ WESTERN CRETE .... ✿✿✿ Chania, ✿✿✿ Samaria Gorge 255
- Excursion 21: ✿✿ VAMOS .... ✿✿ Vamos, ✿ Frangokastello, ✿ Sfakia 269
- Excursion 22: ✿✿ RETHYMNO 277
- Excursion 23: ✿ PHAESTOS - MATALA .... ✿✿ Phaestos, ✿ Matala, ✿ Lake Zarou 289
- Excursion 24: ✿✿✿ KNOSSOS-HERAKLIO 295
- Excursion 25: ✿ ELOUNDA 305
- Excursion 26: ✿✿ EASTERN CRETE .... ✿✿✿ Vai ✿ Aspros Potamos, ✿ Zakros 313

DODECANESE 319

- Excursion 27: ✿✿✿ RHODES 323
- Excursion 28: ✿ SYMI 339
- Excursion 29: ✿✿ PATMOS 345
- Excursion 30: ✿ MARATHI .... ✿ Marathi, Lipsi, Arkii 353

IONIAN ISLANDS 359

- Excursion 31: ✿✿✿ CORFU .... Paxi, Antipaxi, Diapondia Isl. 363

EVVIA, SPORADES & NORTHERN AEGEAN 387

- Excursion 32: ✿✿ SKIATHOS 393

PART IV

CONTINENTAL GREECE 403

- Excursion 33: ✿✿ PELION 407
- Excursion 34: ✿✿✿ DELPHI-ARAHOVA .... ✿✿✿ Delphi ✿✿ Arachova ✿✿ Ossios Loukas 417
- Excursion 35: ✿ LAKE PLASTIRAS .... ✿✿ Lake Plastiras (Tavropos) ✿ Agrafa 427
- Excursion 36: ✿✿ METEORA 431
- Excursion 37: ✿ METSOVO 437
- Excursion 38: ✿✿✿ ZAGOROHORIA .... ✿✿ Ioannina, ✿✿ Perama Cave, ✿ Bourazani 441
- Excursion 39: ✿✿ KASTORIA-PRESPES .... ✿✿ Kastoria, ✿✿ Nymphaio, ✿✿ Prespes 455
- Excursion 40: ✿✿ VERGINA 465
- Excursion 41: ✿✿ THESSALONIKI 471
- Excursion 42: ✿ SITHONIA 483
- Excursion 43: ✿✿✿ MOUNT ATHOS 491

PART V

PRACTICAL INFORMATION GUIDE 501

• General Information • Visa Requirements • Customs • National Tourist Organisation • Greek Embassies • Foreign Embassies in Greece • Greece and the Greeks • Religion • Politics • The Economy • Geography • Plant Life • Animal Life • The Climate • When to go • What to take with you • What to buy • What to eat • Travelling to Greece • Communications • Newspapers and magazines • Health • Entertainment • Major Cultural Events and Festivals • Sports • Bargaining • Public Holidays • Safety • Organisations of Interest to Travellers • Hotels and Rented Rooms • Currency • Weights and Measures • Films and Photographs • Further Reading • The Greek Alphabet • Useful Words and Phrases

INDEX 517

HOW TO USE "BEST"

ONLY
THE BEST
is not simply
one more
guide book.
It is a TRAVEL
INFORMATION
SYSTEM

BEFORE SETTING OUT ON YOUR TRIP

① The table **"Select your Excursion"** (Pages 8 & 9) helps you, with a glance at the column of 22 qualifications (cultural interest, beaches, countryside, restfulness, amenities, entertainment, cost, etc.), to quickly and easily form an opinion on which of the Excursions meets your requirements.

② The same table also gauges every one of the **43 Best excursions** separately, on the basis of each criterion. If for instance you wish to combine beaches, antiquities, comfort and entertainment, Excursion 15 (Mykonos-Delos) will head your list. If however you want a quiet, inexpensive holiday with good beaches away from it all, you'll choose Excursion 30 (Marathi).

③ Having taken your pick, you can look at the **large folding map** to see if this trip may be combined with other **Best** excursions, so as to estimate

Name of the **broader area**
11   Area colour code / Number of the excursion you have picked
Detailed map of the area
Sights evaluated with colour code and numbered in the order in which you will see them
☂   At-a-glance **beach evaluation**
■   **Location of the Excursion**
Best's tips and opinion on the excursion
❶   **Colour code of sights**, step by step, corresponding to the map
Colour photographs next to the relevant text
SYMBOLS ARE SHOWN ON BOOKMARK

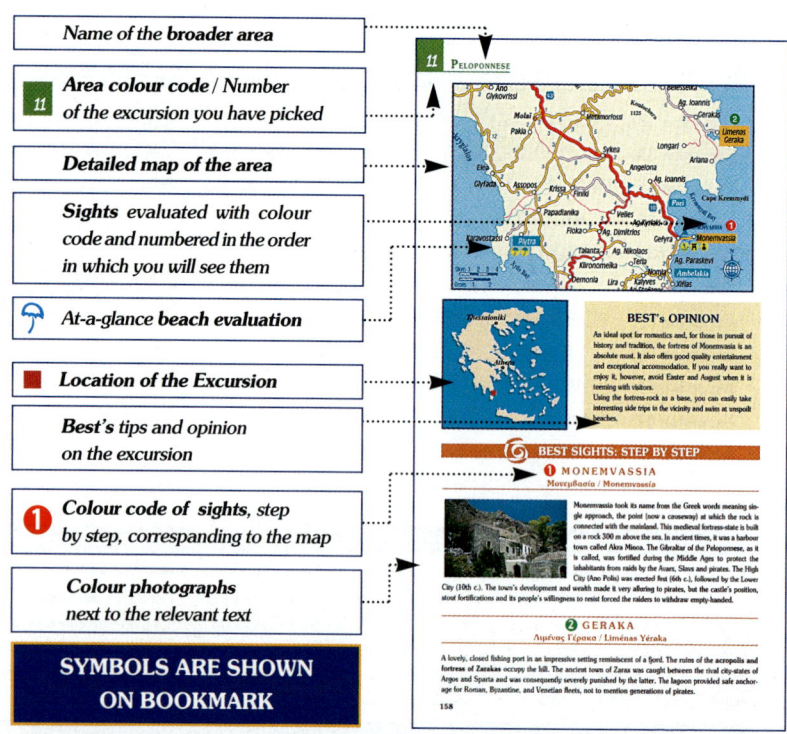

STEP BY STEP

how much time you wish to spend on each.

④ Turning to the pages of the **Best** excursion you have chosen, you'll find the **district's hotels**, often with a photograph, and always with prices and star-rating for excellence and value for money. Following **Best's** advice as to the ideal location of your hotel, you will make your bookings with confidence.

⑤ On the last page of each excursion you'll also find our **Tips** as to how to get there and how to link up the trip you have selected to other **Best** excursions.

ONCE THERE

① At the beginning of the description of every excursion there is a **detailed map of the area** on which all the sights and beaches are colour-coded and evaluated (the codes are explained on the bookmark) so that you can easily and rapidly plan your route and schedule your valuable time.

② The map on the pages of the excursion is **particularly practical** and will be your principal adviser on your tour of the sights, which are numbered in logical geographical order. On the subsequent pages the same order and numbering applies to step-by-step descriptions and photographs of what to see.

③ Every excursion also includes descriptions and photographs of **restaurants** and tavernas as well as suggestions for your **entertainment**.

Name of the Excursion	
Evaluation of beaches corresponding to the map	
Advice on best hotel location	
Evaluation of hotels	
Value for money evaluation of hotels	
Evaluation of restaurants	
Restaurant price range	
Suggestions for entertainment	
Tips & Information	

NOTE: The illustrations are edited examples and do not correspond to the actual pages of the guide

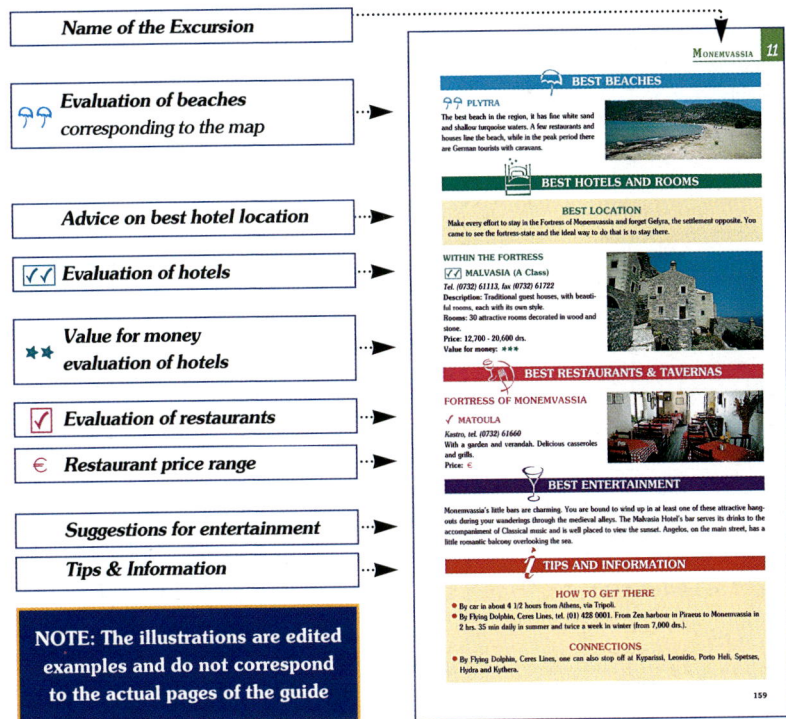

select your excursion

	ATHENS & Environs	1 Nafplio Area	2 Kastania	3 Zarouchla	4 Kalavryta	5 Arcadian Highlands	6 Ancient Olympia	7 Ancient Messene	8 Pylos	9 Mani	10 Mystras	11 Monemvassia	12 Kythera	13 Spetses	14 Hydra	15 Mykonos / Delos
				PELOPONNESE												
CULTURAL INTEREST																
Ancient Sites / Antiquities	●●●	●●●				●●	●●●	●●●	●				●			●●●
Byzantine	●●●	●			●	●●		●		●●	●●●	●				
Forts / Venetian fortifications		●●●			●				●●	●	●	●●				
Neo-Classical / Mansions	●●●	●●●							●					●●	●●●	
Old Town	●●	●●														
Traditional village			●	●	●●	●●			●	●●●			●●●	●	●	●●●
NATURE																
Beaches	●	●				●●	●		●●	●			●●	●●	●	●●●
Scenery / View	●●●	●	●●●	●●	●●●	●●●	●	●●●	●	●●	●●	●●●	●	●	●	●
Lake / Wetland	●		●●	●			●									
Mountain / Ravine	●●		●●	●●	●●●	●●					●●					
Caves	●●			●	●●					●●●						●
Walks / Sports	●●		●●	●●	●●	●●●			●	●●	●●●		●	●	●	
ATMOSPHERE																
Sophisticated / Social	●●●	●			●●		●		●	●			●●	●●●	●●●	●●●
Restful		●	●●	●●	●●	●●●	●●	●●		●	●●	●●	●●	●	●●	●●
Intrepid	●		●●●	●●●	●●●	●●●		●●	●●	●●●		●				
Touristic	●●	●●		●	●		●●	●	●		●●	●●	●●●	●●●	●●●	●●●
CONVENIENCES																
Traditional hotels		●			●	●			●●		●●		●●	●	●●	●
Standard of hotels	●●●	●●	●	●	●●	●	●●	●	●●	●	●●	●●	●●	●●	●●	●●●
Standard of restaurants	●●●	●●		●	●	●●	●	●	●●	●	●●	●●	●●	●●	●●	●●●
VARIOUS																
Entertainment	●●●	●●●				●		●		●		●		●●	●●	●●●
Casino	●●	●														
Cost of Excursion	●●●	●●●		●	●	●●	●●	●	●●	●	●●	●●	●●	●●	●●	●●●

	17 Sifnos	18 Folegandros	19 Santorini	20 Western Crete	21 Vamos	22 Rethymno	23 Phaestos / Matala	24 Knossos / Heraklio	25 Elounda	26 Eastern Crete	27 Rhodes	28 Symi	29 Patmos	30 Marathi	31 Corfu	32 Skiathos	33 Pelion	34 Delphi / Arahova	35 Lake Plastiras	36 Meteora	37 Metsovo	38 Zagorohoria	39 Kastoria / Prespes	40 Vergina	41 Thessaloniki	42 Sithonia	43 Mount Athos
		•••	•		•••	•••		•	•••								•••								•••	•••	
•			•	•	•			•••	•	•	•••			•		•	•••	•	•••		•••			•••		•••
	•	•	•••		•	•••	•			•••	•	•••		•						•••				•••		•
•	•								•••	•••		•				•						•				
			•••		•					•••																
•••	•••	•••		•••						•	•••	•••	•			•••	•••	•			•••	•••			•	•••
•	•	•	•••		•••	•••		•	•••	•	•	•••	•••	•••	•				•••		•••	•••			•••	
•	•	•••	•••	•	•			•	•	•	•	•••	•••	•••		•	•••	•••	•	•••	•••	•••			•••	
			•									•	•••		•••			•••					•			
		•••				•						•••				•••			•••							•••
	•				•					•			•		•		•								•	
•••	•	•			•		•	•	•••	•••	•••			•••	•••	•••		•					•	•••	
•	•••	•••		•••				•••	•	•••	•	•				•		•		•				•••	•	
•••	•••	•	•••	•••	•••		•	•	•••	•	•••	•••	•	•	•••	•••	•••	•••	•••	•••					•	•••
•••	•	•••	•••	•••	•••	•	•••	•••	•••	•••	•	•••	•••	•••	•••	•••	•••	•	•••	•••	•••			•••	•	•••
•••	•	•••	•	•••	•	•••	•••	•••	•	•••	•••	•	•••	•••	•	•••	•••	•••	•	•••	•••	•••	•	•••	•	•••
•		•••	•••		•••			•••		•		•••		•		•••	•		•••	•••				•••	•	•••
•••	•	•••	•	•	•	•	•••	•	•	•••	•	•••	•	•	•••	•	•••	•	•	•	•	•	•	•••	•••	•••
•••	•	•••	•••	•••	•	•••	•••	•	•••	•••	•	•••	•••	•	•••	•••	•	•••	•	•	•••	•	•	•••	•	•••
•••	•••	•••	•••	•••	•••	•••	•••	•••	•••	•••	•	•••	•••	•••	•••	•••	•••	•••	•••	•••	•••	•••	•	•••	•••	•••
											•••			•										•••		
•••	•	•	•	•	•••		•••		•••	•••	•	•••	•	•	•	•••	•••	•	•	•••	•	•		•••	•••	•••
•••	•••	•••	•••	•••	•••	•••	•••	•••	•••	•••	•••	•••	•••	•••	•••	•••	•••	•••	•••	•••	•••	•	•	•••	•••	•

Detail from Nicholas Gyzis «Clandestine School»

History and Culture Through the Ages

HISTORY & CULTURE

NEOLITHIC ERA	7000-3000 BC
Earliest civilizations in Thessaly, at **Sesklo** and **Dimini**. Stoneware, farming and animal husbandry.  Sesklo unwalled and Dimini walled. Pottery decorated with **linear designs**.	3200-1100 BC

BRONZE AGE	3000-1200 BC
EARLY GREEKS OR PELASGIANS Tribes well-versed in the use of bronze migrate from Asia to Thessaly. Centres of civilization: **Tiryns**, **Lerna** and **Orchomenos**. Rectangular dwellings with foundations built of stone and walls of bricks. **Glazed pottery**.	 *Tiryns*

CYCLADIC CIVILIZATION 
A Mediterranean people who employed bronze. — 3200 BC
Maritime and commercial activities. — 3200-1100 BC
The Cycladic civilization flourishes. — 3000-2000 BC
Settling of refugees from Ionia. — 2100-2000 BC
Cretan domination - Minoan influence. — 1700-1450 BC
Eruption of the volcano of Thera. — 1500-1450 BC
Mycenaean influence. — 1450 or 1100 BC

Dwellings have straight or curved lines. **Figurines** of pellucid Parian marble. Mostly standing female figures, naked.

MINOAN CIVILIZATION — 3200-1100 BC
Early Minoan period — 3000-2100 BC
A significant civilization evolves in Crete.
Middle Minoan period — 2100-1580 BC
Masters of the Aegean sea with principal centres the palace-states of **Knossos** and **Phaestos**, which were unfortified.
Late Minoan period — 1580-1100 BC
Violent earthquakes and the eruption of the volcano of Thera cause a decline hastened by the Achaeans' invasion.

MYTH
The Labyrinth, derived from the word for double axe **labrys**, concealed the man-eating offspring of **Minos's** wife **Pasiphae**, the **Minotaur**, slain by the Athenian hero **Theseus**.

Imposing multi-storeyed palaces with exquisite murals and an advanced sewerage system.
Statuettes, pottery and other objects evidencing the quality of a peerless civilization. Three forms of script and a system of measurement.

The Phaestos disc

History & Culture

MYCENAEAN CIVILIZATION
The Achaeans invade from the north. Seamen and merchants. They speak **Greek** and introduce the **horse**. Centres of civilization: **Pylos, Orchomenos, Thebes, Iolkos, Tiryns** and **Mycenae**.

1600-1100 BC

Palaces are plain and unadorned, with mighty walls later called Cyclopean. Wall painting, sculpture and metalwork depicting scenes of battle, chariots and horses.
The dead are interred in tombs, often vaulted, with their personal belongings.

FIRST FORMATION OF GREEK COLONIES
At **Kimi, Killa, Myrina, Pitani** and **Smyrna**.

1100-800 BC

Appearance of Greek script, 900-800 BC.

TROJAN WAR
The Achaeans conquer Troy, having besieged it for ten years.

1184 BC

MYTH
Homer describes the last year of the Trojan War in the **Iliad**. He tells of the abduction of **Helen** by the Trojan, **Paris**, and the expedition of the Greeks, incited by her husband **Menelaos**, to fetch her back.

The Trojan War and its heroes have been a source of inspiration for many creative artists, both in antiquity and today.

THE DORIAN INVASION

1100-900 BC

Tribes from Thessaly armed with **irons weapons**, descend on Argolis, Lakonia and Messenia in the Peloponnese.
Achaean civilization destroyed.

GEOMETRIC PERIOD

1000-700 BC

Geometric-style art flourishes.
Hesiod's epic of precepts.
Homer writes the **Iliad** and the **Odyssey**.

750 BC

SECOND FORMATION OF GREEK COLONIES
Sicily, southern Italy, Macedonia, Thrace and **Black Sea**.

800-401 BC

Lyric poetry at its peak (650 - 450 BC)
Kallinos, Tyrtaios, Solon, Theognis, Archilochos, Alkaios, Sappho, Anakreon, Alkman, Simonides, Pindar and others.

HISTORY & CULTURE

ARCHAIC PERIOD	900-600 BC
ANCIENT SPARTA A warlike tribe of **Dorian origin**, governed by the laws of **Lykourgos**. Hereditary monarchy and three classes of citizens. Three **Messenian Wars**. Reform (centralized regime). The **first Olympic Games** take place.	900-700 BC 743-455 BC 610 BC 776 BC
ANCIENT ATHENS Of **Ionian origin**, with an initially aristocratic regime. **Draconian code** of legislation. **Solon's** reforms. **Peisistratos** comes to power. **MYTH** The gods **Athena** and **Poseidon** contended for the city. The goddess of wisdom took it under her protection and gave it her name. Greek philosophy flourishes in the thought of **Thales**, **Anaximandros, Anaximenes, Pythagoras, Heraklitos**.	700-527 BC 624-621 BC 594 BC 561-527 BC

Poseidon

Athena

CLASSICAL PERIOD	480 - 338 BC
ATHENS **Kleisthenes** establishes a democratic regime. Battle of **Marathon**. Battle of **Thermopylae**. Naval battle of **Salamis**. Naval battle of **Artemision**. Battle of **Plataea**. The Golden Age of Pericles.	508 BC 490 BC 480 BC 480 BC 479 BC 479 BC 480-404 BC

Tragedians: **Aeschylus, Sophokles, Euripides**.
Comedians: **Aristophanes**.
Philosophers: **Empedocles, Anaxagoras, Democritos, the Sophists, Socrates**.
Historians: **Herodotos, Thucydides**.

Sculptors: **Pheidias, Myron, Iktinos, Kallicrates, Zeuxis**.
Doric and **Ionic** style columns in temples.
The architectural marvel of the **Acropolis**.

History & Culture

PELOPONNESIAN WAR 1st Period Invasion of Attica by the Spartan King **Archidamos**. Peace of **Nikias**. 2nd Period **Sicilian** campaign. Defection of **Alcibiades** to Sparta following his sentencing to death in absentia. The Athenians meet with disaster. 3rd Period Alcibiades recalled to Athens. The Athenians are defeated at **Aigos Potamoi**. **Lysandros** attacks Athens. Democarcy loses to rule by the few (oligarchy). The **Thirty Tyrants**.	**431-404 BC** **431-421 BC** **415-413 BC** **407 BC** **405 BC** **404 BC**

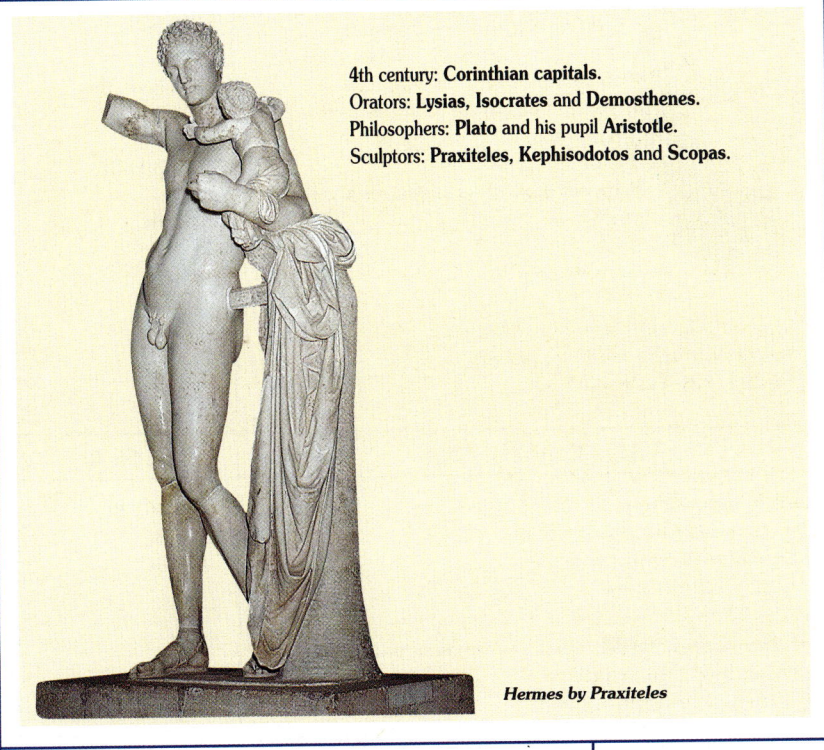

4th century: **Corinthian capitals**.
Orators: **Lysias, Isocrates** and **Demosthenes**.
Philosophers: **Plato** and his pupil **Aristotle**.
Sculptors: **Praxiteles, Kephisodotos** and **Scopas**.

Hermes by Praxiteles

SPARTAN HEGEMONY Peace of **Antalkidas** for the Greek city-states. Historian: **Xenophon**. Artists: **Apelles** and **Protogenes**.	**404-382 BC** **386 BC**
THEBAN HEGEMONY Thebes turns against Sparta, led by **Pelopidas** and **Epaminondas**. The victory of **Leuktra**. Battle of **Mantineia**. Comedians: **Philemon** and **Menander**.	**382-359 BC** **371 BC** **362 BC**

HISTORY & CULTURE

MACEDONIA 3rd Sacred War. **Philip II** destroys Olynthos, having been victorious in successive battles. Peace of **Philocrates**. 4th Sacred War. Defeat of the allied armies at **Cheronea**. **Philip** is **assassinated** by Pausanias. His son **Alexander the Great** accedes to the throne. Annihilation of **Thebes**. *Philip II* The **Persian** campaign. Victory at **Granikos**. The Gordian knot. Battle of **Issos**. **Egypt** greets Alexander as liberator. The city of **Alexandria** is founded and the famed Museum and Library are built. Battle of **Gaugamila** definitively crushes the Persian army. Expedition to **India**. **Illness** and **death** of the youthful conqueror, at the age of 33. *Alexander the Great* Sculpture by **Lysippos** of the head of Alexander. Vaulted tombs with a wealth of funeral gifts. Palaces at **Pella** and **Vergina**.	359-323 BC 355-346 BC 348 BC 346 BC 339-338 BC 338 BC 336 BC 336 BC 335 BC 334 BC 333 BC 333 BC 332-331 BC 331 BC 327-325 BC 323 BC
HELLENISTIC ERA	**323-146 BC**
Conflicts and weakness of the states of the successors. The country is divided into confederacies. Macedonia becomes a Roman province. **Pergamon** a centre of culture, with altars and monuments. **Rhodes** develops in every area. 4 Schools of Philosophy at **Athens**. Characteristics of **Hellenistic art**: vigour and verve, inner dynamism and sophistication.	323-301 BC 301 BC 148 BC

HISTORY & CULTURE

ROMAN DOMINATION	146 BC-330 AD
Edict of **Mediolanum** (religious tolerance).	313 AD
Constantine becomes emperor.	323-337 AD
Founding of **Constantinople**.	330 AD
The Romans are influenced by the Greek spirit.	

BYZANTIUM	324-1453 AD
EARLY BYZANTINE PERIOD	324-642
Julian in conflict with the Christians. Assassinated in battle.	361-363
Theodosios the Great.	379-395
Christianity the official state religion.	381
Olympic Games abolished.	394
Justinian I, Emperor.	527-565
Together with his wife **Theodora**, a former prostitute, he suppresses the **Nikas Sedition**.	532
Re-establishment of the state following a series of campaigns. Significant codification of legislation.	533-555
Herakleios, Emperor.	610-641
Victories in battles with the Persians. Successive heresies give rise to religious clashes.	622-628
Construction of **Agia Sophia** at Constantinople by **Anthemios** and **Isidoros**.	

Daphni monastery.

MIDDLE BYZANTINE PERIOD	642-1204
The empire in deadlock, resolved by the **Isaurians**.	717
Iconoclasm, provoking the edict of **Leo the Isaurian**, results in the destruction of countless works of art.	726-843
Icons are permitted again.	843
The Macedonian dynasty of **Basil I, Leo VI the Wise** and **Nikephoros II Phokas**.	867-969
Ioannis Tsimiskis usurps the throne, having murdered Phokas.	969-976
Basil II The Bulgar-Slayer.	976-1025
The **Komnenos** dynasty wages war against the Seljuk Turks.	1081
The **Angeli** dynasty hastens state decline.	1185
Fourth Crusade, Frankish **Conquest of Constantinople**.	1204

HISTORY & CULTURE

LATE BYZANTINE PERIOD The Franks parcel out the Byzantine state among the leaders of the 4th Crusade. **Michail Palaiologos** retakes Constantinople and reconstitutes a weakened Byzantine empire. **Constantine Palaiologos** confronts Mohammed II. Fall of Constantinople to the Ottoman Turks.	1204-1453 1204 1261 1453

> **Byzantine churches**: built with linear brick, domes and vaulted ceilings. They consisted of a **narthex** or vestibule, the **naos** or central church proper, and of the **ieron** or sanctuary.
> **Byzantine devotional art**: portable icons, frescoes and mosaics.

THE VENETIANS AND FRANKS IN GREECE	**1204-1715**
For extended periods, Franks and Venetians rule over the Ionian islands, Crete, many coastal Greek towns, and the Peloponnese. The famed **Knights of St. John** occupy Rhodes for 200 years until its citadel surrenders to **Suleiman II**. Crete conquered by the Turks. Turks overrun the Peloponnese.	 1522 1669 1715

> The **imposing fortresses** of the Venetians and the Franks, with masonry ramparts, embrasures, battlements and keeps, enhance Greek towns such as **Candia (Heraklion)**, **Nafplion** and **Corfu**, and are generally built on foundations of previously existing ancient or Byzantine emplacements.

OTTOMAN DOMINATION	**1453-1829**
Turks and Venetians vie for Crete. The uprisings of Orloff, and of **Daskalogiannis** in Crete. **Ali Pasha** in Ioannina. Death of **Rigas Ferraios** whose battle-song and activities roused the Greeks. The Philike Etaireia (Society of Philhellenes) formed by **Alexander Ypsilantis**. Ypsilantis launches the War of Independence from Iasio in Moldo-Wallachia.	1645-1669 1769 1788 1798 1814 1821

> Vernacular trends in the architecture of Pelion, Epiros, Mani, the Cyclades and Macedonia.
> The prime of **Cretan literature**.
> **Demotic (folk) songs**.

Ali Pasha

HISTORY & CULTURE

THE GREEK WAR OF INDEPENDENCE	1821-1829
Fired in the Peloponnese, Hydra, Spetses and Psara, it spreads to Continental Greece and the North.	**April 1821**
Archbishop of Patras **Palaion Patron Germanos** hoists the banner of freedom at the monastery Agia Lavra of Kalavryta.	**25.3.1821**
The battles of **Alamana, Gravia, Valtetsi, Vassilika of Dragatsani**. Capture of Tripolis. 1st National Assembly at Epidaurus, presided over by **Alexandros Mavrocordatos**, proclaims independence. **1st siege of Messolonghi**. Annihilation of **Chios**.	**1822**
Dramalis's disastrous campaign. Civil conflict between the military and politicians costs **Odysseas Androutsos** his life. The 2nd Assembly at **Astros** relieves **Kolokotronis** of command of the army, which is entrusted to a tri-partite committee.	**1823**
European philhellenes such as **Santa Rosa**, Lord **Byron** and **Norman** actively participate in the struggle. Annihilation of **Psara** and **Kassos** Naval battles of **Samos** and **Gerondas**.	**1824**
Ibrahim of Egypt lands in the Peloponnese. **2nd siege of Messolonghi**.	**1825**
Epidaurus National Assembly. The exodus from Messolonghi.	**1826**
3rd National Assembly of Troezen. Naval battle of Navarino in which the Great Powers destroy the Turco-Egyptian fleet.	**1827**
Arrival of **Kapodistrias** from Russia.	**1828**
Greece declared an independent state by the London Protocol, signed by the Great Powers.	**3.2.1830**

The writing of **Andreas Kalvos, Panagiotis and Alexander Soutsos, Alexander Rizos - Rangavis, Dionysios Solomos** and **George Zalokostas** was inspired by the nation's struggle.

Palaion Patron Germanos raises the banner of liberation.

HISTORY & CULTURE

CONTEMPORARY GREECE	1829
THE GREEK STATE AFTER THE WAR OF INDEPENDENCE	**1829-1912**
Assassination of the first Governor Capodistrias.	1831
A convention is signed in London and Constantinople, placing on the throne of Greece the Bavarian prince **Otto**, who disembarks at Nafplion.	
Revolution of 3 September.	1832
Establishment of constitutional monarchy.	1843
George I accedes to the throne.	1862
Cretan uprising at **Arkadi**.	1863
Insurrection at **Goudi**.	1866-1869
Eleftherios Venizelos forms a government.	1909
	1911
Stamatis Kleanthis builds the mansion of the Duchesse de Plaisance, **Theophilos Hansen** the Academy, the University and the National Library, **Ernst Ziller** neo-classical buildings influenced by German architecture, such as the Iliou Melathron and the present Presidential Mansion, **Goertner** the former royal palace and **Anastasios Helmis** the Stathatos mansion. **Lysandros Kaftanzoglou, Anastasios Metaxas**, and **Aristoteles Zachos**, are also responsible for major constructions. **Nikiforos Lytras, Nicholas Ghyzis, Constantine Iakovidis**, are the artists of the new generation. **Theophilos** creates his astonishing folk paintings. **Yannoulis Halepas, Dimitrios Philippotis, Michalis Tombros** represent the modern trends in sculpture. Principal authors and poets are **Andreas Laskaratos, Aristoteles Valaoritis, Kostis Palamas, George Vizyinos, Aristomenes Provelengios, Kostas Krystallis** and **Alexander Papadiamantis**.	*Eleftherios Venizelos*
THE BALKAN WARS	**1912-1913**
Greece at war with Turkey.	5.10.1912
Thessaloniki captured by the Greek army.	1912
Following a series of successful engagements, the Greek army and navy take Ioannina.	1913
King George I is assassinated in Thessaloniki and **Constantine** accedes to the throne.	5.3.1913
Bucharest Conference (the Nestos river to constitute the Greco-Bulgarian border).	1913
THE FIRST WORLD WAR	**1914-1918**
Venizelos forms a government in Thessaloniki and organizes a defensive force.	1916
Constantine forced to abdicate, replaced by his son **Alexander**.	1917
Battle of **Skra**.	1918
The **Treaty of Sevres** grants Greece Eastern Thrace, the Aegean islands and sovereign rights in Smyrna. Venizelos loses the election.	1920
The Asia Minor disaster.	1922
The **Treaty of Lausanne** awards Eastern Thrace to Turkey, as well as a section of Western Thrace and Imbros, Tenedos and the Smyrna zone. It also concedes 14 villages of the Korytsa Kaza to Albania.	1923

HISTORY & CULTURE

THE PERIOD BETWEEN THE WARS	1922-1939
Abolition of constitutional monarchy.	1924
Dictatorship of **Theodore Pangalos**.	1925
The **Plastiras** uprising.	1933
Dictatorship of **Ioannis Metaxas**.	4.8.1936
Mussolini's forces invade Albania.	7.4.1939

> **Constantine Cavafy** the Alexandrian, **Kostis Palamas** and **Angelos Sikelianos** are leading lights in poetry. There are also writers such as **Grigoris Xenopoulos** and **Constantine Theotokis**.

2nd WORLD WAR	**1939-1944**
Metaxas obliged to declare war.	28-10-1940
Retreat of the Italian army as a result of victories by the Greeks, who advance into enemy territory, capturing Korytsa and reaching Agii Saranda.	1940
German invasion and occupation of Greece.	
The German occupation, opposed by **strong resistance groups**, cost Greece more than **350,000** fatalities.	1941-1944
Liberation.	12.10.1944

POST-WAR PERIOD	**1944-1974**
Civil war between left-wing guerrillas and the nationalist army which had the support of the British. Defeat of the left-wing forces.	1946-1949
Greece joins NATO.	1951
The **Papagos** government.	1952-1955
Constantine Karamanlis forms a government.	1955-1963
George Papandreou comes to power.	1964
The Novas, Tsirimokos, Stephanopoulos and Kanellopoulos governments.	1965-1967
Dictatorship of George Papadopoulos following a putsch by the military.	21-4-1967
Students take over the Polytechnic School.	17-11-1973
Military coup of the **junta in Cyprus** followed by Turkish invasion.	1974
The Greek and Cypriot dictatorships collapse.	1974

> **Dimitrios Pikionis** and other younger architects are influenced by vernacular architecture.
> Painters: **Hatzikyriakos Gikas, Giannis Tsarouchis,** and **Giannis Spyropoulos** were influenced by the art of **Constantine Parthenis**.
> **Kostas Varnalis, Napoleon Lapathiotis, Elias Venezis, Michalis Karagatsis, Stratis Myrivilis, Nikos Kazantzakis, Nikos Kavadias, Giannis Ritsos**, and the Nobel prize winners **George Seferis** and **Odysseas Elytis**, are some of the writers and poets.
> Theatre reaches new heights with **Emilios Veakis, Marika Kotopouli, Katina Paxinou, Karolos Koun, Alexis Minotis**.

Constantine Karamanlis

History & Culture

At the same time, shined the star of actress and later politician, **Melina Mercouri**.
Film directors: **Alexis Damianos, Nikos Koundouros, Michalis Cacoyannis, Costas Gavras, Elia Kazan** and more.
Some internationally renowned Greek musicians: conductor **Dimitris Mitropoulos**, soprano **Maria Callas**, avant-garde composer **Giannis Xenakis**, composers, **Manos Hadjidakis** and **Mikis Theodorakis**.
Greek shipping magnates dominate the world scene, most notably **Stavros Niarchos** and legendary **Aristotle Onassis**, who married **Jacqueline Kennedy**. After a series of tragic events his enormous fortune has come down to his granddaughter Athena.

Melina Merkouri

Maria Callas

Aristotle Onassis

Mikis Theodorakis

MODERN TIMES

Constantine Karamanlis forms a goverment of national unity.	1974-to present
69% of Greeks vote against monarchy in a plebiscite.	1974
Greece becomes a member of the **European Common Market**.	12-2-1978
The Panhellenic Socialist Movement of **Andreas Papandreou** governs for two four-year terms.	1981-1989
The New Democracy party under Prime Minister **Constantine Mitsotakis** takes power.	1989
Andreas Papandreou is again prime minister.	1993
The vote of the PASOK parliamentary committee proclaims **Kostas Simitis** as prime minister, following Andreas Papandreou's illness.	1996
Under **Prime Minister Kostas Simitis** Greece aims to join the European Monetary Union and effect economic recovery.	1996 to present

Manos Loizos and **Thanos Mikroutsikos**, and others, are representative of popular music trends.
Pianist **Dimitris Sgouros** and violinist **Leonidas Kavakos** acquire international renown.
Theodore Angelopoulos, awarded the 1998 Golden Palm, is the internationally distinguished Greek film director.

Andreas Papandreou

ATHENS & ENVIRONS

ATHENS & ENVIRONS

BEST's OPINION

Athens is one of the world's most culturally endowed cities and holds the promise of cosmopolitan pursuits as well as many entertainment and learning possibilities. These pages may prove illuminating even for Athenians, helping them to get to know their city better. As for visitors, we believe that while exploring Athens may not have the appeal of the other excursions, it is still worth spending two or three days in this historic city to see the Acropolis and its most important museums.

IN BRIEF

Athens is the country's most important cultural, commercial and industrial centre, with some 4 million people living in the capital and its suburbs. Omonia Square is the city's most crowded point, Plaka and Thission are the districts that attract both tourists and locals since they represent the most beautiful and best preserved parts of the old city. Kolonaki, the most chic quarter, is patronized by intellectuals and the fashion-conscious and boasts the most luxurious and expensive shops. Mets is the most up-and-coming neighbourhood, where old neo-classical homes are beginning to be restored and its cultural offerings are multiplying steadily. Kypseli is the third most densely populated district per square metre in the world. The northern suburbs have the most modern high-rise office blocks and shopping centres and they also claim tree-lined streets with large villas surrounded by spacious gardens. The western suburbs are composed of working-class neighbourhoods and the city's factories. Eastern Attica is famed for its tavernas and rotisseries, and it also has a number of summer houses. Southern Attica, from Neo Faliro to Sounion, is the most important summer retreat for both locals and visitors, with its beaches, nightclubs, second homes and luxury hotels. Today's Athens is a chaotic city, crowded, expanding without town-planning principles and with minimal green parks to help its people breathe. Nevertheless, its ancient and more recent monuments, its museums, its sights, its attractive, lively traditional districts, the wonderful sunny Attic climate, and its fascinating past are more than enough reasons to spend some time here.

HISTORY

Athens has been inhabited since the Neolithic era and around 4000 BC the hill of the **Acropolis** and the area around the Ilissos river saw their first settlements. The **Mycenaean period** was as brilliant here as in the Peloponnese. The palace belonging to the city's ruler was built on the Acropolis in the late 15th c. BC. By the late 13th c., fortifications had been erected and the locals were living peacefully with Ionian tribes who had entered the Greek mainland. Four centuries later, the various settlements of Athens were united and the city-state was born. From 1050 to 700 BC, the foundations were laid for a civilization that would contain the seeds of Western thought and art.

During the **Archaic period**, authority passed from the king to the hands of the aristocracy and in 624 BC **Dracon** established a legal system, which was replaced in 594 by that of **Solon**. **Kleisthenes** became chief archon in 508-507 BC, while **Pericles** ruled from 460 to 429 BC. This period would come to be known as the **Golden Age** when Athens rose to its zenith in terms of cultural, intellectual, economic and political achievements. The city became the centre of the ancient world, arousing envy in the Spartans and Corinthians.

Thus in 431 BC, the **Peloponnesian War** broke out between the Spartans and Athenians, with victory eventually falling to the Spartans. In 404 BC the Athenians were forced to destroy their walls and surrender their ships. The Macedonians respected the ancient city although the Athenians resisted their expansionist plans and fought against them at Cheronea in 338 BC. After the Roman conquest, Athens became part of the **Roman empire**. Later, under the emperor Hadrian mainly, it regained some of its former glory. **Franks, Burgundians, Catalans, Venetians** and **Byzantines** took turns ruling it, until it passed to **Ottoman** domination in 1458 AD.

In 1833, the city was liberated once and for all after a series of uprisings. By then it was just a village, devoid of any lustre, yet on 1 December 1834 it was declared the capital of the new Greek state. It was rebuilt according to new specifications and reclaimed its place as the centre of the Hellenic world. It has paid for the privilege with galloping growth since the Second World War when it was flooded with new residents from the Greek countryside seeking jobs, schools and hospitals.

HISTORICAL AREA OF ATHENS

WHY AMONG THE BEST

Because this is the most attractive part of the city, incorporating the inimitable Acropolis, as well as Athens' most significant ancient Greek, Roman and Byzantine monuments.

ATHENS AND ENVIRONS

HISTORICAL ATHENS

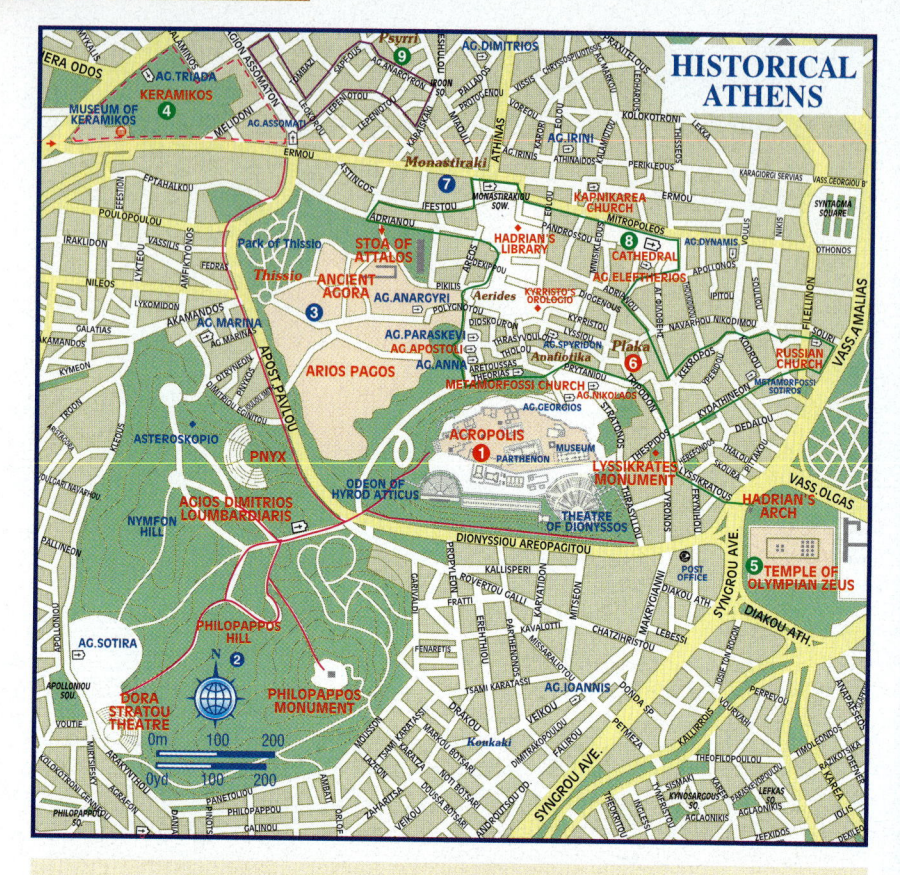

[Map of Historical Athens showing the Acropolis and surrounding area]

BEST's OPINION

Walking is the best way to really appreciate all these sights. Wander around the picturesque streets and the fascinating archaeological areas, crowned by the sacred space of the Acropolis. Follow the three walks we outline below in order to get to know the district without suffering the traffic congestion and the lack of parking facilities.

BEST SIGHTS: STEP BY STEP

FIRST WALK
RED ROUTE ON THE MAP: 5 HOURS

❶ THE ACROPOLIS
Ακρόπολη / Akrópoli

Tel. (01) 3210219, 3214172, 3210219, 9238724
Summer: 8 am-9 pm, winter: 8:30 am-3 pm

IN BRIEF

This unique monument, which represents the ultimate in architectural and artistic expression of the ancient Athenian spirit, occupies a rock 156 m above sea level, which is itself a natural fortress. Entrance to the "high city" is from the west.

HISTORY

The hill was first inhabited in the Neolithic era and the first walls were erected in the mid 13th c. BC. In the course of the Dorian invasion, the city was moved elsewhere and the Acropolis began to be established as a place of worship. It acquired its first temple in the 8th c. BC. Building started on the Parthenon itself, dedi-

HISTORICAL AREA OF ATHENS

cated to Athena, in the early 5th c. BC, only to be razed by the Persians in 480. It was rebuilt during Pericles' rule in just ten years. The monumental entrance to the summit of the holy rock, the **Propylaia**, designed by **Mnesicles**, was under construction from 437 to 432 BC. The Erechtheion was completed twelve years later. These brilliant architectural and artistic achievements of the 5th c. BC were supervised by **Pheidias**, while the designs were the work of **Iktinos** and **Kallikrates**.

The foundations of the temple of Athena Nike were also laid at this time, as were those of the Chalkotheke and the sanctuary of Artemis Vravronia to the south and west of the Parthenon.

The extraordinary **gold and ivory statue of Athena**, Pheidias's masterpiece which stood 13 m high with its base, dominated the centre of the temple of the goddess, and the 9 m high statue of **Athena Promachos**, also by Pheidias, rose imposingly between the Parthenon and the Erechtheion. Of the former, all that is left is a Roman copy, **Athena tou Varvarkiou**, now in the National Museum. The latter was carried off to Constantinople under Justinian, where it was destroyed by fanatic Christians.

In 334 BC **Alexander the Great** dedicated the spoils from his victory at the Granikos river to the Parthenon. In 304 BC the harem of Demetrios Poliorketes (the Besieger) made the sacred temple their home. In 267 AD the Herulean invasion caused considerable damage and the west gate was fortified. In Byzantine times, the Parthenon, Erechtheion and Propylaia were converted into Christian churches. Justinian declared the Parthenon a church consecrated to Holy Wisdom (Agia Sophia); later it was rededicated to the Virgin Mary. The Franks made it a Catholic church, Santa Maria. The Ottomans in turn converted it to a mosque, while the whole Acropolis became a Turkish neighbourhood. By 1463 the Erechtheion was so debased it had become a harem, and the temple of Athena Nike was completely razed. In 1687, during one of the Venetians' battles against the Ottomans, one of Morosini's shells burst over the Parthenon, setting off the dynamite the Turks had stored inside and blowing off the roof. In 1827 a Turkish shell damaged the Karyatids on the Erechtheion, while an earthquake in 1894 wreaked additional havoc.

Today the temples' worst enemy is pollution, which has severely corroded the marble. The Karyatids have been removed to the Acropolis Museum, replaced by copies on site. The ongoing efforts at restoration, which are taking far longer than the original construction, have unfortunately resulted in an Acropolis partially covered with scaffolding, making it much harder for us to imagine what it must have been like. Nevertheless, visitors from the world over still flock to the ancient rock to contemplate this unique specimen of perfection, which shows us that humankind, despite its frailties, can now and then attain greatness.

THE ELGIN MARBLES

Most of the Parthenon sculptures as well as one of the original Karyatids can only be admired in London's British Museum ever since Lord Elgin, on his way home from his tour of duty as ambassador to Constantinople, scooped up a good many splendid works of art, naturally with the Sultan's consent. On your next trip to London, read the caption under one of the Parthenon friezes: "The other horse is still in Athens."

Despite the efforts of former Culture minister Melina Mercouri, the other horse as well as the rest of the Parthenon marbles are, unfortunately, still in London.

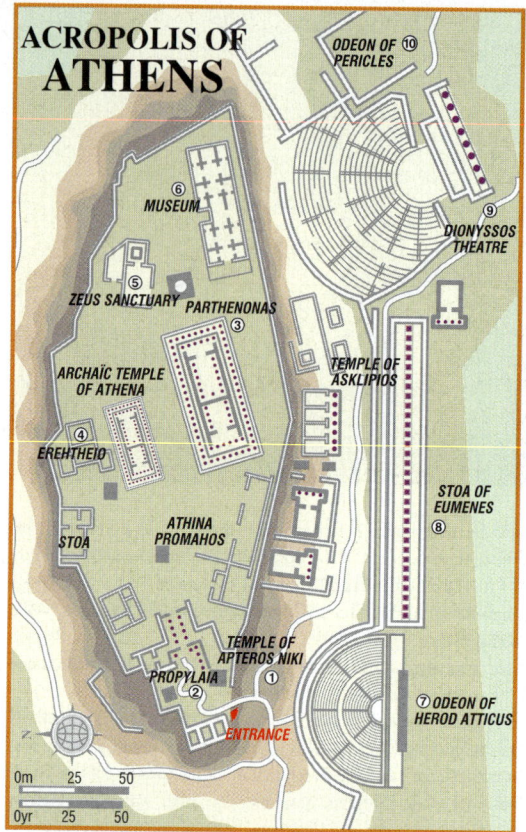

ACROPOLIS OF ATHENS

WANDERING ROUND THE ACROPOLIS

If you look down as you're walking up to the Propylaia, you can see the **Theatre of Herod Atticus**, while just outside the entrance to the museum you'll notice the remains of the **Stoa of Eumenes** and **Theatre of Dionysos** below it.

① ⚬⚬ **Temple of Apteros Nike** (Wingless Victory). A small temple with eight Ionic columns, in which the Athenians placed a statue of Nike without wings to ensure that she would never "fly" away from their city. Today the statue can be seen in the Acropolis Museum.

② ⚬⚬ **The Propylaia.** Built of Pentelic marble, it consists of a central structure with two wings. It was designed by Mnesicles and replaced the earlier Propylon erected by Peisistratos.

③ ⚬⚬⚬ **The Parthenon.** Built between 447 and 432 BC to plans of Iktinos and Kallikrates. An extraordinary combination of Ionic and Doric features, it is 69.1 m long, 30.86 m wide and was surrounded by 46 columns. The temple proper, the sekos, was divided into three aisles, with a double series of columns framing the statue of Athena. The inner columns supported an epistyle with smaller Doric columns, which reached as high as the roof. A frieze depicting the Panathenaic procession in relief ran round the upper part of the outer wall. Its 92 metopes portrayed the battle of the Giants, the battle of Centaurs and Lapiths and other subjects. The pediments were decorated with sculptures representing the birth of Athena and her contest with Poseidon for possession of Athens. The building itself contains not a single straight line and no strictly true perpendicular line either. The stylobate and the epistyle are both gently curved, the columns are a bit narrower at the top than at the middle and lean slightly toward the centre, so that if they were extended indefinitely, they would eventually form a pyramid. This gives the temple a lightness and a unique feeling that it is about to take off.

The Parthenon

④ ⚬⚬⚬ **The Erechtheio.** Built during the Peloponnesian War by Philocles, the temple was shared by Athena and Poseidon-Erechtheus, from whom it got its name. Six female statues, the famous Karyatids, with canisters on their heads as column capitals, support the roof of the temple. Today five copies stand in their place. The originals are in the Acropolis Museum. The sixth Karyatid, thanks to Elgin, can only be seen in London.

Karyatids

HISTORICAL AREA OF ATHENS

(5) ⓖ **The shrine of Zeus.** Very little is left of this temple dedicated to Zeus Polios, to whom sacrifices, the Bouphonia, were brought every summer during the harvest season.

(6) ⓖⓖ **The Acropolis Museum**
Tel. (01) 3236665
🕐 8 am-9 pm (same hours as the Acropolis)

Just outside the entrance is a splendid vantage point for a bird's eye view of the Theatre of Dionysos below.

The museum contains works found during excavation of the Acropolis. The four first rooms have exhibits from the 6th c. BC, such as the ⓖ **pediments** of Herakles with the Lernaian Hydra, the lions savaging a bull, and the demon with three bodies. Here, too, are the ⓖ **Archaic kores** (maidens) and the ⓖ **Moschoforos** (youth with the calf). The 5th room holds the wonderful marble pediment depicting the ⓖ **battle with the Giants** from the days of the Peisistratids. In the 6th room, of special note are the ⓖ **boy of Kritios**, the ⓖ **head of the blond youth**, the ⓖ **kore of Eudikos** and other works dating between 490 and 450 BC. The masterpieces of the Golden Age are displayed in the 7th and 8th rooms. See here the plaster copies of the ⓖⓖⓖ **Parthenon pediments** and ⓖⓖⓖ **frieze**.

The most remarkable pieces in the 9th room are the head of ⓖ **Alexander**, attributed to Leocharos, the statue of ⓖ **Procne** by Alkmenes, a pupil of Pheidias, and the ⓖ **head of old philosopher**.

The youth with the calf.

(7) ⓖⓖ **Theatre of Herod Atticus (The Herodion).** Erected in 161 BC by the Athenian orator and benefactor whose name it commemorates. It can seat 5,000 spectators but most of its marble seats, except for those in the front row, are modern restorations. It hosts all the events of the Athens Festival, as well as a few other concerts and performances throughout the summer.

(8) ⓖ **Stoa of Eumenes.** Constructed in the 2nd c. BC, it took its name from the king of Pergamon, **Eumenes II**, who paid for it. Only its foundations remain, but Athenians used to stroll and discuss in the shade of this 163 m long arcade.

(9) ⓖ **Theatre of Dionysos.** This theatre, which occupies the site of an earlier sanctuary of Dionysos Eleuthereos, is considered to be the oldest yet discovered. Of the original 5th c. BC structure, only the orchestra remains. The movable

Theatre of Herod Atticus

stage and seats were of wood. It was here that the great dramas of the Golden Age had their first performances. The stone seats were added in the 4th c. BC. Measuring 100 m in width, 90 m in depth and possessing 78 rows of seats, of which only two-thirds are extant, the theatre underwent many alterations before it reached its final form.

(10) ⓖ **Odeon of Pericles.** Completed in 443 BC. Its foundations have been only partly excavated. This roofed building with columns was used as a concert hall.

29

ATHENS AND ENVIRONS

❷ PHILOPAPPOS HILL
Λόφος Φιλοπάππου / Lófos Philopáppou

Philopappos Hill was also known as the Hill of the Muses or Mouseion, and naturally it was dedicated to them. To get to it, walk up Dionysiou Areopagitou St., which possesses some of Athens' finest neo-classical buildings, and which runs into Apostolou Pavlou St., where the Filistron restaurant – one of the city's *Best* – is located.

AGIOS DIMITRIOS LOUMBARDIARIS
You'll come to this picturesque church at the foot of the hill.

🌀 THE PNYX
This was where the ancient Athenians assembled to debate politics. Today foreigners congregate here to watch the **Sound & Light** spectacle.

🌀 PHILOPAPPOS MONUMENT
Erected in honour of one of Athens' benefactors, a prince from Syria and Roman consul, this monument at the top of the hill is the tomb of **Gaius Julius Antiochus Philopappus**, whose statue stands in the central niche.

Philopappos Monument

❸ ANCIENT AGORA AND THESEION
Αρχαία Αγορά - Θησείο / Archéa Agorá - Thissío

🌀 ANCIENT AGORA
Tel. (01) 3210185

⏱ *8 am-5 pm, closed Mondays and holidays*

From Apostolou Pavlou St., take Adrianou St., and you'll end up in the Thission district and the archaeological site of the Ancient Agora.

The heart of Athenian daily life, the Agora was the chief meeting place and market throughout antiquity. It was constructed under Pericles and Kimon, after the Persian wars, and ran between the temple of Hephaistos and the stoa of Attalos. After numerous changes and much rebuilding, it fell into disuse during the Byzantine era and attracted little attention until archaeologists began their digs in 1931.

On the west side are the ruins of the **Tholos**, **Bouleuterion** and **Metroon**. Arcades – the **stoa of Zeus**, the **Royal Stoa** and the **Stoa Poikile** – encircled the area, which was traversed diagonally by the Panatheniac Way, the ceremonial road.

Temple of Hephaistos (Thission).

HISTORICAL AREA OF ATHENS

ⓖⓖ THE THESEION (TEMPLE OF HEPHAISTOS)

A 5th c. BC temple dedicated to Hephaistos and Athena, with reliefs inspired by the feats of the Athenian hero king, Theseus. The view from here is quite inspiring.

ⓖ STOA OF ATTALOS

A two-storey arcade built with funds donated by Attalos II king of Pergamon. Restored by the American School, it is now used as a museum for finds discovered in the Agora.

AGII APOSTOLI

Byzantine church built in the 11th c. over ruins of a 2nd c. AD Roman nymphaion.

AREOS PAGOS

This low hill in front of the Propylaia was the seat of the highest court. It was here that the principle of equality of the accused before the law was established. It was implemented for the first time, according to mythology, in the case of the matricide Orestes, whose acquittal was won through Athena's vote.
It is also famous as the place where, in the 1st c. AD, St. Paul preached the tenets of the new religion, Christianity, without however making much of an impression on the Athenians.

❹ THE KERAMEIKOS
Κεραμεικός / Keramikós

148 Ermou St., tel. (01) 3463552
8 am -2:30 pm, closed Mondays and holidays

Continue walking and leave Adrianou Street take Ermou Street until you reach the Kerameikos, the most important cemetery of the ancient Athenians. It lay outside the Sacred and Dipylon gates in the city walls and was so called because of the potters' workshops found in the vicinity.(Take dotted red route)

Kerameikos

ⓖ POMPEION

The space between the two gates, the two most formal of the ancient city, was where the ritual vessels used in the Eleusinian Mysteries were stored.

DEMOSION SEMA

Where the war heros and benefactores were buried. The digs here revealed wonderful vases, funeral offerings and grave stelae.

THE MUSEUM

Grave stelae and offerings from Mycenaean to Roman times.

SECOND WALK
(GREEN ROUTE ON THE MAP: 3 HOURS)

❺ TEMPLE OF OLYMPIAN ZEUS
Στύλοι Ολυμπίου Διός / Stíli Olympíou Diós

Opposite Lyssikratous St., off Vassilissis Amalias Ave., you'll see the tall columns of the ⓖⓖ **temple of Olympian Zeus**, which was the city's largest sanctuary. According to myth it was founded by **Deucalion**. Work started on the temple in the early 6th c. BC. Then under the Peisistratids, four architects – **Antistates**,

Kaleschros, Antimachides and Porinos — began to build a new temple, a project that was revived in 175 BC with the help of Antiochos IV, whose death put a stop to construction. This enormous temple was finally completed during the reign of **Hadrian**, who inaugurated it in 132 AD. It had 104 Corinthian columns, a length of 110.5 m and a width of 43.70 m. Between 253 and 260 AD its destruction began and by the 15th c. only 21 columns were still standing, given that the Turks were fond of crushing them to make white-wash. Today 16 columns are erect, one fallen, to remind us of its former grandeur.

HADRIAN'S ARCH

Emperor Hadrian passed through this arch which stands in front of the temple of Olympian Zeus, for the inauguration. It was built on the boundaries of the old and new city in the 2nd c. AD. On its west side, facing the old city, there is an inscription which says, "Here is Athens, the old city of Theseus", while on the east side, another inscription tell us, "Here is Hadrian's city, not Theseus'", a reference naturally to the expansion the emperor had initiated. The arch also contained statues of both men on either side.

6 PLAKA
Πλάκα / Pláka

Enter Plaka by going up Lissikratous St. Every summer thousands of visitors make a pilgrimage to the city's best preserved 19th c. neighbourhood, with its beautiful restored mansions and charming narrow streets, its lively tavernas, antique shops and interesting nightlife. It's called Plaka because it is flat, as opposed to the neighbouring district Rizokastro, which was built on the sides of the Acropolis. It used to have lots of small houses and almost as many large mansions with spacious courtyards, cut off from view by high walls. According to another version, the area took its name from a large plaque found in Adrianou St. The name initially referred only to one part of the NE tip of the Acropolis, but has later come to mean all the small neighbourhoods that composed old Athens.

LYSICRATES MONUMENT (THE LIGHTHOUSE OF DIOGENES)

This elegant circular edifice stands at the end of Lyssikratous St. Built in 335-334 BC, it formed the base of a bronze tripod which the donor had won as a prize.

THE ANAFIOTIKA

An oasis of peace in the heart of the metropolis, this little quarter of tiny white houses perched just under the Acropolis took its name from the residents of Anafi, a speck in the Aegean, who settled here in the 19th c. Minute squares and picturesque lanes, such as Panos, Theorias and Diogenous Sts., so steep they have stairs, make for a pleasant stroll. You could stop for a meal at **Platanos**, an old-fashioned taverna, which we find to be one of the area's best.

AGIOS NIKOLAOS RANGAVAS

This church on the corner of Stratonos and Prytaniou Sts. was built in the 11th c. by the Rangave family, which gave Byzantium many emperors and patriarchs.

HISTORICAL AREA OF ATHENS

CHURCH OF THE METAMORPHOSIS

This 14th c. church on the corner of Theorias and Klepsydras Sts. is unusual. In its south side, a grotto has been hollowed out of the face of the Acropolis and transformed into a chapel dedicated to St. Paraskevi. Inside you'll notice an Early Christian column capital near the altar.

Tower of the Winds

KANELLOPOULOS MUSEUM

At the corner of Theorias and Panos streets
Tel. (01) 3212313

🕒 8 am-2:30 pm, closed Mondays and holidays

A private collection with interesting exhibits spanning the whole gamut of Greek art from 2500 BC to the early 20th c.

TOWER OF THE WINDS (AERIDES)

Proceed from Dioskouron St., to Areos St., which will lead you to the square where this monument is located. It is called the Horologion or **Clock of Andronikos Kyrrhestes**, after the architect from Syros who built it in the 1st c. BC. It served as a waterclock, sundial and weathervane. Its eight sides are orientated to the eight points of the horizon, which correspond to the eight winds whose names and symbols are carved out of the upper portion. From here there is a good view of the back of the Acropolis.

❼ MONASTIRAKI
Μοναστηράκι / Monastiráki

A delightful district in the heart of the historic centre, Monastiraki (named after a large convent that disappeared a century ago) is a continuation of Plaka. Here you'll find pedestrian streets, old houses, charming little tavernas, cafes and bars. Walk down Adrianou St., which fills up on Sundays with bazaar stalls. For a pause, try the very "in" **Kouti** restaurant, where you can have a bite while gazing at the Acropolis.

Monastiraki, shops

🛍 GIOUSOUROUM

Athens' famous flea market on Abyssinias Square, where Athenians and tourists alike search for lost treasures concealed amongst the flotsam and jetsam of the past and more modern shops. Giousouroum was originally the surname of many of the Jewish junk/antiques dealers in the neighbourhood and there are still a good number of shops with interesting antiques in this area. The **Kafe Abyssinia** on the square is a popular hang-out, a place where a meal can turn into a party.

MONASTIRAKI MARKET

On and around Ifaistou St., you'll discover a host of small funky shops selling everything from folk art to shoes, sandals, old maps, records, antiques, old gramophones and lamps from bygone ships — among other things.

HADRIAN'S LIBRARY

Built by the emperor in the 2nd c. AD, it was a rectangular structure with five rooms and columns at one end. The middle room had niches in the walls for parchments and manuscripts. The patio possessed a cistern, which has since been covered by various buildings. Two of the arcades that encircled the central court were decorated with podiums, which are still intact. The archaeological site is fenced off, so you'll have to be content with admiring it from afar. The Staropazaro mosque, built in 1759, stands alongside the library.

ATHENS AND ENVIRONS

❽ FROM THE CATHEDRAL TO HADRIANS ARCH
Μητρόπολη-Πύλη Αδριανού / Mitrópoli-Píli Adrianoú

Kapnikarea

🟠 THE BYZANTINE CHURCH OF KAPNIKAREA

On an island in the middle of Ermou St., where it is joined by Kalamiotou St., this church dates from the 11th c. and takes its name from Kapnikaris, its founder. It is cruciform in style with a dome supported on four columns. The small narthex, the chapel and the exonarthex with its sharply pointed roofs are later additions.

THE CATHEDRAL (METROPOLIS)

On Mitropoli Square, it was erected between 1839 and 1862 and is where the official religious ceremonies of Athens take place.

🟠 CHURCH OF AGIOS ELEFTHERIOS (PANAGIA GORGOEPIKOOS)

Also known as the little metropolis, this exquisite church stands in the shadow of the cathedral. It was built in the 11th or 12 c. in marble rather than traditional Byzantine brick, using materials – plain and relief plaques – from ancient and early Christian monuments. The frieze over its entrance represents a seasonal calendar and once adorned a 4th c. BC edifice.

THE RUSSIAN CHURCH

From Adrianou St., take Kekropos St., to Filellinon St. This large church of the Sotiras Lykomedes is octagonal in style and dates from the 11th c. It was bought by the Russians in the mid 19th c. and has a marvellous choir, well worth hearing on any religious holiday.

THIRD WALK
(PURPLE ROUTE ON THE MAP: 30 MINUTES)

❾ PSYRRI
Ψυρρή / Psirrí

We suggest you take this stroll in the evening and combine it with a meal in one of Best's tavernas either here or in nearby Plaka.

This large working-class neighbourhood began to take shape around 1840; its first residents were veterans of the 1821 War of Independence and people from outlying districts. But as you may gather from its name (which means louse), it was not renowned for either its cleanliness or its high standard of living. From the end of King Otto's reign up to the late 19th c., it was the lair of a band of rather picturesque thugs who were adept at picking fights and had a weakness for robberies, extortion and other forms of intimidation, until they were removed from the scene by the harsh Colonel Baraiktaris, who had his own novel methods. Today many of the buildings of this once sleazy neighbourhood have been restored and converted into attractive eateries, nightclubs and theatres bordering pedestrian streets. You can enter Psyrri from Ermou St., turning right at Asomaton Square, where Lepeniotou St., will take you to Taki St., which ends at Iroon Square. From there take Agion Anargyron St., onto Sapphous, turn right at Tombazi and then return to Ermou via Agion Asomaton St., This is an area popular with Athenians but which has not yet become touristy.

Psyrri

Contemporary Athens

WHY AMONG THE BEST

Because this includes the superlative Archaeological Museum and all the city's other notable museums, which are among Greece's finest. And because many beautiful neo-classical buildings and a good number of Athens' best hotels, restaurants, cafes and nightclubs are to be found here.

ATHENS AND ENVIRONS

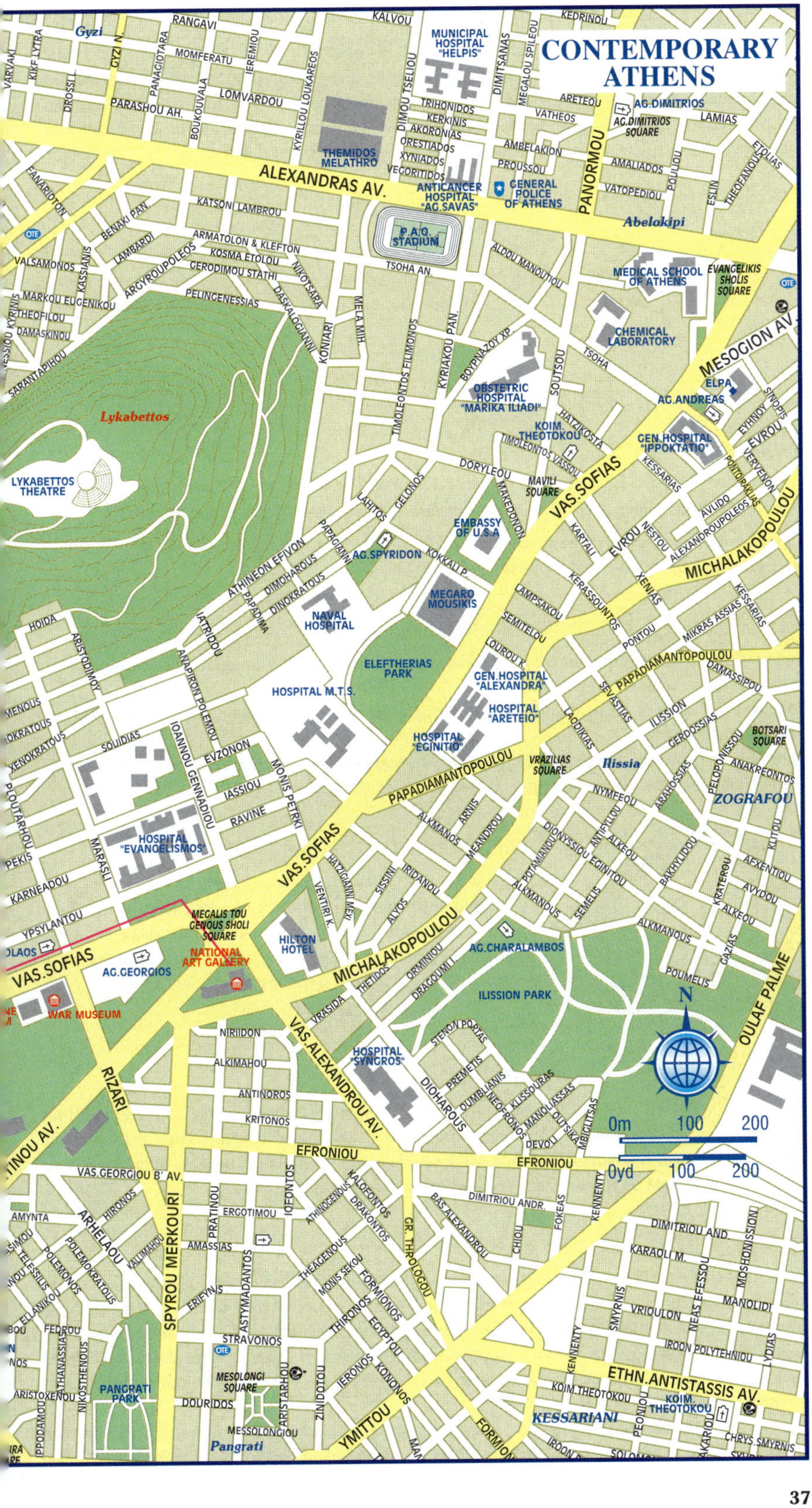
CONTEMPORARY ATHENS
Gyzi
RANGAVI
KALVOU
MUNICIPAL HOSPITAL "HELPIS"
KEDRINOU
MOMFERATU
LOMVARDOU
PARASHOU AH.
THEMIDOS MELATHRO
TRIHONIDOS
KERKINIS
AKORONIAS
ORESTIADOS
XYNIADOS
VEGORITIDOS
ARETEOU
AG.DIMITRIOS
AG.DIMITRIOS SQUARE
LAMIAS
VATHEOS
AMBELAKION
PROUSSOU
AMALIADOS
VATOPEDIOU
PANORMOU
ALEXANDRAS AV.
ANTICANCER HOSPITAL "AG.SAVAS"
GENERAL POLICE OF ATHENS
Abelokipi
KATSONI LAMBROU
P.A.O. STADIUM
ARMATOLON & KLEFTON
KOSMA ETOLOU
GERODIMOU STATHI
TSOHA AN.
ALDOU MANOUTIOU
MEDICAL SCHOOL OF ATHENS
EVANGELIKIS SHOLIS SQUARE
VALSAMONOS
MARKOU EUGENIKOU
THEOFILOU
DAMASKINOU
PELINGENESSIAS
CHEMICAL LABORATORY
MESOGION AV.
ELPA
AG.ANDREAS
Lykabettos
LYKABETTOS THEATRE
OBSTETRIC HOSPITAL "MARIKA ILIADI"
KOIM. THEOTOKOU
GEN.HOSPITAL "IPPOKTATIO"
DORYLEOU
MAVILI SQUARE
VAS.SOFIAS
EMBASSY OF U.S.A
AG.SPYRIDON
MEGARO MOUSIKIS
MICHALAKOPOULOU
NAVAL HOSPITAL
ELEFTHERIAS PARK
HOSPITAL M.T.S.
GEN.HOSPITAL "ALEXANDRA"
HOSPITAL "ARETEIO"
HOSPITAL "EGINITIO"
PAPADIAMANTOPOULOU
VRAZILIAS SQUARE
Ilissia
BOTSARI SQUARE
ZOGRAFOU
HOSPITAL "EVANGELISMOS"
MEGALIS TOU GENOUS SHOLI SQUARE
NATIONAL ART GALLERY
HILTON HOTEL
AG.GEORGIOS
WAR MUSEUM
AG.CHARALAMBOS
ILISSION PARK
OULAF PALME
HOSPITAL "SYNGROS"
VAS.ALEXANDROU AV.
RIZARI
EFRONIOU
0m 100 200
0yd 100 200
N
VAS.GEORGIOU B' AV.
SPYROU MERKOURI
DIMITRIOU ANDR.
KARAOLI M.
MANOLIDI
VRIOULON
IROON POLYTEHNIOU
ETHN.ANTISTASSIS AV.
KOIM.THEOTOKOU
KESSARIANI
STRAVONOS
MESOLONGI SQUARE
PANCRATI PARK
DOURIDOS
MESSOLONGIOU
Pangrati
YMITTOU
FORMIONOS

ATHENS AND ENVIRONS

BEST's OPINION

The modern city of Athens may appear vast, but its sights, apart from the Archaeological Museum, are all concentrated near the centre at short distances from one another. We suggest you take a taxi from your hotel as far as the museum and, once you've visited it, ask another taxi to take you to Klafthmonos Sq. From there you can easily walk to all the other landmarks, following the route outlined in red on the map.

BEST SIGHTS: STEP BY STEP

❶ ARCHAEOLOGICAL MUSEUM
Αρχαιολογικό Μουσείο / Archeologhikó Moussío

44 Patission St.
Tel: (01) 8217717, 8217724

Summer: Monday 12:30 am-7 pm, Tuesday-Friday 8 am-7 pm, Saturday & Sunday 8 am-3 pm, Winter: Monday 10:30 am-5 pm, Tuesday-Sunday 8 am-2:30 pm; closed on holidays

Housed in a neo-classical building designed by the 19th c. Bavarian architects, Lanke and Ziller. The exhibits trace ancient Greek history from prehistoric to Roman times.

ⓖ NEOLITHIC AND CYCLADIC ART (7000-1100 BC)

Prehistoric Greece in the Neolithic era and the early and middle Bronze Age is represented by finds displayed in the first three rooms on the ground floor.
The north hall contains examples of Neolithic workmanship, such as the terracotta figurines and **gold jewellery** from Limnos.
The Cycladic rooms are very impressive, with such statuettes as the ⓖ **marble figure of a naked woman**, the ⓖ **Flute**, - and the ⓖ **Lyre - player**, and the **frescoes** from Milos.

ⓖⓖ MYCENAEAN ART (1900-1100 BC)

The central hall is filled with exquisite finds, mostly from tombs, including ⓖⓖ **the gold death masks**, ⓖ **jewellery**, ⓖ **weapons** and ⓖⓖ **pottery**. Be sure to seek out the wonderful ⓖⓖ **rhyton in the shape of a bull's head**, which is contemporary with the one found in the small palace at Knossos, and which you can see at the Museum of Heraklio.

ⓖⓖ GEOMETRIC AND ARCHAIC ART (7TH C.-450 BC)

These finds include the astonishing larger-than-life marble ⓖⓖⓖ **Kouroi**, from Attica, Milos, Megara and Boeotia, the ⓖⓖ **statues of seated women**, the ⓖⓖ **standing female statue of Nikandra** from Naxos, which was discovered on Delos, ⓖ **remains of the frieze from the temple of Aphaia on Aigina** and ⓖⓖ **grave stelae with relief sculptures**.

ⓖⓖⓖ SCULPTURES FROM THE CLASSICAL ERA (5TH-4TH C. BC)

Room 15 is where you'll find two of the most outstanding sculptures in the museum's collection: the extraordinary bronze statue of ⓖⓖⓖ **Poseidon of Artemesion** and the ⓖⓖ **relief from Eleusis** with the figures of **Demeter, Persephone and Triptolemos**. The adjoining halls contain 5th c. BC grave stelae from Attica, such as of ⓖⓖⓖ **Aegesos**, the ⓖ **friezes from the Argive Heraion**, the ⓖ **head of Hera** and the ⓖ **sculpted base of the statue of Nemesis** from Rhamnous. To the west are some smaller rooms with **copies** of works by artists of the Classical period.
The main hall, the museum's central axis, has reproduced an open-air **ancient shrine with its altar and votive offerings**. In room 21 you'll see the ⓖ **Hermes of Andros**, a copy of the ⓖⓖ **Diadoumenos** by

CONTEMPORARY ATHENS

Polykleitos, the 🌀🌀 **bronze galloping horse** from Artemesion and two 🌀 **statues of the Herakleiotisses**. Room 22 contains the famous 🌀🌀 **pediments from the temple of Asklepios** at Epidaurus. The three small rooms that follow are given over to 🌀 **inscriptions** and 🌀 **commemorative sculptures**, while the two adjoining larger halls contain 🌀 **Attic funeral stelae** of the 4th c. BC. In Room 28 look for the 🌀🌀 **relief grave stele of Aristonautis** and the 🌀🌀 **stele with the horse and Aithiopa**. The bronze statue of the 🌀🌀🌀 **youth from Antikythera** is a true masterpiece, and the 🌀 **sculptures by Scopas** from the **temple of Alea Athena** at Tegea and the 🌀🌀 **head of Hygeia** are also exceptional. The 4th c. BC bronze statue of 🌀🌀 **Paris** is possibly the work of Euphranoros. In the next hall, particularly noteworthy are the statue of 🌀 **Themis** from Rhamnous, the 🌀 **relief statue bases** from Mantineia and the 🌀 **sculptures** from Lykosoura.

Bronze galloping horse from Artemesion.

🌀 3RD C. BC-LATE ANTIQUITY

The most interesting works of this period are in room 30: the marble statue of 🌀 **Poseidon from Milos**, three bronze heads, the 🌀 **marble statue of Chairestrates** (3rd c. BC) and the one of **Aphrodite with Pan and Eros**.

🌀 THE KARAPANOS COLLECTION

Located in the east wing, this collection has 🌀 **finds from the oracle at Dodona** and three rooms with 🌀 **Roman sculptures** and 🌀 **Egyptian works**.

THE GARDEN

Relief grave stelae and a remarkable 🌀 **mosaic with the head of Medusa**, from Piraeus.

🌀🌀🌀 1ST FLOOR

Don't miss the wonderful 🌀🌀🌀 **frescoes** from Thera, such as **"Spring"** and the **"Young Boxers"**, or the museum's unique 🌀🌀 **collection of vases** from every period.

Poseidon of Artemesion.

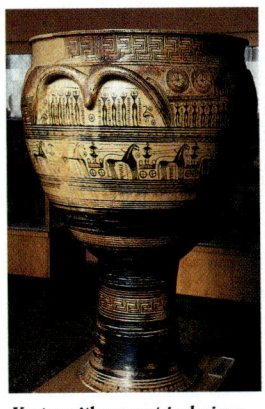

Krater with geometric designs.

Fresco from Thera.

39

ATHENS AND ENVIRONS

❷ OTHER MUSEUMS AND SIGHTS
(Red Route on the map: 1 hour plus museum time)

Starting from Klafthmonos Square and following the red route marked on the map, you will see the rest of Athens' better museums, neo-classical buildings, Byzantine churches, the Parliament, the National Gardens and Kolonaki.

◎ AGII THEODORI

The church was most probably built in the late 11th c., on a site consecrated in the 9th; its outer walls are decorated with pseudo-cufic brickwork (inspired by Arab designs).

Univercity

◎ ◎ THE ACADEMY, UNIVERSITY AND NATIONAL LIBRARY

Three monuments from the early years of neo-classicism, built to plans of the Danish architect, Theophilos Hansen. The foundations for the first were laid in 1859, for the second in 1839, while the third was constructed between 1887 and 1902.

◎ THE OPHTHALMIATREIO (EYE HOSPITAL)

Occupying an impressive neo-classical structure, with a wrought-iron gate containing intertwined crosses.

◎ ILIOU MELATHRON

12 Panepistimiou St. , tel. (01) 3643774
⊙ Summer: 8:30 am-14:45 pm, winter: 8 am-2:20 pm, closed Mondays and holidays

This unusual building, on the corner of Amerikis St., with its exquisitely painted facade and arcades, was built by Ernst Ziller in 1879-81. The former home of the German archaeologist Heinrich Schliemann and for fifty years the headquarters of the Supreme Court (Areos Pagos), it is now the Numismatic Museum.

Tomb of the Unknown Soldier

SYNTAGMA (CONSTITUTION SQUARE)

At Christmas this square boasts the tallest (artificial) tree in Europe. You can watch the changing of the kilted Evzone guard at the Tomb of the Unknown Soldier, inscribed with words from Pericles' Funeral Oration, every hour or two.

◎ ◎ GRANDE BRETAGNE HOTEL

A superb architectural synthesis of neo-classical and Renaissance styles. The hotel, to which an additional five floors were added after World War II, is one of the city's oldest; it has had a fascinating history and a long list of distinguished guests.

Grande Bretagne Hotel

CONTEMPORARY ATHENS

🌀 PARLIAMENT HOUSE

The royal palace built for King Otto between 1836 and 1842 by the Bavarian architect Goertner has housed the Greek parliament since 1933.

THE ZAPPEION-NATIONAL GARDENS

If you wish to walk through the National Gardens, follow Vasilissis Amalias Ave. dotted red route. If not continue on Vasilissis Sophias Ave. and skip the detour.

Parliament House

You can enter the park from Vasilissis Olgas Av., which is dominated by the Zappeion a large neo-classical building, given to the state by Evangelos Zappas for use as a conference and exhibition centre. The former palace's grounds, a legacy of Otto's wife, Queen Amalia, has a great diversity of trees and ponds, green areas and pavillions, and is a lovely refuge from the city's bustle. Stroll along its shaded paths, or sip an iced coffee in its cafe. Follow the signs which will lead you out to the tree-lined Irodou Attikou St., where some of Athens' most expensive and most elegant real estate is located. Opposite you, are the 🌀 **Megaro Maximou**, built in 1924 by Anastasios Helmis for the politician, economist and former prime minister Maximos, and the 🌀 **Proedriko Megaro**, another royal palace, designed in 1890 by Ernst Ziller. The former now houses the prime minister's offices, the latter those of the president of Greece. Return to Vassilissis Sophias Ave. to continue your tour.

🌀🌀 BENAKI MUSEUM

1 Koumbari St. and Vasilissis Sophias Ave.
Tel: (01) 3611617

🕐 *9 am-3 pm. At the time of writing, closed for renovation, scheduled to reopen in May 2000.*

A gift of philanthropist Antonis Benakis, who donated to the state his father Emmanouil's neo-classical mansion and extensive collection of Greek art from prehistoric times on, folk art, costumes, pottery, embroideries, Byzantine and post-Byzantine icons, manuscripts and treasures, as well as objects and documents related to the 1821 War. Also of interest are the collections of 18th c. paintings and engravings, and exhibits of Coptic, Islamic, Turkish and Chinese art. One room also contains the papers of Eleftherios Venizelos.

🌀 KOLONAKI SQUARE

Continuing along Koumbari St., you'll come to the square at the heart of the city's most fashionable district, where some of the priciest boutiques and trendiest cafes and restaurants are located, attracting big names and big money as well as those aspiring to join them. The square's usually crowded cafes are popular with successful artists, models, designers, actors, TV personalities and politicians. This was where the poet Varnalis, the artist Tsarouchis and the composer Hatzidakis, along with other important members of the post-war intelligentsia, used to meet. Return to Vassilissis Sophias Ave. via Neofytou Douka St. in order to continue your cultural ramblings.

🌀🌀 GOULANDRIS MUSEUM OF CYCLADIC AND ANCIENT GREEK ART

4 Neofytou Douka St.
Tel. (01) 7228321-2, fax 7239382

🕐 *10 am-4 pm, Saturdays 10 am-3 pm, closed Tuesdays and Sundays*

Founded in 1986, with the aim of furthering the study and appreciation of early Aegean culture and ancient

41

ATHENS AND ENVIRONS

Greek art generally. The museum's Cycladic collection numbers 350 pieces, including ⓖ **marble sculptures** and ⓖ **vases, pottery,** ⓖ **metal tools and weapons** from the Early Cycladic civilization (3200-2000 BC). The collection of ancient Greek art contains works dating from the 2nd millennium BC up through the 4th c. AD, including ⓖ **ceramics**, ⓖⓖ **sculpture**, ⓖ **metal objects**, ⓖ **jewellery, glass,** ⓖ **terra cotta**, ⓖ **coins**, and a very interesting group of ⓖ **bronze objects** from the 6th c. BC to the time of the Romans. The museum recently expanded into the ⓖⓖ **Stathatos mansion**, another stunning 19th c. building designed by Ziller, with which it is linked via an open-air/glass-roofed corridor. The main entrance to the new wing is on the corner of Vasilissis Sophias Ave. and Irodotou St.. On exhibit here is the ⓖ **Athens Academy's collection**

Stathatos Mansion.

of ancient Greek art and **copies** of Classical Greek **furniture**. The museum also hosts temporary exhibits of variable duration.

ⓖⓖ BYZANTINE MUSEUM

22 Vasilissis Sophias Ave.
Tel. (01) 7231570, 7211027, 7232178
ⓒ *8 am-2:30 pm, closed Mondays and holidays**

Founded in 1914. Housed in a neo-classical mansion constructed like a Florentine palazzo, it contains works of **architecture, sculpture, painting** and **miniatures** from the **Early Christian, Byzantine** and **post-Byzantine eras**. Sculpture from the first two periods are exhibited in the courtyard.

The three rooms on the ground floor have been arranged to resemble churches of the three styles. Thus, there is a ⓖ **three-aisled Early Christian basilica**, a ⓖ **middle Byzantine cross-in-square church with a dome**, and a simple ⓖ **post-Byzantine chapel**. They are decorated with the corresponding sculptures or frescoes, wood carvings and sacramental vessels. On the upper floor you will see ⓖ **icons from the 12th to 16th c.**, the most important being the carved, ⓖⓖ **double faced icon of St. George**, the mosaic icon of the Virgin called the ⓖⓖ **Visitation** and the ⓖ **icon of the Archangel Michael**, painted in the Constantinople style. Also on exhibit are ⓖ **illuminated manuscripts**, ⓖ **frescoes, metalwork** and ⓖ **miniatures, weavings** and **vestments**. The left wing contains icons of the same subject in many different iconographical types, ⓖ **16th c. icons**, ⓖ **naif icons** and ⓖ **Russian devotional paintings**.

42

CONTEMPORARY ATHENS

WAR MUSEUM

Vasilissis Sophias Ave. and Rizari St.
Tel. (01) 7239560

☉ *Tuesdays-Fridays 9 am-2 pm, Saturdays and Sundays 9:30 am-2 pm, closed Mondays and holidays**

Exhibits on Greek military history, such as grave stelae, ☉ **relief plaques from frizes**, historical and **military relics, weapons, uniforms, medals, flags, paintings and sculptures**. See the ☉ **Petros Saroglou weapon collection** and the wonderful ☉ **map collection**.

☉☉ NATIONAL GALLERY AND ALEXANDROS SOUTSOS MUSEUM

50 Vasileos Konstantinou Ave.
Tel. (01) 7235857

☉ *Mondays-Fridays 9 am-3 pm, Saturdays 10 am-4 pm, closed on holidays**

At the junction of Vasilissis Sophias and Vasileos Konstantinou Ave., by the Hilton. The museum comprises several representative collections of Greek painters from the 18th c. to the present, as well as works of foreign artists from the Renaissance to the 20th c. The collections of Greek works include paintings by ☉ **Lytras**, ☉ **Vryzakis**, ☉ **Ghyzis**, ☉ **Volanakis**, ☉ **Iakovidis**, ☉ **Parthenis**, ☉ **Hatzikyriakos-Ghikas**, ☉ **Moralis**, and others. The European collection, composed mainly of Italian paintings, includes works by ☉ **Brueghel the Younger**, ☉ **Veneziano, di Pietro,** ☉☉ **Giordano,** ☉☉ **Caravaggio,** ☉ **Jordaens,** ☉ **Tiepolo,** ☉☉ **Delacroix** and ☉ **La Tour**. Don't miss the four canvases by ☉☉☉ **Dominikos Theotokopoulos**, otherwise known as **El Greco**, and the drawing and engraving collections, from **Durer to Picasso**. The museum also hosts major temporary exhibitions from all over the world.

This marks the end of your cultural tour — which we really do not expect you to complete in one day. It is rather a brief overview of just some of the city's modern sights and museums.

FREE TIME

☉ LYKABETTOS HILL

Take the cable car from Kolonaki up to the top of Lykabettos, the "hill of the wolves", at an altitude of 277 m. There you'll see the church of Agios Georgios and enjoy a splendid view of the asphalt jungle while sipping some refreshment at the cafe. Hardy souls might prefer to walk up (or down) the path.

FESTIVALS AND CULTURAL EVENTS

☉☉ HEROD ATTICUS THEATRE (THE HERODIO)

Dionysiou Areopagitou St., tel. (01) 3231291
Programmes and tickets for the Athens Summer Festival can be obtained at the theatre box office or the Festival Offices at 4 Stadiou St. (in the arcade). The events — dance, opera, concerts, recitals and drama performed by well known Greek and foreign troupes, orchestras and musicians — run from late June to late September (and are rarely rained out). This Roman theatre has hosted such stars as Vladimir Ashkenazy, Margot Fonteyn and Rudolph Nureyev, Maria Callas, ballet companies from Covent Garden to Twyla Tharp and Pina Bausch, and some of the world's finest orchestras. If you can't manage a performance of ancient comedy or tragedy at Epidaurus, try at least to catch one here.

The Alvin Ailey Dance Company.

ATHENS AND ENVIRONS

ⓢ ⓢ ATHENS CONCERT HALL (MEGARO MOUSIKIS)

Vasilissis Sophias Ave. and 115 Kokkali St.
Tel. (01) 7282722, fax 7290174

Not too far from the centre of town, the Athens Concert Hall boasts state-of-the-art technology and acoustics. It was designed by a consortium of foreign and Greek consultants to correspond to the stringent demands of contemporary audiences and performers and can be considered one of the finest in the world. Apart from the main hall, Filon tis Mousikis (Friends of Music), which seats an audience of 2,000, it contains a smaller hall seating 500, a music library, recording studios, a restaurant and a foyer in which exhibitions of various kinds are held. It also houses an ultramodern conference centre on a par with the best. The "Megaro" schedules concerts of all kinds (from classical music of all periods to jazz, folk and even tango) performed by world class soloists, groups and orchestras, operas and ballet companies throughout the year, except in summer. All of its spaces are accessible to wheel-chairs.

ⓢ SOUND & LIGHT

Tel. (01) 3226442

This spectacle may be viewed from the Pnyx on Philopappos Hill opposite the Acropolis. It utilizes impressive lighting of the ancient buildings to emphasize the high points in the history of Athens in English, French and German, a performance which lasts 45 min. The events will be radically revised in the year 2000.

OPEN-AIR CINEMAS

One of the great pleasures of a Greek summer evening is watching a film in one of the country's open-air cinemas. In Athens alone there are dozens, several together in some neighbourhoods, at least one in others. Many of them possess bars and little tables, where you can have a drink and a snack in the interval. You can even smoke, if you have the habit.

LYKABETTOS FESTIVAL

Lykabettos Hill, tel. (01) 3271154

The theatre here is the scene of many, usually pop, concerts with famous Greek and international performers, and a few plays. Every summer, the events start in June and continue into September, attracting tourists and locals alike.

PETRA THEATRE

The old quarry at the end of Petroupoleos St.
Tel. (01) 5012402, 5055390

An impressive open-air theatre built into the cavity of an old quarry, it was opened in 1982 when Melina Mercouri was minister of Culture. Since then it has hosted adventurous classical and pop concerts, ballet and theatre performances. Leading personalities and artists, such as the Bolshoi ballet, have appeared on the stage of this newish theatre.

PLAKENTIAS FESTIVAL

4 Georgiou Athanasiadi St., Pendeli
Tel. (01) 8042575, 8040000

Built in the 19th c. by the architect Kleanthis for the mysterious Duchess of Plaisance (Plakentias), the setting of this festival is a neo-Gothic "castle". Every July and August, it hosts concerts ranging from the pre-Baroque to the late 20th c., mostly performed by Greek artists. In the past, composers Theodorakis and Hatzidakis, the two giants of Greek popular music, appeared here.

ATHENS ENVIRONS

WHY AMONG THE BEST

Because of the impressive ruins of the temple of Poseidon at Sounion, the nightlife, the beaches and the splendid hotels at Vouliagmeni. And because of the wonderful drive along the coast between Athens and cape Sounion, the national park on Mt Parnis (Parnitha) and the beautiful old monasteries of Kessariani and Dafni.

ATHENS AND ENVIRONS

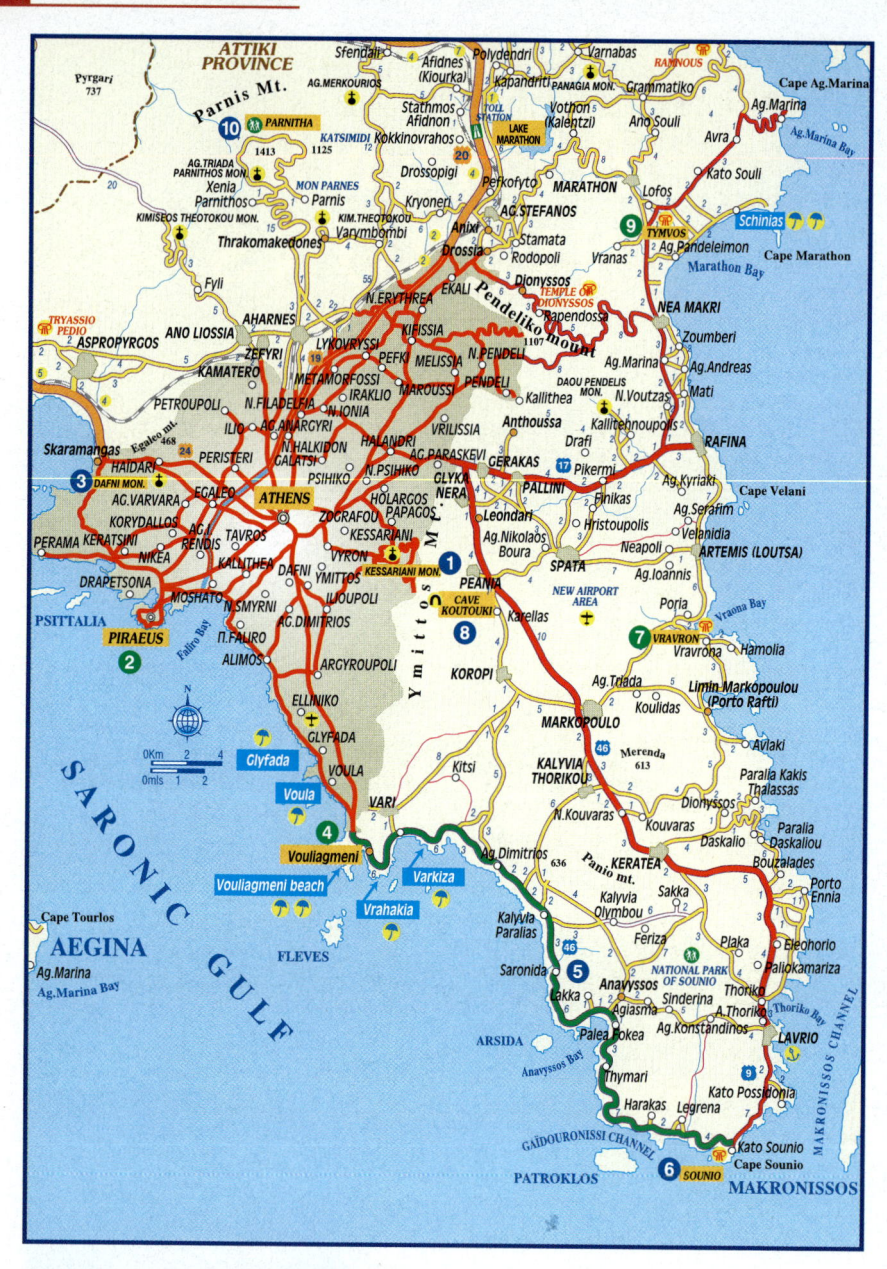

BEST's OPINION

For this excursion, if you don't have your own transport, you can join one of the organized tours offered by various travel agents. If your time is limited and you have no special interest in archaeology, then you need to do no more than take the drive between Vouliagmeni and Sounion, which is the most exciting in this region, preferably in the late afternoon.

ATHENS ENVIRONS

BEST SIGHTS: STEP BY STEP

❶ KAISARIANI MONASTERY
Μονή Καισαριανής / Moní Kessarianís

Tel. (01) 7236619

🕒 *8:30 am-3:30 pm*

Built in the 11th c. near the ruins of a temple of Aphrodite, amidst thick vegetation and abundant springs, this is one of the most beautiful spots on Mt Hymettus. The monastery is dedicated to the Eisodia tis Theotokou (Presentation of the Virgin Mary).
Its *katholikon* (main church) is cruciform, with a dome dating back to the 10th c. The narthex contains impressive **frescoes** by Ioannis Hypatiou from the Peloponnese, while the rest of the church is covered with frescoes of the **Cretan School**. The monastery ceased functioning in 1850 and became a popular spot for summer outings until the late 19th c. It was restored recently. The water from its spring spouts from a marble fountain in the shape of a ram's head. If you like walking, extend your visit to the half-ruined **Asteri monastery**, altitude 545 m, by following the road that leads to the top of the mountain.

❷ PIRAEUS
Πειραιάς / Pireás

Greece's largest harbour, Piraeus is the country's third largest city, and the port of Athens, with which it has by now merged.
At **Zea Marina** or **Passalimani** (the Pasha's harbour), the bay between Kastella and Freattyda, you can see some of the world's largest and most luxurious yachts.
Kastella is the most charming of Piraeus's neighbourhoods, built on a steep hill overlooking **Mikrolimano** (formerly Tourkolimano), where you can eat

Mikrolimano

fresh fish or sip a cool drink with a **view** of the marina. If you have time, take a look at the foundations, near Agios Nikolaos, of one of the ancient boathouses *(neoria)* that used to line the three harbours of Piraeus, and then visit the city's two museums, the **Naval Museum** and the **Archaeological Museum** next to the remnants of the **ancient theatre of Zea**.

❸ DAFNI MONASTERY
Μονή Δαφνίου / Moní Dafníou

Tel. (01) 5811558

🕒 *8:30 am-3 pm*

Founded in the late 5th c., it was destroyed and then rebuilt in the 11th c. Its Byzantine *katholikon*, dedicated to the Assumption of the Virgin, is decorated with exceptionally fine **mosaics**. The crenellated **walls**, ramparts and towers that surround it were erected in the 6th c. by the emperor Justinian. The site was originally occupied by a temple of Apollo, which Alaric's Goths vandalized in AD. 395. The monastery declined during the Ottoman occupation when it suffered considerable damage. It was occupied by Cistercian monks, a branch of the

47

ATHENS AND ENVIRONS

Benedictine order, for more than two hundred years. At other stages in its history, it has served as a police station, an isolation ward for cholera victims, and a psychiatric hospital. It was restored in 1893 and remains one of the finest examples of Byzantine architecture.

❹ VOULIAGMENI
Βουλιαγμένη / Vouliagméni

Sandy beaches, where beach-parties are sometimes held, waterfront cafes, marinas hosting, superb yachts and a beautiful lake of extraordinary depth and therapeutic properties. You can stay at the Astir chain's marvellous hotels here, along with many of the world's notables. Visit "Laimos" Vouliagmenis, i.e. the "neck" or pine-clad peninsula, where the ruins of a 6th c. BC temple share space with more modern constructions. In summer, Athenian nightlife centres around the neighbouring suburbs of Glyfada, Voula and Varkiza.

❺ FROM VOULIAGMENI TO SOUNION

The coast road passes through **Varkiza**, **Agia Marina**, **Lagonissi**, **Saronida** and **Anavyssos**, pretty seaside resort towns overlooking little coves, islets and varied scenery. Try to take this drive in the early evening, around sunset, when the waters of the Saronic Gulf reflect the changing colours and the mountains turn to a soft shade of violet.

❻ SOUNION
Σούνιο / Soúnio

Tel. (0292) 39363

🕒 *10 am-sunset*

A stronghold of the ancient city-state of Athens, Sounion controlled southern Attica, the silver mines of Lavrion and sea traffic in the vicinity. The ruined 🎧 **temple of Poseidon** is surrounded by a double fortification wall with Doric propylaia (entrances) and porticoes. The first temple was built in 490 BC, only to be demolished by Xerxes. 444 BC seems to have been the year when construction began on the new temple, Doric in style with six columns front and rear, thirteen on the sides, set on a high base surrounded by three flights of steps. Two pairs of columns precede the pronaos and opisthodomos (areas in front and behind the interior or cella). The sekos (inner wall) possessed no internal supports and the architrave projected over part of the outer peristyle, leaving room for a continuous inner frieze lining all four sides of the interior. The frieze bore sculptures in relief of the 🎧 **battle with the Giants**, the 🎧 **exploits of Theseus** and the 🎧 **battle of the Lapiths and Centaurs**. The sanctuary was abandoned in the 1st c. AD. Since then many passersby, including Lord Byron, have scratched their names onto its columns. It was restored to its present form in the early 20th c.

❼ VRAVRONA
Βραυρώνα / Vravróna

Tel. (0299) 27020

🕒 *8 am-2:30 pm, closed on Mondays and holidays**

A medieval watch - tower marks the site of the ancient sanctuary of **Artemis Vravronia**, goddess of childbirth. Beside the ruins of the 5th c. Doric temple, there is a small shrine dedicated to Agamemnon's daughter Iphigeneia, and a cave. The 🎧 **museum** contains many unusual children's toys, because the sanctuary was the site of a festival for young girls.

ATHENS ENVIRONS

⑧ KOUTOUKI CAVE
Σπήλαιο Κουτούκι / Spíleo Koutoúki

Precipitous cave 510 m up the east slope of Mt Hymettus. Discovered by a shepherd looking for a lost goat, it descends to a depth of 38.5 m. Follow the signs at the village of Paiania.
The phantasmagorical cavern, in a natural decorative setting of all manner of columns, stalactites and stalagmites has become even more impressive with the aid of hidden coloured lights and stereophonic Vivaldi.

⑨ MARATHON
Μαραθώνας / Marathónas

Archaeological site, tel. (0294) 55462
Museum, tel. (0294) 55155

☼ *8 am-2:30 pm, closed on Mondays and holidays**

A must for history buffs wishing to see the **tumulus** of the Athenians slain in the battle of Marathon in 490 BC. The funeral mound is 8 m high and 180 m in circumference. The original relief of the **Marathon warrior** is in the Athens Archaeological Museum; the white marble stele you'll see here is a copy. The small **museum**, next to another tumulus where the Plataeans were buried, has finds from the Neolithic to Roman eras.
The artificial **Lake Marathon**, in the wild, thickly wooded hills above, is one of the sources of the Athenian water supply.

⑩ MT PARNIS
Πάρνηθα / Párnitha

Information: Parnitha-Aharnes Forestry Service, tel. (01) 2440003
Ef Zin (Adventure travel agency), tel. (01) 7216285
Trekking Hellas, tel. (01) 3310323-6

Rising to 1,413 m, a mere 40 km from Athens, Parnitha was designated a national park in 1961.
You can approach it easily by a number of paved roads. Attica's last intact forest has an impressive variety of trees and plants, including firs, pines, arbutus, holm oak, holly and more than a thousand other species. It is also a wildlife sanctuary, with deer, foxes and a multitude of other animal species, as well as a variety of birds. Still virtually unexplored despite its proximity to Athens, Parnitha is a beautiful mountain with gorges, running water, thick woods and springs, which promise moments of tranquillity and relief from the hot, noisy city. There are alpine refuges at **Bafi** and **Flambouri**, as well as hiking paths, many of which are in good condition, signposted and well-marked. The mountain also has interesting cliffs for abseiling, as at **Arma**, **Flambouri** and **Megalo Armeni**, not to mention dozens of marvellous picnic spots.
The peaks of **Kyra**, **Lagos**, **Avgo**, **Xerovouni**, **Flambouri** and **Platy Vouno** are all climbable. At Mavrovouni, the hotel **Mont Parnes** with its casino is popular with gamblers.

FREE TIME

ⓖ KIFISSIA-NORTHERN SUBURBS

Kifissia, 15 km from Syntagma Square, is the place to go if you want to shop in designer boutiques, ride in a horse-drawn buggy, dine on international cuisine in a swanky restaurant or take a stroll through tree-lined streets flanked by imposing mansions, some in flamboyant turn-of-the-century style and some modern.

ATHENS AND ENVIRONS

⛳ GLYFADA GOLF COURSE

On Konstantinou Karamanli St. (formerly Pronois), beyond the airport, in Glyfada
Tel. (01) 8946820, 8945727

Covering 600,000 sq. m (150 acres), this 18-hole, 72 par course is 6,500 m long. It was constructed by the National Tourist Organization in 1963 and has 800 members. It is open nearly all year round and is the best maintained golf course in Greece, a bonanza for foreign visitors who may have to wait hours for a chance to play at their own clubs back home. Besides the club house, it has all the other essential auxiliary facilities.

🏖 BEST BEACHES

While Attica's beaches are not the best in Greece, they can be considered among the world's finest in proximity to a national capital.

🏖 GLYFADA - VOULA

Voula

Run by the National Tourist Organization, the entry fee also gives you access to tennis and basketball courts, refreshment stands, restaurants and umbrellas, as well as the sandy beach. It's proximity to Athens guarantees crowds.

🏖🏖 VOULIAGMENI

The "in" beach, where the elite congregate though the Astir Palace Hotel has a rather "chilling" entrance fee. Sandy, shallow, dotted with pedalos and water sports enthusiasts, it is recommended for those who want to cool off while socializing. Tennis, volleyball and basketball courts, a gym, sauna, playgrounds, three bars, a restaurant, waterslide, water-skiing and wind-surfing are all on offer at this and the adjoining beach.

🏖 VRAHAKIA

Between Vouliagmeni and Varkiza, choose your own rock ("Vrahaki" in Greek) above a little cove for a swim in clean water and relative privacy.

🏖 VARKIZA

Sandy beach, also run by the National Tourist Organization, with tennis, volleyball, basketball, playgrounds, a restaurant, waterslide and a school for water-skiing and wind-surfing.

🏖🏖 SCHINIAS

Schinias

Infinitely long beach backed by pinewoods growing down to the sand. The sea is shallow, ideal for kids. You can take shelter under the trees, roam till you find a less crowded patch of sand for a picnic at water's edge, or simply be content eating fish in one of the many beach tavernas.

ATHENS & ENVIRONS

- **BEST HOTELS**
- **BEST RESTAURANTS & TAVERNAS**
- **BEST ENTERTAINMENT**
- **TIPS AND INFORMATION**

ATHENS & ENVIRONS

BEST HOTELS

BEST LOCATION

On your first visit to Athens, a hotel within walking distance of Syntagma (Constitution) Square would probably be the most convenient. But if sightseeing is not your top priority, you might want to combine summery seaside activities with quiet moments at one of the exceptional hotels of the Astir chain at Vouliagmeni. Should you decide to remain in the centre of Athens with your car, make sure your hotel has parking facilities.

PRICES

The hotel prices mentioned below are the official ones set by the National Tourist Organization for double rooms, at low and high season, with breakfast. Since owners are allowed to modify the prices, always try to negotiate them.

CENTRE: SYNTAGMA SQUARE AND PLAKA

✓✓✓ GRANDE BRETAGNE
(Luxury Class)

Syntagma Sq.
Tel. (01) 3330000, 3314444, fax 3228034
Open: All year round

Description: One of the world's most famous hotels. A 19th c. building in traditional British style, it has hosted many major figures of the past two centuries. Its decor, luxurious and grandiose, still evokes a bygone era. It is ideally placed for sightseeing.
Rooms: 394 rooms, with marble bathrooms, telephone, music, TV, A/C and mini bar.
Special features: Restaurant, bar, conference hall. Pets upon request.
Price: 93,000-144,000 drs.
Value for money: ✱
Credit cards: American Express, Visa, Mastercard, Diners

✓✓✓ N.J.V. ATHENS PLAZA
(Luxury Class)

2A Vassileos Georgiou St., Syntagma
Tel. (01) 3255301-9, fax 3235856
Open: All year round

Description: Luxurious public areas decorated with hand-chiselled stonework. Between the Acropolis, the historic/shopping districts of Athens and Kolonaki.
Rooms: 182 rooms with bath, telephone, TV, A/C and mini bar.
Special features: Restaurant, WEB-TV, bar and conference hall. Pets upon request.
Price: 121.000 drs.
Value for money: ✱✱
Credit cards: American Express, Visa, Mastercard, Diners

✓✓ DIVANI PALACE ACROPOLIS
(Luxury Class)

19-25 Parthenonos St.
Tel. (01) 9229650-9, fax 9214993
Open: All year round

ATHENS & ENVIRONS

BEST HOTELS

Description: Situated below the Acropolis. The impressive remains of part of a Themistoclean wall have been cleverly incorporated in a specially constructed area in the hotel basement.
Rooms: 253 rooms with bath, telephone, music, TV, A/C and mini bar.
Special features: Restaurant, bar, pool, conference hall and roof garden.
Price: 97,000-162,000 drs.
Value for money: ✷
Credit cards: All

✓✓ ROYAL OLYMPIC (Luxury Class)
28-32 Diakou St.
Tel. (01) 9226411, 9220185, 9224518, fax 9233317
Open: All year round
Description: Opposite the temple of Olympian Zeus. Built in the 70s but since renovated.
Rooms: 304 rooms with bath, A/C, TV, telephone and mini bar.
Special features: Restaurant, parking, bar, conference hall, pool.
Price: 59,000-76,000 drs.
Value for money: ✷✷
Credit cards: American Express, Visa, Mastercard, Diners

✓✓ ELECTRA PALACE (A Class)
18 Nikodimou St.
Tel. (01) 3241401-7, fax 3241875
Open: All year round
Description: View of the Acropolis, the ancient Agora and Lycabettus Hill from the upper floors.
Rooms: 106 rooms with bath, A/C, TV, telephone and mini bar.
Special features: Restaurant, parking, bar, pool, conference hall and roof garden.

Price: 39,800-48,400 drs.
Value for money: ✷✷
Credit cards: All

✓ ELECTRA (A Class)
5 Ermou St.
Tel. (01) 3223222-6, fax 3220310
Open: All year round
Description: Renovated in 1993. Near Syntagma, with impeccable service.
Rooms: 110 rooms with bath, TV, telephone, A/C and mini bar.
Special features: Restaurant and bar.
Price: 39,800-44,800 drs.
Value for money: ✷✷
Credit cards: All

✓ AMALIA (A Class)
10 Amalias Ave.
Tel. (01) 3238792-9, fax 7290439
Open: All year round
Description: Centrally located, with a view of the National Gardens.
Rooms: 98 rooms with bath, TV, telephone, A/C and mini bar.
Special features: Restaurant, bar, conference hall and roof garden.
Price: 50,600 drs.
Value for money: ✷✷✷
Credit cards: American Express, Visa, Mastercard, Diners

✓ ESPERIA PALACE (A Class)
22 Stadiou St.
Tel. (01) 3238001-9, fax 3238100
Open: All year round
Description: Situated at the very heart of town. Entirely renovated, and with as many conveniences as possible for the guests.

ATHENS & ENVIRONS

BEST HOTELS

Rooms: 185 rooms with A/C, bath, TV and telephone.
Special features: Restaurant, bar and conference room.
Price: 49,500-58.000 drs.
Value for money: ✸✸
Credit cards: All

ATHENS GATE (B Class)

10 Syngrou Ave., Makrygianni
Tel. (01) 9238302-9, 9238781-2, 9237493, fax 3259952
Open: All year round
Description: All the modern amenities, near the centre of town, but traffic noise can be a bother if you leave your window open.
Rooms: 104 rooms with bath, A/C, TV, telephone and mini bar.
Special features: Restaurant, bar, conference hall and roof garden.
Price: 31,000-41,000 drs.
Value for money: ✸
Credit cards: Mastercard, Visa, American Express, Diners

LYCABETTE (C Class)

6 Valaoritou St.
Tel. (01) 3633514-7, fax 3633518
Open: All year round
Description: Centrally located, small, inexpensive and clean.
Rooms: 39 rooms with bath, A/C, TV, telephone and mini bar.
Special features: Pets upon request.
Price: 21,000-25,300 drs.
Value for money: ✸✸✸
Credit cards: All

PLAKA (B Class)

7 Kapnikareas & Mitropoleos Sts.
Tel. (01) 3222096-8, fax 3222412
Open: All year round
Description: In Plaka, good service, clean and quiet.
Rooms: 67 rooms with bath, A/C, TV, telephone and mini bar.
Special features: Restaurant, conference hall, roof garden. Pets upon request.
Price: 16,500-28,000 drs.
Value for money: ✸
Credit cards: All

HERMES (C Class)

19 Apollonos St.
Tel. (01) 3235514-6, fax 3232073
Open: All year round
Description: In Plaka, clean with spacious rooms and well-tended public areas.
Rooms: 45 rooms with bath, A/C, telephone.
Special features: Restaurant, pets upon request.
Price: 21,200-30,000 drs.
Value for money: ✸
Credit cards: American Express, Visa, Mastercard, Diners

ACHILLES (C Class)

21 Lekka St.
Tel. (01) 3233197, 3225826, fax 3222412
Open: All year round
Description: Modern, no-frills hotel, near Syntagma Sq. on a quiet street.
Rooms: 34 rooms with bath, TV, A/C, telephone and mini bar.
Special features: Pets upon request.
Price: 15,000-24,000 drs.
Value for money: ✸
Credit cards: Visa, American Express, Mastercard

LESS CENTRAL HOTELS

✓✓ ATHENS HILTON (Luxury Class)

46 Vasilissis Sophias Av.
Tel. (01) 7250301, 7281000, fax 7253110
Open: All year round
Description: Athens' first international chain hotel, the Hilton opened up new prospects for Greek tourism. Cosmopolitan atmosphere. Views of the Acropolis and Lykabettus Hill from its balconies.
Rooms: 453 rooms with bath, A/C, TV, telephone and mini bar.
Special features: Restaurants, parking, bars, pool, conference hall, roof garden. Pets upon request.

ATHENS & ENVIRONS

BEST HOTELS

Price: 136,200-163,400 drs.
Value for money: ✱
Credit cards: All

✓✓ SAINT GEORGE LYCABETTUS
(Luxury Class)

2 Kleomenous St., Dexameni Sq.
Tel. (01) 7290711-18, fax 7247610
Open: All year round

Description: On Lykabettus Hill with the best panoramic view of Athens as far as the sea and beyond.
Rooms: 167 rooms with bath, A/C, TV, telephone and mini bar.
Special features: Restaurant, parking, bar, conference hall, pool, roof garden.
Price: 56,300-94,300 drs.
Value for money: ✱✱
Credit cards: All

✓✓ ANDROMEDA (A Class)

22 Timoleontos Vassou St.
Tel. (01) 6466362, 6437302-4, fax 6466361
Open: All year round
Description: Small, elegant hotel behind Mavili Sq. (near the US embassy), it is ranked among the 200 best small hotels in the world. The decor combines contemporary objects with antiques in superlative taste.

Rooms: 30 rooms, with bath, A/C, TV, telephone and mini bar.
Special features: Restaurant, bar and conference hall.
Price: 107,000-127,000 drs.
Value for money: ✱✱✱
Credit cards: All

✓✓ DIVANI CARAVEL
(Luxury Class)

2 Vasileos Alexandrou St.
Tel. (01) 7253725-43, fax 7253770-7236683
Open: All year round

Description: Completely renovated, within walking distance of the shopping and business districts.
Rooms: 471 rooms with bath, TV, A/C, telephone and mini bar.
Special features: Restaurant, parking, bar, pool, conference hall, roof garden.
Price: 102,000-172,000 drs.
Value for money: ✱✱
Credit cards: All

55

ATHENS & ENVIRONS

BEST HOTELS

✓✓ HOLIDAY INN (Luxury Class)
50 Michalakopoulou St.
Tel. (01) 7248322-29, fax 7278600
Open: All year round

Description: Discreetly luxurious, friendly, helpful staff.
Rooms: 188 rooms with bath, A/C, TV and telephone.
Special features: Restaurant, parking, bar, pool, conference hall, roof garden. Pets upon request.
Price: 80,000-110,000 drs.
Value for money: ✱
Credit cards: Visa, Mastercard, American Express, Diners

✓ HERODION (A Class)
4 Rovertou Galli St., Makrygianni
Tel. (01) 9236832-6, fax 9235851
Open: All year round
Description: A pleasant hotel with stone decoration, clean and comfortable. Stunning view of the Acropolis from the terrace. A bit far from the centre but near the entrance to the Acropolis.
Rooms: 90 rooms, with bath, A/C, TV, telephone, mini bar, safe and hair dryer.
Special features: Restaurant, bar, conference hall and roof garden.
Price: 34,700-46,700 drs.
Value for money: ✱✱
Credit cards: All

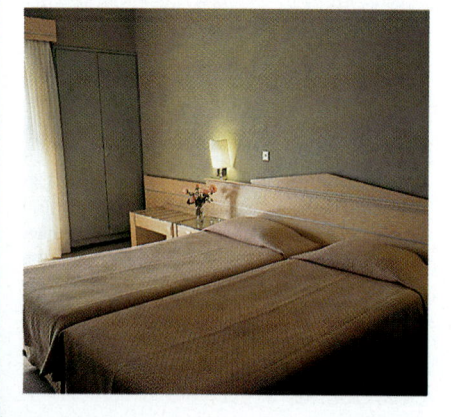

✓ TITANIA (B Class)
52 Panepistimiou St.
Tel. (01) 3300111, fax 3300700
Open: All year round
Description: With luxurious decoration, modern technology and amenities, near the historic and shopping district, but on one of Athens' busiest streets.
Rooms: 398 rooms, with bath, A/C, TV, telephone and mini bar.
Special features: Restaurant, parking, bar, conference hall and excellent roof garden restaurant. Pets upon request.
Price: 31,600-39,000 drs.
Value for money: ✱✱✱
Credit cards: All

✓ PARK (Luxury Class)
10 Alexandras Ave., Pedio tou Areos Park
Tel. (01) 8832711-9, fax 8238420
Open: All year round
Description: Big, modern hotel with a view over the Pedion tou Areos (Mars Field), a lovely green park though far from most sights. Very comfortable.
Rooms: 143 rooms with bath, A/C, telephone, TV and mini bar.

ATHENS & ENVIRONS

BEST HOTELS

Special features: Restaurant, parking, bar, roof garden. Pets upon request.
Price: 59,000-77,000 drs.
Value for money: ✽✽
Credit cards: All

ZAFOLIA (A Class)

87-89 Alexandras Ave.
Tel. (01) 6449012, 6449002, fax 6442042
Open: All year round
Description: Modern hotel with all the expected facilities and good service. Its location is a disadvantage.
Rooms: 191 rooms with bath, telephone, music, TV, A/C and mini bar.
Special features: Restaurant, pool, conference hall, roof garden.
Price: 39,400 drs.
Value for money: ✽✽
Credit cards: All

GOLDEN AGE (A Class)

57 Michalakopoulou St.
Tel. (01) 7240861-9, fax 7213965
Open: All year round
Description: Built in the 70s, attractive decor, warm, hospitable atmosphere. But the location is not a plus.
Rooms: 122 rooms with bath, telephone, TV, A/C and mini bar.
Special features: Restaurant, bar, conference hall.
Price: 36,000-40,000 drs.
Value for money: ✽
Credit cards: All

ATHENIAN INN (C Class)

22 Haritos St., Kolonaki
Tel. (01) 7238097, 7239552, 7218756, fax 7242268
Open: All year round
Description: Small, unpretentious hotel near Kolonaki Sq., and its bars, boites and boutiques.
Rooms: 28 rooms with bath, TV, telephone and mini bar.
Special features: A/C.
Price: 24,800-31,350 drs.
Value for money: ✽
Credit cards: Visa, American Express, Diners

CHRISTINA (B Class)

15 Petmeza & Kallirrois Sts.
Tel. (01) 9215353, fax 9215569
Open: All year round
Description: Built in 1973 and renovated in 1996-97, a good hotel in a less good location.
Rooms: 93 rooms with bath, A/C, telephone.
Special features: Restaurant, and conference hall.
Price: 40,000 drs.
Value for money: ✽
Credit cards: All

ILISSIA (B Class)

25 Michalakopoulou St.
Tel. (01) 7244051-6, fax 7241847
Open: All year round
Description: Modern hotel with all the amenities. Not luxurious but satisfactory.
Rooms: 91 rooms with bath, telephone, TV, A/C and mini bar.
Special features: Bar and conference hall.
Price: 30,500-35,800 drs.
Value for money: ✽
Credit cards: American Express, Visa, Mastercard, Diners

ACROPOLIS VIEW (C Class)

10 Webster St., Philopappou
Tel. (01) 9217303-5, fax 9230705
Open: All year round
Description: Under the Acropolis, in the historic district.
Rooms: 32 rooms with bath, A/C, TV and telephone.
Special features: Roof garden. Pets upon request.
Price: 25,000-37,000 drs.
Value for money: ✽
Credit cards: Visa, Mastercard

ATHENS & ENVIRONS

BEST HOTELS

SYNGROU AVENUE

✓✓✓ ATHENAEUM INTERCONTINENTAL (Luxury Class)

89-93 Syngrou Ave.
Tel. (01) 9206000, fax 9243000
Open: All year round

Description: Exceptionally attractive luxury hotel with exemplary amenities and service, meeting all the demands of both business travellers and vacationers. Only disadvantages its distance from Athens' major sights.
Rooms: 587 rooms with bath, A/C, TV, telephone and mini bar.
Special features: Restaurants, parking, bars, conference hall, pool, roof garden.
Price: 91,400-165,000 drs.
Value for money: ✹✹
Credit cards: American Express, Visa, Mastercard, Diners

✓✓✓ LEDRA MARRIOTT (Luxury Class)

113-115 Syngrou Ave.
Tel. (01) 9347711, fax 9358603
Open: All year round

Description: Exceptional accommodation, sumptuous decor. Too bad the location isn't better.
Rooms: 259 rooms with bath, TV, telephone, A/C and mini bar.
Special features: Wonderful restaurants, parking, bars, conference hall, pool and roof-garden.
Price: 89,000-145,000 drs.
Value for money: ✹✹✹
Credit cards: All

✓✓ ATHENS CHANDRIS (Luxury Class)

385 Syngrou Ave.
Tel. (01) 9408000, fax 9403424
Open: All year round
Description: Good hotel with up-to-date amenities and service. Frequent venue for conferences and special events owing to its range of well-organized spaces. Quite a distance from the major sights.
Rooms: 386 rooms with bath, A/C, TV, telephone and mini bar.
Special features: Restaurant, parking, bar, pool, conference hall and roof garden restaurant in summer.
Price: 100,000-130,000 drs.
Value for money: ✹✹
Credit cards: All

NORTHERN SUBURBS

✓✓ PENTELIKON (Luxury Class)

66 Deligianni St., Kefalari
Tel. (01) 6230650-6, fax 8010314
Open: All year round
Description: Originally a 1920s mansion. Renovated and decorated in English style with antiques, works of art, silver and old chandeliers, it

ATHENS & ENVIRONS

BEST HOTELS

combines a timeless atmosphere with contemporary luxury.
Rooms: 44 rooms with bath, TV, telephone, A/C and mini bar.
Special features: One of Athens' best restaurants, parking, bar, pool, conference hall.
Price: 124,700 drs.
Value for money: ✻
Credit cards: American Express, Visa, Mastercard, Diners

✓✓ THE KEFALARI SUITES
(A Class)

1 Pendelis & Kolokotroni Sts., Kifissia
Tel. (01) 6233333, fax 6233330
Open: All year round

Description: Neo-classical architecture. Each suite has its own decor and colours. Serene atmosphere which takes you back to the 19th century. Small reception area.
Rooms: 12 suites with bath, kitchenette, A/C, telephone, mini bar, veranda, safe, music, tv and internet.
Special features: Breakfast room and jacuzzi.
Price: 850,000-180,000 drs. Without breakfast.
Value for money: ✻
Credit cards: All

PIRAEUS

CAVO D' ORO (B Class)

19 Vasileos Pavlou St., Kastella
Tel. (01) 4113744-5, fax 4122210
Open: All year round
Description: Simple hotel with wonderful sea-view.
Rooms: 74 rooms with bath, A/C, TV in some rooms and telephone.
Special features: Restaurant, bar, conference hall, roof garden. Pets upon request.
Price: 23,000-26.000 drs.

Value for money: ✻
Credit cards: All

CASTELLA (B Class)

75 Vasileos Pavlou St.
Tel. (01) 4114735-37, fax 4175716
Open: All year round

Description: Fully renovated hotel with modern decor and view of Mikrolimano.
Rooms: 32 rooms with bath, A/C, TV, telephone and mini bar.
Special features: Restaurant, bar and roof garden.
Price: 34,500-37,800 drs.
Value for money: ✻
Credit cards: All

MISTRAL (B Class)

105 Vasileos Pavlos St., Kastella
Tel. (01) 4117150-4117675, fax 4122096
Open: All year round

Description: Above Mikrolimano, modern hotel with friendly, polite personnel.
Rooms: 80 rooms with bath, TV, A/C and telephone.
Special features: Restaurant, parking, bar, pool, conference hall and roof garden.
Price: 25,000-29,500 drs.
Value for money: ✻
Credit cards: Visa, Mastercard, American Express

ATHENS & ENVIRONS

BEST HOTELS

SOUTHERN SUBURBS
VOULIAGMENI

✓✓ ASTIR PALACE (Luxury Class)
Vouliagmeni
Tel: (01) 8902000, 8960211, fax 8962579, 8962582
Open: All year round
Description: A very large and luxurious hotel complex amid greenery, with view of the sea. It consists of three hotels, the Aphrodite Astir Palace, Arion Astir Palace and Nafsika Astir Palace.
Rooms: In total 571 rooms with bath, A/C, TV, telephone and mini bar.
Special features: Restaurant, parking, bar, areas for athletics, pools, conference rooms and water sports.
Price: 80,000-120,000 drs.
Value for money: ✻✻
Credit cards: All

✓ ARMONIA (A Class)
1 Armonia St.
Tel: (01) 8963304, 8960105, 8963184, 8960030, fax 8963698
Open: All year round
Description: Modern hotel in the cosmopolitans coastal area of Vouliagmeni with a view over the Saronic Gulf. Many conference rooms with the latest equipment. The hotel organizes many seminars and congresses.
Rooms: 116 rooms, with bath, telephone, music, TV and A/C.
Special features: Restaurant, parking, bar, pool, and conference rooms.
Price: 35,000-58,000 drs.
Value for money: ✻
Credit cards: All

VOULA

✓✓ BLAZER SUITES (A Class)
1 Alkyonidon St., Voula
Tel. (01) 9658801-7, fax 9658808
Open: All year round
Description: A modern hotel complex without flashy decoration, up-to-date on all facilities, lends itself to both vacationing and business visits. Near the sea and the airport.
Rooms: 28 suites with A/C, bath, TV, telephone and wide balconies with seaview.
Special features: Parking, bar, pool, tennis court, water sports and conference room.
Price: 60,000-80,000 drs.
Value for money: ✻✻
Credit cards: All

ALTERNATIVES

RIVA (A Class)
114 Michalakopoulou St., Pangrati,
tel. (01) 7706611-5, fax 7708137
Price: 47,000 drs.

DELICE (A Class)
3 Vassileos Alexandrou & Brassida, Pangrati, tel. (01) 7238311-4, fax 7238311
Price: 22,000-27,500 drs.

ATHENS ACROPOL (A Class)
1 Pireos St., Omonia Square, Athens,
tel. (01) 5231111-18, fax 5231361
Price: 67,000 drs.

LAGONISSI RESORT (Luxury Class)
Lagonissi, tel. (0291) 23911-25
(01) 3229489, 3223111, fax (0291) 24534
Price: 91,000 drs.

EDEN BEACH HOTEL CLUB (A Class)
47th km Athens-Sounio road, Anavyssos,
tel. (0291) 60031-41, fax 60043
Price: 16,000-27,300 drs.

ATHENS & ENVIRONS

BEST RESTAURANTS & TAVERNAS

PRICES
For Athens in particular, the price categories in restaurants are very different from those in the rest of Greece because of the higher standard of living in the capital. Take the following as guidelines for a meal for two: € up to 20,000 drs., €€ 20,000-30,000 drs., and €€€ over 30,000 drs.

HISTORICAL AREA OF ATHENS

✓✓ PIL POUL
51 Apostolou Pavlou and Poulopoulou Sts., Thission Tel. (01) 3423665

The most beautiful terrace in Athens with an unimpeded view of the Acropolis. Impressively converted old mansion. Mediterranean haute cuisine created by chef Servatka. Try the stuffed lamb with feta and hot goat cheese wrapped in prosciutto. Excellent service amidst a luxurious ambiance.
Price: €€€

✓✓ SYMPOSIO
44 Erechthiou St. (opposite Herod Atticus Theatre), tel. (01) 9225321

Exceptional open-air setting in summer, warm, stylish interior in winter, in an old mansion in Makrygianni. Emphasis on seafood and creative Mediterranean cuisine with Italian flavours predominating. Unforgettable carpaccio made from sea bream.
Price: €€€

✓✓ GURU BAR
10 Theatrou Sq., tel. (01) 3246530

An appealing little bar in the heart of town. The loft has velvet sofas and an exotic atmosphere. Genuine Thai dishes. Reservations needed several days in advance.
Price: €€

✓✓ STOUS EPTA ANEMOUS
17 Astingos and 1 Thissiou Sts., Monastiraki, tel. (01) 3240386

Attractively decorated, discreet, refined ambiance. Chef Tselepis makes wonderful original dishes using Mediterranean ingredients with a French touch, like his terrine of roasted vegetables with goat cheese.
Price: €€

✓✓ KITRINO PODILATO
Iera Odos and 116 Keramikou Sts., tel. (01) 3428462

Trendy restaurant in the up and coming Gas Works area. Emphasis on Mediterranean cuisine with some hints of fusion. Try the fish with nettles and mallow or lamb and sliced aubergine.
Price: €€

✓✓ BALTHAZAR
27 Tsoxa St., tel. (01) 6412300

The better for having been renovated. Lively bar. In the restaurant charismatic chef Christoforos Peskias likes to play with "ethnic" ingredients. Baby octopus on a bed of split yellow pea puree and caramelized onions is a favourite.
Price: €€

ATHENS & ENVIRONS

BEST RESTAURANTS & TAVERNAS

✓ KAFE ABYSSINIA
Avyssinia Sq., Monastiraki, tel. (01) 3217047

Tables outdoors and indoors, warm, friendly atmosphere and service. Rebetika (Greek blues) sung by a remarkable female vocalist. You'll love the mussel pilaf and, for a grand finale, try the kaimaki ice cream with morello cherries and shaved almonds.
Price: €

✓ FROURARCHEIO
6 Agion Anargyron St., Psyrri, tel. (01) 3215156

Tasteful decor utilizing stone and wood. Lovely courtyard in summer. Good music and impeccable service.
Price: €€€

✓ ZAFIRIS
2 Propylaion St., tel. (01) 9215182

An old house opposite the Herod Atticus Theatre. An owner with personality. VIPs at every table. Superb service. Try the game, stuffed chicken and wild boar with olives. One of the best taverna in Athens with a history stretching back to the turn of the century.
Price: €

✓ TADE EFFI ANNA
72 Ermou St., tel. (01) 3213652

Impressive dining room in an old house. Mediterranean cuisine influenced by Greek traditional cooking. Marvellous salads and an intriguing stuffed chicken with a pistachio crust.
Price: €€

✓ MAMACAS
41 Persefonis St., Gazi, tel. (01) 3464984

In this originally styled place you can eat delicious pies and tasty soutzoukakia (meatballs with cumin-flavoured tomato sauce), while rubbing elbows with the rich and famous.
Price: €

PLATANOS
4 Diogenous St., Plaka, tel. (01) 3220666

Old fashioned taverna patronized by intellectuals and artists who appreciate its legendary moussaka and good home cooking. One of the best in Plaka.
Price: €

XYNOS
4 Angelou Geronda St., tel. (01) 3221065

Traditional Plaka taverna, one of the best. Moussaka, spaghetti with meat sauce and nostalgic music.
Price: €

ATHENS & ENVIRONS

BEST RESTAURANTS & TAVERNAS

FILISTRON
23 Apostolou Pavlou St., Thission,
tel. (01) 3467554
In summer it has a lovely terrace with a view of the Parthenon. The appetizers, like aubergine Amorgos-style and wild greens pie, are beautifully prepared, the service excellent, the barrel wine very good, and the prices reasonable.
Price: €

ZEIDORON
10 Taki and Agion Anargyron Sts., Psyrri Sq.,
tel. (01) 3215368

Hangout where people drink ouzo and watch each other. Unexceptional cuisine.
Price: €

KOLONAKI AREA

✓✓✓ BOSCHETTO
Alsos Evangelismou, across from the Hilton.
Tel. (01) 7210893

Set in an idyllic park, the utmost in luxury and "nouvelle" Italian creations. Famous for its risotto, but that's not all. Refined ambiance, a favourite with politicians and celebrities.
Price: €€€

✓✓✓ KIKU
12 Dimokritou St., Kolonaki, tel. (01) 3647033
Best place for Japanese sushi and sashimi in Athens. Minimalistic decor and layout, flawless service. Wonderful tuna sashimi and raw shrimp. Delicious sake. Very expensive and quality to match.
Price: €€€

✓✓ RATKA
30 Haritos St., Kolonaki, tel. (01) 7290746

Genuinely old bar-restaurant. Casual atmosphere, small but cosy, friendly service. Once "in" with the rich and famous, it now also attracts publicity-seekers. Specializes in Asian cuisine, with sushi and tempura that rival Kiku's, but try the fantastic meat cooked on a tile and the wonderful desserts. We love this place. So different and so good.
Price: €€

✓✓ ABREUVOIR
51 Xenokratous St., Kolonaki, tel. (01) 7229106
The oldest French restaurant in Athens. Classic menu, classic luxury, classic atmosphere and frogs' legs as good as we've tasted. Excellent fish dishes and wine cellar. Tables under the trees in summer.
Price: €€€

✓✓ OLIVE GARDEN
Roof garden, Hotel Titania, 52 Panepistimiou St.,
tel. (01) 3838511
Superb Mediterranean cooking, prepared with great finesse. Views of the city and the Parthenon from the

ATHENS & ENVIRONS

BEST RESTAURANTS & TAVERNAS

roof garden adorned with olive trees, lavender and thyme shrubs.
Price: €€

✓✓ TUTTI A TAVOLA
8 Spefsippou St., Kolonaki, tel. (01) 7257756
Genuine Italian trattoria in a cosy, hospitable basement. Fantastic antipasti, wonderful fresh pasta and meat Italian style.
Price: €€

✓✓ THE KITCHEN-THALASSINOS
The old Thalassinos has been transformed into a fusion restaurant and its neoclassic decor is now post-mod "design". The presence of Costas Tsingas in the kitchen guarantees an interesting gastronomic experience, as his sauces and garnishes appear in whatever mad combination strikes his fancy.
Price: €€

✓✓ CASA DI PASTA
30 Spefsippou St., Kolonaki, tel. (01) 7233348
Ageless Italian restaurant, rather pricey, but with good service and wonderful pasta dishes based on traditional recipes. The fettucine with lobster is a must.
Price: €€

✓✓ ROCK & ROLL
6 Loukianou and Ypsilantou Sts., Kolonaki, tel. (01) 7217127. Closed in summer.
Christoforos Peskias has taken over the kitchen of this well-known bar restaurant, adding to

Mediterranean-inspired haute cuisine to the usual bar staples. **Price:** €€

✓✓ SALE E PEPE
34 Aristippou St., Kolonaki, tel. (01) 7234102
The wine cellar in this restaurant is excellent. A cosy, attractive place with innovative dishes for Greece, such as noodles smothered in rabbit ragout, linguini with clams and rabbit with porcini.
Price: €€

✓ IL PARMIGIANO
3 Grivaion St., Kolonaki, tel. (01) 3641414

Small but luxurious nook in winter, pleasant garden in summer. Exceptional service. Italian cuisine. Tomato sauce almost ubiquitous. Fresh fish and lobster.
Price: €

LESS CENTRAL RESTAURANTS

✓✓✓ SPONDI
5 Pyrronos St., Pangrati, Tel. (01) 7520658
One of the finest restaurants in Athens. Atmospheric surroundings, understated luxury, with medieval touches, brick and refectory tables. In summer tables are set on a multi-tiered terrace cooled by old fash-

ATHENS & ENVIRONS

BEST RESTAURANTS & TAVERNAS

ioned ceiling fans. Exceptional wine cellar and fusion cuisine, with such dishes as foie gras with confit of onions, lamb sweetbreads with caramelized onions, millefeuille of squid with pesto, and lamb shanks with apple puree and calvados sauce.
Price: €€€

✓✓ MEZZO-MEZZO
58 Syngrou Ave., tel. (01) 9242444

The ultimate in glamorous bar-restaurants. Here Japanese flavours blend with Mediterranean and the latest American trends flirt with classic French tradition. Trying to win accolades for gastronomy and wine, while remaining the most "in" and flamboyant hangout in the capital. Impressive two-storey space with its own style, it also fancies itself an art gallery.
Price: €€€

✓✓ KONA KAI
115 Syngrou Ave., tel. (01) 9347711
Asia and Polynesia have made their mark in the Ledra Marriott hotel. Exceptional service, slightly touristy atmosphere. Try the shrimp tempura, lighter than air and succulent at the same time, the best spring rolls in Athens and the fantastic won ton with cheese. The Thai "souvlakia" are unforgettable.
Price: €€€

✓✓ KALLISTI
137 Asklipiou St., tel. (01) 6453179
Hospitable rooms, retro atmosphere, antiques. Traditional dishes with a modern, imaginative touch. Friendly service. Try the stewed spinach beet, stuffed aubergines and kaimaki ice cream with bergamot preserves and caramel sauce.
Price: €€

✓ VLASSIS
Pasteur and Hadzikosta Sts., Mavili Sq., Tel. (01) 6463060

Where the artists and actors go, in an old house with an atmosphere to match. Simple but flawlessly prepared dishes. Fresh fish, appetizers, delicious roast kid with potatoes.
Price: €

✓ EL GRECO GRECO
6 Fthiotidos St., off Kifissias Ave., Ambelokipi. Tel. (01) 6480089
Gracious, hospitable surroundings. Traditional Constantinople touches combined with modern gastronomic trends. Stuffed piglet and fresh seafood are among the specialities. Original appetizers, such as anchovies stuffed with tarama and wild fennel rissoles.
Price: €€

✓ IPPOKRATOUS
166 Ippokratous St., tel. (01) 6425305
Aesthetically pleasing, friendly and quiet place. An interesting guide to traditional Greek tastes, such as kavourmas (a meat dish from Thrace), Epirot pies, Naxos stuffed squid, and so forth.
Price: €€

✓ SUSHI BAR
Varnava Sq., Pangrati, tel. (01) 7524354

ATHENS & ENVIRONS

BEST RESTAURANTS & TAVERNAS

Minimalistic but with a difference. Well-prepared sushi and sashimi at more reasonable prices than usual.
Price: €€

✓ CHRYSSA

81 Dimofondos and Aioleon Sts., Ano Petralona, tel. (01) 3412515
Discreet, aristocratic ambiance, international cuisine and irreproachable service. The salads steal the show and the gnocchi with red caviar and gorgonzola is a real winner.
Price: €€

✓ O KITRINOS SKIOUROS

21 Dimitressa St., Ilissia, tel. (01) 7211586

Brazilian bar-restaurant with a cosy atmosphere. Decorated with flair, next to a green park. Try the Caipirinia cocktail made with the Brazilian national drink, cachassa, and the feijoada (black beans, meats and garnishes), while listening to the rhythms of Brazil.
Price: €

✓ O TZITZIKAS KI O MERMINGAS

4 Papadiamanti Sq., Ano Patissia, tel. (01) 2232376 and at Georgiou A and 26 Aischylou Sts., Halandri, tel. (01) 6810529
Good ouzeri serving appetizers in a congenial atmosphere. Home-cooked treats, tsipouro (like raki), and cockerel stewed in wine. End the meal with galaktoboureko (a kind of custard pie) drenched in sour cherry preserves.
Price: €

ANATOLI

60 Ipirou St., tel. (01) 8254101
Genuine Turkish restaurant. The place looks like your corner pizzeria but the service is friendly. Anatolian music sets the stage for real Turkish kebabs, lachmatzoun, juicy pies made with pastourma and lamb doner kebab (gyro).
Price: €

SEOUL HOUSE RESTAURANT

8 Evritanias St., Ambelokipi, tel. (01) 6924669
Simple Asian restaurant with good service. Don't miss the dumpling soup, the rice with egg, and meat barbecued in the Korean way.
Price: €

BARBA-YIANNIS

94 Emmanouil Benaki St., Exarchia, Tel. (01) 3300185

Classic old-fashioned cook-house, where dozens of fresh, delicious ready-cooked dishes await a steady stream of faithful customers. Among the treats, rich meat balls and juicy roast pork. The barrel wine is quite drinkable, too.
Price: €

KOUTOUKAKI

35 Lydias St., Kaisariani, tel. (01) 7258418

ATHENS & ENVIRONS

BEST RESTAURANTS & TAVERNAS

Reed mats on the walls, old barrels, folk music, the scent of grilling meat, cheerful atmosphere, words of winey wisdom and an eccentric, appealing host – in short, all the ingredients of a traditional dive. Try the beets with garlic and anchovies marinated in oil scented with coriander. Very good red wine from the barrel.
Price: €

TRATA
7-9 Anagennisis St., Kaisariani Sq.

One of the best fish tavernas in Athens in a genuine, no-frills setting. Delicious fish soup (wrongly called bouillabaisse), fantastic grilled langoustines, lavish salads. Ask for a large sargos (bream) if there is one.
Price: €

PANORMITIS
117 Panormou St., Ambelokipi, tel. (01) 6996480
Hospitable, cosy spot with fireplace on the upper storey of an old house. Good appetizers; don't miss the oven-baked aubergines.
Price: €

KINA
72 Evfroniou St., Ilissia, tel. (01) 7233200
The city's first Chinese restaurant, it continues to produce good food at reasonable prices. The soup with pickles and pork is marvellous.
Price: €

APHRODITE
12 Konitsis St., Goudi, tel. (01) 7752467
Cypriot cuisine in its most classic form served in a hospitable, extremely rustic spot, occasionally accompanied by live music. Try the seftalies (Cypriot grilled meatballs), pickles, potatoes with coriander and kolakassi.
Price: €

NORTHERN SUBURBS

✓✓✓ VARDIS
66 Deligianni St., Kefalari, Kifissia,
Tel. (01) 6230650-6
In this luxury restaurant in the Pentelicon Hotel, chef de Grigio creates haute cuisine with an intensely Mediterranean flavour, inheriting Greece's only Michelin star from his predecessor chef Feuerbach.
Price: €€€

✓✓ COSMOS
8 Omirou St., Neo Psychiko, tel. (01) 6729150

Where the elite meet, this is actually two places under one roof. One is a comfortable, luxurious bar with music for young tastes (ee), while the other (eee), more serious, doubles as an art gallery. Both have improved gastronomically, and the service is good, but they're very pricey indeed.
Price: €€

✓✓ RENA TIS FTELIAS
28 25th Martiou St., Neo Psychiko,
Tel. (01) 6743874
Sui generis cuisine. Conventional upmarket atmosphere. The eccentric patroness supervises both menu and service. Emphasis on excellent ingrediens with some superlative dishes, such as savoury pies and roast kid. The creamy sweets are few but mouth-watering. Children are not welcome!
Price: €€€

✓✓ SAIPAN
9 K. Varnali St., Halandri, tel. (01) 6850644
Perhaps the best Peking duck in Athens. Oozing with opulence, highly professional service. Fairly conventional decor, cosy atmosphere, but the bill is less friendly.
Price: €€€

ATHENS & ENVIRONS

BEST RESTAURANTS & TAVERNAS

✓✓ FONTANINA DI TORRE

Kifissia Tower, corner Kassaveti and Kyriazi Sts., tel. (01) 8017635

Swanky Italian restaurant in Kifissia's shopping land, with an elegant tiny courtyard and interiors decorated with antiques. Helpful service, excellent prosciutto al forno. Don't pass up the fettuccine with shrimps and zabaglione sauce.
Price: €€

✓✓ GEVSEIS ME ONOMASIA PROELEFSEOS

317 Kifissias Ave., Kifissia, tel. (01) 8001402

Elias Mamalakis, a writer and gourmet, and enologist Panos Zouboulis have converted this old Kifissia mansion into a welcoming, attractive, simply decorated place where one feels like their privileged guest. Try the cockerel with blackberry sauce, dogfish with saffron and spinach beet with garlic and oil, to mention just a few of their homely yet original creations. Superb wine cellar.
Price: €€

✓ SPUNTINO

6 Omirou St., Neo Psychiko, tel. (01) 6745203 and at 13 Markou Botsari, Glyfada, Tel. (01) 8941649

Charming garden in Psychiko and delightful interiors in Glyfada, for two different encounters with the varied tastes of a good, genuine Italian restaurant. The spaghetti alla pescatore is exquisite, the ravioli with ricotta a revelation and the pasta with lobster more than notable. The vast variety of antipasti lend themselves to happy "snacking" – which is what "spuntino" means.
Price: €€

✓ ALTAMIRA

28 Perikleous St., Maroussi, tel. (01) 6128841

Multi-ethnic cuisine with Indian, Mexican, Arab and Asian flavours predominant. The garden is extremely pleasant in summer, the interiors decked out with tasteful "ethnic" motifs.
Price: €€

✓ ROYAL THAI

12 Zirini St., Kifissia, tel. (01) 6232322-3

Thai cooking. Ceremonial service and well-prepared dishes. Along with the soup tom yung and the better known satays, the Royal Thai offers a generally high standard and wide selection of Thai dishes.
Price: €€

✓ IL PARMIGIANO

254 Kifissias Ave., Halandri, tel. (01) 6778765

Small but luxurious nook in winter, pleasant garden in summer. Exceptional service. Italian cuisine. Tomato sauce almost ubiquitous. Fresh fish and lobster.
Price: €€

✓ HOCHLIDAKI

21 Pendelis Ave., Halandri, tel. (01) 6848043

Timeless Anatolian-type restaurant, specializing in "little dishes" ("mezedes"), with the accent on flavours from Constantinople. Try the succulent saganaki (the Greek equivalent of Welsh rarebit) with "pastourma" (paper-thin cured camel or beef slices) and sausage, cheese pies, and mussels stuffed with rice, sultanas and pine nuts.
Price: €

ATHENS & ENVIRONS

BEST RESTAURANTS & TAVERNAS

✓ KIPOS TIS EDEM

12 Ghini St., Dourou Sq., Halandri,
tel. (01) 6853580

Lebanese specialities in the heart of Halandri, served in a little old house surrounded by greenery. Among the treats are Arab pies, tabbouleh, hummus, kibbe, capping a rich variety of wonderful choices. Reservations essential.
Price: €

✓ DEALS

20 Dim. Vassiliou St., Neo Psychiko,
Tel. (01) 6773183

Trendy, sophisticated, lively and noisy, perfect for public relations and people watching. Emphasis on fashionable, especially Italian, tastes. For a splashy finale, have the chocolate fondue with fresh fruit.
Price: €€

✓ ENOTECA

35 Pendelis Ave., Vrilissia, tel. (01) 6138651

Old house converted into a simple, attractive restaurant with an enormous wine cellar and a few, well-prepared dishes, such as pork with green olives. Both the staff and the owner are on the unconventional side.
Price: €

REMVI

64 Aristotelous St., Halandri,
tel. (01) 6810507, 6834202

Beautifully decorated, cosy rooms in two old houses with fireplace. International cuisine and fresh fish. You'll appreciate the service, which is among the city's most attentive. Lovely patio for summer and special room for non-smokers.
Price: €€

DIM SUM

46 Adrianiou St., Neo Psychiko,
tel. (01) 6873327-8

Modern setting for dim sum (Chinese dumplings), such as char kaou (steam shrimp dumplings), though a bit lacking in variety. The chow mein is excellent.
Price: €

PYRAMIDES

60 Drosias-Stamatas Ave., tel. (01) 6417712

Egyptian grill-house. Family atmosphere, delicious food, low prices. Tasty meats served with large hot pieces of Arab bread.
Price: €

PIRAEUS

✓✓✓ VAROULKO

4 Deligianni St., tel. (01) 4112043

Chef Lazarou continues to triumph in this Piraeus temple to seafood, which is one of the city's finest and most creative. The dining area is both discreetly elegant and comfortable. Let the experienced waiters guide you through the menu (but insist on having a look at it or the bill may come as a shock). Don't miss the seafood en papillotte, the baby squid with pesto and the classic steamed monkfish.
Price: €€€

✓ KOLLIAS

3 Stratigou Plastira St., Tambouria,
tel. (01) 4629620

Fish taverna that is winning more and more approval for its beautifully fresh and unusual

BEST RESTAURANTS & TAVERNAS

seafood, including rare molluscs and sea urchins. Try the outstanding octopus krassato (with wine sauce) and squid fried with their ink.
Price: €

✓ THE PIRAEUS YACHT CLUB (ISTIOPLOIKOS OMILOS PIREOS)

At the south end of Tourkolimano, Tel. (01) 4134984

Stunning view from Kastella over Faliron Bay. Congenial service, pleasant atmosphere. Try the risotto with octopus and the paella.
Price: €€

MIKROLIMANO

This delightful little yacht harbour in Piraeus has naturally not escaped the notice of the crowds. Early on it became a tourist attraction, like Plaka, and along with its undeniable picturesqueness, visitors were introduced to "Greek seafood". Some time ago it was possible to eat well in many of the tavernas that line the Mikrolimano waterfront. A few of the older ones are still in business, such as **Zorbas**, **Zephyros** and **Kalyva**. Unfortunately, however, none of them has remained genuine, at least as far as cooking is concerned. Amidst the shouts and coaxing of the waiters who try to solicit your custom, one taverna stands out – **Jimmy and Fish (!)**, which produces fairly decent food.

Jimmy and Fish (!)

SOUTHERN SUBURBS

✓✓ KIOUPIA

50 Ioannou Metaxa St., Glyfada, tel. (01) 8943146 and at Poltitia Sq., Politia, Kifissia, tel. (01) 6206433

A feast of 60 dishes inspired by traditional Greek cooking. Rustic luxury. Service discreetly adjusted to your mood.
Price: €€

STROFILIA

2 Sokratous St., Voula, opposite the Voula High School, tel. (01) 8958255

Traditional food in an authentic atmosphere. Try the meatballs "keftedes" Kozani style, tomato keftedes in the manner of Santorini, chickpea keftedes a la Sifnos and "sarmadakia" from Kassos (a variation on dolmades – stuffed vine leaves).
Price: €

VIETNAM

91 Achilleos St., Amfithea, tel. (01) 9881417

Classic Cantonese cuisine, adapted to western tastes. Mundane setting more than compensated for by the Peking duck.
Price: €

VALENTINA

235 Lykourgos St., Kallithea, tel. (01) 9431871

This spot resembles an old-fashioned kafeneion, but the menu will surprise you. Try the home made noodles, borscht, piroshki and extra-tender roasts.
Price: €

ATHENS & ENVIRONS

BEST ENTERTAINMENT

In the evening, Athens puts on another face and transforms herself into a delightful, ebullient hostess who can provide every possible kind of entertainment and amusement. In any case, her citizens are famed for their nocturnal activities, as they spill out into the streets with the greatest of ease to exhaust every opportunity for a good time.

The city that never sleeps is equally fond of Greek and foreign novelties, simple tavernas and expensive restaurants, coffee bars and nightclubs, winter outings and summer all-nighters.

For coffee and your first drink, Kolonaki is the place. You'll discover lots of bars lining the pedestrian streets of Haritos and Delfon, Tsakalof and vicinity. In **Exarchia** you can plan your nightlife in the cafes surrounding the square, where you'll meet up with the city's intellectuals and fringe youth. Here there are charming little bars in old mansions with quiet gardens. In **Plaka**, have a coffee or an ouzo in a romantic setting, often with a view of the Acropolis. Or check out the music clubs where some of the best Greek vocalists display their talents. In the **National Gardens**, at the exit onto Irodou Attikou St., a cool cafe serves soft drinks and tasty cheese-pies until the sun goes down. In **Thission**, especially on Irakleidon St., stylish new bars and eateries are opening all the time in splendidly decorated converted houses. While in **Psyrri**, the mezedopoleia (where you can choose from dozens of appetisers) vie for the claim of liveliest atmosphere and trendiest clientele. **Gazi** – the old gas works – is an up-and-coming area where the nightclubs and restaurants are reaching new heights of quality and inspired design. In **Piraeus** take a refreshing stroll for coffee, or a bite to eat in Mikrolimano or the charming old neighbourhood on Kastella hill above it. As for the nightclubs, you can choose from among Greek, rave, house, trans, techno and anything else your heart desires, until dawn. In winter the nightclubs tend to be clustered around the centre – in the vicinity of Ermou St. and Amerikis Sq.. In summer, though, they move out to the southern coast, followed by thousands of Athenians, to Glyfada, Voula and the neighbouring coastal suburbs, almost always near the sea so you can have an early dip before returning home. Remember that these kinds of hangouts are constantly changing and that sometimes their doors open only if you're wearing the right attire. There's nothing wrong with flirting but too extreme behaviour will be rewarded with eviction. The drinks are usually untampered with, and the areas above and below the tables are the most entertaining to watch, especially when the young start doing their thing. Match your tastes with the selection of the BEST spots we suggest below. And have a great time!

Monastiraki

Thission

CAFE
DA CAPO
1 Tsakalof St., Kolonaki, tel. (01) 3602497
CIAO
2 Tsakalof St., Kolonaki, tel. (01) 3647665
STOA COOPER
101 Patission & Kodrigtonos Sts. (inside the arcade), tel. (01) 8253932
LUCKY STRIKE
24 Fokionos Negri St., Kypseli, tel. (01) 8253913
BASEBALL
190 Alexandras Ave., Ambelokipi, tel. (01) 6460555
CAFE FOLIE
156 Kifissias Ave., Neo Psychiko, tel. (01) 6740264
FLOCAFE ESPRESSO BARS
118 Kifissias Ave., tel. (01) 6497220
14 Fokionos Negri & Drossopoulou Sts., tel. (01) 8230755
OSTRIA
10 Poseidonos St., Alimos, tel. (01) 9852350
CORTE
30 Ioannou Metaxa St., Glyfada, tel. (01) 8941871
EGOMIO
10 Zissimopoulou St., Glyfada, tel. (01) 8949454

ATHENS & ENVIRONS

BEST ENTERTAINMENT

BARS
STAVLOS
10 Irakleidon St., Thission, tel. (01) 3467206, 3452502
BAILA
43 Haritos St., Kolonaki, tel. (01) 7233019
ASTRON
Taki 3, Psyrri, tel. 0977 469356
INOTECA
Avissynias Sq. 3, tel. (01) 3246446
FOLIE
4 Eslin St., Ambelokipi, tel. (01) 6469852

CLUBS (Winter)
SODA
161 Ermou St., Thission, tel. (01) 3456187
KINGSIZE BEDROOM
3 Amerikis Sq., tel. (01) 3232500, 3232506
KALUA
6 Amerikis Sq., tel. (01) 3608304
PRIVILEGE
3 Voukourestiou St., tel. (01) 3232723, 3232776
PRIME
Vouliagmenis Ave. 22, tel. (01) 9246688-9

Banana Moon

BANANA MOON
56 Patriarchou Ioakeim St., Kolonaki, tel. (01) 7251771
TANGO
9 Kifissias Ave., Filothei, tel. (01) 6850740-1
CAMEL
268 Vouliagmenis Ave., tel. (01) 9716145

CLUBS (Summer)
BANANA MOON
1 Vasilissis Olgas St., Zappeion, tel. (01) 3215414
PRIME
4, A' Beach, tel. (01) 8953973
PRIVILEGE
Poseidonos St., Elliniko, tel. (01) 9852995
PLUS SODA
Poseidonos St., Glyfada, tel. (01) 8941300
CUBANITA HAVANA CLUB
Third glyfada Marina, tel. (01) 8942788

CAMEL
25 Pergamou St., Glyfada, tel. (01) 9650879
TANGO
4 Alkyonidon St., Voula, tel. (01) 8956577
BO
8-10 Alkyonidon St., Voula, tel. (01) 8959645
ISLAND
Limanakia Vouliagmenis, tel. (01) 9653563
YACHT CLUB BAR
Tourkolimano, Piraeus, tel. (01) 4134084

JAZZ-BLUES-FUNK-ETHNIC
HALF NOTE
17 Trivonianou St., Mets, tel. (01) 9232460, 9213310
CUBANITA
Karaïskaki 28, Psyrri Sq., tel. (01) 3314605
ASANTE
78 Damareos St., Pangrati, tel. (01) 7560102
PALENQUE
41 Farandaton St., Goudi, tel. (01) 7718090, 7487548

REBETIKA (Greek Blues)
STOA ATHANATON
19 Sofokleous St. and Stoa Athanaton,
tel. (01) 3214362, 3210342
APTALIKO
6A-6B Ironda St., Old Olympic Stadium,
tel. (01) 7258648
BOEMISSA
19 Solomou St., Exarchia, tel. (01) 3843836
REBETIKI ISTORIA
181 Ippokratous St., Exarchia,
tel. (01) 6424937
FRANKOSYRIANI
57 Arachovis St., Exarchia, tel. (01) 3800693
MOUSIKES SKIES
Eftihidou & 4 Athanasias Sts., Plastira Sq., Pangrati, tel. (01) 7261465
PALIA MARKIZA
41 Proklou St., Pangrati, tel. (01) 7225074

LIVE GREEK MELODIOUS MUSIC
ZOOM
39 Kydathinaion St., Plaka, tel. (01) 3225920, 3245595
PANSELINOS
101 Adrianou St., Plaka, tel. (01) 3247575, 3247252
MEDOUSA
2 Makri St., Makrigianni, tel. (01) 9218120, 9218272
MOUSIKI SKINI PIREA
Asklipiou and Kastoros, Pireas, tel. (01) 4120510-11

ATHENS & ENVIRONS

BEST ENTERTAINMENT

IERA ODOS
18-20 Iera Odos St., tel. (01) 3428272
STAVROS TOU NOTOU
37 Tharipou St., Neos Kosmos,
tel. (01) 9226975, 9239031
ARCHITEKTONIKI
8 Minoos St., Neos Kosmos, tel. (01) 9014428
ALSOS
In Pedion Areos Park, entrance from Evelpidon St., tel. (01) 8212271, 8252172
SFENDONA
22 Alexandras Ave., tel. (01) 8253991-2
ENNEA OGDOA
40 Alexandras Ave., tel. (01) 8821095
TABOO
42 Andinoros St., tel. (01) 7224244
METRO
33 Kalvou & Ghizi Sts., tel. (01) 6461980, 6439089
GYALINO MOUSIKO THEATRO
143 Syngrou Ave., tel. (01) 9316101-4
DIOGENIS STUDIO
259 Syngrou Ave., Nea Smyrni, tel. (01) 9424267
13 FENGARIA
61 Agiou Meletiou & Patission Sts. (Stoa Broadway), tel. (01) 8655100, 8659859

MUSIC HALLS
LIVE BOUZOUKI AND DANCING ON TABLES (winter)
ROMEO
4 Kallirrhois St., temple of Olympian Zeus, tel. (01) 9224885, 9232648
PAPAGAYO
37 Patriarchou Ioakeim St., Kolonaki, tel. (01) 7240736
NEOS APOLLON
22 Vouliagmenis Ave., tel. (01) 9246688-9
APOLLON PALACE
279 Syngrou Ave., tel. (01) 9425754
LA NOTTE
10-12 Kifissias Ave., Maroussi, tel. (01) 6846139
ASTERIA
The Glyfada Astir, tel. (01) 8944558

MUSIC HALLS (summer)
BIO-BIO
Glyfada, tel. (01) 8941300, 8944166
ASTERIA
The Glyfada Astir, tel. (01) 8944558
ROMEO
1 Ellinikou St., Glyfada, tel. (01) 8945345

BAR-RESTAURANTS
ROCK & ROLL
6 Loukianou & Ypsilandou Sts., Kolonaki, tel. (01) 7217127
AQUA STADIUM
10 Irakleidon St., Thission, tel. (01) 3467206, 3452502
AISOPOU MYTHOS (wine bar)
Irini and Filias, tel. (01) 4834190-1
BARA CLUB
Patriarchou Ioakeim & 23 Ploutarchou Sts., Kolonaki, tel. (01) 72217178

Bara

EXO
Markou Mousourou, tel. (01) 9235818, 9237109
JACKSON HALL SPIRIT
4 Milioni St., Kolonaki, tel. (01) 3616098, 3616546
CAPRICE
1 Fokilidou St., Kolonaki, tel. (01) 3619646
ROCKWOOD
2 Vasileos Irakliou St., tel. (01) 8216400
CRAFT ATHENS
205 Alexandras Ave., tel. (01) 6462350, 6451112
JACKSON HALL FILOTHEI
236 Kifissias Ave., Filothei, tel. (01) 6728053-4
NEW YORK-NEW YORK
Ioannou Metaxa & 18 Pandoras Sts., Glyfada, tel. (01) 8946323

BOUZOUKI JOINTS
VARELADIKO
Distomou & 1 Zanni Sts., Piraeus, tel. (01) 4227500-2
KARPOUZI
Polytechniou & 34 Syntagmatos Sts., Piraeus, tel. (01) 4126074

POP CONCERT HALLS
RODON
24 Marni St., tel. (01) 5247427
PIRAEUS MUNICIPAL THEATRE
(Dimotiko Theatro Piraia)
4 Agiou Konstantinou St., tel. (01) 4194550

ATHENS & ENVIRONS

TIPS AND INFORMATION

HOW TO GET THERE

Athens has an international airport with direct flights from many places around the globe. Your travel agent will inform you of the options.

By ship (increasingly fast and modern) from Ancona, Brindisi and Bari (Italy) which will land you in Patras on the west coast of Greece, with or without your own car or motorbike. From Patras, if you don't have your own transport, take the train, OSE, tel. (061) 639108, or the intercity bus, KTEL, tel. (061) 273936.

CONNECTIONS

With Athens or Piraeus as a starting point you can get to anywhere you want in Greece by whatever means. Choose one of our Best excursions and see the *How to Get There* directions at the end of each excursion.

BEST TIPS

HOW TO GET AROUND: While Athens is a big city in terms of both population and area, the spots of most interest to visitors are all located conveniently near each other. Try to walk around the centre so that you get acquainted with the many faces of Athens – ancient, Byzantine, neo-classical and modern. Avoid driving as much as possible because the traffic is horrendous and parking very problematic. As for seeing the sights in the environs of Athens, it would be worth hiring a car for a day or two, so that you can plan your programme the way you choose. Otherwise, ask your hotel or a travel agent to recommend some organized tours to the sites you may be interested in.

Taxis:
Approximately 15,000 taxis circulate in the streets of Athens, but be careful, because although the fares are the lowest in Europe, they often overcharge, despite heavy penalties. Ensure the meter is on and pay that amount plus legal extras displayed on the dashboard. Taxis are unofficially allowed to collect more than one party on the way. You will have to accept it even if you don't like it.

Public Transport:
- The **electric train** runs from Piraeus port, through the city of Athens (and its historic centre), to its northern suburbs (Kifissia). It operates from 5 am to 12 midnight. Fare: 120-180 drs.
- **Trolleys** and **buses** run on frequent schedules throughout the city. They operate from 5 am to 12 midnight. Fare: 120 drs.

BEST SEASON: Athens, a cosmopolitan town, is lively and interesting all year long. However, the weather is at its best in either spring or autumn, while the streets are less crowded in summer if you can bear the heat.

BEST BUYS: You can find literally everything in Athens, at pretty good prices. Most visitors restrict their purchases to furs and jewellery, both of which are among the best in the world in terms of quality and cost, Greek wines and imported clothing.

Ermou St. is a good place to shop for clothes, shoes and fabrics, whereas Voulis St., which crosses it, is the centre of the fur trade. Around Ermou and Voukourestiou Sts. are some of the city's finest jewellers. For more eclectic shopping, investigate the boutiques of Kolonaki, but the prices are higher there.

USEFUL TELEPHONE NUMBERS

ATHENS	(01)
Municipality	195
Tourist Bureau	3271300-1
Athens Festival	3235582, 3221459
Tourist Police	171
Police	100
Traffic Police	5230111
Ambulance Service	166
Hospitals	106
Pharmacies	107
OTE Information	131

Intercity Bus Station, Kifissou	5124910-1
Intercity Bus Station, Liossion	8311434
Railroad (OSE) Stations	
Larissis Station	5240601, 5240646-8
Peloponnisos Station	5131601
Airports	
East Airport	9699111
West Airport (**Olympic**)	9269111
Port Authorities	
Piraeus	4511311, 4172657, 4226000-4
Rafina	(0294) 22487, 28888

THE PELOPONNESE

PELOPONNESE

BEST's OPINION

The Peloponnese for some inexplicable reason is one of the least tourist-oriented regions of Greece. And yet its landscape is stunningly varied, it is of enormous cultural interest, and its west coast possesses some of the longest, most beautiful beaches in the country.

IN BRIEF

The climate generally is mild and while some areas are extremely lush, others are quite arid. There are high mountains, such as Taygetos and Helmos, the fertile plains of Argos, Tripolis and Evrotas, and long, sandy beaches. The architecture varies greatly, depending on the location and purpose, and shows a diverse assortment of influences. Its important archaeological sites, traditional settlements and castles attract visitors in every season.

HISTORY

The Peloponnese has had a particularly significant and continuous history, traces of which are visible everywhere. It gave birth to a large portion of Greek mythology, the civilization and might of Tiryns and Mycenae, the wealth and art of Corinth, the martial skill of the Spartans and the Olympic Games. The Peloponnese is a land that many sought to conquer. Its soil has been the site of bloody battles and innumerable wars: the descent of the Dorians, Greek tribes (1100-900 BC), who fought until they wiped out the Achaeans, the local clashes between neighbouring city states, the exhausting thirty-year struggle between Athens and Sparta and, finally, the Romans' savage conquest (sack of Corinth 146 BC). With the decline of Rome, the land was swept by invading Goths, Slavs, Avars, Normans and pirates, until the early 13th c. when the Frankish Crusaders made it their kingdom. They divided it into fiefs and constructed castles for protection against the Byzantines, Venetians and other enemies.

It took the Byzantines 150 years of struggle to win back most of their lost territory and to found the Despotate of the Morea with its capital at Mystra. Their regime was short-lived, however. After the fall of Constantinople (1453), the Ottomans were quick to take over the Peloponnese and most of the rest of Greece. Any areas held by the Venetians continued to thrive, but the rest witnessed massacres and destruction, and the population fled. Many sought refuge in the Ionian islands, Hydra, Spetses, the Cyclades and even Smyrna, which had already begun to prosper. It was in the Peloponnese that the Greek revolution began in 1821 and that the most important battles were won against the Turks, which finally led to independence.

PLACES OF INTEREST BEYOND THE "BEST" EXCURSIONS

PATRAS / Πάτρα / Pátra

Patras is the largest city in the Peloponnese (175,000 inh.) and its administrative, industrial and commercial centre. Its big harbour is an important transit hub for trade with Western Europe, via the ports in Italy. Ferries also connect Patras with the Ionian islands. To see Patras at its liveliest, plan your visit to coincide with the famous 🌀🌀 **carnival**, the third largest in the world after Rio and Venice. Take time out to see the **Archaeological Museum**, the **Castle** and the **Roman Odeon**, the 🌀 **Upper Town** and, to the south-west of town, the 🌀 **Achaia Clauss wine factory**.

Patras Carnival

🌀🌀 KALOGRIA / Καλογριά / Kalogriá

33 km west of Patras

A unique **wetlands habitat** with **stunning beaches** and azure waters. The endless Kalogria beach stretches for 20 km, framed by the 🌀 **Strofylia pine forest**.

Kalogria

THE NAFPLIO AREA

✺ Mycenae ✺ Epidaurus
✺ Nafplio ✺ Ancient Corinth

WHY AMONG THE BEST

For the picturesque and romantic old town of Nafplio and its impressive, well-preserved forts. For the very significant archaeological sites of the area, the Epidaurus Festival and the interesting museums. What's more, for the good food and pleasant little bars.

1 PELOPONNESE

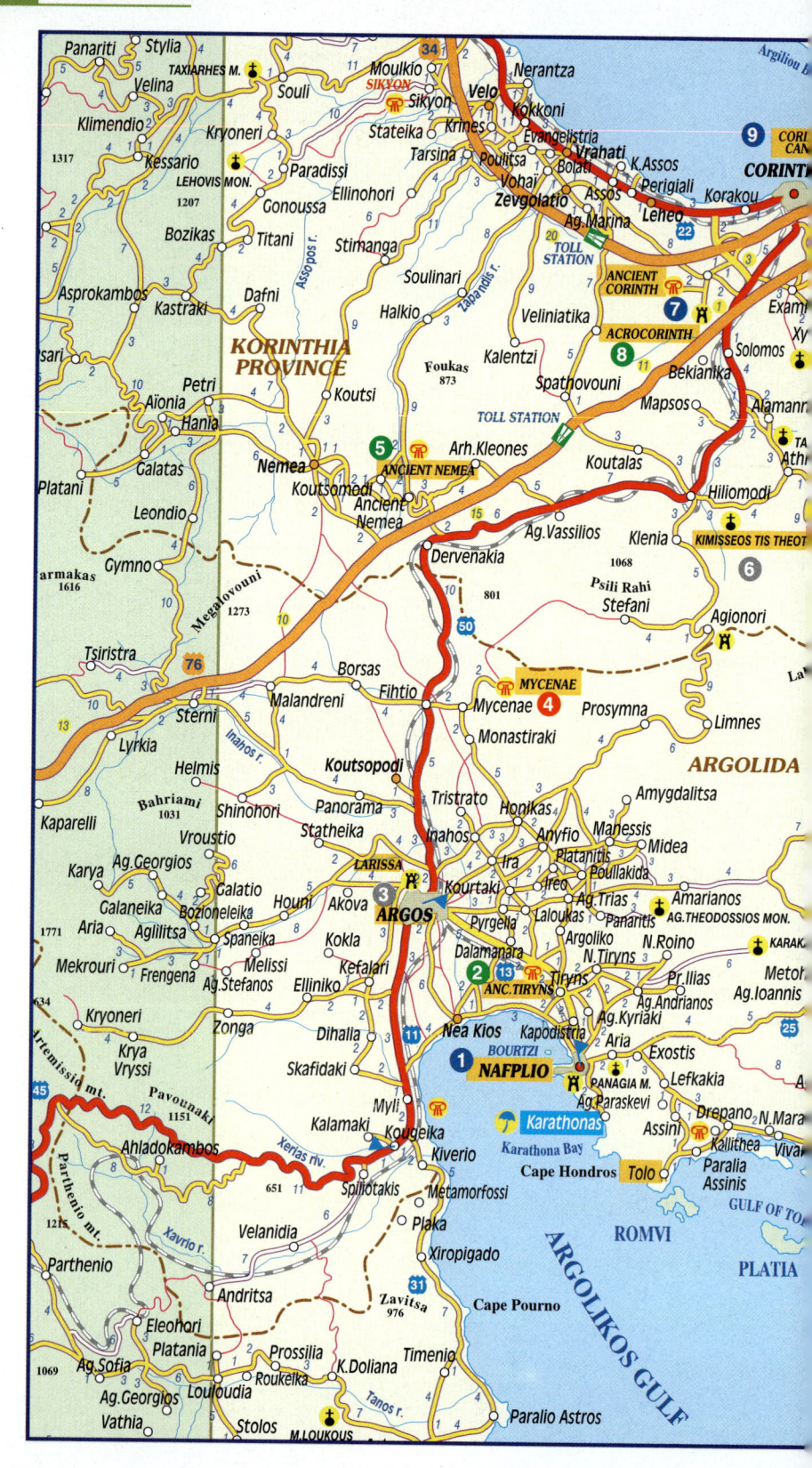

THE NAFPLIO AREA   1

1 PELOPONNESE

BEST's OPINION

Nafplio is not far from Athens, which adds to its attraction even for just a weekend trip. It is a good place for exploring in all seasons and you can also combine it with other worthwhile **Best** excursions in the Peloponnese. Moreover, the highly developed tourist infrastructure and satisfactory transport conditions facilitate access and movements. The only disadvantage is the mediocre beaches, overcome however by an excursion to Porto Heli (see **Excursion 13**).

BEST SIGHTS: STEP BY STEP

❶ NAFPLIO
Ναύπλιο / Náfplio

Nafplio has 20,000 inhabitants and is divided into the old and the new town. The old town was built mainly in the days of the governor **Ioannis Capodistrias**, at the beginning of the 19th c, but buildings still exist from the Venetian era. The new town is an ordinary Greek town with no special assets, so stroll about the old, historical quarters with their neo-classical buildings, charming squares and majestic forts.
Nafplio has known tourism since the first decades of the century. It is a colourful town with culture and history and tallies entirely with the standards of the demanding modern visitor for accommodation, meals and entertainment.

MYTHOLOGY

According to the myths, the founder of ancient Nauplia was **Nauplios**, son of Poseidon, and the city took part in the Argonauts' expedition.
Better known, however, was to be another **Nauplios**, a great expert in naval arts and father of **Palamedes**, who was an inventor, doctor, astronomer, poet, mathematician and philosopher. Palamedes' misfortune was that during the Trojan war he clashed with Odysseus, who slandered him as collaborating with Priam, resulting in **Palamedes** being put to death before the walls of Troy. To avenge his death, Nauplios seduced the wives of the Greek princes one by one, but failed in the case of Penelope, the wife of his great enemy.

HISTORY

The city developed until the 7th c. BC, when it was destroyed by the Argives. It was re-established in the Hellenistic era. In Roman and Byzantine times, it suffered invasion by the Avars, Goths, Slavs and Albanians. It passed successively from the domination of the Franks (1212) into the hands of the Venetians (1389), who reinforced the walls of Acronafplia (1470) and fortified the little island in the entrance to the port, Bourtzi. The city was then adorned with grand buildings in the Renaissance style of the period, some of which still exist.
In 1540, after a three-year siege, Nafplio fell to the Ottomans; in 1686 it returned to Venetian domination until, in 1715, the Ottoman Turks came back, to remain until 1822, when it was liberated by the Greeks.
The city became the capital of the newly established Greek state and the centre of political developments. In September 1831, in the forecourt of the church of Agios Spyridon, the first governor of the nation, **Ioannis Capodistrias**, was assassinated.
In January 1833 Nafplio welcomed the first king of Greece, **Otto of Bavaria**, with the three-member committee who were his guardians until he came of age.
The city continued to play an important role in political developments until 1834 when the capital was transferred to Athens.

Ioannis Capodistrias

THE NAFPLIO AREA 1

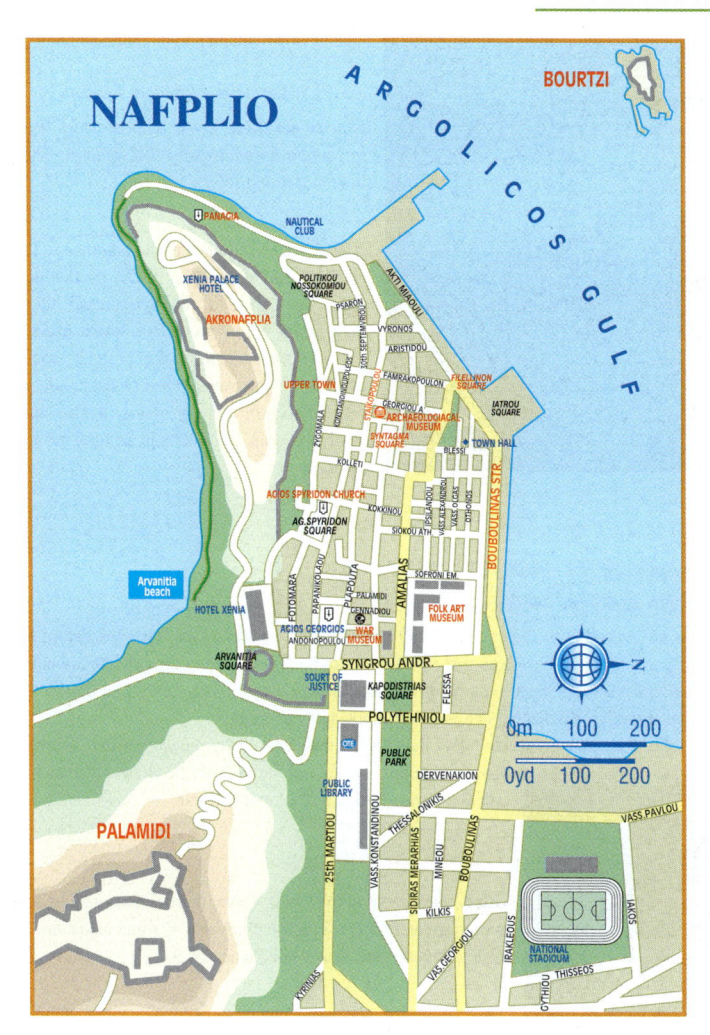

WHAT TO SEE

🌀🌀 PALAMIDI

Tel. (0752) 28036

🕐 Mondays-Fridays 8:30 am-6 pm, Saturdays & Sundays 8 am-2:30 pm, closed on holidays*

How to get there: In your car or by taxi. If you are up to walking it, take the way up the thousand or so steps cut into the rock, starting at Arvanitias Square (Plateia Arvanitias). You may be sure that the spectacular view unrolling at your feet will more than compensate you.
The fort has a small canteen.

This famous Venetian fort was constructed by the engineers **La Salle** and **Giaxich** (early 18th c.) The top of the hill, at an altitude of 216 m, is crowned by the seven ramparts named after ancient heroes.

Although it was considered impregnable, it changed hands several times and after Greece's liberation, was used as a prison. You can even see the cell in which the hero of the Greek War of Independence, **Theodoros Kolokotronis**, was held. In the lower rampart named Miltiades, long-term convicts were imprisoned.

Also do not miss a visit to the historic **chapel of Agios Andreas**, built in Venetian times.

81

1 PELOPONNESE

◎◎ BOURTZI

☼ *8:30 am-5 pm, closed on holidays**

How to get there: *By small boat which leaves the jetty in Nafplio harbour every five minutes. They ferry you over in 3-4 min (500 drs.)*

A small rock island-fort at the entrance to the port, 450 m from land, fortified in **1473** by the Venetians, on plans by Cambello, and connected to the fort at Acronafplia by a heavy chain which prevented enemy shipping from entering the port. It was used as a dwelling for the executioners of the condemned prisoners in Palamidi, among others. It also operated as a hotel for a time. Occasionally, cultural events take place there.

◎◎ FOLK ART MUSEUM

1 Vass. Alexandrou St., tel. (0752) 28379, 25267
☼ *9 am-2 pm, closed on Tuesdays and holidays**

The museum was closed at the beginning of 1997 for renovations. Make sure it is open before going there. In 1981 it was awarded the European prize of Museum of the Year. Among the exhibits are collections and objects covering the entire Greek heritage, principally in the domain of costumes and fabrics. At the same time it has developed an interesting line in publications and discography.
Part of the collection, concerning the life of the child, is exhibited at the railway station. There you will see figures of puppet shows and Karaghiozi (the Greek Mr. Punch of a Punch-and-Judy show), toys, school material, etc.

◎◎ UPPER TOWN

Stroll in the alleys of the Upper Town, beneath Acronafplia, and be transported to another era. You will come across stone mansions, small picturesque squares and flower-filled courtyards.

◎ ACRONAFPLIA

How to get there: *By car or on foot from Nikitara square to the old town. Walk up the incline leading to the fort of Acronafplia. Do not fail to have a cup of coffee at the* **Xenia Palace** *with its* ◎◎ *vista over Bourtzi.*

Nafplio's acropolis is at the foot of Palamidi, with which it communicated by a secret passage. When the Venetians captured Nafplio, there were two forts: the eastern or Frankish and the western or Roman. The Venetians built their fort on the eastern side and the five cannons placed there were called the «**Five Brothers**».

Upper Town

◎ SYNTAGMA SQUARE

Syntagma Square, the heart of the city for many years, is a handsome and spacious pedestrian-precinct square with well-preserved elegant buildings.
Besides the **Archaeological Museum**, you will see two traditional Turkish mosques: **the old mosque**, a school in Capodistrias' time – today a cinema – and the **Vouleftiko** (**Parliamentary**), so named because this is where the first Greek Parliament convened.
It was here that in 1834 Theodoros Kolokotronis was condemned to death.

THE NAFPLIO AREA 1

ⓖ ARCHAEOLOGICAL MUSEUM
Syntagma Sq., tel. (0752) 24690

🕘 *8:30 am-3 pm, closed on Mondays and holidays**

It was built in **1713** by the Venetians, to serve as a naval depot. Nowadays it houses finds from Tiryns, Mycenae, Asine and Corinth. See the **ceramic figurines** from Mycenae (1300 BC), **the Prince of Asine**, the unique **bronze armour** and the **proto-helladic cooler** – an early frigidaire! – from Tiryns. The ⓖ **building** itself is noteworthy.

STAIKOPOULOU STREET

A commercial street with attractive houses, shops and tavernas. Take a look at the little shop with the figures from the shadow-theatre which is there. Not far away you will see the Komboloi (or "Worry-Bead") Museum. In it, all kinds of strings of beads are exhibited and sold.

ⓖ AGIOS SPYRIDON CHURCH
Agiou Spyridona Sq., at Papanikolaou St.

Staikopoulou Street

It was built in 1702. You can still see today, next to the portal, the hole made by one of the bullets fired by the assassins of **Ioannis Capodistrias**, one of the most significant Greek statesmen of the 19th c. The interior of the church was decorated with copies from great Italian painters, of which one is still preserved: Leonardo da Vinci's **Last Supper**.

BOUBOULINA STREET

The street by the sea along the port, with many cafes, bars, restaurants and shops.

WAR MUSEUM
Amalias Ave., tel. (0752) 22591

🕘 *9 am-2 pm, closed on Mondays and holidays**

Formerly the location of the first Greek military academy. You will see exhibits from recent Greek history.

Bouboulina Street

ALSO WORTH SEEING

- ⓖ **Philhellinon Square**, with fine and well-preserved historic buildings.
- The **church of Agios Nikolaos** (architect Augusto Sagredo, 1713).
- The churches of the **Genessi tis Theotokou** and of the **Metamorphossis** also called Frangoklissia.
- In the quarter of Pronia, **Siegel's lion**, which was erected there by order of Otto to commemorate the Bavarians who succumbed to the plague of 1834.
- The monastery **Agia Moni Areias** (4 km east of Nafplio), founded in 1143 by Leon, bishop of Argos & Nafplio. Initially it was a convent, but fear of pirates led to it being fortified and turned over to monks. See the **central nave**, one of the most representative examples of Byzantine art.

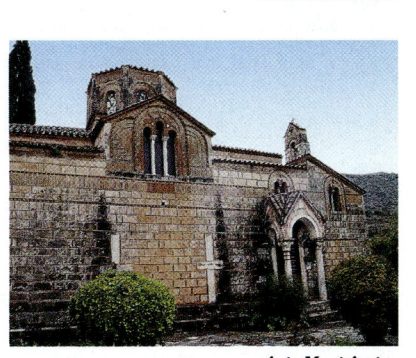

Agia Moni Areias

83

PELOPONNESE

FREE TIME

Walk: Tour of Acronafplia-Arvanitia (30 min)
The paved road round the fort starts at the western end of Akti Miaouli. After the Yacht Club and the stone arch, you will be on Arvanitia beach. Do not miss the reverential atmosphere of the chapel of the Panagia.

Tour of the Town (by little train or carriage)
The little train and two horse-drawn carriages start from the port and follow a route passing by the town sights.

Nafplio Festival
Information: tel. (0752) 23332, 27869
Organized every July by the municipality at Bourtzi, Palamidi and Agios Georgios, featuring classical music, exhibitions and theatre.

❷ ANCIENT TIRYNS
Αρχαία Τίρυνθα / Archéa Tíryntha

Tel. (0752) 22657

8 am-7 pm, closed on holidays*

According to myth, the heroes of Tiryns are connected to Argos and Mycenae. The first king mentioned is Proetos, for whom the Cyclopes constructed the walls (14th c. BC) The cyclopean masonry contains **stone blocks** weighing 13 tons, while some section have a thickness of 17 m. After the central gateway you will encounter the famous **tunnels of Tiryns**, long, narrow subterranean galleries which helped the defenders under siege. Also see the **palace**, with its **propylaea**, **courtyard** and **large mansion** and be sure to see the **floor of the bath made of a single slab of stone**.

❸ ARGOS
Άργος / Árgos

A mighty city of antiquity founded by King Danaos. Its power was at its peak in the 7th c. BC. It is the site of one of the most **ancient theatres** of the 5th c. BC, in which municipal assemblies took place. Argos today is a prosperous farming town of 23,000 inhabitants.

ARCHAEOLOGICAL SITE
Tel. (0751) 76585

8 am-5 pm, closed on Mondays and holidays*

See the ruins of the Roman baths and the Odeon and climb the hill of Larissa to the Theatre and Fort.

THE THEATRE (4th c. BC)
It was huge – 20,000 seats! Reconstructed by the Roman emperor Hadrian (2nd c. AD), it has 92 rows of seats, while the diameter of the proscenium stage is 137 m!

THE FORT OF LARISSA
In the enclosure of the acropolis you will see the traces of two temples: of **Zeus Larissaios** and of **Athena Poliados**. There are remnants of Mycenaean walls and of 4th c. BC fortifications. In the Middle Ages, it was the residence of the Frankish rulers, who reinforced the fortifications, as was also done later under the Ottomans. On the eastern side is the 10th c. **Panagia ton Vrahon monastery**.
It was built on the site of the ancient temple of Hera Akraia and destroyed at the time of the Ottoman domination.

THE NAFPLIO AREA

④ MYCENAE
Μυκήνες / Mikínes

Tel. (0751) 76585. For guides, tel. (01) 3220090, 3229705
8 am-7 pm, closed on holidays*

The majority of the finds excavated can be seen at the Athens National Archaeological Museum (see **page 38**)

HISTORY

It was the German archaeologist **Heinrich Schliemann** who in 1876 brought to light the greatest centre of the Achaeans: the acropolis of Mycenae. The city which was built by the mythical Perseus, and ruled by kings such as **Atreus** and **Agamemnon** developed a vigorous civilization from 1600 BC, reached its peak of glory in 1400 BC and began to decline following the appearance of the Dorian tribes, finally to be destroyed by the Argives (468 BC). "**Mycenae, rich in gold**" as Homer described the city, thanks to its communication with Minoan Crete, was able to extend its sphere of influence throughout the entire Peloponnese (14th-11th c. BC) as well as northern Greece, reaching Asia Minor and Sicily. The kings of Mycenae, as evidenced by archaeological finds, were known even to the Assyrians, Hittites and Pharaohs of Egypt.

MYTHOLOGY

The palace of Mycenae hosted all the events described in the famed myths of the House of Atreus, which inspired the great poets and dramatists of antiquity.
Here **Clytemnestra** killed her husband, King **Agamemnon** returning victorious from Troy, with **Cassandra** by his side. Here **Orestes** avenged his father's murder, killing his mother and her lover **Aegisthus**, to be punished in turn by the **Furies**, who persecuted him.

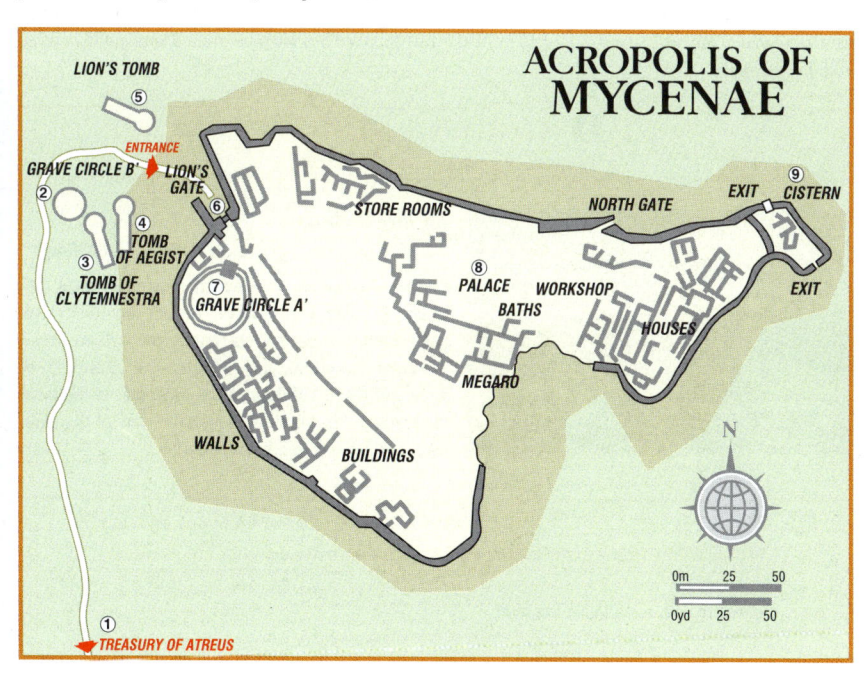

CONDUCTED TOUR
OUTSIDE THE ACROPOLIS

① ⓖⓖⓖ **Treasury of Atreus or tomb of Agamemnon:** The impressive beehive tomb-monument, of the same date as the Lion Gate, is the best constructed and the most recently discovered. It is the only one of the 9 tombs with a second room at the side where previous burials were transferred. The inner monolith lintel of the entrance weighs 120 tons! There is no doubt that this was the tomb of a dynasty.

1 PELOPONNESE

Treasury of Atreus

② ⊚ **Grave circle B**: 14 royal shaft graves. Significant gold funeral gifts were found.

③ ⊚ **Tomb of Clytemnestra**.

④ ⊚ **Tomb of Aegisthus**.

⑤ ⊚ **Tomb of the Lions**.

THE ACROPOLIS

⑥ ⊚⊚⊚ **Gate of the Lions**: The gateway to the acropolis. An imposing portal of the 13th c. BC with the **most ancient sculptured monument**, atop the mighty cyclopean walls of Mycenae.

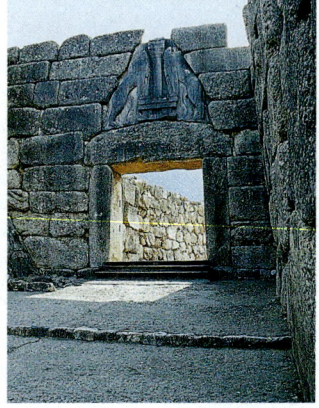

Gate of the Lions

⑦ ⊚ **Grave circle A**: A group of 6 royal graves. Important finds were made here, such as gold masks, swords and gold jewellery.

⑧ ⊚ **Palace**: Built at the top of the acropolis, it consists of a central courtyard, to the south of which is the great staircase, and to the east, the megaron itself. This consists of the anteroom (propylon), the entrance leading to a long narrow room, the antechamber, and the chamber, the largest and most formal room, decorated with fine frescoes and with a large hearth in its centre.

⑨ ⊚⊚ **Cistern (Persia Krini)**: An extraordinary technical achievement. An underground passage leads to the cistern within the wall, at a depth of 18 m. Water was supplied by clay pipes from a spring 400 m away from the acropolis.

---

❺ ANCIENT NEMEA
Αρχαία Νεμέα / Archéa Neméa

Tel. (0746) 22739

🕗 8:30 am-3 pm, closed on Mondays and holidays*

Ancient Nemea is a noteworthy archaeological site where the **Nemean Games**, athletic contests, took place every two years. You can see the well-preserved ⊚ **ancient stadium**, the ⊚ **baths**, the ⊚ **temple of Zeus** and the ⊚ **exhibits in the museum**. In the town of Nemea a few km away, enjoy the view of the plain with its vineyards and buy some wine.

---

❻ KIMISSEOS TIS THEOTOKOU MONASTERY
Μονή Κοιμήσεως της Θεοτόκου / Moní Kimísseos tis Theotókou

A 12th c. monastery with remarkable frescoes.

---

❼ ANCIENT CORINTH
Αρχαία Κόρινθος / Archéa Kórinthos

The wealth and luxury of Corinth were proverbial to the other awe-struck Greeks. Following the coming of the Dorians, Corinth became a great naval power with numerous colonies such as Syracuse and Corfu among others. Some one thousand (!) priestesses of Aphrodite, the most famous being **Lais** (pronounced La-is), lived in the city, undertaking to initiate visitors to the secrets of love. When Athens prevailed as the dominant power,

THE NAFPLIO AREA

and due to the conflict between Athens and Sparta with ensuing constant warfare, Corinth gradually declined until it was destroyed by the Romans in 146 BC.
In 44 BC, the emperor Augustus rebuilt the city, adorning it with grand buildings. Little by little, Corinth began to develop again and under the rule of Hadrian and Herod Atticus retrieved its former prestige.
There, in 52 AD, St. Paul the Apostle preached Christianity. In the following years repeated barbarian invasions, and finally the earthquakes of 521 AD completely flattened the city.

Roman mosaic

ARCHAEOLOGICAL SITE AND MUSEUM

Tel. (0741) 31207
8 am-7 pm, closed on holidays*

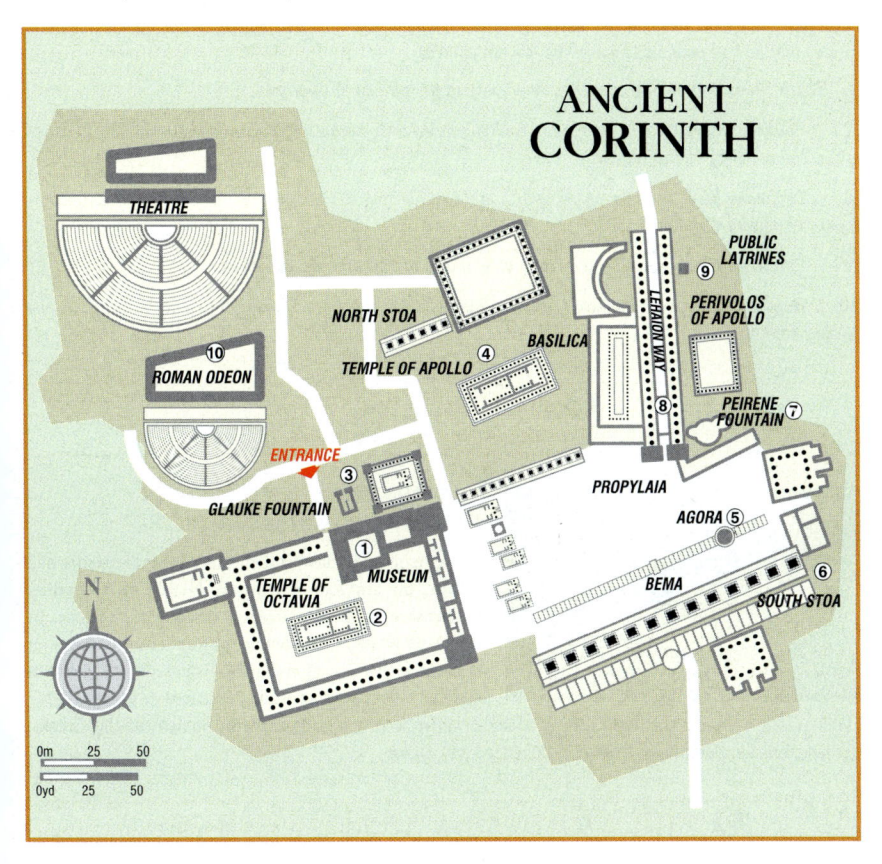

ANCIENT CORINTH

Archaeological Museum

① **Museum:** Significant exhibits, mainly from the Agora of Ancient Corinth and also from the broader district. In one of the two large rooms, examples of the Archaic and Classical eras are shown, as well as some of the renowned **Corinthian vases**, much sought-after throughout the then known world. Ask to be shown the marble inscription "Hebrew synagogue" and have opened for you the locked room containing the **models of the human body** which were dedicated to Asklepios.
The museum was built with funds of the American School of Classical Studies, which also undertook the excavations.
In the courtyard, notice the reliefs of battle scenes with the Amazons and the Giants and others.

87

1 PELOPONNESE

Temple of Octavia

② **Temple of Octavia:** The three marble columns belong to the majestic temple dedicated to the sister of the emperor Augustus.

③ **Fountain of Glauke:** Into its waters, Glauke, the Corinthian princess bride, fell consumed by the poisoned veil sent to her as a bridal gift by Medea, because she was to marry Medea's husband Jason.

④ **Temple of Apollo:** An Archaic temple of 540 BC, one of the most ancient in Greece, with monolithic Doric columns of limestone. It was the only construction the Romans conserved when they rebuilt the city.

⑤ **Agora:** The central square with shops, public buildings and the bema or podium from which orators addressed the public. Here sat the Roman governor Gallio when St. Paul defended himself against the accusations that he had preached against the Roman emperor.

⑥ **South Stoa:** Built in 338 BC, after the victory of King Philip at Cheronea.

⑦ **Fountain of Peirene:** A sumptuous building faced with marble and decorated with statues. Restored in the 2nd c. AD by Herod Atticus.

⑧ **Lechaion Way:** A street paved with marble connecting the ancient port of Lecaion to the central square of ancient Corinth.

⑨ **Public Latrines:** Some seats of the public toilets of that time are still there.

⑩ **Roman Odeon:** Built by Herod Atticus, seating 3,000. There are traces next to it of the Greek theatre seating 18,000.

❽ ACROCORINTH
Ακροκόρινθος / Akrokórinthos

Tel. (0741) 31207

8 am-7 p.m., closed on holidays*

The acropolis of ancient Corinth. Here were sanctuaries and temples, the best known being the **temple of Aphrodite**. Wherever there was a temple to the goddess of love, its priestesses usually followed and the fort became famous for its erotic nights. Its imposing walls show the fortifications made by those who successively captured it, principally the Franks (13th c.) and Venetians (17th c.). Fierce battles were fought beneath its battlements by Greeks, Romans, Franks, Byzantines, Normans, Venetians and Turks.

❾ THE CORINTH CANAL (ISTHMUS)
Ισθμός / Isthmós

Across this narrow neck connecting the Saronic and Corinthian gulfs, the ancient Corinthians had constructed a "diolkos", a corridor along which, with ropes, slaves drew only small, light, ships along a wooden track. Nero, in 67 AD, was first to attempt to open the channel, but the project was completed only in 1893. The canal is 6 kms long, the sides reaching 70 m high, width 14-21 m and depth 8 m below sea-level. You can visit the hamlet Isthmia on the eastern side of the canal and see the little bridge which is submerged every time a ship passes.

❿ ISTHMIA-ARCHAEOLOGICAL SITE
Ίσθμια - Αρχαιολογικός χώρος / Ίsthmia - Arheologikós Hóros

Near Isthmia, one of the 4 major Panhellenic athletic games of ancient times used to take place. You will see traces of the substantial **stadium**, the **theatre**, **ruins of temples** and remnants of the **Roman walls**. The museum exhibits interesting finds.

THE NAFPLIO AREA

⑪ FROM THE CANAL TO EPIDAURUS
Ισθμός - Επίδαυρος / Isthmós - Epídavros)

A route with many bends, but a varied landscape with pine forests and marvellous views to the Saronic Gulf. A better choice than the Athens-Tripoli highway. It takes longer, but the scenery will compensate you.

⑫ KORFOS
Κόρφος / Kórfos

A fishing village on the bay of Sofiko with several tavernas by the sea. For a swim, choose one of the three little beaches with limpid waters to the right of the village, to which you have to go by boat. An ideal spot for a day trip from Athens.

⑬ AGNOUNDOS MONASTERY
Μονή Αγνούντος / Moní Agnoúndos

A Byzantine monastery of the 11th c. with excellent 18th c. frescoes.

⑭ OLD EPIDAURUS - SMALL THEATRE
Παλαιά Επίδαυρος - Μικρό Θέατρο
Paliá Epídavros - Mikró Théatro

Tel. (0753) 41249
On the site of the present village of Old Epidavros there stood the city of Ancient Epidaurus. Excavations have brought to light traces of a **Doric temple**, an **ancient cemetery** and remains of **Roman walls**. A few years ago on the peninsula the marble-built and well-preserved 👁 **small theatre** (4th c. BC) was discovered. It held 6,000 spectators and today, after 23 centuries of silence, is again the scene for cultural events.

⑮ ANCIENT EPIDAURUS
Αρχαία Επίδαυρος / Archéa Epídavros

Tel. (0753) 22009
🕐 8 am-7 pm, closed on holidays*

👁 👁 👁 THE GREAT THEATRE
The most famous theatre of antiquity was built, according to Pausanias, in about 300 BC by the Argive architect and sculptor **Polykleitos the Younger**. It is one of the best-preserved ancient theatres, renowned for its incomparable **acoustics**, the result of particularly advanced technical expertise for that period.
It was the only theatre to maintain its circular stage in the Roman period, while the others were made semi-circular. Its original capacity was for about 6,000 spectators. In the 2nd c. BC, the upper bank of tiers was added and the number of spectators considerably increased. It was destroyed three times: by Sulla's soldiers (the Romans later rebuilt it), by the Visigoths and by the Byzantine emperor Theodosios. The Ionic columns of the stage no longer exist, but the perfect acoustics have lost none of their quality. It is built on a slope of Mt Kynortion, which acts as resonator, so that sound reaches the highest tiers.

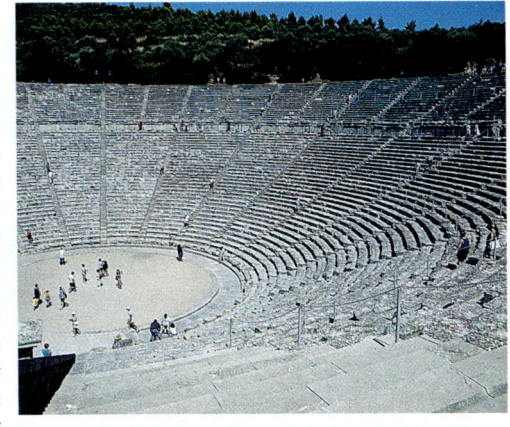

1 PELOPONNESE

ⓖⓖⓖ EPIDAURUS FESTIVAL

Information on the season and programme of performances as well as tickets: Theatro Epidavrou, tel. (0753) 22006 EOT (Greek National Tourist Organization), tel. (01) 3221459, 4 Stadiou St., Stoa Spyrou Miliou, Athens.

How to get there: By bus (KTEL), 100 Kifissou Ave., Athens, tel. (01) 5134588. On performance days there are departures at 5:15 pm, return at close of performance. There are also three daily departures from Nafplio.

In summer, the theatre presents performances within the **Epidaurus Festival**. Well-known Greek and foreign companies present celebrated works by the great ancient Greek dramatists Aeschylus, Sophocles, Euripides, Aristophanes and others. Don't miss at least one of these extraordinary events!

ⓖⓖ SANCTUARY OF ASKLEPIOS

This is in a pine grove not far from the theatre. It was the principal sanctuary of the god of healing, Asklepios, and reached its apogee in the 4th c. BC. There are many interesting architectural monuments in the area such as the second sanctuary at the back of the theatre, the **temple of Apollo Maleata**, where the faithful washed their hands and made their first sacrifice. You will see the gymnasium, the ruins of the **Kotyos Portico** and the **small wrestling ring** (palaistra). The remnants of the **temple of the goddess Artemis** are still visible, also of the large **guest-house** and the **"avaton"** ("not to be trodden") where the sick awaited the apparition of the god Asklepios. The **rotunda** (tholos) was the sanctuary's most resplendent edifice, erected by **Polykleitos the Younger**, while on the base of the principal building, the ⓖ **temple of Asklepios**, the work of the architect **Theodotos** (375-380 BC), there once stood the renowned chryselephantine (gold and ivory) statue of the god.

Asklepios

MUSEUM OF ANCIENT EPIDAURUS

Tel. (0753) 22009

🕐 8 am-7 pm, Monday 12-7 pm, closed on holidays*

Finds from the Asklepion are exhibited in the three rooms: ceramic decorative objects, surgical instruments of the period, sculptures and the capital of a column, by Polykleitos the Younger.

OTHER THINGS TO DO

Loutraki Casino: Καζίνο Λουτρακίου / Casíno Loutrakíou
A few km north of the Corinth Canal, at the entrance to the town of Loutraki. For the daring who wish to try their luck.

⛱ BEST BEACHES

The region is not known for its beaches. The better ones are far away whereas the nearer ones will not entirely please you. If you are not up to lengthy distances, make do with what we have to propose. If you are not satisfied, then it is worth visiting the quiet yet smart Porto Heli and its colourful coves.

⚓ KARATHONAS

This sandy beach with eucalyptus trees is the best nearby choice. Except that in summer it is thronged with people.

Karathonas

⚓ SALADI

A lovely long beach. Unfortunately a massive hotel spoils the setting. If you follow the coastal dirt track to the north, you will discover attractive little coves, but beware of sea urchins!

THE NAFPLIO AREA

ARVANITIA
An organized beach beneath the fort of Acronafplia. Likely to be crowded.

TOLO
A summer resort, well-developed for tourism, but chaotic. Although it has a fine beach, especially in high season it is very crowded.

IRIA
South of Nafplio. A nice beach with greenery reaching to the shore.

BEST HOTELS AND ROOMS

BEST LOCATION
We suggest you select a hotel in Nafplio's old town. Most sights are within easy reach, while your expeditions in the area will not be more than an hour away. Nafplio's better hotels are few so you should make you reservations in good time.

PRICES
The hotel prices mentioned below are the official ones set by the National Tourist Organization for double rooms, at low and high season, with breakfast. Since owners are allowed to modify the prices, always try to negotiate them.

NAFPLIO

✓✓ XENIA PALACE (Luxury)
Kastro Acronafplias, Nafplio
Tel. (0752) 28981-5, fax 28987
Open: All year round
Description: A hotel complex situated in town near the fort of Acronafplia. Its great advantage is the ❢❢ **spectacular view**. Unfortunately it is managed by the state and also gives an impression of endless size and impersonality.
Rooms: 96 rooms, most with A/C and telephone.
Special features: Restaurant, bar, pool, parking and gift shops.
Price: 41,000-58,300 drs.
Value for Money: ✱
Credit cards: All

Xenia Palace

✓✓ BYRON (A & C Class)
2 Platonos St., (opposite Agios Spyridon), Nafplio
Tel. (0752) 22351, fax 26338
Open: All year round
Description: An elegant building, in traditional style and good taste.
Authentic traditional furnishings.
Rooms: 17 rooms with room service. Ask for one in the new (neo-classical) wing and choose one with a view.
Special features: A veranda with view of the town and fort.
Price: 27,200 drs.
Value for Money: ✱✱
Credit cards: All except Diners and Alpha Card

✓✓ AMALIA (A Class)
3 km north of Nafplio
Tel. (0752) 24401, fax 24400
Open: All year round
Description: Large hotel complex in neo-classical style, of the well-known Amalia Hotels chain. It is unfortunately outside the town.

PELOPONNESE

Rooms: 175 rooms with A/C, telephone and radio.
Special features: 3 restaurants, bar, TV room, shops, pool, garden, conference room and parking.
Price: 50,600 drs.
Value for Money: ✦
Credit cards: All

Amalia

✓ OMORFI POLI (C Class)
5 Sofroni St., Nafplio
Tel. (0752) 21565, 21485
Open: All year round
Description: Neo-classical building converted to a small and cosy hotel. In good taste and certainly the best for its price.
Rooms: 9 rooms tastefully decorated and with personality.
Special features: There is an attractive coffee-shop.
Price: 17,000 drs.
Value for Money: ✦✦✦

Omorfi Poli

Credit cards: Visa

ACRONAFPLIA (C Class)
Old Town, Nafplio
Tel. (0752) 24481, fax 24076
Open: All year round
Description: Consists of five small hotels in different parts of the old town.

Rooms: A total of 30 rooms. Most are tasteful, some with bath and some not. Some big and some small. Very good for their price are the rooms in Terzaki Street, even though there is a shared bathroom.
Price: 6,000-18,000 drs., Without breakfast.
Value for Money: ✦✦
Credit cards: Visa

OUTSIDE NAFPLIO

✓ MARGARITA (A Class)
Korfos
Tel. (0741) 95480, fax 95404
Open: February-October
Description: A modern hotel in good taste consisting of 5 separate buildings surrounded by greenery, 10m from the sea.
Rooms: 36 pretty rooms with A/C, TV, mini bar, telephone, balcony, most with sea view.
Special features: Pool, bar, restaurant and parking.
Price: 20,300-29,500 drs.
Value for Money: ✦
Credit cards: Visa, Diners, Ethnocarta

ALTERNATIVES

AMPHITRYON (A Class)
Akti Miaouli, Nafplio, tel. (0752) 27366-7, fax 25850
Price: 19,400-25,000 drs.

AGAMEMNON (B Class),
3 Akti Miaouli St., Nafplio, tel. (0752) 28021, fax 28023. **Price:** 17,800-18,600 drs.

VENUS
Korfos, tel. (0741) 95279 & fax
Price: 17,000 drs., Without breakfast.

Should you not be able to get a room in one of the hotels of our selection, one of the travel agents listed below may be able to help you:
Yiannopoulos Travel, 18 Syntagma Sq.,
tel. (0752) 28054
Zafiris Tours, 9 Thessalonikis St.,
tel. (0752) 22221, 21205
Staikos Tours, 50 Bouboulinas St.,
tel. (0752) 27950, 22444

THE NAFPLIO AREA

BEST RESTAURANTS & TAVERNAS

NAFPLIO
One of the town's great assets is its many and excellent restaurants and tavernas.

✓✓ VASSILIS
Staikopoulou St., tel. (0752) 25334
A taverna with a delightful traditional atmosphere, good Greek food and grills.
Price: €€

Vassilis

✓✓ ARAPAKOS
Bouboulinas St., tel. (0752) 27675
With a view on the port. Neo-classical building, open for lunch and dinner but make reservations. Fish and Greek cooking in a pleasant room seating 70. Excellent service.
Price: €€

✓✓ STELARAS
Bouboulinas St., tel. (0752) 28818
Fish and Greek food at lunch and dinner-time. Agreeable classical music.
Price: €€

Stellaras

✓ MARKEZINIS
Staikopoulou St., tel. (0752) 23785
Plain Greek food, good waiters, courteous owners, only 24 places, tables outside and inside. Locals recommend it. Speciality: cod with garlic sauce.
Price: €

✓ TA FANARIA
Staikopoulou St. in a side-street, tel. (0752) 27141
A charming taverna with good food and reasonable prices. In summer, out of doors under trees.
Price: €

✓ OMORFO TAVERNAKI
Kotsonopoulou & 1 Vass. Olgas Sts., tel. (0752) 25944
Cosy, good food and friendly service.
Price: €

PALIO ARCHONTIKO
7 Siokou St., tel. (0752) 22449
Not a large choice but well-cooked food, good service, friendly owner. In summer, live guitar music in the side-alley.
Price: €

Palio Archontiko

ELLAS
Syntagma Sq., tel. (0752) 27278
Nafplio's oldest restaurant – a hundred years old. Spacious, excellent Greek specialities, open for lunch and dinner.
It had an international reputation, was mentioned in the *New York Times*, but we found it to have rather deteriorated.
Price: €

1 PELOPONNESE

OUTSIDE NAFPLIO

✓ LEONIDAS
Ligourio - Epidaurus, tel. (0753) 22115
A good taverna, favourite venue for actors after the festival performances. **Price:** €€
If you can't get a table, try the cheaper **Asteria**.

SELANA
Korfos, tel. (0741) 95236
Very fresh fish at good prices. Tables by the sea, at the edge of the village.
Price: €

BEST ENTERTAINMENT

Most cafes and bars are in Nafplio, concentrated in Plateia Syntagmatos, Bouboulinas Street and Akti Miaouli. *Best* suggests: the **Lyrikon** for Greek coffee made the traditional way on embers; the **Agora**, the venue for the young; the **Pantheon** for coffee and delicious walnut cake; the **Akteon** for pastries and a fine view and the **Kafenion** with its attractive decor. Also the bars **Anadromi**, **Lykeio** and **Vetto** for the night hours. In summer the bigger nightclubs are all on the Nafplio-Kios coastal road.

i TIPS AND INFORMATION

HOW TO GET THERE
- Ideally in your own car from Nafplio to be able to travel around the many significant sights of the area.
- By Minoan Flying Dolphins (hydrofoil). Information: tel. (01) 4280001-4113108. 4 hrs from the port of Zea in Piraeus to Nafplio (from 4,600 drs.). Summer only.
- By intercity bus, KTEL, 100 Kifissou Ave., Athens, tel. (01) 5134588 (from 2,550 drs.).
- By train (OSE Stathmos Peloponnissou), Athens, tel. (01) 5131601 (from 1,400 drs.).

CONNECTIONS
- By Minoan Flying Dolphin, tel. (0752) 28054. In summer months Nafplio is connected to the Argosaronic Gulf islands, to Porto Heli, Ermioni and Tolo.
- By intercity bus, KTEL, tel. (0752) 27323. From Nafplio to Sparta, Corinth, Tripoli, Kalamata and Megalopolis.

BEST TIPS

HOW TO GET AROUND: In Nafplio's old town, on foot, as the streets are narrow and parking space hard to find. For out of town sightseeing, if you haven't got a car we suggest you hire one for a day or two.
Other solutions:
- The Argolis intercity bus, KTEL Argolidas, frequent departures, 10 Syngrou St., Nafplio, tel. (0752) 27323.
- Day trips from Nafplio with travel agents:
  Giannopoulos Travel, 18 Syntagma Sq., tel. (0752) 28054
  Zafiris Tours, 9 Thessalonikis St., tel. (0752) 22221, 21205
  Staikos Tours, 50 Bouboulinas St., tel. (0752) 27950, 22444

BEST SEASON: The region is suitable for excursions year round, though it would be a good idea to combine your trip with the summer festival season at Epidaurus, to experience a theatrical performance in the ancient theatre.

BEST BUYS: Do not fail to try the Nemea wines, renowned for their quality. In the little shop in Staikopoulou Street, you can buy shadow-play figures and in the little string-bead museum, an unusual string of worry-beads will relieve your anxieties!

USEFUL TELEPHONE NUMBERS

NAFPLIO 0752	Tourist Bureau..24444
Municipal Office...23330	Traffic Police..22972
Tourist Police...28131	Port Authority..27022
Police 27776	Taxis...23600, 24120

KASTANIA

Kastania **Lake Doxis**
Lake Stymphalia

WHY AMONG THE BEST

For the natural beauty of Corinthia's highlands. For the marvellous routes between the towering heights of Mts Kyllini (Ziria) and Aroania (Helmos). For the dense fir and pine forests. For the enchantment of Lake Doxis and the Feneos plateau, the Stymphalian plain, Kastania and the many charming villages of "Corinthian Switzerland" as it is called by its admirers.

PELOPONNESE

BEST's OPINION

In recent years the region has become more widely known. It is the place for ardent nature-lovers, as well as for those who want to escape from the city for a few days to ramble in mountainous country, in an unspoiled natural environment. In winter you'll often encounter the delights of snowscapes in the mountains and on lakeshores, although occasionally the snow may hamper your movements.

BEST SIGHTS: STEP BY STEP

❶ FROM PSARI TO KALIANI
Ψάρι- Καλιάνοι / Psári- Kaliánoi

The colour green in a glory of all its variations and shades. On this route you'll encounter flatlands, plains encircled by mountains, steep cliffs with clambering vineyards, chestnut and plane trees, also a winding brook.

❷ LAKE STYMPHALIA
Λίμνη Στυμφαλία / Límni Stimfalía

The lake is known from the days of mythology. This is where **Heracles** (Hercules) destroyed the **Stymphalian Birds**. Today the water level varies, depending on the time of year, and it is surrounded by reed-beds. On its northern side there are the ruins of the **acropolis of ancient Stymphalos**, as well as remnants of **walls**, **an aqueduct** and **temples**. The village of Stymphalia is of no particular interest.

❸ LAFKA
Λαύκα / Láfka

A small village of traditional architecture, one of the most attractive of the region, in a ravine covered in fir trees. There is a square with cafes and tavernas. Walk to the top of the village and continue your **hike** from there, following the path along the stream and into the ravine.

④ KASTANIA
Καστανιά / Kastaniá

The most pleasant village of the district and ideal for a stay. It is on the slopes of Ziria, in a ravishing **landscape** smothered in lush chestnut, fir, plane and pine trees. It is not developed for tourism but there are some tavernas and the only worthwhile hotel of the region. Nature-lovers will find here many options for walks and hikes.

⑤ GOURA
Γκούρα / Goúra

A large village hardly touched by the passage of time, at an altitude of 930 m, with a view over the plain and the fir-covered slope. Nowadays it is a minor administrative centre for the region. See the **traditional buildings** and the **church** in the well-preserved square, enjoy a cup of coffee in **Bekiari's** charming kafenio (cafe) behind the church.

⑥ FENEOS
Φενεός / Feneós

When you reach this small idyllic village, stop a while above the road to look at the cluster of handsome well-preserved stone houses. A few kilometres to the south-west, on a hill, traces have been found of the fine ancient city of **Pheneos**, known from Homer. The city declined in Roman and Byzantine times and disappeared from the pages of history.

⑦ FROM FENEOS TO LAKE DOXIS
Φενεός- Λίμνη Δόξης / Feneós-Límni Dóxis

Time required: about one hour.
A practicable dirt road for a superb route with an unbelievable variety of trees. At some point you may think yourself lost, but if you continue, you will find the **dam** before you. From its top you will enjoy the vista over calm green **Lake Doxis**, reflecting the surrounding mountains in its waters. One of the loveliest spots in Greece. Many travellers have mentioned the lake, which was at times seen dry (Pausanias, 176 AD) or had a depth of 50 m (1859). The subterranean passages or drains let the water out of the plateau but the inhabitants nonetheless suffered floods. The church on the little island is dedicated to **Agios Fanourios**. Walk around the lake along the path. The entire region lends itself to enjoyable hikes as well as to picnic sites.

⑧ MONASTERY OF AGIOS GEORGIOS FENEOS
Μονή Αγίου Γεωργίου Φενεού / Moní Agíou Georgíou Feneoú

A 17th c. three-storeyed monastery on the hill above the lake. In the years of Ottoman domination it functioned as a **clandestine school**. In the church, a basilica with an eight-sided dome, you will see interesting **frescoes** by the icon-painter Panagiotis, influenced by the Cretan school. There are notable relics as well as valuable manuscripts and vestments. The **view** from the glass-paned balconies of the upper floors is stupendous. From this height you have a view over the entire Feneos plateau, the slopes of the Aroania mountains, Lake Doxis and the Dourdouvana mountain peak.

BEYOND THIS EXCURSION
FROM FENEOS TO ZAROUCHLA *(See Excursion 3)*
Φενεός- Ζαρούχλα / Feneós-Zaroúchla. *Time required: about one hour.*

PELOPONNESE

BEST HOTELS AND ROOMS

BEST LOCATION

The region does not have good hotels. Make reservations ahead of time at the only decent hotel, the **Xenia** at Kastania.

PRICES

The hotel prices mentioned below are the official ones set by the National Tourist Organization for double rooms, at low and high season, with breakfast. Since owners are allowed to modify the prices, always try to negotiate them.

✓ XENIA KASTANIAS (B Class)

Kastania, tel. (0747) 61283-5, (01) 6645304
Open: All year round
Description: Stone-built of 1978, amidst fir trees. Pleasant atmosphere, although state-owned and somewhat neglected.
Rooms: There are 17 simple but comfortable rooms with bath.
Special features: Fireplace in the lounge, restaurant and parking.
Price: 16,000 - 24,140 drs., half-board obligatory.
Value for Money: ✷
Credit cards: None

ALTERNATIVES

STYMPHALIA (E Class) *Stymphalia, tel. (0747) 22072, 22058.* **Price:** 14,600 drs.
LAFKA GUEST HOUSE *(Xenonas Lafkas), Lafka, tel. (0747) 31220.* **Price:** 7,200-10,800 drs.

BEST RESTAURANTS & TAVERNAS

In Kastania you can have a meal at the **Xenia hotel restaurant** or at the **Steki**, a taverna with good food, fireplace and pleasing view from the veranda.
In Stymphalia there are tavernas under the plane trees, with brooks running beside them. We propose **Pestrophes** (The Trouts) where you can choose from live fish.
At Karteri, south west of Kastania, **Leonida's**, grill has resisted plastic chairs and also has a few simple rooms for the night.
Price: All €

TIPS AND INFORMATION

HOW TO GET THERE

- By your own means of transport, so as to stop where you wish and enjoy the natural beauty spots. If it is a 4-wheel drive, you will not be hampered by the dirt roads. For rental we advise you to hire a car before reaching Stymphalia as there is no branch office there.
- Organized excursions: Trekking Hellas, tel. (01) 3310323
- By intercity bus from Athens, KTEL, 100 Kifissou Ave., tel. (01) 5129232
- By intercity bus from Corinth, KTEL Corinthias, tel. (0741) 24581

BEST TIPS

BEST SEASON: All seasons in good weather. Relatively tranquil and cool in the summer if you wish to escape from the masses.

USEFUL TELEPHONE NUMBERS

KASTANIA .... (0747)
Community 61268
Police 61211

ZAROUCHLA

Zarouchla   Lake Tsivlou

WHY AMONG THE BEST

Because of its landscape. Unspoiled and with very little tourism. Because of the traditional character of its villages, the drives one can take through its magnificent forests and its walks. People who enjoy Greece's mountains consider the district one of the country's most beautiful.

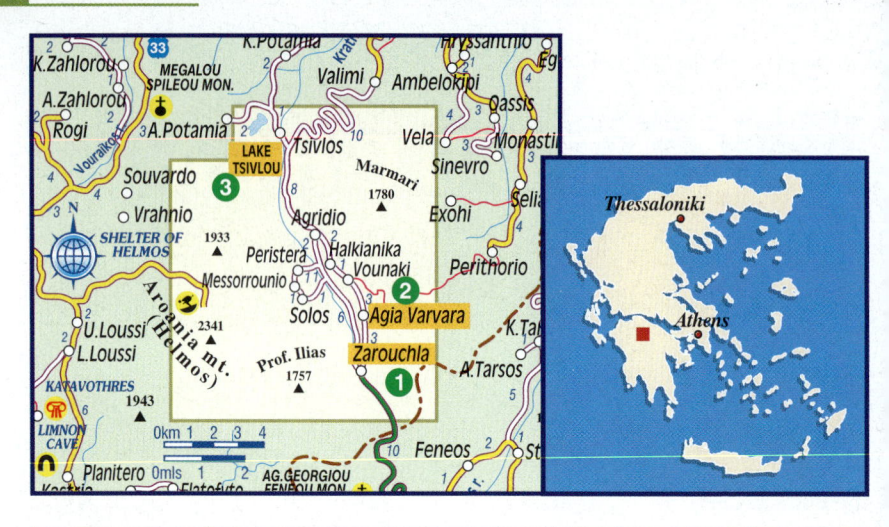

3 PELOPONNESE

BEST's OPINION

A place for adventure. For 4-wheel drives and cross-country bikes over unpaved roads and through small, untouched hamlets up in the mountains, amidst thick fir and pine forests, ravines and slopes, rivers, streams and springs. Lake Tsivlou will take you by surprise. Most of all, you'll love getting lost on trails that don't exist on any map, but will take you to the ski centre on Helmos, to Kalavryta or to Feneos, which are described below.
The district is becoming more and more popular, so make sure you reserve your room ahead of time.

BEST SIGHTS: STEP BY STEP

❶ ZAROUCHLA
Ζαρούχλα / Zaroúchla

A traditional village spread out in the open valley, in a splendid 〞〞 **setting** with a great variety of trees (mainly plane-trees and firs). The area has an abundance of running water, thanks to the **Kryoneri spring**. This is a wonderful option for a quiet weekend, with many possibilities for walks or drives. In winter the village is often snow-covered.

❷ AGIA VARVARA
Αγία Βαρβάρα / Agía Varvára

A village with many traditional features. In the 19th c. its residents were much sought-after as builders. It occupies a mountain slope, 5 km from Zarouchla, and is well worth a visit. This is a good place to stay if you can't find a room in the **Pyrgos of Zarouchla**.

❸ LAKE TSIVLOU
Λίμνη Τσιβλού / Límni Tsivloú

A bit before (2 km) you arrive at this small lake, you will come to a dirt road which will lead you to its pale green waters surrounded by

Agia Varvara

steep, fir-covered slopes. It cannot however compare with the beauty of the nearby lake Doxis. There are picnic benches on its banks and a canteen, which is unfortunately in very poor taste and spoils the setting.

FREE TIME
HIKING: THE SOURCE OF THE STYX
(Mavroneri waterfall)

Lake Tsivlou

This is a difficult hike which we do not recommend to the inexperienced. The paths are tricky, turning into slippery scree in places and blocked by snow in winter. The intrepid should ask the villagers in Zarouchla about path conditions and other details.

Set off from the village of Peristera in the direction of the Styx valley, and from there to Xirokambos (the ski centre) and then to Neraidorahi (2,238 m). It is about three to four hours' walk to the Styx waterfall.
One of the daughters of Oceanus, Styx, helped Zeus win in his battle against the Giants. To show his gratitude, Zeus gave her the right to be the guarantor of the oaths of the immortals. This oath was sacred and any deity who violated it was condemned to ten years of severe punishments. During the first year, the god was not permitted to breathe or to partake of the divine nourishment, ambrosia and nectar. From the second to the tenth year, he/she had to live in isolation and was not permitted to join in Olympian counsels. Thetis washed her son Achilles in the waters of the Styx to make him invincible.
The waters, most abundant in winter and spring, fall from the peak of Neraidorahi and form two small waterfalls. At the point where they fall, there is an opening in the rock, which the ancients believed to be one of the entrances to Hades. Don't linger here: there is a danger of rock-slides.

BEYOND THIS EXCURSION
FROM ZAROUCHLA TO FENEOS
Ζαρούχλα-Φενεός / Zaroúchla-Feneós
Time required: about one hour for the 15 km. (See Excursion 2).
A dirt road for vehicles with high road-clearance such as a 4-wheel drive. There is snow in the winter and with rain it gets muddy and you might get bogged down. In fair weather conditions though, you will enjoy a wonderful route through dense forest with tall firs. Ideal for hikers. Shortly after Zarouchla there is an organized playground and picnic area.

BEST HOTELS AND ROOMS

BEST LOCATION
Try for the **Pyrgos of Zarouchla** despite the difficulties of finding a room there. It is the best choice so make your reservation well in advance.

PRICES
The hotel prices mentioned below are the official ones set by the National Tourist Organization for double rooms, at low and high season, with breakfast. Since owners are allowed to modify the prices, always try to negotiate them.

PELOPONNESE

☑ PYRGOS OF ZAROUCHLA

Zarouchla
Tel. (0696) 51252, (01) 5445596, fax (01) 6440416
Open: All year round
Description: A beautiful stone pension. Built on a high spot, it has a marvellous view. Its owners open only if they can let all the rooms, which is difficult in midweek. If you're thinking of going for a weekend, then make sure you have a reservation.
Rooms: The pension has 4 rooms, with central heating and a fireplace.
Price: 22,000 drs.
Value for money: ✻
Credit cards: None

ALTERNATIVES

HELMOS
Zarouchla, tel. (0696) 51243, (01) 7517555.
Price: 9,500 drs. Without breakfast

EPAMINONDAS MAHAIRAS ROOMS
Zarouchla, tel. (0696) 51218, 22931.
Price: 6,000-10,000 drs. Without breakfast

CHRISTOS ARFANIS PENSION
Agia Varvara, tel. (0696) 34095. **Price:** 8,000 drs.

BEST RESTAURANTS & TAVERNAS

Zarouchla has a few tavernas. Try **Mahairas** for its wild greens and charcoal grills in clean surroundings. In Agia Varvara, the **Tzaki** (fireplace) on the village square is a good bet, but it is not always open during the week.
Price: All €

TIPS AND INFORMATION

HOW TO GET THERE

- This itinerary is recommended only for those with a motorcycle or car, preferably with 4-wheel drive.
- The road as far as Zarouchla, via Akrata on the Corinthian Gulf, is good, but the dirt road to the surrounding areas is fairly rough, particularly in winter.
- Because exploring in the region is the aim of this excursion, make sure your vehicle is in good condition and has a full petrol tank.

BEST TIPS

BEST SEASON: Lovely all year round, as long as the weather is good.

USEFUL TELEPHONE NUMBERS

ZAROUCHLA .... (0696)   Community Office 51266   OTE 51311

Kalavryta

⁶⁶⁶ Cog-Wheeled Railway (Vouraikos Gorge)
⁶⁶ Kalavryta

WHY AMONG THE BEST

Because of the Vouraikos Gorge which you can go through either on foot or by cog-wheeled railway. Because of the historic monasteries of Agia Lavra and Mega Spileon and also Mt Helmos and the impressive cave of the Lakes (ton Limnon) at Kastria, the Aroanian springs and the ski resort.

4 PELOPONNESE

BEST's OPINION

Kalavryta is fashionable in the winter months and in early spring because of its ski resort. Most visitors are winter-sports fans, mainly from Athens and Patras, enjoying a weekend full of fun and action. The marvellous natural scenery and old monasteries are a special attraction for all age-groups.

BEST SIGHTS: STEP BY STEP

① KALAVRYTA
Καλάβρυτα / Kalávryta

At an altitude of 750 m on a slope of Mt Helmos, a historic chief town still preserving features of its heritage. It was the site of the ancient city of Kinetha, destroyed in 220 BC by Aetolians, later by Philip V, King of Macedonia, and finally devastated by Goth and Slav invasions. It was a barony in the days of the Frank overlords and when liberated with the assistance of Mystra, passed to the Paleologues. In 1460 it fell to the Turks when they captured the fortress of Oria (on the hill above the town) and was again twice destroyed in the course of the War of Independence. The greatest tragedy to befall the town in modern times occurred on 13 December 1943 when Nazi troops massacred the entire male population (over 1,400 men above the age of thirteen). Today Kalavryta is a modern town of 2,000 inhabitants, the district's commercial centre and is rapidly expanding its attractions for tourists.

❷ COG-WHEELED RAILWAY - VOURAIKOS GORGE
Οδοντωτός (Φαράγγι Βουραϊκού) / Odondotós (Farángi Vouraikoú)

Diakofto cog-wheeled railway, tel. (0691) 43206
Kalavryta cog-wheeled railway, tel. (0692) 22245
Departures from Diakofto to Kalavryta daily at 8 am, 10:30 am, 1:15 pm and 3:45 pm. Weekends: 9 am, 11:30 am, 2:15 pm and 4:45 pm. Departures from Kalavryta daily 9:15 am, 11:45 am, 2:30 pm and 5 pm. Weekends 10:15 am, 12:45 pm, 3:30 pm and 6 pm. Duration about one hour, tickets 1,000 drs. one way and 1,750 drs. return. Phone to confirm departure times.

The cog-wheeled railway starts at Diakofto, stops at **Zahlorou** and continues to Kalavryta. It is the only one of its kind in Greece, in operation since 1896, with pinions to prevent it sliding back on the steep gradients. The route is one of the loveliest in the country, climbing through the gorge above the Vouraikos river, unfolding scenery of unmatched beauty to the traveller's marvelling eyes. Enormous cliffs down to the river bed, little valleys, bridges and, midway, Zahlorou's abundant greenery, where there is a stop. You can take a walk in the forest and have a cup of coffee or a meal in one of the tavernas under towering plane trees. There are also rooms for rent for anyone wishing to spend the night.

Zahlorou

❸ MEGA SPILEON MONASTERY
Μονή Μεγάλου Σπηλαίου / Moní Megálou Spiléou

Tel. (0692) 23130, 22401
An eight-storey monastery built into the cliff-face at an altitude of 924 m. It was founded in the 4th c. by two monks and is considered one of the oldest and best-known in Greece. The surroundings are stunning and it can be reached either by car or on foot by the path from Zahlorou. The monastery was first destroyed in 840 by the iconoclasts and again in 1460 and 1640 by the Turks. In 1934 it burned down and in 1943 was demolished by the German occupation troops. See the icon in relief of the **Panagia tis Chryssospiliotissas**, made of wax and gum mastic, **one of four works attributed to Saint Luke**. The church has significant frescoes dated 1600, manuscripts, bibles and reliquaries.

❹ AGIA LAVRA MONASTERY
Μονή Αγίας Λαύρας / Moní Agías Lávras

Tel. (0692) 22363
Founded in the 10th c. by the monk **Athanassios Athonitis**, it played an important role in the period of the Greek War of Independence of 1821. Several times destroyed by the Turks and then by Ibrahim when he invaded the Peloponnese, it also suffered great damage by the Nazi troops, but was always rebuilt by the monks. It contains numerous valuable relics and a library with antique manuscripts. It was here that the banner of freedom was raised on 18 March 1821.

5 UPPER AND LOWER LOUSSI
Άνω και Κάτω Λούσοι / Áno ke Káto Loússi

A short detour will take you through these villages where fine old mansions have been preserved.

6 LIMNON CAVE
Σπήλαιο Λιμνών / Spíleo Limnón

16.5 km from Kalavryta at the village of Kastria, tel. (0692) 31001, 31588, 31633
*9:30 am-4:30 pm, extended in summer and on holidays**

A cavern on three levels with thirteen tiers of lakes, galleries and passages presenting an astounding spectacle of stalagmites and stalactites hanging from the roof which is sometimes as high as 30 m, in extraordinary shapes. It was discovered in 1964 by Kastrian villagers and the lower level contains finds of great palaeontological interest: human and animal fossils, among which a specimen of Hippopotamus Anticus. The first level is unfortunately not accessible to visitors because of on-going excavations, but you can see one of the lakes (length 37 m, width 10 m and depth 5.5 m) and the beginning of the rim of the second. The lakes are separated by a dam 2.5 m high.

7 PLANITERO
Πλανιτέρο / Planitéro

Gorgeous scenery with thousands of plane trees, and streams, where you will see the famous springs of the Aroanios river, a trout farm and an artificial lake with real swans. Although popular with tourists, the area has not lost its charm. At numerous tavernas you can have delicious salmon and trout caught on the spot. They are open winter and summer and for lunch and dinner. To avoid the throngs arriving by coach, for a more expensive coffee, meal or fresh fish, go to **Laleoussa**, for ready-cooked dishes, grills and trout, where there are canvas chairs rather than the plastic of the others.

Hike
It is an ideal spot for walking and hiking by the river, which has water all year round.

8 FROM NEOHORI TO KRINI
Νεοχώρι-Κρήνη / Neohóri-Kríni

This 🅶🅶 route takes you through superb woods surrounded by mountain peaks, leading to the 🅶 **Makellaria monastery** built on a huge smooth pinnacle of rock reminiscent of Meteora. Continue on to the village of Krini to round off your experience of a truly exceptional landscape.

9 MAKELLARIA MONASTERY (KIMISSIS TIS THEOTOKOU)
Μονή Μακελλαριάς (Κοίμησης της Θεοτόκου) / Moní Makellarías (Kímissis tis Theotókou)

An 18th c. marble inscription indicates that the monastery was founded by Belissarios, the renowned general of the time of the Byzantine emperor Justinian, and gives the date as 532. The nave consists of two small churches of the 18th c., Agia Triada and Panagia. The monastery has a modest collection of relics on show.

OTHER THINGS TO DO

🅶 SKI RESORT
15 km from Kalavryta, tel. (0692) 22174, 22661
8:30 am-3:30 pm

KALAVRYTA 4

Stretching from Xirokambos (altitude 1,700 m) to Neraidorahi (2,347 m), on the northern slopes of Mt Helmos, the resort has ski instructors and 12 runs for all aptitudes with 7 lifts (5 T-bars and 2 chair-lifts) of a total length of 25 km. The reception building, with a cafeteria and parking lot, is at Xirokambos, from where the lift to Vathia Laka (1,850 m) starts. There is also a National Tourist Office pavilion with public rooms, a cafe and restaurant, first aid station, and a store for the rental and purchase of skiing equipment. A refuge for mountain climbers is located at 2,100 m.

BEST HOTELS AND ROOMS

BEST LOCATION

The pensions of Kalavryta are preferable to the hotels and offer better value, unless you wish to stay in the centre of town. High season is winter because of the ski resort.

PRICES

The hotel prices mentioned below are the official ones set by the National Tourist Organization for double rooms, at low and high season, with breakfast. Since owners are allowed to modify the prices, always try to negotiate them.

✓✓ FANARAS (A Class)

Tel. (0692) 23665, fax 23667
Open: All year round

Description: A recently-built pension in the upper town with a panoramic view.
Rooms: 9 apartments and 2 twin-bed rooms decorated in local traditional style, with kitchen, fireplace and balcony or wide veranda. View of the slopes with fir-trees and vista in the round of the town.
Special features: Independent central heating, TV and telephone. Parking.
Price: 12,000-18,000 drs.
Value for money: ✳✳✳
Credit cards: None

✓✓ DRYADES (A Class)

Tel. (0692) 23840, fax (061) 621076
Open: All year round except July and 20/8 - 20/9.

Description: Pension with much charm, 200 m from the square, view of Kalavryta.
Rooms: The rooms are new, with TV, telephone and taped music.
Price: 17,000-20,000 drs. without breakfast
Value for money: ✳✳
Credit cards: Visa

✓✓ APHRODITES INN (A Class)

Tel., fax (0692) 23600, 23418, (094) 758595
Open: All year round

107

Description: On the road to the ski resort, 2 km out of Kalavryta. A pension with a difference, at the edge of the forest in peaceful and green surroundings.
Rooms: 10 rooms with heating, telephone and TV.
Special features: Parking. If you like riding, lessons are available and outings are organized with docile horses. Make the arrangements when you book.
Price: 17,000-26,500 drs.
Value for money: ✱ ✱
Credit cards: None

ALTERNATIVES

THETIS HOTEL (A Class)
Tel. (0692) 22605. **Price:** 10,000-20,000 drs.

FILOXENIA HOTEL (B Class) *tel. (0692) 22422, 22290, 22493, fax 23009.* **Price:** 18,500-25,000 drs.

For inexpensive rooms to rent, contact the National Tourist Organization (EOT) for information: tel. (0692) 23418.

BEST RESTAURANTS & TAVERNAS

KALAVRYTA
✓ **ALLES GEFSIS**
Tel. (0692) 22615
It is well named "Other Flavours", an exact description of the food, which is totally unusual.
Worth a visit to check it out.
Price: €

You'll also find good food at the tavernas **To Tzaki**, tel. (0692) 22609, **O Elatos**, tel. (0692) 22541, and **To Steki**, tel. (0692) 22629. **Price:** All €

BEST ENTERTAINMENT

There are many classy cafes in Kalavryta, most of them in the central square. Next to the railway station under the plane trees you can feast on delicious hot deep-fried dough-huts (loukoumades). We can unreservedly recommend **Gri-gri** for coffee, breakfast, home-made cheese and custard pies; **Milo**, next to the hospital, a cosy bar with good Greek and international music; the **Deer Hunting Pub**, in British style, on the side street off Taki Georgakopoulo St. and the **Arhondiko** with Greek music, behind the church. There is also **Skiniko** on Helmos Square and finally **Xefandoma**, formerly the **Cinema Club**.

TIPS AND INFORMATION

HOW TO GET THERE
- In your own car if you wish to see the region the lesser known sports.
- If you want to join an organized tour, contact the following travel agents:
  Pyramis, tel. (01) 3254975.
  Travel Day, in collaboration with Key Tours, tel. (01) 3246701.
- By intercity bus (KTEL), 100 Kifissou Ave., Athens, tel. (01) 5134588.
- By rail, OSE Stathmos Peloponissou, Athens, tel. (01) 5131601. To Diakofto by Intercity and from there by cog-wheeled railway.

BEST TIPS

HOW TO GET AROUND: If you do not have your own car, public transport and taxis will get you to your general destinations.

BEST SEASON: In winter if you ski or wish to combine a trip with entertainment, but pleasant at any time of year.

BEST LOCAL FOOD: Dough-huts at **Yianni Gerou's** little cafe at Kalavryta railway station. Alexopoulos' yoghurt at the **Proino** and cheese pie at **Vardakastanis'**. Finally, lovers of preserves will find the **Ermidi family** white-heart and wild morello cherries treat.

USEFUL TELEPHONE NUMBERS

KALAVRYTA	(0692)	Police	23333
Town Hall	22390	Hospital	22366, 22222, 22724

Arcadian Highlands

Stemnitsa · Loussios Gorge · Dimitsana
Karytena · Vytina · Andritsena

WHY AMONG THE BEST

Because of the routes through forests and mountain slopes; because of the beautiful and historic mountain villages Vytina, Dimitsana, Stemnitsa, Karytena and Andritsena; because of the hikes in the entrancing landscape of the Loussios river with its gorge and monasteries; because of the temple of Apollo Epikourios at ancient Bassae.

5 PELOPONNESE

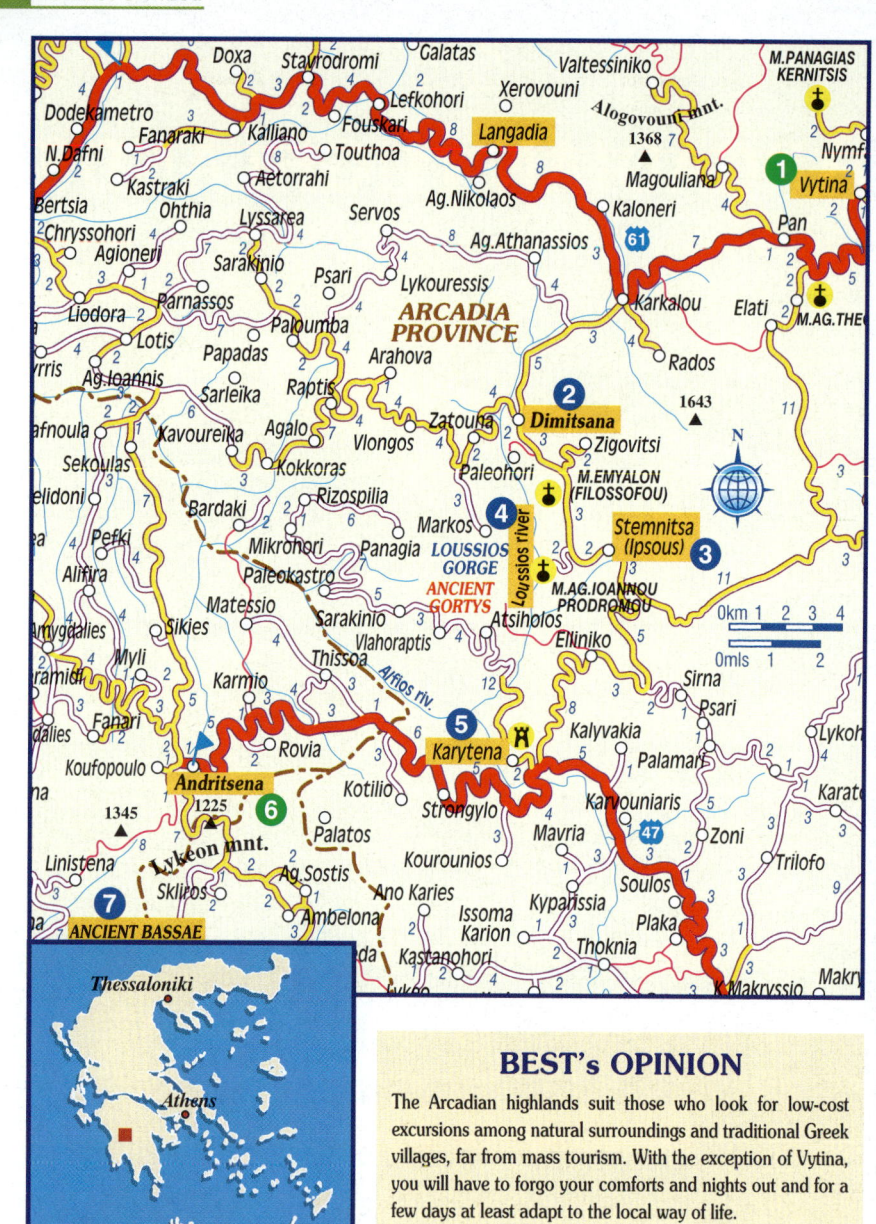

BEST's OPINION

The Arcadian highlands suit those who look for low-cost excursions among natural surroundings and traditional Greek villages, far from mass tourism. With the exception of Vytina, you will have to forgo your comforts and nights out and for a few days at least adapt to the local way of life.

BEST SIGHTS: STEP BY STEP

❶ VYTINA
Βυτίνα / Vytína

A mountain village on Mt Menalo, altitude about 1,033 m. It is thickly wooded and its excellent climate has long made it a favourite destination for Athenians. It is the best organized of all the district's villages, at the expense however of its local colour. Vytina is also known for its wood-carvings.

ARCADIAN HIGHLANDS 5

WHAT TO SEE

The **church of Agion Apostolon** and nearby, built on a rock, the **monastery of Panagia tis Sfiridas**. It also served as a clandestine school in the days of Ottoman domination.

❷ DIMITSANA
Δημητσάνα / Dimitsána

A historic chief town built like an amphitheatre on Mt Menalos, above the Loussios river. At this spot there once existed the ancient city of **Tefthis**. There are scattered remains of **cyclopean walls** and the ruins of the acropolis at **Kastro**. Dimitsana flourished under the Franks and remained prosperous under the Turks. It played an important role in the years of the Greek War of Independence of 1821 because of its **90 gunpowder** factories and was the birthplace of prominent figures in the struggle for liberation. Strong traditional features are preserved and the visitor can admire the **cobblestone alleys** and **stone-built mansions**, in harmony with the splendid surroundings.

WHAT TO SEE

The houses of the **Patriarch Gregorios V** and of **Paleon Patron Germanos**, the fine library, the folk art collection, the **historic churches of Agios Efthymios**, of **Agios Georgios** and of **Agios Ioannis**, as well as **Mustafa's fountain**.

⑥⑥ HYDRAULIC POWER MUSEUM
Μουσείο Υδροκίνησης / Moussío Idrokínissis

☉ Summer 10 am-2 pm, winter 10 am-4 pm and 5-7 pm, closed on Tuesdays and holidays*

The most striking of Dimitsana's sights. Three types of mill are worked by the river whose spring is next to the chapel above the museum: gunpowder and flour-mills and a tannery. You'll get an idea of how our ancestors coped with their requirements.

❸ STEMNITSA
Στεμνίτσα / Stemnítsa

A chief village in a scenic spot on the slopes of Mt Menalos, among four ravines. It prospered greatly in Byzantine times and was renowned for the **bells** crafted by its artisans. Later, due to its **metal works**, it developed into one of the major commercial and artisans' centre of the region. It was also a **centre of gold and silver-smithery**, for which it has today a technical school.
For about one month during the War of Independence Stemnitsa was the capital of Greece.

Stemnitsa

WHAT TO SEE

Other than strolling about the **picturesque alleys** with **stone mansions**, in the square you can see an admirable **stone belfry** and the **churches** of **Panagia Bafero** (12th c.), **Agios Nikolaos** with 14th c. frescoes and the **Tris Ierarches** with 18th c. frescoes.

Panagia Bafero

111

5 PELOPONNESE

MUSEUM OF FOLK ART / Λαογραφικό Μουσείο / Laografikó Moussío
Tel. (0795) 81252

Mondays, Tuesdays, Fridays 4-6 pm, Wednesdays, Thursdays, Sundays 11 am-1 pm, Saterdays 11 am-1 pm and 4-6 pm

In the **Hatzi mansion**, near the hotel **Trikolonio**. You will see **workshops for traditional handicrafts**, very good **Byzantine icons**, and ceramics, wood-carvings, embroideries, traditional costumes, etc.

❹ LOUSSIOS GORGE
Φαράγγι Λούσιου / Farángi Loússiou

How to get there: The road from Elliniko is a passable dirt road. After the 3rd km, at the first crossroads, there are road signs pointing left for Ancient Gortyna (1 km) and right for Moni Prodromou (4 km), Stemnitsa (14 km) and Dimitsana (17 km). Go to Ancient Gortyna first and then to Moni Prodromou. Should you set out to hike from Dimitsana or Stemnitsa, it is advisable to ask the inhabitants for information about the paths, which are not signposted.

One of the most **impressive gorges** in Greece. For 5 km you will delight in sights unique for their stupendous landscape, combining the luxuriant vegetation of holm-oak, maple, cedar and plane trees, with gulches, crags, superb monasteries and the River Loussios with its secret waterfalls. The region satisfies all tastes and degrees of stamina: of both hikers and ordinary walkers.

① **Agios Andreas** / Άγιος Ανδρέας / Áyios Andréas: A single-aisled domed 12th c. Byzantine chapel.

② **Kokkori Bridge** / Γεφύρι Κόκκορη / Yefíri Kókori : A splendid stone bridge over the Loussios river. It is worth stopping here to enjoy the surroundings. There is a good road as far as the bridge and you can leave your car here and walk on by the path. The river-banks under the bridge are an ideal picnic spot.

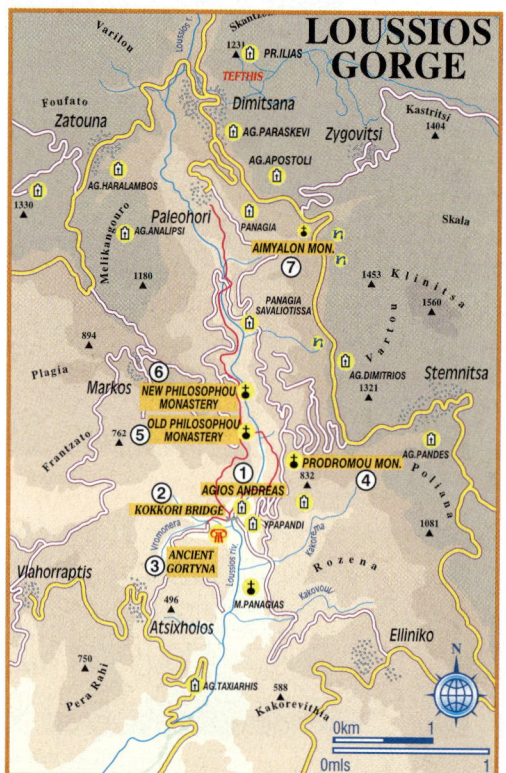

③ **Ancient Gortyna** / Αρχαία Γόρτυνα / Archéa Górtyna: Near the chapel and bridge are the ruins of one of the principal ancient Arcadian cities. Unfortunately little is extant today. However, on the banks of the Loussios you will see the ruins of the walls, the dwellings, the baths and sanctuaries, the most important among them that of Asklepios.

④ **Monastery of Agios Ioannis Prodromos** / Μονή Αγίου Ιωάννη Προδρόμου / Moní Agíou Ioánni Prodrómou: It was founded in 1167 and built in the hollow of a rock overhanging the ravine. A few monks live there who will welcome you, guide you round the library and show you the noteworthy devotional paintings kept in the monastery.

⑤ **Old Philosophou Monastery** / Παλαιά Μονή Φιλοσόφου / Paliá Moní Philosóphou: A historic monastery built in 967 but abandoned nowadays. It was for a time a spiritual centre for the resistance against the Ottomans and a clandestine school.

⑥ **New Philosophou Monastery** / Νέα Μονή Φιλοσόφου / Néa Moní Philosóphou: Take the little path from the Old Monastery

ARCADIAN HIGHLANDS 5

and some 300 m further along at the lip of the ravine you will come across the New Philosophou Monastery (17th c.) The monastery operates, is occupied by monks and was recently restored. Guests are welcome.

⑦ **Aimyalon Monastery** / Μονή Αιμυαλών / Moní Emialón: By car, take the Stemnitsa-Dimitsana road and after the crossroads to Zygovitsi bear left to reach the monastery. It was built at the beginning of the 17th c. above a wooded ravine. Nowadays it has two monks. See the excellent wall paintings dating back to 1608.

Ancient Gortyna

HIKES
Routes proposed:
1. Dimitsana-Moni Philosophou (clandestine school). Duration 1hr 30 min.
2. By car to Moni Philosophou and walk from there to Moni Prodromou. Duration 1 hr.
3. Stemnitsa - Moni Prodromou - Ancient Gortyna - Atsiholou Bridge. Duration about 3 hrs.

Moni Prodromou

SPORTS
There is also rafting, kayaking, canoeing etc. in the region. Information:
Vytina Forestry Service, tel. (0795) 22213.
Organized excursions to the Loussios gorge: Trekking Hellas, tel. (01) 3310323, Alpine Club, tel. (01) 7212773.

Aimyalon Monastery

❺ KARYTENA
Καρύταινα / Karítena

Dramatic, enchanting scenery, in the saddle of a green hill with a castle at its top (450 m). When the Franks arrived in the Peloponnese (13th c.) Hugues de Bruyeres built the castle and the town became a barony and capital of the province of Gortynia. It gradually flourished but in 1459 fell to the Turks, then to the Venetians and to the Turks again in 1715 until its independence. Karytena today is more impressive from a distance, as there are about 150 inhabitants left and the dereliction is noticeable.

WHAT TO SEE
Wander through the narrow alleys with the deserted stone houses giving it an aspect of a ghost village. There are about **40 churches**, the most significant being the **Byzantine church** of **Agios Nikolaos** with 13th c. frescoes and famous 14th c. **bell-tower**, and the church of **Zoodochos Pigi**. Unfortunately besides the abandoned houses the historic castle too is crumbling.

⑥⑥ ARCHED BRIDGE OF KARYTENA
Τοξωτή Γέφυρα Καρύταινας / Toxotí Yéfira Karítenas

In the ravine by the river Alpheios and just below the new bridge you will see the lovely arched stone bridge, a watermill and the chapel featured in the 5,000 drachma notes. It is worth getting out of the car to follow the path and enjoy the rare beauty of this sight.

5 PELOPONNESE

❻ ANDRITSENA
Ανδρίτσαινα / Andrítsena

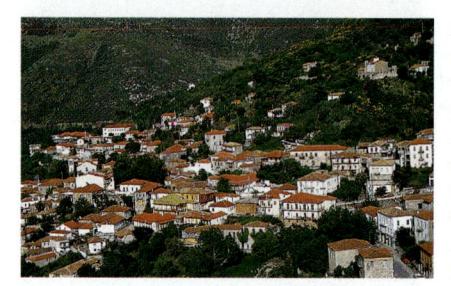

A mountain village built on a slope, with **traditional architecture**, a large square and **charming alleyways** worth a stroll, the only way to admire the grandeur of the old houses. See the **churches** of **Agios Therapontas**, of **Agios Nikolaos**, **Agios Athanasios**, **Agia Varvara** and the **Taxiarchon chapel**. Also do not miss the **library**, formerly a primary school, in the village centre. It contains rare documents of historic importance and an archive of the struggle of 1821. There are also archaeological finds from excavations in the area.

❼ ANCIENT BASSAE (TEMPLE OF APOLLO EPIKOURIOS)
Αρχαίες Βάσσες (Ναός Επικούρειου Απόλλωνα) / Archées Vásses (Naós Epikoúriou Apóllona)

Tel. (0626) 22254

From sunrise to sunset, closed on holidays*

A perfectly conserved temple, the work of **Iktinos** – one of the two architects of the Parthenon – now standing under a huge tent among wild mountains and at an altitude of 1,100 m. It was built about 410-400 BC by the inhabitants of the nearby ancient city **Phygaleia** in honour of Apollo Epikourios (the assister) who saved them from the plague which broke out during the Peloponnesian war. The temple has a single **colonnade all round**, is externally in **Doric** style with internal **Ionic** elements, and at the southern end of the recess there is also the first example of a **Corinthian column**. The dimensions are 38,24 x 14,48 m and it is mainly of limestone and marble. It consists of a **first room, cella,** and **recess (adyton)**, with 6 columns on the facade and 15 on the sides. In the recess, according to Pausanias, there was an enormous bronze statue of Apollo. The slabs of the cella frieze and the metope, depicting scenes of battles between Greeks and Amazons, and Centaurs and Lapiths, are in the British Museum in London.

BEST HOTELS AND ROOMS

BEST LOCATION

We suggest that you stay in Dimitsana although it does not have the best hotels. It is however in the centre of the district and will facilitate your touring. If you are more interested in a better hotel you had better make Vytina your base. It is not the prettiest village but is satisfactorily organized for tourism. You should also know that the hotel **Xenios Zefs** due to open in Dimitsana, may prove to be the best of the region. Telephone the Tourist Police, tel. (0795) 31660 to make sure it is in operation.

PRICES

The hotel prices mentioned below are the official ones set by the National Tourist Organization for double rooms, at low and high season, with breakfast. Since owners are allowed to modify the prices, always try to negotiate them.

ARCADIAN HIGHLANDS 5

VYTINA

✓✓ MENALON (B Class)
Tel. (0795) 22217, (0945) 851125

Open: All year round
Description: It is in the centre of the village and is the best of the whole district. Newly built, it has pleasant public areas with fireplaces, and on the walls pictures from the gallery of its Athenian owner.
Rooms: 7 suites and 41 rooms with bath and telephone.
Special features: Bar and pleasant garden.
Price: 16,000-20,000 drs.
Value for money: ✱✱✱
Credit cards: None

MAGOULIANA VILLAGE
13 km NW of Vytina, altitude 1,300 m

✓ KOSMOPOULOU GUEST HOUSE (A Class)
Tel. (0795) 82350-2, fax 82352

Open: All year round
Description: Two-storeyed traditional private house built in 1920, operating as a pension since 1982. Has a yard with pine-trees and vista of the fir forest of Mt Panos.
Rooms: 14 rooms furnished in traditional style, private shower and telephone.
Special features: Restaurant with fireplace and parking.
Price: 16,524 drs.
Value for money: ✱
Credit cards: None

STEMNITSA

TRIKOLONION (A Class)
Tel. (0795) 81297, fax 81483
Open: All year round
Description: The only hotel in Stemnitsa. Composed of two old mansions now joined together. Attractive exterior and simple interior.
Rooms: 20 rooms with heating and telephone.
Special features: Restaurant, breakfast and television room.
Price: 10,200 drs.
Value for money: ✱
Credit cards: None

DIMITSANA

ROOMS VASSILI TSIAPA (A Class)
Tel., fax (0795) 31583
Open: All year round
Description: Small family pension.
Rooms: 5 comfortable rooms, clean and new, with private kitchenette, TV and bath.
Special features: Parking, public lounge with fireplace. Pleasing atmosphere and very good for the price.
Price: 9,000-12,000 drs. without breakfast.
Value for money: ✱✱✱
Credit cards: None

ALTERNATIVES

DIMITSANA HOTEL (C Class) *Dimitsana, tel. (0795) 31518-31520, fax (071) 239065.*
Price: 16,000 drs.

BEST RESTAURANTS & TAVERNAS

The best restaurants are in Vytina, such as **Klimataria**, tel. (0795) 22226, and **Aidonia**, tel. (0795) 22224. You can also have a meal at **Oenotherapeftirio**, tel. (0795) 22898, or **Koutouki tou Gianni**, tel. (0795) 22202, by the exit of the village. For baked pasta there is **Stavro Yavi**, tel. (0795) 22747. At Dimitsana the best taverna is **Trypa**, tel. (0795) 31595, which, albeit a hole-in-the-wall as its name indicates, is tastefully decorated and has good food. Stemnitsa has few tavernas and unfortunately none of note. At Andritsena **Giorgi**, tel. (0626) 22004, is preferable but you will find other tavernas with good food. **Price:** All €

Aidonia

BEST ENTERTAINMENT

The only place in the region to have fun is Vytina. In the other villages you will have to be content with traditional cafes (kafenions). At Vytina, to enjoy yourself, go to **Sirio**. In Dimitsana have a cup of coffee at **Vrahos**, with a magnificent view, and in Karytena sit a while in the pleasant square under the pines.

TIPS AND INFORMATION

HOW TO GET THERE

- A private car is certainly preferable also to serve for your local movements.
- For an organized tour, contact travel agents:
  Trekking Hellas, tel. (01) 3310323 and
  Manos Tours, tel. (01) 3645511

BEST TIPS

HOW TO GET AROUND: In your car, and if you don't have one, it's a good idea to hire a jeep so as to be able to enjoy the region's potential. Many natural beauty spots are hidden on dirt roads, especially at the Loussios gorge and it would be a pity to miss them.

BEST SEASON: At all times of year the countryside will delight you.

BEST BUYS: In Stemnitsa there are various interesting items of jewellery.

BEST LOCAL FOOD: Country noodles, **trahana** (cracked wheat boiled with milk and dried), cheeses, honey and pastries. It is worth sampling the local grilled meats. In Stemnitsa, **Argyri's** pastries. In Dimitsana delicious bakery bread and **myzithra cheese**.

USEFUL TELEPHONE NUMBERS

VYTINA (0795)	Police 81236
Town Hall 22329	Rural Clinic 81277
Police 22207	
Rural Clinic 22222	**KARYTENA** (0791)
	Town Hall 31214
DIMITSANA (0795)	Police 31205
Town Hall 31237	Rural Clinic 31300
Police 31205	
	ANDRITSENA (0626)
STEMNITSA (0795)	Town Hall 22236
Town Hall 81237	Police 22209

ANCIENT OLYMPIA

WHY AMONG THE BEST

Because the birthplace of the Olympic Games, Ancient Olympia, is a place to return to again and again. And once you have done the tour of this most significant archaeological site, you can go on to Kaiafas where there is a magnificent beach and well-known spa.

PELOPONNESE

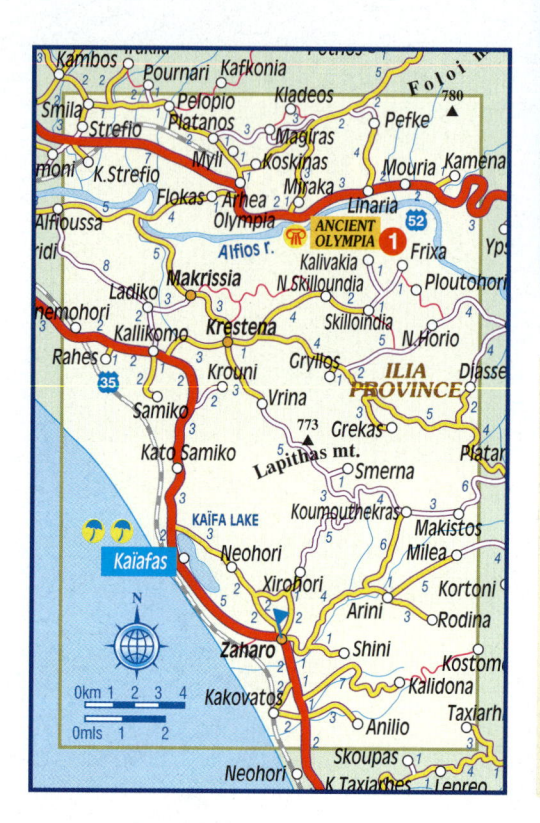

BEST's OPINION

This excursion is not proposed as a mere holiday trip — it's more of a pilgrimage into time immemorial, which will rouse your awareness of the spirit and history of the Olympic Games. But as the ancient monuments are in ruins, spend a little time reading up on the history or take a reputable guided tour, which might be one organized by a travel agent. After a couple of days in Olympia, if you have time, pick a neighbouring **Best** excursion and continue on your way.

BEST SIGHTS: STEP BY STEP

❶ ANCIENT OLYMPIA
Αρχαία Ολυμπία / Archéa Olympía

The sacred grounds of Olympia, one of Greece's most renowned archaeological sites the world over, lie in an enchanting setting in the valley between the hill of Kronios and the confluence of the Alpheios and Kladios rivers.

Early Christian basilica

OLYMPIC GAMES

MYTHOLOGY

We are told in myths that the gods first competed in the age-old stadium. At that time the god Kronos was worshipped in the area, later to be supplanted by his son Zeus to whom this sacred site was dedicated. The games were originally instituted by the first king of Elis, Aethlios. His son Endymion continued the tradition as did King Augeias (who summoned Hercules to clean out his stables). After a time, the games were forgotten, but were again reinstated by the great king of Elis, Iphitos, in accordance with a pronouncement by the oracle of Delphi. According to legend, Hercules (Herakles) took part in the games and won at wrestling and at the "pankration" combining wrestling and boxing.

ANCIENT OLYMPIA

HISTORY

The monuments in the **Altis**, the sacred grove, began to be erected in the 10th-9th c. BC. In the 7th-6th c. the first monuments were built to accommodate the ever-increasing demands of the sanctuary, as it is estimated the games began in 776 BC, after the Dorians had gained supremacy and the worship of Zeus was established. Votive offerings have however been found dating to the 10th c. BC, statuettes of humans and horses, indicating that chariot races had already been taking place at that time. Homer in fact mentions the prizes as "Athla". The games were reorganized by the king of Elis **Iphitos**, by **Kleisthenes of Pissa** and by **Lycourgos of Sparta**. These three together instituted the **"sacred truce"** for the city-states to suspend any hostilities for the duration of this great athletic event (something being attempted again today). Initially the truce lasted one month but was extended to three. Any city not adhering to the truce was heavily fined. The districts of Olympia and Elis were declared sacred and access was prohibited to armies and armed men generally. The Olympiads were held every four years and all the principal Greek cities took part. Later on, the cities of Ionia and Sicily also followed suit. They originally lasted one day – the duration of the sole contest for the winner of the simple sprint (**the Stadion**) – but as fresh contests were added, the days were increased to five. Before 752 BC, champions were awarded the prize of an apple or a bronze tripod, later however they were crowned with a wreath of wild olive from the tree **Kallistefanos Elaia** (beautiful-crowned olive) which grew near the temple of Zeus and symbolized fair competition or sportsmanship. This wreath was the greatest honour that could be granted to an athlete, his family or his home town. This is why, for the reception of the victor, his fellow-citizens would tear down part of the walls of their town for him to make his entrance. The contests were divided into **gymnastic** and **equestrian**. Gymnastic were the Stadion (192 m); Diavlos (double course 192 m x 2), Dolihos (long course 192 m x 24), Pali (wrestling), Pentathlon (long-jump, discus, javelin, sprint and wrestling), Pygme (boxing); Pankration (wrestling and boxing), Hoplites Dromos (running in armour), Dromos Stadiou (one-stade-long race), Pali/Pygme/Pankration Paidon (youths' wrestling, boxing and combination). Equestrian were the Ippodromia keliton (horsemanship races), Synoris (two-horse chariot race), Tethripou/Synoris /Ippodromia polon (four / two / colts chariot race and horse-race with colts). Prizes were awarded to the owners of the horses, not the charioteers. The Olympic Games were at their peak from the 6th to 4th c. BC. The athlet-

Nike by Paionios

Lions' heads

Heraion

119

Peloponnese

ANCIENT OLYMPIA

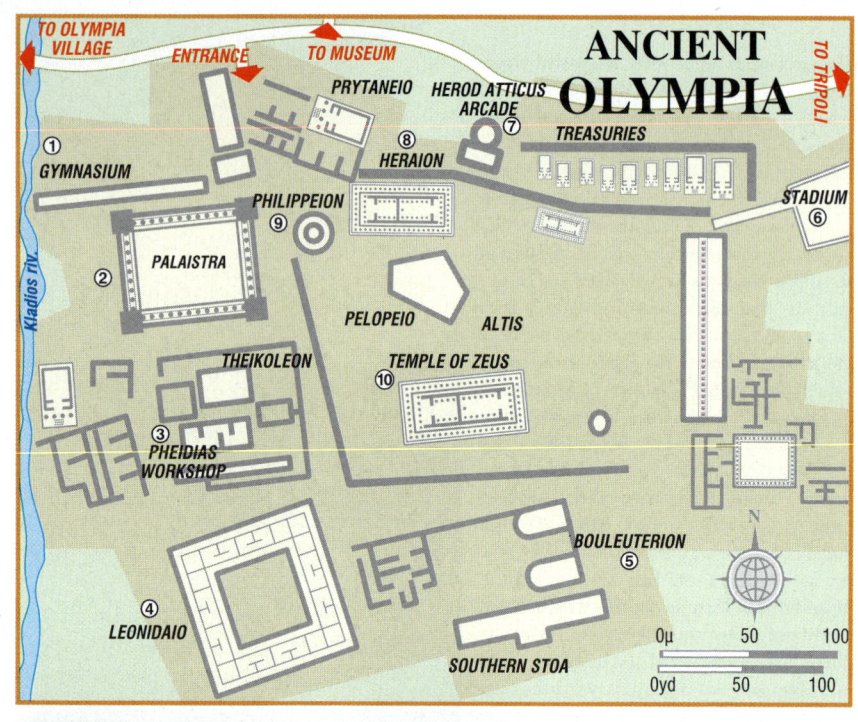

Map labels:
- TO OLYMPIA VILLAGE
- ENTRANCE
- TO MUSEUM
- TO TRIPOLI
- PRYTANEIO
- HEROD ATTICUS ARCADE ⑦
- TREASURIES
- ① GYMNASIUM
- ⑧ HERAION
- STADIUM ⑥
- PHILIPPEION ⑨
- ② PALAISTRA
- Kladios riv.
- PELOPEIO
- ALTIS
- THEIKOLEON
- TEMPLE OF ZEUS ⑩
- ③ PHEIDIAS WORKSHOP
- BOULEUTERION ⑤
- ④ LEONIDAIO
- SOUTHERN STOA

Gymnasium

Palaistra

ic events were accompanied by great religious feasts which added much to the prestige of ancient Olympia. In the 4th c. the games lost their sacred character and became purely athletic. Under Roman domination, Roman citizens and emperors began to take part and become Olympic champions, after first being naturalized as Greeks upon recognition of their Greek origin.

In 85 BC, Sulla, in need of funds to confront Mithridates, plundered the treasuries of the sanctuaries. There was a brief period of resurgence under the emperors Augustus (30 BC-14 AD) and Hadrian (117-138 AD). The games continued until 393 AD when the Byzantine emperor Theodosios by decree prohibited idolatrous feasts. A few years later, in 426, Theodosios II decreed the destruction of heathen temples. The area was then subjected to further destruction and pillage until its total devastation. Toward the end of the 19th c., attempts were made to revive the Olympic Games, the most significant being those of the **Zappas Foundation**. The French baron **Pierre de Coubertin** achieved their re-establishment in 1894. The first international Olympiad took place at Athens in 1896 and in 2004, 108 years later, the Games will come home again.

ANCIENT OLYMPIA 6

ARCHAEOLOGICAL SITE

Tel. (0624) 22517

☺ *8 am-5 pm, weekends 8 am-2:30 pm, closed on holidays**

For a guided tour of Olympia as recommended above, make arrangements ahead of time at your hotel, at the archaeological site, at the museum or at the Athens Guides' Association, tel. (01) 3220090, 3229705 for a private guide, who will charge about 20,000-25,000 drs.

① **Gymnasium**: Constructed in the 2nd c. BC, near the Kladios river. The athletes of the sprint and pentathlon trained in its open-air space. In bad weather they were under cover in the porticoes. It was rectangular in shape with Doric columns.

② **Palaistra (Wrestling School)**: A square building of the 3rd c. BC. The courtyard was surrounded by Ionic columns. Beyond the porticoes were rooms such as the Elaiothesio where the athletes oiled themselves, the Konistirion where they dusted themselves with dust or sand and the Ephebeion where youths trained with their coaches. At the NE corner there was a 1.40 m-deep cistern for bathing.

③ **Pheidias' workshop (Byzantine church)**: An Early Christian, triple-aisled basilica of the 5th c. AD which was built on the foundations of Pheidias' workshop. In the course of excavation, moulds – pottery casts – were found, which had been used for the chryselephantine (gold and ivory) statue of Zeus.

④ **Leonidaion**: The sanctuary's guest-house. It was built in 350 BC, funded by Leonidas of Naxos. A building with two storeys, dimensions 80 x 83.51 m, surrounded by a portico of 138 Ionic columns.

⑤ **Bouleuterion**: This is where the Olympic Parliament convened and official documents were kept. It was built in the 6th c. BC with successive alterations until the 2nd c. BC. Here also stood the altar of Zeus Orkios, holding the thunder-bolts, and it is where athletes and their coaches, after the sacrifice of a boar, gave the customary oath before commencement of the games.

⑥ **The Stadium**: Gymnastic contests were held here. The athletes and judges entered by the **Krypte** (3rd c. BC), the vaulted gateway with antechamber and Corinthian columns which was the official entrance to the stadium.

The stadium is 212.5 m long, (the track 192 m) and 28.5 m wide. It had no seats other than the Exedra, the podium for the judges, and the altar of the goddess Demetra Hamyna, where sat the goddess's

Pheidias' workshop (Byzantine church)

Bouleuterion

Entrance to the stadium

6 PELOPONNESE

Temple of Zeus

priestess, the sole woman permitted to be present at the games. The gradients surrounding the stadium could take up to 40,000 spectators.

What we see today is the third stadium (4th c. BC). The first, of the Archaic period and the second, of the 5th c. BC were in the grove of Altis, beginning approximately in front of the great altar. However when the religious element diminished and the Olympic ideal was replaced by professional sport, the new stadium was constructed outside the Altis.

⑦ 🌀 **Exedra of Herod Atticus** or **Nymphaion**: The sanctuary's water supply, constructed in 160 BC, with funds of Herod Atticus. There were various statues of Romans round it and in the middle of the semi-circular reservoir, the statue of a bull.

⑧ 🌀🌀 **Temple of Hera or Heraion**: One of the most ancient temples in Greece (600 BC). In Doric style, with a single row of columns all round, it originally had wooden columns but when it was later rebuilt they were replaced by others of shell limestone. The **statue of Hermes by Praxiteles**, now exhibited in the museum, was found in the recess of the temple. The stone head of the sacred statue of Hera is also extant. In Roman times, the most valuable votive offerings were kept here.

⑨ 🌀 **Philippeion**: This circular construction with an Ionic peristyle or colonnade all round, was an offering by King Philip of Macedonia for his victory at the battle of Cheronea (338 BC). It was completed after his death (336 BC) by his son Alexander the Great. The interior contained five chryselephantine (gold and ivory) statues of Philip's royal family.

⑩ 🌀🌀 **Temple of Zeus**: The most grandiose of the monuments of the Altis was built in the middle of the 5th c. BC. It was the work of the Elian architect Livon, with a single row of columns in the Doric style all round, 13 at the sides and 6 at the front and back. Its dimensions were 64.12 x 27.66 x 20.25 m. At the back of the recess was the masterpiece of the gigantic **chryselephantine statue of Zeus on his throne**, Pheidias's greatest work, considered the first of the Seven Wonders of the world. In 393 AD, the statue was transported to Constantinople where, they say, it was destroyed in a fire of 474 AD. The sculptures of the temple's pediments are exhibited in the musem of Olympia.

🌀🌀🌀 ARCHAEOLOGICAL MUSEUM OF OLYMPIA

Tel. (0624) 22742

🕑 Mondays 8 am-2:30 pm, Tuesdays-Fridays 8 am-5 pm and weekends 8 am-2:30 pm, closed on holidays*

Many remarkable exhibits are on view in the rooms of this notable museum. You'll see among others the celebrated 🌀🌀🌀 **statue of Hermes by Praxiteles** (330 BC), carrying the newborn **god Dionysos**, the 🌀🌀 **heads of the statues of Hera** and of 🌀 **Athena**, the 🌀🌀 **ceramic statue of Zeus abducting Ganymede**, 🌀 **Miltiades' helmet**, the 🌀 **statue of Nike (Victory)** by Paionios, the **stamp collection of the Olympic Games**, the unique **sculptures from the pediments** of the temple of Zeus, the bronze busts of griffins, and more.

MODERN OLYMPIA

The village of Nea Olympia has developed thanks to tourist activity in Ancient Olympia. It is pleasantly situated among greenery, and although it is nothing special, it also has no modernistic eyesores.

Hermes by Praxiteles

ANCIENT OLYMPIA 6

BEST BEACHES

🏖🏖 KAIAFAS

The longest in Greece, 50 km of continuous sandy beach in front of a pine forest. There is **free camping** in the wood, where you will be undisturbed. Most people gather at the tavernas and cafes around lake Kaifas spa. In the woods round the beaches there are several km of dirt roads ending at the rail tracks which have become magnets for rabish. Look for your campsite elsewhere. For swimming the best places are to the left and right of the fort, on the beach opposite the thermal springs, and the beach of Zaharo which also has a taverna.

BEST HOTELS AND ROOMS

BEST LOCATION

It is definitely worth staying in Olympia for at least a night, where you will be close to the antiquities, the sole but also most important sight of the area.

PRICES

The hotel prices mentioned below are the official ones set by the National Tourist Organization for double rooms, at low and high season, with breakfast. Since owners are allowed to modify prices, always try to negotiate them.

OLYMPIA

✓✓ EUROPA BEST WESTERN
(A Class)

Tel. (0624) 22650, 23650, 22700, 23700, fax 23166

Open: All year round
Description: On a hill above Ancient Olympia, with a view to the Arcadian mountains and the Alpheios valley. It is managed by two young brothers and has the warmth of a family business and friendly atmosphere.
Rooms: 42 rooms with A/C, telephone and TV.
Special features: Dining-room seating 200, with marble flooring and wooden ceiling, tennis court and pool. Walks in the countryside and excursions to nearby sights are organized. Horse riding may be available on request. If you are interested, ask if there are horses available for riding.
Price: 24,500-32,000 drs.
Value for money: ✸✸
Credit cards: All

✓✓ AMALIA (A Class)

Tel. (0624) 22190, fax 22444
Open: All year round
Description: A little way out of the village, a plain

modern building surrounded by greenery. Its many and large public areas give a sense of luxury. One of the Amalia hotel chain.
Rooms: 160 rooms with A/C, telephone and radio.
Special features: Restaurant, cafeteria, bar and shops.
Price: 50,600 drs.
Value for money: ✱
Credit cards: All

ALTERNATIVES

ANTONIOS (A Class)
Olympia, tel. (0624) 22348, fax 22112
Price: 40,000 drs.

HOTEL PELOPS (C Class)
Olympia, tel. (0624) 22543, 22792, fax 22213
Price: 17,000 drs.

BEST RESTAURANTS & TAVERNAS

Have a meal at **Klavdio's**, at the edge of the village by the stream. Romantic atmosphere and good food. **Amvrosia**, next to it, is of no worse quality but not so well situated. At Miraka, 4 km from Olympia, there is the taverna-grill **Drossia**, tel. (0624) 22311, with home-cooked food and cordial service. At Linaria, 7 km from Olympia on the Tripoli road, go to **Kanellopoulos'** for delicious chicken.

Drossia

TIPS AND INFORMATION

HOW TO GET THERE

- In your own car from Athens via the national highway Athens-Corinth-Patras. From there, on the main roads to Amaliada-Pyrgos-Olympia (total 329 km).
- Should you wish to join an organized excursion with guide, contact the following travel agents:
  Pyramis, 3 Kydathineon St., Syntagma Sq., tel. (01) 3254975.
  Travel Day, in collaboration with Key Tours, 3-5 Lekka St., Syntagma Sq., tel. (01) 3246701, or your habitual bureau for alternatives.
- By intercity bus, KTEL, 100 Kifissou Ave., Athens, tel. (01) 5134110.

BEST TIPS

HOW TO GET AROUND: If you do not have your own transport, on foot or by taxi. The distances are not great.

BEST SEASON: All year round for the archaeological site and in summer for the beaches of the area, which are among the best in Greece. They are so extensive that however many people there are, you'll still be able to find your own peaceful spot.

USEFUL TELEPHONE NUMBERS

OLYMPIA	(0624)	Tourist Police	22550
Town Hall	22250	Police	22100

ANCIENT MESSENE

WHY AMONG THE BEST

Because this is a relatively unknown corner of the Peloponnese, with important archaeological sites and picturesque but forgotten monasteries. But also because it can be combined so easily with other interesting excursions in the region.

PELOPONNESE

BEST's OPINION

The trip to Ancient Messene will be a pleasant surprise for those who have already seen the more famous attractions of Greece and are seeking something new. We also recommend it to travellers who happen to be in the vicinity and have time for exploring. The area is not really holiday-oriented, but it makes for a good short excursion or interesting weekend.

BEST SIGHTS: STEP BY STEP

❶ ANCIENT MESSENE (OR ANCIENT ITHOME)
Αρχαία Μεσσήνη (ή Αρχαία Ιθώμη) / Archéa Messíni (or Archéa Ithómi)

The village of **Mavrommati** lies at the foothills of Mt Ithomi, on the site of Ancient Messene and amidst the ruins.

Ancient Messene

HISTORY

Ancient Ithomi was the acropolis of Messene and was fortified as early as the 8th c. BC. The residents of the area used to take refuge within its walls to escape the belligerent Spartans.
In 740 BC, the Spartans, wishing to gain control of its fertile lands, began the first of the **Messenian Wars**, which were to continue, off and on, for some three hundred years until the Messenians had either surrendered or fled the district (460 BC).
In 371 BC, the battle of Leuktra took place

here. The Thebans led by Epaminondas, along with the Argives and the Arcadians, crushed the Spartans. Immediately afterwards (369 BC), Epaminondas built a new well-fortifed city in the strategic position held by the original town of Ithomi, in order to withstand the Spartans' retaliation. It was settled by those Messenians who had joined forces with the Thebans, freed helots and many former residents of the region who had been living in exile in Sicily.

The new city became the most prominent in the area and continued to prosper until 146 BC, when it succumbed to the Romans. Its stout fortifications protected its citizens until a catastrophic raid by the Goths in 395 AD. The survivors abandoned the city and it was never reinhabited.

THE ARCHAEOLOGICAL SITE OF ANCIENT MESSENE-ITHOME

Tel. (0724) 51201, the site is open continuously.

A museum is being built in the village of Mavrommati.
Major finds are constantly being discovered; they have been preserved until now under debris brought down by the nearby river. The architecture of the magnificent monuments leads many archaeologists to believe that they may have rivalled those of Ancient Olympia.

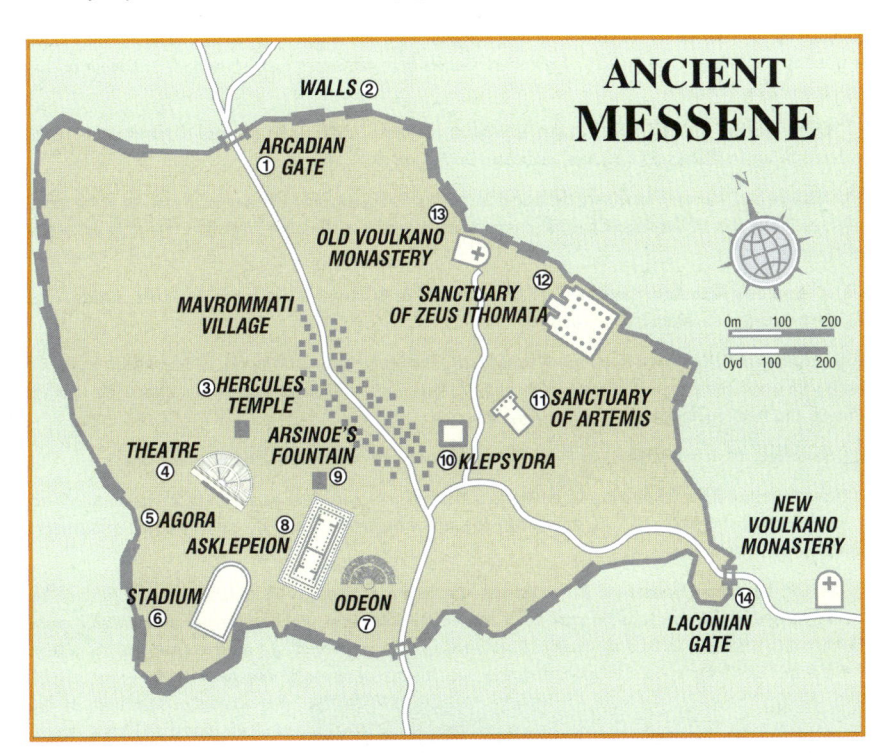

① **Arcadian Gate:** One of the city's four extant gates. It has two entrances, an outer and an inner one.

② **The walls:** Particularly impressive fortifications of the 4th c. BC, 9 km long and 3 m thick, punctuated with solid two-storey four-sided towers.

③ **Temple of Heracles** (Hercules): This temple was discovered in 1997, during excavation of the west stoa of the Gymnasium. Exceptional statues by the sculptor Damophon were found here. This famous artist (2nd c. BC) was re-

Arcadian Gate

PELOPONNESE

The walls

sponsible for many statues in various Greek cities and it was he who repaired the gold and ivory statue of Zeus in ancient Olympia.

④ **Theatre:** With tiers, landings and orchestra, similar in form to the large theatre at Epidaurus. The theatre served the needs of the 40,000 people who lived in Messene at its peak.

⑤ **Agora:** Sacred edifices with cult statues of gods, such as Poseidon, Aphrodite and the "Mother of the Gods", a work by Damophon.

⑥ **Stadium:** Today all that remains is the "horseshoe" of the track. Mid-way along the east side and in front of the spectators' seats stood a stone throne belonging to the city's high priest. Games were performed here in the nude in honour of Asklepios and Zeus Ithomata.

⑦ **Odeon (Small Theatre):** Next to the Asklepeion complex. Designed for displays of rhetoric and political, artistic and cultural performances, dedicated to the god Asklepios.

⑧ **Asklepeion:** Imposing sanctuary dedicated to the god Asklepios and to Messene. The layout of the buildings resembles that of the large Christian monasteries. A temple of Messene Hegemone stood in the centre of the inner court.

⑨ **Arsinoe's Fountain:** The large fountain dedicated to Arsinoe, the mother of Asklepios, stands in the north-east part of the monumental complex.

⑩ **Klepsydra (Kallirhoe Fountain-Mavro Mati):** This spring supplied the city and buildings within the walls with water and was particularly useful in time of siege. According to ancient local tradition, the nymphs Ithome and Neda took care of the infant Zeus here.

⑪ **Sanctuary of Artemis:** Thought to have been dedicated to Artemis Limnatida ("of the lake").

⑫ **Sanctuary of Zeus Ithomata:** According to a Messenian legend, Zeus was born in Ithome and thus acquired the attribute "Ithomata". Initially, before the arrival of the Achaeans, the sanctuary was dedicated to the Pelasgian god Ithomata.

⑬ **Old Voulkano Monastery:** The monastery was built in the 8th c. with material from the ruins of Ancient Messene. It was in operation until 1626 and on the south-east side one can see an enormous stone block, which originally formed the base of a statue of Zeus. A very rough dirt road leads to the monastery, but it is well worth the effort. The monastery was once a place of refuge for escaped slaves.

It is situated at an altitude of 926 m on Mt Ithomi and has a stupendous ☺☺☺ **view**.
On descending, you will pass the Laconian Gate of Ancient Messene before arriving, on the other side of a thick wood, at the New Voulkano Monastery, built in 1712. The new monastery has monks and also takes in guests.

⑭ **Laconian Gate:** It owes its name to the fact that it faces Laconia. It was fortified with two strong towers of which only traces remain.

Old Voulkano Monastery

ANCIENT MESSENE 7

② ANDRIOMONASTIRO
Ανδριομονάστηρο / Andriomonástiro

A ruined monastery surrounded by plane-trees by the bed of a small river. Wonderful architecture and scenery, but the monastery has been abandoned and you cannot view the interior. It was built during the reign of the Byzantine emperor Andronikos Palaiologos and under its sanctuary there is a spring. It consists of three churches conjoined, with three sanctuaries and three altars. The monastery's feast day is August 6. It is an ideal place for a picnic.

③ KYPARISSIA
Κυπαρισσία / Kiparissía

A seaside market town, which has become the tourist and business centre of the Trifylia region. It is separated into the **Upper City** (Ano Polis), with traditional buildings, and the more modern **Lower City** (Kato Polis).

WHAT TO SEE

The eastern hill was the site of the prehistoric acropolis, which the Theban general Epaminondas, and later the Byzantines, fortified. The Franks built a strong **medieval castle** here, too. One can see traces of Venetian and Ottoman additions. The houses in the vicinity of the castle have retained their old, interesting architectural features.

The Upper City

BEST BEACHES

KALO NERO
A large beach bordered by greenery. With its sand and clear waters, it is conveniently close to the **Oasis** hotel.

BEST HOTELS AND ROOMS

BEST LOCATION

There are no good hotels or rooms in the area except for the **Oasis** hotel at Kalo Nero near Kyparissia. Our advice therefore is to spend the night there or at some hotel listed in another nearby *Best* Trip.

PRICES

The hotel prices mentioned below are the official ones set by the National Tourist Organization for double rooms, at low and high season, with breakfast. Since owners are allowed to modify the prices, always try to negotiate them.

129

PELOPONNESE

KALO NERO
(NORTH OF KYPARISSIA)

✓✓ OASIS (B Class)
Tel. (0761) 72561-2, fax 72563
Open: All year round
Description: Tasteful hotel complex. Built in 1994 in lush surroundings right on the sea. Recommended for quiet holidays and well placed for trips to many sights in the area.
Rooms: 32 studios and 4-person suites with kitchen, telephone, A/C and balcony with sea view.
Special features: Pool, hydromassage, poolside bar, taverna and beach bar.
Price: 27,100-47,100 drs.
Value for money: ✽✽
Credit cards: Visa

MAVROMMATI

ZEUS
Tel. (0724) 51025, 51005
Open: All year round
Description: Simple guest house.
Rooms: 4 clean and comfortable rooms.
Price: 12,000-15,000 drs. Without breakfast
Value for money: ✽
Credit cards: None

BEST RESTAURANTS & TAVERNAS

Kyparissia has several acceptable restaurants. We recommend the **Mouragio**, tel. (0761) 23314, for fish and **Platanos** (a taverna on the road to the castle), tel. (0761) 24349.
At Mavrommati the **Ithomi taverna**, tel. (0724) 51298, next to the **Zeus** guest house, has grills and ready-cooked dishes. **Price:** All €

TIPS AND INFORMATION

HOW TO GET THERE
- By car, to be able to move around.
- Otherwise by air to Kalamata with Olympic Airways, tel. (01) 9663363, or by train (OSE), tel. (01) 5131601, or intercity bus (KTEL), tel. (01) 5124910.
- In Kalamata you can hire a car to continue your trip.

BEST TIPS

HOW TO GET AROUND: Definitely with your own transport, because there is no other way of reaching the monasteries.

BEST SEASON: From March to the end of October but also throughout the year.

USEFUL TELEPHONE NUMBERS

MAVROMMATI	(0724)	Town Hall	22280
Community Office	51294	Police	22500
Rural Clinic	51219	Hospital	22222
		Pharmacy	23832
KYPARISSIA	(0761)	Taxis	22666

PYLOS

Methoni   **Pylos**
   Koroni

WHY AMONG THE BEST

Because this is an extremely beautiful but relatively overlooked corner of Greece, with well preserved fortresses, charming fishing villages with an island atmosphere, fascinating archaeological sites and good beaches. The region lends itself to low-cost holidays, since mass tourism has fortunately not yet been made aware of its existence.

8 PELOPONNESE

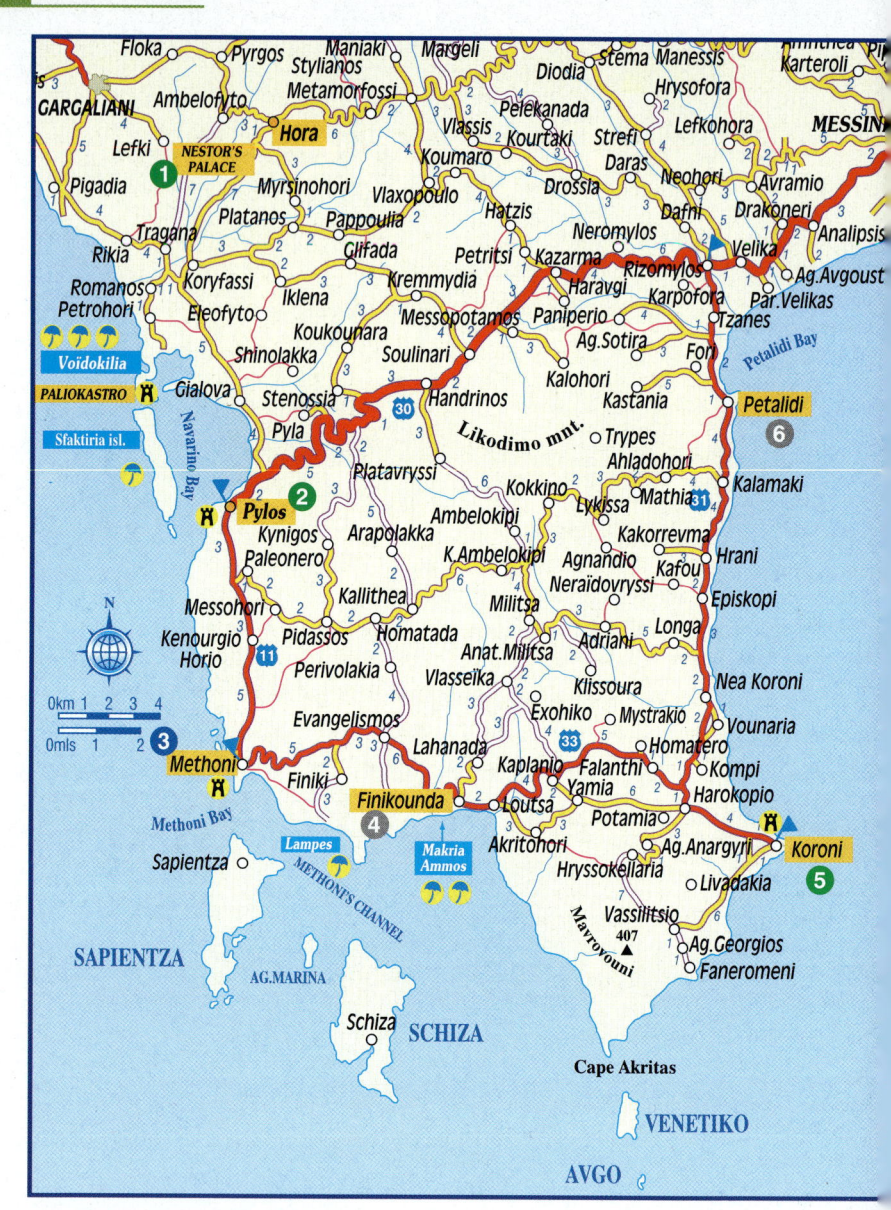

BEST's OPINION

German campers were amongst the first to discover the delights of Messenia, this left leg of the Peloponnese. They discovered peaceful residents, be they farmers or fishermen, inexpensive but good quality holiday facilities, a variety of things to see, and clean, unspoiled beaches. The climate is mild and the scenery is dominated by vineyards and olive groves. The medieval castles provide an easy introduction to the region's rich history and even at the height of summer you are sure to find a beach to your liking since there are so many to choose from.

PYLOS 8

BEST SIGHTS: STEP BY STEP

❶ NESTOR'S PALACE
Ανάκτορο του Νέστορα / Anáktoro toú Néstora

MYTHOLOGY

Nestor, King of Pylos, was one of the richest, strongest and most respected leaders of the Greeks during the Trojan War. Homer describes him as the wisest of them all and his account of Nestor's reception of Odysseus's son, Telemachus, at this palace is one of the high points of the *Odyssey*.

ARCHAEOLOGICAL SITE
Mycenaean Palace of Epano Englianos
Tel. (0763) 31437
☉ 8 am-2:30 pm, closed on Mondays and holidays*

Bath tub in Nestor's Palace

Built in 2000 BC on a plan similar to the architecture of the palaces of Crete and the Argolid (Mycenae and Tiryns), it appears to have been destroyed in a fire around 1200 BC, no doubt by the invading Dorians. It was a two-storeyed building, lavishly decorated with frescoes. Clay **tablets** inscribed in **Linear B**, the earliest form of Greek writing, were found in the ruins. Not far from the hill, lies an imposing vaulted tomb. Make sure to see the **throne room**, the queen's chambers with her **bath** and **hearth** and the **workshop** where scented oils for anointing the body were prepared.

MUSEUM
Hora Trifylias, tel. (0763) 31358
☉ 8:30 am-2:30 pm, closed on Mondays and holidays*

Exhibits from the palace and excavations in the area. **Pottery**, **fresco fragments**, and **objects of everyday use**, as well as **gold jewellery** and wine cups.

❷ PYLOS
Πύλος / Pílos

Built on a steep slope that descends to the harbour, it was planned by French engineers under General Maison in 1829 when it adopted the ancient name of Pylos. Previously, the Venetians had called it Navarino, the historic bay, whose entrance is almost blocked by the island of **Sphaktiria**, leaving only the south channel navigable. In 425 BC the Athenian general Demosthenes took 292 Spartans prisoner after a long siege, breaking the myth that they always fought to the death.

Pylos

The battle of Navarino
In October **1827**, the united fleets of Great Britain, France and Russia, headed by admirals **Codrington**, **Derigny** and **Heyden**, virtually annihilated the Turko-Egyptian fleet commanded by Ibrahim Pasha. The 26 allied ships with a force of 1,270 cannons demolished the 82 enemy ships possessing 2,400 cannons. In all, 6,000 Ottoman troops were lost, 174 allies. This victory contributed decisively to the Greeks' eventual independence.

8 PELOPONNESE

Niokastro

WHAT TO SEE

ⓖ MUSEUM OF NIOKASTRO (or NEO KASTRO PYLOU)

Tel. (0723) 22010, 22448

⊙ 8:30 am-3 pm, closed on Mondays and holidays*

Interesting, well-preserved fortress overlooking the town. It was erected by the Turks in the 16th c. and rebuilt in 1829 by General Maison. Today it houses the **Institute of Underwater Archaeology**. A mosque converted into a gothic-style church of the **Metamorphossi tou Sotira** stands within its walls. ⓖ **Paliokastro** is at the opposite edge of Navarino Bay. It is worth visiting the wonderful nearby beach of ♀♀♀ **Voidokilia** and **Nestor's Grotto**, where traces of neolithic life have been found.

ⓖ TRION NAVARCHON SQUARE

Pretty square with cannons and plane-trees. Most of the town's nightlife and tavernas are concentrated here.

---

❸ METHONI
Μεθώνη / Methóni

A small town behind the Venetian castle, which sits upon the ruins of the ancient city of **Mothoni**, a well-known harbour in antiquity. Mentioned in Homer, it took its name from the "Mothonas lithos", a stretch of rock beginning at the coast and sinking into the sea like a reef. The imposing castle is a Venetian construction and has been a prime factor in the town's development, past and present. Today, the former fishing village has accommodation and shops and one can swim at the nearby beaches, or at the long town beach with its fine sand.

WHAT TO SEE

ⓖⓖ THE FORTRESS OR KASTRO

Built by the Venetians in the 13th c., it was a primary port of call on the trade route to the eastern Mediterranean. The flourishing harbour town was captured by the Ottomans in 1500, retaken by the Venetians in 1615 and finally reverted to the Turks (1715-1828). Even under the Ottomans it continued to thrive, thanks to agricultural commerce with France.

BOURTZI

A small fort occupying an islet linked by a causeway to the larger castle. It was built by the Turks in 1500, who used it as a prison and execution site.

❹ FINIKOUNDA
Φοινικούντα / Finikoúnda

Fishing hamlet on the cape opposite the islet of Schiza with a fine ♀♀ **beach** and some small tavernas. A quiet place for a peaceful holiday.

❺ KORONI
Κορώνη / Koróni

A medieval town surrounding an impressive **fortress** which incorporates a monastery. Tourism has been slow to catch on here and it has managed to retain its local colour which is reminiscent of a Cycladic island. Its nightlife thrives in the pleasant tavernas and little bars on the waterfront.

WHAT TO SEE
THE FORTRESS
Open every day and still inhabited. Also built by the Venetians, who considered it and Methoni their two eyes on the Eastern Mediterranean trade routes. Take a walk around the gardens and homes in the **castle precinct** and don't miss the **monastery of the Timios Prodromos** which follows the Julian Calendar. The best time to visit is early morning or sunset.

Koroni fortress

❻ PETALIDI
Πεταλίδι / Petalídi

A summer resort on the shore of the Gulf of Kalamata on the site of **ancient Koroni**. Parts of the walls and other structures have been found on the hill above it. It too boasts a **Venetian castle**, in ruins however, as well as a Byzantine **church of Agios Nikolaos**. An **enormous beach** stretches from Petalidi all the way to Kalamata.

BEST BEACHES

🌂🌂🌂 VOIDOKILIA
One of Greece's most splendid beaches, near Paliokastro on a closed bay in the shape of a crescent moon whose two ends are dominated by steep rocks. The beach is full of sand dunes, while the sand becomes very fine as you approach the sea. Ideal in May, June and September but best avoided in July and August, when it is swarming with people, caravans and all forms of vehicle, that clog the narrow road.

🌂🌂 MAKRIA AMMOS
A wide beach with coarse sand and clear water, a favourite of wind-surfers, where you can hire surfboards.

🌂 SPHAKTIRIA
Sandy beach at the back side of the island. Accessible by caique from Pylos.

🌂 LAMBES
East of Methoni on the road to Finikounda. Pleasant beach with a taverna in a lovely natural setting.

BEST HOTELS AND ROOMS

BEST LOCATION
Pylos if you crave action, Finikounda if you need peace and quiet.

PRICES
The hotel prices mentioned below are the official ones set by the National Tourist Organization for double rooms, at low and high season, with breakfast. Since owners are allowed to modify the prices, always try to negotiate them.

PELOPONNESE

PYLOS
✓ KARALIS BEACH (B Class)
Tel. (0723) 23021-2, fax 22970

Open: April-October
Description: A plain, spotlessly clean hotel at the edge of Pylos town with a view to the fort and the sea, also to a copse of cypresses. Its location makes it an excellent choice.
Rooms: 14 rooms with bath.
Special features: Restaurant and parking.
Price: 22,000-24,000 drs.
Value for money: ✻✻
Credit cards: Visa, Mastercard, Eurocard

METHONI
✓ ACHILLEAS HOTEL (B Class)
Tel., fax (0723) 31819

Open: All year round
Description: Newly built (1997) in the neo-classical style, agreeable and well kept.
Rooms: 13 comfortable rooms.
Special features: Bar and breakfast room.
Price: 15,500-21,000 drs.
Value for money: ✻✻✻
Credit cards: None

✓ AMALIA HOTEL (B Class)
Tel. (0723) 31193, fax 31195
Open: April-October
Description: Large, two-storeyed hotel on a hillside just outside town on the east side of the waterfront, with views of the fort and the town.
Rooms: 34 rooms and bungalows.
Special features: Restaurant, bar, parking.
Price: 13,600-20,300 drs.
Value for money: ✻
Credit cards: Visa, Mastercard

FINIKOUNDA
TOMARA STUDIOS
Tel. (0723) 71442
Open: April-October
Description: Built in 1995. Right on the beach.
Rooms: A few rooms with kitchen and telephone.
Price: 12,000-29,000 drs. Without breakfast
Value for money: ✻
Credit cards: None

HOTEL PORTO FINISSIA (C Class)
Tel. (0723) 71358, 71458, (01) 9621167
Open: April-October
Description: Two-storeyed neo-classical building, in the village and right on the beach.
Rooms: 27 rooms with bath, A/C, telephone and music. Ask for a room with a seaview.
Special features: Breakfast room, TV and cocktail bar.
Price: 12,000-18,000 drs.
Value for money: ✻
Credit cards: None

KORONI
✓ HOTEL DIANA
Tel & fax (0725) 22312
Open: All year round
Description: Small, attractive hotel in town.
Rooms: Tasteful rooms with fridge, TV and A/C.
Special features: Cafe-bar on the ground floor.
Price: 12,000-18,500 drs.
Value for money: ✻✻
Credit cards: None

HOTEL DE LA PLAGE (B Class)
Tel. (0725) 22401, fax 22508
Open: April-October
Description: Simple, cared-for hotel with a lawn and other greenery, right on the beautiful beach.
Rooms: 32 rooms.
Special features: Restaurant and bar.
Price: 21,600 drs.
Value for money: ✻
Credit cards: None

PYLOS 8

CHRANI, KORONI

✓✓ PARIS STUDIOS MAISONETTES
(A Class)
Tel. (0725) 32124, fax 32110, tel. (01) 4908816, fax (01) 4911623
Open: All year round
Description: Luxurious holiday village complex with modern architecture not far from the beach.
Rooms: 17 particularly well-appointed rooms with kitchen and telephone.
Special features: Pool, playground, mini-market, coffee shop, restaurant and snack bar.
Price: 19,000-32,000 drs.
Value for money: ✱✱✱
Credit cards: Diners

PETALIDI

✓✓ SUNRISE (A Class)
Tel. (0722) 32122, fax 31799

Open: March-October
Description: Large hotel complex, traditional architecture, right on the beach.
Rooms: 204 bungalows and 47 rooms with bath, telephone, minibar, TV and A/C.
Special features: Heated pool, tennis, verandas, restaurant and scuba diving school.
Price: 20,000-33,500 drs.
Value for money: ✱✱
Credit cards: All

ALTERNATIVES

NAVARONE
Petrohori, tel. (0723) 41572-4, fax 41575
Price: 13,000-20,200 drs.

KARALIS
26 Kalamatas St., Pylos, tel. (0723) 22960.
Price: 22,000-23,000 drs.

12 THEOI
Pylos, tel. (0723) 22179, 22324.
Price: 6,000-11,000 drs. Without breakfast

BEST RESTAURANTS & TAVERNAS

PYLOS
Pylos offers many gastronomic choices.

✓ 1930
Tel. (0723) 22032
Exceptional restaurant in interesting surroundings.
Price: €€

✓ O GRIGORIS
Tel. (0723) 22621
On the town square. Stone decor and courtyard in the rear. Delicious casserole dishes and charcoal grills.
Price: €

TA ADELFIA
Tel. (0723) 22564
On the coastal road. Pleasant surroundings, tables by the sea. Fish and ready-cooked dishes.
Price: €€

O Grigoris

4 EPOCHES
Tel. (0723) 22564
Fish taverna on the beach.
Price: €€

137

You can also go to the **Platanos** cafe, tel. (0723) 22342 and **Navarino** cafe ouzeri, tel. (0723) 22772. They are on the square under the planetrees. Traditional.

METHONI

Most of the town's tavernas are concentrated along the waterfront square.

✓ ELENA

Tel. (0723) 31773
An attractive taverna with potted plants and old Ali Baba jars. Greek cuisine.
Price: €

✓ KLIMATARIA

Tel. (0723) 31544
On the square, a traditional taverna. Greek cuisine.
Price: €

RESTAURANT VENETICO

Tel. (0723) 31205
Pasta, pizza and grills in an alley of the town.
Price: €

KORONI

In Koroni the best place to eat is on the waterfront, at the **Anastasia**, tel. (0725) 22594 and **Flisvos**, tel. (0725) 22033, tavernas and in the **Kangelarios** ouzeri, tel. (0725) 22648. **Price:** All €

BEST ENTERTAINMENT

Nightlife in the area is liveliest in Pylos, in Trion Navarchon square. **Sunset** and **Legitimus** are the hottest spots at the moment. Outside town, **Zoglo** or **Gigi's** with a pool are also "in". In Koroni, try the **Astra Club** on Memi beach, **Poseidon**, **Remezzo** and **Ichos ke Fos**.

i TIPS AND INFORMATION

HOW TO GET THERE

- With your own transport if you want to tour the region.
- By Olympic Airways from Athens, west airport, to Kalamata (10,000 drs.), tel. (01) 9363363.
- You can hire a car in Kalamata.
- By intercity bus (KTEL), 100 Kifissou Ave., Athens, tel. (01) 5134293.

CONNECTIONS

- By intercity bus (KTEL) from Kalamata to neighbouring destinations, tel. (0721) 22851, 23145.

BEST TIPS

HOW TO GET AROUND: If you don't have your own transport, the region is adequately served by local buses and the distances are relatively small.
In summer, one-day excursions are organized from Kalamata by the Zafiropoulos travel agency, tel. (0721) 95400, 94032.
BEST SEASON: Early summer when it's peaceful and green and the beaches are all yours. But even in August it is not as crowded as much of the rest of Greece.
BEST BUYS: Olive oil, wine and pastelli (sesame candy).

USEFUL TELEPHONE NUMBERS

PYLOS	(0723)	Pharmacy	31140
Town Hall	22221	Taxis	31333
Police	22316	**KORONI**	(0725)
Hospital	22315	Community Office	22221
Pharmacy	22228	Police	22422
Taxis	22555	Rural clinic	22208
METHONI	(0723)	Pharmacy	22200
Community Office	31255	Taxis	22195
Police	31203	**FINIKOUNDA**	(0723)
Rural clinic	31456	OTE	71329

MANI

WHY AMONG THE BEST

Because visitor will be impressed by the medieval villages perched on the mountain-tops and by the wild, rocky scenery. They can see the famous Diros and Alepotripa caves, the rugged beauty of Cape Tainaron and the Viros gorge at Kardamyli before staying at one of the extraordinary and well-preserved tower-guest houses.

PELOPONNESE

MANI 9

BEST's OPINION

If you go to Mani, be aware that you have chosen a peaceful holiday – though you'll be constantly on the go – on the search for and discovery of history and heritage. If you haven't much time, keep to the sights between Kardamyli and Vathia. If you do, a tour of Mani is very much worthwhile, particularly because it includes the Laconian Gulf's remarkable beaches of Scoutari and Mavrovouni.

IN BRIEF

Mani is the name of the middle prong of the southern Peloponnese, extending to the slopes of Mt Taygetos (Taígetos) and forming a notional triangle from Kalamata to Cape Tainaron and Gytheion. The peninsula is about 72 km long and no wider than 28 km. The inhabitants, numbering 22,000, engage in farming, fishing, commerce and catering to tourists. The climate is dry in the uplands, hot and humid on the coast. There are 250 villages and hamlets in Mani, 800 towers and six castles. The predominant impression is of a landscape extraordinarily grim, stony, waterless and barren, consisting of stark jagged mountains plunging precipitously to the sea and countless **stone tower dwellings** and **Byzantine churches**.

Maniots have always been fired by a strong sense of independence and profound patriarchal family ties. If any member of a family were to suffer an insult, it resulted in a feud, a "**vendetta**" – frequently bloody – involving the entire family of the offended (and offending) party. The idiosyncracies of Mani's past history and the severity of its bizarre customs forced almost every family to have its own defensive tower to live in, its own chapel and cemetery. Poverty and the consequences of such rifts among the great and powerful families forced many to emigrate to other parts of Greece and abroad – some to Corsica, whose descendants constituted Napoleon's bodyguard – and quite a few became pirates.

HISTORY

In the Dorian era (11th c. BC), the Spartans, not wishing to be absorbed into the local population, differentiated among their subjects, segregating them into the "provincials", enjoying civil but not political liberty, and the "helots" or serfs. The region fell to the Romans in the 2nd c. BC, and then in the days of Byzantium endured a number of barbarian incursions, the worst of them Alaric's in 395 AD. On these occasions the Maniots took refuge on Mt Taygetos, whence they always ferociously fought every conqueror.

The Franks dominated the region in the 13th c., but they were soon ousted by the Byzantines. After two centuries of warfare, the Turks overran the Peloponnese, but Mani retained its autonomy and was among the first to go to battle for the liberation of Greece.

BEST SIGHTS: STEP BY STEP

❶ FROM KARDAMYLI TO AREOPOLIS
Καρδαμύλη-Αρεόπολη / Kardamíli-Areópoli

Coming from Kalamata you will be met by a splendid first sight of medieval Mani, with a view to the sea over the tiled roofs of the stone Maniot mansions of Kardamyli. If you are lucky, the sun will be setting and the palette of colours will enchant you.

KARDAMYLI

It was once the harbour for ancient Sparta with which it communicated by the Viros gorge. Kardamyli is one of the better-preserved villages in the traditional style of Mani, sufficiently geared for tourism, and has tavernas and shops. Wander around **Old Kardamyli** to see some of the fine towers, ancient and medieval ruins, the church of **Agios Spyridon**, the **graves of the Dioscuri** and the **Mourtzinos tower**.
Next to the village there is also a nice beach,

Agios Spiridonas

PELOPONNESE

Ritsa. If you want to go for a hike through the remarkable ⓖ **Viros gorge**, to experience its fierce magnificence closely, be properly clad and shod, and walk to the **sources** of the Viros river (2 1/2-3 hrs).

ⓖ FROM KARDAMYLI TO AREOPOLIS

The route is of particular interest with much to see. The main coastal road takes you to the foothills of Mt Taygetos toward striking **Proastio** with fine churches and seaview, then to picturesque **Stoupa**, which is where Nikos Kazantzakis met Alexis Zorbas. On the hill nearby there are the ruins of the **Frankish castle of Lefktron or Beaufort**. The way continues on to **Agios Nikolaos**, a pretty harbour with stone houses, some tavernas and the beach of Agios Dimitrios 3km to the south. You then go through **Platsa**, where there is the splendid 10th c. church of ⓖ **Agios Nikolaos**, and **Nomitsi**, a little farther south of Platsa on a hill with a vista to the sea, where you can see the Byzantine ⓖ **church of the Metamorphossis** (11th c) with its notable and well-preserved ⓖ **frescoes**. Not far from there, the village of **Thalames** with its small Ethnological & Historical museum, and **Langada**, a hamlet of stone houses, are worth taking a look.

Shortly before Areopolis, you will come to ⓖ **Itilo**, the regional capital, a village of 500 inhabitants in the traditional style, on the ruins of the ancient city of the same name mentioned in Homer's *Iliad*. As in several other Greek cities, in Itilo too, the locals maintain that the great poet of antiquity was born there. Take the path which will lead you in about half an hour to the **fort of Kelefa**. It was built by the Ottomans to keep the district under control. It is an imposing sight from afar, but little has survived other than a few towers and the contour of the rampart. Continue on to ⓖ **Limeni**, a small bay, harbour for Areopolis, and worth a visit. It is a scenic spot of the Mani, a charming fishing village where you can rest a while and see the **Mavromichali family's tower** before having a meal at **Taki's** taverna.

Agios Nikolaos

Mavromichali family's tower

ⓖ AREOPOLIS

Mani's capital. The name is derived from the god Ares. With traditional architecture, many towers and churches, in a superb setting, it is one of the more representative examples of Mani's singularities. It's the commercial and administrative centre, with lively tourist activity, hotels, shops, tavernas and a few bars. In its narrow flagged alleys you will find tower-dwellings and the historic **church of the Taxiarchon** of the 17th-18th c. with excellent ⓖ **frescoes**.

Church of the Taxiarchon

❷ FROM AREOPOLIS TO THE DIROS CAVES AND VATHIA
Αρεόπολη – Σπήλαια Διρού – Βάθεια / Areópoli – Spílea Diroú – Váthia

Leaving Areopolis, you go to **Pirgos Dirou**, a cluster of small hamlets with many well preserved towers but also a lot in ruins. See there the **Sklavounakos tower** and the **churches of the Taxiarchon** and of **Agia Marina**. You can pop into the **Museum** with **neolithic finds** discovered in the district. Some of the little villages are built above the subterranean, and as yet largely unexplored, galleries of the famous **Diros caves**.

🌀🌀🌀 DIROS CAVES / Σπήλαια Διρού / Spílea Diroú

Tel. (0733) 52222-3
☺ *Summer 8 am-6:30 pm, winter 8 am-2:30 pm
Duration of tour 30min, waiting time max. 30min.*

The biggest is the navigable lake-cavern **Glyphada** or **Vlyhada** with 2.5 km of galleries, chambers with stalactites and stalagmites and an underground river flowing among them. It's an extraordinary experience to tour it, on foot and by boat. In the great chamber **Oceanos**, the water can be as deep as 30 metres! It's one of the world's largest and most noteworthy caves. Exploration has not yet been completed as new sections are constantly being discovered. East of Vlyhada

Diros caves

is the **Alepotrypa**, which had been lived in by prehistoric man as evidenced by the number of finds made by speleologists. There is a 450 m-long gallery with a central lake-cave. A self-service cafeteria, restaurant and snack bar are outside the cave and should you wish to have a swim while in the area, go to the adjacent pebble beach.

🌀🌀 FROM DIROS TO VATHIA

Going in a southerly direction, on the right you will come to the village of **Harouda** with its admirable 11th c. 🌀 **church of the Taxiarchon**. Further on is the bay of **Mezapos** with an attractive village of the same name, while on cape Tigani you'll see the ruins of the **Frankish castle of Great Maina** (13th c.). 🌀 **Stavri** is reached through a stunning mountain landscape dotted with crumbling towers and ruins. See the church of **Episkopi** (12th c) with interesting frescoes,

Kita

and then on to 🌀🌀 **Kita**, an especially striking village full of historic towers and old churches. A must for a visit. See the **stone Maniot mansions** and the domed Byzantine church of 🌀 **Agion Sergiou ke Bacchus** (12th c.). On the Kita-Gerolimenas road, be sure to stop at **Ano Boularii** with a lovely view, well-preserved tower-dwellings (**Pyrgos Anemodoura**) and the churches of **Agios Stratigos** (11th c.) and **Agios Panteleimon** (10th c.)
🌀 **Gerolimenas** is a little port with a waterfront hamlet, on the peninsula near the ruins of the ancient city of Ippola. Modern construction has unfortunately spoiled the traditional local colour but the surroundings are nonetheless a pleasant respite for the traveller in Mani.

🌀🌀 VATHIA

A superb monument of a town with traditional old stone towers and houses. Vathia is under preservation, with a church, a square, fortified dwellings and a small war museum. Some of its larger houses have been converted into guest-houses. A stay there is definitely a special experience.

Vathia

❸ FROM VATHIA TO LAGIA
Βάθεια-Λάγια / Váthia-Lágia

If you head toward **Marmari** and **Porto Kagio**, you must see **Cape Tainaron** or **Kavo Matapa**. At its edge, you will find the little harbour Porto Sternes where you can visit the **sanctuary** of **Poseidon Tainarios**. There, next to the dilapidated **chapel** of the **Asomatos** you'll see the **cave of Hades** (in Greek "tou Adi"), one of the entrances to the underworld, according to the ancient Greeks. You then go through **Porto Kagio**, a fisher-

Porto Kagio

PELOPONNESE

Lagia

Tzanetakis Tower

mans' village where the sole worthwhile sight is its vast enclosed bay. Continue to **Lagia**, a village sprawled on a hill, in competition with Kita for its **well-preserved towers**. Have a stroll through the pleasant alleys.

❹ GYTHIO
Γύθειο / Gíthio

Situated at the foot of Mt Koumaros, it has been inhabited since prehistory. It was once a Phoenician colony, the navy yard of ancient Sparta (destroyed by the Athenians in 455 BC) and a major commercial port for the Romans. It is today an attractive, lively, tourist-oriented seaside town combining traditional architecture with many neo-classical buildings. Visit the **Tzanetakis tower**, now the **Mani Historical** and **Ethnological Museum**, on the little pine-covered island **Kranae** or **Marathonissi**.

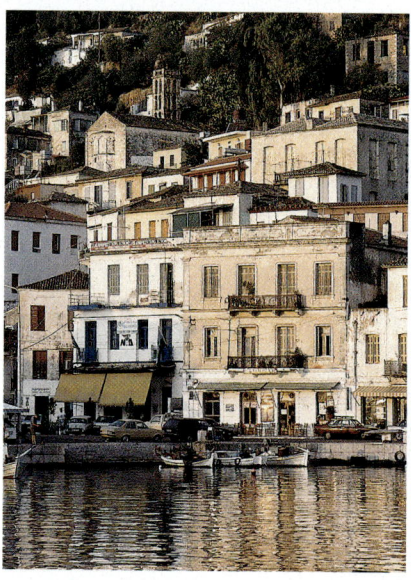

Gythio

OTHER THINGS TO DO

HIKES

The well-known European foot-path E4 crosses the region. From Gythion, it's a 7hr hike to the Taygetos refuge via Kastania and the monastery of Panagia Giatrissa. For more information: Gythion Forestry Service, tel (0733) 22255, Trekking Hellas, tel (01) 3310323-6. At Karavostassi (Itylo) you can ask Mr. Giorgos Kalapothakis, tel. (0733) 51194, for information about excursions, also at the bookshop of Mr. Dimakogiannis, who knows the area well.

BEST BEACHES

SCOUTARI

Three sandy beaches with unpolluted seas. The middle and northern are the best. There is also a nice little taverna.

MAVROVOUNI

A large resort village and one of the best beaches of Mani. It is organized, with water sports.

MARMARI

In southern Mani, before reaching Cape Tainaron you will come across three consecutive beaches on a big enclosed bay. Choose the third, divided by two small spits of land. Sandy in and out of the sea, it is considered the best in the area.

ᑎᑎ STOUPA

Two exceptional beaches with fine sand, **Stoupa** and, even better, ᑎᑎ **Kalogria**, white sands, shady trees, small and quiet tavernas and a few rooms for rent. In high season parking is a problem.

AGIOS NIKOLAOS
A small shingle beach near Stoupa.

Kalogria

BEST HOTELS AND ROOMS

BEST LOCATION

Since distances between the sights are not great, you have two choices: one is to pick a hotel for your entire stay. In this case the best location is in the district between Itylo, Limeni and/or Areopoli.
The second choice is to move from point to point, so as to enjoy the variety of the changing landscape as well as of different guest-houses. In this case Kardamyli, Stavri or Vathia and Gytheion are the most attractive.

PRICES

The hotel prices mentioned below are the official ones set by the National Tourist Organization for double rooms, at low and high season, with breakfast. Since owners are allowed to modify prices, always try to negotiate them.

KARDAMYLI
✓ KALAMITSI HOTEL (B Class)
Tel. (0721) 73131-3, fax 73265

Open: April-October
Description: Situated a little outside the village, in an olive grove, with seaview. Built in 1989 in Maniot style.
Rooms: 26 charming rooms and isolated bungalows with telephone and fridge.
Special features: Taverna.
Price: 24,500-26,000 drs.
Value for money: ✱
Credit cards: Visa, Mastercard

ITYLO
✓✓ PORTO VITILO HOTEL
(B Class)
Tel. (0733) 59270, 59220, (01) 9709076,

fax (0733) 59210.
Open: All year round
Description: At Karavostassi, on the shore of Neo Itylo. Excellent, one of the most tastefully done guest-houses with a very cordial owner.
Rooms: 24 rooms with A/C, canopied beds, antique telephones and balconies with a good view of the mountains and sea.
Special features: Restaurant, good service and parking.
Price: 18,000-23,000 drs.
Value for money: ✱✱
Credit cards: None

PELOPONNESE

✓ PIRGOS ALEVRA
(A Class)

Tel. (0733) 59388, (01) 6645023
Open: All year round
Description: A very attractive guest-house with well tended garden, on a hill and view of the sea. The owner is a well-known film director. An excellent place for a family holiday.
Rooms: 5 rooms with A/C – three with kitchen – balcony and seaview.
Special features: Pool and veranda with a magnificent vista.

Price: 15,000 drs.
Value for money: ✱
Credit cards: None

LIMENI

✓✓ LIMENI VILLAGE
(B Class)

Tel. (0733) 51111
Open: All year round
Description: A large bungalow group with good reproductions of 18 Maniot towers.
Rooms: 33 rooms
Special features: Fine view, a pebble beach with rocks, water sports and parking.
Price: 22,000-27,000 drs.
Value for money: ✱✱
Credit cards: None

AREOPOLI

✓✓ LONDAS (A Class)

Tel. (0733) 51360, fax 51012
Open: All year round.
Description: Restored and well decorated tower-guest-house. It belongs to an artist and an architect who have made their statement, in very good taste.
Rooms: 4 rooms (three twin- and one three-bed) with particular personality and cosy atmosphere. Make reservations well ahead.

Special features: Sitting- and dining-room at visitors' disposal. Pets upon request.
Price: 22,000 drs.
Value for money: ✱✱
Credit cards: None

STAVRI

✓✓ PIRGOS TSITSIRI
(B Class)

Tel. (0733) 56297-8, fax 56296
Open: April-October
Description: A Maniot tower, renovated in 1988 in the traditional style, with a pleasant garden.

Rooms: 20 rooms with A/C.
Special features: Whether staying there or not, take a look at the restaurant with its remarkable arches.
Price: 16,900-20,600 drs.
Value for money: ✱✱
Credit cards: None

VATHIA

✓✓ VATHIA TRADITIONAL GUEST HOUSES

Tel. (0733) 55244
A village under preservation in traditional architecture. The guest-houses no longer belong to the state and the matter of ownership has not yet been clarified. An excellent choice for a stay, but to be sure, call them before going.

GYTHEIO
✓ **AKTAIO (B Class)**
Tel. (0733) 23500, 22484, fax 22294
Open: All year round
Description: A grand, listed building on the coast road of town.
Rooms: 24 rooms with A/C, TV and balcony with view to the sea.
Price: 17,000-21,000 drs.
Value for money: ✱
Credit cards: Visa, American Express

ALTERNATIVES
LELA'S ROOMS
Kardamyli, tel. (0721) 73541. **Price:** 10,000 drs.
PATREARHEAS (B Class)
Kardamyli, tel. (0721) 73660,73366, fax 73660.
Price: 16,000-18,000 drs.
KARDAMYLI BEACH (C Class)
Kardamyli, tel. (0721) 73180-3, fax 73184
Price: 18,500-22,500 drs.
PIRGOS KAPETANAKOU (A Class)
Areopoli, tel. (0733) 51233, fax 51401
Price: 12.000-14.000 drs. Without breakfast

BEST RESTAURANTS & TAVERNAS

There is a good choice of eating-places in the region. In Kardamyli and Areopoli, you'll find some excellent tavernas and restaurants. In the mountain villages, you will find local specialities, but go at a reasonable time if you want to find anything open. In the coastal villages Porto Kagio, Limeni and Gerolimenas you will enjoy fresh fish caught by the local fishermen.

KARDAMYLI
✓ **KYRIA LELA**
Tel. (0721) 73730, 73541

Good ready-cooked food, without a wide choice, in a truly delightful setting with trees, flowers and a view of the rocky shore.
Price: €€

ELIES
Tel. (0721) 73140
A pleasant taverna on Ritsa beach. Greek cuisine.
Price: €

LIMENI
✓ **O TAKIS**
Tel. (0733) 51327

An attractive fish taverna by the sea. The real thing, perhaps the best in the area, with pleasant staff, quick service, fresh fish and lobster.
Price: €€

AREOPOLI
✓ **BARBA-PETROS**
Tel. (0733) 51237
Barba-Petros is next to the church of the Taxiarchon, open for lunch and dinner. The best taverna of Areopoli in a pretty courtyard with good hors d'oeuvre, ready-cooked dishes and grills.
Price: €

GEROLIMENAS
AKROGIALI
Tel. (0733) 54204
The hotel's taverna. With fresh fish and lobster from the local fishermen.
Price: €€

GYTHEIO
TAVERNA NISSI
Tel. (0733) 22830
On the islet Kranae with a view of Gytheio. Little tables around an 80-year-old ficus and good Greek food.
Price: €€

BEST ENTERTAINMENT

This is not the place for swinging nightlife.
In Kardamyli, there is an interesting stone-built little bar, the **Aman**, for a drink with pleasant music. Gytheio has the agreeable bars **I Navaghio** and **Kafepotopoleio**, for a cup of coffee or drinks while looking over the sea to the town.

Aman

TIPS AND INFORMATION

HOW TO GET THERE
- By car in 5 hrs from Athens on the national highway Athens-Corinth-Tripoli-Kalamata and from there to Kardamyli.
- By Olympic Airways from Athens, west airport, to Kalamata (10,000 drs.), tel. (01) 9363363. Olympic Airways, Kalamata, tel. (0721) 22274.
- For an organized tour, go to the travel agents Trekking Hellas, 7 Philhellinon St., Athens, tel. (01) 3310323, and Marathon Tours, 87 Acadimias St., Athens, tel. (01) 3835136, 3818069.
- By rail, OSE Athens, tel. (01) 5131601. From Piraeus or Athens to Kalamata, via Argos-Tripoli or Patras-Pyrgos.
- By intercity bus, KTEL, 100 Kifissou Ave. Athens, tel.(01) 5124913.
- If you don't have your own transport, you can hire a car in Kalamata to continue to Mani.

BEST TIPS
HOW TO GET AROUND: Definitely by your own transport or with an organized tour.

BEST SEASON: The best time of year for Mani is spring or autumn. But it's a good place for a trip all year round.

BEST BUYS: Olive oil, olives, sausages and honey.

USEFUL TELEPHONE NUMBERS

KARDAMYLI	(0721)	Taxis	51382
Community Office	73265	**GYTHEIO**	(0733)
Police	73209	Town Hall	22210
AREOPOLI	(0733)	Police	22100
Community Office	51239	Hospital	22001
Police	51209	Port Authority	22262

MYSTRAS

⁶⁶ Mt. Taygetos ⁶ Ancient Sparta

WHY AMONG THE BEST

For the stunning medieval/Byzantine fortress-state of Mystras, whose impressive buildings led foreign travellers to believe they had discovered ancient Sparta. For the gorges, plane trees, springs and fir forests on Mt Taygetos. And for the ruins of ancient Sparta, the city of the legendary warriors, which are also worth a visit.

BEST's OPINION

The main reason for visiting the region is to explore the once glorious fortress-state of Mystra. But for nature-worshippers and hikers, Mt Taygetos still offers possibilities for remarkable walks in the areas that were not destroyed by the huge fire of 1998.

BEST SIGHTS: STEP BY STEP

❶ SPARTA / Σπάρτη / Spárti

The Franks built medieval Sparta near the ruins of the ancient city-state. The new town gradually declined, in contrast to Mystras, which flourished during that period. It was rebuilt according to new plans under King Otto in 1834, when the modern Greek state was founded. Today's Sparta is a modern town, the capital of Lakonia, the administrative and commercial centre of the prefecture, nicely laid out and with several neo-classical buildings still standing. Here you'll find plenty of entertainment possibilities in the many cafes and bars situated around the main square.

WHAT TO SEE

ARCHAEOLOGICAL MUSEUM

71 Agiou Nikonos St., tel. (0731) 28575

🕒 8 am-3 pm, closed Mondays and holidays*

Housed in an attractive neo-classical building. Exhibits include the mosaic of Perseus slaying Medusa, Hellenistic sculpture and valuable Mycenaean finds from Amyklai.

❷ ANCIENT SPARTA / Αρχαία Σπάρτη / Archéa Spárti

The city is famed in history for its military prowess and the harsh laws formulated by Lykourgos. Sparta had an aristocratic regime, as both the tyranny and the direct democracy of Athens were detested. The intense rivalry between the two powerful city-states led to the calamitous Peloponnesian War (431-404 BC) which ended with Sparta's victory. Following a period of decline, the city began to prosper again under Roman domination, until it was destroyed by a strong earthquake, while a fierce attack by the Visigoths under Alaric (3rd c. AD), gave it its death-blow. Among the ruins of ancient Sparta, you'll see the **Acropolis**, the **sanctuary of Artemis Orthia**, where Spartan boys won a prize for endurance under flogging, the temple of **Athena Chalkioikos** and part of the **Roman theatre**. You will also see the walls, 8-10 km in perimeter, which the Spartans were forced to erect at the onset of the city's decline.

MYSTRAS 10

❸ MYSTRAS
Μυστράς / Mystrás

The walls of Mystras (or Mystra) enclose six centuries of rich and important history that kept Greek civilization alive during a long and dark period (1200-1830).
The cultural development of this fortress-state played a noteworthy role in the formulation of humanist theories and artistic trends in 15th c. Europe.

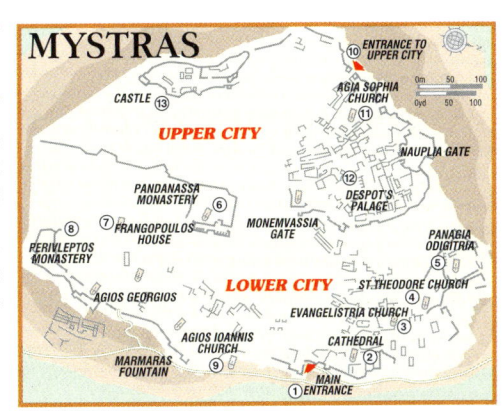

MYSTRAS map:
- ENTRANCE TO UPPER CITY (10)
- AGIA SOPHIA CHURCH (11)
- CASTLE (13)
- UPPER CITY
- NAUPLIA GATE
- PANDANASSA MONASTERY (6)
- DESPOT'S PALACE (12)
- FRANGOPOULOS HOUSE (7)
- MONEMVASSIA GATE
- PANAGIA ODIGITRIA (5)
- PERIVLEPTOS MONASTERY (8)
- LOWER CITY
- ST. THEODORE CHURCH (4)
- AGIOS GEORGIOS
- EVANGELISTRIA CHURCH (3)
- AGIOS IOANNIS CHURCH
- CATHEDRAL (2)
- MARMARAS FOUNTAIN (9)
- MAIN ENTRANCE (1)

HISTORY

At the top of the hill of Mystras, on a northern slope of Mt Taygetos, 6 km NW of Sparta, the Frankish leader Guillaume de Villehardouin constructed a fortress in 1249 which was called **Oriokastro**, "the most beautiful ("oréo" in Greek) castle in the Peloponnese". When he was taken prisoner by the Byzantines, he was obliged to cede it to them in exchange for his freedom. Under the governance of the Katakouzenes and Palaiologues, Mystras soon grew into a major cultural centre and the **Despotate of the Morea (1348-1460)** was founded there. The fortress was transformed into a large Byzantine fortress-state with palaces, mansions, grand churches and monasteries. After the fall of Constantinople, the Peloponnese also fell into the hands of the Ottoman Turks. In the 17th c. the region was briefly under Venetian control but the Turks returned in **1715**. Mystras managed to survive until **1825**, when the fortress-state was completely destroyed by the Egyptian armies of Ibrahim Pasha, who attempted to quell the Greek War of Independence. Mystras was abandoned and never resettled, since the new Sparta was built shortly thereafter.

THE FORTRESS-STATE

Tel. (0731) 83377

◷ *Summer 8 am-7 pm, winter 8 am-3 pm*

The ruined city is divided into three zones: the **Lower City** (Kato Hora), the **Upper City** (Pano Hora) and the **Castle**, at the summit. Try to start your tour early, particularly in summer when the sun can be scorching. Allow at least 3 hrs.

The Despot's Palace

◎◎ LOWER CITY

The neighbourhoods which were created in the 13th c., when the city began to grow and attract residents from ravaged Sparta and the nearby villages. The Lower City was also fortified, but under the Ottomans, houses continued to be built outside the walls in the **Exo Poli** or **Exo Hora**.

◎◎◎ UPPER CITY

This is where the upper classes lived in Mystras. The houses of the nobles were constructed on the north side, those of the bourgeoisie on the south side. You can walk from the Lower City to the Upper City, through the Monemvassia Gate, but you can also get there by car. There is a road that will take you right to the main entrance of the Upper City.

◎ THE CASTLE

The walk up to the castle takes about half an hour. Apart from the chance to explore the ruined fortress, you'll be rewarded by the marvellous view of the whole region.

The Castle

PELOPONNESE

THE TOUR

① **Main entrance:** This takes you to the Lower City.

② 👁👁 **Cathedral (Agios Dimitrios, 13th c.):** A splendid majestic basilica with superb frescoes. The two-storeyed west wing houses a small Byzantine Museum with interesting sculptures, inscriptions, Byzantine icons and the coats of arms of Isabella Lusignan, consort of Michail Katakouzinos.

③ **The Evangelistria Church (15th c.)**, with fine frescoes of the period.

④ 👁 **Agii Theodori Church:** Cruciform 13th c. church, with exceptional architecture and sculpted decoration. The once sumptuous frescoes are now in very poor condition.

⑤ 👁 **The Panagia Odigitria or Afentiko (early 14th c.):** Church with an unusual design, a combination of the basilica and cruciform pattern with five domes. Interesting frescoes and sculpted decoration.

⑥ 👁👁 **Pandanassa Monastery (15th c.):** Mystras' best preserved monastery. With ceramic decoration and frescoes dating back to 1428, dedicated to the Virgin by Ioannis Frangopoulos.

⑦ **The Frangopoulos house (early 15th c.):** Ioannis Frangopoulos, a kind of prime minister to the despotate, lived here.

⑧ 👁👁 **Perivleptos Monastery (14th c.):** Little remains but the church, which is decorated with the most beautiful frescoes in Mystras, executed during the rule of Michail Katakouzinos.

⑨ **Agios Ioannis Church:** Make sure you see the excellent fresco of the Crucifixion (15th c.)

⑩ **Entrance to the Upper City.**

⑪ 👁 **Agia Sophia Church (1350):** Simple two-columned church, with an unusual Byzantine design. The remains of the sculpted decoration are poor but its paintings are wonderful.

Agia Sophia

Panagia Odigitria

⑫ 👁👁 **The Despot's Palace:** An enormous ruined complex of palatial buildings. The NE wing was built by the Katakouzenes (13th c.), the NW wing by the Palaiologues (15th c.).

⑬ 👁 **The Castle:** First to be built on the hill. One can see the ruins of the original Frankish fortress, the cistern and the keep. It was the regional governor's residence.

❹ MT TAYGETOS (FROM TRYPI TO THEOTOKOS)
Ταΰγετος (Τρύπη-Θεοτόκος) / Taígetos (Trýpi-Theotókos)

Trypi, a small village at the start of the **Kaiada** gorge, marks the start of a wonderful route that will take you to the legendary steep precipice where the ancient Spartans disposed of infants born with defects preventing them from serving the state efficiently as warriors.

After Theotokos, on the road to Kalamata, the 1998 fires have tragically marred the beauty of the landscape.

MYSTRAS 10

BEST HOTELS AND ROOMS

BEST LOCATION
Try to stay in the nice, comfortable hotels in Sparta, where you'll be near some night spots. However, if you prefer quiet and a view of the fortress-state, then Mystra would be a better choice.

PRICES
The hotel prices mentioned below are the official ones set by the National Tourist Organization for double rooms, at low and high season, with breakfast. Since owners are allowed to modify the prices, always try to negotiate them.

SPARTA

✓✓ MENELAION (B Class)
C. Palaiologou 91, Tel. (0731) 22161, fax 26332
Open: All year round
Description: Although it's a B Class hotel, it is probably the best in Sparta. Neo-classical building with pleasant, renovated public areas. Be sure to book ahead.

Rooms: 48 rooms with A/C, telephone and TV. Many have been renovated recently.
Special features: Restaurant, parking, and pool.
Price: 23,000 drs.
Value for money: ✷✷✷
Credit cards: Visa, Mastercard

✓ MANIATIS (C Class)
C. Palaiologou 72, Tel. (0731) 22665-9, fax 29994
Open: All year round
Description: Don't be misled by its appearance, it's much nicer inside. Recently renovated, with soothing colours and pleasing decor. Exceptional for its class; be sure to book ahead.
Rooms: 80 small but comfortable rooms, with A/C, TV and telephone.
Special features: Restaurant.
Price: 22,000 drs.
Value for money: ✷✷
Credit cards: All except Diners

MYSTRA

✓ BYZANTION (B Class)
Tel. (0731) 83309, fax 20019
Open: April-October
Description: Recently renovated hotel with a very advantageous location, next to Mystra. Ask for a room with a view of the city ruins.
Rooms: 22 rooms with A/C, telephone and TV.
Special features: Restaurant and parking. Pets upon request.
Price: 25,000 drs.
Value for money: ✷
Credit cards: Mastercard, Visa

TAYGETOS

CANADA HOTEL (CHALET)
Tel. (0721) 76281
Open: All year round
Description: Located at Tsiliboves, 22 km from Sparta, on the way to Kalamata. Chalet with a peaked wooden roof surrounded by firs. The owner is a Greek from Canada. Ideal for undemanding nature-lovers.
Rooms: 9 small but clean and tidy rooms. The reception area is a bit messy.
Special features: Restaurant and central heating.
Price: 5,500 drs.
Value for money: ✷
Credit cards: None

153

ALTERNATIVES

LEDA (A Class) *Sparta, tel. (0731) 23601-3, fax 24493.* **Price:** 30,300 drs.
SPARTA INN (C Class) *Sparta, tel. (0731) 21021, 21421, fax 24855.* **Price:** 17,700-19,100 drs.
APOLLO (C Class) *Sparta, tel. (0731) 22491, fax 23936.* **Price:** 14,800-17,800 drs.

BEST RESTAURANTS & TAVERNAS

✓ AKROLITHI

Sparta, Street of the 118 & Orthias Artemidos St.
Traditional small taverna with courtyard, vine-shaded pergola, and good food. Evenings only.
Price: €

✓ KERAMO

Mystra, at Parori, tel. (0731) 82855
Wonderful location, amongst plane trees, springs and a waterfall. Wooden tables and good cuisine. Lunch and dinner. **Price:** €

✓ BOURLOKAS

Mystras, tel. (0731) 82666
In a pretty courtyard with bougainvilleas and flowers. It serves Greek food, for lunch and dinner.
Price: €

✓ GIANNOPOULOS

Magoula, tel. (0731) 29275
Not much in terms of atmosphere, but your first bite will tell you how great the cooking is here. Pizza and grills of superlative quality. Perhaps the best food in the whole area. **Price:** € €

✓ KOUPITSA

On the road between Sparta and Kalamata at the 24th km, tel. (0721) 76015
Country taverna on the roadside, in a delightful spot filled with plane-trees and running water.
Whether in winter, next to the fireplace, or in summer, the setting is wonderful. Clean, serving both grills and home-cooking, hospitable hosts and impeccable service.
Price: €

TIPS AND INFORMATION

HOW TO GET THERE

- By car, Via the Corinth-Tripoli National Road and then to Mystra and Sparta (271 km). Or rent a car upon your arrival in Sparta.
- To join an organized tour, contact the travel agents: Trekking Hellas, tel. (01) 3310312, Marathon Tours, tel. (01) 3835136, 3818069, 3841684 and Pafsanias, tel. (01) 3820535, 3809016.
- By intercity bus from Athens (KTEL), terminal at 100 Kifissou St., tel. (01) 5134588.

BEST TIPS

BEST SEASON: Mystra is worth visiting at any time of the year.

USEFUL TELEPHONE NUMBERS

SPARTA ....(0731)	KTEL Sparta 26441
Town Hall 26517	**MYSTRA** ....(0731)
Tourist Police 20492	Municipal Office 83368
Police 26229	Police 83315
Hospital 28671	Taxis..83450

Monemvassia

WHY AMONG THE BEST

Monemvassia is not simply just another destination. Apart from the awe you'll feel walking up the amazing stone-paved alleys of the medieval, Byzantine and Venetian fortress-state, you will also have the unique opportunity of living in the wonderful old stone mansions that have been converted into pensions, dining, taking strolls and doing your shopping amongst Venetian houses, with views over the Myrtoon Sea.

PELOPONNESE

BEST's OPINION

An ideal spot for romantics and for those in pursuit of history and tradition, the fortress of Monemvassia is an absolute must. It also offers good quality entertainment and exceptional accommodation. If you really want to enjoy it, however, avoid Easter and August when it is teeming with visitors.
Using the fortress-rock as a base, you can easily take interesting side trips in the vicinity and swim at unspoilt beaches.

BEST SIGHTS: STEP BY STEP

❶ MONEMVASSIA
Μονεμβασία / Monemvassía

Monemvassia took its name from the Greek words meaning single approach, the point (now a causeway) at which the rock is connected with the mainland. This medieval fortress-state is built on a rock 300 m above the sea. In ancient times, it was a harbour town called **Akra Minoa**. The Gibraltar of the Peloponnese, as it is called, was fortified during the Middle Ages to protect the inhabitants from raids by the Avars, Slavs and pirates. The High City (Ano Polis) was erected first (6th c.), followed by the Lower City (10th c.). The town's development and wealth made it very alluring to pirates, but the castle's position, stout fortifications and its people's determination to resist, forced the raiders to withdraw empty-handed.

The inhabitants even devised a law on taxation, the **Aviotikon**, whereby the fortunes of those who died without heirs were left to the community and used to maintain and strengthen the walls.

In 1147, Monemvassia successfully held its own against the Normans, but in 1249 it surrendered, after a three-year siege, to the Frankish conqueror of the Peloponnese, Guillaume de Villehardouin. He employed a large amount of military equipment, 3000 infantry, 8000 cavalry and

Entrance gate

MONEMVASSIA

cut off the fortress from access to both sea and land. The population surrendered only on condition that they would be accorded the same rights as the Franks. Ten years later, Guillaume was defeated by the Byzantines in the battle of Pelagonia and after three years in captivity, gave them three of his most important fortresses in the Peloponnese, Monemvassia, Mystra and Maina (1269). The Palaiologues granted Monemvassia many trading privileges which made it wealthy and powerful. The emperor Andronikos II Palaiologos spent 20 years in exile in the city, until he was returned to his throne in Constantinople. At that time the fortress-state had 8,000 houses and 40 churches. In 1292, the city was tricked into opening its gates and then sacked by the former Catalan admiral and would-be pirate, Roberto de Lauria. When the emperor Ioannis Katakouzinos founded **the Despotate of the Morea**, he included Monemvassia within its jurisdiction. From 1460 to 1464, the fortress-state fell under the authority of Pope Pius II who vainly attempted to convert the population to Catholicism. The Venetians followed (1464) until they were forced to hand the state over to the Vizir of the Peloponnese (1540). In 1690, the Venetians reconquered the area under the leadership of Admiral Morosini and remained there until 1715, when they were obliged to sell the fortress-state to the OttomanTurks. They in turn ruled Monemvassia until the outbreak of the Greek War of Independence in 1821, when Greek besiegers compelled them to surrender.

Monemvassia was a major trading centre and port-of-call for the ships that used to ply the Mediterranean. It was also known for its fabled **Malmsey** wine which was much sought after in the royal courts of Europe. The fame of its wines and tavernas endured until the 1950s.

Today, after lying abandoned for about two decades, the medieval city-state is very much alive and has become a favourite among tourists.

WHAT TO SEE

Strolling through the narrow lanes in the fortress surrounded by beautiful Byzantine buildings is a unique experience. Walls bearing the scars of countless sieges, structures left behind by the Venetians, cobbled paths and imposing mansions from medieval, Byzantine and Venetian times — all make for hours of fascinating exploring.

① *The poet's house.* This is where Yiannis Ritsos (1909-1990), one of modern Greece's best loved poets, was born. His tomb lies in the little cemetery on the side of the rock, along the road up to the fortress.

② *Mosque.* A 10th church that was converted by the Turks into a mosque. Located in the main square, it now houses the town's museum.

③ **Christos Elkomenos.** A three-aisled domed basilica, this is the cathedral church of

Christos Elkomenos church

Monemvassia. It was erected under Andronikos II Palaiologos and is situated on the main square. The interior contains the thrones of Andronikos and his wife, while on the icon screen you will see an exact copy made in 1700 of a wonderful icon portraying Christ in chains (elkomenos), the original of which was stolen a few years ago after having first been hacked to pieces. Fortunately it was found and repaired and can now be seen in the Byzantine Museum in Athens.

④ **Panagia Myrtidiotissa**. A small 18th c. church. The facade contains a relief sculpture of the two-headed eagle, symbol of Byzantium, which originally adorned a Byzantine church erected during the Frankish occupation (13th c.).

⑤ **Panagia Chryssafitissa (16th c.)**. Tradition maintains that the icon travelled on its own to Monemvassia from the village of Chryssafa near Sparta. It is considered to have miraculous properties.

⑥ **Agios Nikolaos (17th c.)**. Above the Chryssafitissa church. Built by a physician philosopher, it was never consecrated because a workman was killed during its construction.

⑦ 👁👁 **Agia Sophia (14th c.)**. In the 👁 **Pano Kastro (Upper Castle/Acropolis)**, at a point where one can marvel at the 👁👁 **splendid view** over the boundless Myrtoon Sea. This is an eight-sided church with a dome, erected by the wife of Andronikos in memory of Agia Sophia in Constantinople. It is the only monument in the Upper City in a good state of preservation.

Agia Sophia church

Other churches: There are 35 more churches on the promontory, including **Agia Anna** (14th c.), **Agios Dimitrios** near the main gate, and **Agii Apostoli**, the chapel in the cave of the rock.

❷ LIMENAS GERAKA
Λιμένας Γέρακα / Liménas Géraka

A lovely, enclosed fishing port in an impressive setting reminiscent of a fjord. The **ruins of the acropolis and fortress of Zarakas** occupy the hill. The ancient town of Zarax was located between the rival city-states of Argos and Sparta and was consequently severely damaged, especially by the latter. The lagoon provided safe anchorage for Roman, Byzantine, and Venetian fleets, not to mention generations of pirates. The Hydriot and Spetsiot ships that besieged the Turks in Monemvassia also took refuge here in bad weather.

Today it is a small hamlet with some excellent fish tavernas, such as **Lazarakis**, **Diamantis**, and the ouzeri, **Apothiki** (in an old warehouse).

BEYOND THIS EXCURSION

ARCHANGELOS
Αρχάγγελος / Archángelos

Fishing hamlet with a few inhabitants in a pretty little cove with clean, tranquil waters. It can be reached via the road from Neapolis and has adequate accommodation and tavernas.

GERAKI
Γεράκι / Yeráki

The guards of the Archaeological Service will show you around. Ask them in town to open the churches for you and let you into the fenced fortress precinct, or call before you go, tel. (0731) 71393.

Historic market town with 1,400 inhabitants at the foothills of Mt. Parnon.
It is worth seeing the churches of **Agios Athanassios (12th c.)**, the **Evangelistria (11th c.)**, **Agios Nikolaos (13th c.)**, **Agios Sozon (12th c.)**, and **Agios Ioannis Chryssostomos (13th c.)**. All the churches have fine frescoes dating between the 12th and 15th c. The **Evangelistria** contains the most important.

THE FORTRESS-STATE OF GERAKI

Built by the Franks, this fortress was even larger than that of Mystra and acted as the intermediate communication post, using signals and fires, between the fortresses of Mystra and Monemvassia. It later passed to the Byzantines and the Turks.
Worth visiting are the churches of **Agios Georgios (11th c.)** which predates the castle and has remarkable icons, the Byzantine church of **Zoodochos Pigis**, the **Archangelos** and **Agii Anargyri**.

KYPARISSI
Κυπαρίσσι / Kiparíssi

An interesting detour will take you to this picturesque coastal village with its three traditional neighbourhoods (Vryssi, Paralia and Mitropoli). It began to attract attention during the Turkish occupation, when Spetsiots fleeing from the Turks took refuge there. The place grew quickly after Greek independence but before long much of the population was forced to emigrate in order to survive. The village has a modicum of tourist facilities in the form of rooms for rent, tavernas and lovely beaches. A good place for a quiet holiday and walks on the slopes of Parnon.

BEST BEACHES

Apart from Plytra, the region is not noted for its beaches. We have selected the best options for a cooling swim in the hottest hours of the day.

PLYTRA

Plytra

The best beach in the region, it has fine white sand and shallow turquoise waters. A few restaurants and houses line the beach, while in the peak period there are German tourists with caravans. To get there, take the road to Sykea-Molaoi and turn after Sykea towards Asopos.

PORTELLO

Portello

Just below the fortress of Monemvassia, with clear, deep water. Rocks paved with plaques to facilitate sunbathing.

AMBELAKIA

Below the village of Nomia. The pebbly beach is not particularly inviting but it is close to Monemvassia and is good enough for a quick dip.

PORI

Long, narrow and clean but not much more.

PELOPONNESE

BEST HOTELS AND ROOMS

BEST LOCATION
Make every effort to stay in the Fortress of Monemvassia and forget Gefyra, the settlement opposite. You came to see the fortress-state and the ideal way to do that is to stay here, even if it means rearranging your dates in order to get a room.

PRICES
The hotel prices mentioned below are the official ones set by the National Tourist Organization for double rooms, at low and high season, with breakfast. Since owners are allowed to modify the prices, always try to negotiate them.

WITHIN THE FORTRESS

✓✓ MALVASIA (A Class)
Tel. (0732) 61113, 61160, 61323, fax 61722
Open: All year round
Description: Traditional guest-houses, located at three points in the old town, with beautiful rooms, each with its own style. Perhaps the best place to stay in Monemvassia. The reception office is on the main street. Of the three buildings, try to stay in the **Malvasia Hotel**, where there is a bar.

Malvasia

Rooms: 30 attractive rooms decorated in wood and stone. With A/C, fireplace and a sea view.
Special features: Exceptional bar on the ground floor and breakfast-room.
Price: 13,400-46,400 drs.
Value for money: ✻✻✻
Credit cards: Visa

✓✓ BYZANTINO (A Class)
Tel., fax (0732) 61351, fax 61254
Open: All year round
Description: Traditional buildings scattered around the Kastro. The reception office is on the main street.
Rooms: 9 attractive, comfortable rooms with A/C and telephone.
Special features: The lovely **Enetiko** bar.

Price: 20,000-35,000 drs.
Value for money: ✻✻
Credit cards: Visa

✓ ARDAMIS (A Class)
Tel. (0732) 61886, 61887, (071) 233 532, fax (0732) 61886
Open: All year round
Description: Spacious, beautiful and luxurious apartments and rooms.
Rooms: 5 rooms with A/C, TV, telephone, kitchen and verandas with a view of the sea, plus old-fashioned marble bathtubs, picturesque windows and romantic stone turrets.
Special features: Courtyard for coffee or cocktails.
Price: 28,000 drs. Without breakfast

Ardamis

MONEMVASSIA   11

Value for money: ✱✱
Credit cards: Visa, Alphacard

✓ GOULAS (A Class)
Tel. (0732) 61707, (01) 6135988
Open: All year round
Description: Renovated in 1996. The hospitable

Goulas

owner, Kyria Filio, also publishes the *Voice of Monemvassia*, the local newspaper.
Rooms: 5 rooms (3 doubles, 1 apartment, 1 triple) with another two under construction. With minibar, A/C and telephone. The best rooms are nos. 4 and 5, with verandas overlooking the sea.
Price: 16,000-18,000 drs. (no breakfast, with a different price for each room).
Value for money: ✱✱
Credit cards: Diners, Visa

✓ KELLIA (A Class)
Tel. (0732) 61520, fax 61767
Open: All year round
Description: Renovated in 1990 and run by the National Tourism Organization.
Rooms: 12 rooms with private shower, fans, radi-

Kellia

ators, telephone and sea view.
Price: 23,000 drs.
Value for money: ✱
Credit cards: None

AT GEFYRA, OPPOSITE MONEMVASSIA

✓✓ LAZARETTO (A Class)
Tel. (0732) 61991-3, fax 61992
Open: All year round
Description: Just across the bridge to Monemvassia but outside the fortress, it is the best of all the hotels, except for its location.
Rooms: 14 rooms with telephone, TV, minibar. The suites also have a kitchen.
Special features: Restaurant, cafe-bar, gym and conference hall.
Price: 25,000-30,000 drs. Without breakfast
Value for money: ✱
Credit cards: Visa

ALTERNATIVES

KATE'S APARTMENTS, *Monemvassia Kastro*.
Tel. (0732) 61772, fax 61027.
Price: 15,000-35,000 drs.

BEST RESTAURANTS & TAVERNAS

There are only three in Monemvassia and they are all on the main street. In peak periods make sure to reserve a table. The restaurant owners collaborate to make sure one of them is always open in winter.

✓ MATOULA
Kastro, tel. (0732) 61660
With a garden and veranda. Delicious casseroles and grills.
Price: €

Matoula

161

✓ TO KANONI

Kastro, tel. (0732) 61387
Lovely taverna with verandas, terrace, good Greek cuisine and fish.
Price: €

MARIANTHI

Kastro, tel. (0732) 61371
Good food, less desirable location.
Price: €

BEST ENTERTAINMENT

Monemvassia's little bars are charming. You are bound to wind up in at least one of these attractive hangouts during your wanderings through the medieval alleys.

The **Malvasia Hotel's** bar serves its drinks to the accompaniment of classical music and is well - placed to view the sunset. **Angelos** on the main street, has a little romantic balcony overlooking the sea, classical music from breakfast on. The owner has a good sense of humour and is happy to answer any questions about rentals, etc. On the main street you'll come across the gorgeous cafebar **Byzantino**. For a livelier atmosphere, try the **Enetiko**, frequented by the young.

Byzantino

TIPS AND INFORMATION

HOW TO GET THERE

- By car in about 4 hrs 30 min. from Athens, via Tripoli.
- By hydrofoil, Minoan Flying Dolphins (from 7,000 drs.), tel. (01) 3244600, 4280001, daily in summer and twice a week in winter from Zea harbour in Piraeus to Monemvassia in 2 hrs 30 min.
- For organized tours from Athens: Marathon Tours, tel. (01) 3835136, 3818069, 3841684, Pafsanias, tel. (01) 3820535, 3809016
- By intercity bus (KTEL Lakonia), from Peloponnissou Station, Athens, Tel. (01) 512 4913, KTEL in Monemvassia, tel. (0732) 61432, 61274.

CONNECTIONS

- By hydrofoil , Minoan Flying Dolphins, one can also stop off at Kyparissi, Leonidio, Porto Heli, Spetses, Hydra and Kythera.

BEST TIPS

HOW TO GET AROUND: If you are only interested in seeing Monemvassia, then take the hydrofoil and walk around the old fortress. If you'd like to explore the countryside and other destinations, then a car is definitely advisable.

BEST SEASON: Monemvassia is ideal for a long weekend any time of year, even at Easter and in August, if you can find a room in the fortress.

USEFUL TELEPHONE NUMBERS

MONEMVASSIA .... (0732)	Police 61210
Town Hall.. 61222	Port Authority 61266
Clinic.. 61204	Malvasia Travel... 61752

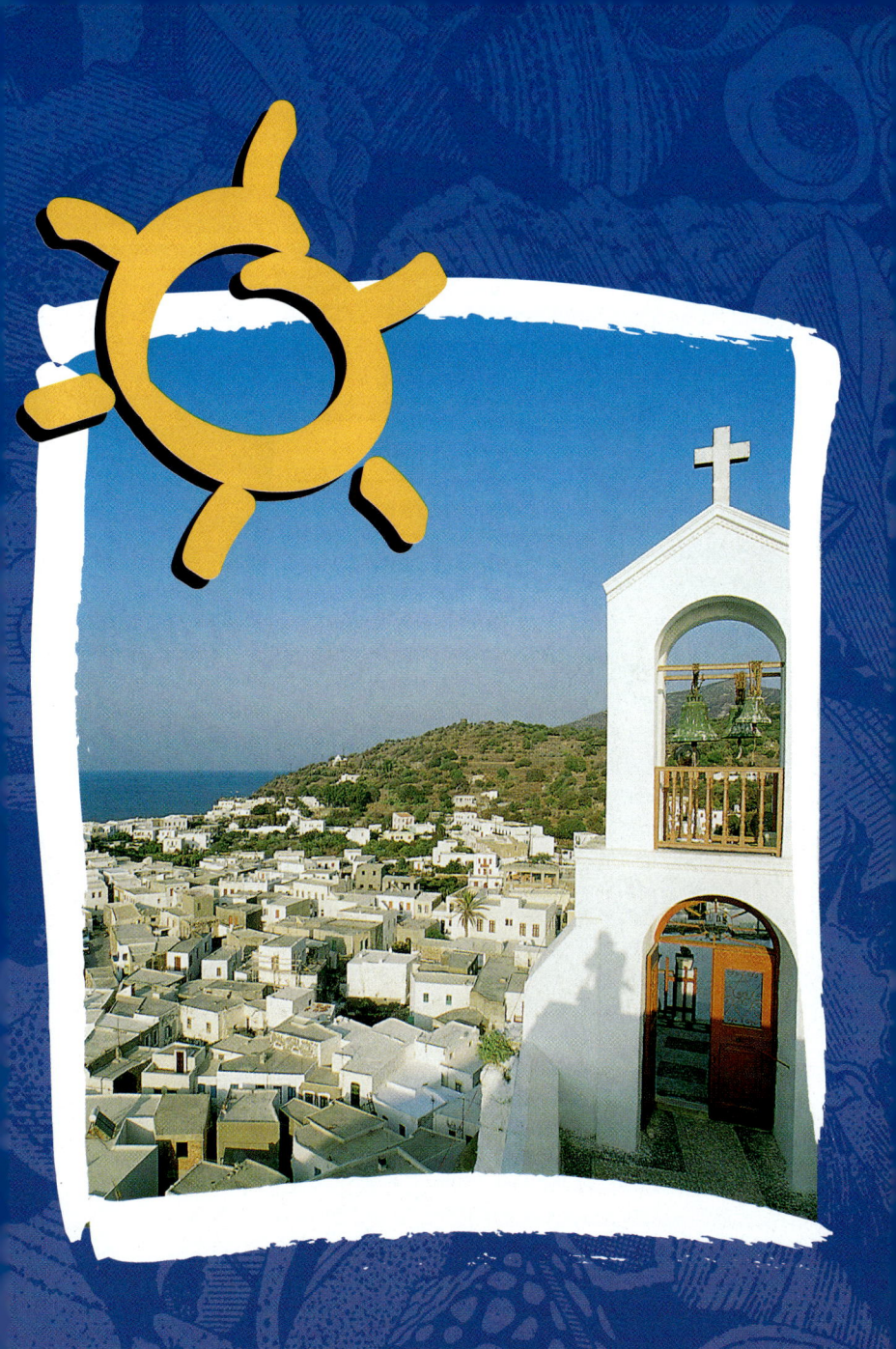

The Greek Islands

The Greek Islands

More than two thousand islands adorn the Greek seas. Of those, 170 are inhabited, home to no more than 10 percent of the country's total population.

That string of pearls, the Cyclades, with their barren, rocky hills and blinding white houses; the fertile Sporades, with their endless stretches of golden sand; the Argosaronic islands, with their rich maritime history; the Northeastern Aegean islands, with their ancient mystical origins; the Dodecanese with its aristocrat, Rhodes, and the devout Patmos; the Ionian islands, with their European culture echoing with serenades; timeless Crete with its fascinating contrasts, and Cyprus, violently torn from its ethnic roots, birthplace though it was of Aphrodite, goddess of love and union.

> **Island: Land surrounded on all sides by sea or lake.**

Almost all of them bearing female names, these islands have germinated civilizations from the dawn of time, such as the Cycladic and Minoan, and have been the birthplace of many artists: the erotic Sappho, the lyrical Alkaio, Elytis who won the Nobel prize for poetry, the exuberant Kazantzakis, Psycharis who wrote the people's language, the devout Papadiamantis, the lofty Valaoritis, Solomos the sublime and the greatest of them all, epical Homer.

Each island in its way seduces the senses of the visitor, enchanting him with magical sunrises, superb sunsets, jagged coastlines alternating with picturesque bays where fishing boats gently rock under the bright sunlight, damp winters of solitude and boisterous blue seas with the brilliant sun reflecting its rays off glistering sands and sparkling white houses. Their quaint squares in the heart of the villages where eternal plane trees spread their shade beside crystal-clear springs, the tortuous windings of cobbled lanes, the small white-washed churches dedicated to their patron saints precariously clinging to a mountainside, pine-clad or bare. There are also fortresses built by Venetians in the Ionian islands, the Cyclades and Crete, by Knights of the Hospital of St. John of Jerusalem in the Dodecanese and by the Genoese in the Northeastern Aegean, proudly flanking noble castles or massive stone mansions which housed the fighting-men of the West and the the shipmasters of the Aegean.

The islands relate legends and folklore. They spring to life with colourful customs and festivities, ecstatic carnivals, the festive Assumption day, the pious Easter celebrations when streets and homes are white-washed, eggs are dyed red and traditional cookies are backed.

Their intoxicating drinks exhilerate – "raki" from Crete, "ouzo" from Mytilini, "tsipouro" from Naxos, "masticha" from Chios and seductive wines from Samos or Zakynthos– while they exude the scents of salt, pine, sizzling fish, fumes of incense and night-blossoming flowers.

They bewitch their visitors with irresistible spells, making them dream, like Odysseus, as they bid farewell, of the "nostimon imar", the day of return.

The Islands of the Argosaronic Gulf and Kythera

ARGOSARONIC GULF AND KYTHERA

BEST's OPINION

The diversity of landscape and the wealth of things to see, from emerald green Poros to the bare rock of Hydra and the antiquities of Aegina, made so accessible by the frequent hydrofoil service linking all the islands and some mainland destinations, are sure to give the traveller a host of memorable experiences, even during the course of a one-day excursion.

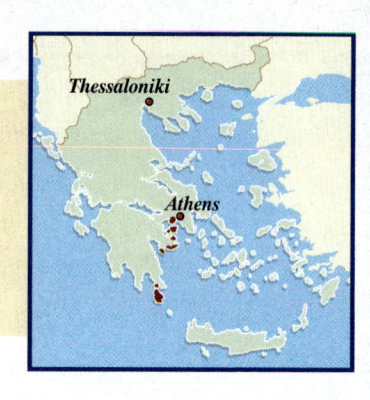

IN BRIEF

The Argosaronic Gulf has five large islands – Salamis, Aegina, Poros, Hydra and Spetses – three smaller ones – Angistri, Dokos and Moni – as well as the spa towns of the Peloponnese, Porto Heli and Methana. Kythera, although culturally tied to the Ionian islands, belongs administratively to the prefecture of Attica, as do the rest.

HISTORY

From early on, the inhabitants of these islands became masters in sailing and trading. Aegina and Salamis were important city-states in antiquity, reaching their peak in the 7th and 6th c. BC, while Hydra and Spetses followed suit in the 18th and 19th c.
The islands were repeatedly subjected to conquests until they were united with the rest of Greece.

THE ARGOSARONIC ISLANDS

The *Best* of these islands are described in the following excursions: ⓖⓖ **Kythera** & ⓖ **Elafonissos** (*Excursion 12*), ⓖⓖ **Spetses** (*Excursion 13*) and ⓖⓖⓖ **Hydra** (*Excursion 14*). Your time permitting, it would be worth visiting others as well.

Temple of Athena Aphaia

ⓖ AEGINA / Αίγινα / ́Egina

An ancient naval power, for a brief period Aegina was the capital of the new Greek state after its liberation from the Turks. Today it has about 7,000 inhabitants, some lovely scenery, of fertile soil which favours its famous pistachio plantations, and several ancient sites. Among the most impressive sights are the well preserved ⓖⓖ **Doric temple of Athena Aphaia** (5th c. BC) and the ⓖ **convent of Agios Nektarios**. It is however short of good and clean beaches.
Nearby ⓖ **Angistri**, with 650 inhabitants and plenty of pine trees, is a tranquil holiday spot with deserted beaches visited by quite a lot of pleasure craft.

ⓖ POROS / Πόρος / Póros

The wooded island of Poseidon is separated from the Ermioni peninsula by a very narrow, almost lagoon-like channel. If you don't visit Poros, make sure you have your camera ready when your boat passes by on the way to Hydra. It has 4,000 inhabitants and is a favourite with photographers because much of it is still unspoilt. The famous ⓖ **lemon forest** ("lemonodasos") is located on the mainland opposite. The calm sea round Poros is ideal for water-skiing, but there are no good beaches.

Poros

KYTHERA

◦◦ Kythera   ◦◦ Elafonissos

WHY AMONG THE BEST

Because although Kythera is one of the most beautiful islands, its tourist development is still in its infancy. Because you will be enchanted by the old traditional villages, now mostly abandoned to the ravages of time, the medieval castle at Hora with a view of Kapsali and to sea, the greenery alternating with ravines and the peerless beaches with crystal-clear waters.

ARGOSARONIC GULF AND KYTHERA

BEST's OPINION

Kythera will definitely not disappoint you, particularly if you take the trouble to explore. The best place to stay is in the southern part (Hora, Kapsali, Livadi) and take short trips from there to the delightful hamlets of the interior.

IN BRIEF

Many of the inhabitants have emigrated to Australia, which they call "Greater Kythera" and a lot return to the island in the summer. The terrain is mountainous, with one extensive cultivable plain between two ranges. The population is about 3,000, working for the tourist trade, fishermen and farmers.

Visitors are charmed by the scenery, the Cycladic and Venetian villages, the monasteries, rocky coves and fine sand beaches. The climate is mild and there is scant rainfall. There are three harbours: Diakofti, new, large and protected from the winds, Agia Pelagia, until recently the island's port, and finally Kapsali, where pleasure boats moor alongside fishing boats.

HISTORY

There are finds at Kastri demonstrating the presence of Cretans in 2000 BC and Mycenaeans in the 14th c. BC. Later, it was successively dominated by Athenians, Spartans and Romans. In the Byzantine period it was often overrun by pirates until, in 1207, it came into the hands of the Franks and in 1363 of the Venetians, who fortified the sites of Mylopotamos, Kapsali and Agios Dimitrios (Paliohora). In 1537 Kythera's evolution was brought to a halt by the greatest disaster in its history: the pirate raid of Barbarossa. Venetian supremacy was overthrown by Napoleon in 1797, but a year later the Russian fleet forced the French garrison to surrender. There followed English domination from 1809 and eventually in 1864 Kythera was incorporated into Greece.

BEST SIGHTS: STEP BY STEP

There is one main road in Kythera which crosses it from north to south. As a slight detour is necessary to see most of the principal sights, we have made a selection of short trips to save you travelling on narrow roads to no purpose.

❶ SOUTHERN KYTHERA
Νότια Κύθηρα / Nótia Kíthira

The main points of interest are Hora and Kapsali, the island's lovely scenery and the spectacular vistas.

◎◎ HORA

This charming "capital" of Kythera dominates from a height, with its Cycladic architecture and the once mighty ◎ **medieval fortress** of the 13th to 15th c. It has about 600 inhabitants and receives its share of the island's tourism.

Strolling in Hora's lanes and about the castle is a pleasure, culminating in the fantastic ◎◎ **view** of Kapsali, while just off shore you can see the islet of **Hitra** or **Avgo** (the Egg) emerging where the goddess Aphrodite was born, according to the myth.

The hamlet clustering round the castle still contains houses from the days of the Venetians and the British, such as the **residence of the Venetian governor** (later that of the British Commissioner), as well as Byzantine churches.

Visit the small **Archaeological Museum** at the edge of Hora, tel. (0735) 31739, open 8:30 am-2 pm, closed on Mondays and holidays*.
It exhibits finds from the Minoan and Classical periods, Byzantine icons and Venetian coats of arms.

Alley in Hora

ARGOSARONIC GULF AND KYTHERA

Kapsali

🌀🌀 KAPSALI

On the way down from Hora to Kapsali it's worth making a stop on the left hand side of the road at the **chapel of Agii Akindyni** to enjoy the splendid panorama. Kapsali is a sheltered natural harbour divided in two by a little peninsula, the most photographed and the most **popular spot** of the island for the numerous Greek and foreign visitors, with the most shops, cafe-bars and tavernas. Nevertheless, the big beach of the harbour is not the best place for a swim, since there are incomparably more beautiful ones on the island. Do not fail to visit the cave with the **chapel of Agios Ioannis tou Gremou** of the 16th c., in the rock face above Kapsali, at the edge of the pine forest. This is where tradition places St. John the Divine as beginning the writing of his Revelation.

A hired boat will take you across to the striking rocky island, **Hytra** or **Avgo**, where there is an impressive **cave with stalactites** and, if you are lucky, maybe a seal or two. Choose the hour of sunset when the enormous rock takes on an unreal dimension.

🌀 LIVADI AND 🌀🌀 KATO LIVADI

Livadi is a village of traditional architecture with 300 inhabitants and grand houses from the days of the British presence in the island. In **Kato Livadi** see the 🌀🌀 **Katouni bridge**, the biggest stone bridge in the Balkans, 150 m long, with 13 arches, built by the British engineer McFale in 1822. If you have time, visit the **Byzantine Museum** (open: 10 am-2 pm) with mosaics and icons. There is a road from Kato Livadi to the nice beach of **Kombonada**.

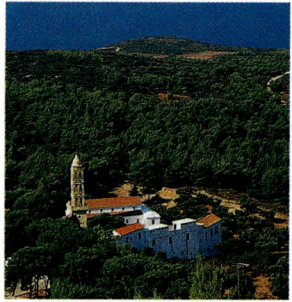

MYRTIDION AND AGIA ELESSA MONASTERIES

The 🌀 route to the 🌀 **Myrtidion monastery** has many natural attractions to offer and particularly just before Myrtidia where you should watch the 🌀🌀 **sunset** from Stavros. The monastery's icon is considered by the faithful to have miraculous powers.

Before Drymonas, a village with local colour near the bay of Melidoni, you'll see atop a towering rock of 433 m, the **monastery of Agia Elessa**. The 🌀🌀 **vista** along the way as well as from the plateau at the end of the 🌀 road (4 km), is superb. The monastery is dedicated to a local saint, a girl who, legend has it, was butchered by her father for having embraced Christianity.

Myrtidion monastery

❷ CENTRAL KYTHERA
Κεντρικά Κύθηρα / Kentriká Kíthira

This is where the traditional villages of the interior are to be found, where once the inhabitants of the island fled to take refuge, hiding from the pirates.

🌀🌀 MYLOPOTAMOS

A small and verdant village with an attractive square and abundant flowing waters next to which the watermills of the island used to be. At the spot called Neraida, in the Fonissa gully, there is a 🌀 **waterfall**. Enjoy a cup of coffee or a meal in the old-time *kafenio* (cafe)-restaurant in the village square.

🌀 **Kato Hora Mylopotamou** is a fascinating ruined hamlet with a **Venetian fort**, chapels and cobbled lanes. If you are there in the afternoon you may see a spectacular 🌀🌀 **sunset**. The beach of Limnionas is close by.

Finally, it is worth seeing the 🌀🌀 **cave of Agia Sophia** inside a 60 m high rock, which has enchanting pools and chambers with stalactites and stalagmites in curious shapes. It can be visited from June to September, 10 am-2 pm, tel. (0735) 33754, 31213.

Waterfall

KYTHERA 12

VILLAGES OF THE INTERIOR

Of the many traditional villages in the region, we singled out **Aroniadika**, a picturesque hamlet where there are rooms for rent; the specially colourful **Aloizianika**; **Frilingianika** which has a handsome stone church; **Zaglanikianika**, where Belgian visitors to the island have already begun buying houses; and **Mitata** with the impressive crevasse formed in 1903 by the violent earthquake which convulsed the island. There you'll find plenty of streams and the nectarines called Aphrodite's breasts. In August a wine festival takes place here. At **Palaiopoli**, located before Avlemonas, lie the ruins of **Skandia**, a major ancient city-port, destroyed by the eruption of the volcano of Santorini. Archaeologists believe this was where the temple of Aphrodite stood, visited by Paris and Helen of Troy.

Avlemonas is an idyllic fishing village of 80 inhabitants and a beautiful narrow and protected harbour with a small **Venetian fort** at its entrance, as well as boats, fishing caiques and tavernas serving fresh fish.

Going to Diakofti along a short stretch of road, if you drive to the top of the mountain, on your right you will reach the **chapel of Ai-Georgi tou Vounou**. The excavations in the district revealed a **Mycenaean sanctuary** on the crown of a hill. The way back takes you to the same road for Diakofti but you can turn off in the direction of Aroniadika and drive up the mountain to the monastery of **Agia Moni**, from where the **view** is beautiful..

Aroniadika

Mitata

Avlemonas

---

❸ NORTHERN KYTHERA
Βόρεια Κύθηρα / Vória Kíthira

The north side of the island is scenic and less touristic, with the exception of the town and harbour of Agia Pelagia. The most interesting sight of the area is **Paleohora**.

POTAMOS AND VILLAGES IN THE ENVIRONS

Potamos is the island's biggest town with about 700 inhabitants and Kythera's commercial centre, with a fine tree-shaded square and a pine copse. On the way out of Potamos continue on to **Karava**, a verdant village on a steep slope, with a stream. For a swim, go to the deserted little beach at Cape **Spathi** or to **Fournous**. Returning, pass by **Gerakari** and **Petrouni**, two delightful villages in traditional style. The road to Gerakari takes you through the island's biggest forest with pine and eucalyptus trees. **Logothetianika** is noted for it's church clock and the roast kid served at **Karydies** taverna.

PALAIOHORA

8 km east of Potamos, at the top of a rocky outcrop there are the **remnants of Byzantine buildings** and of the **churches of Palaiohora**, which used to be the island capital. The lay-out of the fortified town plan is reminiscent of Mystra and Monemvassia. It was built in the 13th c. between two gullies so as to be concealed from pirates. However, the pirate Barbarossa found it and razed it to the ground, massacring its 5,000 inhabitants in one night and taking the rest as slaves. Visit it at sunrise or sunset. Entrance is free and you can go there any time you want. The ruins and the scenery are striking and the **view** of the gullies breathtaking. This is also where the **gorge of Kakia Langada**, 100 m deep, begins, ending at a beach.

ARGOSARONIC GULF AND KYTHERA

❹ ELAFONISSOS

We propose Elafonissos to those who like exotic beaches. ☂☂☂ **Simos**, with dunes and cedars, is perhaps the most fabulous beach in Greece, unless there is a south wind, and if you are not bothered by the tourist crowds in August.

All the island's activity is concentrated in the village and port. There is a considerable local fishing fleet and many fish tavernas on the waterfront. For a stay we suggest the **Hotel Elafonissos** (see **Best hotels and rooms**)

Simos

☂ BEST BEACHES

Kythera's sea is considered the most unpolluted of the Mediterranean. There are many wonderful beaches where even in peak season you will find no crowds. Most are not organized, nor do they have any tavernas, so be equipped with an umbrella, water and something to eat.

☂☂☂ KALADI

On the road to Avlemonas, before Paleopolis turn right at the sign. The last bit of roadway is difficult to negotiate. Park where the dirt track ends and walk down the steps to Kaladi beach, enjoying the marvelous view as you go. After you've had a first dip, walk to the end of the next beach to look at the spectacular rock formations and caves.

☂☂ FYRI AMMOS

A lovely big beach with coral pink pebbles and coral breeding-ground. It's the best near Kapsali and preferred by many who know Kythera well. There is also a canteen.

☂☂ KYRIAKOULOU

A tiny sandy cove with beautiful colours in the water. You get there by caique from Kapsali.

☂ SPARAGARIO

Opposite Kapsali. Glistening pebbles in a narrow cove surrounded by rocks. You can go by car (parking after the bridge and walking 5 min along the path) or by pedalo from Kapsali.

☂ MELIDONI

A charming bay with sand and crystalline waters. It is not as close as it seems but it attracts crowds and pleasure-craft. It has a canteen and umbrellas. Avoid it in August when it can be overcrowded or go to the smaller and quieter beach next to it.

☂ AGIOS NIKOLAOS (SPATHI)

A pretty little cove, ideal for hermits.

☂ PALAIOPOLI

A striking beach with a long stretch of sand, caves and lots of bathers. On the way from Palaiopoli to

KYTHERA

Avlemonas, near the road, you'll come across another good 🏖 beach, long and peaceful.

🏖 KOMBONADA
An good large beach with caves.

🏖 HALKOS
A cove surrounded by tall rocks honeycombed with caves. A nice, small beach with turquoise waters. There is a canteen.

OTHER BEACHES
🏖🏖 **Kalami** at Kato Hora Mylopotamou is marvellous, but only for the intrepid (access with a rope).
🏖 **Fourni** is near Karava and 🏖 **Kakia Langada** is the diminutive beach at the end of the ravine of the same name (by a dirt track from Agia Pelagia).

BEST HOTELS AND ROOMS

BEST LOCATION
The entire island is both beautiful and interesting, but it is advisable to stay in the southern part between Hora and Kapsali, where the natural attractions are combined with many things to see, as well as offering the majority of options for meals and amusement.

PRICES
The hotel prices mentioned below are the official ones set by the National Tourist Organization for double rooms, at low and high season, with breakfast. Since owners are allowed to modify the prices, always try to negotiate them.

HORA
✓ MARGARITA (C Class)
Tel. (0736) 31711, 31694, fax 31325
Open: April-October
Description: A grand old house in the local architectural style, with a fine veranda and view of the sea.
Rooms: 12 rooms with bath, A/C, telephone and taped music. The front rooms have a sea view.
Special features: Bar, garden and a safe for valuables.
Price: 14,000-25,000 drs.
Value for money: ✱ ✱
Credit cards: Visa, Mastercard

KAPSALI
✓✓ RAIKOS (C Class)
Tel. (0736) 31629, 31766, fax 31801, (01) 8964322
Open: June-September
Description: On a hill between Hora and Kapsali, a recently-built hotel complex with features of Cycladic and Venetian architecture. Care was taken with the interior decoration and the view is magnificent to Hora, the castle and the sea. You need a car.

Rooms: 24 rooms with bath, telephone, A/C and fridge. Some have a balcony with a view of the sea and the fort.
Special features: Parking, swimming pool, bar and a safe.
Price: 18,000-27,000 drs.
Value for money: ✱✱
Credit cards: Visa, Mastercard

✓ VASILIS VILLAS (B Class)
Tel. (0736) 31125, 31356, fax 31553

Open: Easter-October
Description: Cycladic and Venetian styles
Rooms: 13 self-contained studios with bath, kitchen, telephone and veranda with splendid sea view.
Special features: Parking, garden. Pets upon request.
Price: 14,950-21,850 drs.
Value for money: ✱✱
Credit cards: Visa

✓ PORTO DELFINO (B Class)
Tel. (0735) 31940, 31941 fax 31939
Open: April-October
Description: Just outside Kapsali, a small and simple hotel complex on a hill with a lovely view of Kapsali and Avgo.
Rooms: 22 rooms with bath, A/C, telephone and balcony.
Special features: Restaurant, bar, garden and a safe.
Price: 27,000-31,000 drs.

Value for money: ✱
Credit cards: Visa

AGIA PELAGIA
VERNARDOS (C Class)
Tel. (0736) 34205, fax 34206
Open: All year round
Description: A small modern hotel with a home-like atmosphere and a superb view.
Rooms: 16 rooms with A/C, satellite TV, telephone and small fridge.
Special features: First-class breakfast buffet with traditional specialities.
Price: 22,000-29,000 drs.
Value for money: ✱✱
Credit cards: None

TRADITIONAL LODGINGS
We have selected three attractive traditional guest houses in renovated old buildings, with 4 to 7 rooms with bath, welcoming owners and reasonable prices.

TA KYTHERA (B Class) Manitohori, Tel. (0736) 31563. **Price:** 12,000-14,000 drs.

KAMARES (B Class) Aroniadika, tel. (0736) 33420. **Price:** 10,000-14,000 drs. Without breakfast

ROUGA (C Class) Aroniadika, tel. (0736) 33596, fax 33130 **Price:** 11,000-17,000 drs.

ELAFONISSOS
HOTEL ELAFONISSOS (C Class)
Tel. (0734) 61268, 61210
Open: Whit Monday-September
Description: Small, unpretentious hotel.
Rooms: 11 rooms with bath and balcony with sea view.
Special features: Snack bar.
Price: 9,000-10,000 drs. Without breakfast
Value for money: ✱
Credit cards: None

BEST RESTAURANTS & TAVERNAS

HORA
✓ MYRTOO
Tel. (0735) 31705
Good Greek food in a pretty garden. Summer and winter.
Price: €

KAPSALI
✓✓ YDRAGOGEIO
Tel. (0735) 31065
On the right as you come to Kapsali. Quiet, with excellent service, a splendid view, delicious "ethnic"

food and music. It is pleasant at all times of day, at sunset and by moonlight. Specialities: peppery blended cheese, pies, vegetarian moussaka (aubergines layered with fillings). **Price:** €€

✓✓ ANDONIS O MAGOS

Tel. (0735) 31407-8
Fresh fish and ready-cooked dishes on the waterfront. **Price:** €€

✓ KOUKOS

Tel. (0735) 31794
On the curves of the road between Hora and Kapsali. The typically Greek ouzo – anise-flavoured spirits – is served with the habitual appetizers which are very tasty here. The view is great. **Price:** €

✓ ARTENA

Tel. (0735) 34173
Flavourful Greek cooking and fish, on the beach. **Price:** €€

KALAMOS

✓ PHILIO

Tel. (0735) 31549
A first-rate family-managed taverna in a pretty, terraced garden with dry-stone retaining walls and concealed lighting in the trees. Home-cooked food, hors d'oeuvre and cockerel a speciality. **Price:** €

LIVADI

✓ TOXOTIS

Tel. (0735) 31780
Good restaurant, grills and "seftalia" the Cypriot "hamburger". Open summer and winter. **Price:** €

MITATA

MICHALIS

Tel. (0735) 33626
A kafeneio – the old fashioned cafe – with ready-cooked dishes, grills, and a view of the plain. **Price:** €

PALAIOPOLIS

✓✓ SKANDIA

Tel. (0735) 33700

Traditional restaurant under the poplars, with good food, an agreeable ambiance and, often, live music. **Price:** €€

AVLEMONAS

✓✓ SOTIRIS

Tel. (0735) 33722

A fish taverna of repute. Speciality: pasta with lobster. Also try the lobster either poached or stewed with tomato, fish dishes and lobster pilaf. The place is generally crowded. **Price:** €€

✓ KORALI

Tel. (0735) 34173
Fresh fish, caught by the owners themselves. Next door to Sotiris. **Price:** €€

DIAKOFTI

✓ MANOLIS

Tel. (0735) 33252
Freshly-caught fish, exceptional lobster and lobster pilaf. **Price:** €€

POTAMOS

✓✓ PANARETOS

Tel. (0735) 31206
The tables are out of doors, on the central square of Potamos, next to the National Bank. An old-style taverna with exceptional cooking. Try the fricassee of lamb with lettuce. Open summer and winter. **Price:** €

KARAVAS

✓✓ AMIRALI

Tel. (0735) 33513
Next to the springs, in a lovely setting amidst the plane trees. 50 different appetizers and sea food dishes. **Price:** € €

PLATIA AMMOS

✓ VARKOULA

Tel. (0735) 34224
A taverna on a large rock with a sea view to Mani. Tasty home cooking and live Greek music. In very hot weather one of the cooler spots in the evening. Reservations essential. **Price:** €

LOGOTHETIANIKA

✓ **I KARYDIES**

Tel. (0735) 33664
Excellent Greek cooking and a garden with walnut trees and live music. **Price:** €

✓ **KYRA-MARIA**

Tel. (0735) 33211
Taverna where the food is good and the fish is fresh, cooked by Kyra Maria herself. **Price:** €

BEST ENTERTAINMENT

Kythera does not offer much in the way of nightlife. Most bars and nightclubs are in Kapsali on the waterfront. When in Hora go to **Mercato** for coffee, breakfast and pancakes as well as for drinks with good music in the evening. In Kapsali, coffee and breakfast are good at **La Spiaggia**. The delightful traditional cafe **Alexandros** is at Potamos. **Grossa Ponta** in Kapsali is the place for those who want a change of pace from the peace and quiet of Kythera, or you could try the **Shaker**. On the main road to Potamos at the turn-off for Fratsia and the nightclub **Pritanio**. For Greek music the **Amoroso** is at Logothetianika.

TIPS AND INFORMATION

HOW TO GET THERE

- By air from Athens, west airport, by Olympic Airways (11,000 drs.), tel. (01) 9363363.
- By Dolphin Sea Lines hydrofoil from Zea, Piraeus, in 5 hrs (from 8,100 drs.), Piraeus agency, tel. (01) 4280001 and Athens agency, tel. (01) 3244600.
- By ferry from Piraeus in 7 hrs (from 4,150 drs.) Piraeus Port Authority, tel. (01) 4511310.
- By ferry from Neapolis to Elafonissos, weekdays only, in 10 min (600 drs.), Neapolis Port Authority, tel. (0734) 22228. Also by ferry from Pounda (8 km before Neapolis) to Elafonissos. Pounda Harbourmaster, tel. (0734) 61177.

CONNECTIONS

- By Dolphin Sea Lines hydrofoil from Kythera to Gerakas, Kyparissi, Leonidio, Monemvassia, Porto Heli and Spetses. In summer to Neapolis, Tiros and Hydra. Kythera agency, tel. (0735) 31390, 33748.
- By ferry from Kythera to Githion, Neapolis and Kastelli Kissamou in Crete.
- By small boat from Kapsali in Kythera to Neapolis and Gythion. Kythera Port Authority, tel. (0735) 31222, Neapolis Port Authority, tel. (0734) 22228 and Gythion Port Authority, tel. (0733) 22262.

BEST TIPS

HOW TO GET AROUND: Definitely in your own car. If you haven't got one you can hire a car or scooter to get around in the island. Don't be deceived by the distances in km marked on your map. Although they are not great – the island's central thoroughfare is only 27 km – the peculiarities of the terrain's configuration and the tortuous roads make for much longer drives than you calculate. For organized tours contact the travel agents Porfyra Travel, tel. (0735) 31888-9.

BEST SEASON: From Easter to September except August.

BEST LOCAL FOOD: Try the kid with tomato, lobster pilaf and the island's thyme honey, also the rusks (**ladopaximada**) from the bakery at Karvounades.

CHURCHES-MONASTERIES: The keys of the old churches are kept by the Archaeological Service. Phone if you want to visit them, tel. (0735) 31195.

USEFUL TELERHONE NUMBERS

KYTHERA	(0735)	Port Authority	33280-31222
Town Hall	31213	**ELAFONISSOS**	**(0734)**
Police	31206	Community	61238
Rural Clinic	31243	Rural Clinic	61294

SPETSES

°°Spetses °Porto Heli

WHY AMONG THE BEST

Because of its wonderful mansions built in the 18th c. when Spetses was in its prime, many of which have been beautifully restored. Because of the thick pinewoods that cover a good part of the island and the picturesque Paliolimani, the old harbour, filled nowadays with elegant yachts. Finally, because Spetses attracts Athenian high society.

13 ARGOSARONIC GULF AND KYTHERA

BEST's OPINION

Spetses is the island for a fun long-weekend away from the stress of city life. It is amply endowed with pleasant places to stay and have a meal, while its night life is renowned in Greek circles. Being so close to Athens, it has long been a favourite holiday spot for residents of the capital, many of whom have second homes there.

Spetses, as well as Costa and Porto Heli on the mainland across the way attracts lots of Greek VIPs. The area is an "in", spot among the rich and famous and their privileged children. But this doesn't mean ordinary mortals can't have a good time there, too. The back side of the island and the coast opposite have many good beaches and "private" coves, and there are restaurants, bars and nightclubs for every taste.

SPETSES 13

BEST SIGHTS: STEP BY STEP

❶ SPETSES
Σπέτσες / Spétses

Spetses has 3,500 inhabitants. More than half the island is covered with pinetrees that grow down to the water's edge. Even the areas that were burned in the fires of a decade or so ago are recovering. The town itself has landmark status and the use of cars is severely restricted on the island.

HISTORY

Ancient Pityoussa (pine-covered) was first inhabited in the Early Helladic era (2300 BC), as various scattered remains have shown. Relics of the Mycenaean, Classical, Roman and Byzantine periods have also been found, though the island was ravaged by the Saracens in the 9th c. During the Frankish occupation, Spetses was under Venetian rule and later passed to the Ottoman Turks.

In the 18th c., many of the islanders entered the wheat trade and their expertise in shipping soon evolved into a strong, powerful and important merchant fleet. In those days, Spetsiot ships ploughed the waves from the Mediterranean and Black seas to the Baltic and even the Americas.

Despite the relative autonomy they enjoyed under the Turks, the Spetsiots took part in the abortive Orloff uprising in the Peloponnese in the 1770s and suffered serious reprisals as a consequence. Those who had been exiled to Kythera fought on until they were granted amnesty and permitted to return.

Spetses is most famous for the role it played in the War of Independence, when together with Hydra and Psara, it supplied a major part of the Greek fleet. In recognition of its role, Capodistrias, the first governor of Greece, rewarded the island with two representatives in the fledgling parliament.

After the War of Independence, the centre of trade moved to Syros and later to Piraeus, and Spetses fell into a decline until the early 20th c., when it gradually became a favourite summer resort for Athenians, and by the 70s a very popular destination among tourists.

WHAT TO SEE

THE OLD HARBOUR (Palió Limáni)

This natural harbour was purely residential until a few decades ago. Now, along with the mansions lining the waterfront, there are many restaurants, tavernas, bars and nightclubs. In the inner harbour (Baltiza), traditional caiques are still made, looking somewhat incongruous amongst the scores of sailing and motor yachts seeking a mooring on summer weekends and throughout August.

The Old Harbour

BOUBOULINA LASKARINA'S HOME / MUSEUM

Tel. (0298) 72077

9:30 am-8:30 pm, on the last long weekend before Lent and from 25/3 to 8/10, 12-14 guided tours every 45 min.

This 300-year-old mansion belonged to Bouboulina, the legendary admiral/heroine of the War of Independence (1821). Today it has been converted into a non-profit-making museum containing her furniture and personal possessions. There are guided tours in English several times a day (see poster in Dapia and near the museum); they are an amusing and informative introduction to the island's most brilliant period.

Bouboulina Laskarina's home / museum

DAPIA

This is the island's hub, where the boats dock and everyone meets to plan their day. The word means fortified place and its high walls still have cannons protruding from them. It is literally lined with cafes, which are full from early morning to late at night, with visitors young and old.

Dapia

179

ARGOSARONIC GULF AND KYTHERA

Poseidonio Hotel

ALSO WORTH SEEING

- **The Spetses Museum,** the fortress-like mansion that belonged to Hatziyiannis Mexis, another Revolutionary hero, has two museums as of September 1998. The upper floor is devoted to exhibits from the War of Independence, folklore and a few ancient finds, while the ground floor houses Greece's first permanent exhibition devoted to underwater archaeology.
- **Agios Nikolaos,** a 17th c. church with its lovely, pebble-mosaic courtyard and serene interior is the most beautiful in Spetses. Legend has it that Napoleon's brother once lived secluded within this former monastery.
- **The church of Agia Triada** at the highest point in town.
- **The Anargyros mansion** at the back of Dapia, built at the turn of the century by the island's greatest benefactor.
- **The grand Poseidonion Hotel,** another of Sotirios Anargyros's contribution to the island. This was all the fashion before World War II and during the 60s.
- **The Anargyrios College,** the buildings and campus also endowed by Anargyros, where novelist John Fowles taught the sons of Greeks and wrote *The Magus* in his spare time.

FREE TIME

Circuit of the island
Large caiques make the "round the island" tour for about 1,500 drs., stopping for swims at various coves and at the large organized beach of Agii Anargyri Prophhitis Ilias. The best known caique captain is Big George.

A hike: From Dapia to Prophitis Ilias
Walk up to the ridge of the hill through the pinewoods, from Vrellos on the coast, skirting ravines until you reach the church of Prophitis Ilias. From there, you'll have a 360 degree view of the sea and the Peloponnese and you'll have it all to Prophitis Ilias.

The Armata
On the second Saturday in September, the locals re-enact the historic naval battle against the Turks of 1822. The spectacle is preceded by folk dancing and speeches and finished off with fireworks. The event attracts crowds and so many yachts are anchored offshore that it's as good as a boat show.

❷ PORTO HELI
Πόρτο Χέλι / Pórto Héli

A summer holiday spot built around a large protected bay that fills up with sailing yachts. The mild climate, fine beaches and easy access from Athens has led to the building of many (some spectacular) second homes in the area. There are many hotels, tavernas and bars to choose from.

BEST BEACHES

The island has relatively good beaches, but *Best* reserves its stars for the beaches sprinkled around the indented shores of the Porto Heli area, which are less frequented than those on Spetses. In many cases, trees line the water's edge, providing much-needed shade, and the water is invariably clean.

BEACHES ON SPETSES

☂ AGIA PARASKEVI
The island's best. Pebbles, sand and pines for shade. Though lacking umbrellas and facilities, it has a canteen and attracts both caique passengers and the Chriscraft set. The "Magus' house" still occupies the hill above the beach.

SPETSES

LIGONERI
A pretty little cove west of town, with pebbles, sand and pine trees.

AGII ANARGYRI
The most organized beach on Spetses, the biggest and the most popular. Many caiques come here and it is also served by the island's bus. Water sports are offered and there are two tavernas. Beyond the far end, is the ⛱ Bekiri cave, where Spetsiots hid from the Turks; get a mask and swim in.

XYLOKERIZA
No tavernas or umbrellas. A very pretty, unspoiled beach and not too crowded, either.

AGIA MARINA
Patronized by the young and the British. Not far from town, it has a bar and restaurant where music plays day and night. Reached by caique or a 1/2 hr walk.

BEACHES AROUND PORTO HELI

⛱⛱⛱ KORAKIA
This may seem a bit too far to go, but it's unquestionably the best beach in the area. A small promontory cuts the large stretch of sand in two and there is an islet offshore floating in turquoise waters. A splendid setting, few people and totally unspoilt.

⛱⛱ AGIOS EMILIANOS
A lacy coastline punctuated by numerous small coves. Little bays with sand and pebbles in lovely natural surroundings. Take your pick according to the weather, the number of people and your mood.

⛱⛱ KOSTOULA
A narrow but marvellous sandy beach with shallow water. Ideal for children. The turquoise reflections make it seem like a South Sea paradise. Bring your own umbrella and picnic.

BEST HOTELS AND ROOMS

BEST LOCATION
We recommend that you stay in or near the town, because the main way of getting around is on foot. We make an exception in the case of the **Lefka Palace** (the old **Xenia**), which has been recently renovated and combines a lovely setting and sea view with a pool and a decent little beach. A good choice for families with young children.

PRICES
The hotel prices mentioned below are the official ones set by the National Tourist Organization for double rooms, at low and high season, with breakfast. Since owners are allowed to modify the prices, always try to negotiate them.

✓✓✓ NISIA
(Luxury Class)

Tel. (0298) 75000, (01) 3462879, fax (0298) 75012
Open: All year round
Description: Just west of Dapia, around the corner from the Poseidonion. Indisputably the most attractive, luxurious and expensive hotel on the island, it's hard to believe that it was originally a 19th c. factory building.
Rooms: 20 rooms and 10 suites with TV, telephone, A/C, fireplace and kitchen.
Special features: Pool, sea view, gardens, exceptional restaurant, bar and special play-area for children.

Argosaronic Gulf and Kythera

Price: 33,000-54,000
Value for money: ✻✻
Credit cards: All

✓✓ ZOE'S CLUB (Luxury Class)

Tel. (0298) 74447-8, fax 74093
Open: May-October

Description: Neo-classical architecture, up a narrow lane 10 min from Dapia.
Rooms: 22 rooms, 4 suites, 3 luxurious maisonettes, with telephone, TV, A/C and kitchen.
Special features: Pool, bar and special play-area for kids.
Price: 28,000-35,000 drs.
Value for money: ✻✻
Credit cards: Visa

✓✓ SPETSES (A Class)

Tel. (0298) 72602-4, fax 72494
Open: April-October
Description: Everything you'd expect from a hotel of this category. Its capable owner has managed to maintain its initial high standards. West of Dapia on the coast at Kounoupitsa.
Rooms: 77 rooms.
Special features: Sea view and a pretty little beach. Telephone, TV, A/C, restaurant, snack bar and water sports.
Price: 30,600-41,500 drs.
Value for money: ✻
Credit cards: All except American Express and Diners

✓ LEFKA PALACE (A Class)

Tel. (0298) 72311, (01) 9225943, fax (0298) 72161
Open: All year round
Description: Recently renovated, surrounded by 25,000 sq m of pine woods. Located west of town beyond the College.
Rooms: 80 beautiful rooms, with telephone, TV, A/C and fridge.
Special features: Tennis courts, pool, beach and bar. Ideally set up for families.
Price: 33,000-49,000 drs.
Value for money: ✻
Credit cards: Visa

✓ VARLAMIS

Tel. (0298) 74983, fax 74825
Open: Easter-September

Description: Above the Old Harbour near Haralambos's former taverna. Quiet location, near the centre and reasonably priced, an excellent choice.
Rooms: 11 apartments (2-4 people), with kitchen, telephone and TV.
Special features: Pool and bar.
Price: 21,800-27,600 drs.
Value for money: ✻✻✻
Credit cards: Visa

VILLA CHRISTINA (B Class)

Tel. (0298) 72218
Open: May-October

Description: Two old mansions with simple, tastefully furnished rooms. At a quiet spot in the centre of town.
Rooms: 12 clean and comfortable rooms.
Special features: Pretty courtyard with bar, trees and flowers. View from the upper house which has studio apartments.
Price: 17,100-19,600 drs.
Value for money: ✻✻✻
Credit cards: None

ALTERNATIVES

VALLIA (C Class) Spetses, tel. (0298) 74059, fax 74064
Price: 13,000-18,000 drs. Without breakfast

PORTO HELI (A Class) Porto Heli,
Tel. (0754) 51490-4, fax 51549 Price: 41,000-64,000 drs.

SPETSES 13

BEST RESTAURANTS & TAVERNAS

IN TOWN

✓✓ NISIA
Tel. (0298) 75000
Attractive restaurant with superb cuisine in the hotel Nisia. **Price:** €€€

✓✓ PATRALIS
West of Dapia, near the Spetses Hotel, Tel. (0298) 72134
Perhaps the best place for fish on the island. Original dishes, impeccable service. **Price:** €€€

LAZAROS (GALERA)
At Kastelli (above Dapia), tel. (0298) 74144
Clean, good simple food and excellent barrel wine. Open only for dinner, tables out on the street. Specialities: hamburgers (Greek style), grilled meat and kid with lemon sauce. **Price:** €

OLD HARBOUR

✓ BYZANTINO
Tel. (0298) 72870

Good, moderately priced mezedes (appetizers). 200-year-old building with a lovely terrace overlooking the old harbour. Very popular. **Price:** €€

✓ EXEDRA (BETTER KNOWN AS SIORAS)
Tel. (0298) 73497

The "in" place in the Old Harbour, though it may not look it. Excellent Greek fare, fresh fish, as well as good grills and casseroles. Its chef cooks the best red mullet in miles around. **Price:** €€€

✓ LIOTRIVI
Tel. (0298) 72269

Bar-restaurant-pizzeria. Serving Italian dishes, in a converted olive press next to the sea. The old millstones lend atmosphere. **Price:** €€

✓ MOURAGIO
Tel. (0298) 73700

Next to the sea, with romantic lighting and quality cuisine. **Price:** €€

✓ TREHANDIRI
Tel. (0298) 72122
Where the elite meet. Luxury taverna serving fish, lobster and grills. Pretty courtyard/veranda with view. **Price:** €€€

OUTSIDE TOWN

PORTO HELI

The three best restaurants here are all at the northwest end of the port. **Papadias**, tel. (0754) 51322, has fresh fish and excellent service, **La Casa Vecchia**, tel. (0754) 52422 has a romantic atmosphere to go with its Italian menu, and **Rota**, tel. (0754) 51243 serves French cuisine. **Price:** All €€

BEST ENTERTAINMENT

Spetses comes alive at night and there's a multitude of places to make the most of it, whatever your age or pocketbook. In the Old Harbour, the **Figaro** bar/disco (by now an institution), housed in an old boat house (karnagio), still attracts crowds after midnight, **Brachera** specializes in music of the 60s and 70s, while **Papagayo**, another good old standby, plays Greek music. In Dapia, try the **Paradosiako Kafenedaki**, where those in the know hang out, and the **Spetsa bar** near Agios Mamas, the town beach. **Blueberry Hill**, a favourite of the younger set day and night, occupies a hill above the beach after the College and before you get to Ligoneri. At Agia Marina, **Paradise Beach** right on the sea serves charcoal-grilled meals and salads all day long. The beach is equipped with reclining chairs and umbrellas, the restaurant has palm trees and a lawn, and Greek and foreign music wafts through the breeze nonstop. Across the street is **Tzortzis**, 40 years young and still brightening up the night with live Greek music, made cooler by air conditioning.

TIPS AND INFORMATION

HOW TO GET THERE

- By Minoan Flying Dolphins (hydrofoil) from Piraeus (Zea and Akti Tzelepi in the main port) in 2 hrs, from 5,000 drs., Piraeus agent, tel. (01) 4280001.
- By ferry from Piraeus, daily in summer, less frequently in winter, in 5 hrs, from 2,500 drs., Piraeus Port Authority, tel. (01) 4226000-4.
- One reason Spetses is so popular with Athenians is because it's just a 3 hr drive away. Take the national road to the Corinth Canal and from there get on the road towards Epidaurus and follow the signs to Kranidi, Porto Heli and Kosta, where you can either pick up a sea taxi, ferry or caique to take you across. Even by slow boat, the distance is a matter of minutes.

CONNECTIONS

- By Minoan Flying Dolphins (Glyfada) all year, from Spetses to Poros, Hydra, Geraka, Porto Heli, Ermioni, Leonidio, Monemvassia, Kythera. And in summer, to Aegina, Methana, Elefsina, Isthmia, Nafplion, Neapolis, Tolo and Tyros, as well. Spetses agent, tel. (0298) 73141.
- By ferry from Spetses to Ermioni, Hydra, Poros, Methana and Aegina. Spetses Port Authority, tel. (0298) 72245.

BEST TIPS

HOW TO GET AROUND: Spetses has a few Mercedes taxis, two buses, a fleet of caiques, sea taxis (speedboats), bicycles and motorbikes for hire and even horse-drawn carriages, if you don't feel like walking. Caiques in Dapia do regular beach runs every day in season and the sea taxis are available round the clock. There are so many motorbikes buzzing around Spetses that in summer the local authorities try to limit the hours they are allowed on the coast road and inside the town limits. Check the rules with the rental agency; a small motorbike should cost 3,000 drs. per day. But most key spots are well within walking distance. The taxi rates start from 1,000 drs. A trip around the island will cost you about 10,000 drs., but 1,500 drs. will get you to Agia Marina. The oldest (and very reliable) taxi driver in Spetses is Elias, tel. (094) 605784. For 300 drs. you can board the caique bound for the beach at Kosta, 10,000 drs. per hour may get you one for your exclusive use. One bus leaves for Ligoneri from in front of the Poseidonion Hotel, the other goes to Agii Anargyri on the back side of the island from Agios Mamas. Bicycles can be rented for 2,000 drs. a day, and finally, the sea taxis, which can carry up to 8 passengers, have a price list posted in their cabins for all destinations round the island and across the way.

BEST SEASON: From March to November. In August, Spetses is packed, be warned.

BEST LOCAL FOOD: Fish a la Spetsiota (baked in the oven with tomatoes and onions) is renowned all over Greece, and so are the almond paste sweets called **amygdalota**, which are sold in Dapia.

USEFUL TELEPHONE NUMBERS

SPETSES .... (0298)	Clinic 72472
Town Hall 72225	Port Authority 72245
Police 73100	Sea Taxis 72072

HYDRA

WHY AMONG THE BEST

Because of the unique architecture of its stone mansions and the barren, rocky landscape. Because there is a ban on motorized vehicles and there is only donkey traffic in the lanes. Because of its respect for tradition, apparent everywhere – in the hotels, restaurants, the mode of entertainment, even when strolling in the town – giving each aspect of your visit a special quality.

ARGOSARONIC GULF AND KYTHERA

HYDRA

BEST's OPINION

Hydra's rugged and romantic beauty has made it a favourite with artists for many years now. Because it is a cosmopolitan, but also a very discreet island, it's a favourite with many international jet-setters.
A major advantage is its easy access and short distance from Athens, and the possibility of visiting the neighbouring islands in the space of a couple of days. Its greatest drawback is that there are no good beaches. The standard of tourism is high and for that reason, Hydra may not be suitable for low-cost holidays. However, if you avoid the summer season, you'll enjoy your trip more and spend less money.

IN BRIEF

Hydra is located 35 n mi. from Piraeus and has approximately 2,800 inhabitants, most of whom work in the tourist trade. Apart from the marvellous architecture, the island has about 365 churches, a great variety of plants, innumerable cats (the local council feeds 200) and a yacht club, offering swimming, water polo, sailing and canoeing.
In summer, Hydra is flooded with its regular Athenian visitors, as well as tourists who arrive on cruise ships and yachts.

HISTORY

Hydra's first inhabitants called it **Hydrea**, because of the island's abundant springs. In 1500 AD, inhabitants of the Peloponnese settled in Hydra, in order to avoid the Turks, who, however, seized the island in 1715. Hydra had already begun to develop into a merchant marine power and gained the good will of the Turks, who granted them autonomous status. During the Napoleonic Wars, the Hydriots' ships monopolized food supplies in the Mediterranean area and broke through

HYDRA

the British blockade of French ports. Grain smuggling brought enormous wealth to the island and unprecedented development. Most of the mansions and a great number of large ships were built at that time. A Merchant Marine Training School was established, while Greece's finest teachers taught at the island's schools. In those days, Hydra had a population of 35,000 and approximately 200 ships, armed with cannon. Following Greece's liberation and the advent of steamships, Hydra's maritime supremacy fell into decline and the majority of Hydra's inhabitants were forced to emigrate.

Tsamados mansion

BEST SIGHTS: STEP BY STEP
❶ HYDRA TOWN
´Υδρα / ´Idra

The town of Hydra is built in the shape of an amphitheatre on the rocky slopes of the steep hills enclosing its harbour. The stone mansions dominate the town, with their austere, imposing architecture. The narrow, winding, quiet streets frequently lead to steps ascending between the elegant homes with their yards and small gardens.

MANSIONS

Many of the mansions are inhabited and some are open to the public. You can find their location on the town-plans available. The ⊚⊚ **Tsamados mansion** on the east side of the harbour houses the oldest Merchant Marine Training School in the world, still in operation today. The ⊚⊚ **Tombazis mansion** accommodates students from the Athens School of Fine Arts in summer. The ⊚⊚ **mansion of Pavlos Koundouriotis** (Greece's first president) functions as a museum, with exhibits from the 1821 Greek War of Independence. Also worth seeing are the 19th c. ⊚ **Rafalias**

Tombazis mansion

Pharmacy, and among others, the stately homes of **Boudouris**, **Georgios Koundouriotis** (Greece's first prime minister), **Lazaros Koundouriotis**, **Georgios Voulgaris**, **Admiral Miaoulis**, and the **Town Hall**.

MONASTERIES AND CHURCHES

The **convent of Agia Efpraxia** is an hour's walk outside the town, in a beautiful setting. The **monastery of Prophitis Ilias**, built in the 19th c., offers a marvellous view from the hill and is reached on foot or by donkey. There is also the **Zourva monastery** as well as **Agia Triada** (1704), a monastery with only a few monks close to Prophitis Ilias. Women are not permitted to enter this monastery. Worth seeing too are the **church and Monastery of Kimissis tis Theotokou** (1770), with a splendid marble icon screen, bell-tower and clock. It is situated at the harbour entrance and houses municipal offices. **Agios Ioannis** is the island's oldest church, with wonderful 18th c. frescoes, while high up on the hill is the **Hydra cathedral**.

FREE TIME

Festivals and local events: On June 21 the **Miaoulia**. From June 7-13, the **International Puppet Festival**. On August 15 the **Assumption of the Virgin Mary**.
Donkey-ride in the lanes: Just the thing for an amusing morning.
Gardenia: A summer open-air cinema with a different box-office hit every day, to spend a quiet evening.

BEYOND THIS EXCURSION

A trip by hydrofoil to the nearby islands Poros and Spetses or to Porto Heli. You can also go further afield to the medieval town of Monemvassia, or the island of Kythera.

ARGOSARONIC GULF AND KYTHERA

BEST BEACHES

Hydra is not particularly good for swimming. Except for Mandraki, there is no other sandy beach, and the few beaches are crowded and noisy. The best solution is to dive from the rocks wherever you like along the road to Vlyhos or to go by caique to the Peloponnese coast opposite. Peaceful and pretty rocks can be found on the islets close to the port. At the rear end of the island, the sea is crystal clear and there are also a few seals.

VRAHAKIA

Located on the western edge of town, under the cannons. If you manage to pick your way through the bodies of sunbathers, you'll dive into clear, deep water from rocks that have been levelled with concrete for sun bathing. Afterwards, you can enjoy coffee at **Spilia**.

MANDRAKI

A sandy beach, but nothing special, with facilities and sea sports. There is also a small village and the **Miramare Hotel** restaurant.

KASTELLO

Go by hired boat or regular caique to Kaminia and then on foot. You'll find yourself on a beach with lots of pebbles and even more children. However, it'll do.

VLYHOS

Beautiful setting, with a picturesque village and a beach offering facilities. There are also three tavernas to choose from.

LIMNIONIZA

Hydra's prettiest beach, on the rear side of the island. Peaceful, with shady trees. You can go by foot, if you're up to a hike, after visiting the **monastery of Agia Triada** (women not permitted to enter), or make a day-trip with a caique from the port (3,000 drs., without food).

AGIOS NIKOLAOS

Tranquil bay with clear water, on the south side of Hydra. You can go there on a day excursion, with the caique that sails around the island.

BEST HOTELS AND ROOMS

BEST LOCATION

All the major sights are in the town of Hydra. Your feet will be your main – and probably the only – form of transport, unless you prefer a donkey. A hotel near the harbour would be the most convenient, but if you don't mind going up and down steps, then we recommend some pensions that offer a magnificent view.

PRICES

The hotel prices mentioned below are the official ones, set by the National Tourist Organization for double rooms, at low and high season, with breakfast. Since owners are allowed to modify prices, always try to negotiate them.

HYDRA TOWN

✓✓ BRATSERA (A Class)
Tel. (0298) 53971, fax 53626
Open: March-October

Description: Built in 1860, it is a former sponge factory, with smart, tasteful Hydriot decor. The island's best hotel.
Rooms: 23 fully-equipped rooms, traditional furnishings, built-in beds or iron bedsteads with a canopy, telephone, A/C and TV.
Special features: Swimming pool, outstanding restaurant and bar.
Price: 27,000-41,000 drs.
Value for money: ✱✱
Credit cards: Visa, American Express, Diners, Mastercard

✓✓ ORLOFF (A Class)
Tel. (0298) 52564, 52495, (01) 5226152, fax 53532
Open: March-October

Description: Stately 1789 mansion, with a warm atmosphere. An excellent choice, in an ideal location of the town.
Rooms: 9 rooms with telephone, TV, A/C and refrigerator (only in large rooms).
Special features: Courtyard, restaurant and reception in beautifully designed public areas.
Price: 30,000-35,000 drs.
Value for money: ✱
Credit cards: All

✓ MIRANDA (A Class)
Tel. (0298) 52230, fax 53510
Open: March-October
Description: Tasteful and aesthetic, this former captain's mansion was built in 1810 and is a typical example of Hydriot architecture. However, it has been a little neglected in the past few years.
Rooms: 14 rooms, with ceilings painted by Venetian and Florentine artists.
Special features: Art gallery and breakfast in the attractive garden.
Price: 19,000-30,000 drs.
Value for money: ✱
Credit cards: Visa

✓ BOUAGIA PENSION (B Class)
Tel. (0298) 52869, fax 54083
Open: February-October (the rest of the year by arrangement)

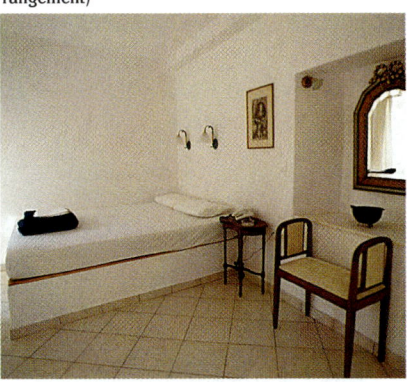

Description: A small and pleasant guest house with hospitable owners, 600 m from the port.
Rooms: 5 very good rooms with A/C, telephone, TV and a stunning view from the veranda.
Price: 22,000-24,000 drs.
Value for money: ✱
Credit cards: Visa

✓ HOTEL MISTRAL (B Class)
Tel. (0298) 52509, 52184, fax 53412
Open: April-October
Description: Stone mansion, at the port.
Rooms: 19 rooms, half of them with TV.
Special features: Modern facilities, good service and breakfast in the picturesque paved courtyard.
Price: 22,800-36,380 drs.
Value for money: ✱
Credit cards: Visa

✓ IPPOKAMBOS (C Class)
Tel. (0298) 53453, 52184, fax 53454
Open: April-October

Description: The island's first bank was once housed here.
Rooms: 16 simple rooms with A/C, telephone, TV and refrigerator. Numbers 21-24 are best, as they have a veranda with a view.
Special features: Courtyard.
Price: 19,000-25,000 drs.
Value for money: ✹✹
Credit cards: Visa

ALKYONIDES (A Class)
Tel. & fax (0298) 54055, 59983
Open: All year round

Description: New, well-designed building, in a quiet corner just a few metres from the port. Plain and clean.

Rooms: 10 rooms, of which only one has television. In winter, there is central heating.
Price: 15,000-17,000 drs., without breakfast
Value for money: ✹✹✹
Credit cards: None

MANDRAKI
✓ MIRAMARE HOTEL (B Class)
Tel. (0298) 52300, fax 42301
Open: April-October
Description: Quiet hotel, away from the bustle of Hydra town. Small rooms, built of stone, in bungalow style, next to the sea.

Rooms: 28 rooms with A/C and telephone.
Special features: Tennis court, restaurant and beach with facilities, including water sports.
Price: 24,000 drs.
Value for money: ✹
Credit cards: Visa

ALTERNATIVES
GRECO (B Class)
Tel. (0298) 53200, fax 53511 **Price:** 17,500-19,500 drs.

HYDRA (C Class)
Tel. (0298) 52102, fax 53085 **Price:** 16,000-18,000 drs.

HYDRIZA (B Class)
Tel. (0298) 52349. **Price:** 18,000-25,000 drs.

BEST RESTAURANTS & TAVERNAS

✓✓ BRATSERA
Tel. (0298) 53971
In an elegant setting, round the swimming pool of the exemplary hotel of the same name. An expensive restaurant, ideal for discerning customers.
Price: €€€

✓ GEITONIKO (CHRISTINA)
Tel. (0298) 53615
Located in town, it is better known as **Christina** to the island's Athenian residents. It's very popular,

Bratsera

HYDRA

so booking is necessary. If you're patient with the service, you'll be rewarded with a plain, but delicious meal. Pleasant, tasteful environment, with a veranda.
Price: €

✓ ZIDORON
Tel. (0298) 54115

Features traditional Greek appetizers. A place with real personality, it offers only a few tables, a small courtyard, soft music and tasty snacks.
Price: €

✓ PYROFANI
Tel. (0298) 53175

At Kaminia, but accessible, with new tastes and sweets. The owner, an architect from Athens, pays a lot of attention to the cooking and the service.
Price: €

✓ XERI ELIA
Tel. (0298) 52886

In Hydra town. Traditional taverna with tables in the square. Simple, but good food.
Price: €

STROFILIA
Tel. (0298) 54100

Neo-classical building, with ceiling-fans and marble tables. Inexpensive, with excellent dishes.
Price: €

SUNSET
Tel. (0298) 52067

Large, touristy, but in a perfect location, with a view of the cannons. Fish, good Greek cuisine and a stunning sunset.
Price: €€

BARBA-DIMAS
Tel. (0298) 52967

One of the top choices for those familiar with Hydra. Tasty appetizers and a wonderful view.
Price: €

KONDYLENIA
Tel. (0298) 53520

At Kaminia. The great view and delicious fresh fish make it ideal for lunch.
Price: €

TRIA ADELFIA
Tel. (0298) 53253

In town. A plain, traditional taverna, in a pretty yard with trees.
Price: €

KRYFO LIMANI
Tel. (0298) 52585

Small, accessible taverna in town, with a little courtyard and good food. Located next to the Barba Dimas taverna.
Price: €

CAPRICE
Tel. (0298) 52454

Small taverna with Greek-Italian dishes and wonderful music.
Price: €

Xeri Elia

ARGOSARONIC GULF AND KYTHERA

BEST ENTERTAINMENT

Hydronetta

A quiet island by day, Hydra is transformed at night. It offers entertainment for all tastes, ages and moods. In the "hangouts", nightlife continues well into the early morning hours. The **Piratis** is the island's trademark, with a long tradition of nightlife on Hydra. However, the most attractive and "in" bar is the **Amalour**, with lively music, and spaghetti or sandwiches for those who want a snack with their drinks. If you want to swim next to the rocks, visit the **Spilia**, a cafe-bar with music, open all day. The **Hydronetta** is ideal for watching the sunset and for swimming near the rocks, with discreet music and a pleasant atmosphere all day. In addition, try the **Saronikos** near the port, with Greek music; the **Lagoudera**, a historic spot on the rocks, next to the sea, on the western point of the harbour; the **Cavos**, a disco-bar, with Greek and foreign music; the **Heaven**, on the hill, with a view, featuring Greek and foreign music; the traditional **Nautilos**, for Greek-style entertainment, and the **Issalos**, for beer, coffee and snacks.

TIPS AND INFORMATION

HOW TO GET THERE

- By hydrofoil, Minoan Flying Dolphins, from Piraeus (Zea and Akti Tzelepi) in 1 hr 30 min (from 3,650 drs.), Piraeus Agency, tel. (01) 4280001. Athens Agency, tel. (01) 3244600.
- By ferry from Piraeus in 3 hrs 30 min, (from 2,000 drs.), Piraeus Port Authority, tel. (01) 4226000-4.
- By car, along the National Athens-Corinth Highway, to Ermioni. From there, to Hydra by hydrofoil in 20 min, or sea taxi, tel. (0298) 53690.
- One-day cruise excursions with the M/V Giorgis, tel. (01) 9249720. Departures from Trocadero.

CONNECTIONS

- By Minoan Flying Dolphins hydrofoil from Hydra to Poros, Spetses, Ermioni, Porto Heli. In summer to Aegina, Methana, Elefsina, Geraka, Isthmia, Kyparissi, Leonidio, Monemvassia, Neapoli, Nafplio, Tolo, Tyro, Kythera. Hydra Agency, tel. (0298) 54053.
- By ferry from Hydra to Aegina, Methana, Poros, Spetses, Ermioni. Hydra Port Authority, tel. (0298) 52279.

BEST TIPS

HOW TO GET AROUND: As you can't drive a vehicle in Hydra, you can use a sea taxi for long distances, tel. (0298) 53690, or one of the caiques waiting in the port. Fares (up to 8 passengers): 1,500 drs. to Kaminia, 2,200 drs. to Mandraki, 2,200 drs. to Vlyhos, 3,000 drs. to nearby islets, 4,500 drs. to Molos, 6,000 to Kondomina-Vlaheika, 8,500 drs. to Bisti. For one-day excursions, ask for details at a tourist office. You can take a one-day trip to Agios Nikolaos and Limnioniza, on the other side of Hydra. Don't forget to take food with you.

BEST SEASON: Spring or September. In summer the island is crowded, with all the pleasant and unpleasant consequences this entails.

BEST BUYS: The island's well-developed tourist infrastructure and the islanders' long experience with high-income visitors means quality is a priority in restaurants, cafes, and shops. Try the Pavlos family's Hydriot yoghurt and the famous Tsangaris almond sweets.

USEFUL TELEPHONE NUMBERS

HYDRA	(0298)	Tourist Police	52205
Town Hall	52210	Hospital	53150

The Cyclades

CYCLADES

BEST's OPINION

If you haven't visited the islands and your time is limited, *BEST* suggests that you restrict yourself to the Cyclades. The possibilities for easy island-hopping, the marvellous beaches, the choice of popular, sophisticated, and quiet islands, the stark white architecture and the Cycladic light, along with the extraordinary archaeological sites at Delos and Santorini are sure to appeal to even the most demanding tourist.

IN BRIEF

The ancient Greeks named them the Cyclades because they seemed to form an imaginary circle round the sacred island of Delos. The circle begins with Kea (Tzia) and ends with Andros, passing through Amorgos, Anafi, Sikinos, Folegandros, Ios, Santorini, Milos, Kimolos, Sifnos, Serifos, Kythnos, Syros, Tinos, Mykonos, Paros, Antiparos, Naxos and the smaller Cyclades – the Koufonissia, Schinoussa, Iraklia and Donoussa. The islands belong today to the Cyclades prefecture, whose capital and administrative centre is Ermoupoli on Syros.

The islands have a dry Mediterranean climate with little rain and only a small amount of cultivable soil. Figs, prickly pears, vines and, in some places, olives do well here.

The inhabitants used to be seamen and fishermen, with a few tending flocks or farming, but the rapid growth of tourism has created numerous new positions in hotels, shops, restaurants and recreation.

The architecture of the Cyclades is generally typically Aegean. Each island has its **Hora** or capital with narrow, flagstone-paved lanes, white houses, tiny churches and some small Venetian castle, while the hills are dominated by abandoned windmills.

These islands will appeal to every kind of tourist, whether they be lazy or restless, lovers or loners.

HISTORY

According to myth, the Cyclades were nymphs until Poseidon in a rage transformed them into islands. The astonishing, exquisitely simple marble figurines found on some of them pointed to the existence of the important Cycladic civilization (2500 BC). The islands developed trade and cultural exchanges with the Minoan empire and later with the Mycenaeans.

The establishment of Delos as a sacred island contributed to the prosperity of all the Cyclades (7th-4th c. BC), but that began to dwindle with successive conquests by the Macedonians, the Ptolemies of Egypt and the Seleucids, the Rhodians and finally the Romans. Later, like the rest of Greece, the Cyclades were not spared attacks by invading Goths, Slavs and Avars. Eventually they passed into the hands of the Byzantines and when Constantinople fell to the Franks, the Venetian Marco Sanudo assumed power over most of the islands, incorporating them into the Duchy of Naxos. While under Venetian rule, many of the islanders converted to Catholicism, particularly in Syros and Tinos. In the 16th c. they became part of the Ottoman empire, except for a short span – 1770-1774 – when they were under Russian protection.

In the course of the Greek War of Independence, some islands participated actively in the struggle, while others did not because, owing to the existence of the Catholic community, they found themselves under French protection. The Treaty of London (1830) united the islands with the new Greek state.

CYCLADES

THE CYCLADES ISLANDS

BEST has described six of these islands in detail: ⊚⊚⊚ **Mykonos** and ⊚⊚⊚ **Delos** *(Excursion 23)*, ⊚⊚⊚ **Santorini** *(Excursion 24)*, ⊚⊚ **Paros** *(Excursion 26)*, ⊚⊚ **Sifnos** *(Excursion 27)* and ⊚⊚ **Folegandros** *(Excursion 25)*, but you should not think that the other wonderful islands have much less to offer.

⊚⊚ SYROS / Σύρος / Síros

The island has about 16,700 inhabitants and its capital ⊚⊚ **Ermoupoli** is the business and administrative headquarters of the Cyclades. An elegant town spread over two hills, it reminds one of a European town of the last century. Each hill has a different character: the lower one with its neo-classical mansions and public buildings, its spacious squares and the gracious ⊚⊚ **Vaporia district** where the Orthodox reside, while the Catholics are concentrated in the walled medieval city, ⊚ **Ano Syros**. At ⊚ **Finika** and **Dellagratsia** (Poseidonia) there are a few stately homes left over from the mid 19th c., when Syros was Greece's busiest port.

While there are plenty of sandy beaches, the best ones are found on the west coast between Cape Grammata and Finika and Megas Gialos. Caiques leave from Kini and Ermoupoli for the lovely deserted beaches to the north-west. Ermoupoli has a casino if you're feeling lucky.

Ermoupoli

⊚ ANDROS / Άνδρος / Ándros

The greenest of the Cyclades, Andros has some 10,000 inhabitants and is known for its **mineral springs** at Sariza, which produce enough water for export, and its world-class shipowners. It has an attractive, non-touristy **Hora** with several **neo-classical buildings** and a vestigial Venetian castle, villages with magnificent villas, some distinguished churches, a few ancient stones at Paliopolis, Zagora and elsewhere, and some outstanding museums, the ⊚ **Archaeological** and the ⊚ **Museum of Modern Art**, both donated by the Goulandris family, and the **Naval Museum**.

Visit the 10th c. **Panachrandos Monastery** and the villages of **Menites**, **Katakilo**, **Arni** and **Lamyra**. The most accessible beaches are along the coast between **Gavrio**, the main port, and **Batsi**; those on the east coast are apt to be windswept.

Batsi

⊚ TINOS / Τήνος / Tínos

The holy island of Orthodoxy, where every August on Assumption Day thousands gather to make the pilgrimage to the ⊚⊚ **Evangelistria church**. Tinos is full of superb examples of vernacular architecture and has produced a great number of notable **sculptors, marble carvers** and **painters**. Among the island's most characteristic features are the ubiquitous ⊚ **dovecotes** which surround its charming unspoilt villages, such as ⊚⊚ **Panormos**, with its many marble craftsmen. The **monastery of Kechrovouni**, one of the largest in Greece, a masterpiece of Cycladic architecture.

Tinos is not known for its beaches. But although none are spectacular you will have no trouble finding a pleasant spot for a swim, especially on the southwest coast from Stavros to Agios Ioannis and around the areas of Panormos and Kolymbithres to the north-east.

Evangelistria church

195

CYCLADES

🌀 KEA (TZIA) / Κέα (Τζια) / Kéa (Tzia)

Kea, a mountainous island with a few fertile valleys and picturesque coves, has only 1,700 permanent residents. It is a quiet island, a good place for family holidays. The pretty 🌀 **Hora**, also called Ioulis, the port (Skala), and cosmopolitan **Vourkari** and **Koundouros** attract the most visitors, predominantly Athenians. **Spathi** is one of the island's better beaches, while the **coves** south of Koundouros and north of Poesses are also good. But in order to get to the best ones, one needs one's own boat or a caique from Skala.

Ioulis

🌀 KYTHNOS / Κύθνος / Kýthnos

A waterless island with bare mountains and few green patches, it is best known for its two exceptional **mineral springs**. It has 1,500 inhabitants, the interesting 🌀 **Dryopis cave** (Katafyki) and several good beaches at its many coves, mainly near **Kanala** and **Meriha**.

Kythnos

🌀 SERIFOS / Σέριφος / Sérifos

A lovely island with 1,400 inhabitants. The dazzling white 🌀 **Hora** perched on the ridge of a hill above the port is its main attraction, while there are exquisite white chapels scattered about the ruins of its Venetian castle. The rocky coast is punctuated with small bays, the trees sprouting from its ravines streak the bare slopes with green ribs. Other sights include the **Taxiarches monastery** near the village of Galani, the 10th c. Byzantine **church of the Panagia** and the **Cyclops cave** at Koutala.

Serifos has no really spectacular beaches, but the coves round the island, mainly in the east, from Livadi to Agios Ioannis, or north-west at Sykamia, are more than just pleasant.

Hora of Serifos

🌀🌀 MILOS / Μήλος / Mílos

Although quarrying has blighted the landscape to some degree, you should not be put off visiting this large and, in many ways, stunning island. With 5,500 inhabitants, it has a lovely Hora called 🌀 **Plaka**, many things to see and exceptional ☼☼☼ **beaches** that compare favourably with those of Mykonos.

The famous 🌀🌀 **catacombs** are located in the vicinity of Klima, while the celebrated **statue of Venus**, pinched by the French and now adorning the Louvre, was discovered near the remains of the some 2,000 tombs. There is an exact copy in the island's **Archaeological Museum**. On the road to the **Venetian castle**, on Profitis Ilias hill, there is a ruined **ancient theatre**.

The **best beaches** on the island are at ☼☼☼ **Agios Giannis** and the coves just to the north of it, but they are hard to reach. More interesting are ☼☼ **Kleftiko** with its surrealistically shaped rocks, a **watery "Meteora"**, and the ☼☼ **grotto of Papafranga** near Fylakopi.

Kleftiko

CYCLADES

🌀 KIMOLOS / Κίμωλος / Kímolos

A quiet, mountainous island with a picturesque 🌀 **Castle-Hora**. With 800 inhabitants, delightful churches, clean beaches, it's a fine place for a peaceful holiday. Among the sights are the **Vromolimni** and **Konssolina** 🌀 **caves**, the ruins of the ancient fortified settlement at **Palaiokastro** and the traces of a **sunken ancient city** near the pointed rocks of Asprogremna. The best beaches lie on the south coast, from Ellinika to Alyki.

Hora of Kimolos

🌀 NAXOS / Νάξος / Náxos

The isle of Dionyssos and Ariadne is the largest of the Cyclades, with high mountains, fertile valleys and charming villages. Naxos has **15,000** inhabitants, a long ancient, Byzantine and medieval history, and the strongest musical tradition of these islands.

Among its many landmarks are the imposing **Portara**, the entrance to a long-vanished temple of Apollo, and its well preserved 🌀 **medieval castle** in the upper Hora, where you'll find the **Archaeological Museum**. Particularly beautiful are the mountain villages in the interior, **Kato**, **Mesi** and 🌀 **Pano Potamia**, while 🌀🌀 **Apiranthos** is one of the most attractive and biggest villages in the Cyclades. The best beaches, ♀♀ **Plaka** for example, are situated a bit south of Agia Anna, while the deserted shores on the north of the island are worth attempting only on a windless day.

Portara

🌀 AMORGOS / Αμοργός / Amorgós

Rectangular in shape, Amorgos is a steep, dry island with **1,700** inhabitants. Its exciting landscape combined with its conspicuous lack of development make it a favourite with hikers and self-reliant types who don't need discos to be happy. Many of its visitors are young and casual, content with its laid-back pace.
The 🌀 **Hora** with its fortress, tiny Byzantine churches, windmills and view over the Aegean rank among the most beautiful in the Cyclades. The 🌀🌀 **approach** to the stunning white 🌀 **Hozoviotissa monastery**, tucked into the wall of a sheer cliff 300 m high, has no equal.
The beaches of Amorgos are not memorable; the best are concentrated in the coves on the south-west tip of the island, opposite the islet of Petalidi.

Hozoviotissa monastery

🌀 IOS / ΄Ιος / ΄Ios

Ios (inh. **1,450**) has plenty of facilities for its crowds. It became a legend in the 70s, a hippy's paradise with lots of bars, beach bars, nudist beaches and an exotic nightlife. The 🌀 **Hora** is picturesque with its 14th c. castle, cubist houses and small churches. Local tradition maintains that one of the **graves** found in the archaeological site in the vicinity of Plakotos was none other than **Homer's**. On an island renowned for its beaches, the best are 🌀 **Mylopota**, the string of sandy coves at ♀♀ **Manganari bay** and in the north-east (♀ **Tris Klissies**, ♀ **Louka**, **Kalamos**) and ♀♀ **Psathi**, with its engaging taverna on the hill above.

Manganari bay

CYCLADES

ⓖ SIKINOS / Σίκινος / Síkinos

A small, serene island with only 300 inhabitants, unspoilt Sikinos appeals to those in search of peace and quiet.

Its lovely ⓖ **Hora** has a **church** dedicated to the **Pantanassa** and stately stone houses, many of which are abandoned. Take a look at the deserted fortified **Chryssopigi monastery** and the island's **three caves, Mavri Spilia, Drakondospilies** and **Drakofrydo**.

There are a few beaches on the south coast, none of them particularly good.

ⓖ ANAFI / Ανάφη / Anáfi

An isolated island far from the world of organized tourism. It has 290 inhabitants and an extremely beautiful ⓖ **Hora** with tiny Byzantine churches, several windmills, a castle and houses with vaulted roofs. The only way to get around Anafi is on foot, since the single road is the one between the port and the Hora.

Sikinos

Among the things you should look for are the ⓖ **Panagia tis Kalamiotissas Monastery** on Prassia bay, the ⓖ **Drakondospilia Cave** (near the monastery), ⓖ **Vagia**, the only place on the island where there is greenery and running water, the sunken ancient town at **Katalimatsa** and the remains of the **temple of Apollo** at Kastelli.

The best beaches are sandy and are all in the south part of the island.

Anafi

ⓖⓖ THE SMALL EASTERN CYCLADES
Μικρές Ανατολικές Κυκλάδες / Mikrés Anatolikés Kykládes

This is a cluster of both inhabited and deserted islets between Naxos and Amorgos. Their unspoilt landscapes and exceptional 99 **beaches**, mainly on Pano and Kato Koufonissi and Donoussa, make them ideal holiday spots for nature worshippers.

ⓖ **Iraklia** (95 inh.) is a small fertile island with lovely beaches and translucent water. It has two caves, the more interesting being the ⓖ **cave of Polyphemus the Cyclop (Ai Giannis)**, which is among the largest in the Aegean. Its spectacular chambers measuring 2,000 sq. m in area contain stalagmites and stalactites of amazing beauty, as well as a little lake. Also with a few permanent residents are ⓖⓖ **Donoussa** (120 inh.), ⓖ **Pano Koufonissi** (230 inh.), a former pirate haven, ⓖ **Kato Koufonissi** (5 inh.) and ⓖ **Schinoussa**. All enjoy very good beaches. Amongst the uninhabited islands, Keros is the best known as having been one of the main centres of the prehistoric Cycladic civilization; the others are Antikeros, Dryma, the 3 Makaries and Daskalio. The main islands have regular ferry connections with Naxos, Amorgos and Piraeus.

Donoussa

Pano Koufonissi

MYKONOS
DELOS

WHY AMONG THE BEST

Because Mykonos is a world class destination. Because here you'll find the international jet set mingling with the rest of us and not being given special treatment, whether seeking an umbrella on the beach or a table in the trendiest restaurant. Because Mykonos combines its gorgeous beaches with dazzling Cycladic architecture and an endless variety of places to stay and things to do.

15 CYCLADES

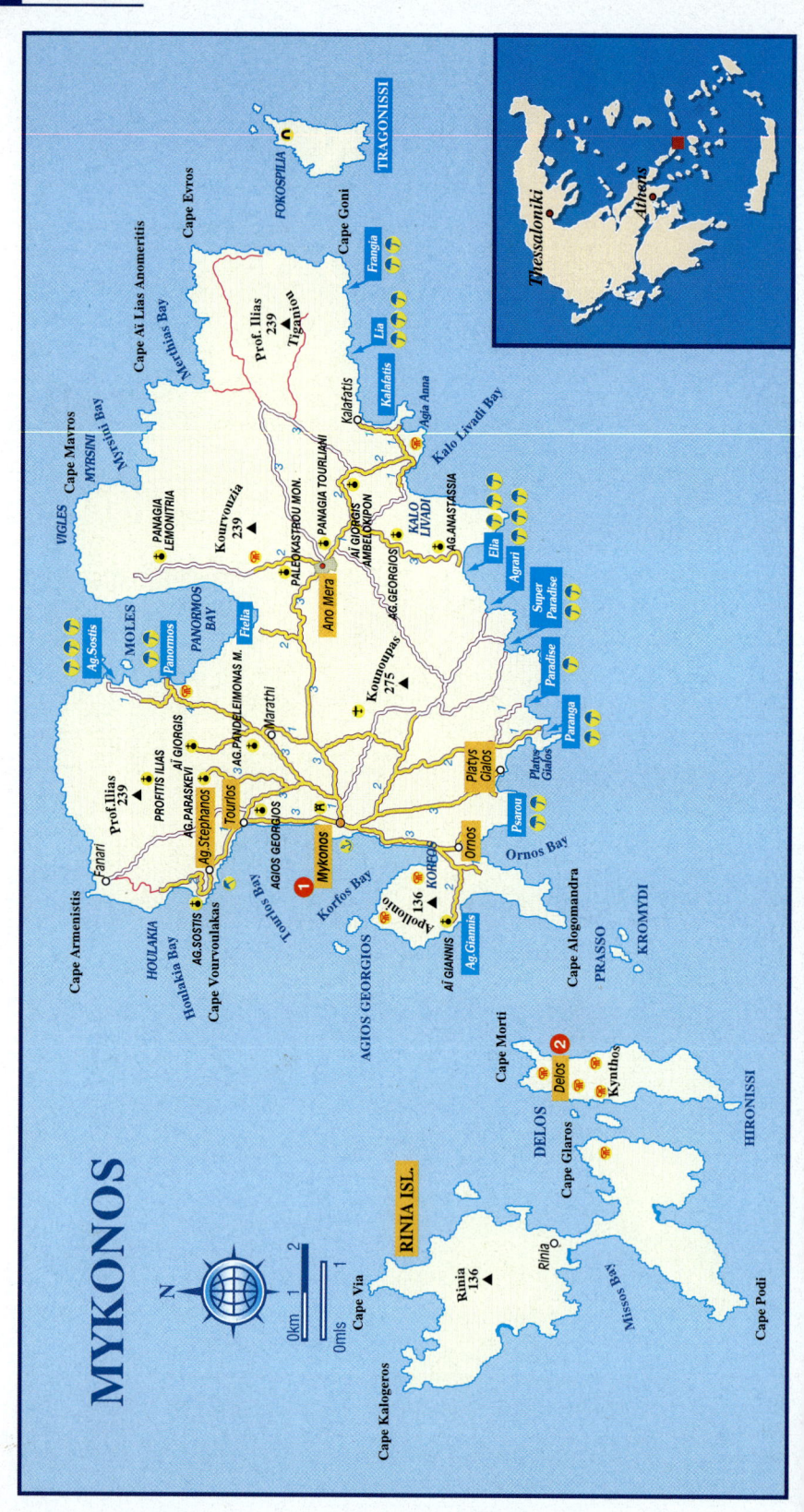

MYKONOS

MYKONOS - DELOS

BEST's OPINION

Young or old, you have to go to Mykonos at least once in your life. Only if you can't bear crowds or the idea that the island has been transformed into one big entertainment centre would you be justified in not going. But visiting the Greek islands without seeing Mykonos is like travelling to the United States and bypassing New York.

BEST SIGHTS: STEP BY STEP

❶ MYKONOS
Μύκονος / Mýkonos

Mykonos, one of the north-eastern Cyclades, lies in the centre of the Aegean and is home to 5,500 permanent inhabitants. Its climate is typically Mediterranean, with mild, fairly dry winters and blustery north winds in summer that make the heat more bearable. An island of low hills, it is stony and arid with very little vegetation.

For centuries Mykonos lived under the shadow of its neighbour, Delos, which in antiquity was the most sacred island in the Greek world. In our own day, it is a major archaeological site. In the past, travellers used Mykonos as a base for visiting Delos, until they were eventually bewitched by its own charms and natural beauty. It gradually began to be known abroad and the rapid growth of tourism soon made it an international summer resort. Now, the tables are turned and Delos is in the shadow of Mykonos.

Today the island is exceptionally well equipped with facilities for tourists and offers an enormous range of entertainment possibilities. Most of its beaches are among the most beautiful in Greece. And among its habitues are some of the planet's most famous personalities, not a few of whom have built lovely vacation homes. From the architectural point of view, only the ☺☺☺ **Hora** (main town/port) is of particular interest. Nevertheless, ☺ **Ano Mera**, the island's sole village apart from Hora, and the new, small summer settlements built on protected coves, are worth a look. These include **Ornos** and **Ai-Giannis**, with its restaurants, hotels and bars, **Agios Stephanos**, **Tourlos** and **Platys Gialos**.

HISTORY

The island took its name from a legendary hero called Mykonos. Like most of the Aegean islands, it was a member of the 1st and 2nd Athenian Confederacy. In 166 BC the Romans conquered the Cyclades, after which Mykonos enjoyed a certain prosperity, which came to an abrupt end with the destruction of the sanctuary on Delos by Mithridates (88 BC). After the fall of Constantinople to the Franks, the Venetians governed the island (1207-1537) until it was devastated by the notorious Turkish admiral, Khaireddin Barbarossa. During the Ottoman occupation, the islanders were engaged in shipping and trade and dabbled in piracy on the side. Led by the heroine Manto Mavrogenous, they sent their experienced crews to fight in the war of Independence. After the liberation of Greece, in the early 19th c., the Mykonians rebuilt their merchant fleet and slowly began to grow wealthy. The replacement of sails by steam nipped their economy in the bud and many islanders were forced to emigrate in order to survive. Mykonos was one of the first Greek islands to attract tourism in the mid 50s and has held its popularity ever since among sophisticates.

WHAT TO SEE

☺☺☺ HORA / MYKONOS TOWN
Χώρα Μυκόνου / Hóra Mykónou

This is a gem of a town, a prime example of Cycladic architecture. Even the noted architect-town planner Le Corbusier admired its harmony and the artistry of the self-taught master builders who constructed it over time. Today a listed settlement, it consists of narrow, whitewashed alleyways, tiny churches, white houses with brightly painted woodwork and marvellous windmills. The pelican you'll see eating fish in the port is one of a series named Petros; he's the island's mascot.

Petros the pelican

15 CYCLADES

Matogianni

The main street, 👁️👁️ **Matogianni** with its chic shops, cafes and bars, is where the island's pulse throbs. Apart from the attractive things you'll see as you stroll around the 👁️👁️👁️ **Hora's winding lanes**, you'll also have the chance to shop or window-shop in the fabulous, but pricey, boutiques, which carry all the most exclusive name brands. Among them are the outstanding Greek jewellers. By day the pace in the Hora is slow and calm. But once the sun sets, the picturesque alleys fill to bursting with the people who come to Mykonos just to check out its celebrated nightlife.

👁️👁️ LITTLE VENICE - ALEFKANDRA

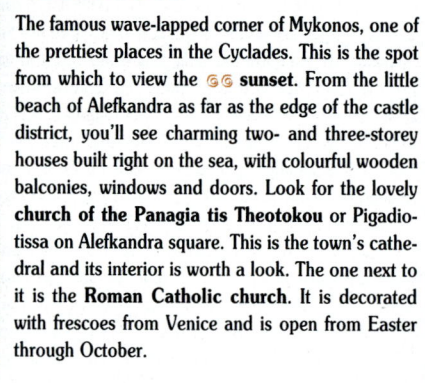

The famous wave-lapped corner of Mykonos, one of the prettiest places in the Cyclades. This is the spot from which to view the 👁️👁️ **sunset**. From the little beach of Alefkandra as far as the edge of the castle district, you'll see charming two- and three-storey houses built right on the sea, with colourful wooden balconies, windows and doors. Look for the lovely **church of the Panagia tis Theotokou** or Pigadiotissa on Alefkandra square. This is the town's cathedral and its interior is worth a look. The one next to it is the **Roman Catholic church**. It is decorated with frescoes from Venice and is open from Easter through October.

👁️👁️ PANAGIA PARAPORTIANI

This church got its name from the fact that it stands at the small entrance (paraporti) to the medieval fortress. Though building started in **1425**, it was not completed until the 17th c. Consisting of five small churches, four on the ground level and one raised, it is a superb example of local vernacular architecture.

Panagia Paraportiani

ALSO WORTH SEEING

● **Archaeological Museum**
Tel. (0289) 22325
🕐 *8 am-2 pm, closed on Mondays and holidays**

Housed in a neo-classical building of 1901, south of the harbour, it contains exhibits of pre-Classical and Classical pottery, figurines from various periods, Hellenistic and Roman sculpture and inscriptions. Many of the finds come from the necropolis of Rinia, the island next to Delos. Look for the **clay jar** with scenes from the Trojan War (7th c. BC).

● **Folk Art Museum**
Tel. (0289) 22591
🕐 *April-October, 8 am-2 pm*

An interesting museum which opened in 1962 in the former home of a sea captain. It contains collections of local weaving, knits, embroideries, pottery, traditional costumes, maritime instruments and old furniture. Among the exhibits you'll see the first Petros the pelican, stuffed. He was the island's mascot for three decades. Also part of the museum are the restored 16th c. windmill, the threshing floor and the dovecote, all in the vicinity.

MYKONOS - DELOS

• Naval Museum
Tel. (0289) 22700

April-October, 10:30 am-1 pm, 6:30-9 pm

Opened in 1985, this museum is housed in a traditional Cycladic building of the 19th c. Here you'll see models of ships from the early Minoan period to the 19th c., maritime instruments, maps and documents, ancient coins with naval motifs of the 5th c. BC, as well as marble copies of grave steles from Delos and Mykonos, among other things.

• The windmills
Near the castle erected in the 13th c. by the Venetian ruler of Mykonos, Andrea Ghizi.

• The Town Hall
A neo-classical building constructed in 1785 to house the Russian consulate, and **Ta Tria Pigadia** (the Three Wells), which were, until 1956, the town's only source of water.

OUTSIDE MYKONOS TOWN

ANO MERA

A small inland village with tavernas on its pretty *plateia* where you can eat meat grilled over charcoal or fresh fried **loukoumades** (doughnut relatives) and honey in one of the sweet-shops.
Near the square you'll see the **monastery of Panagia tis Tourlianis**, which was founded in the 16th c. but took its final form in 1767. It has an attractive bell-tower and interesting relief scenes on its carved wooden icon-screen. The monastery's modest museum contains relics, ecclesiastical treasures and Byzantine icons.

❷ DELOS
Δήλος / Délos

How to get there: Daily departures 8-10 am by boat from Mykonos harbour. Return, 12-2 pm.

A small, rectangular, waterless and uninhabited island with low hills, 2.5 mi SW of Mykonos. Delos is one of the most important archaeological sites in Greece, full of ruined houses, temples, statues and mosaics.
The island developed a notable civilization during the Mycenaean period (1580-1200 BC) and from 700 BC it was the centre of the worship of Apollo, the god imported by colonists from the Ionian shores of Asia Minor in about 1000 BC. Here, according to myth, Leto finally came to rest and gave birth to Apollo, while his sister Artemis was born on the nearby island of **Rinia**. The divine offspring had been fathered by Zeus and, ever vindictive, his jealous wife Hera had pursued Leto relentlessly all over the Aegean. Every five years great festivals, the **Delia**, were held in honour of Apollo on his sacred island. They included musical competitions. The Athenians made the island the centre of the Athenian Confederacy (478 BC). From 250 BC until 166 BC Delos was under Roman rule. During that time it grew into a prosperous trading port. In 88 BC it was destroyed by the Pontic King Mithridates, who was at war with the Romans. After that, one disaster followed another, mostly in the form of pirates and antiquity smugglers.

CYCLADES

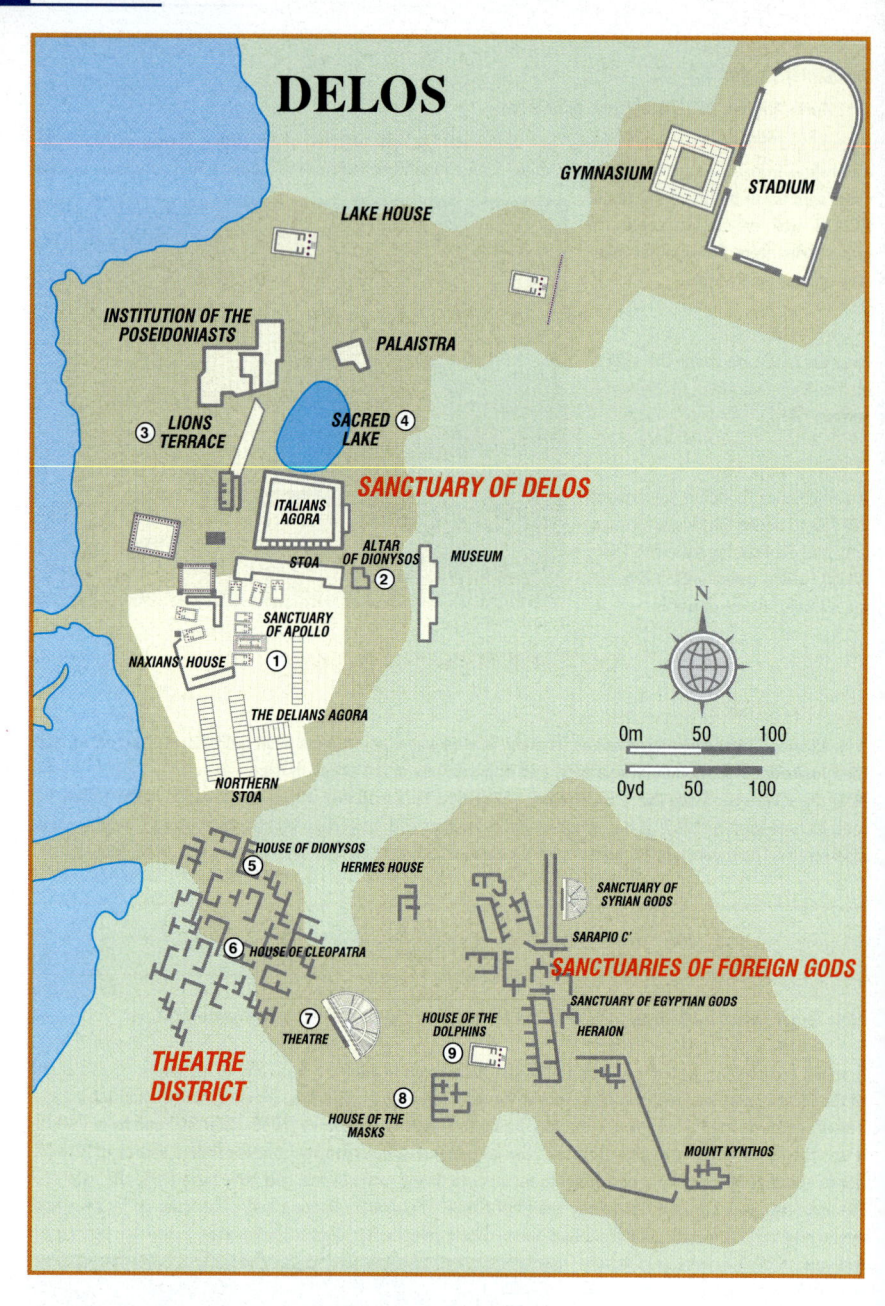

DELOS

🌀🌀🌀 THE ARCHAEOLOGICAL SITE

Tel. (0289) 22259

🕗 8 am-3 pm, closed on Mondays and holidays*

The whole island is one vast archaeological site of inestimable significance. Explore it with a guide or follow **BEST's** route describing the most important ruins. For your convenience, we have divided the site into three large areas: the **Sanctuary of Delos/Sacred Lake**, the **Theatre District**, and the **Sanctuaries of the Foreign Gods**.

MYKONOS · DELOS 15

THE SANCTUARY OF DELOS / SACRED LAKE

The most important ruins in this district are:

① ⓖ **The temples of Apollo**: There were three temples dedicated to Apollo: the temple of the Delians, the temple of the Athenians and the older limestone temple.

② ⓖ **The Altar of Dionysos**: Remains of a huge phallic monument (300 BC).

③ ⓖⓖ **The Lion Terrace**: The famous lions of Delos, a gift of the Naxians (7th c. BC). Once there were nine, now there are five.

④ ⓖ **The Sacred Lake**: The place where Apollo was born. Today the lake is waterless. This quarter also contains the agora of the Italians, the temple of Leto, the small Dodekatheon, dedicated to the Twelve Gods, etc.

Lion Terrace

THE THEATER DISTRICT (ANCIENT TOWN)

⑤ ⓖⓖ **House of Dionysos**: Here you'll see the mosaic floor depicting the god Dionysos riding a winged tiger.

⑥ ⓖ **Cleopatra's House**: A 2nd c. BC building, which took its name from two headless statues of Cleopatra and the Dioscuri that were found in it.

⑦ ⓖ **The Theatre**: Built in the 2nd-3rd c. BC, it could seat 3,000-5,000 spectators. Also see the enormous ⓖ cistern next to it.

Theatre

⑧ ⓖⓖ **House of the Masks**: A 2nd c. BC dwelling supposed to have been an actors' residence. The mosaics, apart from the one portraying Dionysos riding a panther, show various satyrical and comic masks.

⑨ ⓖⓖ **House of the Dolphins**: A house with the marvellous mosaic with the dolphins, a work of Asklepiades from Syria.

SANCTUARIES OF THE FOREIGN GODS

This is where the **sanctuaries of the foreign gods** – Sarapis and Isis, the **Syrian deities** – and the little theatre were located. From the back of the theatre, a path leads in 45 min to the sacred mount Kynthos where the ruins of the temples of Zeus Kynthios and Athena Kynthia are and from which there is a fabulous ⓖ view.

House of the Masks

ⓖⓖ ARCHAEOLOGICAL MUSEUM

Tel. (0289) 22259

☼ 8 am-2 pm, closed on Mondays and holidays*

Containing interesting exhibits found on the island. Take a look at the statue of Artemis with the Hind, the statue of Apollo, and the pottery and kouroi of the 7th c. BC. The original statues of the lions will also be on view here soon.

House of the Dolphins

205

CYCLADES

OTHER THINGS TO DO

- **Watermania** (**near Elia beach**) A private recreation park for adults with kids. It covers 60,000 sq m and includes water slides, pools, restaurants, a mini-club for children, a diving school, etc. Open: April-October, tel. (0289) 71685.

- **Go Carts** There is a go-cart track on the road between Hora and Ano Mera. It's a mecca for the young.

Watermania

BEST BEACHES

The beaches of Mykonos rank among the best in the Aegean, in Greece, and perhaps in the world. July and August are surely the worst time to visit them, but in June and September, you'll find the weather better and the crowds reduced. Some may even be deserted. Most of the best beaches are on the south coast, sheltered from the prevailing northerly winds, the "meltemia". You can get to these beaches, including Paranga, Paradise, Super Paradise, Agrari and Elia, by caique from Platys Gialos for 1,000 drs. per person round trip.

LIA

Exceptional beach with turquoise water, umbrellas and relatively few people, mostly those in the know. For a good meal, you can choose between ✓ **La Luna**, tel. (0289) 72150, with an ethnic atmosphere, and the excellent fish taverna, ✓✓ **Lia**, tel. (0289) 71015, for fresh fish and live lobster.

AGRARI

Perhaps the most picturesque beach in Mykonos, Agrari has coarse sand and organized facilities for water sports and sunbathing. It is also one of the least crowded, since it's not on the bus route. A favourite with celebrities. You can lunch at the simple, inexpensive taverna (self-service) on the sea or have a coffee or a drink at the beach bar.

ELIA

The island's most beautiful, this beach offers water sports, umbrellas, and **two good tavernas**. Unfortunately, chaotic building and too many people have somewhat spoiled the surroundings.

AGIOS SOSTIS

An exquisite, large sandy beach, one of the few on Mykonos that is not organized. It's a paradise for

MYKONOS - DELOS

nudists and boat owners. Hoping you're lucky enough to find a table, don't miss a meal at ✓✓ **Vassili's taverna**, among the most charming on the island. Grilled chicken and pork chops are among its specialities.

SUPER PARADISE

One of the most famous beaches in the Aegean. This very pretty beach is preferred by the gays and the younger set. If you like swimming and swinging at the same time, music blasting from the bars and you're not put off by crowds, then this is the place for you. You can have a coffee, a drink or a snack at **Coco's Club**, on a rise at one end of the beach, or start living it up from 6 in the afternoon at the bar at the other end.

PSAROU

A nice, organized beach, fairly protected from the wind, but very, very crowded. This is a big favourite among Athenians and their families. You can eat at the ✓✓ **Psarou taverna**, tel. (0289) 24871, one of the in hang-outs at midday, which is one reason why it's so expensive.

PARANGA

Lounge chairs and umbrellas in the sand. A lot of foreigners come here. There are two tavernas, but if you want to eat well, we recommend the **taverna** on the adjoining beach of Agia Anna.

PANORMOS

A rather beautiful sandy beach with no umbrellas or water sports. But with **Andoni's** taverna.

FRANGIA

One of the island's best and most deserted, with coarse sand. You can only get here by boat or rented caique.

PANORMOS

It's not a bad beach, but because of the camping site, it does get crowded. Old timers avoid it.

KALAFATIS

One of the most organized on Mykonos, it has water sports, a scuba diving school and a beach bar. Popular with the younger set. It's worth coming just to eat lobster and fish at the very attractive ☑ **Spilia**, tel. (0289) 71205, in the shelter of a rock and with a few tables on the sea.

FTELIA

The wind-surfers' favourite. We don't recommend it for swimming, but it's ideal if you like the challenge of strong winds. **Chrysantho's taverna** is a fine choice for spaghetti with scampi.

AI-YIANNIS

It's worth coming here, mainly because you can combine a swim at a decent beach with a meal at **Christo's** taverna. He serves fresh fish and grilled octopus in a delightful setting with hand-made furniture. Christos himself is also a sculptor.

OTHER BEACHES IN THE VICINITY

RHENIA (MEGALI DELOS)

Rhenia is one hour away by excursion caique from Mykonos. It has **wonderful beaches** and is a great place if you've got your own boat.

TRAGONISSI

A deserted island, 1 mile east of Mykonos, it has sea caves where monk seals hide.

CYCLADES

BEST HOTELS AND ROOMS

BEST LOCATION

If you're going to Mykonos for the nightlife and entertainment, then you should stay in the Hora and avoid having to walk back to your hotel in the wee hours. If, however, you've a quieter holiday by the sea in mind, then pick one of the hotels we recommend below.

PRICES

The hotel prices mentioned below are the official ones set by the National Tourist Organization for double rooms, at low and high season, with breakfast. Since owners are allowed to modify the prices, always try to negotiate them.

MYKONOS TOWN / HORA

✓✓ BELVEDERE (A Class)
Tel. (0289) 25122, fax 25126
Open: April-October

Description: One of the best hotels, with a marvellous view, if you want to stay in Hora.
Rooms: 40 rooms and 6 suites, with bath, hair dryer, telephone, A/C, TV, music, mini bar and balcony with view. Internet access and fax connections offered.
Special features: Underground parking, a good restaurant ✓ **Remvi**, car and motorbike rentals, room service, dining room, snack bar, room safes, money changing, baby sitters, laundry and ironing services, pool, gym with jacuzzi, steam bath, etc.
Price: 36,500-100,000 drs.
Value for money: ✱
Credit cards: Visa, American Express, Diners, Mastercard

✓✓ SEMELI (A Class)
Tel. (0289) 27466, fax 27467
Open: All year round
Description: Built in 1996 in traditional style, completely in tune with the island scale. The helpful and hospitable staff will please even the most demanding.
Rooms: 41 rooms and 3 suites, with bath, A/C, TV, mini bar, hair dryer, telephone, sitting-room and balcony.
Special features: Parking, bar, room safe, pool, pool bar, child care, laundry service, breakfast room, jacuzzi.
Price: 44,000-66,000 drs.
Value for money: ✱✱
Credit cards: All

✓✓ CAVO TAGOO (A Class)
North of town
Tel. (0289) 23692, fax 24923
Open: April-October
Description: Built in traditional style across the Tourlos rock, very close to the harbour. Deep blue and white predominate, along with local stone.
Rooms: 67 rooms and 5 suites-maisonettes, with

MYKONOS · DELOS

bath, telephone, A/C, TV, mini bar and sea view.
Special features: Restaurant, room service, pool with bar, car and motorbike rentals, etc.
Price: 53,000-78,000 drs.
Value for money: ✱
Credit cards: Visa, American Express, Diners, Mastercard

✓ ROHARI (B Class)
Tel. (0289) 24391, fax 24307
Open: April-October
Description: One of Mykonos' better hotels, it fits in with the local architecture and has a panoramic view over the town and the Aegean. For years it has been a favourite among Athenians.
Rooms: 60 rooms, with bath, telephone, fridge and TV.
Special features: Parking, pool with bar, breakfast room, snack bar, conference hall, etc.
Price: 15,000-31,000 drs.
Value for money: ✱✱✱
Credit cards: Visa, American Express

OUTSIDE TOWN

✓✓✓ MYKONOS BLUE
(Luxury Class)
Psarou, Platys Gialos
Tel. (0289) 27900, fax 27783
Open: April-October
Description: Above beautiful Psarou beach. A new luxury hotel complex belonging to the Grecotel chain, in traditional style. One of the island's best, with a cosmopolitan atmosphere, impeccable service and a sea view.

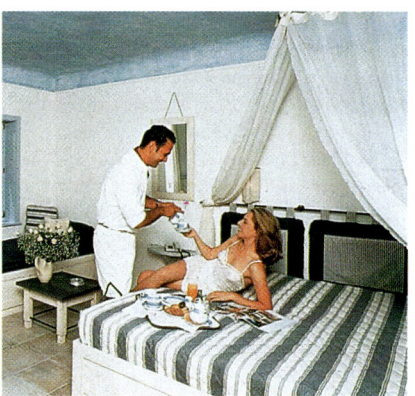

Rooms: 102 very attractive bungalows, with A/C, TV, telephone, radio, mini bar and hair dryer.
Special features: Two exceptional restaurants, the **Piitis tou Aigaiou** and **L'Archipel**, bar, pool with bar, room safes, conference hall, children's pool, gym, sauna, ping pong, water sports, etc.
Price: 121,300 drs.
Value for money: ✱✱
Credit cards: Eurocard, Visa, American Express, Diners

✓✓✓ SANTA MARINA (A Class)
Ornos, Ai-Yiannis
Tel. (0289) 23220, fax 23412
Open: April-October
Description: A luxurious hotel complex, one of the most sophisticated in Mykonos, the choice of celebrities who come with their yachts. Built amphitheatrically on 20,000 sq. m of hillside overlooking Or-

nos Bay. It consists of the main building, bungalows and private villas in tasteful Cycladic style. We have heard, however, that the service is a trifle slow.
Rooms: 60 spacious rooms, 30 suites and luxury villas with private pool. With A/C, TV, telephone, radio, hair dryer, mini bar and safe.
Special features: Private marina, pool with bar and restaurant, conference hall, gym, sauna, beauty salon, mini market, shops, tennis courts, ping pong, water sports, parking, etc.
Price: 75,000-115,000 drs.
Value for money: ✽✽
Credit cards: Visa, American Express, Diners, Mastercard

✓✓ PRINCESS OF MYKONOS (A Class)

Agios Stephanos
Tel. (0289) 23806, fax 26690
Open: April-October
Description: A small hotel in traditional style with modern furnishings and a view of the sea.
Rooms: 38 rooms with A/C, telephone, TV, radio, mini bar, and hair dryer.
Special features: Restaurant, bar, snack bar, room safe, pool with bar, sauna, etc.
Price: 25,000-61,000 drs.
Value for money: ✽✽
Credit cards: Visa, Diners, Mastercard

✓✓ KIVOTOS (A Class)

Ornos
Tel. (0289) 24094, fax 22844
Open: May-October
Description: Cycladic architecture, a synthesis of white and stone. On Ornos Bay overlooking the sea. Member of the Small Luxury Hotels Association.
Rooms: 26 rooms and 4 suites, with elegant old furniture, A/C, TV, telephone, radio, mini bar, hair dryer and safe.
Special features: Restaurant, bar, gym, pool with bar, sauna, mini market, ping pong, etc. Guests can take trips on board the hotel's private boat.
Price: 59,000-108,000 drs.
Value for money: ✽✽
Credit cards: Visa, American Express, Diners, Mastercard

✓ APOLLONIA BAY (A Class)

Ai-Yiannis
Tel. (0289) 27890-5
Open: April-October
Description: Opposite the port, next to Ai-Yiannis beach with a view of Delos. Austere Cycladic architecture, built of stone. 
Rooms: 29 rooms with telephone, A/C, TV, music, mini bar and room service.
Special features: Parking, buffet breakfast, bar, snack bar, pool, laundry service, safe, etc.
Price: 32,000-59,000 drs.
Value for money: ✽✽✽
Credit cards: All

✓ PETASOS BEACH (A Class)

Platys Gialos
Tel. (0289) 23437, 24204, fax 24101
Open: April-October

Description: Traditional architecture, with modern amenities. Near the coast at Platys Gialos with a sea view.
Rooms: 82 rooms with A/C, satellite TV, telephone, radio, mini bar and hair dryer.
Special features: Restaurant, bar, snack bar, safes, conference hall, pool with bar, gym, sauna. etc.
Price: 29,800-53,500 drs.
Value for money: ✹✹
Credit cards: Visa, American Express

✓ KOUROS (A Class)
Tagoo
Tel. (0289) 25381, fax 25378
Open: April-October
Description: Built on a small hill with a view of the sea. A fine hotel that successfully marries the rock of the landscape, stone construction and the colour white.
Rooms: 25 rooms with telephone, A/C, TV, radio, mini bar and hair dryer.
Special features: Bar, snack bar, safes, pool with bar.
Price: 33,000-59,000 drs.
Value for money: ✹
Credit cards: All

MYKONOS BAY (B Class)
Vryssi area
Tel. (0289) 23338, fax 24524
Open: April-October
Description: On the road to Ornos, blue and white decor. On the so-so beach of Megali Ammos; patronized by the young.
Rooms: 31 rooms with telephone, A/C, TV, radio and fridge.
Special features: Bar, snack bar, safes, pool with bar, etc.
Price: 20,000-36,000 drs.
Value for money: ✹✹✹
Credit cards: Visa, Mastercard, American Express

HOTEL SUNRISE
Agrari
Tel. (0289) 72201, 72013, fax 72203
Open: May-October
Description: Built in 1998 right on the superb Agrari beach, with sea view. A good, moderately priced hotel.
Rooms: 33 rooms with bath, TV, fridge and A/C.
Special features: Pool, free transport to Hora in the evening.
Price: 27,000-44,000 drs.
Value for money: ✹✹✹
Credit cards: Visa

ALTERNATIVES

SAN MARCO (A Class) *Houlakia, tel. (0289) 27172, fax 25376.* **Price:** 33,000-59,000 drs.

ANDROMEDA (A Class) *Hora, tel. (0289) 24712.* **Price:** 25,000-35,000 drs. Without breakfast

GOLDEN STAR (A Class) *Hora, tel. (0289) 23883.* **Price:** 32,000-59,000 drs.

MYKONIAN INN (D Class) *Hora, tel. (0289) 22663, 23420.* **Price:** 17,000-36,000 drs.

DESPOTIKO (B Class) *Despotika, Hora, tel. (0289) 22009, 24600.* **Price:** 29,000-41,000 drs.

ILIO MARIS (B Class) *Despotika, Hora, tel. (0289) 23755, fax 24309.* **Price:** 30,000-55,000 drs.

PETASOS (B Class) *Hora, tel. (0289) 22608, 22739, fax 24101.* **Price:** 18,900-39,600 drs.

POSEIDON (B Class) *Hora, tel. (0289) 22437, 24441-2, fax 23812.* **Price:** 27,000-44,000 drs.

MANOULA'S BEACH (C Class) *Ai-Yiannis, tel. (0289) 22900, fax 24314.* **Price:** 18,600-43,600 drs.

ELENA (D Class) *Hora, tel. (0289) 23457, 24134.* **Price:** 19,200-32,300 drs.

NAZOS (D Class) *Hora, tel. (0289) 22626, 22904.* **Price:** 16,000-30,000 drs.

TERRA MARIA (D Class) *Hora, tel. (0289) 24212-3, fax 24604.* **Price:** 20,000-29,000 drs.

If you don't find a room in one of the hotels we've recommended, then perhaps one of the following travel agencies can help you:
Mykonos Accommodation Center, Tria Pigadia, Hora, tel. (0289) 23408, 23160, fax 24137
Blue Moon, Mykonos Harbour, tel. (0289) 26730-2, fax 23276

BEST RESTAURANTS & TAVERNAS

Mykonos has a lot of very good restaurants, and a good many visitors for whom gastronomy is a top priority. So, don't forget to make your reservations. Most restaurants in town are closed for lunch since people would rather eat in the beach tavernas (see *Best Beaches*) and in Ano Mera. Try not to get impatient with restaurant service; the waiters are polite but they can't always cope with the heavy demand.

HORA / MYKONOS TOWN

✓✓✓ KATRIN'S
Tel. (0289) 22169

One of the most famous and oldest restaurants on the island and one of the best in Greece. Classic French and Greek cuisine, excellent service. Evenings only.
Price: €€€

✓✓ PHILIPPI
Tel. (0289) 23470

Historic, sophisticated spot with good food and a lovely garden. The Greek music often produces the right atmosphere for dancing. Get a table near the bar if you want to be part of the action. Evenings only.
Price: €€€

✓✓ CAPRICE
Tel. (0289) 26083

In Little Venice, sharing the space with the bar of the same name. Tables on the water's edge and good traditional dishes. Evenings only.
Price: €€

✓✓ CHEZ MARIA
Tel. (0289) 27565

International and Greek cuisine with local specialities in a lovely garden. Fast, good service.
Price: €€

✓✓ YVES KLEIN BLUE
Tel. (0289) 27391

Good Italian cuisine, artistic decor, a few tables inside and outside and wonderful service. Be sure to reserve ahead. And don't miss the risotto. Evenings only.
Price: €€€

✓✓ SALE PEPE
Tel. (0289) 24207

Italian restaurant. Small, but superb cooking. The service is apt to be slow, so just relax.
Price: €€

✓✓ MAMACAS
Ag. Anna, Tel. (0289) 26120

Set in a pretty white patio with palm trees near the main square, Mamacas offers the good greek cuisine it has in it's Athens restaurant under the same name.
Price: €€

✓ SESAME KITCHEN
Tel. (0289) 24710

In a narrow lane near the Naval Museum. A few tables indoors and out, but rather original dishes based on vegetables and rice. Try the fantastic onion pie. Evenings only.
Price: €€

✓ REMVI

Tel. (0289) 25122
One of the island's newest restaurants, in the Belvedere Hotel.
Good food and a pleasant setting.
Price: €€€

✓ APALLOOSA

Tel. (0289) 27086

Mexican style and menu with latin music. Unfortunately, there are only a few tables on the small veranda overlooking the street, so be sure to reserve well ahead, or else you'll be sitting indoors. Evenings only.
Price: €€

✓ TAVERNA O NIKOS

Tel. (0289) 24320
Famous for its excellent Greek cooking. Usually there are lots of people waiting for a chance to taste Nikos's wonderful casserole dishes. This is perhaps the best taverna in Hora and definitely the best value for money.
Price: €

OUTSIDE TOWN

ANO MERA

A pleasant place at both midday and the evening is the square in Ano Mera, where there are several nice tavernas serving grills and ready-cooked food. One good, inexpensive choice would be ✓ **Apostolis' taverna**, tel. (0289) 71760, which has decent service and delicious little meatballs (keftedakia).

MATHIOS

Tourlos
Tel. (0289) 23344, 24984
Taverna with good Greek food.
Price: €

🍸 BEST ENTERTAINMENT

Start your day with a fine cup of coffee and a fantastic breakfast at the **Angyra** or the **Astra** on Matogianni Street.
Around 6 pm, after your swim, move on to **Super Paradise** and join the liveliest party on the island. Then take yourself into town, to Little Venice, for a look at one of the most gorgeous sunsets in Greece at the **Caprice bar**, which has the best fruit juices around and the coolest music. Also in Little Venice, there's the **Kastro Bar** with lots of atmosphere, a wonderful view and classical music, and the **Veranda**.
After dinner, head back to Matogianni Street. Everybody else will be doing the same. Have a first drink at **Uno**, which is slowly beginning to replace the famous Vengera which closed down, and then go on to **Aroma** for coffee and a sandwich. You could continue at **Anemous**, which plays Greek and foreign music, or at **Angyra** across the way. In any case, the clientele at both places make the street impassable. The same happens a few metres further on at **Pierro's**, one of the town's best known gay bars.
Astra is one of the most "in" places on the island and celebrities seem to flock there. If you like rock music, then **Argo** is for you. You could continue your evening at the **Remezzo-Mercedes Club**, at the far end of the harbour, where the latest foreign hits are played and the view is wonderful. But if you'd rather have

Caprice

15 Cyclades

Greek music, then you mustn't miss **La Notte**, with live music, on the port.
But if you want to escape the madding crowds and you like music from the 60s and 70s, then you'll appreciate the **7 Sins**, off Manto Mavrogenous square. While for those who'd prefer to wind up the evening with some rave music and stay out till dawn, **Cavo Paradiso** on Paradise Beach is one of the best known after-hours clubs.

🛈 TIPS AND INFORMATION

HOW TO GET THERE

- By air from Athens west airport with Olympic Airways (19,100 drs.), tel. (01) 936 3363. In summer from Thessaloniki ("Macedonia" airport) with Olympic Airways, tel. (031) 228 880 and with Air Manos, tel. (01) 3233562-4.
- By Dolphin Sea Lines (hydrofoil) from Rafina in 2 hrs. 45 min. Rafina agency, tel. (0294) 25100.
- By Minoan Lines Sea Jet (high speed boat) from Rafina in 2 hrs. 30 min., Rafina agency, tel. (0294) 23561.
- By Minoan Lines (high speed boat) from Piraeus in 3 hrs., Piraeus agency, tel. (01) 408 0006-13.
- By ferry from Rafina in 4 hrs. 15 min. (from 4,200 drs.), Rafina agency, tel. (0294) 23561.
- By ferry from Piraeus in 5 hrs. 45 min. (from 4,600 drs.), Piraeus Port Authority, tel. (01) 422 6000.

CONNECTIONS

- By air from Mykonos, with Olympic Airways, to Santorini, Rhodes, Heraklio, tel. (0289) 22490.
- By Dolphin Sea Lines (hydrofoil) from Mykonos to Amorgos, Andros, Ios, Donoussa, Iraklia, Pano Koufonissi, Schinoussa, Naxos, Paros, Santorini, Syros, Tinos. In summer, also to Serifos, Sifnos, Karystos. Mykonos agency, tel. (0289) 22853.
- By Minoan Flying Dolphins hydrofoil to Milos, Naxos, Paros, Sifnos, Syros, Tinos. Mykonos agency, tel. (0289) 22322. By Speed Lines high speed boat to Amorgos, Anafi, Ios, Iraklia, Pano Koufonissi, Schinoussa, Naxos, Paros, Santorini, Sikinos, Syros, Folegandros. Mykonos agency, tel. (0289) 23284.
- By Minoan Lines (hydrofoil) to Andros and Tinos. Mykonos agency, tel. (0289) 23284.
- By ferry to Paros, Syros, Amorgos, Donoussa, Iraklia, Pano Koufonissi, Schinoussa, Naxos, Syros, Tinos, Evdilo (Ikaria), Fourni (near Ikaria), Lipsi, Patmos, Andros, Santorini, Serifos, Sikinos, Sifnos, Folegandros. Mykonos Port Authority, tel. (0289) 22218.

BEST TIPS

HOW TO GET AROUND: With your own transport or by taxi, which are virtually unavailable during the peak season. The best solution is to rent a car or a scooter as soon as you arrive on the island. There are public buses to many of the hamlets.

BEST SEASON: From April through October. The best months are May, June and September. Avoid August unless you like commuter trains at rush hour.

USEFUL TELEPHONE NUMBERS

MYKONOS	(0289)	Police	22235
Town Hall	23261	Port Authority	22218
Municipal Information Office	22201	Clinic	22274
Tourist Police	22482	Clinic (Ano Mera)	71395

Paros

Paros Antiparos

WHY AMONG THE BEST

Because, second to Mykonos, Paros is the favourite island of society and young people in particular. It has beautiful beaches, good hotels for all budgets, and countless bars and nightclubs ensuring lively and enjoyable nights out. It is of course also a mecca for wind-surfers.

CYCLADES

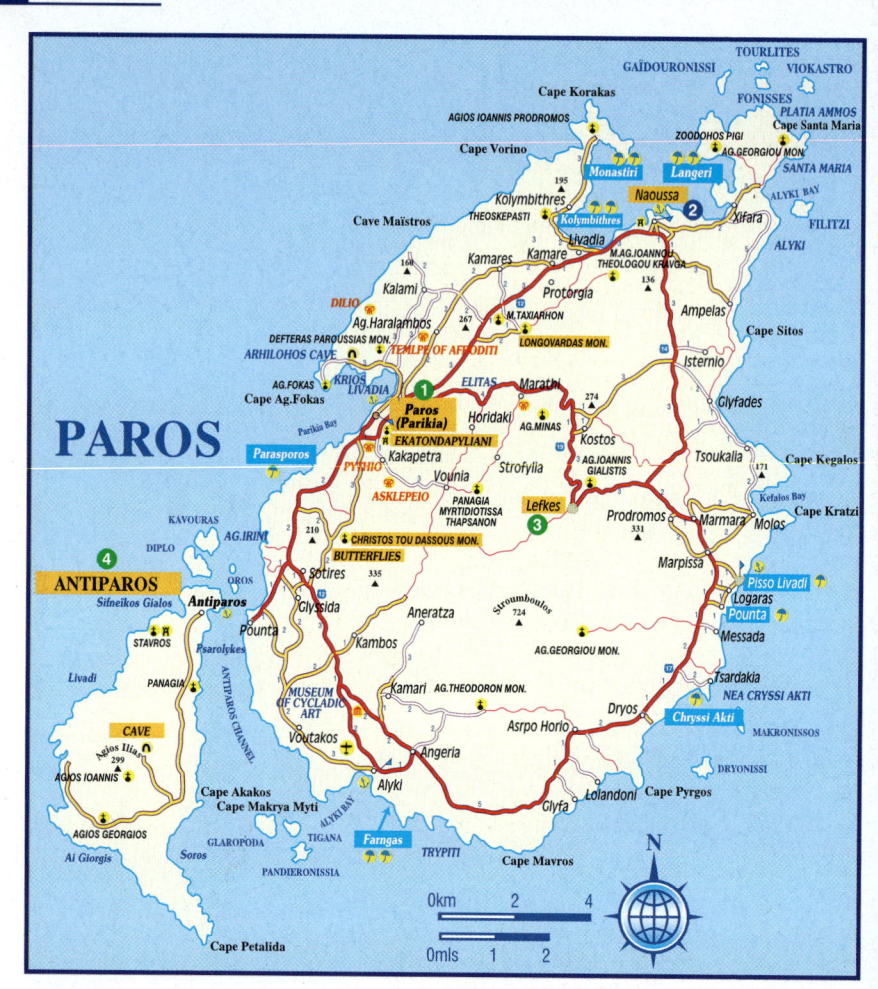

BEST's OPINION

The island is considerably developed for tourism and it isn't only its natural beauties which have made it so fashionable among the young. The locals have taken care to organize its infrastructure well, cleverly exploiting the high cost of a stay at neighbouring Mykonos. The island has two aspects: its tourist side in Parikia or Naoussa, with their crowded beaches and beach bars, and the other featuring the traditional local colour of the tranquil villages of the interior, still ticking over in the peaceful pace of island life. Nonetheless Paros is not so much the place to go for a quiet time as it is to take part in the tumultuous gaiety of its nightlife.

IN BRIEF

Paros is at the centre of the Cyclades, its population about 8,000, and the inhabitants are mostly employed in the tourist trades although they are of course also fishermen and farmers. The three major centres of Parikia, Naoussa and Lefkes concentrate the greater number and the remainder live in the many villages and hamlets scattered all over the island. The configuration is mainly mountainous but there are cultivable valleys with market gardens, vineyards and olive groves.

PAROS **16**

HISTORY

At the time of the Minoan empire Paros was a maritime centre of importance and one of the major centres of Cycladic civilization. Its development was due to the quality of its much sought-after Parian marble which was used to build many significant temples and for works of art such as the **Hermes of Praxiteles** and the **Venus de Milo**. Paros was the birthplace of the great sculptor **Skopas** and of the poet **Archilochos**.

In the 8th c. BC the island was a maritime power with considerable colonies. Its decline began in the 3rd c. BC and in the years of Byzantium it suffered devastating inroads by Goths (267 AD) and Slavs (675 AD).

The Venetian Marco Sanudo captured Naxos, Paros and the neighbouring islands in 1207, founding the **Duchy of the Aegean**. Paros then flourished again, until the appearance of the Ottomans in the Aegean sea in the 16th c. In the course of clashes between Venetians and Turks the island suffered devastation, while its ports became the prey of pirates. It took part in the War of Independence of 1821 against the Turks, and was incorporated in the newly-constituted Hellenic state a little later.

BEST SIGHTS: STEP BY STEP

❶ PARIKIA
Παροικιά / Parikiá

With a population of 3,000, it is the island's capital and port, with intense tourist activity mainly concentrated along the waterfront. The alleys and the **castle quarter** have all the characteristics of Cycladic architecture, with arches, medieval vaulted passageways, snow-white little houses with bougainvilleas and delightful chapels, most noteworthy among them that of **Agios Constantinos** and **Eleni**, with its blue cupola, at the fort.

CHURCH OF THE EKATONDAPYLIANI (KATAPOLIANI)

A major Byzantine monument, the paragon of the island. An Early Christian church founded in the reign of Byzantium's first emperor, Constantine the Great (280-337 AD), it consists of three parts and its name derives from the one hundred (Greek: ekato) openings it is supposed to have, of which they say 99 have been identified to date. Worth noting are the **marble iconostasis** and the **icon of the Kimissi** (Dormition), and especially the **icon of the Panagia** (Our Lady), said to have miraculous powers and attributed to **Saint Luke the Evangelist**. There is a small museum in a cell of the courtyard with religious relics and icons.

ARCHAEOLOGICAL MUSEUM

Tel. (0284) 21231

8:30 am-3 pm, closed on holidays*

Neolithic finds and figurines, examples of the great artistic skill of the Proto-Cycladic civilization of 6000 BC from the excavations on **Sialangos** island in the narrow channel between Paros and Antiparos. You can see the portion of the **Parian Chronicle** (Pariou Chronikou) containing a relation of events with took place between the 16th c. BC and 262 BC, the statue of **Wingless Victory** (Apteros Nike) by the sculptor **Skopas** (5th c. BC) and the **relief depicting the wedding of the poet Archilochos** (6th c. BC).

❷ NAOUSSA
Νάουσα / Náoussa

A seaside fishing village of 1,700 inhabitants with a very attractive harbour at the entrance of which there are the semi-submerged ruins of a small Venetian fort of the 15th c. In recent years Naoussa has evolved into an important tourist centre where most of the social life of Paros is concentrated, with lots of boutiques and chic bars. Stroll around in the charming lanes of the town, in the Agios Dimitrios quarter by the sea, and see the fine churches of ⓖ **Agios Ioannis Theologos** and ⓖ **Kimissi tis Theotokou**. Enjoy, finally, a cup of coffee, or have a meal at one of the island's good fish tavernas next to gently rocking yachts providing a pleasant contrast to the multi-coloured fishing caiques.

❸ LEFKES
Λεύκες / Léfkes

A delightful peaceful mountain village of 700 inhabitants, with a lot of **greenery**, built like an amphitheatre in a small valley. There has been some increase in recent years in tourist activity, bringing with it shops in good taste and excellent options for accommodation. Explore the picturesque paved alleys between attractive white houses, chapels and shady squares with old-style kafenions - cafes. See the majestic ⓖ marble church of **Agia Triada**. When leaving, we propose you take the road leading to the top of **Profitis Ilias**, Paros's tallest mountain (771 m). The ⓖⓖ **route** is balmy with the scent of thyme and every sort of wild flower and will offer you a spectacular ⓖⓖ **vista** in the round to nearly all the islands of the Cyclades. Lefkes is connected to the villages **Prodromos** and **Marmara** by an old Byzantine cobbled road (kalderimi), which is a very pleasant walk.

❹ ANTIPAROS
Αντίπαρος / Andíparos

How to get there

- By small boat from Parikia in 30 min (without your car).
- By ferry in 10 min (with your car) from the village of Pounta, 8.5 km west of Parikia, the closest for crossing to Antiparos (not to be confused with the beach of Pounta which is on the eastern side of the island).

Antiparos is approximately half a nautical mile from the western coast of Paros. It is a small, quiet island well able to offer its visitors the tranquillity they wish but which also has a humming nightlife. There are several good little bars, fish tavernas and traditional "ouzeri" where this typical Greek drink is served with appetizers, so that it is an ideal alternative as well as less expensive, for those who are unimpressed by or tired of the social whirl of Paros. The population of Antiparos is of about 850, living in the only village of the island built around the Venetian ⓖ fort, an excellent example of fortification of the 15th c.

Do not fail to see the famous ⓖⓖ **cavern** of the island (open daily from 10:30 am to 3:45 pm), to a depth of 70 m, which still bears traces of the celebrities who have been there in the past, and enjoy swimming from the fine beaches of ⚲ **Psaralikes**, ⚲ **Panagia**, ⚲ **Soros**, ⚲ **Ai-Georgi** and, when there is no north wind, ⚲⚲ **Livadi** and ⚲ **Sifneikos Gialos**.

As a place to stay we can suggest ✓✓ **Kouros Village**, tel. (0284) 61084-5, or ✓ **Kastro**, tel. (0284) 61423 and ✓ **Madalena**, tel. (0284) 61365. Price: All 8,000-15,000 drs.

You will find good food at ✓ **Georgios Marianos's** taverna in the middle of the main street, for Greek cooking and grills, also at ✓ **Kastro**, where they serve appetizing hors d'oeuvre and ready-cooked dishes, as well as at the ✓ **Kouros** restaurant at the hotel of the same name, Greek and international cuisine.

For a good cup of coffee and breakfast, ✓ **Margarita's** on the main road is the place to go, while ✓ **Navagio's** the spot for either breakfast or an afternoon drink. Afterwards you can take your pick of the little bars around the square before winding up at **Mariano**, **Mylos** or **La Luna**.

PAROS 16

WHAT ELSE TO DO

- The ancient marble quarries are located near the hamlet of Marathi (5 km from Lefkes. This was the source of the pure white marble used in so many great temples, celebrated statues and even Napoleon's tomb. The old galleries, stone supports and a few ancient inscriptions scratched into the walls are still intact. Parian marble was sought after for its translucency as light penetrates up to 3.5 cm below the surface.
- The Valley of the Butterflies is 6 km south of Parikia. A small valley with dense vegetation and lots of streams, it is the chosen mating grounds for the multicoloured Jersey tiger moth. Each spring and summer they gather in their millions, clinging to the branches and leaves of the trees. Some 2 km to the north, the 18th c Christou tou Dasous nunnery, perched on a ridge, offers a splendid view. Only women admitted.

Valley of the butterflies

- The **Longovardos monastery,** one of the island's most significant, is an imposing collection of buildings in the shape of the cross (1638). The domed church in the centre of the courtyard is built in Cycladic style and is filled with frescoes (17th c). Only men admitted.

● **Festivities - Local Events**

15 August, at **Parikia**: The feast day of the Panagia Ekatondapylianis, the island's biggest religious event, is celebrated with a procession behind the icon, fireworks and merrymaking.

23 August, at **Naoussa**: Illuminated fishing caiques reproduce the inhabitants' repulsion of the Turkish admiral/pirate Barbarossa in 1537. Followed by feasting on fish, music, dancing and plenty of wine.

Longovardas monastery

BEST BEACHES

If you think you'll find deserted beaches on Paros you're on the wrong island. The fun in Paros begins with the morning (more likely midday) sortie to the beach, with many thronging to the beach bars rather than bathing in the sea. Nevertheless, there are always a few relatively quiet spots reserved for those who enjoy more privacy.

KOLYMBITHRES

A series of little beaches protected from the wind, with extraordinary sculpted rocks. It is usually crowded here, especially at the height of summer. But you should see the place, even if only once. You can get there from Naoussa either by road or by motorboat.

MONASTIRI

A sandy beach with turquoise waters in a pretty little cove. It's a little bit beyond Kolymbithres and also sheltered from the wind. Popular with the young because of its good bar-restaurant, also called Monastiri. Loud music, high spirits and racquets. Also accessible by boat from Naoussa.

219

CYCLADES

🏖🏖 LANGERI

Exceptionally beautiful, long sandy crescent on the closed bay of Naoussa. The smaller beach on the northeast tip is less crowded and has about 10 umbrellas. You can get there by motorboat from Naoussa in 15 minutes. Take along provisions because there's no canteen.

🏖🏖 FARANGAS

Follow the many and well placed signs along the dirt coastal road from Aliki to this lovely, peaceful, fairly small beach with fine sand and clear water. It also has a decent, quiet beach bar. There are several other good unfrequented little beaches in this area (southeast Paros), such as Trypiti, which you can get to on foot or by boat.

🏖🏖 SANTA MARIA

A charming beach divided into two by a pretty mini-promontory. Although it's likely to be crowded, it's large enough that it doesn't matter. It boasts a diving school, water sports concessions and two fish tavernas. Accessible by road or boat from Naoussa.

🏖 POUNTA

Where the young meet for a dip with a loud beat, fun and adrenaline, bursting from one of the best known and biggest beach bars in the Cyclades. Incidentally, the small sandy beach has umbrellas, a few trees and good swimming.

🏖 KALOGEROS

Narrow but decent beach with few people and no unwelcome extraneous intrusions. Next door, the shallow waters of Molos beach are ideal for small children.

🏖 MESADA

A bit to the south of Pounda, Mesada couldn't be more different. There's no canteen, no umbrellas and it's quiet.

🏖 NEA CHRYSSI AKTI (TSARDAKIA)

The windsurfers' beach. This is where the international windsurfing championships take place every August. If wind doesn't madden you, you've come to the right place.

🏖 PARASPOROS

The best beach in the vicinity of Parikia. Sandy, organized and with a good bar. Those without wheels can get there and to the equally attractive organized beach of Martsello by boat from town.

BEST HOTELS AND ROOMS

BEST LOCATION

If you want to live it up in Paros you had better stay in pretty Naoussa. That's where the golden youth congregate for entertainment. Parikia has less "class" but it too is full of people, nightspots and throbbing with life. For a less hectic holiday, the inland village of Lefkes would be a better bet.

PRICES

The hotel prices mentioned below are the official ones set by the National Tourist Organization for double rooms, at low and high season, with breakfast. Since owners are allowed to modify the prices, always try to negotiate them.

PARIKIA

✓✓ IRIA (Class A)
Tel. (0284) 24145, fax 21167

Open: April-October
Description: Spread out over 22,000 sq. m, it's located 3 km from Parikia and only 100 m from Parasporos, a BEST beach. Built in traditional Cycladic style, it even houses an art gallery.
Rooms: 67 bungalows and suites, with veranda, A/C, bath, telephone, TV, taped music and mini bar.
Special features: Parking, a good restaurant, bar, pool, sports facilities.
Price: 25,000-54,000 drs.
Value for money: ✿✿
Credit cards: All

✓✓ PETRES (C Class)
Tel. (0284) 52467, 52589, 52759

Open: April-October
Description: With Aegean style architecture and decorated in good taste. Conveniently close to both Naoussa and the sea (500 m), it also has a fine view.
Rooms: 16 large rooms, with veranda, bath, A/C, mini bar, taped music and telephone.
Special features: Parking, bar, pool, roof garden, marvellous Greek cuisine and a folk art museum. The hotel also has its own bus for to-ing and fro-ing into Naoussa. Exceptional service, friendly owner. Recommended without reservation.

Price: 17,000-26,500 drs.
Value for money: ✿✿✿
Credit cards: Visa, Diners, Eurocard

✓ ARGONAFTIS HOTEL (C class)
Tel. (0284) 21440, 22278, fax 23442
Open: April-October
Description: Small traditional hotel, clean, friendly atmosphere. At the entrance to the market, 50 m from the waterfront.
Rooms: 15 rooms, all with fridge, **telephone**, A/C and veranda.
Special features: Restaurant, cafe-bar and roof garden.
Price: 10,000-17,000 drs.
Value for money: ✿✿
Credit cards: Mastercard, Visa

PAPADAKIS (B CLASS)
Tel. (0284) 51563, 52504, fax 51269
Open: April-October
Description: Traditional hotel, recently renovated, set on a hill 80 m from town.
Rooms: 16 rooms, all redecorated, with fridge, A/C and telephone.
Special features: Pool, TV and breakfast room.
Price: 14,000-25,000 drs. (breakfast 2,000 drs. extra)
Value for money: ✿✿
Credit cards: None

KOLYMBITHRES

✓✓✓ ASTIR OF PAROS (A Class)
Tel. (0284) 51976
Tel. (0284) 51976, 51977-8, fax 51985

Open: April-October
Description: The island's most luxurious and unquestionably finest hotel is housed in a traditional building surrounded by lush gardens. Situated on the north coast of Paros, 3 km from Naoussa, it looks onto a lovely beach.
Rooms: 57 rooms, with verandah, A/C, bath, telephone, TV, taped music, mini bar and safe.

Special features: Restaurant, pool, conference facilities, mini golf, tennis, water sports and parking.
Price: 62,000-86,000 drs.
Value for money: ✹✹
Credit cards: Visa, American Express, Mastercard, Diners

✓✓ PORTO PAROS (A Class)
Tel. (0284) 52010, fax 51720
Open: April-October
Description: Large hotel complex built along the coast at Kolymbithres. Another one in traditional style with a private beach and view over the sea.
Rooms: 131 rooms and bungalows with bath, A/C, bath and TV.
Special features: Water park with 13 slides, restaurant, parking, bar, pool, water and other sports facilities, available for conferences.
Price: 26,500-46,200 drs.
Value for money: ✹✹✹
Credit cards: American Express, Eurocard, Visa, Mastercard, Diners

LEFKES

✓✓ LEFKES VILLAGE (A Class)
Tel. (0284) 41827, 42398, fax 41827

Open: April-October
Description: Situated inland, 4 km from the sea, in the delightful leafy setting, unique on the island, of the village of Lefkes. One of the island's most attractive hotels, it boasts its own folk art collection.
Rooms: 18 rooms, with bath and A/C.
Special features: Parking, restaurant, bar, pool and conference hall. Pets upon request.
Price: 24,000-40,000 drs.
Value for money: ✹✹
Credit cards: Visa, Mastercard, American Express

CHRYSSI AKTI

✓✓ POSEIDON (A Class)
Tel. (0284) 42650, fax 42649
Open: April-October

Description: Restaurant, breakfast room, pool with bar, massage, tennis court, horseback riding, parking, children's pool; car, pleasure boat and helicopter hire plus a windsurfing school and water sports. Excursions organized.
Rooms: Rooms: 26 apartments and 4 suites, with A/C, telephone, TV, taped music, Internet connection and safe.
Special features: Restaurant, breakfast room, pool with bar, massage, tennis court, riding, parking, children's pool; car, helicopter and pleasure-boat hire. Wind-surfing school, water sports and organized excursions.
Price: 20,000-41,000 drs.
Value for money: ✹✹
Credit cards: Visa, American Express, Diners

ALTERNATIVES

AGRAMBELI (Lux Class) *Naoussa, tel. (0284) 53305.* Price: 15,000-30,000 drs.
HOLIDAY SUN (A class) *Pounda, tel. (0284) 91284, (01) 9234897, fax (0284) 91288.* Price: 20,000-36,000 drs.
CHROMA (B class) *Naoussa, tel. (0284) 52690, fax 51630.* Price: 28,000-40,000 drs.
FOTILIA (C class) *Naoussa, tel. (0284) 52582, fax 52583.* Price: 15,000-21,000 drs.
KALYPSO (C class) *Naoussa, tel. (0284) 51488, 52197, fax 51607.* Price: 13,000-20,000 drs.
MANOS (C class) *Naoussa, tel. (0284) 51114, fax 51741.* Price: 16,000-22,500 drs.
CHRISTINA (C class) *Naoussa, tel. (0284) 51017, 51755, fax 51017.* Price: 15,000-22,000 drs.
LILLY APARTMENTS *Naoussa, tel. (0284) 51377, fax 51716.* Price: 25,000 without breakfast
KANALES *Naoussa, tel. (0284) 52044, fax 52045.* Good but too expensive for what it offers. Price: 25,000-39,000 drs.
VILLAS TZANE *Dryos, tel. (0284) 41795.* Five houses, each painted a different colour, with 2 bedrooms, sitting room and kitchen on an estate of 13,000 sq m. Price: 50,000 drs.

BEST RESTAURANTS & TAVERNAS

PARIKIA

✓✓ APOLLON
Tel. (0284) 21875

Good cooking and a pretty garden. Specialities are soutzoukakia – cumin-spiced meatballs – and grilled chicken. **Price:** €€€

✓ HAPPY GREEN COWS (Vegeterian)
Tel. (0284) 24691

In a class by itself. A few tables, even fewer calories, and colourful decor. **Price:** €

✓ PORFIRA
Tel. (0284) 23410

Specialities include seafood, treats that accompany ouzo and sea-urchin salad. Evenings only. **Price:** €

PLATEIA
Tel. (0284) 25175

Just five tables under an enormous tree, next to some small cafes. Ready cooked dishes prepared by French owner. **Price:** €

NAOUSSA

✓✓ POSEIDON
Tηλ. (0284) 51976

Fine restaurant in the excellent Astir of Paros hotel, beside the pool. A wide range of gastronomic de*lights*. **Price:** €€€

✓✓ CHRISTOS
Tel. (0284) 51442, 51901

Classic Mediterranean cuisine with a well-stocked wine cellar and meticulous service. Pleasant garden with works of art and classical background music. **Price:** €€€

✓ TSAHPINIS
Tel. (0284) 51662

Perhaps the best fish taverna in the little port. **Price:** €€

✓ PAPADAKIS
Tel. (0284) 51047, 52504

Excellent taverna run by people who know what they're doing. **Price:** €€

✓ BARBAROSSA
Tel. (0284) 51391

Typical fish taverna-ouzeri on the Naoussa waterfront. Fantastic mussel soup. **Price:** €

✓ PERVOLARIA
Tel. (0284) 51721

Original Greek and Italian creations in a pretty courtyard, with a wood-burning oven in the middle for pizza. **Price:** €

LEFKES

✓✓ LEFKES
Tel. (0284) 42398, 41827

In the hotel of the same name, with excellent traditional Greek cooking and a view over the valley. **Price:** €€

✓ KLARINOS
Tel. (0284) 41608

Simple taverna with exceptional local meat. **Price:** €

MESADA

✓✓ THEA
Tel. (0284) 42653

Attractive setting, wonderful Constantinople style dishes. 70 wines in the cellar, good music and, of course, the view (thea). Between Chryssi Akti and Piso Livadi. Open all year, day and night. Reservations advisable. **Price:** €€

SANTA MARIA

✓✓ KALTSOUNAS
Home cooking by Kyria Maria as well as fresh fish caught by her husband. **Price:** €

BEST ENTERTAINMENT

Paros seems to attract large numbers of young people and the entertainment options are mostly geared to them. In Naoussa, **Sante** is a favourite for coffee and breakfast, while in Parikia the **Balcony** creperie or the **Wired Cafe** for Internet fans are preferred. For a swim with thudding music the most popular beach bars are at the beaches of **Monastiri**, **Pounda** and **Parasporos**. Nightlife is concentrated mainly in Naoussa and Parikia. Good places for that first drink of the evening include the **Agosta** and **Sofrano** bars in Naoussa, or the **Piratis**, **Evinos** and **Kialoa** bars in Parikia. Later the hordes move on to **Del Mar**, **Linardo's** or **Abia** in Naoussa or to **Slalom** or **Splash** in Parikia. The big clubs like **Vareladiko**, **Nostos** and **Priviledge** (sic) are side by side on the Naoussa canal.

TIPS AND INFORMATION

HOW TO GET THERE

- By air from Athens west airport by Olympic Airways (15,000 drs.), tel. (01) 9363363.
- By Minoan Flying Dolphins high speed catamaran from Piraeus in 2 hrs 45 minutes (from 10,000 drs.), Piraeus Agency, tel. (01) 4280001.
- By hydrofoil from Rafina in 4 hrs (from 7,000 drs.), Piraeus Agency tel. (01) 4224980.
- By ferry from Piraeus in 5 hrs (from 4,250 drs.). Piraeus Port Authority, tel. (01) 4226000-4.
- By ferry from Rafina, not in 4 1/2 hrs as advertised but in what can often be 6 hrs and more (from 4,000 drs.). Rafina Port Authority, tel. (0294) 22487, 22300.

CONNECTIONS

- By Minoan Flying Dolphins high speed catamaran from Paros to Naxos, Mykonos, Milos, Serifos, Sifnos. Paros agency, tel. (0284) 21738.
- By Dolphin Sea Lines hydrofoil from Paros to Naxos, Mykonos, Milos, Sifnos, Syros andTinos. Paros agency, tel. (0284) 21738.
- By Speed Lines hydrofoil from Paros to Anafi, Ios, Mykonos, Naxos, Santorini, Sikinos, Syros and Folegandros. Paros agency, tel. (0284) 31390.
- By ferry from Paros to Ios, Donoussa, Naxos, Mykonos, Andros, Tinos, Santorini, Syros, Kalymnos, Karpathos, Kassos, Kos, Lipsi, Leros, Kastellorizo, Nisyros, Patmos, Rhodes, Symi, Tilos, Halki, Astypalea, Evdilos & Agios Kirikos (Ikaria), Fourni, Vathy & Karlovassi (Samos), Skiathos and Thessaloniki. And in summer, with Amorgos and Skyros. Paros Port Authority, tel. (0284) 21240.

BEST TIPS

HOW TO GET AROUND: n your own car, because the island is fairly large and you need to be independent to see it properly. You can of course hire a car on the spot.
BEST SEASON: From May to September. Avoid the month of August here too because the island sinks under the throngs of visitors.
BEST BUYS: Tasteful ceramics made by a couple of potters are on sale at the top of a hill on the road from Parikia to Lefkes. Look for the signpost on the right shortly before Kostos village.
BEST LOCAL FOOD: ry the rafiolia — little round pies with ricotta-like myzithra cheese — karavoles — snails prepared in different ways — and octopus pilaf.

USEFUL TELEPHONE NUMBERS

PAROS .... (0284)	Health Centre 22500
Parikia Community Office............... 21222, 23244	Naoussa Community Office......................... 51220
Parikia Police 23333	**ANTIPAROS**.. (0284)
Tourist Police 21673	Community Office....................................... 61218
Olympic Airways 21900	Police..61202
Paros Airport 91257	Clinic 61219

SIFNOS

WHY AMONG THE BEST

Because Sifnos is a low-key island that respects tradition. You'll have the opportunity of seeing 366 beautiful churches, ancient towers, white Cycladic villages. You can walk to monasteries and swim in the clear waters of its pleasant beaches.

CYCLADES

BEST's OPINION

Sifnos is an ideal island for those who need peace and relaxation. Quality and simplicity are the keynotes of its Cycladic architecture, its hotels and its tavernas. So far, it has managed to avoid mass tourism.

IN BRIEF

Sifnos is located in the middle of the western Cyclades islands. It has 1,900 inhabitants and is surrounded by other islands, which enhance the view and invite you to extend your trip, in order to visit them. The climate is mild Mediterranean, with ample sunshine and low rainfall. Sifnos is quiet all year round, except for August. The island is known for its ceramics, pastries and cooking. You're sure to be pleased with the food, as many Sifniots have worked as cooks on ships, travelling extensively and bringing back flavours from all corners of the earth. Many of its regular visitors are intellectuals and artists. Vehicles are banned in the narrow streets of three major villages – Artemonas, Apollonia and Kastro. Festivals are frequently organized by the island's churches, which are supervised by local families.

HISTORY

Some say that Siphnos, leader of the Ionian colonists (1000 BC), a hero of Attica and the son of Sounios, gave the island its name, but it may derive from the Greek word "sifnós" meaning "hollow", which would refer to the galleries of its famous mines. Herodotus writes that the inhabitants were wealthy because of the gold and silver mines in the Agios Sostis region. Attractive buildings were a feature of their towns, and they had offered the famous **Siphnian Treasury** (530 BC) to the oracle at Delphi. After having been ruled by the Macedonians and Romans, the inhabitants suffered repeated pirate raids and it was then that most of the **beacon towers** were built. During the era of the Crusaders, the Venetian duke Marco Sanudo conquered Sifnos and other Cycladic islands with his galleys. From 1617, the island paid head taxes to the Turks. In 1821, it participated in the Greek War of Independence.

BEST SIGHTS: STEP BY STEP

❶ APOLLONIA
Απολλωνία / Apollonía

The capital and Sifnos' largest village, it extends over three hills, virtually joined to Exambella, Ano Petali and Artemonas. The island's main life is concentrated along the narrow pedestrian street, **Stylianou Prokou**, which begins near the square and ends at the Agios Spyridon church. We suggest you stroll along this street, which offers almost everything. Visit the **Folk Art Museum** on the square (9 am-2 pm and 7-10 pm, closed on holidays*), with a collection of pottery, embroidery, local costumes and weapons from the 1821 revolution and the **church of Stavros** and **Agios Athanassios**, with its frescoes and wooden icon screen. Apollonia's cathedral, **Agios Spyridon**, will also catch your eye and look for the **Chryssopigi icon**, which is considered miraculous. In **Stylianou Prokou**, there is a series of bars and tavernas, as well as elegant shops with clothes, ceramics and jewellery. In Ano Petali, you can see the 18th c. **Panagia tin Ouranofora** (or **Geranofora**) church, built on the ruins of an ancient temple.

Panagia Ouranofora

❷ KAMARES
Καμάρες / Kamáres

Sifnos's main port, in a deep natural bay. Although touristically developed, it has managed to retain its own character. The waterfront is full of hotels, tavernas, bars, shops and pottery workshops. You can swim at the pleasant sandy **beach**, which is shared with the tourist village of **Agia Marina**.

❸ HERRONISSOΣ
Χερρόνησος / Herónisos

An isolated fishing village on the island's northern point, with two tavernas, which serve fresh lobster cultivated there, an attractive pottery workshop and some fishing caiques. There is also a small, relatively good beach. You can get there by a poor road or by caique.

❹ ARTEMONAS
Αρτεμώνας / Artemónas

Village featuring **neo-classical buildings** and **mansions**, with pretty gardens. At the village entrance, is the **church of Agios Konstantinos**, while at the village center, the **Panagia tis Ammou** church with its marvellous icon screen. Several windmills are also located on the top of the hill. If you go up there, you'll have a panoramic view of the surrounding islands and some of Sifnos's villages. Artemonas has elegant boutiques, traditional bakeries, a pottery workshop, and **Theodoros's** famous **pastry shop**. The **walk** from **Artemonas** to **Kastro** takes about half an hour. On the way, visit the **Agios Chryssostomos** church, with its palm tree.

CYCLADES

❺ KASTRO
Κάστρο / Kástro

The most important historical site in Sifnos. A Venetian village was built perimetrically on a hill next to the sea, over the island's ancient acropolis. It was used as a fort against pirate attacks and was Sifnos's capital until 1836. Two narrow roads cross the village — one on the external side of the walls and the other on the inner. You can enter the village through the three arcade-entrances, once called **loggias**. Wander along the narrow alleys within the walls, and feel the trench-like protection offered by the extreme closeness of the houses, constructed almost one on top of the other, both left and right. Note the 👁👁 **ancient columns** and the **coats of arms**. It is interesting from a town-planning point of view that Kastro is the first place in Greece to have introduced **horizontal ownership** of premises. Taking the external perimeter road, you'll find yourself between a spectacular 👁👁 **view** of the sea and the unique architecture of the houses. Walk down the carefully constructed 👁 **path**, and in five minutes, you'll reach the 👁 **Eptamartyros church**, on the rocks overlooking the sea. Here you can swim in the 👁 **clear**, **deep water**. On the return trip, drop in for a cup of coffee or soft drink at the attractive **Remezzo** cafe bar, or have lunch at a taverna. Following the signs, you'll find the **Archaeological Museum** (⏰ 8 am-2 pm, closed on hols*), where the area's ancient finds are on display. On the way out, if you turn right and walk for a while, you'll reach a small gate from where there is a magnificent 👁👁 **view** of the Aegean.

❻ SERALIA
Σεράλια / Serália

Pretty fishing port in the bay under Kastro. You can cool off in the deep, clear waters of the tiny beach.

❼ FAROS
Φάρος / Fáros

A fishing harbour in a deep and sheltered bay, with two beaches, rooms for rent and several tavernas, not particularly noteworthy. Until 1883, it was the island's official port. On the western side, the remains can still be seen of the loading facilities for minerals sent to the mainland for processing. The hamlet got its name from the lighthouse (*faros* in Greek), which is located on the right of the harbour, near the Stavrou monastery. It is a picturesque little village, which attracts a lot of visitors in summer.

❽ CHRYSSOPIGI
Χρυσοπηγή / Chrysopigí

The **Panagia Chryssopigi** monastery is built on a very picturesque promontory, on the foundations of an older church (1650). The **icon of the Virgin** is believed to perform miracles and is linked to numerous traditions. See the old **stone icon screen** with the 1818 marble eagle and admire the magnificent 👁👁 **scenery**. Chryssopigi is the island's patron saint whose feast day is magnificently celebrated on **Ascension Day**, 40 days after Easter, all day, with the island speciality, chickpea soup offered to all comers. For strong swimmers, we suggest you dive into the crystal-clear, deep 👁👁 **waters**, from the rocks or from the smooth stone slabs around the monastery. For those who prefer to avoid the rocks, there is a small pebble beach, about 100 m to the right of the monastery. The excellent **Lembessis taverna** is located in the adjoining bay of **Apokofto**.

SIFNOS

⑨ PLATYS GIALOS

Sifnos' most developed beach, with hotels, tavernas and bars right on the seafront. On the top of the hill, is the **Panagia tou Vounou monastery** (1813) and north-east, the ruins of an ancient structure, the **Aspros Pyrgos**. At the entrance to the bay is **Kypriani** (or **Kitriani**), an uninhabited islet, with only one building, the Panagia tis Kyprianis chapel.

⑩ VATHY

A few kilometres down the road from Apollonia to Vathy, see on the right the old ⓖ **Fyrogion monastery**, with its bakery and olive press. On the way there, are also the ⓖ **ancient** 4th c. BC **towers**, observation posts to warn of enemy attacks. Vathy is an unpretentious little settlement on the island's second largest sandy beach, after Platys Gialos. The

Agios Taxiarchis

beautiful ⓖ **Taxiarchis church**, with its unusual double dome, has been built virtually on the sea. The **panigyri** on Taxiarchi's feast day 5 September, is one of the oldest of the island, attracting flocks of people. With a parking area at the village entrance, Vathy is a good choice for family holidays, as children are free to play without the danger of traffic.

OTHER THINGS TO DO

MONASTERIES

Before setting out, ask a local shopkeeper or taxi driver in the nearest village square when they are open and who has the key.

Panagia tou Vounou

A triple-aisled church built on a hill, with a view of Platys Gialos. It's worth visiting because of its history, its all-white architecture and its interesting old icon screen. See the **icon tis Mahairoussas** and the abbot's quarters, and catch the stunning ⓖ **view** from the verandas. For the romantic, a full-moon visit is recommended.

Prophitis Ilias

A fine 8th c. Byzantine monastery with a marble icon screen in the 12th c. chapel. It's a 90 min walk from Apollonia, but you'll be amply rewarded by the wonderful ⓖⓖ **view**. See the old icon screen, the arched, oblong refectory and the underground arcades, reminiscent of catacombs.

Panagia Poulati

A church with marvellous architecture (1871), impressive bell-towers and a magnificent dome. At the main entrance, see the marble depiction of the Annunciation and the marble eagle with the animals in his talons. On its feast day of **15 August** there is a **panigyri** here, too.
The 20 min walk from Kastro, along the Maina path, is probably the best walk in Sifnos. You can also go by road (3 km from Apollonia).

Theologos tou Moungou

A nunnery, whose operation was banned in 1834, after an order by the new Bavarian rulers of Greece. See the wood-carved icon screen, the floor with the painted two-headed eagle inside the church, the paved courtyards and the prioress's quarters, and enjoy the view of the surrounding villages.

CYCLADES

Agios Chryssostomos Monastery

On the Kastro road, after Kato Petali. A former Venetian fortress which was converted into a church. In 1653, the historic **Fytia** school (the precursor of national education) functioned there. See the iconostasis with the old icons, the two-headed eagle on the floor (1818) and the bishops throne.

EXCURSION BY CAIQUE (FROM KAMARES)

Ask for the owner, Mr. Kambourakis, tel. (0284) 31672, 32375, 33133, who leaves his taverna, **Meropi**, to take visitors on boat excursions, 12,000 drs. to **Gialoudia** and 20,000 drs. to Herronissos, return.
It's a good idea to find other people and split the cost. At **Gialoudia**, you can swim at a deserted pebble beach, although the water is nothing special.
Avoid Vroulidia — which many may recommend, but which is unfortunately strewn with rubbish — and have your next dip in the clear waters in front of the stairs to **Agios Philippos**, once a very pretty little church, spoiled by the recent annexe.

BEST BEACHES

The island's beaches are not outstanding. However, the sea is clean and clear, and the variety of choices available helps avoid crowding. For good swimmers, the beautiful rocks at **Chryssopigi** or at the **Eptamartyros**

Chryssopigi

church, under the Kastro, would be the best choice. Most of the beaches with sand, pebbles or stones, are close to villages. We have listed them in order of preference.

VATHY

A fairly good sandy beach in a bay protected from the meltemi winds. The beach is best on the left side, but — strangely enough — the sea is clearer on the right, in front of the settlement, immediately after the church.

KAMARES

Next to the port, in the village. The beach is a good one and the nearby tavernas offer shade and tasty food.

PLATYS GIALOS

Considered to be Sifnos's best sandy beach. Swimming can be combined with lunch or drinks at the tavernas, snack bars and beach bars on the shore.

FASSOLOU

A quiet, though mediocre beach, with clear water, in the cove next to Faros. Located there, is the taverna of ✓ **Zambelis** who used to be Maria Goulandris's cook in the '60s when Christina Onassis was a frequent guest. He serves ready-cooked dishes and grills.

FAROS BAY

Of the two so-so beaches in the bay, the best one is the most remote, on the right side. The small trees and a taverna offer welcome shade.

SIFNOS 17

BEST HOTELS AND ROOMS

BEST LOCATION
Distances are small, so you have two choices — either stay close to the sea, or select accommodation on one of the hills, offering peace and quiet, plus a view.

PRICES
The hotel prices mentioned below are the official ones, set by the National Tourist Organization for double rooms, at low and high season, with breakfast. Since owners are allowed to modify prices, always try to negotiate them.

APOLLONIA (ANO PETALI)

✓✓ PETALI (C Class)
Tel. (0284) 33024, 33151
Open: May-October
Description: Probably the best hotel in Sifnos, located between Artemonas and Apollonia. However, there is no parking area close by and there are many steps to negotiate. If you notify them on time, hotel staff will be waiting to carry up your luggage. 
Rooms: 6 studios and 4 suites, in a 1,500 sq m area.
Special features: Restaurant with excellent service, lavish breakfast.
Price: 21,000-40,000 drs.
Value for money: ✸✸
Credit cards: Visa

KAMARES

✓ ALKYONIS VILLAS (A Class)
Tel. (0284) 33101-2, 32225, fax 33102
Open: April-October
Description: A fine hotel with emphasis on detail, ideal for those who wish to stay in the port.
Rooms: 9 apartments and one suite, with kitchen, telephone, TV, bath and large verandas, with a sea view.
Special features: Parking.

Price: 15,000-31,000 drs. Without breakfast
Value for money: ✸
Credit cards: Visa, Mastercard, American Express

PLATYS GIALOS

✓✓ ALEXANDROS SIFNOS BEACH (B Class)
Tel. (0284) 71300, 71333, fax 71303
Open: May-September
Description: Cycladic-style hotel complex with bungalows. Excellent choice for those who want a good hotel next to the sea. 
Rooms: 22 rooms with all facilities and large verandas with a view of Platys Gialos. Ask for one of the newly-built rooms. The facilities are the same, but the furnishing is different.
Special features: Swimming pool with a bar.
Price: 21,000-46,000 drs.
Value for money: ✸✸
Credit cards: None

CYCLADES

✓✓ SIMON PLATYS GIALOS
(B Class)
Tel. (0284) 71224, 71324, fax 71325

Open: April-September
Description: Former state-run **Xenia** hotel, now privately owned, which is well known because of visits by Greek Prime Minister Costas Simitis. Of course, if your holiday dates coincide with his, it's unlikely you'll find a room. A distinctive feature of the decor is the wall-paintings by well-known Greek artists.
Rooms: 26 rooms with A/C, TV and bath.
Special features: Parking, restaurant, bar, athletic facilities, conference hall and water sports. Its location at the edge of the beach is an advantage.
Price: 32,000-50,000 drs.
Value for money: ✷
Credit cards: None

FASSOLOU

✓ FASSOLOU (C Class)
Tel. (0284) 33151, fax 32190

Open: June-September
Description: The decor is distinctive for its brass details.
Rooms: 6 rooms with kitchen, telephone, TV, bath and balcony with a view.
Special features: Snack bar.
Price: 15,500-28,000 drs.
Value for money: ✷✷
Credit cards: None

ALTERNATIVES

EFROSYNI (B Class) *Platys Gialos, tel. (0284) 71353.* **Price:** 15,500-20,000 drs.
KALYPSO *Vathy, tel. (0284) 71127, 32043.* **Price:** 11,500-16,000 drs.
GEROFINIKAS *Between Apollonia and Kastro, tel. (0284) 33450.* **Price:** 12,000-20,000 drs. Without breakfast
We warmly recommend the **Aegean Treasure** (Thisavros tou Aigaiou) travel agency, tel. (0284) 31145, 33151, to assist you in finding a room, or to organize a vacation itinerary on the island.

BEST RESTAURANTS & TAVERNAS

APOLLONIA

✓✓ PETALI
Tel. (0284) 33024
Restaurant of the hotel of the same name. Very good service on a veranda with unlimited views and simple Cycladic decor. Attention to detail, good taste very evident.
Price: €€€

SIFNOS

✓ MAMA MIA
Tel. (0284) 33086
Felipe came to Sifnos on holiday and decided to stay. He opened two **Mama Mia** restaurants — the second one is in Platys Gialos — where he serves good Italian food, pasta and pizzas. Pleasant atmosphere in a pretty garden.
Price: €€

ARTEMONAS
✓ LIOTRIVI
On the square, tel. (0284) 32051

One of the island's best tavernas. Traditional style, with delicious Sifniot cuisine. **Price:** €

✓ LEMBESSIS
On the square, tel. (0284) 31303
Famous for its authentic Sifniot cuisine, although the setting is not anything special. The owner's taverna in Apokofto is preferable.
Price: €€

PLATYS GIALOS
KALIMERA
Tel. (0284) 71365
Restaurant-cafe bar on the beach. Open all day, with a happy, lively atmosphere. Large variety of pancakes, pasta, salads and curried chicken. Attractive place for coffee or drinks.
Price: €€

MENELAOS
Tel. (0284) 71210

Behind the **Xenia** hotel, at Platys Gialos, in a beautiful setting with a superb view of the rocks and sea. Friendly service, only ready-cooked food. If you like, you can swim in the small coves under the taverna. **Price:** €

KAMARES
KAPETAN ANDREAS
Tel. (0284) 32356
Tables on the beach, under small trees offering shade and relative coolness. Unfortunately, they don't accept reservations, but it's worth waiting 5-10 min for a table to become available.
Price: €

AI DU PURCONI
Tel. (0284) 31671
Italian delicacies, delicious cuisine.
Price: €€

FASSOLOU
ZAMBELIS
Tel. (0284) 71434
Taverna on the Fassolou beach, with ready-cooked specialities.
Price: €€

VATHY
TSIKALI
Tel. (0284) 31891

On the right side of the beach. A good taverna with reasonable prices for Sifniot ready-cooked food and grilled fish. **Price:** €

APOKOFTOU - CHRYSSOPIGI
✓ LEMBESSIS
Tel. (0284) 31295
The same ownership as the Lembessis taverna in Artemonas. The island's best taverna, with traditional Sifniot cuisine. Unfortunately, it's very well-known, so it's difficult to find a table. **Price:** €

BEST ENTERTAINMENT

Apollonia takes the lead in the island's nightlife. There are good quality bars if you go up Stylianou Prokopou St. There you will find **Isidora**, **Botzi**, **Argo** and **Delfini** (with Greek music). In Kamares you can go to the **Folie** and in Kastro to the **Remezzo**.

Folie

TIPS AND INFORMATION

HOW TO GET THERE

- By Minoan Flying Dolphins from Marina Zeas in Piraeus, in 2 hrs 30 min (from 6,800 drs.), Piraeus Agency, tel. (01) 4280001, Athens Agency, tel. (01) 3244600.
- By Dolphin Sea Lines high-speed passenger boats, only in summer, from Rafina, in 5 hrs (from 3,400 drs.), Piraeus Agency (01) 4224980.
- By ferry from Piraeus in 5 hrs (from 3,300 drs.), Piraeus Port Authority, tel. (01) 4226000-4.

CONNECTIONS

- By Minoan Flying Dolphins from Sifnos to Kimolos, Kythnos, Milos, Mykonos, Naxos, Paros, Serifos, Tinos and Karystos, tel. (0284) 33151, 31145.
- By Dolphin Sea Lines high-speed boats, from Sifnos to Mykonos, Paros, Serifos, Tinos and Karystos, only in summer. Information, Sifnos Agency, tel. (0284) 31217, 32373.
- By ferry from Sifnos to Ios, Kimolos, Milos, Mykonos, Naxos, Paros, Santorini, Serifos, Sikinos, Syros and Folegandros. Information, Sifnos Port Police, tel. (0284) 31617.

BEST TIPS

HOW TO GET AROUND: There are four buses and about 10 taxis for the island's visitors. In addition, you can hire a car or a moped at the larger villages (Kamares, Artemonas and Apollonia).
The buses run regularly to all the island's main points. The distances are small, so many people prefer to walk, especially between Apollonia and Artemonas, or Artemonas and Kastro.

BEST SEASON: For holidays, until early July, there are very few visitors. The island becomes crowded only between July 20 and August 20.

BEST BUYS: Ceramics, textiles, pastries, traditional cheeses and wines.

BEST LOCAL FOOD: Sifnos is famous for its local specialities and several top chefs were born here. Try **revithada** (oven-baked chick-peas with spices, in a ceramic dish) **mastelo** (oven-baked lamb or goat), **baked sweets**, **tyropita** (cheese pie) and **bougatsa** (custard pie) at the Kastro bakery.

USEFUL TELEPHONE NUMBERS

SIFNOS .... (0284)	Police (Apollonia) 31210
Apollonia Community Office 31345	Port Authority (Kamares) 33617
Artemonas Community Office 32388	Health Centre 31315
Information Office (Kamares) 31977	Pharmacy 33033
Room Renters' Association 31333	Taxis 33719, (094) 642680

Folegandros

WHY AMONG THE BEST

Because the town of Folegandros is one of the most enchanting of all the Greek islands. Because the island of Folegandros has modern conveniences without losing its traditional aspect. For peaceful holidays with romantic strolls along the narrow, medieval streets among the unusual fortress-like houses and a view of the infinite blue seascape.

CYCLADES

FOLEGANDROS

BEST's OPINION

Folegandros is our top choice amongst the quieter islands. Its principal attraction is the exquisite Hora, where you'll spend most of your time. Book a room there in advance, take some good books with you and relax in one of the charming squares with the delightful cafes and traditional Greek tavernas serving snacks and tit-bits.

IN BRIEF

The population of Folegandros is about 700. It is a rocky, infertile island, with spectacular cliffs sheer to the sea. The climate is mild, with scant rainfall and windy in summer. The Romans used the island as a place of exile. In the 13th c. it devolved to the duchy of Naxos under the sovereignty of the Venetian Marco Sanudo. It was frequently raided by pirates and in 1617 passed into the hands of the Turks, who went there only to collect taxes. In 1828, together with the other Cyclades islands, it was incorporated with Greece.

BEST SIGHTS: STEP BY STEP

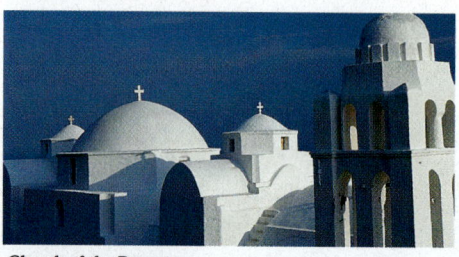

❶ HORA
Χώρα / Hóra

One of the loveliest Cycladic towns, built in and around the island's medieval fort, at the edge of a steep cliff. Ideal for walks along its alleyways and for whiling away your time under the trees of the pretty 〝〞 **squares** full of local colour such as Dounavi Square with three wellheads and its churches, Manolis's

Church of the Panagia

square, Kritikou or Kontarini Square. Stroll in the lanes of 66 **Kastro**, the medieval defence settlement built in 1212 by Marco Sanudo, the governor of the Aegean duchy. The 6 **church of Christos or Pantanassa** is in the fort at the edge of the cliff. The church of the 6 **Panagia (Kimissis Theotokou)** is the most striking church of the island, multi-domed, with a bell-tower, it dominates the peak of Paleokastro above Hora.

OUTSIDE HORA

6 CHRYSSOSPILIA

A beautiful big cave at Paleokastro, with stalagmites and stalactites, which was an ancient place of worship. Access by caique, or by a steep path.

❷ ANO MERIA
Ανω Μεριά / Ano Meriá

Sparsely populated farm settlement built for protection from the winds. See the traditional self-supporting **farmstead** comprising a dwelling, cultivated garden and auxiliary buildings.

❸ KARAVOSTASSIS
Καραβοστάσης / Karavostássis

The island's only port. A small village with some hotels, tavernas, shops and a beach with a few trees.

Kontarini Square

Dounavi Square

Kastro

Monk at Ano Meria

CYCLADES

BEST BEACHES

The main point of interest on Folegandros is Hora. The beaches are mediocre and inaccessible (only on foot or by caique from Karavostassis). The best beach, which also has the easiest access, is ⚲⚲ **Katergo**. Then there is ⚲ **Angali** in Vathy bay, with a taverna and the only beach with a road. If you have time, visit **Livadi** and **Agios Georgios**.

Katergo

BEST HOTELS AND ROOMS

BEST LOCATION
In Hora, because it's the heart of the island. Reserve early.

PRICES
The hotel prices mentioned below are the official ones, set by the National Tourist Organization for double rooms, at low and high season, with breakfast. Since owners are allowed to modify prices, always try to negotiate them.

HORA

✓✓ ANEMOMYLOS (B Class)
Tel. (0286) 41309, fax 41407, tel. (01) 6827777, fax 6823962
Open: May-October
Description: Attractive and welcoming hotel, built in Cycladic style. Ask for a room with a view of the ravine. The best choice on the island.
Rooms: 18 rooms, each with bath and balcony with seaview.
Special features: Parking, bar, pets upon request.
Price: 31,000-45,000 drs.
Value for money: ✱✱
Credit cards: Visa

✓ KASTRO (B Class)
Tel. (0286) 41230, fax 41366
Open: May-September
Description: Traditional hotel, formerly a fortified dwelling built on the edge of a rock, with well-designed interiors.
Rooms: 7 rooms with bath and telephone.
Special features: Room service, roof-garden, with a view of the sea and Hora.
Price: 13,000-18,000 drs. Without breakfast
Value for money: ✱✱
Credit cards: Visa, American Express

FOLEGANDROS

✓ FOLEGANDROS APARTMENTS (C Class)

Tel. (0286) 41239, fax 41166, tel. & fax (01) 3423545
Open: May-September
Description: Pretty hotel built in the traditional-style with special care and attention by its owners, Odysseas and Despina.
Rooms: 19 apartments plus 7 studios, each with telephone, bath, sitting-room and kitchen.
Special features: Veranda with seaview, parking area and room service, pool, pool bar and hydro massage. Pets upon request.
Price: 15,000-26,000 drs.
Value for money: ✤✤
Credit cards: Visa

Credit cards: None

PIGADOS (C Class)

Tel. (0286) 41395, (0945) 476737, fax 41406, tel. (01) 8053695
Open: June-September
Description: A group of independent apartments built in an acre of land overlooking the Aegean.
Rooms: 8 furnished and fully equipped apartments each with bath, kitchen, TV and telephone.
Special features: Courtyard with view to the sea. Pets upon request.
Price: 16,500-22,000 drs.
Value for money: ✤

ALTERNATIVES

ODYSSEAS HOTEL (C Class) *Hora, tel. (0286) 41276.* **Price:** 10,000-19,000 drs. (no breakfast)

AEOLOS BEACH HOTEL (C Class) *Karavostassis, tel. (0286) 41336, fax 41205.* **Price:** 12,000-18,000 drs.

BEST RESTAURANTS & TAVERNAS

- In Hora, you'll enjoy local specialities at ✓ **Pounta**, grills at **Kritikos**, and good Greek dishes at **Melissa**. For fresh fish and local appetizers, try the **Folegandros** *ouzeri*.

Kritikos

Pounta

CYCLADES

- In Karavostassis, you can eat fresh fish next to the sea, at ✓ **Kali Kardia** or ✓ **Kalymnios**.
- In Ano Meria, go to **Iliovasilema** for local specialities: "matsata" or noodles with cockerel, kid or rabbit.
  Price: All €

BEST ENTERTAINMENT

There are many pleasant bars in Hora. Choose among **Astarti** and **Wine Bar**, **Rakentia** with its panorama, or the more youth-oriented **Laoumi**, **Methexis** and **Patitiri**.
For coffee and breakfast, the **Anemomylos** hotel veranda with the incredible view.

Rakentia

TIPS AND INFORMATION

HOW TO GET THERE

- By air from Athens West airport to Santorini, Olympic Airways (from 18,800 drs.), tel. (01) 9363363. From Thessaloniki's Makedonia airport, only in summer, with Olympic Airways (from 27,000 drs) tel. (031) 228880. From Santorini by hydrofoil to Folegandros, Santorini Port Authority tel. (0286) 22239.
- By ferry from Piraeus in 9 hrs (from 4,300 drs.), Piraeus Port Authority, tel. (01) 4226000-4.

CONNECTIONS

- With Speed Lines hydrofoil from Folegandros to other islands, Folegandros Agency, tel. (0286) 22220, 22478, 22940 or Port Authority (0286) 41249.
- By ferries from Folegandros, Folegandros Agency, tel. (0286) 41198, 41221.

BEST TIPS

HOW TO GET AROUND: A central road connects the villages with Hora. There is a bus, so your car is not necessary. Anyway, most beaches are accessed by caique.

BEST SEASON: Easter in Folegandros is exceptionally lovely. Naturally so is summer, with the exception of August.

BEST LOCAL FOOD: Try **matsata**, (traditional home-made pasta with rabbit), especially in Ano Meria.

BEST SHOPPING: Buy **ladotyri** (oil-preserved cheese), **anthotyri** (soft, white cheese) and thyme honey.

USEFUL TELEPHONE NUMBERS

FOLEGANDROS	(0286)	Police	41249
Community Office	41285	Clinic	41222

S ANTORINI

WHY AMONG THE BEST

Because Santorini is simply unique. Created by a volcano, the spectacular rim of the caldera will provide endless hours of contemplation and romance as you gaze at the view while either relaxing on your hotel veranda or strolling through the alleyways between the stunning, brilliant white buildings of the villages, teetering on the edge of the cliff. Ancient Akrotiri adds a cultural dimension to your visit to the island.

Cyclades

SANTORINI (Thera)

BEST's OPINION

Santorini is encapsulated in the 😀😀😀 **view** from the cliff over the 😀😀😀 **caldera**. You should stay on this side of the island no matter what, even if it is more expensive. If you're unable to go up and down steep stairways, it's good to know from the start that on Santorini you won't be able to avoid them. As a consequence, you really should be in good physical condition, or else choose the location of your hotel carefully.

This is an island with something for everyone: couples and newlyweds who want to escape to a romantic hideaway, loners, lovers of archaeology, nature-worshippers, adventurers, night owls and sophisticates. The scenery exudes a fascination better appreciated in tranquillity, which, however, might be somewhat difficult to find during the peak season.

Santorini's beaches are nothing to compare with those of some of the other Greek islands. But they have been created by the volcano and have their own geological interest, as well as red or black sand.

SANTORINI

IN BRIEF

Santorini is one of the southern Cyclades islands. Its **7,000** permanent inhabitants are scattered amongst some ten villages, of which the largest is the capital **Fira**, followed by delightful **Ia**. Most of the islanders work at trade, tourism and fishing, though there is a certain amount of farming inland, for the volcanic activity has made the soil very fertile. Its best known products are its small tomatoes, grown virtually without water, and its vines, which have been a source of sweet wine since antiquity. The climate is mild and very dry.

Santorini owes its dramatic beauty to a volcanic eruption and geological upheavals have left their mark everywhere: the black beaches, the precipice surrounding the caldera, the twisted, colourful rocks and the steep cliffs all give the island a distinctive quality.

In the middle of the caldera, 400 m below the sea, there is an enormous crater, composed of many smaller ones, whose continuous eruptions gradually created the islets in its centre, **Palia** and **Nea Kameni** (the Old and New Burnt Ones).

Santorini's amazing Cycladic architecture is completely in tune with the needs of its people and the presence of the volcano. Visitors are always struck by the **troglodyte house**s tunnelled into the cliff face, the **vaulted churches**, and the neo-classical mansions in Fira and Ia, which were restored after the 1956 earthquake. South of Fira is **Athinios**, the island's harbour where the big ships and cruiseships anchor.

HISTORY

Originally, the island was named Strongyli (Round), because of its shape. The Phoenicians called it Kalliste (Most Beautiful), the Dorians Thera, while Santorini is a corruption of Santa Irini, given it by the Franks in the 12th c. By about 2000 BC, an important civilization had developed on the island. It was closely linked to Minoan Crete, as the archaeologists, who dug its main city **Akrotiri** out from under a thick layer of lava have proven.

Life on the island came to an abrupt halt in the 15th c. BC, when the volcano erupted and the centre collapsed into the sea, forming the **caldera**. The Aegean darkened and a tidal wave 250 m high and moving at 300 km per hour swept over the north coast of Crete and is thought to have brought an end to the flourishing Minoan civilization there. It even reached Egypt. Some scholars associate the catastrophe with the legend of the lost continent of Atlantis.

Thera declared obedience to the Persians during the Persian Wars and later allied itself with the Spartans. In 426 BC, it passed under Athenian control and in subsequent centuries was ruled by the Ptolemies of Egypt and the Romans. In Byzantine times, it belonged to the **Thema of the Aegean**, while the Franks considered it part of the **Duchy of Naxos**, until the Venetians took over. While under western occupation, many of the inhabitants converted to Catholicism. Like most of the Aegean islands, its population was decimated by the Turkish admiral Khaireddin Barbarossa (1537) and it became part of the Ottoman empire in 1579. Two centuries later, a historical quirk put Santorini under Russian domination for four years (1770-1774). It joined the new Greek state in 1832.

BEST SIGHTS: STEP BY STEP

❶ I A
Οία / ´Ia

Here you'll find a cosmopolitan atmosphere, charming **houses** that are half underground, narrow lanes paved with marble flagstones, **two-storey neo-classical mansions**, and attractive bars and restaurants. This is the island's most beautiful village but also the one most geared to tourism. Come here an hour before sunset, sit yourself down on a wall or some bar in the west end of town, near the castle. And you'll be treated to one of the most spectacular **sunsets** you've ever seen. Two stepped paths lead down to the sea: one to the little port of Armeni, where there's a **chapel dedicated to St. Nicholas**, and the other to the small beach of Ammoudi and some fish tavernas.

CYCLADES

☺☺☺ SUNSET FROM IA'S FORTRESS
One of the finest spots from which to view the Aegean.

☺ NAVAL MUSEUM
Tel. (0286) 71156

⊙ 12:30-4 pm, 5-8:30 pm, closed on Tuesdays and holidays*

Here you'll see figureheads, navigation aids and other equipment, watercolours and nautical souvenirs of the 19th c., when many of the islanders were seamen. It was then that most of Ia's mansions were built. In 1821 the Santorini fleet was the third largest in Greece.

❷ IMEROVIGLI-SKAROS-FIROSTEFANI
Ημεροβίγλι-Σκάρος-Φηροστεφάνι / Imerovígli-Skáros-Firostefáni

Firostefani is an extended village on the edge of Fira. Stop here and enjoy the ☺☺ **wonderful view**, take a look at the **church of Agios Gerassimos** and continue your walk for another two kilometres as far as **Imerovigli** (or Merovigli). This is the highest spot on the caldera and the islanders used it as an early-warning system against pirate attacks.

Then go down to **Skaros** (20 min walk), which was the island's capital in medieval times. Unfortunately, there's not much left to admire these days, except for the Venetian castle. If you're a good walker, take the path leading to the white **chapel of the Panagia Theoskepasti**, and be rewarded by the breath-taking ☺☺ view. Between Firostefani and Imerovigli, you'll come to the monastery of **Agios Nikolaos**. It was founded in 1651 by the Ghizis, one of the few Orthodox families who lived in the Skaros castle. When Skaros became deserted, they transferred the monastery to its present location. Its church is unusual in its threefold dedication: to SS Panteleimon and Nicholas, as well as the Source of Life (Zoodochos Pigi).

❸ FIRA
Φηρά / Firá

Fira (or Thera or Hora), the capital of Santorini, is built on the rim of the caldera. Avoid the centre of town with its noisy crowds, tasteless cement constructions and souvenir shops, and wander along the caldera. The wonderful **architecture** and the splendid **view** from the spot known as **Patsouli** will make you forget the clamour.

☺ ARCHAEOLOGICAL MUSEUM
Tel. (0286) 22217

⊙ 8:30 am-3 pm, closed on Mondays and holidays*

Look for the **marble kouroi**, the **kylixes** (drinking cups) decorated with triremes and horses, the **Archaic amphora** and the painted female **figurine of the Mourner**. The museum contains many of the finds from the island's archaeological sites and the excavations are constantly yielding new ones.

ALSO WORTH SEEING
- **The Orthodox cathedral of Ypapandi (Panagia tou Belonia).** The original church was built in 1827 by the Belonia family. After earthquakes toppled it, a new church was erected in its place. The cloisters in the forecourt and the frescoes inside are both of interest.
- **The church of Agios Ioannis,** the Catholic cathedral with its Domo belltower.
- **The Ghizi mansion-Cultural-Exhibition Centre** ⊙ May-September 10:30 am-1:00 pm, 5-8 pm, October 10:30 am-4 pm, tel. (0286) 22244. A beautiful Venetian building, it contains paintings, maps and engravings illustrating moments in the life and history of the Cyclades and Santorini.

SANTORINI

FREE TIME

- **Walk down to Fira port**
  This is the corkscrew road that spirals from Fira to the little cove where the cable car starts from. It takes twenty minutes to descend and half an hour to climb the 600 broad steps cut into the cliff face, with the volcano opposite. If the ascent seems too extreme an exercise, there's always the cable car and the mules.
- **Walk in the medieval district of Frangika.**

❹ AKROTIRI (ARCHAEOLOGICAL SITE)
Ακρωτήρι / Akrotíri

Tel. (0286) 81366

⊙ Summer 8:30 am-5 pm, winter 8:30 am-3pm

The digs conducted by Spyros Marinatos in 1967 confirmed the theory that the eruption of the volcano destroyed the Minoan civilization, and brought to light new evidence related to the life, art and social organization of that period.

At Akrotiri, the archaeologists unearthed an abandoned city with **well-preserved buildings**, **arranged in a discernible pattern** and **linked to a sewage network**, **piazzas** and **flagstone-paved streets**, **multi-storey houses** and **workshops**, **tools** and, fi-

Well-preserved buildings

nally, **works of art** – all from the Minoan era. The discoveries indicate that the inhabitants abandoned their town before the volcano erupted. See the **Sanctuary of the Telchines** and **Building B**, where the exceptional frescoes depicting the **Boxers**, the **Antilopes** and the **Blue Monkeys** were found. The **West House** contained the frescoes of the **Two Fishermen**, the **Priestess**, the **Nile Landscape** and **a miniature frieze of a Naval Campaign**, while the **House of the Ladies** had the **Women and Papyrus** frescoes. Take a look also at **Complex D**, in the rear room (D2) where the fresco **Spring** was found, the three-storey building **Xeste (Villa) 3**, the **Miller's Square** and the **Triangular Square**. Finally, in the **storeroom** you'll see large jars that were found exactly as their owners had left them when they deserted the city. The original frescoes, along with other major finds, were transferred to Athens where they can be seen in the National Archaeological Museum.

❺ EMBORIO (NIMBORIO)
Εμπορειό (Νημπορίο) / Emborió (Nimborió)

In this new village, inside the Venetian castle, there is a beautiful **old**, **listed settlement**, which is slowly being brought back to life. See the medieval lanes, the two **castle portals** still standing in the ruined walls. From here you have a **view** of both sides of the island. The **square tower** on the outskirts of the village protected the inhabitants from enemy attacks.

❻ ANCIENT THERA
Αρχαία Θήρα / Archéa Thíra

Tel. (0286) 22217

⊙ 8 am-2:30 pm, closed on Mondays and holidays*

How to get there: By bus from Kamari.
Guide: Because the site is large, with little or no on-site information regarding the ruins, we propose that you buy the little guidebook or else ask your hotel to find you a guide to show you around.

Theatre

Ancient Thera is located on the west side of Messa Vouno about 350 m above the ancient port of Ia (today's Kamari). The Ptolemies of Egypt used the harbour as a naval base. Messa Vouno belongs to the peaks of Ai-

245

geida, which were not submerged when the Aegean Sea was created. In other words, they pre-date the eruption and collapse of the island's centre.

At the entrance you'll see the chapel of **Agios Stephanos**. Then head towards the ⓖ **sanctuary of Artemidoros of Pergamon** (3rd c. BC), the shrine of the admiral of the Ptolemies, with inscriptions and carvings symbolizing various deities: the eagle-Zeus, the lion-Apollo, the dolphin-Poseidon, the phallus-Priapus. Have a look also at the ⓖ **theatre**, with its Roman additions and view of the sea, the ⓖ **temple of Apollo Karneios** (6th c. BC), and the ⓖ **Gymnasium of the Ephebes**, with baths and an open court for *gymnopaidies*, ritual dances performed by naked youths in honour of the Doric god Apollo Karneios. Some graffiti scratched on the rocks (7th c. BC) mention the names of gods and of admired dancers. One side of the courtyard led into the **grotto of Hermes** and **Herakles**.

Other ruins include the **Quarters of the Ptolemian guard**, the **Agora**, the **temple of Dionysos**, the **Royal Portico** and the **Sacred Way**, the road that started from the southern side of the agora. You'll also see the **Roman baths**, the **Heroon of Thera** near a **chapel dedicated to the Annunciation**, the **sanctuary of Ptolemy III** the **Benefactor** and the **stele of Artemis**.

Near the beginning of the Sacred Way there is a square with an **early-Christian basilica**, occupying the same site as the earlier **sanctuaries of the Egyptian deities** (Isis, Sarapis, Anubis) and of Pythian Apollo.

To the left of the entrance to the archaeological site, a short distance behind the Agora, were the **governor's palace** and the **guards' gymnasium**. Behind them, a small cave has been converted into a chapel of Christ and beyond it, at the entrance to a larger recess, there are **votive niches**, **dedicated to Demeter and Persephone** with a throne cut out of the rock.

OTHER THINGS TO DO

EXCURSION TO THE NEIGHBOURING ISLANDS

By caique from Skala Firon or Ammoudi below Ia (2,500 drs.-5,000 drs.) for a half or whole day. Information from the travel agencies.

Thirassia

Thirassia

The biggest of the islands formed by the volcano. It has some 300 inhabitants and can be reached by caique from Ia and Fira. You'll walk up 250 steps from the little harbour to get to the main hamlet, **Manolas**, which has a magnificent view of the caldera. There is a tunnel-like cave called **Trypiti** in the south part of the island.

Palia Kameni

The islet has hot springs with bluish-yellow water and sulphur.

Nea Kameni

A half hour's walk will get you to the volcano's crater. The ground is extremely hot, so wear appropriate shoes. Hot sulphurous gases billow up from the crater. Between 198 BC and 1950, the volcano has been active 14 times. Here you can enjoy the unique experience of swimming in hot volcanic waters.

WALKS

From Fira to Ia along the ⓖⓖ **spectacular Caldera path** (12 km). Only for the fit, naturally.

PYRGOS-PROFITIS ILIAS

Pyrgos is a village built amphitheatrically on the slopes of Profitis Ilias hill, with a view of the whole island. It has a well-preserved **Venetian fortress**, the Kastelli, a 10th c. church dedicated to the **Dormition of the Virgin** (Theotokaki) and the **monastery of Profitis Ilias** on the hilltop (567 m). Founded in 1711, the monastery was once cenobitic, wealthy and until 1853, off-limits to women. It has an interesting **museum** with precious **ecclesiastical objects** (Cretan icons, codexes, crosses, etc.), a library, and an attractive folk art collection. Pyrgos also has a number of old churches of the 16 and 17th c.: the **Metamorphossis tou Sotiros**, **Ai-Giannis o Theologos**, the semi underground **Agios Nikolaos of Kisira**, **Ta Eisodia tis Theotokou**, **Agios Georgios**, **Taxiarchis Michail**, and others.

SANTORINI

AKROTIRI KOLOUMBOS
Not far from the shore and just 18 m deep is the crater of Santorini's second volcano. It last erupted in 1650, and is visible with goggles and calm sea.

THE NOMIKOS FACTORY
At Akrotiri. More than meets the eye, it's worth taking a little walk around the interior. This old tomato-paste plant still has its original equipment.

BOUTARI WINERY
In the traditional village of **Megalohori**. Take a guided tour of the areas where the wine is produced and taste it as well. Open morning and evening.

HORSE RIDING - MOUNTAIN BIKING
At Kamari, you can rent a horse or go exploring by bike with Lava Trails, tel. (0286) 31165.

BEST BEACHES

Santorini's beaches are not particularly good, since virtually all of them consist of black volcanic sand. As for the sea at the eastern beaches, it is relatively murky, clearer on the south coast. The snorkelling there can be quite exciting.

LEFKI AMMOS
Small but beautiful. Accessible by caique from the shore to the right of Akrotiri, a very agreeable trip. Take a mask and explore the underwater scenery, going around the white islet with the open-ended cave.

KOKKINI AMMOS
(Red) beach near Lefki (white) beach. You can walk there from Akrotiri. There's even a taverna.

VLYHADA
Impressive beach with typical Santorini rock formations protruding from the sea.

PERISSA
The island's best known and most popular. 8 km of black sand with hotels, restaurants, water sports, camping facilities and everything else you can imagine.

PERIVOLOS
Continuation of Perissa. Good and relatively peaceful. Bar and tavernas.

KAMARI
Separated by the peninsula of Messa Vouno from Perissa. Below ancient Thera. Black sand and pebbles. Apt to be crowded.

MONOLITHOS
On the east side of the island. Good beach with facilities for water sports and lots of people.

AMMOUDI
Two hundred steps below Ia, but you can also drive there. Only worth the trouble if you want to combine a dip off the rocks with lunch at one of its tavernas.

BEST HOTELS AND ROOMS

BEST LOCATION

It's worth paying more in order to have a room on the caldera. This is one of the few spots in Greece where a pool is an enormous asset so that you can relax and enjoy the view. The ideal place to stay is Ia, but prices here are higher. On the other hand, Fira attracts larger crowds. For a little peace and quiet, then try Imerovigli or Firostefani. In summer, try to reserve at least two months ahead to get the hotel of your choice. If you intend to take a car, ask if your hotel has parking facilities.

PRICES

The hotel prices mentioned below are the official ones set by the National Tourist Organization for double rooms, at low and high season, with breakfast. Since owners are allowed to modify the prices, always try to negotiate them.

IA

✓✓ PERIVOLAS (A Class)
Tel. (0286) 71308, fax 71309
Open: March-October

Description: The best hotel in Ia. Advantages include parking and not many stairs.
Rooms: 18 rooms with kitchen, bath and veranda.
Special features: Pool with a view of the caldera.
Price: 84,000-98,800 drs.
Value for money: ✱
Credit cards: None

✓✓ CANAVES (A Class)
Tel. (0286) 71453, 71427, 71128, fax 71195
Open: April-October
Description: Recently renovated complex, suspended above the caldera, with many amenities and hospitable staff. 
Rooms: 10 apartments, sleeping from 2 to 6 people. All with their own sitting-room and veranda with view. Equipped with kitchen, telephone and A/C.
Special features: Pool and bar, but most important of all is its car park.
Price: 81,000 drs.
Value for money: ✱✱
Credit cards: Visa

✓ KATIKIES (C Class)
Tel. (0286) 71401, fax 71129
Open: April-November
Description: Complex built in traditional style on the rim of the caldera.
Rooms: 15 apartments with traditional decor, mini bar, radio, telephone and veranda with sea view.
Special features: Stunning pool with a view of the caldera, room service and snack bar.
Price: 53,000-62,000 drs.
Value for money: ✱✱
Credit cards: Visa, Mastercard

✓ IA VILLAGE (A Class)
Tel. (0286) 71114, 71775, fax 71115
Open: 15 April-October

SANTORINI

Description: Complex consisting of semi-basement apartments in traditional architecture with panorama of the caldera. The lady who owns it is very welcoming.
Rooms: 20 apartments with telephone, mini bar and hair dryer.
Special features: Pool with bar, snack-bar and car-hire.
Price: 35,500-43,900 drs. Without breakfast
Value for money: ✔✔✔
Credit cards: Visa

FIROSTEFANI

✔✔✔ TSITOURAS COLLECTION (A Class)
Tel. (0286) 22184, fax 23918
Open: April-October

Description: Lavishly furnished with genuine works of art, large sitting room, bath, telephone and fridge. The decor of each suite was inspired by its name. All of them are very attractive, though they could do with some freshening up.
Rooms: 5 restored suites overlooking the caldera. Each can sleep 2-5 persons.
Special features: Bar and secretarial service.
Price: 120,000-180,000 drs.
Value for money: ✔
Credit cards: Visa, American Express, Mastercard, Diners

✔✔ SUNROCKS (B Class)
Tel. (0286) 23241, fax 23991
Open: April-October
Description: Lovely hotel with helpful staff and marvellous view from the veranda. One of the island's best.
Rooms: 15 rooms with telephone, A/C and view of the volcano.
Special features: Pool, snack bar for breakfast and meals, and hair dryer.
Price: 38,000-76,500 drs.

Value for money: ✔✔✔
Credit cards: American Express, Visa

IMEROVIGLI

✔✔ HELIOTOPOS (A Class)
Tel. (0286) 23670, fax 23672
Open: April-October
Description: Ia in miniature, with traditional troglodyte houses/studios with verandas. All with views of the volcano. It would be perfect if it had a pool.
Rooms: 10 well-maintained apartments with traditional decor, A/C, safe, mini bar and kitchen.
Special features: Bar, dining-room, atrium and library carved out of the rock, and secretarial service for those who want to combine work and pleasure.
Price: 52,000-82,000 drs.
Value for money: ✔✔

Credit cards: Visa, American Express, Diners, Mastercard

✔✔ CHROMATA (A Class)
Tel. (0286) 24850, fax 23278
Open: April-October
Description: Traditional complex of semi-underground apartments with a wonderful view.
Rooms: 17 fully equipped apartments and studios

CYCLADES

for 2-4 people, each with its own courtyard. With hot-cold A/C, balcony, TV, radio, mini bar and kitchen.
Special features: Bar, breakfast room, room service, washing machine, impressive pool built on the brink of the caldera, with a view of the volcano.
Price: 43,000-66,000 drs.
Value for money: ✱
Credit cards: Visa, American Express, Diners, Mastercard

FIRA

✓ ANTITHESIS APARTMENTS (C Class)

Tel. (0286) 25190, 22284, fax 71116
Open: April-October
Description: Delightful small apartment complex with a view, in Fira, near the action. Reserve well ahead. You won't have any service, but it's very good value. Ask for apartment no. 1.
Rooms: 4 apartments with kitchen, bath and veranda.
Special features: Pool with a view of the caldera.
Price: 15,000-33,000 drs.
Value for money: ✱✱✱
Credit cards: Mastercard, Visa

MEGALOHORI

✓✓✓ VEDEMA (Luxury Class)

Tel. (0286) 81796-7, fax 81798
Open: April-October
Description: Especially beautiful, luxurious traditional complex. Santorini's best hotel. Its only drawback is that it has no view of the caldera.
Rooms: 42 small, attractive houses with 1 to 3 bedrooms, equipped with hot-cold A/C, satellite TV, room service, safe, etc.
Special features: Bar and restaurant next to the pool, ✓✓✓ semi-underground restaurant and wine bar, open Jacuzzi pool & bar, art gallery and private beach at Perissa (3 km away – free hotel bus transport). Also pharmacy, laundry service, massage, yoga and gym rooms.
Price: 65,000-177,000 drs.
Value for money: ✱
Credit cards: All

ALTERNATIVES

ASTRA (A Class) Ia, tel. (0286) 23641, fax 24765. **Price:** 42,000-81,000 drs.

FANARI VILLAS (A Class) Ia, tel. (0286) 71008, 71147. **Price:** 60,000-69,000 drs.

LAOKASTI VILLAS (B Class) Ia, tel. (0286) 71343. **Price:** 25,000-50,000 drs.

MUSEUM HOTEL Ia, tel. (0286) 71515, fax 71516. **Price:** 26,000-40,000 drs.

HONEYMOON VILLAS (C Class) Firostefani, tel. (0286) 22895, 23891, fax 23059 **Price:** 39,000-96,000 drs.

GALINI (C Class) Firostefani, tel. (0286) 22095, fax 23097. **Price:** 25,000-30,000 drs.

SANTORINI PALACE (A Class) Fira, tel. (0286) 23705, fax 23705 **Price:** 27,000-47,000 drs.

ARESSANA (B Class) Fira, tel. (0286) 23900-1, fax 23902. **Price:** 26,000-55,000 drs

MELINA HOTEL (B Class) Fira, tel. (0286) 22421, fax 23835. **Price:** 18,000-33,000 drs.

DAEDALUS (C Class) Fira, tel. (0286) 22834, fax 22818. **Price:** 25,600-38,000 drs.

ENIGMA Fira, tel. (0286) 24024, fax 24023 **Price:** 35,000-40,000 drs.

VEGGERA Perissa, tel. (0286) 82060-2, fax 82608. **Price:** 24,000-42,000 drs.

BEST RESTAURANTS & TAVERNAS

IA

✓✓ 1800

Tel. (0286) 71485
In a restored neo-classical mansion, one of the best in Santorini. Lovely setting and good Mediterranean cuisine.
Price: €€€

SANTORINI

✓✓ KOUKOUMAVLOS
Tel. (0286) 23807
Fine international dishes in beautiful surroundings, with a pleasant atmosphere. Also at Fira at the former **Alexandria**. Price: €€€

FIRA
✓✓ ARCHIPELAGOS
Tel. (0286) 22673
Extraordinary casseroles and sweets. A good spot for lunch. Price: €€

Archipelagos

✓ SPHINX
Tel. (0286) 23823
Good food with a superb view. Try the home-made pasta. Price: €€€

SELINI
Tel. (0286) 22249
Bar-restaurant, with good traditional cuisine. Price: €€

FIROSTEFANI
✓ VANILIA
Tel. (0286) 25631
Bar-restaurant with Greek specialities in a traditional building next to a windmill. Price: €

✓ IL CANTUCCIO
Tel. (0286) 22082
Restaurant with good Italian cuisine. Price: €

Il Cantuccio

AKTAION
Tel. (0286) 22336
The oldest restaurant on Santorini. Excellent Greek and local specialities in a room full of paintings (by the owner). Price: €

MONOLITHOS
✓✓ DOMATA
Tel. (0286) 32069
At Agia Paraskevi, near the airport.
One of the finest restaurants on the island, with an imaginative menu. Check first because we heard it may close down. Price: €€€

MEGALOHORI
✓✓✓ VEDEMA RESTAURANT
In the Vedema Hotel, tel. (0286) 81796

Whether or not you're a guest at this hotel, you will certainly appreciate the delicious food served in its restaurant, situated in 300-year-old semi-basement chambers. This is where to satisfy your craving for Beluga. Price: €€€

🍸 BEST ENTERTAINMENT

The lively night-scene is confined to Fira. You'll see a lot of bar-hopping here, people dipping in and out of spots to get a taste of them all. Why not? You could be doing that, too.
In **Fira**, you'll have a good time at **Kyra Thyra**, the island's oldest nightclub with its murals, good music and distinctive atmosphere. **Cavana** is a popular semi-underground wine bar with a Greek flair for fun, while **Casablanca** has classical music for the more discerning. **Koo Club** offers both Greek and foreign music and dancing in a raised cage; the interior is full of the young crowd going wild, the terrace is quieter.
Enigma is one of the island's historic hang-outs, with

Kastro

attractive corners for every age group, and both Greek and foreign music. **Kaviros** is the place for breakfast, coffee, a drink and pancakes at any hour of the day. Finally, don't forget **Franco's**, tel. (0286) 22881 a fantastically situated bar on the caldera, where you can listen to classical music while watching the sun go down. In Ia the **Kastro**, tel. (0286) 71045, is the in spot for a drink and the most spectacular sunset. But go early to be sure of finding a table.

i TIPS AND INFORMATION

HOW TO GET THERE

- By air from Athens west airport to Santorini with Olympic Airways (18,000 drs.), tel. (01) 9363363. From Thessaloniki's Makedonia airport in summer only, with Olympic Airways (27,000 drs.), tel. (031) 228 880.
- By Dolphin Sea Lines high-speed boat from Rafina in 6 hrs, in summer only (8,000 drs.), Rafina Agency, tel. (094) 25100.
- By ferry from Piraeus in 9 hrs (5,400 drs.), Piraeus Port Authority, tel. (01) 4226000. From Thessaloniki in 17 hrs (9,400 drs.), Thessaloniki Port Authority, tel. (031) 531504.

CONNECTIONS

- By air from Santorini with Olympic Airways to Mykonos, Rhodes, Heraklio, tel. (0286) 22493.
- By Dolphin Sea Lines high-speed boat to Ios, Mykonos, Naxos, Paros, Syros, Tinos. Santorini agency, tel. (0286) 22127. By Speed Lines high-speed boat to Amorgos, Anafi, Ios, Iraklia, Pano Koufonissi, Schinoussa, Mykonos, Naxos, Paros, Sikinos, Tinos, Folegandros. Santorini Agency, tel. (0286) 22220.
- By ferry to Ios, Paros, Mykonos, Anafi, Naxos, Sikinos, Kimolos, Kythnos, Milos, Serifos, Syros, Tinos, Folegandros, Astypalaia, Karpathos, Diafani (Karpathos), Kassos, Rhodes, Halki, Heraklio, Skiathos, Volos. And in summer to Skyros. Santorini Agency, tel. (0286) 22239.

BEST TIPS

HOW TO GET AROUND: The ideal way to see the island is to rent a car (15,000 drs. after some haggling). Otherwise, we suggest you rent a motorbike, though the narrow roads make this option a bit risky. Finally, there are local buses making the rounds every hour.
From Fira, a taxi should cost from 500 drs. to Karterados or Imerovigli and up to 2,000 drs. to Perissa. The bus fares vary from 150 to 450 drs., while a donkey ride will cost you 750 drs.

BEST SEASON: From Easter to late October. But don't even think of going there in July and August.

BEST LOCAL FOOD: If you like **fava** (split yellow pea puree), the local product is very good. If you happen upon any **Visanto** sweet wine, do try it. The local table wines are also excellent. Among the island specialities, the tomato **keftedes** (fritters made with the extremely tasty small tomatoes) and **skordomakarona**, spaghetti with garlic, are delicious.

TRAVEL AGENTS

For excursions, tickets and hotel bookings you can contact the following travel agents:
Nomikos Travel, Fira, tel. (0286) 23660
Kamari Tours, Fira, tel. (0286) 22666
The Best of Cyclades, Fira, tel. (0286) 23512, 22622

USEFUL TELEPHONE NUMBERS

SANTORINI .... (0286)	First Aid 71227
Thera Community Office 22231	**Kamari Community Office** 31451
Police 22649	First Aid 31175
First Aid 23123	**Emborio Community Office** 81233
Ia Community Office 71228	First Aid 81222

CRETE

CRETE

BEST's OPINION

If you escape from the frenetic mass tourism on the north coast of the island and closely follow *BEST's* advice, you will be delighted with the landscape and the people of Crete. And, naturally, lovers of ancient sites will have no complaints exploring the important ruins that tell us so much (and so little) about the fascinating Minoan civilization, and which abound in many parts of Crete. The beaches in southern and eastern Crete cannot fail to please from April through October. The Best of the Best of this great island are the old town of Chania, the Minoan palace of Knossos, the Samaria Gorge and the beaches at Elafonissos and Falassarna in western Crete.

IN BRIEF

Located in a particularly strategic position, on the southern tip of Europe, Crete with its 540,000 inhabitants is Greece's largest island. It is divided geographically and administratively into the prefectures of **Heraklion**, **Lassithi**, **Rethymno** and **Chania**. Lapped by the waves of the Cretan and Libyan seas, its coastline measures 1,046 km in length. The long mountain range that splits it down the middle consists of the stark, magnificent **White Mountains**, **Ida** (**Psiloriti**) and **Dikti**. Situated in a seismic zone, it has a warm Mediterranean climate with mild winters on the coast and snow in the mountains. Its fertile hills and valleys are covered with olive, fig, almond, pear, carob, citrus, chestnut, cedar, plane and palm trees, as well as some 2,000 species of plants, of which 131 are indigenous to Crete and one, the Kastrios flower, grows only there and nowhere else.

Crete is a musical island with many dances, like the **syrtos**, **pendozali**, and **sousta**; its chief instrument is the three-string Cretan lyre and its people are known for their **mantinades**, rhymes, for every occasion. Though you will see no women in national costume, the older men still wear their baggy breeches, waistcoat, tasselled kerchief and high boots. Some of the culinary specialities are **savoury cheese pies** baked or fried in a wide variety of shapes, **noodles**, **snails** cooked with rosemary and vinegar, **pork chitterlings**, sweet cheese pies called **kallitsounia**, pancakes with honey known as **sfakian pie** and delicate pastry twirls called **xerotigana**, which are served at most weddings. The locals are fond of downing thimble-sized glasses of fiery **raki**, and the island also has some excellent wines.

Sfakian pie and raki

HISTORY

Cresus, the son of Zeus and legendary ruler of the first inhabitants, the **Eteocretans**, gave his name to the island, which was first settled around 7000 BC, in the **neolithic era**.

The **Minoan civilization** began to develop around 3000 BC. The last period of the **Venetian occupation** was a shining example of Cretan-Venetian cooperation on all levels, but the **Turkish rule** that followed the siege of Candia plunged the island into a period of poverty and rebellion. In **1898**, Crete was declared independent, with **Prince George** of Greece appointed as High Commissioner. In **1905**, **Eleftherios Venizelos** incited an uprising at **Therissos**, opening the door to union with Greece, which was finally realized in **1913**. In **1941**, the Cretans, keeping to their militant traditions, mounted a fierce resistance to the Germans, in the famous **Battle of Crete**.

Eleftherios Venizelos

WESTERN CRETE

ᵒᵒᵒ Chania   ᵒᵒᵒ Samaria Gorge
ᵒᵒᵒ Elafonissos   ᵒᵒᵒ Falassarna

WHY AMONG THE BEST

Mainly because of the Old Town of Chania with its well preserved mansions, the atmosphere of its narrow, winding streets, the picturesque port and the restaurants. Also because of the famous Samaria gorge and the exotic beaches of Falassarna and Elafonissos.

CRETE

WESTERN CRETE 20

CRETE

BEST's OPINION

The prefecture of Chania has to a great extent preserved its authenticity, with a wealth of natural beauty. It is located next to the equally interesting prefecture of Rethymno. If you dream of reasonably-priced holidays with satisfactory facilities, in any season of the year, you will be thrilled by this excursion, which is one of the island's most interesting. However, you should be aware that all the charm of Chania is concentrated in the Old Town (Palia Poli). The new one has been spoilt by excessive use of cement, as is the case in most other Greek cities.

BEST SIGHTS: STEP BY STEP

❶ CHANIA
Χανιά / Haniá

The old port

Located in a bay between the Akrotiri and Onyha peninsulas, it is the capital of Chania prefecture, with 50,000 inhabitants, and is Crete's most beautiful city.
Comprising new and old towns, it attracts tourists from all over the world.

HISTORY

Chania was built on the site of the ancient city of Kydonia, which took its name from Kydon, son of Hermes and Akakallis, the daughter of King Minos. There is evidence of life in the region from as far back as the Neolithic era, and it is known that the city was inhabited during all the periods of Minoan civilization. Up to the 1st c. BC, when it was destroyed and deserted, the city was of great historical importance.
Its traces appear once again in the early 9th c., during Arab rule, when mention is made of the city of Rabd-el-Job, city of cheese, which the Cretans were exporting even then.
In 1205, the Venetians built a city on this site, called Canea, the core of which was composed of the mansions of the first colonists and which developed into western Crete's most important commercial centre. The walls were built in 1252, followed by Kastelli in the 16th c., which was the headquarters of the Venetian guard.
During the last century of Venetian rule, the city flourished economically and intellectually. In 1645, after a two-month siege, it surrendered to the Turks. It became the island's capital city in 1850 and the residence of the general military commander. The Ottomans burnt and looted it, culminating in the three-day massacre in January 1897.
The Greek flag was raised once and for all at Firkas port on December 1, 1913, when Crete was united with the rest of Greece.

WHAT TO SEE

ⓖ ⓖ ⓖ THE OLD TOWN
Παλιά πόλη / Paliá Póli

An extensive self-contained area, with outstanding Venetian buildings, which also incorporate elements of subsequent Turkish interventions. The labyrinthine streets, the arches, the arcades, the houses and the palaces will take you on a journey through time.

WESTERN CRETE 20

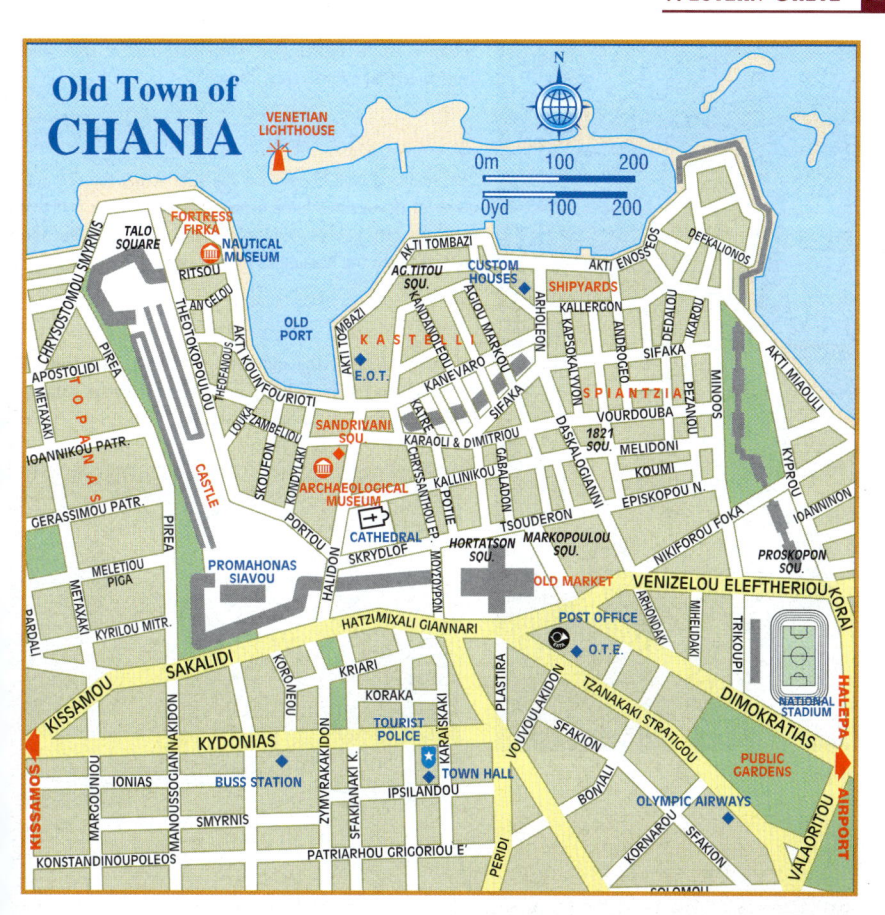

Old Town of CHANIA

[Map of Old Town of Chania]

🎯🎯 Archaeological Museum

25 Halidon St., tel. (0821) 90334

🕐 *8 am-4:30 pm, closed on Mondays and holidays**

Housed in the Venetian church of San Francesco, which is one of the most impressive buildings in the old town.

In the east wing, you will see vases, figurines, jewellery and seals, which were funeral gifts found in necropolises, from post-Neolithic to post-Minoan times. Of special interest is the **collection of Linear A and B tablets**.

In the museum's west wing, on display are funeral gifts from the Geometric period, a section of frieze from the Archaic period, as well as finds from the zenith of Hellenistic times, interesting sculptures from the Asklepeion at Lissos and Roman artefacts.

🎯 The Spiantzia Quarter (Plaza)

The Turkish quarter north-east of the city, with the church of **Agios Nikolaos**, which was turned into a mosque by the Sultan Ibrahim, during the Turkish occupation.

🎯 The Topanas Quarter

The western quarter, with the finest Venetian mansions. Christian merchants lived here during Turkish rule, and the major world powers established their consulates in this district. Head north, as far as the harbour

CRETE

entrance, to the **Firkas** fort, which was built in 1629 and used as a prison for Cretan insurgents.

ⓖ Castle (The Fort)

The medieval wall is open on the side facing the sea and many of its sections have been used for exterior walls of contemporary houses. Now partly ruined, it encircles the old town with the Kastelli as its centre.

ⓖ Shipyards (Neória)

At the harbour of the old town. Venetian 14th-16th c. constructions for shipbuilding or repair of Venetian galleys. Nine of the original 25 have survived.

Mosque

Neoria

ⓖ Old Market

The public market, built on the Marseilles model.

ⓖ Venetian lighthouse

Located at the port entrance, it was originally built by the Arabs and restored by the Egyptians in the 19th c.

Kastelli Quarter

On the eastern side of the port. The Venetian commander's palace and the Pasha's lodgings.

Sandrivani Square

Today's **Eleftherios Venizelos Square**, formed during Venetian times, was a meeting-place for intellectuals in the early 20th c.

ⓖ PUBLIC GARDENS (NEW TOWN)

In 1870, Reouf Pasha created the gardens, designed on European models.

The Old Town

HALEPA QUARTER (NEW TOWN)

In the eastern part of Chania and along Eleftherios Venizelos Square, known for its famous neo-classical mansions, hotels and magnificent villas.

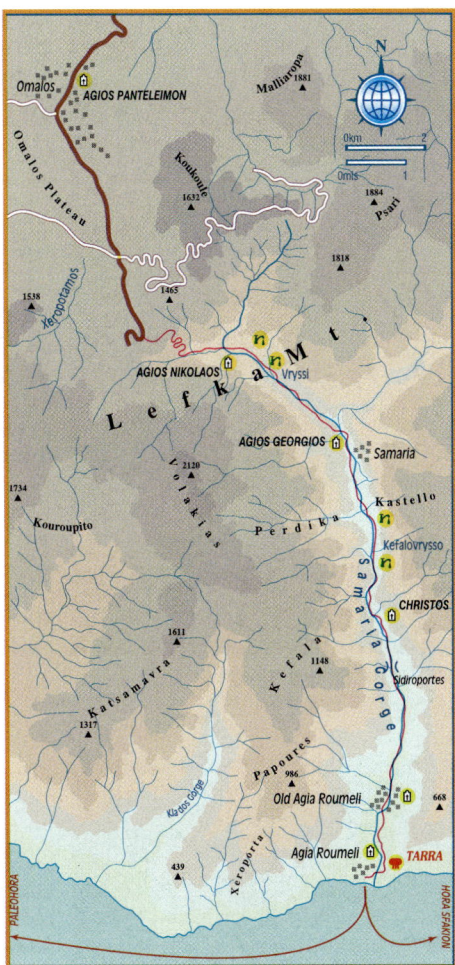

WESTERN CRETE   20

② SAMARIA GORGE
Φαράγγι Σαμαριάς / Farángi Samariás

If you're in good physical shape, don't miss the opportunity to walk through the gorge. It will be an unforgettable experience. However, arm yourself with suitable shoes, thick socks and a canteen. The gorge is 18 km long and ranges in width from 3 to 300 m. Its entrance is at Omalo. Since 1962, it has been declared a national park, and can only be visited between May and October when the river is low. It is one of the most beautiful gorges in Europe. A magnificent natural setting, varying from lush greenery to sheer, imposing rock walls. The walk through takes about 5-7 hrs. The descent into the gorge is by a narrow path called Xyloskala (Wooden Staircase), 1,200 m high. Further down, the narrowest point of the gorge is at the "Tris Portes". You'll emerge at the Agia Roumeli beach, where there are several tavernas. Water can be found at four points during the walk, and in mid-route you'll come across the abandoned village of Samaria, with a police station, a pharmacy, telephone, helidrome and mules for transport to the exit if necessary. If you see the Cretan wild goats, you'll be very lucky (usually everyone has seen them except you!). Lighting fires, staying overnight, smoking, taking plants and hunting are prohibited. From Agia Roumeli, at the exit of the gorge, you can go by boat to Hora Sfakion, Sougia or Palaiohora.

Information
Chania Forestry Service, tel. (0821) 92287
"METAPODIA", tel. (0821) 22701, 22855
Greek Mountaineering Club of Aharnon, tel. (01) 2461528
Greek Mountaineering Club of Chania, tel. (0821) 44677
Chania Ski and Mountaineering Club, tel. (0821) 76520

③ THERISSOS GORGE
Φαράγγι του Θέρισου / Farángi tou Thérissou

It is considered to be a miniature of the Samaria gorge, but you can go through it by car. Travel next to the small river, through thick vegetation with olive and plane trees. At many points, the

Therissos gorge

rock walls rise sheer and imposing. You emerge at Therissos, where you can have a meal at the traditional **Andartis** taverna, tel. (0821) 67551.

❹ AGIA TRIADA TSANGAROLON MONASTERY
Αγία Τριάδα Τσαγκαρόλων / Αγία Triáda Tsangarólon

🕐 *From sunrise to 1 pm and from 5 pm to sunset*

Construction of this impressive monastery, with the splendid tree-lined entrance, first began in 1612 and was completed in 1843, after the Turkish conquest. Its founders were probably the brothers Laurentios and Ieremias, members of the Orthodox Venetian Tsangarolo family. The magnificent facade of the Byzantine church, dedicated to the Holy Trinity, with its double Greek-Roman columns, hints at Renaissance influences. The church is partially covered with frescoes and has a tall bell-tower built in 1864.

The monastery is surrounded by an olive grove and is considered one of the most beautiful on the island.

Agia Triada Tsangarolon Monastery

❺ GOUVERNETO MONASTERY (GDERNETO)
Μονή Γουβερνέτου / Moní Gouvernétou

Crossing a small gorge, you'll arrive at the plateau on which the monastery is situated. Probably built in the early 16th c., its chapel is dedicated to the Lady of the Angels, the Virgin Mary.

The imposing four-sided fort-like wall, with square towers at the corners, protected it from enemy invaders.

❻ AGIOS IOANNIS MONASTERY
Μονή Αγίου Ιωάννη / Moní Ayíou Ioánni

Crete's oldest monastery, it was probably built in the 6th or 7th c. by Saint John (Ioannis) the Hermit, who led an ascetic life in the area. The church is chiselled into the rock of the cave, with only its west side built with stone. It can be reached by a narrow path, north of the Gouverneto monastery, after a 30-min walk.

OTHER THINGS TO DO

GIORGOS PETROULAKIS' RIDING CLUB
Akrotiri
Tel. (0821) 39366
Ponies are available for children. Accomplished riders can participate in excursions and visits to monasteries.

LIMNOUPOLI (WATERPARK)
Varypetro, Chania
Tel. (0821) 33224, 33246, 28465
Waterslides, swimming pools, miniature train, bar, restaurant, scuba diving, mountaineering and whatever else your heart desires, in this refreshing 100,000 sq. m park.

WESTERN CRETE

BEST BEACHES

☂☂☂ ELAFONISSI

Setting out from Chania, enjoy the wonderful 2 1/2-hour drive by car. Be sure to visit the **Chryssoskalitissa monastery**, mainly for its view. When you reach this endless sandy beach – which reminds one of a desert – don't be disappointed if you see crowds and tacky tavernas. Wade through the shallows for another 10 min to the nearby island and choose one of the small coves you'll find there. Those furthest away are isolated even in August at the height of the tourist season.

☂☂☂ FALASSARNA

You'll be impressed by this exotic sandy beach, which is also ideal for children. Go right, towards the rocks nestled in the sand, which create natural divisions for privacy. There are several tavernas above the beach. The ruins of Ancient Falassarna, which are not particularly interesting, are located nearby.

☂☂ GRAMVOUSSA

You arrive by sea, with a private or rented boat from Chania, or on a tour boat from Kastelli. A sandy beach with a Frankish fortress below taken by the Turks in 1692. Snorklers may discover old earthenware jars from shipwrecks. Be sure to take food and water with you. Ballos, just next door, is an exceptional beach.

☂☂ SOUGIA

A picturesque beach with pebbles and deep water. It's possible to rent a room in the village. Discover the section of beach east of the village, after the large rock, and enjoy one of the privileges of Adam and Eve, swimming nude in the crystal-clear deep waters. Choose one of the pleasant village tavernas.

☂☂ AGIOS PAVLOS

Sapphire-blue waters, golden sand and a small church beside the waves. You can come from Paleohora, Sougia and Agia Roumeli by private or hired boat.

☂ PLATANIAS

An infinite stretch of beach, near the city of Chania, but lots of people. There are nearby tavernas.

☂ STAVROS

A small beach at Akrotiri, popular and prettier than Platanias. Meals are available at the village tavernas.

BEST HOTELS AND ROOMS

BEST LOCATION

Without doubt, the best hotel location is the Old Town. However, if you have time and means of transport, the traditional hamlet of **Milia** is worth considering, for a return to the roots.

PRICES

The hotel prices mentioned below are the official ones, set by the National Tourist Organization for double rooms, at low and high season, with breakfast. Since owners are allowed to modify prices, always try to negotiate them.

✓✓✓ CASA DELFINO (B Class)

9 Theofanous St., Old Town
Tel. *(0821) 87400, 93098, fax 96500*
Open: All year round
Description: Restored Venetian-style villa, which belonged to a wealthy Italian and was built in the 17th c. Aristocratic atmosphere, wonderful esthetics, furnishings and interior design.

Rooms: 16 suites, each with A/C, bath, TV, music, telephone, kitchenette and bar. Fax and computer modem facilities. Only the **Nautilus** suite has a view of the harbour.
Special features: Bar and interior courtyard.
Price: 28,000-35,000 drs.
Value for money: ✽✽✽
Credit cards: All except Diners

✓✓ VILLA ANDROMEDA (B Class)

150 Eleftheriou Venizelou St., Halepa
Tel. *(0821) 28300, 28301, fax 28303*
Open: All year round
Description: Neo-classical 1870 mansion, with a view of the sea and the city of Chania. Painted ceilings, marble floors and staircases, carefully selected pieces which comprise the furnishings and the interior decoration. Noisy, because of proximity to street.
Rooms: 8 self-contained suites, each with bath, lounge, kitchenette, mini-bar, TV, telephone and A/C.
Special features: Parking and garden with swimming pool.
Price: 31,000-46,000 drs.
Value for money: ✽✽
Credit cards: Visa, Mastercard, Eurocard, American Express

✓ CASA LEONE (B Class)

1st side-street off 18 Theotokopoulou St., Akti Koundouriotou, Venetian port, Old Town
Tel./fax *(0821) 76762, 56372, (094) 954881*

Western Crete

Open: All year round
Description: Built approximately 600 years ago and restored meticulously to regain its former Venetian splendour.
Rooms: 8 rooms, four of them with a view of the port and all of them with bath and A/C T.V and mini bar. Noisy, due to proximity to the port.
Special features: Courtyard with fountain and a spacious room for drinks and coffee.
Price: 27,000-39,000 drs.
Value for money: ✹✹
Credit cards: Visa, Mastercard

✓ DOMA (B Class)

124 Eleftheriou Venizelou St., Halepa
Tel. (0821) 51772, 51773, fax 41578
Open: March-October
Description: Neo-classical mansion converted into a hotel, with an old-world atmosphere, although it's furnishings and decoration are rather overdone. Noisy, because of proximity to street.
Rooms: 29 rooms, each with bathroom and telephone.
Special features: Sea view and attractive dining-room on the top floor.
Price: 30,000 drs. at all seasons
Value for money: ✹✹
Credit cards: Visa, American Express, Mastercard

✓ AMPHORA (A Class)

2nd sidestreet off 20 Theotokopoulou St. and 49 Koundouriotou St., Venetian port, Old Town
Tel./fax (0821) 93224, 93226
Open: All year round
Description: Built around 1300, its architecture combines Venetian with Turkish elements. It has been beautifully renovated. With a view of the sea from the terrace, romantic furnishings and relaxing environment. Noise from the port.
Rooms: 21 rooms, each with bathroom, heating and, in some, kitchen.
Special features: Restaurant where Cretan cuisine is served, and roof garden.
Price: 23,900-29,000 drs.
Value for money: ✹✹✹
Credit cards: All except American Express and Diners

✓ PORTO VENEZZIANO (B Class)

Venetian port, Old Town
Tel. (0821) 27100, fax 27105
Open: All year round
Description: Impersonal post-war building renovated in modern style, with a wonderful view, well-tended garden and good service.
Rooms: 51 rooms with A/C, telephone and TV. Ask for a room with a view.
Special features: Bar, cafe, parking.
Price: 31,500-37,000 drs.
Value for money: ✹✹
Credit cards: All

✓ NOSTOS (B Class)

42-46 Zambeliou St., Venetian port, Old Town
Tel. (0821) 94743, fax 94740
Description: Built in 1400, it was a church until 1500, and subsequently the palace of a Venetian aristocrat up to Turkish rule. The colour blue is prevalent. Warm, friendly atmosphere. It has a tiny traditional Greek kafeneio.
Rooms: 12 rooms, each with kitchenette, shower, telephone. Numbers 1 and 3 have a view of the port.
Special features: Bar and roof garden.
Price: 18,850-25,100 drs.
Value for money: ✹✹
Credit cards: Visa, Mastercard

Nostos

OUTSIDE CHANIA

✓ MILIA

Vlatos Kissamou
Tel. (0822) 51569
Open: All year round
Description: Traditional settlement built among the ruins of an old farming village, in a valley with a creek and perennial chestnut trees.
The plain dwellings are constructed of stone, wood and tiles, and furnished with traditional simplicity. Cast-iron stoves, boilers with wood for hot water, and solar systems replace electricity.
It's possible to participate in activities on the estate and in cultivating the crops. Ask for information about the 10 walking tours you can take there.
Rooms: The 14 small dwellings can accommodate 25 people.
Special features: Taverna with fireplace in refectory decor, for breakfast and meals.
Price: 14,000-17,000 drs.
Value for money: ✹✹
Credit cards: None

✓ CRETA PARADISE BEACH
(A Class)

Gerani
Tel. (0821) 61315, fax 61134
Open: All year round
Description: Splendidly organized hotel complex for a stay outside the city, with private beach. Located about 10 min west of Chania, its architecture is mainly traditional. The gardens and beach have been awarded the "Gold Star" and the "Blue Flag" respectively. Main buildings and bungalows. 
Rooms: 186 rooms, with veranda or balcony, A/C, central heating, bath, telephone, music, safe, TV, refrigerator.
Special features: 2 restaurants, 2 bars, shops, 2 swimming pools, gym, tennis court, kids' club, satellite TV, chapel, small farm and 4 conference halls.
Price: 36,000-66,000 drs.
Value for money: ✹✹
Credit cards: All

ALTERNATIVES

DOMENIKO (B Class)
71 Zambeliou St., Old Town, tel. (0821) 75647.
Price: 11,000-13,000 drs.

VRANAS STUDIOS
Agion Deka and Kalinikou Sarpaki Sts., Mitropoleos Sq., Old Town, tel./fax (0821) 58618, 43788, 50889.
Price: 9,200-17,250 drs. without breakfast

WESTERN CRETE 20

BEST RESTAURANTS & TAVERNAS

✓✓ ELA
47 Kondylaki St., Old Town
Tel. (0821) 74128

In the ruins of a Venetian house, a setting of great appeal. Touristic, but with interesting Cretan specialities. **Price:** €€

✓✓ DINOS
3 Akti Enoseos St., Venetian port, Old Town
Tel. (0821) 41865
One of the city's oldest fish tavernas, which has been open since 1945 and is famous for its fresh and excellently cooked fish. Order a variety of fish for two.
Open for lunch and dinner. **Price:** €€

✓✓ THALASSINO AGERI
35 Vivilaki St., at the Halepa tannery
Tel. (0821) 56672, 51136

High-class fish taverna with finest quality fish. In summer, book early for a table close to the sea.
Price: €€€

✓ THOLOS
36 Agion Deka St., Old Town
Tel. (0821) 46725
A charming multi-level place set in stone ruins. Not very adventurous from a gastronomic point of view.
Price: €€

✓ TAMAM
49 Zambeliou St., Old Town, tel. (0821) 96080
Originally a Turkish bath. Very good cuisine and pleasant service. Cretan specialities. Preferable in winter, but be sure to book a table. Open all year round for lunch and dinner. **Price:** €€

✓ KARNAGIO
8 Katehaki Sq., Venetian port, Old Town
Tel. (0821) 53366, 45519

Probably the best taverna in relation to value for money. Delicious well-cooked food, smiling waiters, simple interior decoration and a good reputation. Open for lunch and dinner. **Price:** €

✓ BIGAJA
Galatas
Tel. (0821) 32780
Four km from the city of Chania, at Galata, this Turkish restaurant is a pleasant surprise with the exceptionally fine quality of its cuisine and its marvellous dishes. Its appearance discourages only those who do not know it. **Price:** €

PEINALEON
86 Eleftheriou Venizelou St., Chania (new town)
Tel. (0821) 40325
Classically decorated restaurant, which attracts the smart set and offers Greek and Cretan cuisine.
Price: €€€

BEST ENTERTAINMENT

Chania offers numerous opportunities for quality entertainment. Most cafes, bars and nightclubs are in the Old Town. Amongst them, we selected **Gonia ton Angelon** for those who prefer soft music, the **Street Club** for fans of African music, **Mythos** for rockers, **Skala** for rebetika music with a good band and, of course, **Synagogi**, situated in 14th c. ruins which once housed Jewish baths and was also a fortress at one time. This venue has the timeless historic architectural appeal of the days before nightclubs.

It's worth enjoying your coffee or drink at the **Tzamia-Krystalla** art gallery, 35 Skalidi St., which also has a coffee bar. For snacks and coffee Constantinople-style, plus a hookah, go to the **Constantinoupoli**. You'll find the bigger clubs at Platania, including **Mylos**, which was a watermill in 1830, **Neromylos**, with palm trees, pool, sea view and iced coffee, and **Patatrak**, which plays both foreign and Greek music day and night.

Synagogi

TIPS AND INFORMATION

HOW TO GET THERE

- By air from Athens west airport with Olympic Airways (16,500 drs.), tel. (01) 9363363, Air Greece, tel. (01) 3255011, east airport, or with Air Manos, tel. (01) 3233562-4 daily flights. Also by air from Thessaloniki with Olympic Airways (26,500 drs.), tel. (031) 260121, or Air Greece, tel. (031) 244340.
- By ferry from Piraeus to Souda, in 10 hrs (from 4,350 drs.), Piraeus Port Authority, tel. (01) 4226000.
- For organized tours contact Trekking Hellas, tel. (01) 3310323.

CONNECTIONS

- By ferry from Kastelli Kissamou to Gythio, Neapoli and Kythera, tel. (0822) 22024.
- By intercity bus to Rethymno and Heraklio, KTEL, tel. (0821) 93052.

BEST TIPS

HOW TO GET AROUND: By car or taxi. On foot in the Old Town. To the islets, by private vessel, or regular excursion boats which have daily schedules.

BEST SEASON: All year round, but avoid August crowds.

BEST BUYS: At the boot-makers in the Old Town, buy leather goods and traditional Cretan boots, the famous **stivania**. In Chania, you'll discover elegant shops, with jewellery, hand-made kilims, rugs and blown-glass items.

USEFUL TELEPHONE NUMBERS

CHANIA	(0821)	Tourist Bureau	92943, 92624
Town Hall	97777	Port Authority	28388
Tourist Police	73333	Hospital	27000, 27006-9
Tourist Office	59990	Taxis	98700, 98701, 98770

Vamos

Vamos
Frangokastello Hora Sfakion

WHY AMONG THE BEST

Because Vamos is ideally situated in Crete, offering relaxation far from the tourist crowds; after you've completed your cultural outings. But mainly because when staying in this traditional, restored village of stone houses you'll feel that you're returning to a fascinating past.

CRETE

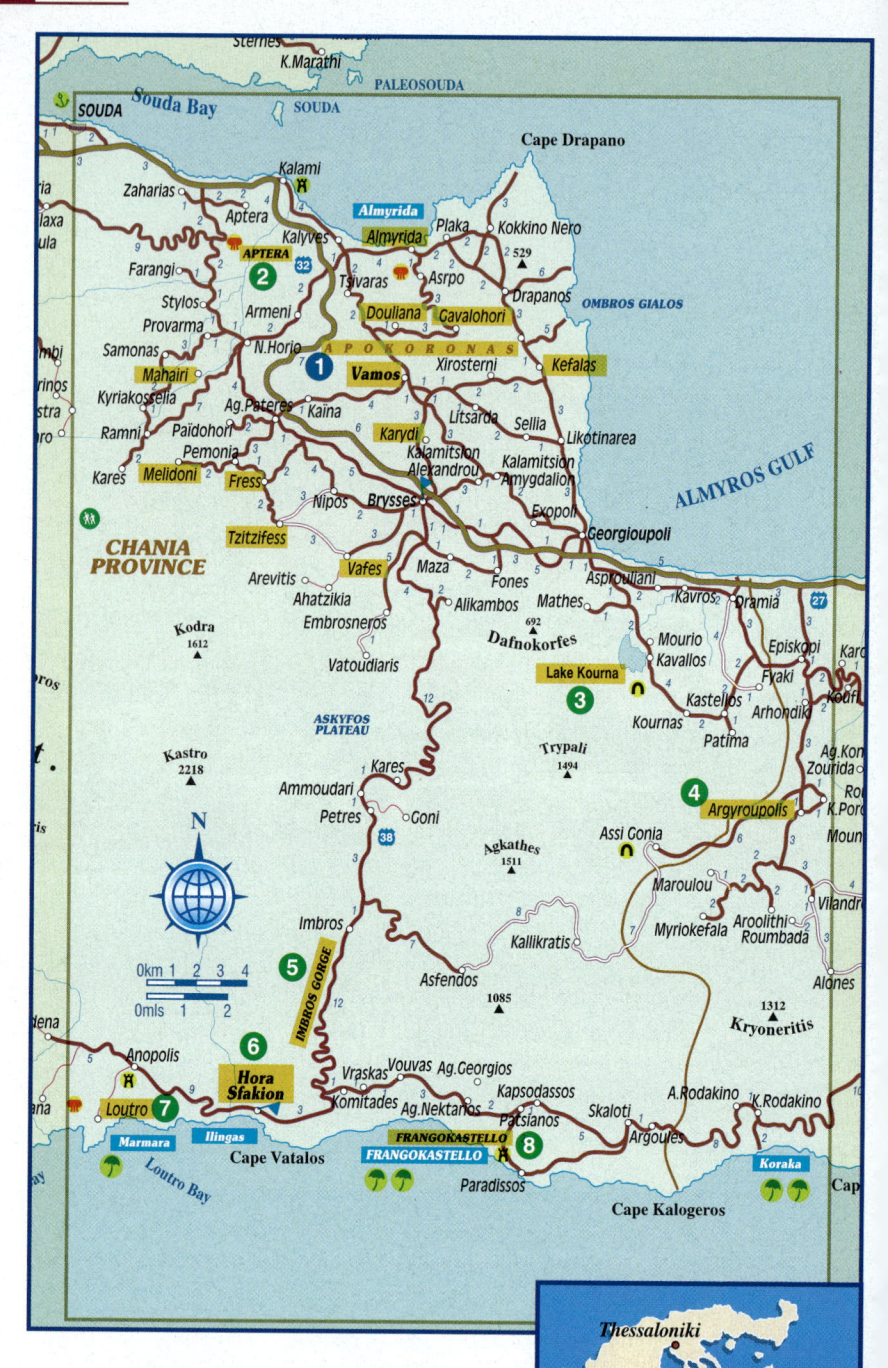

BEST's OPINION

When selecting this trip to Vamos, make sure you appreciate its particularities, because it may appear poorer than others in terms of sightseeing. However, you will find it rich in precious and timeless values, now largely forgotten.

BEST SIGHTS: STEP BY STEP

❶ APOKORONAS
Αποκόρωνας / Apokóronas

VAMOS / Βάμος / Vámos

The Apokoronas provincial capital has 650 inhabitants and was first settled in the mid-8th c.
Today, with sensitivity and effort, the inhabitants have managed to retain the village's traditional atmosphere while bringing it back to life.
Its narrow paved streets, plane trees, park, squares, picturesque cafes and stone houses are exceptionally charming and nostalgically evocative.

KARYDI - METOHI AGIOU GEORGIOU
Καρύδι - Μετόχι Αγίου Γεωργίου /
Karídi - Metóhi Ayíou Georgíou

7 am-3 pm and 4-7 pm, Sundays 4-7 pm, Wednesdays 3-7 pm

In the old village of Karydi, you'll find a group of buildings featuring unique local folk architecture, with Venetian influences: the **Metohi Agiou Georgiou**, a functioning monastery. There is an air of lost splendour about the ruins of the buildings. Of particular interest is the old **olive press** with thirteen arches.

Old olive press

KEFALAS / Κεφαλάς / Kefalás

As you stroll through the alleyways have a look at the numerous old front-doors which have been preserved, the pretty houses and the 16th c. **Timios Stavros church**. One of the village's traditional kafenions would be a good place for a coffee break.

ALMYRIDA / Αλμυρίδα / Almirída

Small, coastal village, frequented by tourists. See the ruins of an Early Christian basilica, of the 5th or 6th c., at the entrance to the village. With a transverse aisle and distinctive architectural features such as the Corinthian capitals and parapet, it is particularly interesting because of its well-preserved mosaic floor, with designs including crosses, stars, geometric shapes, wheels, rosettes and multi-coloured sprigs.

GAVALOHORI / Γαβαλοχώρι / Gavalohóri

A pretty village with interesting sights such as the **domed olive press**, the **Roman cemetery** and the group of **wells** of the Venetian period. At the well laid-out **Folk Art Museum**, the Women's Rural Tourism Association has revived the unique ancient craft of a special kind of lacework, known as **kopanelli**.

DOULIANA / Ντουλιανά / Doulianá

Traditional, village, with narrow streets and beautifully restored houses. You can stay at small hostels and eat at **Ritsa's** taverna.
In the foothills of the white mountains the picturesque villages of Vafes, Tzitzifes, Fres, Melidoni and Mahairi seem oblivious to tourism.

❷ APTERA
Άπτερα / Áptera

*8:30 am-3 pm, closed on holidays**

Even if you're not enthusiastic about ancient monuments, **Aptera**, at Paleokastro, near the village of Megala Horafia is

Itzedin fort, Aptera

worth a visit just to see the shining panorama of the plain and Souda Bay. The town was originally called Paleokastro, and took the name Aptera, or Aptara, from its founder, Apteras or Apteros of legend.
It was **fortified with ramparts**, of which remnants can still be seen. Once an industrial and commercial centre, it guarded the entrance to Souda Bay and in Early Byzantine years was the seat of the bishopric. It was completely destroyed in the 8th c. AD.
On the acropolis, there are the remains of vast **vaulted cisterns** and other public buildings from Roman and Early Byzantine times. The Veneto-Cretan **monastery of Agios Ioannis tou Theologou** and the **Itzedin fort**, from the period of Turkish rule have also been preserved.

❸ LAKE KOURNA
Λίμνη Κουρνά / Límni Kourná

At a height of just 19 m above sea-level, this is Crete's only lake. Its ancient name was **Korissia** and there was a sanctuary here, dedicated to Athena Korissia, according to the chronicler Stephanos Vyzantios. It may however have got its name from the word "kourna" which means "lake". Extending for 600 sq. m and no more than 25 m deep, it lies at the foot of the White Mountains. We suggest you visit it for a picnic or meal at one of the tavernas on its shores. For protection of the lake's ecosystem, it is recommended that you avoid swimming in it. At the adjoining village of Kournas, you can visit the **church of Agios Georgios**, with its significant frescoes of the 12th, 13th and 14th c.

❹ ARGYROUPOLI
Αργυρούπολη / Argiroúpoli

A small village located on the site of ancient Lappa, with streams, small waterfalls, ponds and rich vegetation. The Agyroupoli **springs** supply Rethymno with water.
Leave your car at the entrance to the village and stroll along the picturesque alleys. You can eat at one of the small and cool village tavernas. If you have time, visit the cave-tombs of **ancient Lappa** in their beautiful setting.

❺ IMBROS GORGE
Φαράγγι Ίμπρου / Farángi Ímbrou

About 3 km in length, it is one of the deepest and narrowest in the country and divides the White Mountains from the Angathes region. At some points, the width is only 2 m, while the height of the sheer rock walls reaches about 300 m, which gives you the feeling of going through a tunnel. The vegetation includes cypresses, a variety of other trees and holm-oaks. You can set out by car or on foot from the village of Komitades and you'll end up in the village of Imbros.

❻ HORA SFAKION
Χώρα Σφακίων / Hóra Sfakíon

Located on the shores of the Libyan Sea, with 250 inhabitants, in a barren, wild and rocky region, it was once an important maritime and commercial centre. In the 15th or 16th c. the Venetians built a fort on the hill of Kastelli. The Sfakiots fiercely resisted any enemy invasion, maintained their independence and were prominent in Greece's struggle against Turkish rule. In 1770, this was the base for the commander of the Sfakiot forces, Daskalogiannis or Ioannis Vlahos, who suffered a terrible death at the hands of the Turks, when they publicly flayed him with razors. Here, on April 15, 1821, the flag of the Greek War of Independence was raised. Today's town has lost its former glory and has unconditionally surrendered to the tourist invasion. However, it still retains much of its local traditional architecture and you can see pretty one- or two-storey houses with small openings and enclosed courtyards with wells and outdoor ovens.

Visit the **Panagia Thymiani** church, where the inhabitants of the Sfakia region gathered for their meetings prior to the 1821 uprising, and **Daskalogiannis's cave**, in which the hero had set up the revolution's mint. The cave can be approached only by boat.

❼ LOUTRO
Λουτρό / Loutró

Quaint fishing village, nestled in a cove reachable only by boat or on foot. In the past few years it has attracted more and more travellers looking for unspoilt places for their holidays. All the houses – many of which have rooms for rent – are white, with blue shutters, in a harmony of architecture. At the tavernas, fresh fish and lobster supplied by local fishermen are served, at reasonable prices. You can also visit the **Government House**, the seat of the first government of 1821. Hora Sfakion can be reached in only 30 min, by scheduled boats or by sea-taxi (5,000 drs.), but without your car. For swimming, go to **Marmara**. There are also connections to the island of **Gavdos**.

❽ FRANGOKASTELLO
Φραγκοκάστελο / Frangokástello

Castel Franco, or Agios Nikitas, was built by the Venetians in 1371, probably with material from the adjacent ancient city, for protection against pirates and local insurgents. The beautiful fortress looks like something out of a fairytale, oblong in plan with square towers. In 1828 it was used by the chieftain, Dalianis Hatzimichail, as his operational base. In May of the same year, Mustafa Pasha marched against him with 8,000 infantry, 400 cavalry and 6 cannons. Most of the 666 soldiers and 70 cavalrymen defending the fortress were killed in the subsequent battle, while the remaining few were allowed to leave, armed, following an agreement with the pasha. However, the slain defenders of the fortress were not lost forever. According to a local tale, their shadows – known as **Drossoulites** – appear here in late May or early June, if there is no wind, with the first dew of dawn. In the ghostly form of horsemen, they begin their strange course from the semi-ruined church of Agios Haralambos, disappearing into the sea. This phenomenon has been attributed to reflections from the Libyan coast opposite, which is however 350 km away.

OTHER THINGS TO DO

VAMOS S.A. TOURIST OFFICE PROGRAMMES
Tel. (0825) 23100, 23250, fax 23100
Organized **excursions** and **hikes** to caves, gorges and monasteries. **Lessons** are also available in iconography, ceramics, Greek dances, cooking and Modern Greek. You can also take part in the grape and olive harvests.

WALKING TOURS
"METAPODIA"
Tel. (0825) 22701, fax 22890
Ask for the friendly German, Hansgeorg Hermann, who has a home in Douliana and organizes walking tours.

LOCAL FESTIVITIES AND EVENTS
All the events recommended are held at Vamos
- April is an opportunity to enjoy an evening with raki, snails and wine, well-known as **Hohlidovradia**.
- On June 29, you can watch Cretan dancing and song at the **festival of the Apostles Peter and Paul**.
- In August, exhibitions of folk artists and traditional arts and crafts take place, as well as numerous **evenings with entertainment**, including "**Vamos**" **events**, featuring well-known musicians, dancers and singers.

BEST BEACHES

🌂🌂 FRANGOKASTELLO

500 m east of the castle, leave your car and make your way down the steep dunes to the white sandy beach with exquisitely clear waters.
One end of the beach is isolated and frequented by nudists.

🌂🌂 KORAKA BEACH (RODAKINO)

An excellent beach with sand and crystalline waters. If swimming makes you hungry, there is fresh fish and homemade spinach pie at **Kanakis'** taverna.

🌂 MARMARA

The coves west of Loutro feature beautiful, small beaches with smooth rocks, which both nudists and non-nudists will find ideal for swimming in the crystal-clear waters. You can get there from Loutro with a caique operating regular schedules, by sea-taxi, or on foot in 30 min.

ILINGAS

A good beach with pebbles, only 5 min by car from Sfakia. If you walk westwards for approximately 20 min, you'll reach a nudist beach.

ALMYRIDA

Closer to Vamos, a small beach in the village of Almyrida, surrounded by holiday homes and tavernas. Tourist traffic is brisk in summer.

BEST HOTELS AND ROOMS

BEST LOCATION

Definitely in a traditional pension in Vamos, at the centre for your outings, with adequate facilities for all your needs. Alternatively at Loutro.

PRICES

The hotel prices mentioned below are the official ones, set by the National Tourist Organization for double rooms, at low and high season, with breakfast. Since owners are allowed to modify prices, always try to negotiate them.

✓✓ VAMOS S.A. PENSIONS

Vamos
Tel. (0825) 23100, 23250, fax 23100
Open: All year round

Description: A group of descendants – all of them professionals – of the owners of these 19th c. buildings decided to cooperate to restore them with special care.
Former olive presses, inns and stables have now been converted into pensions, with a capacity of 35 beds. Each lodging has a fireplace, toilet, TV, kitchen and traditionally furnished living-room.
The authentic typical kafeneion, general store and taverna complete the image of nostalgia.
The environment is extremely friendly and makes up for deficiencies in the service.
All pensions have the names of flowers.
Price: 22,000 drs.
Value for money: ✽✽
Credit cards: Mastercard, Visa

VAMOS 21

✓✓ ERGINA & PERY VILLAS

Gavalohori
Tel. (01) 4282377, fax 4282379

Open: April-October
Description: These two villas with Byzantine and Venetian elements of the 16th c., received awards for their excellent restoration work completed in 1986. They are stone-built and the woodwork is of cypress beams.
Each one accommodates 6-8 people. They are fully furnished, with all conveniences, including kitchen, bath, toilet and bedrooms.
Price: 22,000-37,000 drs.
Value for money: ✶✶ without breakfast.
Credit cards: None

✓ PORTO LOUTRO (C Class)

Loutro-Anopoli
Tel. (0825) 91433, 91444, fax 91091
Open: April-October
Description: Through the efforts of Allison – a British woman – and her Greek husband, two separate hotels were built, one up on a hill and the other at its foot. The former is preferable, although both are equally well cared-for. A good choice for quiet holidays next to the sea, far from traffic noise.
Rooms: 23 comfortable and clean rooms.
Special features: Watersports.
Price: 11.000 drs.
Value for money: ✶✶
Credit cards: None

BEST RESTAURANTS & TAVERNAS

✓ I STERNA TOU BLOUMOSIFI

Vamos
Tel. (0825) 23100, 23250

Owned by Vamos S.A., it is housed in a restored 1905 building and operates all year round. Happenings with guitars and songs are frequently organized by its cheerful and friendly group of owners. Cretan dishes are served with a large variety of specialities baked in the wood-oven. It also has a wine-cellar as well as local wine from the barrel. Open all day, it functions as a restaurant for lunch and dinner, and in the morning as a cafe, serving a hearty breakfast. **Price:** €€

DOULIANA TAVERNA

Douliana
Tel. (0825) 23380

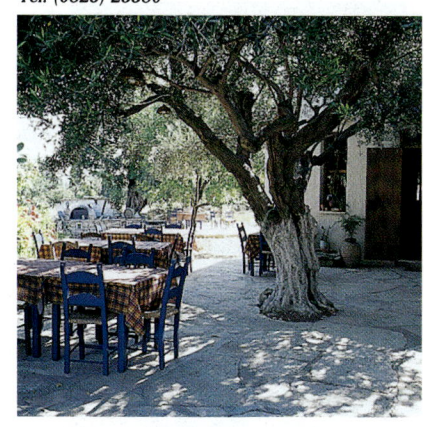

Good Cretan cuisine. Try boureki (baked courgettes, potato and myzithra cheese), snails, Cretan pies, and the delicious bitter-orange preserve, home-made by Ritsa.
Price: €

✓✓ PSAROS

Almyrida
Tel. (0825) 31401
For the finest fresh fish, next to the sea.
Price: €€

275

BEST ENTERTAINMENT

This excursion offers leisurely, low-key entertainment. In the summer, there are events with music and shows featuring well-kown performers. Go to the **Liakoto** cafe in Vamos, in a 19th c. building, which used to be a general store and "kafenion". Today, with the help of Vamos S.A., it has been converted into tasteful premises where you can have a coffee or a drink amidst art work sometimes on show and listen to music.

TIPS AND INFORMATION

HOW TO GET THERE

- By air from Athens west airport to Chania, Olympic Airways (16,500 drs), tel. (01) 9363363, or Air Greece east airport, daily flights, tel. (01) 3255011. Also by air from Thessaloniki's Makedonia airport, Olympic Airways (26,500 drs.), tel. (031) 260121, or Air Greece, tel. (031) 244340.
- By ferry from Piraeus to Souda Bay in 10 hrs (from 4,350 drs.), Piraeus Port Authority, tel. (01) 4226000.
- By intercity bus from Chania to Vamos in less than one hour (550 drs.), KTEL tel. (0821) 93052.

BEST TIPS

HOW TO GET AROUND: You will need a car to reach the villages in the region and to stay in each one for as long as you wish.

Myrovolon

BEST SEASON: Late May and early June. Another good time is Easter, which is celebrated there in the traditional way.

BEST BUYS: The liquor and grocery store **To Myrovolon**, sells mainly **natural products**, packaged and standardized by Vamos S.A. You can buy homemade jams and preserves, handmade pasta, soaps, vinegar and grape syrup. It's worth visiting, if only for the restored 19th c. building, which was a beer hall in the 1920s.
Also at Kokkino Horio you'll find a workshop with **hand-blown glass**, where you can watch the objects being crafted and buy those which take your fancy, Tzombanakis, tel. (0825) 31194. In Gavalohori, you can buy **finely-woven lace** in the traditional **kopanelli** technique.
For the best Sfakian pie, go to **Karkanis'** taverna in the village of Askifos.

USEFUL TELEPHONE NUMBERS

VAMOS	(0825)	Police	22218
Town Hall	22930	Health Centre	22580
Vamos S.A.	23100	Taxis	22202

RETHYMNO

WHY AMONG THE BEST

Because of the attractive Old Town of Rethymno with its Venetian fort, its mosques and picturesque alleys. Because of the wild gorges, enticing beaches and historic monasteries. And of course because of the warm welcome by the locals.

CRETE

BEST's OPINION

This excursion focuses mainly on Rethymno's Old Town. If you wish to combine it with swimming, avoid the crowded and bland organized beaches of the north and go through the remarkable gorges to discover the scenic and fairly untouched beaches of southern Crete. You can combine this expedition with trips to destinations in Chania and Vamos if you have time.

BEST SIGHTS: STEP BY STEP

❶ RETHYMNO
Ρέθυμνο / Réthymno

Rethymno, with 24,000 inhabitants, is on a sandy shore 12 km long. Ancient Rithymna's appearance and architectural style were repeatedly altered, until now at the end of the 20th c. it is divided into the old and new towns. The modern town is a concrete jungle of apartment buildings, but the old maintains the charm which not even the unchecked development of mass tourism can erase.

RETHYMNO

HISTORY

The region was inhabited from prehistoric times but the zenith of the ancient city of Rithymna dates back to the 4th and 3rd c. BC. Here in 1204, the Venetians built a small port and a fortified town, but in 1646 Leo of Venice was defeated by Hussein Pasha.
The town's capture by the Ottomans put an end to any evolution in scholarship and culture and the inhabitants endured a lengthy period of dark oppression which was terminated, after endless struggle, in 1913 when Crete was united with the rest of Greece.

Fortezza

Town of RETHYMNO (map)

🔶🔶 RETHYMNO OLD TOWN
Παλιά πόλη Ρεθύμνου / Paliá Póli Rethýmnou

There is much to admire in the sight of the facades of the Venetian buildings under preservation as you wander about the narrow streets with grand old houses.

🔶🔶 The fortress (Fortezza)

In 1573, after the attack by Oloudj Ali, an Algerian pirate who burned and pillaged the town, the Venetians decided to build a fort

Old Town

with four battlements and three entrances, so as to be protected from attack by sea. On the site of their cathedral you can still see Ibrahim Khan's mosque. If you visit it in the morning you will escape the crowds.

The Venetian Port

A scenic spot ideal for a cup of coffee and a rest from sightseeing, especially at sunset.

Loggia

At the end of Palaiologou St.
A typical Renaissance monument built by the Venetians in the mid 16th c.

Rimondi Fountain

On the north side of Petihaki Sq.
Artistically sculptured and of unusual design, this fountain was erected in 1626 over an older one. Water flows out of the mouths of three lion-heads in relief.

Venetian port

Rimondi Fountain

Archaeological Museum

Himarras St. (opposite the fort), tel. (0831) 54668
Summer 8:30 am-3 pm, winter 8 am-2:30 pm, closed on Mondays and holidays*

Housed in the Fortezza, it contains finds from the Neolithic era until the days of Turkish domination. There are fine examples of ceramic and stone **figurines**, **tools** and stone **jewellery** of the Neolithic age from the Gerani cave, inscribed clay **sarcophagi** and **inscriptions** from Axos and Eleutherna. There is also an excellent **collection** of **Roman statues** and collections of Roman, Greek and Byzantine **coins**.

Agios Frangiskos

Ethnikis Antistasseos St.
A single-aisled basilica with a beautifully carved entrance doorframe and striking architecture, this was the church of a Franciscan monastery.

Church of Kyria ton Angelon

Vernardou St.
A triple-aisled church without a dome, of the order of Dominicans, dedicated to Saint Mary Magdalene.

The Mosques

The **Neratze** mosque in the town's Venetian square has the tallest minaret, while the **Kara Moussa Pasha** and **Veli Pasha** mosques, with their domes and minarets, add an exotic touch.

Neratze mosque

Historical and Folk Art Museum

28-30 M. Vernardou St., tel. (0831) 23398
9 am-1 pm, closed on Sundays and holidays*

Traditional handwoven fabrics, embroideries, jewellery, objects and utensils are housed in an interesting old Venetian house with a lovely garden.

❷ MYLI
Μύλοι / Míli

A delightful isolated village amidst thick vegetation in a gorge with a little stream. Its last inhabitants abandoned it 20 years ago. In the Middle Ages many water mills were built to meet the increasing needs of the district in flour milling. The path, about 300 m long, leading there from the road, is passable and a pleasant walk to the sound of birdsong. If you are seduced by the gorge's beauties, continue your walk to the end of it (four more hours) and if you're hungry, Vangelis's taverna at **Mili**, the only one in the area, will provide something to eat, tel. (0831) 75005, 72021, (0932) 582143.

❸ HROMONASTIRI
Χρομοναστήρι / Hromonastíri

The district's main village, it maintains the atmosphere of olden times and has a lot to see, such as the **Konaki**, the mansion of the Clodio family, later lived in by a Turkish Aga whence its name (Turkish *konak* = home); the fine Byzantine church of **Panagia Kera**, and **Agios Eftyhios**, a Byzantine church with **devotional paintings** of the 11th c. You will come across it 500 m before entering the village, taking the dirt track to the left. Have a rest in the cool and charming square of the village with its cafes.

❹ ARKADI MONASTERY
Μονή Αρκαδίου / Moní Arkadíou

Tel. (0831) 83076

🕗 8 am to sunset

A Byzantine monastery where resistance to the Ottoman occupation was particularly active, due to its strategic position.
The original construction, fortress-like, was built around the 14th c. and the church in 1587.
In the uprising of 1866, women and children, monks and villagers, alongside the revolutionaries, fiercely resisted the forces – 15,000 strong – of Mustapha Pasha for two whole days. As soon as the Turks burst in, the monastery's defenders, the abbot Gavriil at their head, blew up the powder magazine, burying themselves and the enemy under the rubble.
Thus Arkadi, the old monastery built by an unknown monk probably named Arkadios, became the symbol of the Cretans' fight for liberty. The monastery's museum houses a collection of Post-Byzantine icons, religious vessels, weapons from the struggles and an ossuary of its unnamed defenders.

❺ ELEUTHERNA
Ελεύθερνα / Eléftherna

The houses in traditional style, with arched windows and gates are in harmony with a beautiful landscape. Olive trees cover the little hill on which the village is built. There are remnants of the ancient city, Apollonia's, walls, aqueduct and giant reservoirs, and from here comes the Archaic statue of a woman's torso now in Heraklio's archaeological museum.

Spili fountainheads

Kourtaliotiko gorge

Preveli monastery

⑥ MARGARITES
Μαργαρίτες / Margarítes

They say that Queen Margarita, delighted by the beauty of the countryside, built this village, which today has 720 inhabitants, famous for their hospitality and their pottery.

⑦ PANORMOS
Πάνορμος / Pánormos

A seaside village of 370 inhabitants, believed to be on the site of ancient Panormos, the port of Eleutherna, once called Kastelli. The scenery is splendid, but it has long been discovered by holidaymakers who throng the tavernas and bars of the picturesque little bay.

⑧ SPILI / Σπήλι / Spíli

This village is worth a visit mainly for its 25 **fountainheads** which bring the water straight from the top of Mt Psiloritis (Ida). The water flows from the mouths of sculptured lions amid flourishing greenery. Visit the old **church of the Metamorphosis tou Sotira** with **frescoes** depicting the daily life of the damned.

⑨ KOURTALIOTIKO GORGE
Κουρταλιώτικο Φαράγγι / Kourtaliótiko Faránghi

From the village of Koxare, take the road for Asomatos to get to this stunning gorge, with its breathtaking sheer cliffsides.

⑩ PREVELI MONASTERY
Μονή Πρέβελη / Moní Préveli

Tel. (0832) 31246
Summer 8 am-1:30 pm, and 3:30-8 pm, winter 8 am-1:30 pm and 4-6 pm

As you exit the Kourtaliotiko gorge with its dense greenery, you are met by the sight of the monastery perched on the summit of a bare hill. It is dedicated to Saint John the Divine and was founded in the 16th or 17th c. The double-aisled church was built in 1836 and, having been destroyed, renovated in 1911.

If you believe in miracles, see the cross set in gold, with precious stones and wood from the Holy Cross, kept in the church and considered to be miraculous. Also visit the museum and the library of the monastery.

FREE TIME

HIKES

The Happy Walker, *Anthony Pruissen, 56 Tombazi St., Rethymno Old Town*
Tel. (0831) 31390, 52920, fax 52920
This travel agent specializes in excursions and hikes of every degree of difficulty and duration. Sally forth to unexplored

RETHYMNO 22

gorges and forgotten villages, enjoying spectacular routes on foot.
Prices: 6,500 - 8,000 drs. per person.

FESTIVAL
From March to December, the prefecture organizes cultural events including drama, music and dance at the **Erofili** theatre, **Fortezza**, the **basilica of Agios Frangiskos** and the **odeon**.
Information: tel. (0831) 24069, 54224.

BEYOND THIS EXCURSION
SFENDONI CAVE
Σπήλαιο Σφεντόνη / Spílaio Sfendóni

8 am to sunset, closed on holidays*

This cave in the foothills of Mt Psiloritis, between Rethymno and Heraklio and near the village of Zoniana, has remarkable natural phenomena and is considered the island's most spectacular cave. It has four chambers and descends 140 m. Locally they call it Sendoni.

Sfendoni cave

ANOGEIA / Ανώγεια / Anógia
Close to Zoniana and the Sfendoni cave is the village of Anogeia, where during the Ottoman domination revolutionaries established a resistance centre, which was reactivated under the German occupation.
The locals speak in the Cretan dialect, wear their traditional costumes and it is rumoured they never gave up their weapons which reappear as if by magic at weddings, feasts — and also during quarrels.
Have a glass of raki (fiery locally-brewed spirits) at the village cafe and see the admirable local handicrafts in the shops. The path to the summit of Mt Psiloritis (Ida), starts here.

BEST BEACHES

Boat trips from Rethymno to various beaches and caves of the area are organized, lasting from 2 1/2 to 5 hrs. Prices: From 4,000-8,000 drs. However, we suggest you head south for the best beaches of this trip.

PREVELI BEACH (FINIKAS)

At the exit of the **Kourtaliotiko gorge** and at the mouth of the Kourtaliotis river, Preveli beach is one of the island's most attractive.
You'll have to pass along a steep but manageable path over boulders to reach it. Have your camera with you to record the unequalled scenery of the route. The beach, although crowded in summer, has limpid waters and palm trees and if you walk along the riverbed, among lush foliage, you will discover crystal-clear pools of river-water among the boulders, ideal for a dip.

DAMNONI
Were it not for the large hotel complex near it, this sandy beach would be isolated. There is, however, a particularly delightful spot, a smaller beach left of Damnoni and before Ammoudi — reachable by a dirt track. Surrounded by rocks, the waters are transparent and a magnet for nudists. From nearby Plakia beach there are daily departures for Agia Galini and Preveli beach.

CRETE

Damnoni

⛱ TRIOPETRA
A good sandy beach, it has reed parasols and a well cared-for stone-built taverna, the **Apothiki**.

⛱ SOUDA
A beach with sand in Plakia Bay, with palm trees and a taverna popular with the Rethymniots.

BEST HOTELS AND ROOMS

BEST LOCATION
If your stay is to be short we suggest you stay in the Old Town of Rethymno. But for longer stays, it's worth picking one of the Best hotel choices out of town so as to have greater comfort and the sea at your feet.

PRICES
The hotel prices mentioned below are the official ones set by the National Tourist Organization for double rooms, at low and high season, with breakfast. Since owners are allowed to modify prices, always try to negotiate them.

✓✓ PALAZZO RIMONDI (A Class)
21 Xanthoudidou & 16 H.Trikoupi Sts., Rethymno Old Town
Tel. (0831) 51289, fax 26757
Open: All year round
Description: A 15th c. building renovated to meet the requirements of modern visitors without spoiling the atmosphere of the old house.

Rooms: There are 21 suites with A/C, TV, telephone, mini bar, safe and veranda.
Special features: Parking, garden, pool and bar.
Price: 26,000-36,500 drs.
Value for money: ✱
Credit cards: Visa

✓✓ MYTHOS (B Class)
12 Karaoli Sq., Rethymno Old Town
Tel. (0831) 53917, fax 51036 **Open:** All year round

Description: A 16th c. mansion restored in 1993, with antiques, excellent taste and a friendly atmosphere.
Rooms: 10 suites with kitchen, A/C, TV, fridge and telephone.
Special Features: Garden, bar and pool.
Price: 29,000- 58,000 drs.
Value for money: ✱✱✱
Credit cards: All

RETHYMNO

✓ VENETO (A Class)

4 Epimenidou St., Rethymno Old Town
Tel. (0831) 56634, fax 56635
Open: All year round
Description: 13th c. mansion. The oldest part used to be monks' cells while the more recent part dating to early mid-15th or to the beginning 16th c. is Venetian. The restaurant has been restored in better taste than the suites.
Rooms: 4 suites and 5 studios, with A/C, kitchen, telephone, safe, TV and balcony.
Special features: TV room, garden, massage, sauna, bar and the restaurant with the best decor in Rethymno.
Price: 28,000-35,000 drs. **Value for money:** ✹✹
Credit cards: All

✓ FORTEZZA (A Class)

16 Melissinou St., Rethymno Old Town
Tel. (0831) 23828, 55551, 55552, fax 54073
Open: March-October

Description: A modern building with many elements of traditional architecture.
Rooms: 54 rooms with telephone, central heating and balcony.
Special features: Restaurant, snack bar, pool, games room, TV and video room.
Price: 19,000-23,000 drs.
Value for money: ✹✹✹
Credit cards: All

✓ IDEON HOTEL (B Class)

10 Plastira Sq., Rethymno

Tel. (0831) 28667-9, 22346 fax 28670
Open: March-October
Description: An unpretentious hotel built in 1972 and modernized in 1995.
Rooms: 86 rooms with A/C and some with TV.
Special features: Restaurant, bar, garden with pool, small conference room and A/C in all inward-looking rooms.
Price: 15,000-22,700 drs.
Value for money: ✹
Credit cards: All

OUTSIDE RETHYMNO

✓✓✓ GRECOTEL RITHYMNA BEACH (A Class)

Adele, 7 km east of Rethymno
Tel. (0831) 71441, 71002, 29491, fax 71668

Open: March-November
Description: Large hotel complex in traditional style with numerous modern conveniences.
Rooms: 556 rooms, suites and bungalows with telephone, balcony, TV, radio, safe, A/C, fridge and hair dryer.
Special features: Interior and outdoor pools, beach (Blue Flag), parking, tennis courts, shops, hairdresser, bar, 4 restaurants, cafeterias, children's playground, gardens, gym, scuba diving school, bicycle rides, water sports and a centre for the protection of the sea turtle Caretta-Caretta.
Price: 79,700-86,550 drs.
Value for money: ✹✹
Credit cards: All

✓✓✓ GRECOTEL CRETA PALACE (A Class)

Missiria, 4 km east of Rethymno
Tel. (0831) 55181, fax 54085
Open: March-October

Description: In simple and elegant style combining modern and traditional Cretan architecture, a complex surrounded by green gardens.
Rooms: 162 rooms and suites in the central building, 204 bungalows and villas with telephone, balcony, TV, radio, safe, A/C, fridge and hair dryer.
Special features: 3 restaurants, 4 bars, local colour cafe, shops, parking, pools, gym, tennis court, beach, water sports, bicycle rides, scuba diving school, electronic games, billiards. For children from 3 to 12 there are special facilities and specialized staff to ensure they enjoy their stay with lots to do.
Price: 96000-118,000 drs.
Value for money: ✶
Credit cards: All

✓✓ VILLA KYNTHIA (B Class)

Panormos, 22 km east of Rethymno
Tel. (0834) 51102, 51318, fax 51148
Open: All year round
Description: A listed mansion, built in 1898, restored in 1991 with particular care and respect for heritage. 200 m from the seaside.
Rooms: Its most luxurious suites are the 'Artemis' and 'Odyssey', with wall-paintings of the adventures of the Homeric hero. All suites have hot-cold A/C, TV, mini bar, telephone, bath and fridge.
Special features: Inner courtyard with a venerable pine tree, snack-bar and pool.
Price: 29,250-43,550 drs.
Value for money: ✶
Credit cards: None

ALTERNATIVES

ACHILLION PALACE (A Class)
27 K. Giamboudaki St., Rethymno
Tel. (0831) 51502, 54423, fax 51568.
Price: 23,000-28.000 drs.

GRECOTEL EL GRECO (A Class)
Kambos Pigis, 8.5 km east of Rethymno
Tel. (0831) 71102, fax 71215.
Price: 66,000-70,100 drs.

GRECOTEL PORTO RETHYMNO (A Class)
Sikelianou and 52a Venizelou Sts., Rethymno
Tel. (0831) 50432, fax 27825.
Price: 63,000-76,800 drs.

CAPTAIN'S HOUSE
Panormos
Tel. (0834) 51352, (priv.) 23488 (081) 380833
Price: 16,000-18,000 drs.

CRETA ROYAL (A Class)
Skaleta Prinou (12th km)
Tel. (0831) 71902, fax 71962.
Price: 24,500-39,000 drs.

RETHYMNO MARE (A Class)
Skaleta (11th km)
Tel. (0831) 71703, fax 71734.
Price: 28,000-38,000 drs.

ATRIUM (B Class)
30 Portaliou St.
Tel. (0831) 57601-6, fax 57607.
Price: 20,100-30,400 drs.

CRETA STAR (A Class)
Scaleta
Tel. (0831) 71812, 71834, fax 71791.
Price: 19,500-30,000 drs.

BEST RESTAURANTS & TAVERNAS

✓✓ VENETO

4 Epimenidou St., Rethymno Old Town

Tel. (0831) 56634
A beautifully restored 13th c. space under the hotel, with splendid mosaics, fountains, jars, flagged flooring and romantic decor. It once housed monks and now is up to the standard required by the most demanding customer. Service is faultless and the cuisine interesting, with Greek and Cretan specialities.
Price: €€

✓✓ AVLI

22 Xanthoudidou and Rhadamanthous Sts., Rethymno Old Town

Tel. (0831) 26213
Gourmet and aesthetic delights in the superb courtyard of one of the town's best restaurants.
Price: €€

✓ LARENZO

9 Rhadamanthous St., Rethymno Old Town
Tel. (0831) 26780
An imposing Venetian vaulted space with arches. Take your friends and reserve the private room to enjoy an authentic medieval atmosphere undisturbed. Greek dishes, fresh salads, fish dishes and good wine.
Price: €€

KYRIA MARIA

20 Moschovitou St., Rethymno Old Town
Tel. (0831) 29078
In the old town in a picturesque alley, taste typical plain Greek and Cretan food, amidst caged songbirds of all kinds and an especially friendly ambiance.
Price: €

OTHONAS

27 Petihaki St., Rethymno Old Town
Tel. (0831) 55500
A wide variety - 600 - of Greek and international dishes. Try the meat and fish courses and also the pasta.
Price: €

TO ELLINIKON

11 Petihaki St., Rethymno Old Town
Tel. (0831) 52526
For raki (the regional drink), ouzo (like the French pastis) and tasty hors-d'oeuvre in the old town's most central location.
Price: €

TO ARAXOVOLI

34 Iroon Polytechniou Square, Rethymno
Tel. (0831) 52011
Next to the prefecture, it serves delicious Cretan appetizers and fresh fish, has live music and abundant raki.
Price: €

TAVERNA TOU ZISSI

Missiria, 4 km from Rethymno on the old road to Heraklio.
Tel. (0831) 28814
Don't be put off by the ugly modern construction. Locals rate it as one of the best tavernas of the district with excellent charcoal grills and tasty hors d'oeuvre.
Price: €

BEST ENTERTAINMENT

The town's nightlife is mainly shared between the port with its many cafe-bars and nightclubs, and Platania, east of Rethymno, where in summer of all nationalities meet in the big popular waterfront nightclubs.

Follow your impulse but also check out our Best selections. The most «in hangout» of the town is in the Venetian port, the **Fortezza Club**, with house and rave music, and the **Rock Cafe** which will delight enthusiasts of the rock scene.

The **Figaro Cafe**, next to the Folk Art Museum, offers a romantic atmosphere and at Platania the **Opera**, with Greek music, and the universally known **Catarala**, offer nice drinks and even nicer encounters.

Figaro Cafe

TIPS AND INFORMATION

HOW TO GET THERE

- By air from Athens west airport once daily, by Olympic Airways (16,500 drs.), tel (01) 9663363. Rethymno is served by Chania airport and the distance Chania-Rethymno covered by Olympic Airways coaches.
- By ferry from Piraeus in 10 hrs (from 5,250 drs.), Piraeus Port Authority, tel (01) 4226000.

CONNECTIONS

- By intercity bus, Rethymno KTEL, tel. (0831) 22785, to Heraklio, Chania. In summer daily departures for Hora Sfakion.

BEST TIPS

HOW TO GET AROUND: To explore Rethymno's Old Town for the principal sightseeing of this trip, on foot. If you want to visit Arkadi, Moni Preveli and the other beaches and have no car, you can hire a car or go to one of the following travel agents: Ira Travel, tel. (0831) 24466-7, 54674 and Klados Travel, tel. (0831) 54428, 52378, for organized tours in the summer season only.

BEST SEASON: Spring and autumn. The climate is warm enough for sea-bathing. Also a good choice for other times of year.

BEST BUYS: Rethymniot embroidery, ceramics from the village of Margarites and hand-woven fabrics from Anogia.

USEFUL TELEPHONE NUMBERS

RETHYMNO ....(0831)	Port Authority 28971
Town Hall 22245	Taxis 25000, 24000
Tourist Bureau 56350	
Tourist Police 28156	**PANORMOS** ....(0834)
Police 22331	Police 51203
Hospital 27491, 27814	Rural Clinic 51214
KTEL 22659, 22785, 22212	Taxis 51202

Phaestos - Matala

° Phaestos ° Matala
° Lake Zaros

23

WHY AMONG THE BEST

Because it combines the cultural aspect of Phaestos, the important Creto-Minoan palace, with the caves of Matala where hippies once lived next to the truly beautiful beach. And because of its youthful atmosphere and nightlife.

CRETE

BEST's OPINION

If you have time, Matala and Phaestos are worth visiting. However, if you are looking for quality accommodation, select another **Best** excursion in the area and complete your visit to the Matala region on the same day. Distances are not prohibitive.

BEST SIGHTS: STEP BY STEP

❶ MATALA
Μάταλα / Mátala

Matala beach and caves

A small settlement of 300 inhabitants, which is located south-west of Heraklio and has developed, especially in the past few years, with increased tourism. Here, there was once an ancient Cretan town, which in Minoan times was used as Phaestos's seaport and the port of Roman Gortyna.

PHAESTOS - MATALA   23

WHAT TO SEE

CAVES
Tel. (0892) 42315

Summer 8 am-5 pm, winter 8 am-3 pm, closed on holidays*

The caves beside the beach with their strange shapes were probably inhabited by prehistoric people and certainly by groups of Americans from the hippie peace movement in the 1970s. Also found in the caves were graves dating back to Roman and Early Christian times.
Today they are fenced off by the tourist police and staying overnight is prohibited.

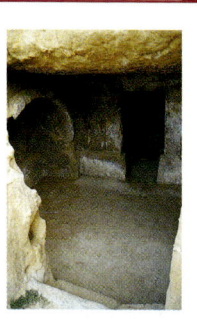

❷ PHAESTOS
Φαιστός / Festós

Tel. (0892) 42315

8 am-6 pm, closed on holidays

After Knossos, this is Crete's most important archaeological site.
According to myth Minos's brother, **Rhadamanthus**, had his luxury palace here.
Its port was initially Kommos and later, Matala. The first palace was built in 1900 BC and the second, after the earthquake, about 1700 BC.
Phaestos is situated on a hill with a wonderful view. The area of the old palace was excavated in 1900, bringing to light valuable finds, including polychrome "Kamares" vases, clay seals and the famous **Phaestos Disk**, which was found in the old palace building complex, in the NE of the palace, and which bears hieroglyphic Minoan writing. The palace architecture is Minoan and its orientation was towards the west, serving religious and practical purposes.

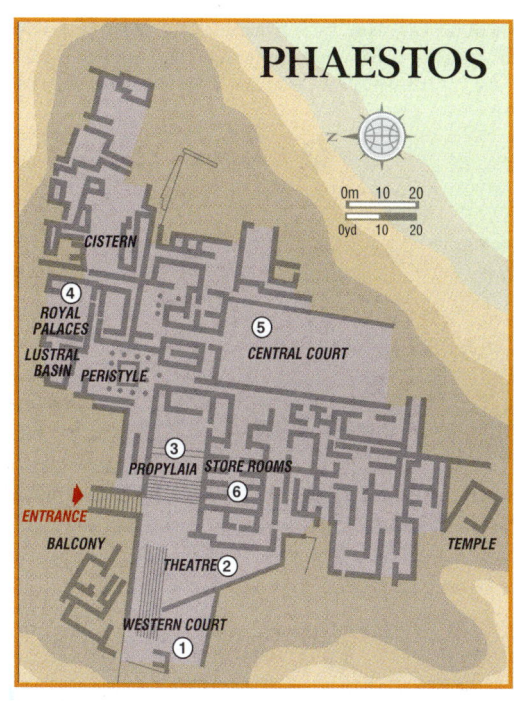

Most of the finds can be seen at the **Heraklio Archaeological Museum** (see Excursion 24)

① **Western court**: An area for public events.

② **Theatre**: Some of the tiered rows can be discerned.

③ **Propylaia**: In the eastern section of the court, you will see the imposing staircase from which we arrive. The stairs, wider in the centre and narrower at the sides, present a majestic picture.

④ **Royal palaces**: To the north, is the king's palace, which has a reception room and bathroom. The queen's palace is in the south. In one of its rooms, the original alabaster bench has been preserved. You will not be able to see the dwellings, which have collapsed.

⑤ **Central court**: Around this are grouped the rooms of the palace, which must have had impressive facades. Meetings, palace events and athletic games would have been held here.

Grand staircase

291

⑥ Storerooms: *Oil, grain and wine were stored in large pottery jars. In the last storeroom on the right, there was a device for collecting the oil which flowed from the containers. Here, archives with clay seals were found.*

❸ ANCIENT GORTYNA
Αρχαία Γόρτυνα / Archéa Górtina

Tel. (0892) 31144

🕒 *8 am-6 pm, closed on holidays**

It enjoyed great prosperity in Ancient and Classical times, as well as during the period of the Roman occupation. It was destroyed by the Saracens in 824 AD and since then remained uninhabited. Excavations began in 1884. Its most important monuments are the Ⓖ **Odeon**, the **northern theatre**, the **acropolis**, the **Temple of Pythian Apollo**, the **church of Agios Titos**, the Ⓖ **sanctuary of the Egyptians**, the Ⓖ **Nymphaion**, the 2nd c. BC **amphitheatre**, the **Great Gate**, the **Hippodrome**, the **cemetery** of the ancient city, the **Agii Deka Tombs** and the **Early Christian triconch**. West of the tombs is the Ⓖ **Archaeological Collection** which includes the area's finds.

❹ LAKE ZAROS (VOTOMOS)
Λίμνη Ζάρου (Βότομος) / Límni Zárou (Vótomos)

North of Zaros, visit the Votomos spring which flows into a very pretty, small, bell-shaped lake. Along the road to the lake, you will come across picturesque tavernas, where you can try delicious trout and salmon. You will also see a water mill among plane trees. Special attention has been paid to the area around the lake, with its benches, children's playground and a restaurant, which would be even more attractive without its plastic chairs. From this point, you can organize **walks to the gorge**, at a distance of 2.5 km, and to **Agios Ioannis**, which is 5.2 km away. At Agios Nikolaos, located 900 m away, you will find an area with water and benches, from which there are marked paths. The walk through the gorge is a fascinating experience. Rest under the shady trees and enjoy the view of the sea.

❺ VRONDISSIOU MONASTERY
Μονή Βροντησίου / Moní Vrondissíou

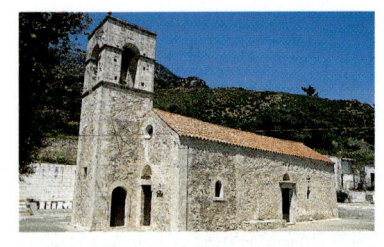

Double-aisled monastery with an extraordinary view.
Its buildings are surrounded by a wall, the bell-tower has been built in Italian style and the aisles are dedicated to Saint Anthony and the Apostle Thomas. It has 14th c. wall-paintings as well as a 5th c. marble fountain, with depictions in relief.
But do not believe the locals, who claim that there are frescoes here and at Valsamonero monastery that have been painted by El Greco (Dominikos Theotokopoulos).

❻ VALSAMONERO MONASTERY
Μονή Βαλσαμόνερο / Moní Valsamónero

Before you set out, find the monastery guard in the village and ask for the keys.
This monastery is located west of Vrondissios monastery, near the village of Voriza, and was an important spiritual centre in the 15th c. It is dedicated to the Virgin Mary, Saint Fanourios and Saint John. The **fres-**

PHAESTOS - MATALA

coes in its church, is all that remains, are particularly interesting in terms of the quality of their design, the variety of subjects and the richness of their colours.
From Voriza you can go **on foot** to the monastery along a smooth dirt road, 2-3 km, with olive groves, plenty of water and beautiful picnic spots.

BEST BEACHES

MATALA
Popular, sandy expanse of beach, next to the village of the same name, with crystal-clear waters, impressive underwater scenery. (See description in **What to See**).

KOMMOS
Large sandy beach, next to the village of the same name.

Kommos

BEST HOTELS AND ROOMS

BEST LOCATION
On this trip, you won't find large hotels with substantial comforts and you'll be confined to two choices. If you prefer to be close to the beach and the nightlife, choose accommodation from our recommendations for Matala. For a quieter stay, we suggest the **Idi** hotel beside the Zaros lake. If you insist on more comfort, you can stay at one of the hotels featured in a neighbouring excursion.

PRICES
The hotel prices mentioned below are the official ones, set by the National Tourist Organization for double rooms, at low and high season, with breakfast. Since owners are allowed to modify prices, always try to negotiate them.

MATALA

✓ ORION (C Class)
Tel. *(0892) 45129, fax 45329*
Open: March-October
Description: On the outskirts of the village, in a tranquil, green environment, ideal for those seeking peace and quiet. Simple, but probably one of the best in the area.
Rooms: 46 rooms with A/C.
Special features: Garden, bar, swimming pool, parking.

Price: 15,000-21,000 drs.
Value for money: ✱

LAKE ZAROS

✓ IDI HOTEL (C Class)
Tel. *(0894) 31301, 31302, fax 31511*
Open: April-October
Description: It began operating in 1980 and is an elegant building featuring stone, wood and the colour white, surrounded by greenery. However, the

service could be better.
Rooms: 59 rooms with A/C, bath, music, telephone and a balcony.
Special features: Garden, bar, restaurant, taverna, swimming pool, mini-golf, tennis court, safe and a trout fishery.
Price: 14,000 drs.
Value for money: ✹✹
Credit cards: Visa, Mastercard

ALTERNATIVES

HOTEL ZAFIRIA (D Class)
Matala, tel. (0892) 45366, 45112, 45747
fax 45725.
Price: 10,800-14,500 drs.

NIKOS (E Class)
Matala, tel. (0892) 45375, fax 45120.
Price: 10,400-12,400 drs.

BEST RESTAURANTS & TAVERNAS

Kivotos

In Matala, you will discover a number of simple, but good, tavernas. You can eat at **The Lions Restaurant**, tel. (0892) 45108, at **Maria's** taverna or, if you are in the mood for a short walk, at the traditional ✓ **Kivotos**, tel. (0892) 42744, which is in the village of Sivas, 10 km from Matala, with oven-baked food and live music every day in the summer. For your entertainment, walk along Matala's main street and make your choice. **Price:** All €

TIPS AND INFORMATION

HOW TO GET THERE

- By air from Athens' west airport to Heraklio with Olympic Airways (18,500 drs.), tel. (01) 9663363 (west airport). With Air Greece, tel. (01) 3255011, and with Cronus Airlines, tel. (01) 3315515, from the east airport, daily flights. Also, by air from Thessaloniki's Macedonia airport with Olympic Airways (26,500 drs.), tel. (031) 260121, with Air Greece, tel. (031) 244340, with Cronus Airlines, tel. (031) 870555, daily flights.
- By ferry from Piraeus to Heraklio (from 5,300 drs.), Piraeus Port Authority, tel. (01) 4226000. From Thessaloniki (from 11,000 drs), Thessaloniki Port Authority, tel. (031) 531505.
- From Heraklio, if you do not have your own transport, take an organized tour to Matala by intercity bus (KTEL), tel. (081) 221765.
- For one-day trips from Heraklio contact the following travel agents:
Creta Travel, tel. (081) 227002, 227003
Cretan Holidays, tel. (081) 342900-10

BEST TIPS

HOW TO GET AROUND: It's fun to walk! Enjoy strolling in Matala and organize hikes in the Zaros district. Other outings by car.

BEST SEASON: March to November, except for August.

USEFUL TELEPHONE NUMBERS

MATALA	(0892)	Clinic	42236
Community Office	45340	Police	45168

KNOSSOS · HERAKLIO

WHY AMONG THE BEST

Because of the Minoan palace of Knossos, a splendid example of one of Europe's oldest and most important civilizations and a place of pilgrimage for visitors from all over the world. Because of the extraordinary exhibits from Knossos, Phaestos and the rest of Minoan Crete in Heraklio's Archaeological Museum.

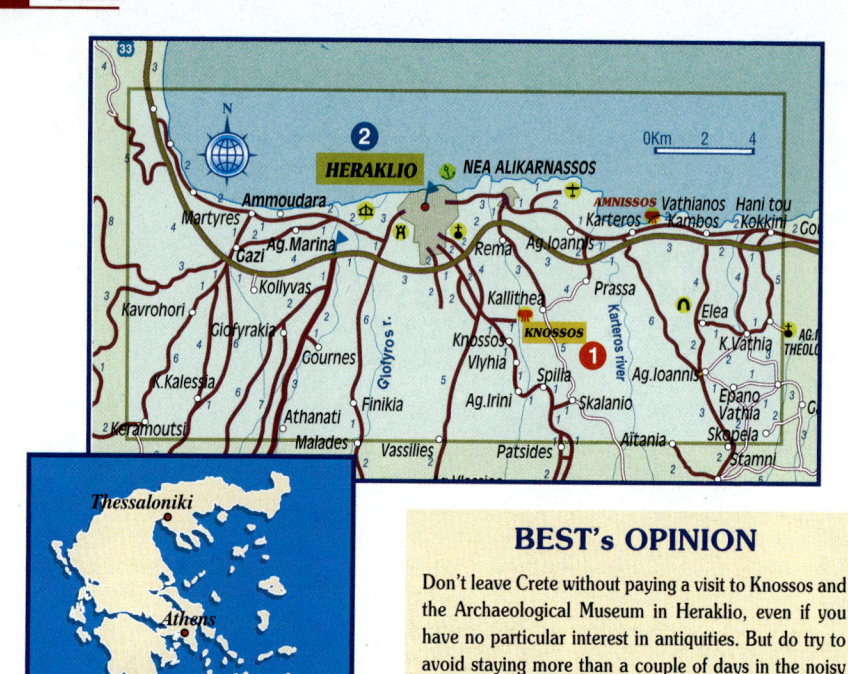

CRETE

BEST's OPINION

Don't leave Crete without paying a visit to Knossos and the Archaeological Museum in Heraklio, even if you have no particular interest in antiquities. But do try to avoid staying more than a couple of days in the noisy jumble of architecturally unacceptable buildings that the city of Heraklio has become. We propose that you see the sights in one day and then move on to another Best excursion.

BEST SIGHTS: STEP BY STEP

❶ KNOSSOS
Κνωσός / Knossós

MYTHOLOGY

In the late 19th c., the British archaeologist **Sir Arthur Evans** brought to light an extremely ancient and exceptionally advanced civilization, that of Minoan Crete. Mythology maintains that its mighty king, **Minos**, failed to keep his promise to sacrifice a magnificent white bull to **Poseidon**, thus provoking the god's rage. In retribution, **Poseidon** instilled in Minos's wife, **Pasiphae**, an uncontrollable lust for the bull which drove her to couple with it. The fruit of this unnatural union was a man-eating monster with the body of a man and the head of a bull, the famous **Minotaur**. Pasiphae concealed her son in a **labyrinth** constructed for her by the celebrated Athenian craftsman, **Daedalus**, and fed him on the bodies of seven young men and women which the Athenians were forced to send every year as tribute to the Cretans. **Theseus**, son of the king of Athens, entered the labyrinth and slew the Minotaur. With the help of Minos's daughter **Ariadne** and her famous ball of twine he managed to find his way out again.

The word **labyrinth** most probably comes from "labrys", the double axe which was the emblem of the Minoan dynasties. Its two curved sides, like the horns of a bull, symbolized the positive and negative force of the **Moon**. Minos was either the ruler of Crete around 1600 BC or a mythical personage who gave his name to a dynasty.

HISTORY

The history of the palace at Knossos begins in about 2600 BC and ends in 1100 BC. The site had been inhabited as early as the Neolithic era and later, in the 3rd millennium BC during what is known as the **Pre-palatial period**, it developed into an important settlement.

The first palace was built before 2000 BC and destroyed in 1700 BC, giving its name to the **Proto-palatial** period. In the **Neo-palatial period**, between 1700 and 1400 BC, a second, grander and more luxurious palace was erected.

KNOSSOS - HERAKLIO

Around 1600 BC an earthquake caused some damage but repairs were made and the life of Minos's subjects continued as usual up to the moment of an even bigger catastrophe, probably the eruption of the volcano on Thera or a savage raid by Achaean invaders from the mainland, which brought to an end the most brilliant era at Knossos. The last, **Post-palatial period** ended in 1100 BC. During this time the palace was rebuilt as the residence of the Achaean rulers. According to **Homer**, **Idomeneus**, the last scion of the Minoan dynasty sailed with 80 ships to join in the **siege of Troy**.

During the Middle Ages, Knossos was a mere village called **Makrys Toichos** (Long Wall).

In 1878 another **Minos**, **Kalokairinos** from Heraklio, started the first archaeological excavations. It was up to Evans, however, to attempt the systematic study and partial restoration which gives us today, 3,500 years later, an idea of how the Minoan palaces, centre of the oldest civilization in Europe, looked and functioned.

ARCHAEOLOGICAL SITE

Tel. (081) 231940

⊙ *8 am-5 pm, closed on holidays**

The archaeological site at Knossos covers **20,000 sq m**. A massive circuit wall with several entrances encircles the palace, which has no fortifications or walls. Its two harbours were probably situated at the mouths of the **Karaitos** and **Amnissos rivers**. The palace was both the residence of the royal family and a major shrine of the Minoan religion.

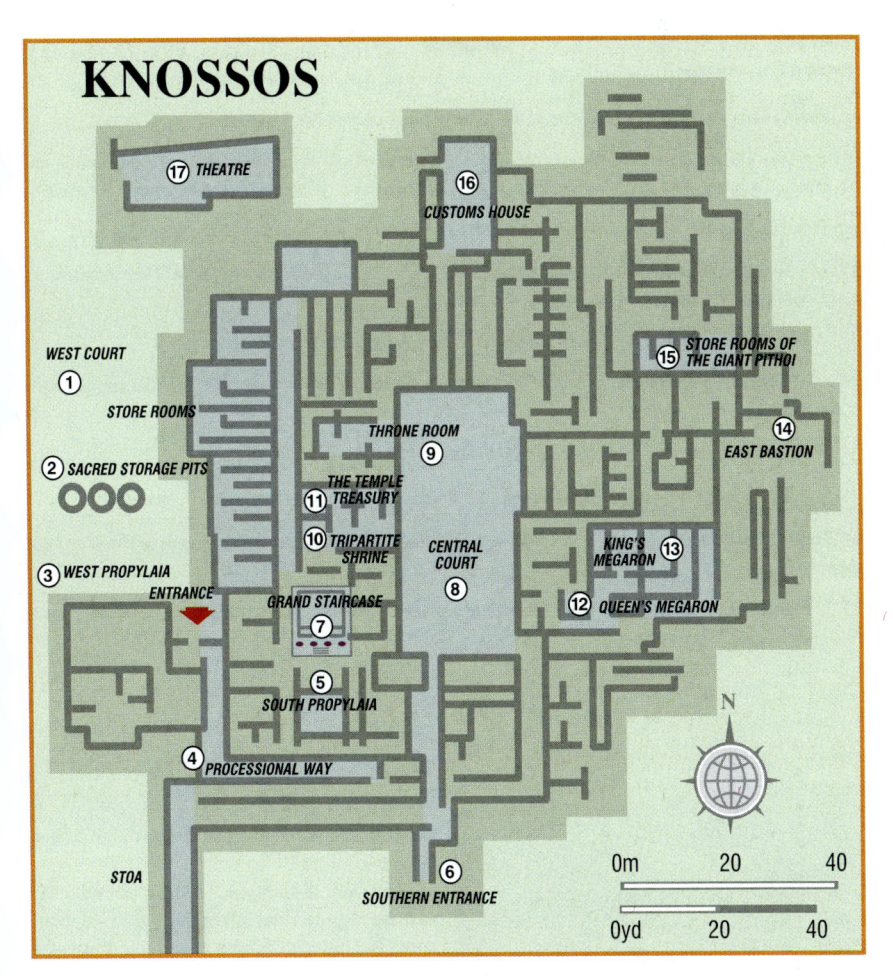

KNOSSOS

- ⑰ THEATRE
- ⑯ CUSTOMS HOUSE
- ① WEST COURT
- STORE ROOMS
- ② SACRED STORAGE PITS
- ⑮ STORE ROOMS OF THE GIANT PITHOI
- ⑨ THRONE ROOM
- ⑭ EAST BASTION
- ⑪ THE TEMPLE TREASURY
- ⑩ TRIPARTITE SHRINE
- ⑧ CENTRAL COURT
- ⑬ KING'S MEGARON
- ③ WEST PROPYLAIA ENTRANCE
- ⑫ QUEEN'S MEGARON
- ⑦ GRAND STAIRCASE
- ⑤ SOUTH PROPYLAIA
- ④ PROCESSIONAL WAY
- STOA
- ⑥ SOUTHERN ENTRANCE

① **The West Court**, which was paved with flagstones, seems to have been the chief meeting/market place.

② **The Sacred Storage Pits**, three walled pits, were probably the depositories of litter from the shrines.

CRETE

The Royal Apartments

③ **The West Propylaia** or **Small Propylaion**, in the south-east corner of the court, was the formal entrance for foreigners. This is where the king most probably received his visitors. The two large rooms immediately after this antechamber had a special red mosaic floor, indicating its use by the ruler.

④ **Processional Way** was separated from the porch with a double-leafed door and was decorated with frescoes showing 350 young men and women bearing offerings to the goddess. An inverted Greek Π in shape, its floor was paved with irregular slabs of green slate and their ended at the central court.

⑤ **South Propylaia** on the left side of the corridor led to the formal state apartments; its entrance was closed by three doors.

⑥ **The South Entrance** has a copy of the fresco of the Prince with the Lilies.

⑦ **The Grand Staircase** with its 12 steps led to the first floor and the royal apartments.

⑧ **The Central Court** lies at the heart of the palace; it was paved with flagstones.

⑨ **The Throne Room** has the original, simple but anatomically shaped royal throne, made from a single block of gypsum, and the stone benches where his courtiers sat. Wingless griffins decorated the walls.

⑩ **Tripartite Shrine**. The central section, with the sacred horns, was higher than the lateral sections.

⑪ **The Temple Treasury**, where the famous figurines of the snake goddess were found. They represent an early lunar divinity worshipped particularly in Crete.

⑫ **The Queen's Megaron** and her private apartments with the famous "flush toilet".

⑬ **The King's Megaron** or Hall of the Double Axes, named for the double axes etched into the walls of the light-shaft.

⑭ **The East Bastion**, with its view of the Kairatos river valley, resembles a tower.

⑮ **The Storerooms of the Giant Pithoi**, the storeroom with its giant jars still in place.

⑯ **The Customs House**, a square hall with large square pillars, which adjoined the palace entrance from the sea.

⑰ **The Knossos Theatre**, perhaps the oldest theatre in the world, has rows of steps on two sides and a royal box. It could seat about 400 spectators.

❷ HERAKLIO
Ηράκλειο / Iráklio

Fort Koules

Heraklio, the capital of Crete and its largest city, has 200,000 inhabitants and attracts another 2 million tourists every year.
Unfortunately, the unsightly buildings erected in the past few decades have badly damaged its appearance. The historian **Strabo** relates that it was the port of Minoan Knossos. In the 9th c. **Moors from Spain** conquered Crete and in 824 constructed a town surrounded by a huge moat (Greek: Handaka),

KNOSSOS - HERAKLIO 24

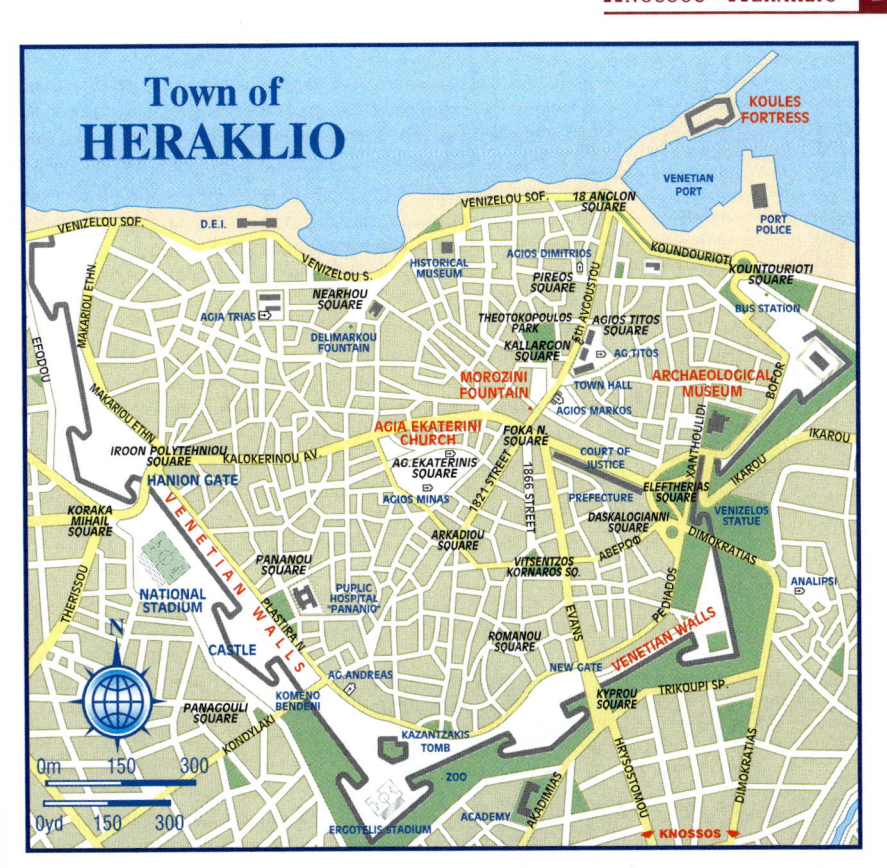

Town of Heraklio map

which became the island's capital but also a pirate lair. The Byzantines conquered it in 960 AD in the time of the emperor **Romanos II**, after numerous attempts. In 1204 the Venetians bought the whole island for one thousand silver marks from the Crusader, **Boniface of Monferrat**. The town was then renamed **Candia** and beautiful public buildings were constructed.

The Ottomans besieged Heraklio for twenty years by land and sea. The blockade decimated and exhausted the population, for lack of food. In 1669 the Venetian leader **Francesco Morosini** decided to surrender to the Turkish General **Kioprulu** on condition that the city's defenders and unarmed population would first be evacuated. The next two centuries were characterized by massacres, uprisings and violence until Crete finally won its independence in 1898. Though foreigners continued to refer to the town (and the island) as Candia, the locals themselves called it Megalo Kastro (Big Fort). In 1822, upon recommendation of the Cretan nominees it reacquired its name of **Heraklio** and was so first referred to by their governor, **Michail Afendoulis**.

WHAT TO SEE

◎◎◎ THE ARCHAEOLOGICAL MUSEUM OF HERAKLIO

1 Xanthoudidou St., tel. (081) 226092
8 am-5 pm, closed on Mondays and holidays*

The finds exhibited here complete the picture of Minoan civilization that the visitor begins to form after a tour of the archaeological sites, especially Knossos and Phaestos.
In room 1 on the ground floor look out for the **steatopygian figurines of a female divinity**, a **marble male figurine**, stone vases and seals with peculiar designs. All the finds here are from the Neolithic and Prepalatial periods.

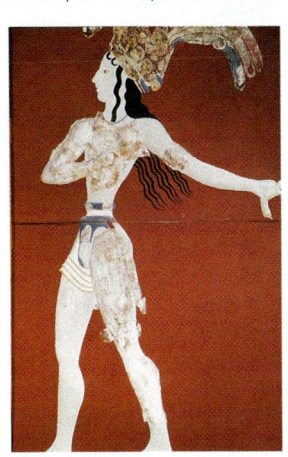

The prince with the lilies

299

CRETE

In room 2 the most interesting finds are the series of vessels with unusual shapes and the votive offerings of male and female **figurines**. Room 3 contains one of the most important finds, the **ceramic Phaestos disc** and Room 4 has the figurines of the **snake goddess**, the **faience girl**, and an ivory figure of the **bull dancer** depicting the moment he attempts to leap over the bull's back. Note also an exceptional example of Minoan stonework, the **rhyton in the shape of a bull's head**, which was a libation vase.

Vases, silver vessels, seals, lamps and figurines, as well as a terracotta **model of a two-storey house** from Archanes, are displayed in Room 5, **gold jewellery and mirrors**, and finds from graves are to be found in Room 6. In Room 7 there are major finds from the Neo-palatial period and interesting jewellery, such as the **pendant with the two bees**.

Room 8 also contains finds from the Neo-palatial period, such as **amphorae** and **vases** from the palace at Zakros and a **rhyton of rock crystal**.

In Room 9 you'll find **vases, rhytons, terracotta figurines** and **examples of miniatures** from eastern Crete. In Rooms 10 - 12 there are objects from the Post-palatial, Sub-Minoan, Early and Late Geometric and Orientalizing periods. Room 13 has **sarcophagi, large jars** and **human skeletons**.

The frescoes from the palace and houses at Knossos are on the first floor. In rooms 14 & 15: the **procession of youths**, the **prince with the lilies**, the **running bull**, the **blue ladies**, the **dolphins**, the **bull-leapers** and of course the so-called **"la parisienne"**, the priestess who delighted her finders with her elegance.

On the same floor, also in room 14, is a wooden model of what the palace at Knossos must have been like and, in Room 16, are the frescoes of the **monkey saffron-collector**, the **leader of the blacks** and the **dancing girl**.

Finally, in Room 20, on the ground floor, take a look at the statue of **Aphrodite**, a copy of Praxiteles' original, and other sculptures from the Classical to Greco-Roman period.

Bull's head rhyton

The blue ladies frescoe

Insert relief of a lion on the Venetian walls

VENETIAN WALLS

Built over a period of one hundred years from 1462 to 1562, they measure 4.5 km in length.

KOULES FORT

At the entrance to the Venetian harbour, built 1523-1540, and impressive even today despite wear and tear.

MOROSINI FOUNTAIN

On Nikiforo Foka square there is a Venetian marble fountain with four lions dated 1628, a work commissioned by the governor general of Crete, Francesco Morosini.

CHURCH OF ST. CATHERINE OF SINAI

Next to the market. Single-aisled, vaulted basilica built in 1600, which contains a collection of icons by Michail Damaskinos of the Cretan School.

KNOSSOS - HERAKLIO

BEST BEACHES

The area has no beaches worthy of inclusion under this heading, but for a quick dip, the beaches east and west of Heraklio, like Amnissou or Ammoudasa, will do. Otherwise pick a beach from one of the excursions to Rethymno, Matala or Elounda.

BEST HOTELS AND ROOMS

BEST LOCATION

The ideal would be to see the sights of Heraklio and Knossos in one day and then spend the night in either Rethymno or Elounda. Failing that one of the city's faceless but efficient hotels will serve as a perfectly decent base.
An alternative would be to stay at **Arolithos**, a traditional hotel in the interior, some 10 km from Heraklio. If you plan to spend several days in the area and you'd like easy access to a beach, then choose from among the fine hotels we recommend under "Beyond this excursion".

PRICES

The hotel prices mentioned below are the official ones set by the National Tourist Organization for double rooms, at low and high season, with breakfast. Since owners are allowed to modify the prices, always try to negotiate them.

HERAKLIO

✓✓ CANDIA MARIS
(Luxury Class)

2.5 km west of Heraklio centre
Tel. (081) 314632, fax 250669
Open: All year round

Description: Built in 1995. Its exceptional, traditional architecture combining brick and marble set it apart from the run of the mill, as do its attractively designed facilities and unusual round pool.
Rooms: 260 bungalows with TV, A/C, and sea view.
Special features: Parking, restaurant, pool, massage, sauna, sports centre, water sports and marine therapy.
Price: 38,400-74,600 drs. (with half board)
Value for money: ✻✻
Credit cards: All

✓✓ APOLLONIA BEACH HOTEL
(A Class)

6 km west of Heraklio centre
Tel. (081) 821646, 821668, 821602, 821624, fax 821433
Open: April-October
Description: A complex with its own beach, which includes a main building, bungalows and model village. The friendly staff, good service, and hospitable atmosphere make up for the fact that the buildings have begun to show their age.
Rooms: 320 rooms and suites, with room service, telephone and A/C.
Special features: Parking, volleyball and tennis courts, gym, pool, water sports, riding, mini golf, conference hall, nightclub, and taverna with Greek dancing every evening.
Price: 23,000-52,000 drs.
Value for money: ✻✻
Credit cards: All

✓✓ ATLANTIS GRECOTEL (A Class)

2 Ygeias St. (next to the Archaeological Museum)
Tel. (081) 229181, 229147, 229103, fax 226265
Open: All year round
Description: Makes for a pleasant stay in comfortable, luxurious and hospitable surroundings.
Rooms: 164 rooms, with room service, A/C, satellite TV, mini bar; most rooms have a panoramic view of the harbour.

Special features: Parking, football, tennis, and other sports, the attractive **Ariadne** restaurant and roof garden with fantastic view, modern conference hall (1,000 sq m). Pets upon request.
Price: 32,000-36,000 drs.
Value for money: ✻✻
Credit cards: All

✓ LATO (B Class)

15 Epimenidou St.
Tel. (081) 228103, 228125, fax 240350
Open: All year round
Description: Simple, modern building with a friendly atmosphere, renovated in 1995.
Rooms: 50 rooms with room service, TV, mini bar, A/C, some with very beautiful balconies overlooking the Venetian castle.
Special features: Parking and conference hall. Pets upon request. 
Price: 25,600-31,400 drs.
Value for money: ✻
Credit cards: All

BEYOND THIS EXCURSION

✓✓✓ ROYAL MARE VILLAGE & ROYAL MARE THALASSO (Luxury Class)

Limenas Hersonissos (30 km east of Heraklio)
Tel. (0897) 22850, 25025, fax 21404, 21664
Open: April-October

Description: Luxurious low buildings in typical Cretan architecture spread out amongst well-tended gardens designed to induce rest and relaxation. Since 1997 the hotel boasts the country's only thalasso (marine) therapy centre, which possesses state-of-the-art French technology. Choose one of the centre's programmes and enjoy the ministrations of its specially trained staff. The beautiful private beach and the many, impeccably organized facilities offered here are additional perks.
Rooms: 415 rooms (24 suites and 101 rooms with direct access to the thalassotherapy centre), with telephone, TV, A/C and safe.

Special features: Parking, 4 tennis courts, mini golf, water sports, 8 pools (1 closed, 2 for kids), archery, restaurant and 2 conference halls.
Price: 63,000-100,000 drs.
Value for money: ✻✻
Credit cards: All

✓✓✓ KALIMERA KRITI (A Class)

Sissi, 45 km east of Heraklio
Tel. (0841) 71603, fax 71598
Open: March-November
Description: The structure of this unusual hotel was inspired by the Minoan style to which some neo-classical features have been added. The bungalows, on the other hand, are based on traditional Cretan architecture. The complex consists of the main building and three attractive "villages", **Agia Varvara**, **Pyrgos** and **Harakas**.

KNOSSOS - HERAKLIO

Rooms: 416 rooms, with room service, TV, telephone, safe, mini bar and A/C.
Special features: Parking, restaurants and tavernas, roof garden, water sports, pools (including an impressive indoor pool), volleyball, gym, private beach, baby sitters/play school with trained personnel, and 2 exceptionally equipped conference halls.
Price: 51,000-74,000 drs.
Value for money: ✹✹
Credit cards: All

☑ AROLITHOS (A Class)

10 km south west of Heraklio
Tel. (081) 821050, fax 821051
Open: April-October
Description: Not your every day, ordinary hotel. Built by Nikos and Aliki Kallergis in 1988, this is more like a traditional, turn-of-the-century hotel. Fifty stone houses with tile roofs surrounded by native bushes and shrubs, cobbled paths, an old smithery, pottery, icon-painting, basket-weaving and carpenter's workshops, an oven, weavers' workshop with looms, a saddle-maker, little bridges over streams, an old fashioned village square and, before your eyes, a whole community from the past has come alive in an area covering about 10,000 sq m. If you're at all nostalgic about bygone days and sometimes think you'd like to look back, then **Arolithos** may be just what you're seeking – a really different kind of holiday.
Rooms: 36 rooms with telephone, some with A/C.
Special features: Parking, restaurant and special tradition-inspired events.
Price: 17,000-21,000 drs.
Value for money: ✹✹
Credit cards: Visa, Mastercard, American Express

BEST RESTAURANTS & TAVERNAS

Heraklio's restaurants, without being exceptional, are nevertheless acceptable, and the best of them offer an interesting range of tastes. They will also give you an introduction to the island's delicious and healthy traditional cuisine.

☑☑ LOUKOULOS

5 Korai St.
Tel. (081) 224435
Italian cuisine in attractive surroundings with a romantic atmosphere provided by antiques, engravings, white tablecloths and candles.
Price: €€€

☑☑ GIOVANNI

12 Korai St.
Tel. (081) 346338
Open for lunch and dinner. The chef loves Italian cuisine but he also makes wonderful Cretan treats. The speciality here is lobster with filet mignon a la cafe de Paris. Light music and nostalgic decor.
Price: €€€

Also the **Giakoumis** and **Ta Grousouzadika** tavernas on Theodosaki street in the old and colourful market serve wonderful lamb chops and other mouth-watering grilled meats. Open for lunch and dinner.
Price: All €

Giovanni

BEST ENTERTAINMENT

In summer the big nightclubs, like **Baracuda** and **Bahalo**, take their high spirits, good drinks and Greek and foreign music out to Ammoudara.

In Heraklio itself most of the entertainment possibilities in winter and in summer are to be found around Korai street. Look for the cafe-bar **Milon tis Eridos** and **Notos**, where you'll find young people and enjoy the lively atmosphere at the bar.

If you're seeking something more traditional, then we recommend the picturesque Turkish cafe, **Koumbes**, near the old market.

TIPS AND INFORMATION

HOW TO GET THERE

Heraklio is connected by direct flights with many European cities. Inquire at your travel agent.
- By air from Athens, with Olympic Airways (18,500 drs.), tel. (01) 9663363, from the west airport. With Air Greece, tel. (01) 3255011, and with Cronus Airlines, tel. (01) 3315515, from the east airport, daily flights.
- By air from Thessaloniki's Makedonia airport, with Olympic Airways, tel. (031) 260121, with Air Greece, tel. (031) 244340, and with Cronus Airlines, tel. (031) 870555, daily flights.
- By ferry from Piraeus in 12 hrs (from 5,300 drs.), Piraeus Port Authority, tel. (01) 4226000.
- And, by ferry from Thessaloniki in 22 hrs (from 11,000 drs.), Thessaloniki Port Authority, tel. (031) 531505.
- For organized tours contact the travel agent Trekking Hellas, tel. (01) 3310323.

CONNECTIONS

- By air with Olympic Airways, from Nikos Kazantzakis airport to Rhodes, Mykonos, Santorini, tel. (081) 229191.
- By ferry to Karpathos, Diafani, Kassos, Rhodes, Halki, Ios, Naxos, Paros, Santorini, Syros, Tinos, Mykonos, Skiathos and Volos. In summer also with Skyros. Heraklio Port Authority, tel. (081) 244856.

BEST TIPS

HOW TO GET AROUND: The best way to see the sights in town is to walk with map in hand, because the locals have the same passion for mazes as their distant Minoan ancestors.

For more distant destinations, the taxis are among the cheapest in Europe. You can get to Knossos for 1,500 drs. and to Hersonissos for 3,500 drs. Buses leave from Morosini Square for Knossos, depositing their passengers at the Archaeological Museum on the return journey. Departures every half hour.

Other solutions:
One-day tours are offered by travel agents, such as:
Creta Travel, tel. (081) 227002-3
Cretan Holidays, tel. (081) 342900-10

BEST SEASON: Every time of year is suitable except July and August when the archaeological site of Knossos and the museum are too crowded to be enjoyable.

USEFUL TELEPHONE NUMBERS

HERAKLIO .... (081)	Tourist Police.. 283190
Town Hall................................. 227102, 221227	Port Authority 244856

Elounda

Mirabello Gulf   Elounda   Agios Nikolaos

WHY AMONG THE BEST

Because of the high standard deluxe hotel complexes in Elounda Bay, which offer visitors a rare experience of a beautiful and luxurious setting, plus excellent service with all comforts. A favourite with the international jet set, celebrities and politicians.

CRETE

BEST's OPINION

This destination is for visitors who demand the highest quality accommodation and can afford expensive holidays. Special attention has been given to the development of quality tourism in the region. If you enjoy social life, sports, luxury and entertainment, you'll be enchanted by the combination of the Elounda hotel complexes with the exciting nightlife offered at Agios Nikolaos. And if you want more action, you can use Elounda as a base for sightseeing in the area.

BEST SIGHTS: STEP BY STEP

❶ ELOUNDA
Ελούντα / Eloúnda

Visitors are impressed by the unique beauty of the rocky coast and the barren, harsh landscape, as they view the Elounda region from the Evangelistria chapel.
Seven settlements, of which only Schisma is located next to the sea, succeeded the Greco-Roman site of ancient Olous, one of the most interesting cities of ancient Crete. A section of Olous sank, following a land subsidence, and the only remains left today are the foundations of some homes, which can be seen in the

ELOUNDA

shallows when the water is calm. Olives and the export of emery — a mineral substance used for grinding — were the mainstays of the local inhabitants, until the large, luxury hotel complexes were built, transforming the region into one of the island's major tourist attractions.

Today, Elounda is the focal point for the top bracket of Crete's tourist traffic, hosting some of the world's rich and famous.

❷ SPINALONGA
Σπιναλόγκα / Spinalónga

You can go to Spinalonga from Agios Nikolaos by boat in 35 min, from Elounda by caique in 20 min, and from Plaka by caique in 5 min. That's islet at the entrance of Elounda Bay, with a Venetian fortress, which was built in 1579 and seized by Kapoudan Pasha in 1715. Following independence, it was for many years a leper colony. The islet's ancient name was Kalydon and the word Spinalonga means "long thorn".

❸ AGIOS NIKOLAOS
Άγιος Νικόλαος / Áyios Nikólaos

The capital of Lassithi prefecture is built around a picturesque lagoon on the north western side of the Mirabello Gulf. A large town with a variety of bars and restaurants, it offers a wide choice of entertainment.

❹ KRITSA
Κριτσά / Kritsá

This pretty village, at the foot of Mt. Kastello is an unspoilt example of traditional Cretan aesthetics. Some 2 km before the entrance to town there is an admirable three-aisled Byzantine church dedicated to the Panagia Kyras, with interesting frescoes from the 14th and 15th century. Visitable daily between 9 am and 3 pm.

❺ LATO
Λατώ / Lató

An ancient Doric city, which was at its peak from the 8th to the 2nd c. BC. It was considered to have been the home of Nearchos, Alexander the Great's admiral.

❻ MIRABELLO GULF
Κόλπος Μιραμπέλλου / Kólpos Mirabéllou

From Agios Nikolaos to Siteia, enjoy a 90 min trip, offering a spectacular view of the Mirabello Gulf. The asphalt road is good, but very winding. Watch along the way, the beautiful little villages nestled in the hills.

⑦ MOHLOS
Μόχλος / Móhlos

A small village by the sea, ideal for a swim and relaxation. You'll find attractive little tavernas for fresh fish on the waterfront.

BEYOND THIS EXCURSION
⑥ LASSITHI PLATEAU

Lassithi plateau

Panagia tis Keras

This fertile mountain plain is at a height of 817 to 850 m with pear, almond and apple orchards. Visit it when its **7,000 windmills** are in operation. Arriving at Psyhro, you can explore the **Dikteo Andro** cave, in which, according to mythology, Zeus was born. Another interesting site is the **monastery of Panagia tis Keras**. Its three-aisled church has 14th and 15th c. frescoes.

BEST BEACHES

The most beautiful beaches in this area are exposed to the north wind.
If you want to avoid choppy seas, you'll have to wait until the wind dies down or check the map for more protected places.

VOULISMA

A pretty, sandy beach, next to Istron, with exquisite, clear blue water.

PAHIA AMMOS

In the village built on the site of the ancient city of Minoa, there is a large, sandy beach, but the sea is frequently rough.

KOLOKYTHA

From the coastal settlement of Schisma, in the Elounda area, you can go swimming opposite, on the island of Kolokytha. It can be reached by boat or by a half-hour walk crossing the bridge.

AGIOS PANDELEIMONAS

A beach at Istron with a picturesque little church, sand and pebbles. To get there, you'll pass through a lush green area, with olive and fruit trees.

PLAKA

Picturesque fishing village, with a small port and pretty beach.

ELOUNDA   25

BEST HOTELS AND ROOMS

BEST LOCATION
Since we selected this excursion mainly for the outstanding hotels at Elounda, which are among the best in Greece, we unreservedly suggest you stay there, if you can afford it. If not, choose another excursion with a richer sightseeing itinerary.

PRICES
The hotel prices mentioned below are the official ones, set by the National Tourist Organization for double rooms, at low and high season, with breakfast. Since owners are allowed to modify prices, always try to negotiate them.

ELOUNDA

✓✓✓ ELOUNDA BEACH
(Luxury Class)
Tel. (0841) 41412-3, fax 41373
Open: April-October
Description: Located 2 km from the village of Elounda. It has rooms and bungalows, with a view of the sea or the garden.
A magnificent, uniquely beautiful hotel complex, which offers outstanding service in a luxurious setting, combined with the privacy and comforts of its elegantly designed, fully-equipped bungalows and plush suites.
It is considered to be one of the finest hotels in Europe, if not the world.

Rooms: 301 rooms, with A/C, TV, telephone. Including bungalows with private swimming pool, which meet the most demanding criteria at prices to match. (in one suite, an overnight stay can cost up to 3,000,000 drs!).
Special features: Restaurant, parking, bar, mini-golf, sports facilities, swimming pool, beach, water sports, sailing club, conference halls, entertainment and health centre.
Price: 72,000-145,000 drs.
Value for money: ✱✱
Credit cards: All except Diners

✓✓✓ PORTO ELOUNDA
(Luxury Class)
Tel. (0841) 41903, fax 41889

Open: April-October
Description: Offers a stunning view of its private beach. Typical traditional architecture, interior decoration and furnishings.
Rooms: 183 rooms and bungalows with A/C, TV, telephone. Many of the bungalows have a private pool.
Special features: Restaurant, parking, golf, roof garden, bar, sports facilities, swimming pool, water sports and conference halls.
Price: 21,000-86,000 drs.
Value for money: ✱
Credit cards: All except Diners

✓✓✓ ELOUNDA MARE
(Luxury Class)
Tel. (0841) 41102-3, fax 41307
Open: April-October
Description: A splendid view of the Aegean, combined with the cool freshness of marvellous gardens. Stone, authentic antiques, the element of tradition and a cosmopolitan atmosphere distinguish this hotel complex which combines luxury and beauty with local colour.

CRETE

Rooms: 108 rooms with A/C, TV and telephone.
Special features: Restaurants, parking, bar, roof garden, sports facilities, swimming pool, water sports, conference hall.
Price: 43,000-97,000 drs.
Value for money: ✱✱
Credit cards: All except Diners

✓✓✓ ELOUNDA BAY PALACE (Luxury Class)
Tel. (0841) 41502, 41702, fax 41783
Open: April-October
Description: Offers a wonderful sea view and a beautiful, luxuriantly green environment.
Rooms: 297 rooms and bungalows with A/C, TV and telephone.
Special features: Restaurant, parking, bar, mini-golf, roof garden, sports facilities, swimming pool, bungalows with private swimming pool, water sports, entertainment centre, sailing club, beauty salon, conference halls.
Price: 61,400-91,200 drs.
Value for money: ✱✱
Credit cards: All

✓✓ GRECOTEL ELOUNDA VILLAGE (A Class)
Tel. (0841) 41802, 41002, fax 41278

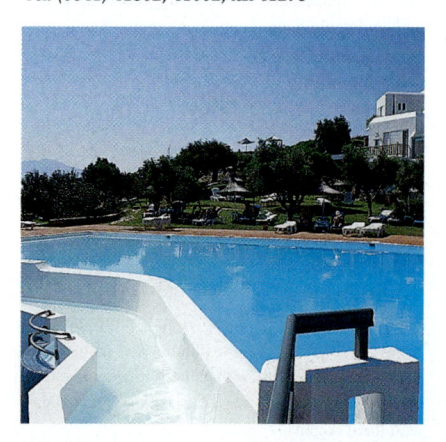

Open: April-October
Description: With a view of Elounda Bay and ample comforts, this fine hotel complex with interesting architecture offers isolated bungalows for those seeking peace and privacy.
Rooms: 162 rooms, with A/C, TV and telephone.
Special features: Restaurant, parking, sports facilities, swimming pool, water sports, roof garden, conference hall.
Price: 66,500-72,000 drs.
Value for money: ✱✱
Credit cards: All

✓✓ PORTO DI CANDIA (A Class)
Tel. (0841) 26811, fax 22367

Open: March-October
Description: It boasts a 65,000 sq. m garden, a warm, hospitable environment, and a meticulously planned design throughout, reminiscent of Spanish architecture. Marvellous view of the sea.
Rooms: 186 rooms with A/C, TV, telephone and kitchen.
Special features: Parking, restaurant, supermarket, sports facilities, water sports and four swimming pools. Pets upon request.
Price: 29,600-94,600 drs.
Value for money: ✱✱
Credit cards: All

AGIOS NIKOLAOS

✓✓ MINOS BEACH (Luxury Class)
Tel. (0841) 22345-9, fax 22548
Open: March-October
Description: Located at a distance of 10 min on foot from the town of Agios Nikolaos, this was the first luxury hotel in the area.
Rooms: 43 rooms with a garden view, 39 rooms and bungalows with a view of Mirabello Gulf and 17 VIP suites which are literally lapped by the sea. All have A/C, TV and telephone.
Special features: Restaurant (known for its French as well as Cretan cuisine), parking, bar, roof garden,

ELOUNDA 25

Olympic-size swimming pool, water sports, conference and congress hall. Pets upon request.
Price: 33,000-98,000 drs.
Value for money: ✷
Credit cards: All

ISTRON
✓✓ ISTRON BAY HOTEL
(Luxury Class)

Tel. (0841) 61303, 61325, 61347, fax 61383
Open: April-October
Description: Located 13 km from Agios Nikolaos and 880 m from the village of Istron. A very special hotel, all-white, with simple but striking architecture, a fantastic 👁👁 **view** of the Mirabello Gulf, beautiful palm trees and a hospitable environment. In addition, it offers superior ✓✓ **gastronomic surprises** in its outstanding restaurants, **Votsala** and **Meltemi**.
Rooms: 145 rooms with A/C, TV and telephone.
Special features: Restaurant, parking, tennis court, games room and pool.
Price: 32,000-54,600 drs.
Value for money: ✷
Credit cards: All

BEST RESTAURANTS & TAVERNAS

ELOUNDA
✓✓✓ OLD MILL
Elounda Mare Hotel

Tel. (0841) 41102-3
With a seating capacity of 20, its cuisine would satisfy the most demanding tastes. Meals are served to the accompaniment of discreet piano music. Book ahead and wear a tie.
Price: €€€

✓✓ YACHTING CLUB
Elounda Mare Hotel

Tel. (0841) 41102-3
Sixty-seat restaurant, with a la carte service, offering special gastronomic delights in exceptionally elegant surroundings.
Price: €€€

✓✓ DIONYSOS
Elounda Beach Hotel

Tel. (0841) 41412-3 
Luxury, excellent service and fine Greek cuisine. Live music accompanies dinner imperative to book.
Price: €€€

✓ MARILENA

Tel. (0841) 41322
A friendly taverna for fish lovers, with good cooking and reasonable prices.
Price: €€

✓ KALIDON

Tel. (0841) 41451

This romantic restaurant is literally situated on the sea, as tables have been placed on a floating platform at Elounda port. Full of atmosphere, with excellent service and a large variety of dishes from both Greek and European cuisine, the Kalidon is the ideal choice for a very special evening.
Price: €

ISTRON

✓✓ VOTSALA & MELTEMI
Istron Bay Hotel

Tel. (0841) 61303, 61347

These restaurants have received awards for their exceptional Cretan cuisine. You'll have a guided tour of different flavours. Cooking lessons also given.
Price: €€

Kalidon

i TIPS AND INFORMATION

HOW TO GET THERE

- By air to Heraklion from Athens with Olympic Airways, tel. (01) 9663363, from the west airport. With Air Greece, tel. (01) 3255011 and with Cronus Airlines, tel. (01) 3315515, from the east airport, daily flights. Also, by air from Thessaloniki's Makedonia airport with Olympic Airways, tel. (031) 260121, with Air Greece, tel. (031) 244340 and with Cronus Airlines, tel. (031) 870555, daily flights. To reach Elounda from the airport, you can rent a car or take a taxi. There are also buses (KTEL) from the port of Heraklion to Elounda.
- By ferry from Piraeus to Heraklio and Agios Nikolaos, Piraeus Port Authority, tel. (01) 4226000, from Thessaloniki to Heraklio, Thessaloniki Port Authority, tel. (031) 531505.

CONNECTIONS

- Ferries from Agios Nikolaos to Karpathos, Kassos and Milos, Agios Nikolaos. Port Authority, tel. (0841) 22312.

BEST TIPS

HOW TO GET AROUND: You will definitely need a private or rented car to get around in the area. There are caiques and boats available daily to visit the pretty islets in the region.

BEST SEASON: The most suitable season for this trip is April to October.

USEFUL TELEPHONE NUMBERS

ELOUNDA	**(0841)**	Tourist Office	22357
Municipal Office	41346	Tourist Police	26900
		Police	22251
ΑΓΙΟΣ ΝΙΚΟΛΑΟΣ	**(0841)**	Port Authority	22312
Town Hall	28286	Taxis	24000

Eastern Crete

Vai · Aspros Potamos · Kato Zakros

WHY AMONG THE BEST

Because the combination of a magnificent beach with a rare grove of palm trees makes Vai one of the absolute musts of Crete. And because of the colourful islets, the wonderful beaches and the traditional architecture of the Aspros river valley villages. And then there are the Toplou monastery and the antiquities of Kato Zakros, all of which constitute the ingredients for a most interesting trip.

CRETE

BEST's OPINION

With the exception of the very popular Vaï which understandably attracts every type of tourist, this trip is addressed principally to those of adventurous spirit, who seek the lesser-known beaches and sights, far from bustling crowds and mass tourism. It is for those who love natural surroundings and hiking, while pursuing an inexpensive holiday without caring about being pampered in big hotels.

EASTERN CRETE

BEST SIGHTS: STEP BY STEP

❶ VAI BEACH
Παραλία Βάι / Paralía Vái

According to legend, Arab soldiers who came to conquer Crete threw out the pips of the dates they were eating while they were here and that from these came this grove of 5000 palms. In fact of course there have been palm trees in Crete at least since Minoan times. It is prohibited to camp overnight within the grove, which covers an area of 60 acres and is protected by fencing under the care of the Forestry Service. In the summer months the wonderfully exotic aspect of Vai is not seen at its best advantage because of the crowds of people. If you get hungry, the taverna on the hill at the edge of the beach offers a good solution and an even better view, if you find a table.

❷ TOPLOU MONASTERY
Μονή Τοπλού / Moní Toploú

Tel. (0843) 61226
8 am-6 pm

The monastery's museum is open from April to October daily from 9 am-1 pm and 2 pm-6 pm. The famed Toplou monastery, twin-aisled, dedicated to the Virgin Mary and to St. John the Divine, was built in the 15th c. in the manner of a veritable fortress. Under the Venetians it was known as Agon Akrotiriani and it acquired the name of "Toplou" in Ottoman days from the Turkish word for cannon: "top". In its prime the monastery had as many as 100 monks but it was devastated in 1821 when twelve monks were massacred in the vaulted entrance, the Lodza gate, by the Turks. Today the visitor will see a fine **windmill**, the **arched doorway** of the entrance, the **stone cells** built into the inner thickness of the fortress walls, old **marble inscriptions**, the admirable **belfry** and the **courtyard** cobbled with pebbles, and **icons** such as that by Ioannis Kornaros, named "Megas ei Kyrie" (Great is the Lord).

❸ GORGE OF THE DEAD
Φαράγγι των Νεκρών / Farànghi ton Nekrón

On the way to Kato Zakros, just after the village of Zakros, on the left, there is a dramatic gorge with sheer cliffsides honeycombed with caves. It is called "ton Nekron" - of the Dead - because the Minoans of Zakros used to bury their dead there in the caves. Go through it on foot, reaching Kato Zakros.

❹ KATO ZAKROS
Κάτω Ζάκρος / Káto Zákros

After a **pleasant drive** from Zakros you come to Kato Zakros, a seaside hamlet with a beach and agreeable fish-tavernas. This is where the great palace of Zakros was discovered. The cisterns found in the palace, one of which was probably a swimming-pool, while the other, with a well, supplied the palace with water, differentiate it from the other Minoan palaces.

❺ HANDRAS - ETIA
Χανδράς - Ετιά / Handrás - Etiá

Here the main point of interest is the nearby ruined medieval village **Voila** (Vo-i-la) as well as the equally ruined hamlet **Etia** on the road to Xerokambos. At Voila see the admirable fort with an arched gateway

Voila, stone fountain

Aspros Potamos

and its only restored construction, the **church of Agios Giorgios** which dates from the 15th c. North of Voila you will discover a remarkable **stone fountain**, which still functions. At Etia you can wander among houses and churches in a relatively good state of preservation and discover a 400-year-old Venetian villa.

❻ ASPROS POTAMOS
Άσπρος Ποταμός / Áspros Potamós

Aspros Potamos is a little valley with lush vegetation where there are two excellent guest-houses in the traditional style. It is near Makrygialo, a tourist village with 500 local inhabitants, which has a number of tavernas and an organized sand beach.

BEST BEACHES

☂☂☂ VAI
A dream of an exotic tropical oasis with a beach of golden sand and crystal-clear deep-blue sea. (*See description under* **Best Sights: Step by Step**)

☂☂ XEROKAMBOS
The easiest way to go is by the asphalt road via Ziros. But if you should wish to enjoy a more scenic route, pick the rough dirt road with no traffic which starts outside Zakros. To the right of the pretty, peaceful, small village there is a good beach interspersed with rocks. Going on to the right you'll find a second little beach with rocks which is even better. Then for the daring there is yet a third, sandy beach with clear blue waters. So don't be put off by first impressions, follow your explorer's impulse and push on. What's more, if you continue on to the right and turn left at the first dirt track you will discover another wildly beautiful and deserted beach. There are tavernas and rooms for rent in the village.

☂☂ KOUREMENOS
A broad unpolluted beach with sand, perfect for sunbathing, swimming and wind-surfing.

☂☂ KOUFONISSI
On the southern side of this attractive little island there are many beautiful, pristine and secluded beaches with sand and limpid shallow waters, ideal for children. You can get there in 45 min taking the speedboat from Makrygialos. Take your lunch with you.

Kouremenos

☂ DIASKARI
East of Makrygialos and slightly off the main road you will come across this beach with clean sand and sea, unfrequented and ideal for a swim.

EASTERN CRETE   26

BEST HOTELS AND ROOMS

BEST LOCATION
There is no doubt that Aspros Potamos and its idyllic setting are of the greatest interest.

PRICES
The hotel prices mentioned below are the official ones set by the National Tourist Organization for double rooms, at low and high season, with breakfast. Since owners are allowed to modify prices, always try to negotiate them.

PALAIKASTRO
MARINA VILLAGE (C Class)
Tel. (0843) 61284, 61407, fax 61285
Open: April-October
Description: A small family hotel built in 1982 and modernized in 1996. It is near Palaikastro beach, one km out side of town in a quiet area.
Rooms: 33 rooms with A/C, telephone and balcony.
Special features: Tennis court, parking, snack bar and pool.
Price: 19,900-23,000 drs.
Value for money: ✹✹✹
Credit cards: None

Aspros Potamos

ASPROS POTAMOS-DIASKARI
✓✓ WHITE RIVER COTTAGES (A Class)
Tel. (0843) 51120, fax 51120
Open: April-October
Description: Amidst pine, olive and carob trees, what in the old days were shepherds' dwellings have been converted, with exemplary reverence for tradition, into apartments for two, three or four persons each. The surroundings, filled with greenery and echoing with birdsong, are a delight. The living spaces are beautifully arranged, featuring mainly elements of stone, rock and wood. Make your reservations well ahead.
Rooms: 13 apartments with bath and telephone.
Special features: Garden, pool, a safe for valuables.
Price: 19,540-36,500 drs., without breakfast
Value for money: ✹✹
Credit cards: Visa

✓ ASPROS POTAMOS
Tel. (0843) 51694, fax 51816
Open: All year round
Description: Not to be confused with the White River Cottages, Aleka's little settlement does not have electricity and has been preserved externally exactly as it was. It will delight romantics who get a thrill out of drinking pure well-water and sitting up late with the soft glow of a paraffin lamp for company.
Rooms: There are 10 cottages.
Price: 6,000-12,000 drs.
Value for money: ✹✹✹
Credit cards: None

317

✓✓ DIASKARI

We 've discovered for you on this beach, two splendid old stone warehouses which have been converted with taste and transformed into superb villas right by the sea. This is a challenge to spend a holiday unlike any other, away from the tourist beaten track. If interested, get in touch with Mr. Gianni Grammatika, tel. (0843) 51282 or with Simply Crete in London tel. 0044-181-9944462.

BEST RESTAURANTS & TAVERNAS

On this excursion, everywhere you'll find small inexpensive tavernas for an adequate meal but none of them special, with the possible exception of Porfira. A little beyond this excursion, it is worth stopping at Anna Bay in the town of Ierapetra.

✓ PORFIRA

Makrygialos, tel. (0843) 52189
The cooking here is in a class apart and the friendly owner will be pleased to give you a guided tour of the gourmet world of Crete. Their unusual dishes, created with love and devotion to tradition, are redolent of nature and appealing to the senses, taking the dinner guests on a flavourful journey to a past originating in Minoan times.
Price: €

OTHER PLACES BEYOND THIS EXCURSION

✓ ANNA BEY

8 Gonnadaki St., Ierapetra, tel. (0842) 27733
A multi-purpose space of excellent design including an area for food and wine and an old-style kafenion and bar.

TIPS AND INFORMATION

HOW TO GET THERE

- By air from Athens (west airport) to Sitia by Olympic Airways (23,100 drs.), tel. (01) 9363363.
- By ferry from Piraeus to Sitia in 12 hrs (from 6,800 drs.) and to Agios Nikolaos in 10 hrs (from 5,750 drs.), Piraeus Port Authority tel. (01) 4511317.
- By intercity bus, Sitia KTEL, tel. (0843) 22272 and from Agios Nikolaos to Vai, tel. (0841) 22234.
- You can hire a car in Sitia or Agios Nikolaos.

BEST TIPS

HOW TO GET AROUND: If you do not have your own car, other than Vai where you can go in an excursion coach, you will need to hire a car.

BEST SEASON: Spring, when everything's in bloom and in the summer months. But if it is your dream to enjoy the sight of Vai as it is never seen by the tourists, go there in spring and autumn.

USEFUL TELEPHONE NUMBERS

PALEKASTRO	(0843)	OTE	61225
Police	61222	**MAKRYGIALOS**	**(0843)**
Town Hall	61204	OTE	51490

The Dodecanese

DODECANESE

BEST's OPINION

The possibility of easy island hopping gives the traveller the chance to pursue a great diversity of interests, especially if the tour is combined with a visit to the Greek and Roman archaeological sites on the coast of Asia Minor. One disadvantage of the Dodecanese is the disappointing beaches, apart from those on Rhodes and Kos and a few scattered exceptions.

IN BRIEF

The Dodecanese are the islands of the south-eastern Aegean just off the coast of Asia Minor. Though Dodecanese actually means "twelve islands", the group consists of fifteen major inhabited ones and several smaller rocks and islets.

The climate is warm with many sunny days and little rain. Some of the islands, the larger ones, are cosmopolitan tourist destinations with luxury hotels, organized beaches and a zippy nightlife, while the lesser known ones tend to be quiet, isolated and laid back.

HISTORY

The origins of life in the Dodecanese are lost in the mists of time. The islands have always straddled the crossroads of civilizations, been conquered and ravaged by waves of easterners moving west and westerners venturing eastwards. They have known periods of geological upheaval, flourishing arts and economic prosperity and times of decline and obscurity.

They were first settled in the Neolithic era (8000-3000 BC) and later by the Phoenicians, Carians, Minoans, Mycenaeans and Dorians. They took part in the Trojan War and later grew prosperous thanks to their skill as sailors and merchants. Forced to surrender to the Persians, they joined the First Athenian Confederacy after liberation (478 BC) and fought on the side of the Athenians during the Peloponnesian Wars. In 408 BC the three most important city-states of Rhodes – Lindos, Kameiros and Ialyssos – united to found the city of Rhodes, an event that transformed the Dodecanese into a powerful centre of trade and culture. Although the islands were initially opposed to Macedonian might, they eventually supported Alexander the Great in his campaign against the Persians.

The Dodecanese remained independent during the unsettled period after Alexander's death and soon allied themselves with the Romans who shortly afterwards conquered Greece (146 BC). In 395 AD they became a province of Byzantium and fell into decline as a consequence of earthquakes combined with barbarian attacks.

After the Fourth Crusade and the fall of Constantinople to the Franks (1204), the islands were divided among Venetian and Genoese dynasties and from 1309 to 1522 they were governed by the Knights of St. John. This was a period of economic and cultural development, which ended abruptly with the Ottoman conquest. The islands managed however to retain a certain autonomy by paying an annual tribute.

They joined the Greek revolution of 1821 against the Turks and were briefly part of the new Greek state, but the Treaty of London (1830) awarded them, together with Samos, to the Ottomans. In 1912, during the Italo-Turkish War, the Italians occupied the Dodecanese and held on to them until 1947. The treaty between Greece and Italy signed in Paris in 1948 returned the islands to Greece.

THE DODECANESE ISLANDS

Although we have selected some islands for inclusion in our Best excursions – ☺☺☺ **Rhodes** (*Excursion 27*), ☺☺ **Patmos** (*Excursion 29*), ☺☺ **Symi** (*Exursion 28*) and ☺ **Marathi, Arkii** and **Lipsi** (*Excursion 30*) – we want to stress that many of the other islands do not lack for great natural beauty and cultural interest.

DODECANESE

ⓖⓖ KOS / Κως / Kos

Kos, the homeland of Hippocrates, is a long narrow island with an excellent road network, **mineral springs** and **large beaches**. It is a popular package tour destination and is aimed at young people hoping to combine sightseeing with an energetic nightlife.

Among its many landmarks are the stately ⓖⓖ **castle of the Knights of St. John**; the ⓖⓖ **Asklepeion**; the ⓖⓖ **Ancient Agora** with its **Sanctuary of Dionysos** and many ruined temples; the ⓖⓖ **Archaeological Museum**; the Roman villa ⓖⓖ **Casa Romana** and the ⓖⓖ **Odeon**. You should also see the enormous ⓖ **plane tree** under which **Hippocrates** is said to have taught, the ⓖ **mosque** and the ⓖ **fountain of Gazi Hassan**.

Don't miss a trip inland to the mountain villages in the area of **Asfendiou**, on the slopes of Mt Dikaion, including ⓖ **Zia**, **Asomatos**, **Lagoudi**, **Evangelistria** and **Agios Dimitrios**. Then continue on to **Pyli** and the deserted Byzantine village of ⓖⓖ **Palaio Pyli** and from there head for **Andimacheia** to see the ⓖ **Venetian castle** that dominates from the hill. Afterwards, ⓖ **Kefalo** and the ruins of ancient Astypalaia, the birthplace of Hippocrates, are worth a visit. The island's best beaches are to be found on this (south) side: ⚲ **Agios Ioannis o Theologos**, ⚲ **Paradissos** and ⚲ **Kamari**. The northern beaches are also good and organized, but they do draw the masses.

Asklepeion

ⓖ KARPATHOS / Κάρπαθος / Kárpathos

Although it is fairly large, has a variety of attractions, pretty beaches and an enormous airport, Karpathos has not yet been exploited for tourism. This makes it a fine choice for an adventurous, peaceful holiday.

Among the sights, we recommend the open air museum ⓖ **Karpathos Park**, ⓖ **Poseidon's Cave**, and the ancient acropolis sitting on the rocky hill.
Take the time to explore the island's beautiful villages, such as ⓖⓖ **Olymbos** or **Elymbos**, the most traditional of them all, with its unusual houses, windmills, local customs and wonderful panegyri (village festival) on the 15th of August.
The best beaches are concentrated around the middle of the island, from Pigadia to Agios Nikolaos on the east coast and from Finiki to Makrys Gialos on the west coast.

Olymbos

ⓖ KASSOS / Κάσος / Kássos

A bare, mountainous and remote island, with a rocky, steep coastline. The **stone mansions** in the lovely villages of **Phri**, **Agia Marina** and **Arvanitohori** are its main attraction, though its scattered windmills, plethora of tiny churches and caves add to its charm. Kassos will appeal to nature lovers, hikers, and spearfishermen, but it has no real beaches. The best place to swim is at the nearby islet of Armathia.

ⓖ KALYMNOS / Κάλυμνος / Kálymnos

The sponge-fishers' island since time immemorial, with mountains and castles, delightful coves, monasteries, and ancient temples. It's a quiet island with relatively little tourism.
ⓖ **Pothia**, the capital and main port, has pastel houses, pleasant public buildings and a ⓖ **sponge processing factory**. Here you'll find the last sponge-fishing fleet in Greece. Going north-west will bring you to ⓖ **Horio**, on a rocky hill with a stunning ⓖⓖ **view** and the nine white chapels which are all that is left of

Pothia

321

DODECANESE

the fortified settlement of **Pera Kastro**. The road continues on past sheltered beaches, and ends at the sleepy fishing hamlet of **Emborio**. The north-east route leads to the fjordlike ⓖⓖ **Vathy Bay** and the **Kefala cave**.

ⓖ LEROS / Λέρος / Léros

Leros is an interesting island with a sharply **indented coastline**, an enormous closed harbour, **Lakki** with its Art Deco **Italian architecture**, medieval castles and decent beaches. It's worth a visit, possible by hydrofoil, if you feel like escaping the resort islands for a bit.
Platanos, the capital, has a ⓖ **Byzantine-Venetian castle** enclosing the church of **Kyra tou Kastrou**, and the picturesque villages nearby, **Pandeli** and **Agia Marina**, the latter with its mini castle, Bourtzi, are worth a look. Then head for the lush, sophisticated ⓖ **Alinda**, going as far as Partheni, next to the airport and near the ancient ⓖ **temple of Artemis**, from where you can visit the islet of **Archangelos** with its beautiful beaches.

ⓖⓖ ASTYPALAIA / Αστυπάλαια / Astypálaia

A fine spot for a peaceful holiday, Astypalaia's ⓖ **architecture** is more reminiscent of the neighbouring Cyclades. The charming ⓖⓖ **Hora** is well worth a visit, with its imposing ⓖⓖ **Venetian castle** lived in from the 13th to 15th c. by the Guerini family. Don't miss the lovely scenery around the ⓖ **Monastery of Agios Ioannis** with its spectacular view, gardens and **mini waterfall**. The best beaches are in the south part of the island.

Hora of Astypalaia

ⓖ NISSYROS / Νίσυρος / Níssiros

A round island with a simmering volcanic crater at its core, its landscape is half green, half lunar. It attracts relatively few tourists who stay no longer than a day or two, but it does have its devotees who return year after year. Strolling through the narrow medieval lanes of its main town, ⓖ **Mandraki**, you can climb up to the ⓖ **Venetian castle** with its ⓖ **monastery Panagia tis Spiliani** and then take a swim at **Hochlakia beach** with its black pebbles. The chief sight is of course the ⓖⓖ **volcano** with a second, double crater and numerous blowholes. There are good ⚓ **beaches** at Giali.

ⓖ TILOS / Τήλος / Tílos

A small island with a long tradition and hospitable residents, a diversified landscape encompassing lush green valleys and steep mountains, churches and archaeological sites. Among the things to see here are the beautiful deserted ⓖ **Mikro Horio**, with its **Agios Panteleimon Monastery** and the **Harkadio cave** where the bones of a prehistoric **dwarf elephant** were discovered. Also worth a look are **Megalo Horio**, with its **castle** occupying the site of the ancient acropolis; there is a fantastic **view** of the sunset from the abandoned church dedicated to the **Archangel Michael**. The best beaches are also near here.

ⓖ HALKI / Χάλκη / Hálki

A tiny barren, waterless island near Rhodes, Halki has also become an international meeting centre for youth from around the world. Its sole village and port is picturesque ⓖ **Nimborio** which has a pretty ⓖ **church** and ⓖ **belltower** dedicated to **St. Nicholas**.

Nimborio

ⓖ KASTELLORIZO (MEGISTI)
Καστελλόριζο (Μεγίστη) / Kastellórizo (Megísti)

The stately **mansions** on this remote island were once home to 15,000 people; since the second world war most of them are deserted hulks. Kastellorizo (pop. 250) is slowly being restored to life and it has a **wild beauty**. Though it has **no cars**, it does have a small airport. Worth visiting are the derelict Venetian ⓖ **Castello Rosso** and its ⓖ **museum**, perched on its red hill, from which there is a wonderful ⓖⓖ **view**. Don't miss a trip to the ⓖ **Blue Grotto** (Galazia spilia/Parasta), where the light plays on the stalactites, and the offshore islets of ⓖ **Strongyli** and ⓖ **Rho**.

322

RHODES

WHY AMONG THE BEST

Rhodes has been included among the BEST mainly due to its old medieval town. But the addition of the antiquities of Lindos, the Byzantine churches and the monastery at Filerimos, as well as the swinging nightlife to be found everywhere, all contribute to make Rhodes a very agreeable destination, as long as you are not put off by the tourist crowds.

27 Dodecanese

RHODES

RHODES

BEST's OPINION

The characteristics which make the island so attractive to tourists are the excellent quality and value of the shopping opportunities, the superbly preserved monuments, the high standard of tourist infrastructure and above all its wonderful climate. The throngs of visitors apart, you will greatly enjoy this trip and it is certain that you can never be bored on an island as large and sophisticated as this one, because you will have a vast choice of things to see and a great variety of entertainment and pastimes.

IN BRIEF

In the Aegean sea, between Karpathos and the shores of Asia Minor, Rhodes – population some 100,000 – shows strong evidence of the influence of western Europe from the days of the Knights and more recent Italian domination. The scenery is composed of lush vegetation, numerous torrents, protected coves as well as wide bays exposed to the wind. The climate is soft and mild with a great deal of sunshine over nine months of the year. Medieval castles, combined with the nightlife, make for a nostalgic evocation of the past, yet with the liveliness of modern times. Tourist facilities are excellent as tourism constitutes the island's principal source of income. The majority of tourists are concentrated in the town of Rhodes, in the Ixia quarter with its sizeable hotels and numerous restaurants, in the Faliraki quarter and in Lindos. The further south one goes, and into the hinterland, the less touristic are the areas to be discovered.

HISTORY AND ARCHITECTURE

Dedicated to the sun god Helios-Apollo, Rhodes, or Ophioussa, or Asteria, Aithraia or Kolimbia – some of the names it bore in times past – acquired its present name in honour of a daughter of Poseidon – the sea god – or, according to others, from the rose, for which the Greek world is «rodho». There is mention in Homer of three ancient cities, Lindos, Ialyssos and Kamiros, which, according to myth, took their names from three princes, grandsons of Helios and were probably founded during the Mycenaean period, surviving to the time of the Dorians. The first inhabitants, back in the days of mythology, were the Telchines, then came the Achaeans and, after 1200 BC, the Dorians. In the 5th and 4th c. the island had 5 major harbours and its statutes constituted the international law of the day. In 70 AD it was subjected to the Romans and later passed to Byzantium. In 515 AD it was destroyed by a violent earthquake, in 1097 it fell to the Crusaders and from 1309 was ruled by the Knights of the Hospital of St. John of Jerusalem, who remained on the island for two centuries. There followed the Ottoman domination and then the Italian, until 1947 when Rhodes was liberated and incorporated into Greece.

BEST SIGHTS: STEP BY STEP

❶ RHODES TOWN
Πόλη Ρόδου / Póli Ródou

With a population of 43,500, the contemporary town of Rhodes was built by the Italians and has a number of interesting neo-classical buildings. Rhodes flourished in 300 BC when it was adorned with exceptional works of art in sculpture and architecture, of which – one of the Wonders of the World – was the Colossus. In the 4th c. BC, the orator Aeschinis, exiled to the island, founded a school attended by major personalities. The Knights of St. John fortified the town and constructed splendid monuments and public works. In 1480, when Pierre d'Aubusson was Grand Master, the town was besieged but not taken. In 1522 the Turks again invaded Rhodes, with an army of 20,000 and 280 ships. After heroic resistance the Grand Master Villiers de l'Isle Adam, whose later death signalled the end of the era of chivalry, was forced to surrender the town to the sultan Suleiman the Magnificent.

DODECANESE

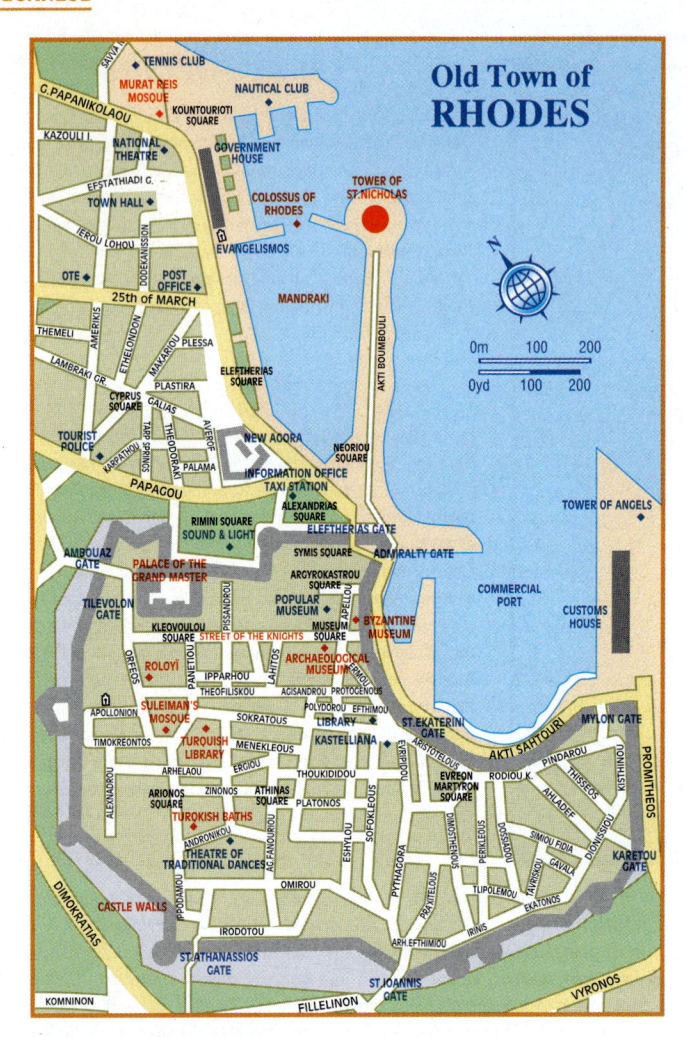

Palace of the Grand Master

🏛🏛🏛 RHODES OLD TOWN
Παλιά Πόλη Ρόδου / Paliá Póli Ródou

Located within the ramparts, in a semi-circle round the port. Only cars with special permits are allowed in. The Greeks and the families of the Franks lived in the southern part, the Jews in the eastern, while the Knights Hospitallers lived in the northern, in the quarter named Castello, with a perimeter wall. Their residences and their hospital are still in an almost perfect state of conservation today. The style is Late Gothic, local limestone was used, with many very apparent western European elements and very little of the architectural heritage of Byzantium and the Orient.

🏛🏛🏛 Palace of the Grand Master
Παλάτι του Μεγάλου Μαγίστρου / Paláti tou Megálou Magístrou

Tel. (0241) 25500, extension 180

🕐 *Summer 8 am-7 pm, winter 8 am-2:30 pm, closed on Mondays and holidays**

A 14th c. construction, at the NW highest point of the medieval town, this also served as the ultimate

RHODES

stronghold in case of invasion. It was abandoned in the days of Ottoman domination and suffered extensive damage from an explosion in 1856. The attempt to restore it was undertaken by the Italian governance, at which time the flooring was covered with Hellenistic and Roman mosaics imported from Kos.

The palace is impressive, decorated with the coats of arms of the Grand Masters. Of particular splendour are the refectory, the halls with the Hellenistic marble trophy and with the cross-vaulted ceiling.

🌀🌀🌀 Street of the Knights
Δρόμος των Ιπποτών / Drómos ton Ippotón

Ascending straight from the port to the palace, it is 200 m long, 6 m wide, and lined by the most imposing and richest buildings of the Knights of St. John. Avoid the crowds, and you will be transported into the past and may even have some mystical communion with someone of the Order.

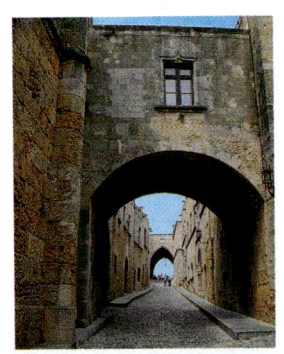

Street of the Knights

🌀🌀 Castle Walls
Τείχη του Κάστρου / Tíhi tou Kástrou

Mighty fortifications to withstand cannon fire transformed the old Byzantine ramparts into an impregnable medieval fort. Its size is grandiose and it is in a fairly good state of conservation, the hallmark of the Old Town's distinctive character.

The coats of arms, stone carvings in relief and the round towers which resisted three major sieges grip the imagination of today's visitor as forcefully as they impressed those who saw them as restored by the Knights, who regularly cared for their maintenance. A broad moat surrounds the walls which have seven entrances, the grandest being the 🌀 **Amboise gate**, with a bridge.

The Amboise gate

🌀🌀 Tower of Saint Nicholas
Πύργος του Αγίου Νικολάου / Pírgos tou Agíou Nikoláou

Open only occasionally, so find out first from the Archaeological Service, tel. (0241) 25500. It stands on the end of a pier opposite Mandraki and was also known as St. Aimé or Adamantos. Construction began in 1464 on the site of the small chapel of the same name, because of the strategic importance of its position. The Turks were never able to capture the tower, which had powerful defence mechanisms.

Archaeological museum

🌀 Archaeological Museum
Αρχαιολογικό Μουσείο / Archeologikó Mousseío

Tel. (0241) 25500, extension 167
☼ *Summer 8 am-7 pm, winter 8 am-2:30 pm, closed on Mondays and holidays**

Housed in the Hospital of the Knights, the substantial, imposing 🌀🌀 **construction** dates from 1440. In the museum, you can see noteworthy vases, tools, sculptures and miniatures, clay sarcophagi, figurines, a fine Rhodian oenochoe (wine jug) of the 7th c. BC, ancient coins, the finds from the acropolis of Ialyssos and funeral offerings from the graves of Kameiros. Also shown are stelae, fragments from temples, Christian mosaics, coats of arms, weaponry, coins and medals. Worth seeing are also the two archaic Kouroi, the stele of Krito and Timaristi, the stele of the dead warrior, the statue of Aphrodite bathing and the two headless statues of nymphs.

Byzantine museum

Suleiman's mosque

Turkish library

🛈 Byzantine Museum
Βυζαντινό Μουσείο / Vizantinó Mousseío

Moussiou Square, tel. (0241) 27657

🕘 8 am-2:30 pm, closed on Mondays and holidays*

The Gothic 🛈 **Church of the Panagia** was erected in 1480 by the Grand Master Pierre d' Aubusson to give thanks to Our Lady for preventing the Ottoman invasion. It was destroyed in the subsequent and fatal siege by the Ottomans. The museum now in it contains splendid frescoes and icons of the Late and Post Byzantine periods. Of special interest are the diptych icons of the Panagia Odigitria of the mid-14th c.

🛈 The Clock / Ρολόι / Rolóyi

Orpheos St.

The clock tower was built in 1852. Climb its stairs and gaze over the town from its height. A cafe-bar of the same name is located there.

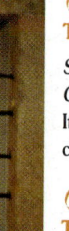

🛈 Suleiman's Mosque
Τζαμί του Σουλεϊμάν / Tzamí tou Suleimán

Sokratous St.
Closed for renovations

It was erected shortly after the siege of 1522, probably on the site of the church of Agion Apostolon and restored in the 19th c.

🛈 Murat Reis Mosque
Τζαμί Μουράτ Ρέις / Tzamí Mourát Réis

Eleftherias Square
Closed

Built on the site of the church of Agios Antonios, it is distinctive for its delicate and elegant minaret. Murat Reis, Suleiman's admiral in the siege of 1522, is buried in the Turkish cemetery.

Turkish Library / Τουρκική Βιβλιοθήκη / Tourkikí Vivliothíki

Founded by Havouz Ahmed Agha in 1794. Among the significant manuscripts stored there is an interesting chronicle of the last siege of the town.

Turkish Baths / Χαμάμ / Hamám

Arionos Square
Tel. (0241) 27739

🕘 Tuesdays 1 pm-6 pm, Wednesdays-Fridays 11 am-6 pm, Saturdays 8 am-6 pm, closed on Sundays, Mondays and holidays*

An oriental atmosphere in an authentic Turkish bath in operation.

COLOSSUS OF RHODES – THE DEER
Κολοσσός της Ρόδου – Ελάφια / Kolossós tis Ródou – Eláfia

It was a bronze statue of Helios 31 m high, the work of Haris, a pupil of Lysippos or of Lahis. It took 12 years to be made, from 302 to 290 BC. There are no records of the statue's position, but it is unlikely that it straddled the two ends of the entrance of the harbour for ships to sail through between its legs, as the legend goes. When the Saracens captured the island they sold it piecemeal as scrap metal. At the place where it was said that the Colossus once stood you will see today two **bronze deer**. They remind the inhabitants that Rhodes was once named Serpent Island (Ophioussa) and that the deer were used to protect them from the infestation of snakes, which they killed with their horns.

The deer

RHODES 27

FREE TIME

👁 👁 SOUND AND LIGHT, AT THE PALACE

An event with music and evocative lighting effects, taking place from April to October in the garden of the Palace of the Knights.

👁 AQUARIUM

With rare specimens of fish, live or not, and sea creatures, for those who are fascinated by marine life.

👁 RODINI PARK

Slightly out of the centre of town, with oleanders, swans, peacocks, abundant streams of water flowing in beds forming little pools and plenty of foliage, this garden is ideal for a respite from the midday heat of summer. See the tomb of the Ptolemies chiselled out of the rock in the cemetery dating back to the 3rd c. BC. For refreshment there is also a restaurant and bar.

Monte Smith

MONTE SMITH

This hill of Agios Stephanos is the acropolis of ancient Rhodes. At its top there are ruins of a temple of Athena Poliados and of Zeus Polieos. It was the registry where the treaties signed by the Rhodians with other cities were deposited.

PLAYBOY CASINO

4 Papanikolaou St., Rhodes town
(in the beautiful former Hotel de Roses), tel. (0241) 97500.

Hot springs of Kallithea

❷ HOT SPRINGS OF KALLITHEA
Θέρμες Καλλιθέας / Thérmes Kallithéas

The spa waters of Kallithea which Hippocrates recommended to his patients are now dry, and the premises of the baths are no longer in operation. There is however a little hamlet nearby, built in 1020.

❸ SEVEN SPRINGS
Επτά Πηγές / Eptá Pigés

The perfect place for relief on hot summer days. The plane trees and other foliage flourish by the springs, which pour into a lake with a waterfall. Organize a picnic or visit the taverna.

Seven springs

❹ LINDOS
Λίνδος / Líndos

Lindos, with 900 inhabitants, is perched on a triangular rock and preserves the local colour of traditional Cycladic architecture, with its blinding-white houses, steep alleys and the plane tree in the square. At the same time, it pays the price of intense tourist development with lots of boutiques, advertisement signs and the crowds which converge here in the summer months. Choose sunset for the time of your stroll around Lindos, when the sun's last rays reflecting off the white-washed houses create magical rainbow hues. The ancient city began to develop during Dorian overlordship

Lindos

329

and reached its zenith in the 6th c. BC when ruled by Kleovoulos, one of the sages of antiquity descended from an ancient royal line. Lindos' most significant ancient and medieval monuments are on its acropolis, a huge rock plunging sheer to the sea. You go up on foot or on donkey-back.

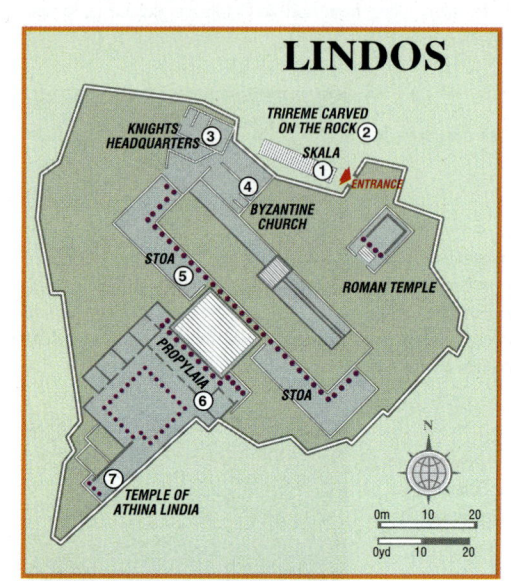

🟢🟢 ACROPOLIS OF LINDOS
Ακρόπολη Λίνδου / Acrópoli Líndou

Tel. (0244) 31258

🕐 Summer 8 am-7 pm, winter 8 am-2:30 pm, closed on Mondays and holidays*

① **Skala:** This leads to the plateau on which the acropolis stands.

② **Triiris (Trireme):** The base of a bronze statue carved into the rock, it has the shape of a ship.

③ **Knight's Headquarters:** An elegant and imposing medieval building.

④ **Byzantine church:** Ruins of the Byzantine church of Agios Ioannis.

⑤ **Stoa:** 88 m wide, in the Doric style, reached by a great central staircase, it has wings jutting at the ends and eight central columns behind which a further stair leads to the propylea.

⑥ **Propylaia:** A wall with five openings, round which there are porticoes and enclosed spaces.

⑦ 🟢 **Temple of Athena Lindia:** In Doric style with four columns in front and four at the back and a length of 22,4 m, dating back to the 4th c. BC, apparently reproducing the architectural structure of an older temple which stood on the same site.

Acropolis of Lindos

🟢 THARRI MONASTERY
Μονή Θάρρι / Moní Thárri

The monastery of Taxiarchis Michail tou Tharri, with an impressive wood-carved iconostasis (rood) and **frescoes** of the 17th c., stands in a wood amid beautiful scenery.

🟢 ASKLEPEION
Ασκληπιείο / Asklipieío

A charming village with white-washed houses below the ruins of the castle. See the Late Byzantine church of the 🟢 **Kimissi tis Theotokou** with interesting frescoes. Next to it is a small devotional and folk art museum.

🟢 FROM MONOLITHOS TO FOURNI
Μονόλιθος-Φούρνοι / Monólithos-Foúrni

Monolithos is a village of 500 inhabitants, in the traditional style, amid olive-planted hills. The architecture of the old stone houses is interesting, and also very attractive are the narrow lanes and steps of particularly picturesque aspect. 3 km out of the village you can visit the Venetian fort, built on an impressive and huge rock. The small pure-white church of Agios Panteleimon is inside the fortress, a semi-ruined chapel and antique cisterns. Enjoy the panorama of the deep blue Aegean from the heights, before taking the road with spectacular vistas and landscape to Fourni where there is a good beach.

The castle at Monolithos

⑧ FROM SEVEN SPRINGS TO SALAKO
Επτά Πηγές-Σάλακο / Eptá Pigés-Sálako

A wonderful route with much greenery, flowing waters and plane trees. You will come across the 15th c. **monastery of Agios Nikolaos Fountouklis**, with fine frescoes. There you'll also discover a delightful picnic spot with a playground, a spring, and the shade of plane trees. Further down there is a cluster of houses built in the years of Italian domination, converted into a sanatorium by Queen Frederika. Today there is a school and a guardhouse, but unfortunately most of it is crumbling. At **Prophitis Ilias** there were two beautiful hotels, the **Elafos** and the **Elafina** (Stag and Hind), famous in the old days but abandoned today. This route will constantly reveal new views of natural beauty as far as your final destination of Salako village.

Profitis Ilias

⑨ ANCIENT KAMIROS
Αρχαία Κάμειρος / Archéa Kámiros

Tel. (0241) 40037
☺ *Summer 8 am-7 pm, winter 8 am-2:30 pm, closed on Mondays and holidays**

Archaeological finds from Mycenaean cemeteries as well as major monuments of the Classical period are evidence of the age-old history of this second ancient city of Rhodes. Its acropolis was on a hill with sheer sides all round, except that which slopes gently down to ancient Milantion, the promontory now called Agios Minas. Here were the private buildings of Kamiros, whereas the public and sacred buildings were on a plateau at the highest point. The most significant remains are from the temple of Athena Kameirados and a Doric portico with double colonnade over 200 m long, erected over a large cistern at the end of the 3rd or beginning of the 2nd c. BC.

⑩ VALLEY OF THE BUTTERFLIES
Πεταλούδες / Petaloúdes

☺ *8 am-5 pm, closed on holidays**

A verdant valley with a stream, plane trees, a path and wooden bridges where you can have a delightful walk of 1 km.
It is worthwhile to go there even if you don't see the kind of moth called **Panaxia**, which come here like clockwork on 15 June to reproduce, leaving again on 30 September. They sleep in the daytime, requiring your respect because they die if you make them fly. After your walk, you can make a stop at the **Petaloudes** cafe-bar.

Valley of the Butterflies

⑪ FILERIMOS
Φιλέρημος / Filérimos

Tel. (0241) 92202
☺ *Summer 8 am-7 pm, winter 8 am-2:30 pm, closed on Mondays and holidays**

Visit the church of the **Kimissi tis Theotokou**, dating

Filerimos

back to the 17th c. and the **chapel of Agios Nikolaos** next to it with 15th c. **frescoes**. Walk along the Dromos tou Golgotha (Calvary), climbing its 134 levels with stone stelae on your right depicting the Passion of Christ, to reach the top of the hill and its grandiose cross.

⓬ ANCIENT IALYSSOS
Αρχαία Ιαλυσσός / Archéa Ialissós

Tel. (0241) 92202

Summer 8 am-7 pm, winter 8 am-2:30 pm, closed on Mondays and holidays*

One of the island's most ancient cities initially inhabited by Phoenicians, from which they were ousted by the trickery of the Greek, Iphiklos. The birthplace –in antiquity called Achaia– of the Olympic champion Diagoras, today it is the meeting point for the various periods of the civilizations of Rhodes. At the highest point of the hill of Filerimos, there are a very few remnants of the ancient temple of Zeus and Athena, in Doric style with four double frontal pillars, dating back to the 3rd or 2nd c. BC. In the 2nd or 3rd c. AD, a triple-aisled Christian basilica with a baptismal font was erected on top of the ruins. On the same spot in the 14th c., the Knights built the church and monastery of the Panagia. On the south side of the acropolis, see the fine Doric fountain of the 4th c. BC, with its four lion-heads.

OTHER THINGS TO DO

GOLF
Tel. (0241) 51256
The Afantou course is unfortunately not in very good condition but still playable. It has 18 holes and par of 72. There is coaching for beginners.

BEST BEACHES

The western beaches are to be avoided when, as often happens in Rhodes, there is a north wind, unless you are windsurfers. Other than Lindos, the eastern beaches are less crowded the farther you go from Rhodes town.

LADIKO
In very green surroundings, a promontory with two creeks. At the farthest, below the canteen, you have the choice of several delightful little coves for a swim from the rocks.
Actor Anthony Quinn bought this land in the sixties when he was filming the *Guns of Navarone*.

KOLYMBIA
Avoid the crowded beach you will find there and go south of the village. Past the fish-taverna ✓ **Limanakia** and in front of a hotel there is a small, attractive and unfrequented pebble beach where you can enjoy bathing.

Tsambika

TSAMBIKA
Between two steep rocks, this is the most popular beach in Rhodes. It is organized, there are canteens and the sands are golden. If you enjoy a view from a height, visit the monastery of **Panagia tis Tsambikas**.

Kolymbia

RHODES

Glystra

⛱⛱ PARALIA LINDOU (LINDOS BEACH)

You can swim, go for water sports or lie under the umbrellas at two sandy, organized beaches, Megalo Limani and Agios Pavlos. There are also canteens if needed.

⛱⛱ GLYSTRA

A lovely little bay with lots of trees and greenery. It has umbrellas and a canteen.

⛱⛱ PLIMMIRI

Follow the dirt path beyond the taverna and pick the spot you prefer with more or less people. It is a long beach with clear waters, sand and pebbles.

⛱⛱ PRASSONISSI

A sandy peninsula at the southernmost point of Rhodes, which the sea covers in winter and which attracts windsurfers. There are two little cafes. To get there, you go a short way along from Kattavia on a practicable dirt track.

⛱⛱ FOURNI

This is your best choice if it isn't windy. The sunsets are gorgeous from here and there is also a taverna at Monolithos.

⛱ FALIRAKI

A long, sandy beach below a series of hotels, very crowded, organized, with umbrellas and water sports.

⛱ AFANDOU

5 km long, pebbly, with fantastic crystal-clear sea. It has been awarded the Blue Flag.

⛱ KALATHOS

3 km long, shingle, a clean sea and a few canteens. It has not been spoiled by mass tourism.

Prassonissi   *Kalathos*

BEST HOTELS AND ROOMS

BEST LOCATION

For the first couple of days, you will want to stay in one of the hotels in the Old Town if you have no car, or nearby if you do, so as to be able to profit as much as possible from its incomparable charm. For the rest of your stay, you can have a relaxing time at one of the hotels on the fine beaches on the east side of the island, where there are calm seas ideal for bathing. You can arrange for your further excursions from there. The best hotels are at Ixia, but it isn't a favourable spot. For the summer book your rooms three months ahead.

PRICES

The hotel prices mentioned below are the official ones set by the National Tourist Organization for double rooms, at low and high season, with breakfast. Since owners are allowed to modify the prices, always try to negotiate them.

OLD TOWN

✓✓✓ RODOS PARK SUITES HOTEL (A Class)

12 Riga Fereou St.
Tel. (0241) 24612, fax 24613
Open: All year round
Description: The best choice for those who can afford it and wish to stay in the town of Rhodes, near the Old Town, and where the staff is friendly and obliging. Member of **Small Luxury Hotels**.

Rooms: It has 30 suites and 30 rooms furnished in excellent taste. All have balconies, several a view to the Palace of the Knights. They have a mini bar, TV and video, fax and computer modem connection, a safe, A/C-ventilation and 24-hour room service. All suites with jacuzzi.
Special features: Restaurant, bar, outdoor bar-restaurant, garden with swimming-pool, gym with sauna, steam bath, jacuzzi, solarium, massage, reception and conference room and parking.
Price: 53,500-83,000 drs.
Value for money: ✹✹
Credit cards: All

✓✓ S. NIKOLIS (E Class)

61 Ippodamou St.
Tel. (0241) 34561, 36238, fax 32034
Open: April-October
Description: In an atmosphere of medieval tradition, this is a particularly well cared-for hotel which has the comforts and quality of A class, although formally being E class. The owner is courteous and cordial, the interior decoration impeccable. The best choice for those who wish to stay in the Old Town.

Rooms: 10 rooms with A/C and TV.
Special features: Parking, restaurant, and bar. Pets upon request.
Price: 46,000 drs.
Value for money: ✹✹✹
Credit cards: Visa, Mastercard

ANDREAS (C Class)

28 Omirou St.
Tel. (0241) 34156, fax 74285
Open: March-November
Description: An unpretentious inexpensive hotel with personality and very welcoming, helpful owner who speaks several languages.
Rooms: 12 small rooms, 6 with bath and 6 without.
Special features: Bar. Telephone, fax, internet.
Price: 18,000-21,000 drs. without breakfast
Value for money: ✹✹
Credit cards: American Express, Mastercard, Visa

CENTRAL

✓✓ GRAND HOTEL SUMMER ASTIR PALACE (Luxury Class)

1, Akti Miaouli
Tel. (0241) 26284, fax 35589, tel. (01) 3243961
Open: All year round

Description: 100 m from the beach, modernized in 1998, it's a good choice for a big hotel in town. Many famous people have stayed here.
Rooms: 378 rooms with A/C, TV and telephone.
Special features: Parking, restaurant, bar, room service, tennis court, swimming pool, roof garden, conference room.
Price: 25,000-41,000 drs.
Value for money: ✹
Credit cards: All

IXIA

✓✓✓ GRECOTEL RHODOS IMPERIAL (A Class)

Tel. (0241) 75000, fax 76690
Open: March-October
Description: One of the biggest, most modern and luxurious hotels in Rhodes, situated above Ixia beach.
Rooms: 402 rooms and suites, with A/C, telephone,

TV, radio, safe, fridge, hair dryer, marble bathroom. All with balcony.
Special features: Restaurant, bar, pool, tennis court, beach volley, gym, sauna, jacuzzi, reception and conference room.
Price: 71,360-90,800 drs.
Value for money: ✱✱
Credit cards: All

✓✓ RODOS PALACE (Luxury Class)

Ialissou Ave.
Tel. (0241) 25222, fax 25350
Open: April-October
Description: A very large imposing hotel complex, above Ixia beach which has been awarded the Blue Flag, it is patronized by VIPs, but also takes in ordinary mortals as guests.
Rooms: There are 785 rooms, with A/C, balcony, bath, telephone, TV, taped music and mini bar.
Special features: Parking, 5 restaurants, 5 bars, card room, 4 pools, 3 tennis courts, water polo, gym, sauna, massage, water sports, conference centre.
Price: 42,500-78,500 drs.
Value for money: ✱
Credit cards: All

EASTERN RHODES

✓✓ ATRIUM PALACE (A Class)

Kalathos
Tel. (0244) 31601, fax 31600
Open: April-October
Description: Near Lindos, in unusual architectural style and interesting interiors, youthful ambiance and a splendid swimming pool. Near a beach.
Rooms: 258 rooms with bath, telephone, TV, radio, mini bar and balcony.
Special features: Parking, restaurant, bar, pool, gym, tennis court, sauna, billiards.
Price: 26,000-48,000 drs.
Value for money: ✱
Credit cards: All

✓✓ RODOS MARIS (A Class)

Kiotari
Tel. (0244) 47000, fax 47051
Open: April-October
Description: Aesthetically pleasing buildings spread over well-tended grounds, next to a wonderful beach, they give a feeling of peace and quiet. Perfect for those who detest noise and crowds.
Rooms: 317 rooms with A/C, TV, telephone, mini bar.
Special features: Parking, restaurant, bar, pool, gym, sauna, tennis and squash courts, water sports and two conference rooms.
Price: 16,000-26,000 drs.
Value for money: ✱✱
Credit cards: All except Diners

✓ MIRAMARE WONDERLAND (Luxury Class)

Ixia-Rhodes
Tel. (0241) 96251, fax 95954
e-mail: mamtour@otenet.gr
Open: April-October
Description: Luxury hotel on the sea, 1.2 km of beach, with beautiful gardens and a little antique train that serves the various parts of the complex.
Rooms: 175 suites with balcony or courtyard, sleeping 2-4 persons. Equipped with kitchenette, fridge, independent temperature controls, telephone, satellite TV and hair dryer.
Special features: Restaurant, bar, tennis court pool, gym, water sports, activities for children supervised by qualified attendants, supermarket and jewellery store.
Price: 50,000-160,000 drs.
Value for money: ✱
Credit cards: All

DODECANESE

CATHRIN HOTEL (A Class)
Ladiko (Faliraki)
Tel. (0241) 85080, 85881, fax 85624
Open: April-October
Description: On a hill above the scenic beach of Ladiko, an inexpensive proposition for family holidays.
Rooms: 160 rooms with A/C, balcony, bath, telephone, taped music. Many rooms with sea-view.
Special features: Parking, restaurant, pool and playground.
Price: 14,000-22,000 drs.
Value for money: ✹✹
Credit cards: All

ALTERNATIVES

RODOS PRINCESS (A Class)
Kiotari, tel. (0244) 47102, fax 47267.
Price: 18,100-27,600 drs.

PARADISE VILLAGE (A Class)
Kallithea, tel. (0241) 67040, fax 67098.
Price: 30,000-46,000 drs.

ESPEROS PALACE (A Class)
Faliraki, tel. (0241) 85734, fax 85744.
Price: 18,000-43,000 drs.

GRECOTEL RODOS ROYAL (A Class)
Faliraki, tel. (0241) 85412, 87571, fax 85091.
Price: 71,800-75,750 drs.

LUTANIA BEACH (A Class)
Kolymbia, tel. (0241) 56295, fax 56441.
Price: 23,000-40,000 drs.

ELENI (C Class)
25 Demosthenous St., Old Town, tel. (0241) 73282, 36690, 29148.
Price: 9,200-11,500 drs.

BEST RESTAURANTS & TAVERNAS

OLD TOWN

✓✓ ALEXIS
18 Sokratous St., tel. (0241) 29347

Fresh fish, seafood and good service. You can order the island's tastiest lobsters, but book ahead.
Price: €€€

✓ DINORIS
14A Mousseiou Sq., tel. (0241) 25824, 35530
Fresh fish and seafood. Try the dressed crab and relish the romantic setting in a medieval lane.
Price: €€€

✓ FOTIS
8 Menekleous St., tel. (0241) 27359
On with the fish-food marathon, delicious dishes for

Dinoris

the fanatic seafood eater have been served here since 1970 in the heart of medieval Rhodes, the outstanding dishes being the seafood and the sea urchin salads, dressed scampi and boutargue (roe pressed grey mullet called avgotaraho).
Price: €€€

OUTSIDE RHODES OLD TOWN

✓✓ PALIA ISTORIA
108 Metropoleos and Dendrinou Sts., tel. (0241) 32421
As the name indicates, this is the story of flavours through the ages, in an authentic and evocative environment with an eye for detail. Visual and gourmet pleasures correspond to the sociability of the owner who used to be an actor and is sure to make

RHODES

you smile. The achievements culminate in spaghetti with lobster and pan-fried spinach.
Price: €€

✓ CAPRICCI
Akti Kanari, tel. (0241) 33395
Superior Italian flavours in a tasteful setting with modern design, next to the sea.
Price: €€

TO STENO
29 Ag. Anargyron St., tel. (0241) 35914
'Ouzeri' serving the traditional appetizers with the aperitif ouzo; they are especially good here.
Price: €

PRYTANION
25 Georgiou Leontos St., Neohorion, tel. (0241) 73291
A music-cafe also serving snacks, in a converted private house with a traditional atmosphere, tasty titbits, wine and skilled folk-musicians.
Price: €

IXIA
✓✓✓ TA KIOUPIA
112 Argonafton St., tel. (0241) 91824, 35056
For the price of 10,000 drs. a head, you can try 60 different dishes we kid you not. Traditional specialities, wood-burning oven, warm atmosphere, many of the dishes prepared before your eyes. Get set for a session of pleasures for the palate in a restaurant that was once rated, as one of the ten best restaurants in the world.
Price: €€€

KOLYMBIA
✓ LIMANAKIA
Tel. (0241) 56240
A view over the blue of the bay, fish straight from the fishing boats, lobsters in the aquarium, delicious hors d'oeuvre and soft Greek music.
Price: €€

LINDOS
✓✓ MAVRIKOS
Lindos Central Square, tel. (0244) 31232
Typical local architecture and a tradition dating from 1933, combined with outstanding quality and the choice of Greek, French and Italian dishes. One of the best, and best-known, of the island. Try the lobster pasta.
Price: €€

🍸 BEST ENTERTAINMENT

Rhodes is as famous for its nightlife as for its castles. The focal point for fun is in Niohori in town, while the big clubs are in Ixia. Romantics will discover quiet nooks in the Old Town, and those of you who look for international contacts should go to Faliraki, where all the tourists congregate.
At Niohori, we propose as the best hangout, the **Del Mar**, with rock, jazz and ethnic music, as well as the **Colorado** with live rock. **La Scala** in Ixia promises a wild night and for tsifteteli oriental undulations there are both the **Melody Palace** at Kremasti and **Elli** next to the prefecture. In the Old Town, the view from **Roloyi** will enchant you, and the **Cafe Chantant**, with its popular and rebetika idiomatic Greek music and song, makes its own statement. When in Lindos, go to **Amphitheatro** with the fantastic view of the town or to **Kioupi**.

DODECANESE

TIPS AND INFORMATION

HOW TO GET THERE
- By air from Athens west airport with Olympic Airways (24,800 drs.), tel. (01) 9363363. From the east airport by Air Greece (23,300 drs.), tel. (01) 3255011-4. From Thessaloniki's Makedonia airport by Olympic Airways (32,000 drs.), tel. (031) 473042.
- By ferry from Piraeus in 15 hrs (from 6,600 drs.), Piraeus Port Authority tel. (01) 4226000-4.

CONNECTIONS
- By air from Rhodes to Karpathos, Kassos, Kos, Kastellorizo, Heraklion, Santorini and Mykonos. Olympic Airways, tel. (0241) 24571-5.
- By hydrofoil of Iptamena Dodekanissou Lines, from Rhodes to Kalymnos, Karpathos, Diafani (Karpathos), Kassos, Kos, Kastellorizo, Nisyros, Simi, Tilos, Halki, Ikaria, and Samos. In summer also to Astypalea.
- By ferry from Rhodes to Astypalea, Karpathos, Diafani (Karpathos), Kalimnos, Kassos, Kos, Lipsi, Leros, Kastellorizo, Nisiros, Simi, Tilos, Halki, Heraklion, Sitia, Lesbos, Limnos, Samos, Chios, Ios, Naxos, Paros, Santorini and Syros.

Lindos

BEST TIPS

HOW TO GET AROUND: The Old Town is visited on foot and you will need at least three hours. For Lindos there are daily departures by public transport (KTEL) and excursions by coach organized by the travel agents Triton, tel. (0241) 21690 and Elafos, tel. (0241) 66543. To see the rest of the island, by hired transport. One day is enough for you to see the majority of the most important sights.

BEST SEASON: All year round except July and August when the island is swamped by crowds and the thermometer rises to tropical heights. Ideal seasons are spring and autumn.

GUIDES: If you want a complete guided tour of the island's sights, contact the Rhodes Guides Association, tel. (0241) 22351.

USEFUL TELEPHONE NUMBERS

RHODES	(0241)
Town Hall	23801
Municipal Tourist Information	35945
Tourist Bureau	23255, 23655, 21921
Tourist Police	27423
Police	23294
Port Authority	28888
Hospital	25555
Taxis	64712, 27666

SYMI

WHY AMONG THE BEST

Because of its 2,500 elegant neo-classical houses, which are the pride and joy of the vigilant Archaeological Service. Because this is a quiet island with a cosmopolitan atmosphere, few cars, hospitable locals and reasonable prices.

DODECANESE

SYMI

BEST's OPINION

It's difficult to get to Symi, since the island has no airport (the one at Rhodes is the closest) and the ferry from Piraeus takes a mere 19 hours! These disadvantages, however, work to the benefit of those who do manage to visit, because Symi has succeeded in escaping the onslaught of package tourism and the chaotic construction that usually accompanies it. Despite its remoteness, the island is not lacking in facilities. Its simple, but good hotels, fine restaurants and nightlife are ample compensation for the trip.

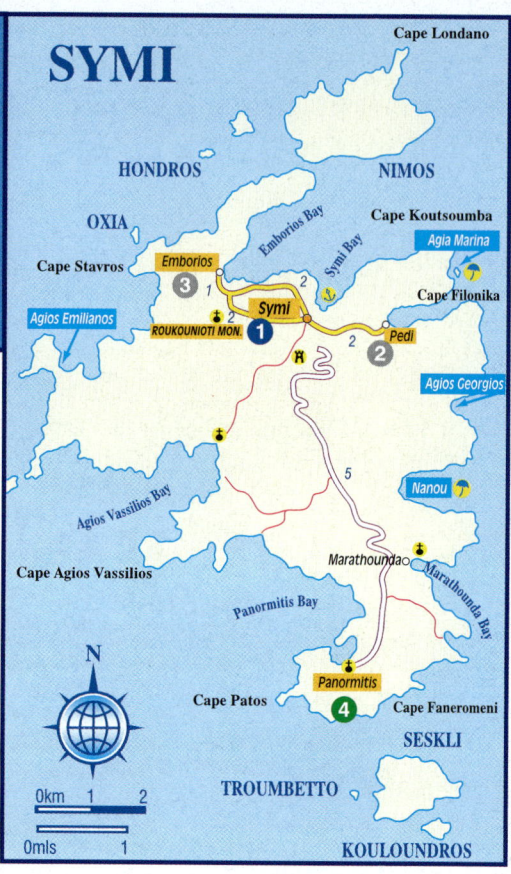

Gialos

IN BRIEF

Symi belongs to the Dodecanese group of islands. Located near the coast of Asia Minor, it has some 2,500 inhabitants, who are involved in the tourist trade and commerce. It used to be an important centre for sponge exports, with a large sponge-fishing fleet. Up to 1930, when synthetic sponges became available, the fleet's activities made the island wealthy enough to support a population of 25,000 people (larger than that of Rhodes). Its town and villages have been declared landmarks and Symi's main attraction is its architecture. The hamlets of Pedi and Nimborio are close to Symi Town and connected to it by regular bus service. The rest of the island, most of it, in other words, is uninhabited and undeveloped. Symi has a temperate climate, with little rainfall, mild winters and many sunny days, while the landscape is mountainous and arid.

BEST SIGHTS: STEP BY STEP

❶ SYMI
Σύμη / Sími

Symi Town consists of two settlements, Gialos (the port) and Horio (the upper town, Ano Symi). The most notable sights in both districts are the superb neo-classical mansions.

🌀🌀 GIALOS

Symi's largest harbour. The entrance is dominated by the municipal **clocktower (1880)**, the **campanile of the Evangelistria church** and the statue of the **Little Fisherman**. At Gialos, you'll also see the stately

Kampsopoulos house (now a restaurant), where on 8 May 1945, General Wagner surrendered the Dodecanese islands to the Allies (commemorated by a plaque). Pay a visit to the **Naval Museum** (10 am-2 pm, closed on Mondays and holidays*), which contains miniature paintings of ships, maps, nautical instruments, as well as sponge-fishing gear (diving suit, etc.).

A sponge shop

HORIO (ANO SYMI)

The town's largest settlement. Charming neighbourhoods with both well-preserved and derelict mansions, picturesque cobbled alleys and views over the port. You won't regret taking the walk from Gialos to Horio, up the 500 steps of **Kali Strata** (the Good Road), because it is flanked by beautiful stone-built houses. Along the way you'll come to the 19th c. **Spetsiata Pharmacy**. Also take time to visit the **church of the Panagia**, with its wonderful frescoes, the **Castle of the Knights** and **Symi's Archaeological and Folklore Museum** (10 am-2 pm daily except on Mondays and holidays*), with its Early Christian, Byzantine and folk culture exhibits.

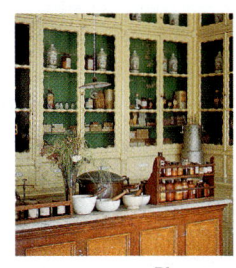

Pharmacy

---

❷ PEDI
Πέδι / Pédi

A little harbour with greenery and a beach. It was a summer favourite with the prosperous families of yesteryear. Along the road to Horio there are traces of a **petrified forest**.

---

❸ EMBORIOS (NIMBORIO)
Εμπορειός - Νημπορίο / Emboriós - Nimborió

Summer houses on a small sandy beach. Visit the **Dodeka Spilea (catacombs)**, twelve underground tunnels used in Byzantine times as an artists' workshop.

---

❹ PANORMITIS
Πανορμίτης / Panormítis

A closed bay dominated by the **monastery of Taxiarchis Michail Panormitis**, the island's patron saint. The monastery has a guest house for 500 pilgrims and the church is filled with Byzantine icons.
The pseudo-baroque bell-tower divides this enormous complex down the middle. Be sure to see the carved **wooden icon screen**, the **icon of the archangel wearing a silver tunic** and the pebble mosaic floor.
The monastery also contains two museums, a **folk museum** and a **collection of ecclesiastical treasures**, as well as a library with old books and manuscripts. You can get to Panormitis from Gialos by car or by boat in 1 hr. Opposite it lies the **islet of Sesklia**, while nearby, at a place called Faneromeni, is the fortified **Megalos Sotiras monastery**.

Panormitis monastery

OTHER THINGS TO DO

ROUKOUNIOTIS MONASTERY
Another fortified monastery, its cruciform church has frescoes painted in the 15th and 18th c.

WALKS
From the Upper Town to the windmills and in Symi's marvellous cypress forest.

341

FESTIVALS - LOCAL EVENTS

Symi Festival: 1st August. The festival ship departs from Piraeus. Free music, literary, theatrical events and happenings with well-known artists and performers participating. Information: Town Hall, tel. (0241) 71302.
May 2nd: The **Koukouma custom**, in which unmarried girls bake and eat a salty pie in the hopes of dreaming of their future husband that night.

BEST BEACHES

Symi has good, though not outstanding, beaches. But the water is always crystal-clear and the high temperatures permit swimming until the end of October.

NANOU

A bay encircled by rocky hillocks. The best and largest beach on the island. Pebbles, umbrellas and a little taverna in the shade of its few trees. Accessible by caique or sea taxi.

AGIA MARINA

On the islet of Agia Marina with the church of the same name. A small beach, with emerald waters, taverna, lounging chairs and sand imported from Rhodes! Reachable by boat from Pedi or Gialo.

AGIOS GEORGIOS

Another small beach in a lovely setting, with a few trees. Access by boat (30 min).

AGIOS EMILIANOS

Picturesque bay with greenery opposite an islet with a monastery. Access by boat (45 min).

BEST HOTELS AND ROOMS

BEST LOCATION

If you like to be in the thick of things, then you should stay in Gialos. If you'd prefer quiet and a lovely view, then Horio would be more appropriate. For family holidays we recommend Pedi, where there is regular scheduled transport to and from Gialos (every hour). To be sure for a room in July or August, you must make your reservation by Easter.

PRICES

The hotel prices mentioned below are the official ones set by the National Tourist Organization for double rooms, at low and high season, with breakfast. Since owners are allowed to modify the prices, always try to negotiate them.

GIALOS

✓ ALIKI HOTEL (A Class)

Tel. (0241) 71665, fax 71655
Open: May-October
Description: Neo-classical three-storey mansion of 1895. Restored, on the sea, with pleasant outdoor areas.
Rooms: 15 rooms, with traditional furnishings, bath or shower, music and telephone. Ask for a room with a view.

Special features: Comfortable lounge, roof garden, bar and hospitable atmosphere.
Price: 28,000-40,000 drs.
Value for money: ✹✹
Credit cards: Visa

✓ NIREUS (C Class)

Tel. (0241) 72400, fax 72404
Open: April-October
Description: Traditional, former public building.

Rooms: 36 rooms, renovated in 1994. Those with the view don't have A/C.
Special features: Veranda and restaurant on the port.
Price: 18,000-25,000 drs.
Value for money: ✹
Credit cards: Visa, Mastercard

FIONA (C Class)

Tel. & fax (0241) 72088
Open: April-October
Description: Well-looked after and with friendly service.
Rooms: 11 rooms, clean, the colour blue predominates.
Special features: Bar, courtyard and splendid view.

Price: 10,000-12,000 drs.
Value for money: ✹✹
Credit cards: None

PEDI

✓ LEMONIA (A Class)

Tel. (0241) 71201, fax 72374
Open: May-October
Description: Small, painted traditional hyacinth blue, with a view of the village and the bay.

Rooms: 6 well-kept rooms, with telephone, ceiling fan, balcony, sitting room and kitchenette.
Special features: Spacious veranda with barbecue.
Price: 16,000-23,000 drs.
Value for money: ✹✹
Credit cards: None

ALTERNATIVES

Why not get together with your friends and rent a lovely old house in Gialos or Horio? For information, call **Kalodoukas Travel**, tel. (0241) 71077. Or else, stay at the Panormitis monastery's guest house, for studio apartment without breakfast, tel 72414.
Price: 8,000-17,000 drs.

HORIO (B Class) Horio, tel. (0241) 71800, fax 71802.
Price: 15,000-21,000 drs.

BEST RESTAURANTS & TAVERNAS

GIALOS

✓✓ MYLOPETRA

Tel. (0241) 72333
Attractive, with traditional decor. Good Mediterranean and Greek cuisine.
Its German owner, a real Hellenophile, could not be more congenial.
Under the restaurant's floor, visible through thick glass, is a 2 m-long ancient tomb dating from about 50 BC. The finds from it are on display in the Rhodes Archaeological Museum.
Price: €€€

☑ ELLINIKON
Tel. (0241) 72455
Greek and Italian cuisine in a well cared-for setting. The wine cellar contains 140 different varieties.
Price: € €

Ellinikon

☑ THOLOS
Tel. (0241) 72033
Serving ouzo and appetizers. Considered the best of its kind on the island. At the far end of Gialos, with a view of the town.
Price: €

At Gialos you will also dine well at **Bella Napoli**, tel. (0241) 72456, with Italian dishes, and at **Mano**, tel. (0241) 72429, which serves fish on the waterfront. **Mythos**, tel. (0241) 71488, also on the port, specializes in appetizers. In Horio, **Giorgo** has delicious ready-cooked meals, while seafood mezedes (hors d'oeuvre), vegetarian food and cockerel with herbs are to be found at **Syllogo (Lefteris)**, tel. (0241) 72148, which boasts a view of Pedi from its veranda. **Price:** All €

BEST ENTERTAINMENT

Though quiet, Symi does not lack nightlife. At Gialos you can choose from amongst many little bars, while at Horio, **Kali Strata**, on the stairs, is the best place and has a stunning view, day and night.

TIPS AND INFORMATION

HOW TO GET THERE
- By air from Athens to Rhodes, with Olympic Airways, from the west airport (from 24,800 drs.), tel. (01) 9363363, or with Air Greece from the east airport (from 23,300 drs.), tel. (01) 3255011-4. And then from Rhodes by ferry to Symi, Rhodes Port Authority, tel. (0241) 22220, 28888, or by Iptamena Dodekanisou hydrofoil, Rhodes Agency, tel. (0241) 24000, 78052.
- By ferry from Piraeus in 19 hrs (from 8,000 drs.), Piraeus Port Authority, tel. (01) 4226000-4.

CONNECTIONS
- Symi is linked by ferry or hydrofoil with most of the Dodecanese islands and some of the Cyclades. Symi Port Authority, tel. (0241) 71205.

BEST TIPS

HOW TO GET AROUND: There are frequent buses between Horio and Pedi. The taxi fare from Gialos to Horio is 500 drs., 600 drs. to Pedi. You can take a caique to the various beaches, the islet of Sesklia or a trip round the island. The excursion price (5,000-9,000 drs. per person) includes a plentiful BBQ, ready-cooked dishes and wine.
Sea taxis: Rent one and organize your own programme.
Walking: Ask the travel agents for a hiker's map of the island.
Excursions: The island's two travel agencies run tours with pick-up trucks to a certain point, followed by a hike down to a beach and return to Gialos by caique.
Kalodoukas Holidays, tel. (0241) 71205.
Symi Tours, tel. (0241) 71307.

BEST SEASON: May, June and September. The winters are dead and the hotels closed.

BEST BUYS: Embroideries, honey, sponges, goat-cheese and spices.

USEFUL TELEPHONE NUMBERS

SYMI	(0241)	Police	71111
Town Hall	71302	Port Authority	71205

PATMOS

WHY AMONG THE BEST

Because of Hora, the island's capital, with its marvellous architecture; because of its treasures of the Orthodox Church and its monasteries; because of its religious tradition and history. But also because of its serene atmosphere.

DODECANESE

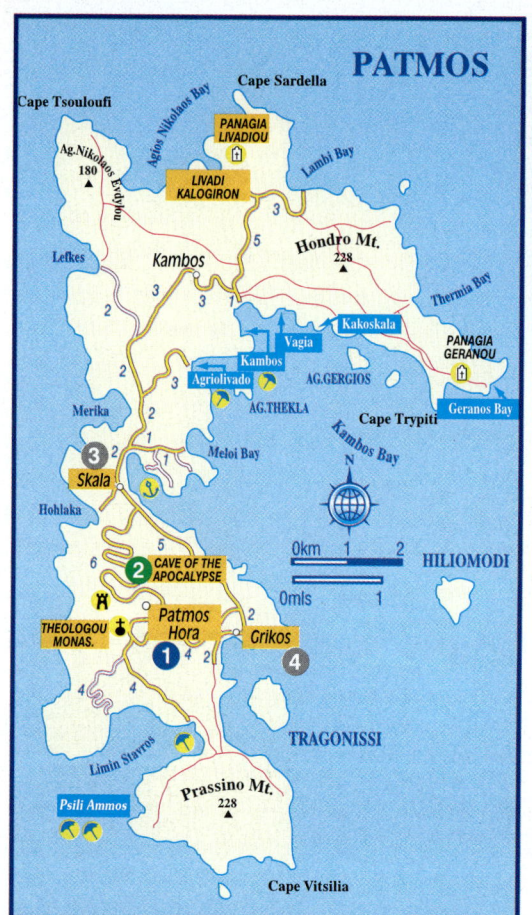

BEST's OPINION

Most visitors to Patmos are either interested in its religious associations or are members of the Athenian and international jet-set seeking a low-profile, high-quality retreat.

Those who arrive on their own yachts are usually guests of the select few who have one of the traditional houses in the Hora and there is also a steady stream of cruiseboats. Patmos beaches are few and not particularly attractive.

If beach life is important to you, then head for the other islands in the vicinity after seeing the sights of Patmos.

IN BRIEF

Patmos is a narrow, irregular strip of volcanic rock only 12,5 km long and mountainous. The climate is mild and summers are cool, thanks to the winds. The locals continue to be involved in farming, fishing and icon painting, in addition to the tourist trade.

HISTORY

Dorians and Ionians were the island's first inhabitants and it was a place of exile during the Roman years. It acquired its first real settlement in the late 11th c. The first person to be exiled here was Orestes, pursued by the Furies after murdering his mother Clytemnestra. He built a temple to Artemis on the spot where in 1088 Christodoulos founded the famous fortress-monastery of St. John the Divine, destroying the temple in the process and using it for building material.

From 1523 to 1912, Patmos was under Ottoman rule, which meant fewer pirate raids and considerable prosperity. In 1713, the Patmian Theological School was founded by the saintly monk and scholar Makarios Kalogeras. Patmos was governed by the Italians from 1912 until 1943. The buildings in the Hora are a very rare example of Byzantine architectural tradition, with their characteristic white facades, ceramic brick floors and external exposed natural stone corners. The stone-built houses, with flat roofs for the collection of rainwater, abut each other and windows are only at a height.

ⓖ BEST SIGHTS: STEP BY STEP

❶ HORA
Χώρα / Hóra

The Hora (pop. 670) grew up around the fortress-monastery of St. John in the late 16th c. It lies due south and above the port of Skala, and is connected with it by a narrow avenue of eucalyptus trees. With its three small squares and dense construction, the village is divided into connecting quarters such as Kritika, Apithia, Allotina and Pezoula. There are many interesting churches of the 15th, 16th and 17th c. to see.
The ⓖⓖ **view** from the Hora over the the island's indented coastline is superb.

WHAT TO SEE

ⓖⓖⓖ MONASTERY OF ST. JOHN THE DIVINE
Μονή του Αγίου Ιωάννη του Θεολόγου / Moní tou Agíou Ioánni tou Theológou

Tel. (0247) 31398
🕒 *8 am-2 pm and 4-6 pm, Thursdays and Sundays*

Under the jurisdiction of the Ecumenical Patriarch, it is a medieval monastic complex surrounded by a fortified polygonal **wall**, studded with tall towers and crenellated battlements for protection against pirates. A **wide stairway** leads to the entrance of the monastery and the **chapel of Agioi Apostoloi**. The main entrance is guarded by two **towers** and the famous projecting barbette, with an opening in the floor through which boiling oil or molten lead could be poured on adversaries. Today only its outer northern wall has been preserved.
The main church or **katholikon** was completed later with various additions of different periods and styles. The buildings line the interior of the circuit wall, leaving open spaces or courtyards, between them which supply light and air. The **cells**, **chapels**, **storerooms** and the other areas are linked by a labyrinthine network of corridors, arcades and stairways.
The courtyard, of stonework with arched cloisters, lies at the heart of the monastery, where you will see a large wooden and a small iron simandro or gong (used in place of bells during Ottoman rule). The old **font** filled with holy water stands on the high stone circular pedestal in its centre. The **katholikon** is of the Greek cross-in-square type, surmounted by a dome supported on four pillars; its ornate icon screen is early 19th c. The chapel of **Ossios Christodoulos** contains an older **icon screen** and **frescoes** by the Cretan Andreas Rindzos, dating back to 1500. The 12th c. chapel of the Virgin, to the right of the main church, has a marble floor with an ancient inscription, an interesting icon screen and the monastery's oldest frescoes, which had been painted over and were not discovered until 1958. The **refectory** or **trapeza** is dominated by the marble-revetted table with spaces carved out for the monks' tableware. Visit the cloistered monastery **library**, which contains, among other things, its founder's Gospel on the original parchments
Finally, don't miss the **Treasury cum museum** with the monastery's icons, heirlooms and relics of saints. The

DODECANESE

monastery is a major centre for research in Byzantine studies and manuscripts; it has two ultramodern studios for restoring icons and approximately 13,000 valuable documents in its archives.

ZOODOCHOS PIGI MONASTERY
Μοναστήρι Ζωοδόχου Πηγής / Monastíri Zoodóhou Pigís

A nuns' convent with two churches in its courtyard, decorated with icons of the 16th-18th c., icon stands, carved wooden icon screens and valuable ecclesiastical vessels.

FOLK ART MUSEUM
Λαογραφικό Μουσείο / Laografikó Mouseío
Tel. (0247) 31360, open from March to October
9 am-2 pm, 5-8 pm (call to make sure)

Housed in the mansion of the gong-striker, which was built in 1625 by masons from Smyrna. Worth seeing are the old furniture, paintings, heirlooms and icons.

Zoodochos Pigi monastery

---

❷ THE CAVE OF THE APOCALYPSE
Σπήλαιο της Αποκάλυψης του Ιωάννη / Spílaio tis Apocálypsis tou Ioánni

Tel. (0247) 31234
7:30 am-1 pm

On the road between Skala and Hora, surrounded by the **Monydrio dedicated to the Apocalypsis**. Go down the few steps to the 18th c. chapel of **Agios Artemios**. To the rear of it, you'll come to the entrance to the **church of Agia Anna** and the **holy cave** where there is also a **chapel dedicated to St. John**. You could also visit the **Patmian Theological School**, today a theological college recognized by the State.

St. John the Divine

THE REVELATION OF ST. JOHN THE DIVINE

Exiled by the Roman emperor Domitian, St. John the Divine came to the island in AD 95 and took refuge in the well-known cave, called the cave of the Apocalypse because this is where he dictated the prophetic text inspired by God to his disciple Prochoros.

---

❸ SKALA
Σκάλα / Skála

The biggest village in Patmos, Hora's port, with modern buildings, lots of shops and the centre of nightlife. To walk up to Hora the old cobbled path is more picturesque than the main road, but be sure to have a torch at night.

❹ GRIKOS
Γροίκος / Gríkos

A small tourist village on a beautiful bay, with an islet at its entrance. Its hotels, rooms and tavernas are all situated on the waterfront.

OTHER THINGS TO DO

LIVADI TON KALOGIRON
Drenched in greenery, with both cypresses and vegetable plots, this delightful valley with its little **church**, the **Panagia tou Livadiou**, is a wonderful place for a walk, followed by a swim at its attractive beach.

BEST BEACHES

With the exception of Psili Ammos, most of the island's beaches are unimpressive, but the water is always clean and clear. You can take your pick from the more remote and relatively empty to the more organized and therefore crowded.

PSILI AMMOS

The only sandy beach on Patmos, and the best. The sea is clean, usually there are some waves.

Accessible by caique or on foot via the main road. The simple taverna here serves good omelettes, stuffed tomatoes and delicious courgette pie.

AGRIOLIVADO

A beach with sand and pebbles. Well organized, with facilities for both the sunbathing crowd and for the more athletic.

KAMBOS

The most sophisticated beach on the island, which in August seems to exemplify the problem of global overpopulation. Shingle for the most part, it becomes sandy once you're in the water. Here you'll find reclining beach chairs for the lazy and water sports for the active. You can also have a meal or coffee and pastries at **George's Place**, tel. (0247) 31881, play backgammon or meet a celebrity.

VAGIA

Deserted, shaded by trees, with pebbles and deep, clear water. Ten minutes' walk from Kambos.

KAKOSKALA

If you don't want to meet a soul, consider walking another kilometre east of Vagia. Here there are two pebbly beaches with trees that are divided by a small promontory. Leave your car by the side of the road and take the path. Bring water and food with you.

LIVADI GERANOU

Opposite two islets, not a particularly good beach, but you can swim to the islands in the company of ducks and geese. A lure for those who know the island.

DODECANESE

BEST HOTELS AND ROOMS

BEST LOCATION

Patmos has no hotels that are particularly noteworthy, and because there are none at all in Hora, you must choose between the port (Skala) if you want to be in the midst of things and the hotels elsewhere on the island if you prefer peace and quiet and beach life.

PRICES

The hotel prices mentioned below are the official ones set by the National Tourist Organization for double rooms, at low and high season, with breakfast. Since owners are allowed to modify the prices, always try to negotiate them.

✓✓ PATMOS PARADISE (B Class)

200 m from Kambos (organized) beach and 4.5 km from Skala
Tel. (0247) 32624, (01) 4224112, (01) 4224119, fax (0247) 32740

Open: May-October
Description: Built on a hill above the bay, typical island architecture with considerable modern amenities. Most rooms have a view from their balcony of the beaches to the south or the bay.
Rooms: 45 rooms and 2 suites, with shower and telephone.
Special features: Parking, pool, water sports, tennis court.
Price: 20,000-43,000 drs.
Value for money: ✱✱
Credit cards: Mastercard, Visa

✓✓ PORTO SCOUTARI (B Class)

Above Meloi bay
Tel. (0247) 33123-5, fax 33175
Open: April-October
Description: One of the island's best hotels, furnished and decorated in traditional style, with exceptional taste and attention.
Rooms: 25 rooms with bath.
Special features: Parking and pool.
Price: 22,000-82,000 drs.
Value for money: ✱
Credit cards: Mastercard, Visa

✓ SKALA (B Class)

Skala
Tel. (0247) 31343, 34034-5, fax 31747
Open: April-October
Description: Traditional island style with a lush flower garden. Ideally situated (50 m from the port), for those who want to be near the action.
Rooms: 150 beds, telephone, shower or bath and balcony with sea or mountain view.

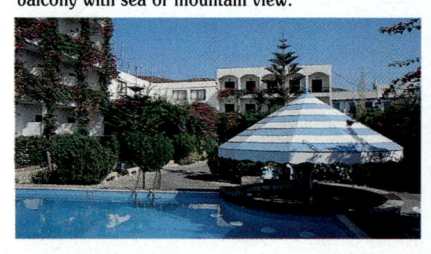

Special features: Pool, terrace with a splendid view of the harbour and Hora, lounge, bar and restaurant.
Price: 14,500-26,000 drs.
Value for money: ✱✱
Credit cards: Visa

✓ PETRA APARTMENTS (C Class)

Grikos
Tel. (0247) 31035, fax 34020
Open: May-October
Description: A small, but warm and hospitable

PATMOS

hotel with attractive decor and furnishings and friendly service.
Rooms: 21 rooms with A/C and bath.
Special features: Bar, roof garden, water sports facilities.
Price: 30,570-43,872 drs.
Value for money: ✱
Credit cards: None

ALTERNATIVES

ROMEOS (B Class) *Skala, tel. (0247) 31962, 34011-3, (094) 769 829, fax 31070.*
Price: 20,000-29,000 drs.

Petra Apartments

BEST RESTAURANTS & TAVERNAS

✓✓ THE PATMIAN HOUSE
Hora, tel. (0247) 31180

The in place that attracts the international jet-set. Striking traditional decor, agreeable hosts and local specialities. Book your table a month ahead!
Price: €€€

✓✓ BENETOS
Sapsilla, tel. (0247) 33089

One of the best on Patmos, with original, sophisticated, Mediterranean recipes, impeccable service, a well-planned, pleasant setting with sea view.
Price: €€€

✓✓ LEONIDAS
Lambi, tel. (0247) 31490

Open for lunch and dinner. Wonderful fish and lobster as well as delicious meat. Fresh vegetables and potatoes from the garden. Their saganaki (fried cheese) doused with brandy is a special culinary experience. **Price:** €€

TO BALKONI
Hora, tel. (0247) 32115

Simple but good taverna with grills and a marvellous view.
Price: €

VANGELIS
Hora, Agias Levias Sq., tel. (0247) 31967

Taverna with average cuisine, but with a gorgeous view from the terrace.
Price: €€

OLYMPIA
Hora, Agias Levias Sq., tel. (0247) 31543

Sitting on the square, watch all the island's world go by. Courteous service.
Price: €

DODECANESE

BEST ENTERTAINMENT

Nightlife on Patmos is concentrated in the Hora and Skala. In Hora, we recommend the beautifully decorated **Stoa** cafe with its tables on Agias Levias Square, for your first drink, and then the **Astivi** cafe-bar, the most «in» place on the island, until 2 am, whereupon nightlife continues in Skala.

In Skala, we pinpointed the unusual cafe **Houston** with its 60s atmosphere and its spoon sweets (preserves eaten by the spoonful), **Arion**, patronized day and night by both locals and non-residents, and the nightclubs **Selini** and **Konsolatos** for night-owls.

Astivi

TIPS AND INFORMATION

HOW TO GET THERE

- By air to Samos (from 14,000 drs.) with Olympic Airways, tel. (01) 9663363. From there by high-speed passenger boat of the Samos Hydrofoil Cooperative (from Pythagorio), Patmos Port Authority, tel. (0247) 31231.
- By ferry from Piraeus to Patmos in 10 hrs (from 6,431 drs.), Piraeus Port Authority, tel. (01) 422 6000.

CONNECTIONS

- By highspeed passenger boat of the Samos Hydrofoil Cooperative from Samos to Kalymnos, Kos, Lipsi, Leros, Ikaria, Fourni Ikarias, Vathy and Pythagorio (Samos). Samos agency, tel. (0273) 25065.
- By highspeed passenger boat of the Dodecanese Hydrofoils Lines to Kos, Leros, Samos, Lipsi, Ikaria, Fourni Ikarias. Kos Agency, tel. (0242) 25449, 25920.
- By ferry to Kalymnos, Kos, Lipsi, Leros, Megisti, Rhodes, Symi, Tilos, Samos, Chios, Naxos, Paros, Syros. Patmos Port Authority, tel. (0247) 31231.
- From Skala you'll find caiques to take you to beaches round the island as well as to the nearby islands of Lipsi, Arkii and Agathonissi.

BEST TIPS

HOW TO GET AROUND: Patmos is a small island and you'll have no trouble getting to the most interesting spots. There are frequent buses to Hora, Skala, Kambos and the beaches of Grikos and Kato Kambos as well as taxis if you don't rent or don't have your own transport. We recommend you hire a motorbike to avoid the parking problem.

BEST SEASON: Patmos is at its best in June and September. The island is dead in winter, but July and August are suffocatingly full of tourists. Easter celebrations are an unforgettable experience, more so at the Zoodohos Pigi monastery than at St. John's because of the crowds. Be sure to book your room well ahead of time.

USEFUL TELEPHONE NUMBERS

PATMOS .... (0247)	Police 31303-31100
Town Hall.. 31235-32278	Motorboats (repairs), S. Kamitsis.... 31115, 31905
Tourist Office 31666	Taxi Rank 31225
Travel Agent Yannis Stratas 31356	Thomas Meris' taxi 33046, (0932) 381107

MARATHI

○ Marathi
Arkii & Lipsi

WHY AMONG THE BEST

As yet mostly overlooked, Marathi is an unexploited small island far from the tourist crowds. With only two small hotels and picturesque tavernas next to the sea, it is ideal for relaxation and contemplation.

DODECANESE

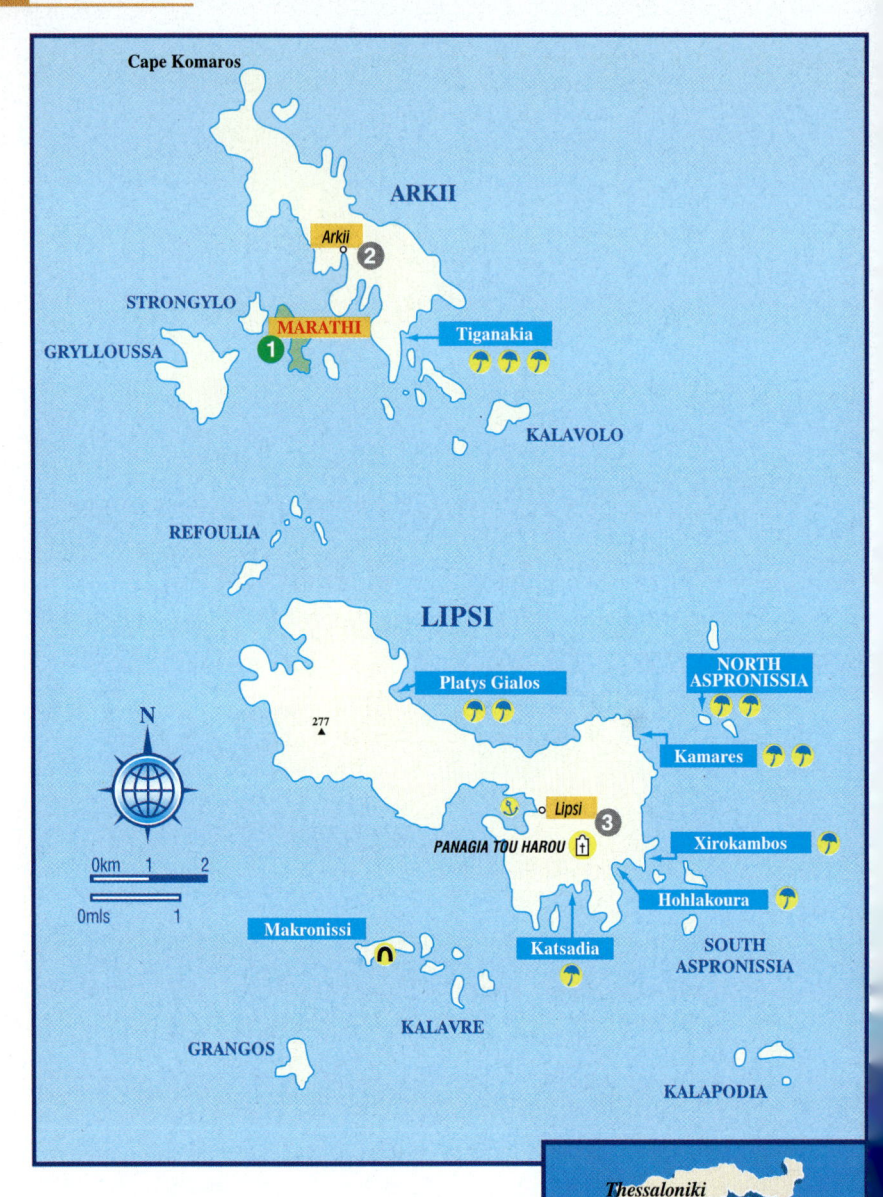

Cape Komaros

ARKII
- Arkii ②
- STRONGYLO
- GRYLLOUSSA
- MARATHI ①
- Tiganakia
- KALAVOLO

REFOULIA

LIPSI
- Platys Gialos
- 277
- NORTH ASPRONISSIA
- Kamares
- Lipsi ③
- PANAGIA TOU HAROU
- Xirokambos
- Hohlakoura
- SOUTH ASPRONISSIA
- Makronissi
- Katsadia
- KALAVRE
- GRANGOS
- KALAPODIA

0km 1 2
0mls 1

Thessaloniki

Athens

BEST's OPINION

The rare combination of beautiful, unspoiled nature and the hospitality, efficiency and care extended by the owners of the simple but functional hotel, **O Pandelis**, makes this trip particularly attractive for those who insist on their basic comforts, but are irritated by the noise and proximity of crowds.

If you belong to this category and particularly if you have a boat, discover this attractive little island, combining your outing with excursions to the neighbouring islets of Tiganakia, Aspronissia, Arkii and Lipsi.

If you don't have a boat, you can still reach Marathi in various ways, from the neighbouring islands, following our instructions.

MARATHI

BEST SIGHTS: STEP BY STEP

❶ MARATHI
Μαράθι / Maráthi

Only eight miles east of Patmos, Marathi is an islet next to Arkii. Both belong to the Patmos municipality. Formerly, the small island had 30 inhabitants who raised cattle and cultivated vineyards. Now, only two families are left, both of whom operate the hotels and tavernas on the island.

The island's only natural greenery are the holm-oaks that dot the hills. However, the verdant oases around the hotels, featuring palm trees, flowers and giant sycamores, make up for this.

Right in front of the two hotels stretches the island's only beach. In spring, Marathi hosts a flock of charming winged visitors, the migrating birds, which stop there on route from Africa to the North.

Naturally, there are very few tourists on Marathi. Only Greek families in July and August, as well as some foreigners during the rest of the year, visitors from pleasure boats, and weekenders who arrive by boat from neighbouring Lipsi.

The island has no roads or cars, and electricity is produced by a generator. However, it is possible to communicate with the rest of the world, as telephone lines were recently installed.

At the top of the hill, you'll find the pretty stone houses, which have been abandoned for decades, as well as the church of **Agios Nikolaos**, with its old icons. Mihalis Kavouras has the key at his hotel.

❷ ARKII
Αρκιοί / Arkií

Fishing islands opposite Marathi, with sparse vegetation of shrubs and tamarisks. It has a safe port, protected by reefs.

There are approximately 20-30 inhabitants, but tourists from Patmos visit the island in summer.

Ask someone from the village to guide you to the **cave**, because it will be difficult for you to find it on your own.

❸ LIPSI
Λειψοί / Lipsí

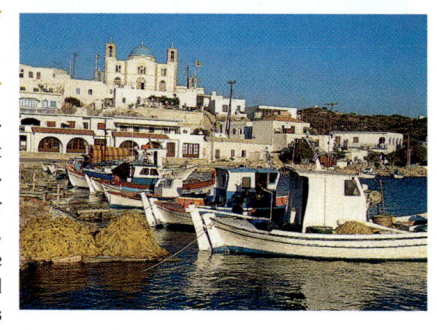

Four miles south of Marathi, and with 650 inhabitants, Lipsi could be your base for this excursion if it had a better infrastructure. It is the region's commercial centre, as well as the connecting point with other islands. The island, only 16 sq. km, is dry and rocky, but with a few trees. In the southern part, there are vineyards, which produce the local sweet, dark red wine. However, it is probably best known for its beaches. Moonlit nights in the small tavernas by the port are very pleasant.

PANAGIA TOU HAROU CHURCH

Built in the 17th c. its "miraculous" icon depicts a Pieta. It is famed for its peculiar lilies which, although dry all summer, sprout buds on August 23, the icon's feast day.

THE PANAGIA CHURCH AT KOUSSELIO

Built on the foundations of a pre-Christian temple. There are marble slabs on its walls which came from the original temple and were used as building material, with Byzantine inscriptions.

BEST BEACHES

Marathi has only one beach, which is in front of the two hotels and is sandy.
Take advantage of the neighbouring islets to discover other pretty beaches.

TIGANAKIA

East of Arkii, with emerald waters, reminiscent of exotic Pacific islands.
An absolute must of the area.

ASPRONISSIA

Three small islands north-east of Lipsi, also with crystal-clear, emerald waters and round, white pebbles. You'll be alone on the beach of the middle islet, but be sure to have water, food and an umbrella with you, as there are no refreshment facilities and no shade.

LIPSI

On the eastern and southern sides of the island, you'll find numerous beautiful beaches, some quite deserted, while others have some facilities available.

Marathi

Kamares

Platys Gialos, with sand, blue-green waters and ducks, and Katsadia, usually protected from the wind, with a good beach and reed beds, are organized beaches with tavernas. Kamares is probably the island's best beach. Xirokambos, a rugged and isolated beach for loners, and Hohlakoura, with pebbles, flat rocks and caves, are also excellent choices for swimming.

MAKRONISSI

You'll catch sight of it as soon as you leave Lipsi port. Half-way along its south side, behind the island, there are caves and a tunnel-like passage through the rocks with spectacular reflections of colours and crystalline waters. To swim, dive off the caique.

Cave at Kamares

MARATHI

BEST HOTELS AND ROOMS

BEST LOCATION
You don't have a wide range of choices. At Marathi you'll stay at one of the two hotels, which are 100 m from one another, and are located on the island's sole beach. If you plan to go in summer, book in May for a room with a veranda.

PRICES
The hotel prices mentioned below are the official ones, set by the National Tourist Organization for double rooms, at low and high season, with breakfast. Since owners are allowed to modify prices, always try to negotiate them.

MARATHI

✓ PANDELIS
Tel. (0247) 32609
Open: May-October
Description: Built in stages, from 1978 to 1990. Pandelis Aimilianos, the owner, originally from Samos, lived for some time in Australia. His children, university graduates speaking impeccable English, help him look after the guests. Their attentive concern creates a pleasant, friendly atmosphere. Toula, his daughter, selects a musical programme to entertain visitors, from morning to night.
Simple, but beautiful, with an ideal location on the beach, offering a view of the boats in the bay. It's our preference.
Rooms: 10 plain rooms with bath.
Special features: The taverna serves breakfast, lunch, dinner and drinks.
Price: 10,500-11,500 drs., without breakfast
Value for money: ✱✱✱
Credit cards: None

MIHALIS KAVOURAS' ROOMS
Tel. (0247) 31580
Open: May-October. Arrangements can be made for winter.
Description: Mihalis formerly worked at hotels in Rhodes. It's a big plus that he owns a boat and organizes excursions to the nearby islands. If he has time, he can even collect you from neighbouring Lipsi. Charges for these services are according to the number of people.
Rooms: 8 simple rooms. Slightly less organized than Pandelis's hotel, but just as clean.
Special features: Taverna for breakfast, lunch, dinner and drinks.
Price: 6,000-7,000 drs., without breakfast
Value for money: ✱✱
Credit cards: None

ALTERNATIVES

APHRODITI
Lipsi, tel. (0247) 41001.
Price: 12,000 drs. without breakfast

KALYPSO (D Class)
Lipsi, tel. (0247) 41242.
Price: 8,800-10,900 drs.

You can contact the Lipsi Community Offices, tel. (0247) 41209, 41333, 41206, for information on accommodation.

BEST RESTAURANTS & TAVERNAS

Mihalis

In Marathi you are restricted to the island's two tavernas: ✓ **Pandelis** – excellent for appetizers, fish and ready-cooked dishes and **Mihalis**, who serves wild kid and fish.
For fresh fish in Arkii, choose among the three fish tavernas available.
In Lipsi, you can eat at one of the tavernas at the port or in the pleasant square, next to the island's church.

TIPS AND INFORMATION

HOW TO GET THERE

If you try this destination, keep in mind that getting to Marathi is difficult, which is why it has remained unspoiled.
- The ideal is to have your own boat.
- If you don't have a boat, ask at your hotel, because of changes in schedules.
- By air from Athens west airport with Olympic Airways, tel. (01) 9363363, to Leros (from 17,800 drs.), Samos (from 14,000 drs.), or Kos (from 18,000 drs.). From Leros or Samos port, you can travel by hydrofoil of Kinopraxia Hydropterigon Samou or of Iptamena Dodecanissou, and by ferry to Lipsi, Leros Port Authority, tel. (0247) 22224, Samos Port Authority, tel. (0273) 27318. From Kos, you can travel to Lipsi only in summer, Kos Port Authority, tel. (0242) 26594-5.
- By ferry from Piraeus to Lipsi, Piraeus Port Authority, tel. (01) 4226000-4.
- By ferry from Piraeus to Patmos, Piraeus Port Authority, tel. (01) 4226000-4. From there, by small boats and by hydrofoil of Kinopraxia Hydropterigon Samou, to Lipsi, Patmos Port Authority, tel. (0247) 31231. Daily in summer, twice weekly in winter.
- From Lipsi, you can reach Marathi and Arkii by caïque.

BEST TIPS

HOW TO GET AROUND: As already mentioned, there are no roads or cars in Marathi, so you'll explore the island on foot. It would be ideal to have your own boat – large or small – and, even better, a motorised rubber boat. This way, you can also explore the beautiful neighbouring islands. If you don't have your own vessel, you can visit them with Mihalis' boat (you'll find him at his taverna), or spend two nights at Lipsi and take one of the excursion caiques, which set out at 10:30am and return at 6pm. Choose the "Black Beauty" which is probably the best, tel. (0247) 41110, 41363, (093) 296775. It will cost you 3,000 drs.

BEST SEASON: June to September but even if you have bookings for August you will have no problem with crowds.

USEFUL TELEPHONE NUMBERS

LIPSI	(0247)		
Town Hall	41209, 41333	Municipal Tourist Information Office	41250
		Police	41222

Ionian Islands

IONIAN ISLANDS

BEST's OPINION

The Italian culture, superb beaches, the Old Town of Corfu and the green, unspoiled landscapes, bring the Ionian islands high up on *BEST's* list of preferences, after the Cyclades.
If you have a boat, the Ionian islands top the list for July and August, as you won't come across the meltemi winds here.

IN BRIEF

The complex of islands located in the Ionian sea, in the west of Greece, are known as the Ionian islands — in Greek as the *Eptanissa* – a chain of the six Ionian islands (Corfu, Paxi, Lefkada, Ithaki, Cephalonia and Zakynthos), as well as Kythera, which is not in the Ionian, but historically belongs to this group. Today, Kythera belongs administratively to the Attica prefecture, together with the Argosaronic islands. For this reason, *BEST* has included it in that group (Excursion 12).
The climate of the Ionian islands is mild and humid. The landscape is usually smothered in greenery, with high, forested mountains and lush vegetation, reaching down to the shores. There is no lack of fertile plains, with citrus trees, olive groves, vineyards and cypress trees. The coastline varies greatly; in some places there are steep cliffs and in others, the sea has eroded the rocks, forming small or endlessly long beaches with fine, white sand.
The number and type of tourists vary from island to island, but the region is especially preferred by Italians, because of its proximity to their country. There are also many of British, French and German visitors. In Corfu, you can find all sorts, from northern European package tours to artists, devotees of alternative tourism and English aristocrats. Celebrities with yachts, as well as recluses, frequent Paxi and Antipaxi, while one can spend peaceful family vacations on Cephalonia and Zakynthos. Ithaki and Lefkada are quiet islands and have been discovered by tourists only in the past few years.
The Ionian islands have regular air and sea connections. Most of them are also inter-connected by shipping lines and have airports.

HISTORY

The Ionian islands took a different historical course from the rest of Greece, from the period of Venetian rule up to their union (1864) with the newly established modern Greek state.
They have been inhabited since prehistoric times, as indicated by Mycenaean finds and references in Homer's *Odyssey*, but they began to develop when settlers from the Peloponnese established themselves there (7th c. BC). The islands' fleets plied the oceans, and the inhabitants prospered as merchants and traders, while they founded colonies as far away as the shores of Spain.
In the wake of the Peloponnesian War, which debilitated the whole of Greece, the Ionian islands began gradually to fall into decline. They were subject to a series of protectors or sovereigns; until they were taken by the Romans, like the rest of Greece (146 BC). Later they passed into the hands of the Byzantines and during the years that followed, they suffered numerous attacks by pirates and barbarians, until Venice placed them under its protection (14th -18th c.). This was followed briefly by French rule (1797-1815) interupted by a short-lived term of nominal indepedence supported by Russia. In 1815, with the defeat of Napoleon, Britain assumed the role of governing the islands.
Four centuries of Venetian rule saved the islands from Turkish sovereignty and gave the Ionian islands the opportunity to keep up with western developments in the arts and sciences. Visitors can easily distinguish the strong influence of Italian art, literature and music on the islands, in the architecture, customs and manners, which became mixed with local tradition. In 1864 the British handed them over to Greece.

IONIAN ISLANDS

BEST EXCURSIONS
Of the Ionian islands, BEST has selected and recommends ⓖⓖⓖ **Corfu** (Excursion 31), together with short trips to ⓖ **Paxi**, ⓖⓖ Antipaxi and the Diapondia islands (ⓖⓖ **Othoni**, ⓖ **Erikoussa**, ⓖ **Mathraki**).
However, these choices do not mean that the other Ionian islands are lacking in natural beauty. For this reason, we also recommend them to those who have more time to spend in the region.

ⓖⓖ CEPHALONIA
Κεφαλλονιά / Kefaloniá
The largest of the Ionian islands, it has 30,000 inhabitants and the highest mountain (Ainos 1,628 m), which boasts a unique, dense ⓖⓖ **black fir-forest** which has been designated a National Park. From its summit, the ⓖⓖⓖ **view** is spectacular, while, the ⓖ **Agios Gerassimos monastery** is situated in the Omalon valley below.

The island has traditional settlements and a luxuriant green landscape, with forests of pine, firs and plane trees. The inhabitants are well-known for their wit and idiosyncracies.

One of Cephalonia's main attractions is the traditional village of ⓖⓖ **Fiskardo**, in a picturesque cove which in summer becomes a cosmopolitan hot-spot, full of yachts. Also worth visiting is ⓖⓖ **Assos**, a small settlement saddling a small peninsula, with a ruined Venetian castle on a peak. The setting is breathtaking, so have your cameras ready. Another impressive sight is the ⓖ **Drogarati cave** with its numerous stalactites and stalagmites, as well as the remarkable ⓖⓖ **Melissani cave**, more than 3 km in length. In the section where the vault has collapsed, a kaleidoscope of colours is created during the early afternoon hours, when the sun is reflected in the waters of its underground lake.

Of Cephalonia's beaches, Myrtos is exceptional, with its white sand and the view of it from the cliffside village of Ano Mera is superb.

ⓖ ZAKYNTHOS
Ζάκυνθος / Zákinthos
A fertile island, the home of great Greek poets and of melodious serenades, it has a population of 35,000, traditional villages, old monasteries and beautiful churches. In a horse-drawn carriage, explore the coastal road, the **Strada Marina** and the town's narrow streets, whose buildings were rebuilt in the Renaissance style of those destroyed in the

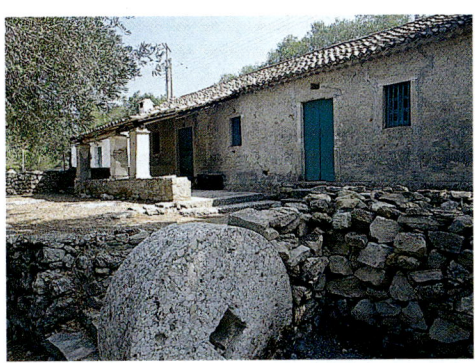

Mathraki, Diapondia Islands

Erikoussa, Diapondia Islands

Fiskardo, Cephalonia

Shipwreck bay, Zakynthos

IONIAN ISLANDS

powerful 1953 earthquake. Visit the **Solomos Museum**, with material relating to the poet, Dionysios Solomos, as well as **prominent Zakynthian** personalities, located in Agios Markos square. In Solomos Square, you'll also find the **Byzantine Museum** and the Renaissance church of **Agios Nikolaos**. On the southern end of the harbour is the 👁👁 **church of Agios Dionysios**, with its wonderful frescoes and the relics of the saint. Zakynthos has some outstanding beaches, like the much-photographed 🌊🌊🌊 **Navagio or Shipwreck bay also called**, in Agios Georgios Kremon, and 🌊🌊 **Gerakas**, which hosts the eggs of the endangered sea turtle, **caretta-caretta**. Not to be missed is a boat excursion to the 🌊🌊 **Galazies Spilies** (Blue Caves), near Volimes, to see one of nature's marvels.

👁 ITHAKI
Ιθάκη / Itháki

The homeland of the legendary Odysseus and his faithful Penelope of the Homer's epic. A special island, with more echoes of myth than actual archaeological sites, it attracts off-beat, casual individualists. It is small compared to the other main Ionian islands, but its scenery is **dramatic** and it is ideal for hiking and touring. On the island there are caves with Mycenaean finds, mountains, forests, dry, stony landscapes and quiet, pebble **beaches**.
For sightseeing, we suggest the 👁 **Grotto of the Nymphs**, or **Marmarospilia**, close to the capital **Vathy**, with stalactites and stalagmites, where according to legend, Odysseus hid the gifts of the Phaeacians, before going to his palace. Also in that area, is the **kastro tou Odysseus**, where Heinrich Schliemann conducted his excavations, finding what he erroneously believed to be the site of the Homeric capital.

👁👁 **Kioni** is a listed, traditional and cosmopolitan harbour, situated in verdant scenery, where yachts anchor, as they also do at the picturesque fishing village of 👁 **Frikes**. Ithaki is not famous for its beaches and this is probably the reason why it has fewer tourists. A good idea is to take a caique to the **Fidaki** and **Sarakiniko** beaches. And even better, if you set out to tour the island, in the middle of the western coast, there is a series of small, deserted coves, divided by attractive rock formations.

Vathy, Ithaki

👁 LEFKADA
Λευκάδα / Lefkáda

Lefkada is connected to the mainland by two bridges which cross the **narrow channel** separating them. It is a mainly mountainous island, with a great deal of natural beauty, areas abounding with plane trees, historical and archaeological sites, as well as beautiful, verdant islets opposite the cosmopolitan port **Nydri**.
These include the famous **Skorpios**, the property of the late shipping magnate, Aristotle Onassis, **Madouri**, with the mansion of writer Aristotelis Valaoritis, and **Meganissi**, with its three caves. In one of these, the **Papanikolis cave**, the famous submarine of the same name concealed itself during World War II.
The island has pretty villages, like 👁👁 **Agios Nikitas**, and is not lacking in outstanding beaches, including the popular 🌊🌊 **Porto Katsiki**, with its white sand and turquoise waters, and 🌊🌊 **Egremnous**, where, although the beach is difficult to get to (250 steps), the sea is superb.
Worth visiting is the 13th c. 👁 **Venetian fortress**, next to the man-made canal, and the 👁👁 **waterfalls** in a gorge in the village of Rahi, 5 km from Nydri.

Porto Katsiki, Lefkada

CORFU

WHY AMONG THE BEST

Because Corfu is attractive as a holiday destination at every season of the year. It has natural beauty, special architectural interest and a sophisticated lifestyle. Because the blend of Venetian, English and French periods and styles in the Old Town, with its castles, stone-flagged alleys locally called 'kandounia' and the arcades will enchant you. And also for the scenic routes through the magnificent countryside with lush green hills and superb deeply indented coastline with its gorgeous beaches.

IONIAN ISLANDS

CORFU

BEST's OPINION

The island's main points of interest are the Old Town, the greenery, the lovely landscape and beaches, as well as the traditional villages of the interior.
If it's peace and quiet you seek, you should avoid the stretches from the town of Corfu as far as Ipsos, Aharavi, Roda and Sidari, and from Benitses to Moraitika and Kavos. The most outstanding scenery of the island is on its west coast, between Paleokastritsa and Agios Gordis.

IN BRIEF

Corfu is the part of Greece closest to western Europe, both geographically and culturally. It was the first area of the country to be conquered by the Romans, who treated their acquisition with benevolence. In the course of its history the island passed through the hands of the Venetians, the French and the British, who also in turn left the stamp of their cultures. The Corfiots have a long tradition in music, theatre and intellectual pursuits. The **Corfu Philharmonic Society** was founded in 1840 and there are today dozens of bands on the island. In 1808 Greece's first university was instituted, the **Ionian Academy** and in 1815 the first **School of Fine Arts**, while the **Reading Society** which continues to flourish to this day, was also the first institution of its kind.

Corfu is 50 km long, 25 km at its widest and produces olive oil, dairy products, fruits and vegetables. The population is 110,000, of which 35,000 inhabit the town. The climate is mild and humid, thus accounting for the rich vegetation with numerous varieties of trees, of which the olive trees — 4,000,000 ! — and cypress dominate in the landscape. The island's size permits its visitors to choose the most suitable spot for a holiday, so that even in the month of August when it is submerged by the hordes of tourists, anyone who so wishes can find tranquillity in isolated areas.

HISTORY

It is said that Corfu is the Homeric island of the Phaeaceans, the kingdom of Alkinoos. According to legend its Greek name derives from the nymph Kerkyra, daughter of the river-god Asopos, or Korkyra, with whom Poseidon, god of the sea, fell in love and whom he brought to the island.

In the 8th c. BC Eretrian colonists arrived and later others came from Corinth. In the subsequent centuries Corfu evolved into a maritime and commercial power, which aroused the anger of the mother city of Corinth. In the naval battle of 644 BC between the two, it was Corfu who won the day. When in 299 BC the Illyrian queen Teuta attacked the island, the inhabitants requested the aid of the Romans who under the command of the consul Fulvius successfully repulsed the Illyrians and for the next five centuries Corfu continued in peaceful coexistence with Rome, becoming a favourite resort of the emperors. In the 4th c. AD the island passed to the Byzantine Empire and began to decline due to repeated attacks by Goths, Normans and Crusaders.

There followed the Venetian domination from 1204, the Byzantine in 1214 and then that of the Angevins, French conquerors of the kingdom of Two Sicilies, in 1267 until the second period of Venetian occupation beginning in 1386 and lasting until 1797. It was thanks to the Venetians that Corfu escaped domination by the Ottomans, despite the latter's sieges and attacks, and followed the evolution of the West in the arts and sciences. In 1797 the island was taken over by the French republicans who publicly burned the Libro d' Oro, the codex of the nobility, and also the deeds of land ownership. However, their poor administration discontented the Corfiots and they turned to Russia, who advocated the independence of the Ionian islands. In 1800, the Treaty of Constantinople created the independent Septinsular Republic which was dissolved in 1807 by the French who this time benefited the island with major public works. After Napoleon's defeat Corfu came into the hands of the British, who also constructed important buildings, roads and the water supply.

Eventually the Treaty of London in 1863 returned Corfu and the other Ionian islands to Greece.

IONIAN ISLANDS

BEST SIGHTS: STEP BY STEP

❶ OLD TOWN
Παλιά Πόλη / Paliá Póli

Originally the plan of Corfu town was drawn up according to the defensive requirements of the times. As it grew, the town clustered round the Spianada (Esplanade): Campiello, Agion Pateron and Agiou Athanassiou quarters, and gradually extended to the suburbs of Garitsa, Mandouki and Sanrokko.

The sight of the buildings as a whole constitutes an impressive blend of different western architectural influences.

Spianada

CORFU 31

Old Town of CORFU

MANDRAKI

OLD FORTRESS

0m 100 200
0yd 100 200

WHAT TO SEE

🌀🌀🌀 SPIANADA AND LISTON

The open space known as the **Spianada** is Europe's second largest square, and for Greece both the biggest and loveliest. It was initially for defence purposes, being bare ground between the citadel and the town. It became a square in **1628** and is now the spot where three of Corfu's major historical periods can be distinguished: in the Old Fort (Palio Frourio), the Venetian; in the Liston arcade the French and in the Palace (Anaktora), the English. Another relic of the past is the cricket matches which still take place on the grassy space. The circular monument in the Ionic style on the south side is the 🌀 rotunda commemorating **Maitland**, the first High Commissioner from 1816-24. In the Spianada in summer the Philharmonic and the bands play in the open air for Corfiot and other music-lovers. The **Liston** with its cafes all in a row is the Greek equivalent of the rue de Rivoli in Paris or the Piazza San Marco in Venice. It consists of multi-storeyed buildings with arcades and Venetian lanterns. They were built in the Napoleonic days (**1807-1814**) by the French to serve as barracks. There was a time when only those families recorded on the lists of the nobility, **Liste d' Or** (Libro d' Oro), were permitted to promenade there, whence its name (list on).

Liston

🌀🌀 THE OLD FORTRESS

The best known of the Venetian citadels, this one is closely linked with Corfu's history.
The Venetians also constructed the sea-water moat, the bastions - designed by Martinengo and Savorgnani - and a network of **underground galleries** for communication between the forts. There were several buildings in it, mainly houses of the aristocracy.
Today it contains one of the island's finest and largest churches, 🌀🌀 **Agios Georgios**, built by the British in **1840**, a basilica with six external Doric columns and which can hold 4,000 people.

The old fortress and Spianada

367

IONIAN ISLANDS

The Palace

🌀🌀 THE PALACE

Palace of SS Michael & George - Museum of Asiatic Art

An English, Georgian neo-classical building on the north side of the Spianada, it is said to be the oldest public building of modern Greece. The country's only **Sino-Japanese Museum** and the **Municipal Gallery** are housed there. The museum has interesting exhibits from Asian countries, and examples of Chinese art from the Neolithic era to the Ming dynasty. In front stands the statue of **Sir Frederic Adam** in recognition of this High Commissioner's work for the benefit of the island.

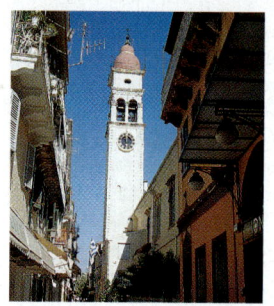

🌀🌀 AGIOS SPYRIDON CHURCH

The church of Corfu's patron saint, whose feast day is on **12 December**. Most impressive is the towering belfry of the basilica, of **1590**, the marble rood, the frescoes, dedications, and relics of the saint in a sarcophagus of **1770**, in gilt and with precious stones. These relics are closely linked to the island's history and religious life.

Agios Spyridon church

🌀🌀 CAMPIELLO QUARTER

An old part of town crammed with multi-storeyed buildings, an endless maze in which it is a pleasure to wander aimlessly. Go by the 🌀🌀 **square of the church of the Panagia tis Kremastis** where the Venetian decrees were executed. Take note of the fine **church of the Kremasti** with its majestic exterior and grand interior, the stone altar screen with a carved vine in relief, and icons in the Italian manner by Spyros Sperantzas (**1771**). In front of the church there is a **Venetian well-head** of 1699, one of the nine cisterns providing water for the citizens when under siege in the years of Venetian domination. Not far is the 🌀🌀 **Church of Agios Nikolaos**, the cathedral of the Great Elders of the Church. The icons of SS Theodora and Kerkyra are attributed to the Cretan painter Tzannes.

Campiello quarter

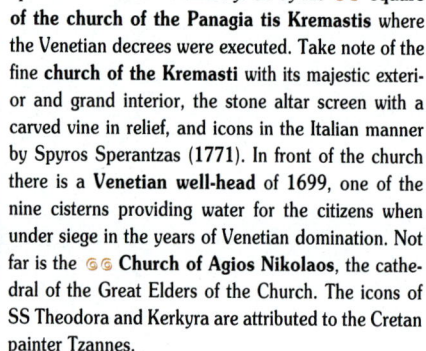

🌀🌀 BYZANTINE MUSEUM IN THE ANTIVOUNIOTISSA

Tel. (0661) 38313

🌀 *8 am-2:30 pm, closed Mondays and holidays**

In Campiello on the Mouragio, in the third side street of Arseniou Street, housed in the renovated late 15th c. church of the Panagia tis Antivouniotissas. It is a basilica in the Ionian island style. The museum, opened in 1984, has icons of the Post-Byzantine period from the 15th to 19th c.

🌀🌀 CHURCH OF AGIOS ANTONIOS & ANDREAS (14th c.)

At 115 Theotoki St., this is the oldest church of the Venetian town. It was rebuilt in 1753, when its aspect was radically altered. Its superb marble altar screen cost 2,110 ducats in its day.

🌀🌀 THE NEW FORTRESS (Néo Froúrio Agíou Márkou)

It is considered one of the major specimens of the technique of fortification architecture. Smaller than the old fortress, it is on two levels, of which the lower protected the harbour and the higher the surrounding countryside. It was partly this fort and partly a tempest which prevented the Turks from capturing Corfu in 1776 and halted their expansionist drive to the West.

ⓖⓖ MOUSTOXYDI STREET (Platí Kandoúni)

This Broad Lane (Strada Larga) was once much wider. Along it you can see the building of the **Ionian Parliament**, once the chamber of deputies and where the union of the Ionian Islands with Greece was voted on 23 September 1863. Nearby is the **mansion** of the noble **Ricci** family from whose balcony, at Carnival time, judges observed the horsemanship contests among the members of the aristocracy.

ⓖ TOWN HALL SQUARE

A lovely square in the centre of the Old Town. The town hall (San Giacomo, 1693) is one of the finest buildings of the Venetian period. Once a club for the nobility, it was converted into the *Opera of the Orient*, the first in modern Greece, in 1720, and became the town hall in 1903.
The ⓖ **Venetian church** of 1632, dedicated to San Giacomo, is the Catholic cathedral. There are some good restaurants in the square.

Town hall square

ⓖ BANKNOTE MUSEUM

Iroon Kypriakou Agona Sq., 1st & 2nd floor of the Ionian Bank
Tel. (0661) 41552
☉ *Monday-Friday 10 am-1 pm, closed on holidays**

It houses an extensive collection of old and contemporary Greek and foreign banknotes. You can also see the first banknote issued by the new Greek state under the Kapodistrias government, value 100 phoenix!

ⓖ IONIAN ACADEMY

On Kapodistriou Street, it was once a Venetian barracks and in 1841 became the seat of the first Greek university, which had operated in the Old Fortress from 1824.

ⓖ READING SOCIETY

At 120 Kapodistriou Street, a Venetian building and modern Greece's oldest cultural foundation, of 1836. It has a well-stocked library with rare manuscripts, etchings and paintings.

ⓖ KAPODISTRIAS MANSION

In Kapodistriou Street. A splendid architectural specimen, built in 1840, with a marble facade, Corinthian pilasters in rose-coloured stone, with capitals. It now houses the interpreters' and translators' department of the Ionian University. Greece's first prime-minister Ioannis Kapodistrias was born in 1776 in the house which formerly stood on this site.

❷ OUTSKIRTS OF CORFU TOWN

ⓖ ARCHAEOLOGICAL MUSEUM

Tennis Club area, on Petrou Vraila & 3 Armeni Sts
Tel. (0661) 30680
☉ *8 am-2:30 pm, closed on Mondays and holidays**

A number of finds excavated on the island are exhibited. Among others, you will see the imposing and huge ⓖⓖ **pediment of the Gorgon** from the temple of Artemis, the ⓖ **head of the statue of Menekrates**, a ⓖ **limestone pediment from Figareto** and the Archaic ⓖ **lion of Menekrates**.

ⓖⓖ CHURCH OF THE APOSTLES AGIOS IASON & SOSSIPATROU

Corfu's oldest church, of the 10th c., is in the suburb called Anemomilos. The church is cruciform, with an octagonal dome and fine masonry, containing large movable icons. It is said that the wife of the Despot of

Mystra, Thomas Paleologos, is buried in the precinct and according to a tradition, the raised stone blocks reaching into the sanctuary behind the screen are the tombs of the two saints.

🌀🌀 KANONI

This is the small peninsula in front of the lagoon of Halikiopoulou and the airport. First enjoy the magnificent 🌀🌀 **view**, pictured on many of Corfu's postcards and then follow the flagged path leading to a concrete bridge crossing onto the island with the Vlahernas monastery.

🌀 VLAHERNA MONASTERY

It was built before 1685 and began to decline in the 18th c. This is where to go to have the best view of 🌀 **Pontikonissi** or to take a boat to the picturesque little island itself.

🌀 PONTIKONISSI

Corfu's emblem, famous from the Swiss artist Boecklin's painting *The Island of the Dead*, and where you'll see the 11th c. 🌀 **Byzantine church of the Pantokrator**.

Vlahernas monastery and Pontikonissi

🌀 MON REPOS

Formerly the summer residence of the High Commissioner Sir Frederic Adam and later of the Greek royal family, it is 65 acres of earthly paradise. The grounds are on Corfu's archaeological site of the ancient city Paleopolis and important finds were made in its NE edge, such as ruins of the **Doric temple of Apollo Korkyraios** (5th c. BC), the island's founding deity. The greatest temple of the island, of the 7th c. BC, dedicated to Hera once stood here but has now disappeared.

Mon Repos

🌀 PALEOPOLIS

Corfu's ancient city, opposite the villa Mon Repos. Very few ruins survive of what were an odeon, an agora, an aqueduct with tall arches, major naval installations, ports and docks and large public baths, of which some remnants can be seen.

The **basilica of Paleopolis**, **Agia Kerkyra**, is the island's **oldest Christian monument**, dating to the 5th c. AD. It suffered extensive damage over the years, the worst from shelling in the second world war. Parts from a Doric temple of Artemis (580 BC) discovered nearby next to the monastery of Agion Theodoron were used in its construction.

🌀 VIDO ISLAND

Reached by boat from the old port (1 n mi) Its ancient name was Ptihia and it once played an important part in Corfu's defences. It was first fortified by the French in 1797-1979 and made impregnable by the British in 1814-1864. The fort was however eventually blown up, according to the provisions of the treaty of the union of the Ionian Islands with Greece. Today it is a tourist resort.

Paleopolis

FREE TIME

IN TOWN

- **Sound & Light:** At the Old Fort. Information, Corfu Tourist bureau, tel. (0661) 37638.
- **Platyteras Monastery:** At the edge of Corfu town, in Mandouki. It contains excellent icons and the tombs of Kapodistrias and Tzavelas.
- **Casino:** Temporarily in the Hotel Corfu Holiday Palace
- **Carriage Ride:** Starting from the centre of the Spianada. It's not cheap (8,000 drs. for 30 min) but worth it on the first day for an impression of the Old Town.
- **Kalypso:** A vessel specially equipped with a glass bottom to see an underwater show of fish and trained seals. Price: Adults 3,000 drs., children 1,500 drs., tel. (0661) 46525.

FESTIVITIES AND LOCAL EVENTS

- The **processions** in honour of St. Spyridon: Holy Saturday, Palm Sunday, first Sunday in November and 11 August.
- **Corfu Festival:** In September, with concerts by orchestras and soloists, ballet, opera and theatre companies from Greece and abroad.
- **Carnival:** The last three Sundays of Carnival in February and March.
- **Petegoletsa:** A tradition for the last Thursday of Carnival when the matrons of Corfu town come out onto their balconies and gossip in the local dialect.
- **Breaking the pots:** On the day before Easter at 11 in the morning the bells of Agios Spyridon sound the summons and from the balconies of the houses in the Old Town, empty or full pots of water, are thrown down into the street. This is said to be an ancient-Greek custom symbolizing the first resurrection (purification) of souls.
- **Barcarole:** On 10 August, illuminated boats in Garitsa Bay re-enact the legend in which Saint Spyridon chased away the Turks who were besieging the town.
- **Celebration of Union** with Greece: 21 May.
- **Cricket:** Matches in the lower Spianada on summer afternoons.
- **Concerts - Events:** Open-air concerts by the local bands, ballet, theatre, etc.

❸ TOUR NORTH OF CORFU TOWN
CORFU TOWN TO PYRGI

Unfortunately intensive tourist development has left but few parts untouched.

KONDOKALI

A sheltered bay before Gouvia. Once a Venetian port, it harbours pleasure craft today. Here also is the fish-taverna ✓ **Gerekos**, one of the best of the island.

GOUVIA

Just after the crossroads for Dassia a short side track takes you to the old Venetian **navy yard**. In the multi-arched vaulted arcades were once slipped the Venetian galleys which protected the Ionian Islands and governed the sea routes of the Mediterranean. Nearby, at the top of the hill of **Kommeno** stands the **polygonal fort** of 1778 with 70 embrasures which guarded this strategic position.

CAPE KOMMENO

The **church of the Ypapandi** at Diamandopetra is a delightful chapel to be seen on the islet of the bay of Gouvia. A short walk or drive of 2 km to the Hotel Corfu Imperial will impress visitors with its variety of greenery, lovely villas in their gardens and the view of the bay of Gouvia.

Church of the Ypapandi

IONIAN ISLANDS

ⓖ CASTELLO AND CASTELLETTO

Kato Korakiana, on the hill above Dassia
The Castello is an imposing Italianate-Gothic mansion built in 1905 by the Italian baron Luca Mimbelli. Before war broke out between Greece and Italy, many royal personages had been guests there. But as soon as hostilities began the Mimbelli family was evicted from Greece and their property confiscated. The renovated Castelletto is in the centre of the park and has been the annexe of the National Gallery since 1992.

ⓖ AGIOS MARKOS

A village with a variety of trees and with charming traditional houses and cafe-bars with views of Mt Pantokrator. There are two **Byzantine churches** to see, the **Pantokrator** with well-preserved **frescoes of 1576** and **Agios Merkourios** with **frescoes** of 1075.

ⓖ SPARTYLAS

A detour shortly beyond Pyrgi. The road climbs the hill to the cafe-restaurant ✓ **Agnandio** where the friendly owner, Theophilos, will find a table for you to relish the ⓖⓖ **panorama** of the indented eastern coastline all the way to Corfu town. The ⓖⓖⓖ **view** is even better if you continue on to the peak of Mt Pantokrator where there is a **monastery** of the same name.

---

❹ TOUR OF NORTH-EASTERN CORFU
PYRGI - AGIOS STEPHANOS - KASSIOPI - PERITHIA - NYMPHES

All the way to Kassiopi this is one of the most splendid routes of the island. The road is in good condition above the little coves with their slopes covered in vegetation reaching down to the small pebble beaches. It is reminiscent of the Corniche of the Cote d' Azur and possibly even lovelier. As soon as you are past the Kouloura crossroads, stop to enjoy the ⓖ **vista**. All along the route the Albanian mountains will form the backround. You will eventually reach the hamlet ⓖ **Nissaki** with a colourful pebble- ⚲ **beach** on which there is a taverna so you can enjoy a pleasant combination of a swim and a meal.

ⓖ AGNI

A charming little harbour where the cypress and olive trees grow down to the sea. We picked the taverna **Agni** for seafood freshly caught by the owner who is a fisherman. Inexpensive and spotless in delightful surroundings.

ⓖ KALAMI

A small beach with clear waters, excellent for those who prefer pebbles. Attractive surroundings and tavernas.

Kalami

ⓖ KOULOURA

A pretty harbour with a curved mole, fishing smacks and plenty of foliage. You can see there the fortified Venetian house of the Gennatas family, formerly the Quartano mansion. In 1537 in the course of a massive incursion by the pirate Barbarossa, a quarter – 22,000 – of the inhabitants of the island were captured, among them the seven year-old daughter of that Venetian family, Kalli Quartano. The little girl's good looks and intelligence procured her an aristocratic upbringing and in time she became the wife of the Sultan Selim II and mother of Sultan Murad III - she was the Valide Sultana Nur Vanu. She did what she could to help the Greeks and on her death she was given Christian burial in Agia Sophia.

ⓖⓖ AGIOS STEPHANOS

A village with traditional architecture and a small port for fishing- and pleasure-boats. It stands amidst olive groves, next to ⚲ **Kerassia** beach. It's especially worth visiting for a meal in one of the tavernas on the waterfront. We chose the **Efkalipto**.

KASSIOPI

Nowadays a charming little town with a lively tourist trade, it has been inhabited since antiquity and was known for its ancient theatre and temple of Kassios Zeus. Pyrrhos king of Epiros, founded it in 281 BC and the city used to be second in importance in Corfu. A promontory divides it in two and on the low brow of the hill there are still today the ruins of the castle named **Pyrgos** which the Angevin French erected on the remains of a Roman fort. There is an interesting **medieval church** to see, the **Panagia tis Kassopitras** which was built in the early days of Christianity over the ruins of the temple of Kassios Zeus. It was ravaged by the Ottomans and later rebuilt by the Venetians in 1580.

On one side of the town there is the small harbour and the beach is on the other. You'll find little bars in good taste, also diminutive attractive beaches easily reached on foot.

OLD OR UPPER PERITHIA

An abandoned hamlet on the slopes of Mt Pantokrator. Enchanting mountain scenery with stunning stone houses and rich vegetation. You can eat at the shady taverna **Palia Perithia** in the middle of the village.

NYMPHES

One of Corfu's traditional villages. 1 1/2 km from it, beautifully situated amid the foliage, is the **abandoned monastery of the Pantokrator tou Askitariou** dating to 950. Ask the village priest for the key and start out on the practicable dirt track (50 m from the cemetery) through dense olive groves. You can see there some exceptional wall paintings, the chapel of the Evangelistria and hewn into the rock the **hermitage** of the first monk to live there, Artemios Paisios.

Outside the village is the **church of the Estavromenos**, of unusual aspect with two domes. The second is the bigger, and hexagonal.

Old Perithia

---

5 TOUR OF NORTH-WESTERN CORFU
SKRIPERO - SIDARI - KAVADADES - ARKADADES - ANGELOKASTRO - PALEOKASTRITSA

This route takes us through pleasant villages to scenery of unparalleled beauty with sublime panoramas which reaches its apex as we approach Paleokastritsa.

SKRIPERO - ANO KORAKIANA

Skripero is worth a stop to enjoy the **vista** and stroll in its alleys. There are more than 30 churches in the village of Ano Korakiana in the traditional style of architecture.

SIDARI - AKROTIRI DRASTIS

Stop a moment to see the famous **Canal d'Amour**, which is worth it if only out of interest in its geology and then immediately set off again. September might be a time to enjoy it because in other summer months the place seethes with umbrellas and tourists.

If you are interested in the unusual geological structure of rock formations, continue on to the neighbouring village of Peroulades and follow the rough dirt track starting from the square down the hill to **Cape Drastis** for a secluded swim in this peculiar **landscape**.

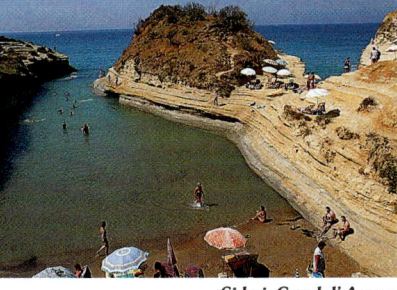

Skripero

Sidari, Canal d'Amour

IONIAN ISLANDS

FROM PEROULADES TO ANGELOKASTRO

After Peroulades you can take a detour from the coast road and the long sandy beach of Agios Stephanos, choosing the narrow but good road of the interior leading to the village of **Kavadades**. From there, with minimal deviations, you can pass through the villages of **Rahtades**, **Daphne**, **Aspiotades** and **Kastellanous**. These are not overrun by tourists and show the true aspect of Corfu and its nature. From Kastellanous you can approach Angelokastro either via Troumbeta or the village of Pagi, where the route is more beautiful but the condition of the road much worse.

ⓖ ANGELOKASTRO

A Byzantine fort built on a sheer cliff at 300 m. As many as 4,000 people from the environs could find shelter here in times of peril. Genoese pirates in 1403, Saracens, even the terrifying Suleiman in 1537, were baffled and departed! There is visual contact from the fort with the forts of Corfu for the purpose of signalling. The Venetians however ceased to make use of it from the 18th c., leaving but a minor guard and the British later abandoned it. The paved road from Angelokastro leads to **Bella Vista** with its cafes, definitely a place to stop! Even before ordering take a look at the ⓖⓖⓖ **view**. Paleokastritsa and its neighbouring creeks with their steep slopes down to a translucent sea will take your breath away. The road downhill from Lakones through olive groves prolongs the enchantment of this route until you reach Paleokastritsa.

Paleokastritsa from Bella Vista

Paleokastritsa

Pelekas

ⓖⓖⓖ PALEOKASTRITSA

Second to Corfu town, the island's best-known spot. It has been a famous resort since between the World Wars. Tradition places here the palace of King Alkinoos, father of Nausicaa. The ⚑ **beach** is less stupendous than the ⓖⓖⓖ **scenery**, with its creeks and the extraordinary turquoise colours of the sea, despite the graceless constructions in the vicinity. Unlike the old days, the waterfront tavernas appear to us to cater to throngs of famished tourists. At the top of the hill you can see the **Byzantine fortress-monastery of the Panagia tis Paleokastritsas**.

Spend a little time on a boat trip with an outboard engine (3,000 drs. per person) to the three grottoes and the relatively peaceful beaches nearby - in particular the beach of ⚑⚑ **Liapades**.

ⓖⓖ MONASTERY OF THE PANAGIA TIS PALEOKASTRITSAS

Founded in 1228, this monastery has a collection of Byzantine icons of the Cretan School, a parchment manuscript bible of the 12th c., devotional books and vessels, a Stone Age axe of 7000 BC and the bones of some sea-monster washed ashore centuries ago.

❻ WESTERN CORFU
ERMONES - PELEKAS - SINARADES - AGIOS GORDIS

A short route of special beauty through green scenery and traditional-style villages with views of hills, craggy cliffs and the sea. This is also the part of Corfu with the best ⚑⚑⚑ **beaches** *(see Best Beaches)*. The outstanding villages are Pelekas, Sinarades and Ano Garouna, known for its stone-masons.

ⓖⓖ PELEKAS

The place from which to watch the glorious ⓖⓖⓖ **sunset** from the top of the hill where **Kaiser** Wilhelm II had his **observatory**.

ⓖ SINARADES

A village with delightful alleys and tiled roofs. Note the 15th c. **Venetian church belfry** and visit the interesting **Folk Art and Historical Museum** to see exhibits of local costumes, tools, a cobbler's workplace, the model of a fishing craft called **papyrella** and a reproduction of the interior of a typical village dwelling of central Corfu.

---

❼ TOUR OF SOUTH-WESTERN CORFU
AGIOS MATTHEOS - FORT GARDIKI - LAKE KORISSION - ARGYRADES

A trip which will take you up hill and down dale to villages with local colour and splendid ♀♀ **beaches** for an opportunity to get away from the crowds *(see Best Beaches)*.

ⓖ AGIOS MATTHEOS

A village built as an amphitheatre in the foothills of Mt Gamilios or Prassoudi. At the top of the hill there is the 4th c. **monastery of Christos Pantokrator** and a **Paleolithic cave** in which were discovered the bones of large prehistoric animals, tools and fossilized foods of Paleolithic man of 30,000 BC. A good ♀ **beach** of the same name is nearby.

FROURIO GARDIKIOU - FORT GARDIKI

3 km from Agios Mattheos. Although not large, it was one of the mightier strongholds of the SW part of the island in medieval days. Octagonal, with eight towers and three gates. You'll see the imposing central gateway, the ruins of six of the towers and remnants of the ramparts.

ⓖ LIMNI KORISSION - LAKE KORISSION

A route worth taking for its varying landscapes, from the dense vegetation in the north to the sand dunes of this lake and fine views south. It is a long narrow lagoon extending over 6,000 acres. A little wooden bridge at the outlet to the sea leads to a wood with rare plants such as white lilies and 14 species of orchid.

Lake Korission

ⓖ ARGYRADES

A chief village on a hill, with Venetian architecture at the higher part and the pleasant beaches **Agios Georgios** and **Issos** below.

❽ TOUR OF SOUTH-EASTERN CORFU
ACHILLEIO - BENITSES - MESSONGI - CHLOMOS

Unfortunately in this southern area of Corfu, Benitses, Messongi, and Kavos in particular, there has recently been a surge of low-budget mass tourism, a pity because it is full of the most lovely olive groves and spots of natural beauty.

IONIAN ISLANDS

🌀🌀 ACHILLEIO

The palace, renovated a short time ago, was built in the last century (1891) for the empress Elizabeth of Austria-Hungary. The ravishing and melancholy Sissy, whose turbulent life and tragic end inspired novelists and film makers, could find in the Achilleion the peace she craved. She was assassinated in Geneva in 1898 by an Italian anarchist, whereupon the palace was bought by Kaiser Wilhelm II of Germany as a holiday home where he stayed from 1908 to 1914. It is a very grand building with formal gardens, Renaissance statues, works of art, verandas, ponds and fountains which will bring to mind scenes from the James Bond film For Your Eyes Only. Note the **statue of the Dying Achilles** by the German sculptor E. Herter and also the well-known oil by the Austrian painter F. Matz, the **Triumph of Achilles**. Today the palace is a museum of the personal belongings of the Empress and the Kaiser.

BENITSES

Once a retreat for the select few, nowadays the crowded beach, water sports and nightclubs have turned it into a paradise for organized tourism. By the main road there are the ruins of the baths of a 3rd c. Roman villa and also the **Kaiser's bridge**, built for him as his private pier.

🌀🌀 CIRCUIT: MESSONGI - AGIOS DIMITRIOS - CHLOMOS - PETRITI - MESSONGI

A route with a spectacular 🌀🌀 **vista** of olive trees, the village of Kato Spileo with the taverna **75 Skalopatia** (Steps), tel. (0661) 75028, with good Greek cooking and from its terrace a 🌀 **panorama** of the Messongi region. See the pretty village of **Agios Dimitrios** on the edge of the cliff and go on to 🌀🌀 **Chlomos**. Leave the car in the square and stroll in this traditional southern Corfiot village. The 🌀 **view** from the **church of the Taxiarches** is splendid. From there you will get to the attractive fishing village Petriti and back again to Messongi on a narrow road between the coast and the wooded slopes. On the way you will see the hamlet Boukari which has a nice taverna by the sea, the **Potamaki**.

Chlomos

OTHER THINGS TO DO

🌀 **Golf:** On the pleasant plain of Ropa at Ermones, tel. (0661) 94220, Athens, tel. (01) 6923028. An 18-hole course, PAR 72, length 6,803 yds/6,221 m.
It was awarded a prize as one of the best in Europe but today we find it neglected. Suitable for beginners (coaching given) and advanced players. There is a cafe-bar, restaurant and shop with equipment for rent.
Green fees: All day 14,000 drs., 18 holes 12,000 drs., 1 week 57,500 drs.
Riding: At Ermones in the Ropa valley next to the golf club, tel. (0661) 94220.
Daily from 8:30 am-3 pm. From 2,000 drs. a head for two hours. Horses and ponies for children, beginners and experienced riders. Rides out into the countryside.
Aqualand: At Agios Ioannis, 7 km west of town, tel. (0663) 52963
Open: May to October.
18 acres of water slides for kids and grown-ups. With a restaurant, cafeteria, bar, boutique, mini market and parking.
Day trips: For day trips from Corfu town, Kassiopi, Ipsos, Agios Stephanos, Paleokastritsa, Lefkimi, ask the following travel agents for information:

Perakis-Sotirakis, tel. (0661) 38690
Sarris Cruises, tel. (0661) 35317
Leonditsis, Sidari, tel. (0663) 95248

Cosmic, Kassiopi, tel. (0663) 81624
Corfu Port Authority, tel. (0661) 30481
Corfu National Tourist Bureau, tel. (0661) 37638, 3973

MORE TRIPS

BOAT TRIPS

From Corfu harbour to ⊚ **Paxi**, ⊚⊚ **Andipaxi**, ⊚⊚ **Parga** and Albania. Also to the **Diapondia Nissia**, the islands of ⊚⊚ **Othoni**, ⊚ **Erikoussa** and ⊚ **Mathraki**.

⊚⊚ DIAPONDIA ISLANDS

They are off the shipping routes and for lovers of peace and quiet. Beautiful and clean beaches, greenery everywhere in a landscape with olive and cypress trees, few trippers and a relaxed atmosphere. Most of the inhabitants have emigrated or moved to Corfu.

⊚⊚ Othoni

An enchanting leafy little island with very varied scenery. It has two hamlets and 150 inhabitants. The small, exquisite sandy beach **tou Frantzeskou to koukouli** at the foot of a precipice is unforgettable. And definitely do not miss the white sands for which the fantastic beach ♀♀♀ **Aspri Ammos** is named (access only by boat). They say it was in the cave here that the nymph Calypso dwelt, who seduced Ulysses and made him forget Penelope - for a time.

⊚ Erikoussa

The most organized for tourism and with the most conveniences of the Diapondia islands. Green hills and wonderful seaside. Seven tiny villages, most of them built on a height for fear of pirates. A half hour's walk will get you to the beach of **Faros** or **Fikki** or to **Pranghini** (by a footpath).

⊚ Mathraki

Diminutive and delightful. Little houses with flower-filled gardens, a taverna on the waterfront and two hamlets with rooms for rent, cafes and restaurants. Gorgeous beaches with fine sand.

⊚ PAXI

Here is all the loveliness of the vegetation of the Ionian islands encapsulated. Before entering the harbour you will see the two picturesque islands of **Agios Nikolaos** and **Panagia**. Then the natural beauty and the charm of the villages **Lakka**, **Longos**, **Magazia** and **Ozias** await you. The population of the island is about 2,500. Besides the many and splendid beaches: **Glyfada**, **Planous**, **Ahai**, **Kipos**, **Monoderi**, **Haramis** and **Lakkos**, you also have to see the amazing **rocks with the wind holes**.

⊚⊚ ANDIPAXI

Reached by speed- and fishing-boat from Paxi and Corfu. A hamlet, a few little tavernas, a hundred inhabitants, a small harbour (Agrapidia), vineyards and ♀♀♀ **exotic beaches with fine sand**, among the most beautiful in Greece. If you have a boat at your disposal, you can be sure you have found your paradise on earth.

IONIAN ISLANDS

🏖 BEST BEACHES

There is an exceptional variety of beaches in Corfu, from tiny coves to beaches with sand or pebbles stretching for miles and from isolated to jet-set beaches.
BEST has selected eleven, judging by their natural surroundings, conveniences as well as the numbers and sort of people who frequent them.

🏖🏖🏖 MYRTIOTISSA

Corfu's most beautiful beach, in a steep-sided wooded cove. Pines, banana trees, sand and tranquillity generally because access by a very poor dirt road attracts mostly nature-lovers and nudists. The scenery is superb. The **monastery** you will see there is the **Panagia Myrtidiotissa** (14th c.).

Myrtiotissa

🏖🏖 GLYFADA

A lovely beach, organized and frequented by high society. It is near Pelekas and popular with young people. There are several hotels there, rooms to rent, tavernas, a number of beach bars, umbrellas and water sports. The parking lot is often full up.

Glyfada

🏖🏖 KONDOGIALOS

The road here from Pelekas or Gialiskari takes you through a lush green landscape until you arrive at this sandy beach which, although organized, with eating places and water sports, has preserved its natural environment relatively unspoiled.

Kondogialos

🏖🏖 GIALISKARI

A beach with sand and pine trees right down to the water among steep rocks. The hotel provides a parking lot, umbrellas, a snack bar and taverna.

Gialiskari

🏖🏖 PRASSOUDI

A transparent sea surrounded by a green landscape. The environment is untouched, despite the sandy beach, easy parking space and two tavernas. Although a lot of people go there you will not be bothered. More peaceful is **Skydi beach**, 200 m away with sand and tavernas.

Prassoudi

Halikouna

🏖🏖 HALIKOUNA

Along the wetlands of Lake Korission the unspoiled sand beach of Halikouna stretches for miles. From the north side, at Alonaki, a decent dirt track takes you over the dunes to the narrow channel between the lake and the sea. There is an agreeable fish-taverna, **Alonaki**, on the northern part and the south side is just as attractive and is reached from Linia. Concerts also take place on Halikouna beach in the summer.

Kerassia

🏖🏖 KERASSIA

The best beach on Corfu's north-eastern coast, in colourful surroundings. Smooth boulders on the shore, sand in the sea, clean waters, umbrellas and a blue flag award.

Barbati

🏖 BARBATI

For those who prefer a pebble beach or have decided to stay north of town, Barbati is a good choice with all the facilities of an organized beach: tavernas, parking, umbrellas, water sports, etc.

Drastis

🏖 AKROTIRI DRASTIS (SIDARI)

At the village of Peroulades. If you want a secluded place for a swim, go down the dirt track from the square to 🟡 **Cape Drastis**, an unusual 🟡🟡 **landscape** with natural swimming pools, or go to **Perouladon beach** a short way down from the village.

🏖 AGIOS GORDIS

Wooded slopes down to a sandy bay in superb 🟡🟡 **scenery**. This is one of Corfu's prettiest beaches but uncontrolled building has choked the area. To park there is an adventure although the village has much to offer in the way of nightlife. From the spot just above Agios Gordis called **Aerostato** just outside Sinarades the 🟡🟡 **view** is magnificent.

Issos

🏖 AGIOS GEORGIOS (ton Korission) - ISSOS

The crowds thronging this splendid sand-beach diminish the farther you go to the right. Equally good is 🏖 **Issos** beach next to it, with its dunes.

IONIAN ISLANDS

BEST HOTELS AND ROOMS

BEST LOCATION
As the town of Corfu and its outskirts has the most to offer we suggest you stay in or near it. If you want to be near the sea you can stay at the capes Kontokali or Kommeno, north of town, or at one of the hotels west of the centre of the island, a little farther away but where the seaside is wonderful.

PRICES
The hotel prices mentioned below are the official ones set by the National Tourist Organization for double rooms, at low and high season, with breakfast. Since owners are allowed to modify the prices, always try to negotiate them.

CORFU TOWN

✓✓✓ CORFU PALACE (Luxury Class)
2 Dimokratias Ave.
Tel. (0661) 39485-7, fax 31749
Open: April-October

Description: It is considered as the best in the centre of town. This restored hotel has a long tradition in having the hospitality of the english aristocracy.
Rooms: 110 rooms with A/C, TV, bathroom, hair dryer, radio and sea view.
Special features: Luxury, excellent service, large pool, garden, tennis court, water sports, ✓✓ **restaurant**, taverna and parking.
Price: 30,000-76,000 drs.
Value for money: ✻
Credit cards: All

✓✓ CAVALIERI (A Class)
4 Kapodistriou St.
Tel. (0661) 39336, fax 39283
Open: All year round

Description: A splendid 17th c. mansion renovated in 1993 although not entirely successfully. Nevertheless it is considered a classic and one of the best in town, in a prime position on the Spianada. Rooms with view of the Spianada and of the sea.

Rooms: 48 rooms with A/C, TV, well furnished in traditional style mini bar and telephone.
Special features: Superb view also from the roof garden.
Price: 26,000 - 35,000 drs.
Value for money: ✻
Credit cards: All

BELLA VENEZIA (C Class)
4 Zambeli St.
Tel. (0661) 44290, 46500, fax 20708
Open: All year round
Description: A neo classical restored mansion of the 19th c. in good taste and comfortable.
Rooms: 32 rooms with A/C, TV and telephone.
Special features: Lovely garden, snack bar, breakfast room, friendly atmosphere and excellent value.
Price: 19,200-29,000 drs.
Value for money: ✻✻
Credit cards: Diners, American Express, Mastercard, Visa

CORFU

KANONI - MON REPOS

✓✓ CORFU HOLIDAY PALACE
formerly HILTON (Luxury Class)

2 Nafsikas St.
Tel. (0661) 30041, 36540-9, fax 36551
Open: All year round
Description: A large, imposing modern construction, beginning however to show its age. One of Corfu's classic hotels in a splendid location close to town.
Rooms: 273 rooms with A/C, telephone and balcony with view.
Special features: The casino is here temporarily and musical evenings with piano playing are organized in the bar. Tennis court, water sports, 3 restaurants, 3 bars, 2 pools, beach, yacht basin and parking.
Price: 41,000 - 56,000 drs.
Value for money: ✱
Credit cards: All

✓ ARHONDIKO (C Class)

Tel. (0661) 36950, 37222, fax 38294
Open: All year round
Description: In Garitsa. A simple old building with an attractive exterior and wooden floors.
Rooms: 29 nicely furnished rooms with bath, telephone, TV and fridge.
Price: 19,500-50,000 drs.
Value for money: ✱
Credit cards: Visa

NORTH-EASTERN CORFU

✓✓ KONDOKALI BAY
(Luxury Class)

Kondokali
Tel. (0661) 99000-2, 90500, fax 91901
Open: April-October
Description: In an idyllically peaceful spot 6 km outside town. Modernized in 1996, it consists of a main building and bungalows.
Rooms: 243 rooms and bungalows with A/C and telephone.
Special features: A fine swimming pool, 2 beaches, 2 tennis courts, water sports, children's playground, restaurants and beach taverna.
Price: 27,900-52,400 drs.
Value for money: ✱✱
Credit cards: Visa

✓✓✓ GRECOTEL CORFU IMPERIAL (Luxury Class)

Kommeno, tel. (0661) 91481-91490, fax 91881
Open: April-October
Description: Situated on beautiful Cape Kommeno. Don't be put off by its external appearance (it used to be managed by the state). It was renovated in 1994 and as soon as you go inside you will be struck by the first-class decor of Corfu's best hotel. Spacious lobbies and well laid-out outdoor areas where the bungalows are.
Rooms: 308 luxurious rooms with A/C, bath, telephone, TV and hair-dryer.
Special features: 3 private beaches on a privately-owned peninsula, pools, tennis courts, water sports, 3 restaurants, 3 bars and parking.
Price: 110,700 drs.
Value for money: ✱✱
Credit cards: All

✓✓ GRECOTEL DAPHNILA BAY (A Class)

Daphnila (Dassia)
Tel. (0661) 90320-4, fax 91026
Open: April-October
Description: In a pleasant spot on the slope of an olive grove, half an hour out of town. A building in the traditional style and bungalows. The interior has been redecorated in good taste. A beautiful, well-tended garden.
Rooms: 260 rooms with A/C, bath, telephone and TV.
Special features: Pool, tennis club, water sports school, modern thalassotherapy center, restaurants, bar, mountain biking, workshop, night club and parking.
Price: 76,000-81,000 drs.
Value for money: ✱

Credit cards: All

✓ ETRUSCO ROOMS
Kato Korakiana (Dassia)
Tel. (0661) 93342
Open: Easter - 20 October
Description: An attractive small building among foliage in an estate.
Rooms: 8 rooms with bath and balcony.
Special features: A hospitable atmosphere and an excellent restaurant.
Price: 8,000-12,000 drs. without breakfast
Value for money: ✹✹
Credit cards: Diners, Visa, Emborocarta

WESTERN CORFU

✓✓ PELEKAS COUNTRY CLUB (A Class)
Pelekas
Tel. (0661) 52239, fax 33867
Open: April-October
Description: On two floors, a traditional mansion in the middle of a wooded estate a few km from Pelekas. The ideal choice for peaceful contemplation in a natural environment of rare beauty.

Rooms: 14 rooms with bath, kitchen, TV and telephone.
Special features: Parking, tennis court, pool and stables.
Price: 72,500 drs. throughout the season.
Value for money: ✹✹
Credit cards: All

✓✓ LOUIS GRAND HOTEL (A Class)
Glyfada
Tel. (0661) 94140-5, fax 94146
Open: April-October
Description: A huge old hotel modernized internally in 1997. Its great advantage is the superb beach of Glyfada in front of it. 4 km from the golf course and riding club.

Rooms: 242 rooms with A/C.
Special features: Swimming pools, water sports, tennis court, restaurants, bar and parking.
Price: 18,500-47,500 drs.
Value for money: ✹
Credit cards: Visa, Mastercard, American Express, Diners

✓ CASA LUCIA
On the way to Palaiokastritsa (12 km)
Tel. (0661) 91419, fax 91732
Open: April-October
Description: A delightful group of buildings of an old converted olive press. Flagged paths surround pretty, small houses with local colour and there is an idyllic garden with a swimming pool in the middle. A hotel unlike any other.

Rooms: There are 10 little houses/bungalows each washed in a different colour and particularly well cared-for both inside and out. Pastel colours, comfortable interiors with the use of wood to make them cosy and home-like. All have a small private garden and kitchen and space for two or for a family.
Special features: Well arranged public rooms, large garden, pool, day-trips arranged.
Price: 16,000-19,000 drs. without breakfast
Value for money: ✹✹✹
Credit cards: None

AKROTIRI BEACH (A Class)
Palaiokastritsa
Tel. (0663) 41237, 41275, fax 41277
Open: April-October
Description: Built in the style favoured in the '70s without anything special except its location on a cape with marvellous views on both sides. Probably the best near Palaiokastritsa.
Rooms: 127 rooms with telephone and balcony with sea view.
Special features: Two beaches (one sandy and one rocky), swimming pool, water sports, restaurant,

bar, A/C in public areas, parking.
Price: 26,400 - 43,000 drs.
Value for money: ✱
Credit cards: All

ELENA (B Class)

Ermones
Tel. (0661) 94131-3, fax 94633
Open: May-October
Description: A small well-designed hotel, 120 m from the beach, 1 km from the golf course.
Rooms: 28 rooms with A/C, telephone and balcony with sea view.
Special features: Garden restaurant, bar, pool, children's playground and parking.
Price: 16,000-20,000 drs.
Value for money: ✱
Credit cards: Visa

ELLY BEACH (A Class)

Liapades (before Palaiokastritsa)
Tel. (0063) 41455, fax 41479
Open: May-October
Description: A square white building with large picture-windows overlooking the beach. A good choice if you want to be near the sea.
Rooms: 44 rooms and bungalows with balcony and sea view.
Special features: Restaurant, water sports and parking.
Price: 14,500-20,200 drs.
Value for money: ✱✱✱
Credit cards: Diners

SOUTH-EASTERN CORFU

✓✓ SAN STEFANO (A Class)

Benitses
Tel. (0661) 71112-8, 36036, fax 72272
Open: April-October
Description: A big hotel 11 km outside the town of Corfu, below the Achilleio in 34 acres of greenery with lovely views. A good choice for young people seeking the nightlife of Benitses.
Rooms: 220 rooms with TV, telephone and A/C, also 30 bungalows with A/C and kitchen.
Special features: A friendly owner and courteous staff. There are very good special price offers such as 7,500 drs. for a double room in June. It is about to be modernized and may house the casino. A 540 sq. m pool, water sports, tennis courts, bar, restaurants, mini market, conference centre and parking.
Price: 24,000-41,000 drs.
Value for money: ✱✱
Credit cards: All

ALTERNATIVES

LOUIS CORCYRA BEACH (A Class)
Gouvia, tel. (0661) 90196, fax 91591
Price: 23,000-51,000 drs.

CORFU CHANDRIS (A Class)
Renovated - good choice
Dassia, tel. (0661) 97100-4, fax 93458
Price: 26,000-66,000 drs.

GIALISKARI PALLAS (A Class)
Gialiskari (Sinarades), tel. (0661) 54401, fax 54724
Price: 16,400-23,200 drs.

CLUB MEDITERRANEE IPSOS
Ipsos, tel./fax (01) 3254674.
Price: 52,500-145,000 drs.
Weekly for one person full board.

NISSAKI BEACH (A Class)
Nissaki, tel.(0663) 91323, 91540, fax 22079
Price: 17,000-45,000 drs.

ERMONES BEACH HOTEL (A Class)
Ermones, tel. (0661) 94241, fax 94248
Price: 19,000-36,000 drs.

PANTOKRATOR (B Class)
Barbati, tel. (0663) 91005, fax 91004
Price: 12,600-17,950 drs.
Half board obligatory

ALEXIOU (B Class)
Barbati, tel. (0663) 91383, fax 91087
Price: 13,000-19,500 drs.

ATHINA ERMONES GOLF (C Class)
Ermones, tel. (0661) 94236, fax 94605
Price: 15,000-18,400 drs.

VALLEY
Palaiokastritsa, tel. (0663) 42012.
Price: 10,000-12,000 drs. Excellent value.

BEST RESTAURANTS & TAVERNAS

CORFU TOWN

✓✓ CORFU PALACE
2 Dimokratias Ave, tel. (0661) 39485-7
In the hotel Corfu Palace, Greek and international cuisine, first-rate service and a view to the fort and the town.
Price: €€€

Corfu Palace

☑ VENETSIANIKO PIGADI
Plateia Kremastis, tel. (0661) 44761
If the food were as good as its 👁👁 **location** this would be Corfu's best.
Price: €€€

Venetsianiko Pigadi

✓ TO DIMARHEIO
Plateia Dimarchiou, tel. (0661) 39031
Very good international and Greek food, Corfiot specialities, pleasantly situated and agreeable ambiance and surroundings.
Price: €€€

Chambor

✓ REX
66 Kapodistriou St., above the Liston arcade, tel. (0661) 39649
The best for lunch in town.
Price: €€

✓ LA FAMIGLIA
In the kandouni (Alley) tou Bizi, tel. (0661) 30270
Small and of good quality, refined cuisine, pleasant atmosphere and a variety of flavours.
Price: €

✓ GIANNIS
43 Ag. Iasonas & Sossipatro St., Anemomylos tel. (0661) 31066
Make your selection from the pots simmering in the kitchen. Good and inexpensive. Pretty courtyard with pergola.
Price: €

✓ IL GIARDINO

Il Giardino

4B Vraila St., tel. (0661) 30723
The town's best Italian restaurant. Comfortable, with a special ambiance, a garden and music.
Price: €€

CORFU

✓ FALIRAKI

Below the palace, at Faliraki, tel. (0661) 30392
By the sea, good Greek and Italian cooking.
Price: €€

Faliraki

✓ NAUSICA

Kanoni, tel. (0661) 44154
Restaurant serving delicious home-cooking. Pleasant garden in a lovely setting. Fireplace in winter.
Price: €

MANDOUKI QUARTER

Opposite the harbour
A series of tavernas here serve good meals at reasonable prices. The oldest and best is ✓ **Bekios**, tel. (0661) 25946, opposite the port with the best grills in simple surroundings.
Price: €

OUT OF TOWN

✓✓ ETRUSCO

Kato Korakiana, in the Dassia area, tel. (0663) 93342

The island's best Italian restaurant of the island. A choice of seafood, home-made pasta and authentic Italian desserts prepared by the chef/owners Monica and Ettore Bottrini. Open evenings only.
Price: €€

✓ TRYPAS

In the village of Kinopiastes, southwest of town, tel. (0661) 56333
It was started by the grandfather and the grandson keeps it now. Always full, is considered a must! Even better in winter, because in summer it caters more to tourists, with the Corfiot dance groups which accompany your meal.
Price: €€

Trypas

✓ ROULA

At Kondokali, tel. (0663) 91832
In a wonderful spot next to the sea. Attractive surroundings and the best fish on the island.
Price: € €

Etrusco

Roula

385

IONIAN ISLANDS

BEST ENTERTAINMENT

Art Cafe

The most **popular bars** are concentrated round the Spianada, on the Liston or in Kapodistriou Street. **Cofinetta** is a good piano-bar on the Spianada, with appetizers and ouzo, open from morning to night. Well placed, with a pleasant atmosphere. At **Kochlia**, the 'in hangout' of the island's youth, you can have an excellent cup of coffee and sandwiches with pleasant music. The **Rondo**, in Ethnikis Antistasseos Street, has rock music and a relaxed atmosphere. In the gardens of the palace you'll find the **Art Cafe** of the Corfu municipality for good coffee, drinks, ice cream or pastries, especially at lunch-time. In the evening, before starting out on a round of the nightclubs, everybody goes to the **Magnet**. In summer, most nightclubs are a little beyond the Neo Limani (New Port) on the coastal road at the exit of town towards Kondokali. You have a choice of the **Coca Club** on Ethnikis Antistasseos Street, the preferred hangout of young people, with techno sound and an electric atmosphere, or the **Sax** next door with a nice garden and techno-rave-trance music. This is where you'll find everybody after three in the morning. A bit further out is Apocalypsis, in neo-classical architecture with antique statuary, a garden with swimming pools and two thousand people dancing to the sound of techno. Very 'in' with the Italians.

TIPS AND INFORMATION

HOW TO GET THERE
- By air from Athens west airport with Olympic Airways (19,000 drs.), tel. (01) 9363363. Also from Thessaloniki by Olympic Airways (18,000 drs.), tel. (031) 260121.
- By car from Athens, by ferry between Rion - Antirion, and Igoumenitsa - Corfu, or by ferry from Patras to Corfu (from 5,500 drs.) in 9 hrs, Patras Port Authority, tel. (061) 341002.
- By intercity bus (KTEL) 100 Kifissou Ave., Athens, tel. (01) 5129443.
- For organized tours contact Trekking Hellas, tel. (01) 3310323-6.

CONNECTIONS
- By ferry from Corfu to Paxi, Palaiokastritsa, Sagiada Thesprotias, Albania and Italy. In the summer to Cephalonia. Corfu Port Authority, tel. (0661) 32655.

BEST TIPS

HOW TO GET AROUND: We suggest you hire a car or scooter for two or three days. But be careful, because although the roads are good they are narrow.

BEST SEASON: All year round for Corfu town and our excursions, if you don't mind rain. For sea bathing, from June to September. At Easter and Carnival Corfu has much to offer because of the many cultural and religious events.

BEST BUYS: Buy some **kum-kwat** (kumquat) liqueur made from a miniature Japanese orange which was imported by the British from China.

BEST LOCAL FOOD: You should try all three of the best-known Corfiot specialities: **Pastitsada**, macaroni with beef in a tomato sauce; **bourtheto**, fish in a hot red sauce and **soffrito**, veal filets with garlic and parsley in a tasty sauce seasoned with vinegar.

USEFUL TELEPHONE NUMBERS

CORFU	(0661)	Tourist Agency	21251
Town Hall	39553	Police	39509
Tourist Police	30265	Hospital	36044
Tourist Information Bureau	37520	Taxis	38811

Evvia, Sporades and North-Eastern Aegean Islands

EVVIA, THE SPORADES AND THE N.E. AEGEAN ISLANDS

BEST's OPINION

Many of the islands in this section (especially Samos) could have been included among the *Best*. But the shortness of their season, the coolness of the NE Aegean sea and their relatively poor accomodation, shifted the balance in favour of some other destinations, apart from 👁👁 **Skiathos**. (*Excursion 32*).

IN BRIEF

Evvia

Greece's second largest island after Crete has a very varied green landscape and several interesting historical monuments from antiquity, the Byzantine era, and the period of Frankish and Venetian domination.

The Sporades

Each one of these islands is distinctly different and rich in tradition. **Skiathos** and **Skopelos** attract large numbers of summer tourists, while **Alonissos** and **Skyros** are relatively quiet, except in August.

North-Eastern Aegean Islands

These islands constitute Greece's eastern borders. Originally they were joined to the coast of Asia Minor. They were first settled by Ionian tribes and reached their zenith, culturally and politically, in early antiquity. Here philosophy, music, sculpture, poetry and the arts all flourished. These islands share a common history as well as some physical characteristics. They all have beautiful coastlines, alternately rocky or sandy, sometimes lush, sometimes barren, and all have archaeological sites which attract a growing number of visitors. They are linked by regular ferry services, both to Athens and to one another, and most of them have airports, too.

BEST SIGHTS: STEP BY STEP

EVVIA / Εύβοια / ´Evia

A long, narrow island running parallel to the east coast of Central Greece, it is connected to the mainland near its middle at Halkida, where there is a **bridge** over the **Evripos channel** — one of the few places in the Mediterranean which has a **notable tide**. Evvia has had a long history. Its ancient city-states peaked in the 5th c. BC and were destroyed during the Roman conquest. They flourished again during the Byzantine era, after which the island fell to the Franks, Venetians and Turks. It was liberated in 1830. The landscape of Evvia is infinitely varied. Barren, stony and mountainous in the south, the north is thickly forested and green. One can explore Evvia by following **three routes** starting out from Halkida, the island's capital. Of the various sights in Halkida, we suggest a walk to the **Kastro district** with its Folklore Museum, a visit to the town's **Archaeological Museum**, and a walk along the waterfront, next to the **Evripos bridge**.

Halkida

First route: Northern Evvia

Heading north out of Halkida, a detour after Nea Artaki will take you to **Politika**, where you should take a look at its square shaded with plane trees and its beach. Getting back onto the main road, follow the signs to the lovely seaside town of **Limni** and the venerable **Galataki convent** set amidst superb, lush scenery near a series of sandy beaches. A little way up the coast, between the mountains and the sea, is the village of **Rovies**, still attractive despite tourist development. **Aidipsos**, a spa town, is next on the route. It's only worthy of a stop if you feel like bathing in its sulphurous hot springs. Otherwise, continue on until you come to the turn-off for **Gregolimano** with its wonderful 🏖🏖 **beach**. To get to it, however, you have to go through the entrance to the **Club Med**. Returning to the main road again, you can complete your tour of northern Evvia,

EVVIA, THE SPORADES AND THE N.E. AEGEAN ISLANDS

passing through Istiaia and driving as far as **Gouves** with its 18th c. Drosini Tower, once owned by the Greek poet Georgios Drosinis, the World War II defences and the medieval castle. This area contains some of the best beaches in Evvia. The remainder of the circuit trip back to Halkida will give you the opportunity to enjoy some lovely forested scenery.

Second route: From Halkida to Karystos

Taking the road south of Halkida, the first place worth a stop is **Eretria**, a summer resort for both ordinary and wealthy Athenians. Here you can see the ruins of the ancient city and theatre and the finds displayed in the excellent **Archaeological Museum**. Driving along the coast will bring you to the industrial town of Aliveri and then to **Dystos**, once a lake, now a marsh surrounding an overgrown ancient acropolis. After this, the road crosses farming country dotted with little villages, eventually arriving at **Styra**, where there are some strange ancient stone constructions, known locally as **Dragonhouses**, on the mountainside. **Karystos**, at the end of our tour, is a port town, organized on a grid, with a few neo-classical buildings, some good fish tavernas and pleasant beaches, overlooked by the Venetian fort, **Castello Rosso**.

Third route: Crossing the mountains from Halkida to Kymi

On this route, after you reach Nea Artaki, proceed to the picturesque village of **Steni** in the foothills of **Mt Dirfys**, which lends itself to hikes and climbs. Push on to the mountain village of **Stropones** with its lovely square and venerable plane tree, kafenions and tavernas. From here you can continue on to the attractive stone houses of **Kymi** and its port, where the boats leave for Skyros, though the road condition deteriorates.

THE SPORADES

ALONISSOS / Αλόννησος / Alónissos

A green island with numerous coves and beaches with fish tavernas. Surrounding the nearby uninhabited islands is the **National Sporades Sea Park**, where a small population of the protected monk-seal lives. If you are lucky you might also see dolphins. It is worth joining one of the daily group excursions to the park, which also stop at the island of **Kyra Panagia** for a swim. The **Hora** (Old Alonissos), being restored on its high hill, and the tree-lined port, Patitiri, are where most visitors to the island stay. But the main attraction is the **beaches**. Those close to town can get crowded, so try the ones you can only get to by caique. In season, caiques also make trips to the deserted offshore islets where there are even better **beaches**.

Alonissos

SKOPELOS / Σκόπελος / Skópelos

Beautiful **Skopelos Town** (Hora, 6,500 inhabitants) has the most distinctive architecture of the Sporades; its slate roofs, half-timbered upper floors and white walls are less austere but very similar to those found in nearby Pelion. The island is well-wooded and famous for its many **charming churches** and fascinating **monasteries**. Take a stroll around the town's **cobbled streets**, climb up to the **Kastro neighbourhood** with its splendid view, and visit the local potters' workshops. The countryside inland is also worth a look with its characteristic two-storey stone **cottages**. And spend at least one day exploring the beaches and villages along the one and only road connecting Hora with Glossa, an unspoilt hill village at the other end of Skopelos. Although the beaches are nothing compared to those in Skiathos, every year more people find they are an adequate complement to the island's pleasures.

Skopelos

SKYROS / Σκύρος / Skíros

Skyros can almost be considered two islands, its two halves

Skyros

EVVIA, THE SPORADES AND THE N.E. AEGEAN ISLANDS

being so different. Most of its **3,000** inhabitants live in the northern half, which is wooded and fertile, while the south half is barren, mountainous and wild. This least developed island of the Sporades is famous for its **traditions** – carved wooden furniture, delightful pottery, embroideries – and its miniature **ponies** (only 1 m high). As you wander round the main town, **Horio**, take a peek into any open door you come across for a glimpse of the famous Skyrian decorated living room and hearth; perhaps an elderly occupant will stop knitting on her stoop and invite you in for a sweet, if it's not August which is the only time Skyros is crowded. The **architecture** in Horio resembles that of the Cyclades with its clusters of small, white cubic houses and flower-filled courtyards, picturesque squares and dozens of old churches. As you walk up to the **Venetian castle**, which shares the top of the hill with the ancient **acropolis of Lykomedes**, the **houses** become larger and more impressive and the **view** is superb. The island's port, **Linaria**, midway between the two halves, has a number of good fish tavernas, while the best beaches are to the south-west and north-east, though the latter can be windblown. Those on the north-west are pine-shaded but stony. Skyros is also known all over Greece for its **Carnival** traditions, which may have their origin in Dionysiac revels. The men dressed in goatskin masks and shaggy cloaks dance through town with an infernal clanging from the sheepbells worn around their waist. Must be seen to be believed.

NORTH-EASTERN AEGEAN ISLANDS

LESVOS OR MYTILINI / Λέσβος (Μυτιλήνη) / Lésvos (Mitilíni)

Lesvos (ancient Lesbos) gave birth to many distinguished musicians and poets, such as Sappho, Arion, Terpander, Alcaeus, as well as to one of the Seven Sages of antiquity, Pittakos the Mytilenean. Theophilos, the 19th c. naif painter, was also born here. The island is covered with thick vegetation and countless olive groves, while its shores are indented with innumerable coves and promontories. The **town of Mytilini** is known for its churches, its **mansions** built in neo-classical, Bavarian or Provencal style, its museums and the **fortress** constructed under the Byzantine emperor Justinian and extended by the Genoese. Be sure to visit **Molyvos** (or Mithymna) with its imposing castle and fine stone mansions and **Thermi** with its fortified tower-houses. **Sykaminia**, a traditional village on a hill where the 20th c. writer Stratis Myrivilis was born, also has a charming port, **Skala Sykaminias**. The village of **Mandamados** is known for its pottery and the **Taxiarchis Monastery**. At Petra climb up to the 18th c. chapel of the **Panagia Glykophiloussa**. **Perivoli Monastery** and **Andissa** are also worth a visit. The picturesque village of **Sigri** is just the place for a quiet holiday, having both lovely beaches and abundant fish. At the top of an extinct volcano is the **Ypsilou Monastery**, near one of the islands most celebrated sights, the **Petrified Forest**, a phenomenon dating back some 20-22 million years. **Skala Eressou** with its extended beach was the birthplace of the lyric poetess Sappho. Kalloni Bay is where the famous Lesvos sardines are caught, while the resort of **Plomari** produces exceptionally fine ouzo. Finally, don't miss beautiful **Agiassos**, on the slopes of Mt Olympos, with its monastery dedicated to the **Panagia Vrefokratoussa**. Lesvos has plenty of beaches but the water is icy and they don't match up to the sights. For this reason, you might want to schedule your visit at some time other than summer.

Molyvos, Mytilini

CHIOS / Χίος / Híos

The birthplace of many notable ancient and modern Greeks, Chios was famous in antiquity for its sculpture school during its most influential period, the 6th c. BC. During the Middle Ages, the island knew prosperity once again, thanks to the extremely lucrative trade in **mastic** (the aromatic crystals produced by the sap of a tree that grows only in southern Chios, and gives the chew in chewing gum). In March 1822, in retaliation for their joining the movement for independence, the Turks slaughtered much of the population, an event that has been immortalized in Delacroix's painting, **The Massacre of Chios**. **Chios Town**, the island's capital and main port, is spread out along the east coast. Levelled by an earthquake in 1881, most of its buildings date from this

Mesta, Chios

390

EVVIA, THE SPORADES AND THE N.E. AEGEAN ISLANDS

century. It does have an interesting market street and museums and an outstanding **Genoese castle**. Among the main attractions of the island are the medieval **Mastic villages** (Mastichohoria), 20 walled villages built by the Genoese rulers in southern Chios during the 14th and 15th c. as protection against raids by pirates and Turks. They include the famous **Pyrgi**, whose facades are painted with bands of geometric designs known as *xysta*, **Mesta** and **Olymbi** — all examples of imposing defensive architecture with the walls of houses doubling as fortifications. The ruined village of **Anavatos**, a listed settlement, is considered the Mystra of Chios. Near Karyes, above Chios Town, are **Nea Moni**, a monastery where memories of the slaughter are still very much alive, and **Avgonyma**, one of the prettiest villages on the island. **Kambos**, a fertile valley with gardens and citrus groves, is where the wealthy aristocrats built their sumptuous homes in the good old days of Chiot prosperity. Nearby is the **monastery of Agios Minas**, where 3,000 Chiots perished in the Turkish massacre of 1822. Other places to visit include **Volissos** with its ruined Byzantine castle and the **monastery of Agia Markella**, north-west of which is the village of Agios Galame, where the **Agiogaloussaina cave** has traces of Stone-Age occupation. It contains two churches, Agiogaloussaina at the entrance and Agia Anna in the interior. The island does not have exceptional beaches but it does lend itself to ecotourism, hiking and quiet, high-quality holidays.

IKARIA / Ικαρία / Ikaría

The island took its name from **Ikaros**, who plunged into the sea when his wax wings started to melt after flying too near the sun. It was known in antiquity for its mineral springs (spas at **Agios Kyrikos** and **Therma**) and for its wines. In recent years more and more visitors are discovering the island's formidable beauty and crystalline seas. In some of the mountain villages, one must adapt to the local rhythms of everyday life, since the islanders seem to sleep most of the day and stay up all night. **Agios Kyrikos**, the island's capital and main port, is within walking distance of many beaches apart from the good town

Hora, Ikaria

beach, while others are accessible by caique. The second port, **Evdilos**, on the north coast, is built on a promontory and has narrow alleyways and blooming courtyards. Up on the mountain are the **villages of Messaria**: Akamatra, Dafni, Steli and Petropouli, with wonderful views over the Ikarian sea. See the Byzantine **castle of Nikaria** in the village of Kosiki and visit the lush mountain villages of **Mavrato**, **Oxea** and **Mileopo**. There are other lovely villages to be seen on the **Rahes** plateau as you continue on to the fishing port of **Armenisti**. Pretty beaches line the coast; among them delightful **Na** with its river and its ruins and **Mesakti**. In order to enjoy the swimming even more, you can escape on a caique to quieter beaches. It is also worth taking a short trip to the island cluster of **Fourni**, about an hour from Agios Kyrikos, where there are other good beaches.

SAMOS / Σάμος / Sámos

One of the great powers of antiquity and birthplace of the celebrated mathematician Pythagoras and the pre-Socratic philosopher Aristarchus, who was the first to formulate the theory of the earth's rotation. Today it is still known for the sweet **wine** that its vineyards have been producing since ancient times. The village of **Vourliotes**, where there is also a **monastery dedicated to the Panagia Vrondiani**, produces the most wine. The island has two high mountains and is thickly wooded with pine, olive, plane and citrus trees, which have unfortunately been decimated in recent years by repeated fires. Samos or **Vathy**, situated on a deep, sheltered bay, is the most important port. Here you will see sev-

Pythagorio, Samos

eral **neo-classical mansions** from the last century when the island knew a degree of self-government and prosperity; these include the Town Hall, the Gallery of Fine Art and the old Parliament. Also worth seeing are the **Archaeological Museum**, the **marble lion** and the **church of Agios Spyridon**. **Karlovassi**, the island's second port, also possesses some lovely mansions and churches. But Samos' most picturesque and lively port is **Pythagorio**, where many yachts are moored and excursions are offered to other islands in the vicinity as well as Kusadasi/Ephessos on the Turkish coast. Not far from Pythagorio is the **tunnel of Eupalinos**, the 6th c. BC conduit that is considered one of the greatest technical feats of antiquity. Also of interest are the **Roman baths** and the **temple of Hera**. **Kokkari** is one of the main tourist resorts on the is-

391

EVVIA, THE SPORADES AND THE N.E. AEGEAN ISLANDS

land with tavernas and nightlife. From here you can climb the second highest mountain, **Ambelos** (1,150 m), through lovely scenery. A trip to **Mt Kerki** (1,440 m) will take you through the verdant mountain villages of **Kallithea**, **Agia Kyriaki** and **Drakaious**, where you will see 8th c. churches and have a meal under humongous plane trees. Near the sea, at the foot of the mountain, are the **caves of Pythagoras** and **Sarandaskaliotissa** (of the 40 steps) with the **church of the Panagia** inside it. From the summit of the mountain, there is a stupendous **view** of many of the Cyclades and Dodecanese. Samos is blessed with many superb **beaches** with fine sand and cool, clear water.

LIMNOS / Λήμνος / Límnos

Myrina, Limnos

According to myth, Limnos was the island of god Hephaistos. It's a place for a quiet holiday, with an abundance of natural beauty, volcanic soil, beaches, traditional buildings and archaeological sites. Its roads are also surprisingly good. **Myrina** (or **Kastro**) is the island's capital and main port. As you wander through its flagstone lanes, take a look at the stone houses around **Romaikos Gialos** (Roman beach), to the north of the harbour. Most of the town's nightlife is concentrated here, while the south end has several fish tavernas. Climb up to the imposing **medieval castle** and enjoy the **view**. **Moudros**, an attractive large village, lies at the back of the bay of the same name, which is one of the safest anchorages in the Mediterranean. Other spots to visit include **Kondia** and the archaeological sites of **Kabeirion** on Cape Tigani, where the Philoctetes' grotto is located, and **ancient Hephaistia** nearby. **Ancient Poliochni** at Kaminia is also of interest, while Limnos' two lakes, **Asprolimni** and **Hortarolimni**, and the village of **Kondopouli** are also worth a look. At **Plaka** there are mineral springs. Near Myrina you'll find some good beaches, such as sandy **Kaspaka** surrounded by high rocks, while other good beaches are to be found on the east coast.

NORTHERN AEGEAN ISLANDS

THASSOS / Θάσος / Thássos

Ancient Thassos

An island of picturesque villages and lush vegetation, beaches with crystal-clear waters, and lots of tourists. The main road follows the outline of the coast, giving visitors the chance to enjoy **lovely scenery** all the way around the island. The fires of the past few years have ravaged enormous tracts of vines, olive and pine trees, but efforts are being made at reafforestation. Not far from the port, the **archaeological site** with its 3rd c. BC **theatre** is the scene of a summer festival. The pretty villages of **Ano Prinos** (Megalo Kazaviti), **Potamia**, **Sotira** and **Theologos** are all worth a visit. You can take your pick from many nice beaches as you tour the island.

SAMOTHRAKI / Σαμοθράκη / Samothráki

Fonias Gorge, Samothraki

A green island with lakes, rivers, waterfalls and the highest mountain in the Aegean, **Mt Fengari** or **Saos** (1,600 m). Samothraki has not yet been discovered by mass tourism and is an ideal place if you enjoy nature and want to get away from it all. The traditional buildings of the main town, Hora, are built amphitheatrically under the remains of a Genoese **castle**. Among the island's many landmarks, one that stands out is the little waterfall in the **Fonias** or **Krya Vathra gorge**, which has created small pools encircled by rocks and plane trees. **Paleopolis** is where ruins of various ancient structures have been excavated, the most important being the **sanctuary of the Cabeirians**, the centre of the well-known ancient mystery cult. It was here that the **Nike (Victory) of Samothrace**, now in the Louvre, was discovered. You can see a copy in the Archaeological Museum. The island does not have good beaches, but you will certainly find places to swim on the south coast.

SKIATHOS

WHY AMONG THE BEST

Mainly because of the colours of its sea and the number and beauty of its beaches, some deserted and others popular. Because of its pine woods, so pleasant for walks, its monasteries and the fortress with the ruins of the old capital. And also because of its opportunities for trips to neighbouring islands and vast choice of entertainment.

SKIATHOS

BEST's OPINION

The escalation of mass tourism in recent years obliged the Skiathians to build some rather rough and ready accommodation premises, fortunately mostly concentrated on the main road between town and Koukounaries. The rest of the island, particularly towards the north, still preserves its natural scenery intact. Sightseeing and cultural events in Skiathos may be restricted but visitors to the island will have a lot to enjoy on their holiday. August should be avoided, when the number of tourists surpasses the island's capacity.

IN BRIEF

It is the nearest of the Northern Sporades islands to the mainland, just 3 n mi from the shores of Pelion and 38 from Volos. Its approximately 5,000 inhabitants live mainly in the town. Skiathos combines a richly green landscape – the terrain is smothered in pine trees and has much arable land – with gorgeous seascapes. It is also a stopping place for many rare migratory birds and there are two small lakes, one at Agios Andreas and the other at Strofylia.

The natural environment offers its visitors an ambiance of relaxation and serenity, although there is no lack of action in the evening hours. We recommend it to young people, couples especially, as well as for family holidays.

HISTORY

Skiathos was colonized in the 8th c. BC by Euboeans and prospered thanks to its alliance with Athens in the 4th c. BC, but successive wars in the ensuing centuries brought about a decline. In Roman times it was a pirates' lair, in 1204 it was taken over by the Venetians and in 1538 it was laid to waste by Barbarossa. Skiathians took part in the War of Independence of 1821 against the Turks. Since the 1960s the tourist development of the island has rocketed.

BEST SIGHTS: STEP BY STEP

❶ SKIATHOS TOWN
Πόλη Σκιάθου / Póli Skiáthou

Skiathos town, the island's sole agglomeration, is spread out on the sides of two hills. It isn't of any particular architectural interest, but has charm because of the traditional appearance of its houses. The inhabitants, either working in the tourist business or farmers and fishermen, keep up their traditions on religious feast-days and other festivities. The town has two ports, divided by the promontory on which stands the fort of Bourtzi. Much of the town's life is on the waterfront.

WHAT TO SEE

BOURTZI

A wooded hillock, the tongue of land dividing the harbour. On it, the Venetian fortress was built in 1207 by the aristocratic Ghizi family, and in 1906 Andreas Syngros, the national benefactor, funded a primary school which is a cultural centre today. It has an open-air theatre seating 800 where the annual **Aegean Festival**, takes place, featuring drama, music, shadow-plays, etc. Tel. (0427) 23717

PAPADIAMANTIS' HOUSE

🕙 10 am-1 pm

The house of one of the greatest modern Greek authors, on the main road near the harbour, is a museum of his personal possessions, a diminutive but faithful example of the simplicity of life before tourism.

❷ EVANGELISTRIA MONASTERY
Μονή Ευαγγελίστριας / Moní Evangelístrias

The island's sole operating monastery, founded in 1704 by monks from Mount Athos on a superb site. This is where the first Greek flag in its present form was designed and hoisted, before the 1821 upheaval. There is a museum with icons, relics and a library. On 15 August the Epitaphios of the Panagia, a religious practice unique in Greece, is celebrated here.

③ PANAGIA KOUNISTRA
Παναγία Κουνίστρα / Panayía Kounístra

An exquisite 17th c. monastery with a rich historic past on the NW side, easy to access by a good tarmac road, where the miraculous icon of the **Panagia Ikonistra**, the island's patron, was discovered. Her feast day is celebrated on 21 November and the icon is kept in the cathedral of the Three Hierarchs in Skiathos town.

④ THE FORT
Κάστρο / Kástro

How to get there: It's an hour from town by small boat. If you're driving, bear in mind that after the road ends you have a 30 min walk, worth it for the splendour of the scenery.

Skiathos' most notable monument, the mute witness of turbulent days gone by. It was erected in the mid-14th c. on a huge rock and here the inhabitants took refuge from pirate raids. In 1453, under Venetian hegemony for the second time, Kastro was the island's sole town but after it was abandoned in 1829, the dwellings and chapels fell into ruins, the walls crumbled and the bridge disappeared. Today there is little but remnants.

OTHER THINGS TO DO

- **Boat Trips:** Caiques depart from the harbour making the island's circuit. This and other trips to islands in the vicinity, Skopelos or Alonnissos, are interesting.

- **Dolphin Diving Center:** On Nostos beach, at Tzaneria. Anyone with a scuba diving certificate can experience here the fascination of the sea bed. There are also programmes for beginners. Tel. (0427) 22520.

- **Skiathos Horse Riding Centre:** At Koukounaries, above Lake Strofylia. Riding out to mountain tops and along scenic paths. Tel. (0932) 268179.

- **Donkey ride to the Evangelistria monastery - church of the Taxiarchis:** Through the outskirts of town, olive groves and dense pine woods to the monastery. While returning, a **panorama** unfolds of the town and nearby islands. Information from the travel agents Heliotropos, tel. (0427) 22430, 21736 and Mare Nostrum, tel. (0427) 21793.

- **Walks:** Wander in the cobbled alleys of the town where you'll discover some charming churches. Also set out to the woods and visit the monasteries and historic monuments.

- **Galleries:** The folk art boutiques **Archipelagos** and **Varsakis**, in particularly cared-for interiors, have objects that could well be museum pieces.

Koukounaries and Strofylia Forest

BEST BEACHES

Skiathos is famed for its 62 beaches. Some are sophisticated and organized, some quiet and solitary but nearly all are extraordinary.
Organized beaches are on the south side, where most people go, but on the north side they are untouched —except for a couple of canteens— and wonderful for bathing when it isn't too windy.

NORTHERN BEACHES

🌂🌂🌂 LALARIA

One of the loveliest in Greece, with smooth boulders, striking rock formations like the enormous **Petra** with its centre arch and blue-green waters. Access is by boat only, from the harbour or in your own. There is nothing there, so take your food and water.

🌂🌂 XERXES BAY

A good beach with two decent tavernas. Easy to get to and uncrowded.

🌂🌂 MANDRAKI

Exotic beach with sand and unpolluted waters north of Koukounaries. You can get quite close by car and then walk for 15 min. A canteen and a few umbrellas.

🌂 KEHRIES

Small Kehria

Two peaceful and attractive beaches, one small and one large, surrounded by forested hills. There are tavernas in the area. The smaller is the prettier, with an impressive rock, grass and wooden tables under the olive trees. Appropriately named "paradise", locally.

SOUTHERN BEACHES

🌂🌂🌂 KOUKOUNARIES

One of Greece's best and best-known beaches, 1 km long. A protected ecosystem and a uniquely beautiful combination of thick-growing Aleppo pines, the lagoon of Strofylia connected to the sea by a channel, golden sands and translucent sea. It attracts crowds, especially in August and is organized with water sports, umbrellas and a snack bar. At Panagioti's by the yacht basin you can hire an outboard dinghy for 14,000-15,000 drs. per day.

🌂🌂 LITTLE AND BIG BANANA

Little Banana

The smaller is the nudists' beach, organized, with umbrellas and a canteen, a fine beach and greenery; the bigger is also organized and sandy, with clear waters, two tavernas and water sports.

🌂🌂 VROMOLIMNOS

The «swinging» beach where a lot of partying goes on. Organized, with beach bars and a pleasant taverna. 🌂🌂 **Agia Paraskevi** next to it is as good but quieter.

🌂 AGIA ELENI

Organized sand beach, with a canteen and two tavernas. Turquoise seas against a lush green background.

SPORADES

⛱ COVES

You'll find small solitary coves between Koukounaries and Troulos with trees for shade. Lovely surroundings, ideal for romantics and courting couples.

THE ISLETS OPPOSITE

Outside Skiathos harbour, they are a good choice especially in August and accessed by boat from the harbour.

⛱⛱⛱ TSOUGRIA

Reached in 20 min by the boat which leaves port every morning. Delightful scenery and shallow water. The northern beach is unspoilt and lovely but difficult to get to because of reefs. There is an organized beach on the west side in a green and charming spot with wonderfully fine sand and clear azure sea. Umbrellas and a canteen which also has fresh fish caught by the owner. Do not fail to see the **chapel of Agios Floros** with its unusual architecture, and the **old house** with the abandoned **Konialides olive press** containing the rusty remains of its machinery.

⛱ ARKOS

A little islet with sand to the top of the hill. No crowds, clean, and with an excellent taverna in the shade of its pergolas.

BEST HOTELS AND ROOMS

BEST LOCATION

The best of Skiathos is its beaches and wooded hills while the hotels in town are not exceptional. We therefore suggest you stay in a hotel of our selection on one of the southern beaches, except if you'd rather be near the nightlife with a hotel in town.

PRICES

The hotel prices mentioned below are the official ones set by the National Tourist Organization for double rooms, at low and high season, with breakfast. Since owners are allowed to modify prices, always try to negotiate them.

✓✓ SKIATHOS PRINCESS (ELISABETH) (Luxury Class)

At Agia Paraskevi, 8 km from town
Tel. (0427) 49226, 49369, (01) 3242152
Fax (0427) 49459, (01) 3233667
Open: April-October

Description: Can be recommended as a really good hotel. Surrounded by gardens and on one of the loveliest beaches.
Rooms: 104 rooms with veranda, 23 junior and 4 luxury suites. Taped music, mini bar, A/C, marble bathroom.
Special features: Parking, restaurants, cafeteria, tavernas and pool bar, tennis court, sauna, jacuzzi, 2 swimming pools, conference room, gift boutique, hairdresser, organized excursions and water sports.
Price: 23,000-35,000 drs.
Value for money: ✷
Credit cards: Visa, American Express, Mastercard, Diners

✓✓ ATRIUM (A Class)

In the Platanias area, 9 km from town
Tel. (0427) 49345, 49376, fax 49444

Open: May-October
Description: The hotel with the island's most attractive architecture and interior decoration with impeccable public rooms, on a steep, pine-covered hill with a superb view. The best choice, although we were unimpressed by the service.
Rooms: 75 rooms resembling monastic cells, with wide verandas, A/C, bath and shower, telephone and the suites have a mini bar.
Special features: Pool, restaurant, pool bar, lounge, billiards, gym, parking and gift boutique.
Price: 21,000-39,500 drs.
Value for money: ✽✽
Credit cards: Visa, American Express, Mastercard

✓ MUSES (B Class)

Koukounaries
Tel. (0427) 49384, 49438-9, fax 49440
Open: May-October
Description: An unpretentious small hotel amidst greenery.
Rooms: 45 rooms with shower, radio, telephone and balcony with fine view.
Special features: Restaurant, bar, parking, garden. Pets upon request.
Price: 21,100-33,410 drs.
Value for money: ✽
Credit cards: Mastercard, Visa

✓ TROULOS BAY (C Class)

Troulos
Tel. (0427) 49390-1, 49375, fax 49218, 21791
Open: May-October
Description: Smallish and charming in a cordial and quiet environment with the sea at your feet. Care has been taken with the public areas, which open onto Troulos beach and the staff is courteous. It has been awarded the "small and friendly hotel" Thomson prize for three consecutive years. The best inexpensive choice.
Rooms: 43 plain but spacious rooms with telephone.
Special features: Restaurant, bar and well-tended garden.
Price: 16,000-32,000 drs.
Value for money: ✽✽✽
Credit cards: Visa, American Express, Mastercard

✓ PLAZA HOTEL (B Class)

Kanapitsa Bay
Tel. (0427) 21971-4, fax 22109
Tel. (01) 8964300, fax 8964301
Open: May-October
Description: In a lovely setting of olive and pine groves, 100 m from Kanapitsa beach and well placed for water sports.
Rooms: 80 twin-bed (20 with A/C) with bath, shower, balcony with sea view, mini bar, telephone and taped music. Family suites have a bed- and sitting-room, two bathrooms, TV, mini bar, telephone and taped music.
Special features: Pool, restaurant, taverna, bar, cafeteria, pool bar, roof garden, gym, sauna, massage, billiards, safe, parking and a tennis court close by.
Price: 25,000-41,000 drs.
Value for money: ✽
Credit cards: Visa, Mastercard

✓ ESPERIDES (A Class)

At Achladies, 3 km from town
Tel. (0427) 22535, 22245, fax 21580
Open: May-October
Description: A big old hotel overlooking the beach, with a splendid view. The interiors completely renovated in 1995-6. Perfect for peace and quiet.
Rooms: 180 spacious rooms with A/C, bath, telephone, radio and balcony.
Special features: Parking, pool, garden, tennis court, snack bar, restaurant, satellite TV room, conference room capacity 250, hairdresser, playground, gift and folk art boutiques.
Price: 27,000-42,000 drs.
Value for money: ✽
Credit cards: Visa, American Express, Mastercard

✓ ALKYON (B Class)

Skiathos town
Tel. (0427) 22981-85, fax (0427) 21643,
tel. (01) 3632575, 3634826
Open: All year round
Description: The best in Skiathos town. It is surrounded by courtyards and gardens.

Rooms: 88 rooms with A/C, mini bar, bath, shower, telephone, taped music, TV in 17 of the rooms.
Special features: Pool, garden, snack bar, breakfast room, roof garden with view of the island. Excellent service.
Price: 14,000-27,000 drs.
Value for money: ✹✹
Credit Cards: Visa, American Express, Mastercard, Diners

✓ 9 MUSES

At Agios Antonios (above Achladies)
Tel. (0427) 21837, fax 21249
Open: April-October and by request at other times.
Description: 2 beautifully decorated villas of 120 sq. m, on a hill with a wonderful view of the sea. Each has 3 bedrooms, 3 bathrooms, fully equipped kitchen and satellite TV. Ideal for groups of 4, 6 or 8. Transport necessary.
Special features: Pool, parking and well-arranged outdoor spaces for eating, sun-bathing, etc.
Price: 46,000-92,000 drs.
Value for money: ✹✹
Credit cards: None

ALTERNATIVES

SKIATHOS PALACE (Luxury Class)
Koukounaries, tel. (0427) 49700-6, fax 49666.
Once the flagship of Skiathos hotels, its only advantage today is its prime location.
Price: 29,200-58,900 drs.

POTHOS (D Class)
Skiathos town, tel. (0427) 22694, 21304, fax 23242.
Price: 22,000-33,000 drs.

ASTORIA (C Class)
Troulos, tel. (0427) 49385-6, fax 49361.
Price: 15,000-23,000 drs.

PANORAMA (C Class)
Koukounaries, tel. (0427) 49382, fax 49383.
Price: 31,000-42,000 drs.

BEST RESTAURANTS & TAVERNAS

SKIATHOS TOWN

✓✓ KARNAGIO

On the waterfront at the east end of town.
Tel. (0427) 22868

The island's best restaurant in an old traditional house, with a friendly atmosphere, in a flagged courtyard with soft lighting. A wide variety of typical dishes and specialities, lobster, fish, courgette flowers, shrimp cooked in sea-water, anchovy fillets and avocado cocktail.
Price: €€

✓✓ ASPROLITHOS

Korai and Mavrogiali Sts., behind the high school.
Tel. (0427) 21016

A big old stone house with a pretty courtyard. Local specialities and fresh seafood, pleasant surroundings, first-class service. Speciality: shrimp with artichokes, beef a l'etouffe, fish Spetsiota with onion and tomato and paper-wrapped lamb. Reservations a necessity.
Price: €€

SKIATHOS 32

✓ ANEMOMYLOS
At the town's highest point, tel. (0427) 21223
The building (a converted windmill) is over 150 years old. Enchanting atmosphere, lovely view and fantastic sunsets. Good food and service.
Price: €€

✓ STAMATIS
On the harbour steps, tel. (0427) 22924, 21468

A good, touristic, popular taverna with view of the port. Greek cooking, fresh fish and variety of hors d'oeuvre.
Price: €€

✓ SUMMER PALACE
Evangelistrias St., tel. (0427) 24516
For Chinese food.
Price: €

✓ GERANIA
Papadiamandi St., tel. (0427) 22178
Greek and international dishes in an agreeable setting.
Price: €€

MEDITERRANEO
Port, tel. (0427) 21627
Greek cuisine and traditional Easter soup (magiritsa) on a roof garden.
Price: €€

TARSANAS
Plakes area, tel. (0427) 21251
Excellent fish soup, plain decor but beautiful location with view of the sea and the rocks that surround it.
Price: €

LE BISTROT
Tel. (0427) 21627
Fish, pizza, ready-cooked dishes. Stunning view of the harbour. Book ahead.
Price: €€

OUT OF TOWN

✓ ANGELOS
On Arkos island

No electricity but lit by fires for a unique ambiance. The lobster is superior.
Price: €€

✓ HORIO
Koukounaries, tel. (0427) 49520
Home-like atmosphere and village decor. View of the wood and Koukounaries lake. Wood-oven. Specialities: Pizza, grilled fish and oven-baked pasta.
Price: €

ANATOLI STA KALYVIA
On the road to Evangelistria, tel. (0427) 25431
A small traditional restaurant with village-style stonework and blue and white colours. Very good if not extensive choice of dishes home-cooked by the owner, courgette and Asia-Minor style minced-meat croquettes as well as grills. The place to see the island's most fabulous sunsets, with a view of Skopelos.
Price: €

AGNANDIO
On the road to Evangelistria, tel. (0427) 22016
An isolated house on a slope, with a splendid view of town and harbour. Country cheese pie and fresh fish. Evenings only.
Price: €

BEST ENTERTAINMENT

There is swinging nightlife in Skiathos town on the eastern waterfront. *Best* proposes the night-club **Remezzo**, with tables by the sea and soul, funky, disco, Greek music and happenings, guest DJs and groups from England. Nearby are **Cavo**, the **BBC** and **Kalua**.

On the other end of the waterfront, the cafe **Oasis** is the meeting place, becoming a bar in the evening. On the harbour's west side there is **Jimmy's Bar** with pop music and unadulterated drinks in a quiet spot by the water. **Borzoi** is in Papadiamandi Street, the best-known hangout in town, once an olive press whose machinery adds to the interior decoration. If it's hot, sit in the courtyard.

TIPS AND INFORMATION

HOW TO GET THERE

- By air from Athens west airport with Olympic Airways (from 13,300 drs.), tel. (01) 9363363.
- By hydrofoil of Minoan Flying Dolphins from Volos in 1hr 15 min (from 5,514 drs.), Athens agency, tel. (01) 3244600. To Volos by intercity bus, KTEL, 260 Liossion Ave., Athens, tel. (01) 8317147.
- By hydrofoil of Minoan Flying Dolphins from Agios Konstantinos in 1hr 25 min (from 5,743 drs.). Athens agency, tel. (01) 3244600. To Agios Konstantinos by Minoan Flying Dolphins coach, departing from Syntagma Square, 3 Philhellinon St., Athens, tel. (01) 3244600.
- By ferry from Volos in 2 hrs 50 min (from 2,663 drs.), Volos Port Authority, tel. (0421) 3888.
- By ferry from Thessaloniki in 5 hrs 30 min (from 4,300 drs.) in summer only, Thessaloniki Port Authority, tel. (031) 531505.

CONNECTIONS

- Hydrofoil of Minoan Flying Dolphins all year round from Skiathos to Alonnissos, Glossa (Skopelos), Aidipsos, Limni, Pefki, Halkida, Volos, Trikeri, Agios Konstantinos. In summer to Skyros, Kymi, Stylida, Ai-Gianni, Platania, Thessaloniki, Marmaras, Moudiana, Porto Carras. Skiathos agency, tel. (0427) 22018.
- By ferry all year round from Skiathos to Alonnissos, Skopelos, Glossa (Skopelos), Volos, Trikeri, Agios Konstantinos, Mykonos, Paros, Santorini, Tinos, Thessaloniki, Heraklio. In summer to Kymi, Skyros, Naxos, Siros. Skiathos Harbour Master, tel. (0427) 22017.

BEST TIPS

HOW TO GET AROUND: If you do not have your own car or scooter nor can hire one, don't worry. There are regular bus departures in every direction until late. From 20 June to 20 September from 7 am-3 am every 12 min five buses depart to local destinations.

The main harbour is in Skiathos town with caiques departing for Skopelos, Alonnissos and for the neighbouring islets, Tsoungria and Arkos.

Caiques depart from the western harbour for the island circuit (2,000-3,000 drs. per person).

If you wish to hire a boat for the day, contact **Dina**, tel. (0427) 22697.

BEST SEASON: From Easter to end September, August best avoided.

USEFUL TELEPHONE NUMBERS

SKIATHOS	(0427)	Information for cultural events	23718, 23702
Town Hall	22233	Heath Centre	21640
Tourist Police	23172	Taxis	22376, 22049

Continental Greece

CONTINENTAL GREECE

BEST's OPINION

Though this is the largest geographical area in Greece, it is the least developed for tourism owing to its cooler, rainier summers, but also because most of its archaeological and cultural monuments are more widely scattered and less well known than those in the rest of Greece.

But for these same reasons the landscape of its various districts has suffered far less damage at the hands of arsonists and land developers, so plant and animal life has been left to flourish. Many of these places have not been included in our detailed excursions because they lack the accommodation and amenities expected by the average traveller. Yet for more adventurous and tougher souls, Continental Greece offers many opportunities for unforgettable experiences. To help you plan a trip more easily, we list here the areas with the greatest interest in terms of nature and culture.

STEP BY STEP

Here we give a few suggestions for exploring the most interesting parts and best sights of Continental Greece which have not been included in the *Best* excursions, but which can easily be combined with one or more of them.

THE MOUNTAINS

OLYMPUS / Όλυμπος / Ólimbos

On the borders of Pieria and Larissa prefectures, the country's highest mountain rises to 2,917 m. The ancients imagined it as the residence of their gods, and with its dramatic peaks, dense forests, running streams and deep ravines it is still a wild, magical paradise worthy of divine occupants.

If you dream of following in the bootsteps of Boissonas, Baud-Bovy and Kakalos who were the first to reach its highest summit, **Mytikas** or **Pantheon**, in 1913 (and left marvellous photographs to prove it), then you should take a car or taxi from Litohoro as far as **Prionia**. At **Stavros** (900 m), you will find a refuge and members of the Greek Mountain-climbing Association of Thessaloniki who will be happy to guide you.

There is a **ski centre** at Vrysopoules, at an altitude of 1,800 m, with one run, a lift and a chalet. Information: Elassona Skiing and Mountain-climbing Association, tel. (0493) 23467.

TEMPE / Τέμπη / Témbi

A favourite among 19th c. poets, this narrow valley cut by the Pinios river connects the plain of Larissa with Macedonia. As one of the few passes leading to southern Greece, it was well trodden by the armies of Xerxes and Alexander. Take a moment to visit the **church of Agia Paraskevi** with its cave. It is also possible to take a 30 min ride on the "Love boat" for 4 km down the river.

AMBELAKIA / Αμπελάκια / Ambelákia

This listed village has gone down in history as the place where the world's first industrial cooperative was founded in the 18th c. Located on the slopes of Mt Kissavos (ancient Ossa) overlooking Tempi, it has some beautiful buildings from that period – see the **Schwarz mansion (1787)** with its porcelain fireplace, Anatolian wood carvings and painted walls and ceilings. After you've admired the setting, the old stone houses with half-timbering and the flagstone lanes, sit in one of the cafes on the square and enjoy the view.

Schwarz mansion

CONTINENTAL GREECE

◎ TZOUMERKA (ATHAMANIKA MOUNTAINS)
Τζουμέρκα (Αθαμανικά Όρη) / Tzoumérka (Athamaniká Óri)

This impressive mountain range consists of Mts **Pachtouri** (1,976 m), **Kakarditsa** (2,429 m) to the west of Trikkala prefecture, and **Katafidi** (2,393 m) at the northern tip of Arta prefecture. The paths to the summits are well marked. The villages of **Vourgarelli** and **Katarrakti** are worth a visit to see the waterfalls.

KARPENISSI / Καρπενήσι / Karpeníssi

Built 1,000 m up the slopes of Mt Velouchi, the capital of Evritania prefecture is a good base for exploring the Alpine scenery surrounding it and the pretty villages nestled among the chestnut, pine and fir trees. Among the villages, **Gorgianades** is a delight with its plane trees and gurgling brooks. Other stops could include **Megalo Horio**, **Domnista**, **Koryschades**, **Granitsa**, east and west **Frangista** and **Prousso** with its famous monastery dedicated to the **Panagia Prousiotissa**. The artificial lake with its lacy coastline, ◎ **lake Kremaston** fed by the Acheloos River, is a local beauty spot. Its bridges, which connect Aitolia with Evrytania, at **Episkopi** and **Tatarna**, are among the largest in the Balkans. The **Karpenissi Ski Centre**, tel. (0237) 23506, at an altitude of 1,800-2,050 m, has 13 runs, three lifts, one tow and a children's lift, a lodge, rental shop and instructors. It's a good alternative to crowded Parnassos.

Karpenissi

◎ NAFPAKTIA HIGHLANDS
Ορεινή Ναυπάκτια / Oriní Nafpaktía

The hamlets north of Nafpaktos, built on slopes ranging from 700 to 1,000 m in altitude, surrounded by greenery, plane and fir trees, brooks and streams are really off the beaten path. If you come here, don't miss the **Ambelakiotissa monastery**, where you can also spend the night, the superb **Platanos** forest and the **Chryssovou** caves.

Nafpaktia Highlands

LAKES–WILDLIFE RESERVES–WETLANDS

◎◎ LAKE KERKINI / Λίμνη Κερκίνη / Límni Kerkíni

A unique area of wetlands 35 km from Serres and 80 km from Thessaloniki, in the north part of the Strymon valley, Kerkini is protected by the Ramsar Convention. To get there, follow the dirt road 16 km from Kerkini village as far as the Lithotopos dam. The **drive** alone is worth the trip, and once you arrive you will see thousands of birds. Special boats are available to bring you closer.

◎◎ THE EVROS DELTA
Υδροβιότοπος Έβρου / Idhroviótopos Évrou

The delta of the river that forms the border between Greece and Turkey and flows into the gulf of Thrace is a unique wildlife refuge covering 100 sq km and protected by the Ramsar Convention. More than **300 species of birds** either live or migrate here, making an incredible spectacle in spring and autumn. The Feres Municipality, tel. (0551) 22211, organizes trips with special boats into the wetlands. Information can also be obtained from WWF Greece, tel. (0551) 22124.

The Evros Delta

CONTINENTAL GREECE

ⓖ DADIA FOREST / Δάσος Δαδιάς / Dhássos Dhadhiás

Also in the Evros region, near the Turkish borders, 14 km from Soufli and 66 km from Alexandroupolis, this is a truly unique park. This majestic pine forest covering 72,5 sq km is of enormous ecological significance since it is home to more than **120 species of rare predatory birds**. You can spend the night here, tel. (0554) 32630 and watch the raptors from special observation posts.

COASTAL TOWNS

ⓖ NAFPAKTOS / Ναύπακτος / Náfpaktos

A picturesque town, 42 km east of Messolonghi, built along the sea and up a wooded hill, overlooked by a well-preserved ⓖⓖ **Venetian castle**, one of the most beautiful in Greece. It is famous for being the site of the naval **battle of Lepanto** where in 1571 the Ottomans suffered a catastrophic defeat at the hands of allied Christians, commanded by Don John of Austria. The small **port** is still surrounded by Venetian walls and turrets. A good base for exploring the Nafpaktia mountain villages.

Nafpaktos

ⓖⓖ PARGA / Πάργα / Párga

A romantic small town 68 km north-west of Preveza, set in a picturesque environment, whose charms in summer are less obvious because it is overrun by Greek holiday-makers. Take a stroll through the back streets and visit the **medieval district** and castle. Caiques leave for the beach of **Platys Gialos tou Valtou** and go up-river against the current to the antiquities and **Necromandeio** at Acheroussia.

ARCHAEOLOGICAL SITES

ⓖ THE NECROPOLIS AND NECROMANDEIO
Νεκρόπολι και Νεκρομαντείο / Nekrópoli ke Nekromandío

45 km north-west of Preveza, near the village of Messopotamo and the delta of the Acheron River alongside Lake Acheroussia. This was where Hermes was meant to have guided the dead into the dark kingdom of the Underworld for the price of one obol. There is a building here with corridors and basement rooms that tradition maintains was one of the four entrances to Hades.

ⓖ DION / Δίον / Díon

Near the village of Dion, 17 km south of Katerini, this was a site sacred to the Macedonian kings, including Alexander, who prayed to **Zeus** before setting out to conquer the world. The original town covered 350,000 sq. m (88 acres) and one can still walk on its flagstone streets to see the ⓖ **ruins** of Hellenistic buildings, shops, workshops, a Roman baths complex, shrines to Eastern goddesses like Isis, and an **Early Christian basilica**. The main attraction here is a villa with a perfectly preserved ⓖ **mosaic floor** depicting the god Dionysos in a chariot. The museum contains marble ⓖ **sculptures** of the Hellenistic and Roman period and a **mosaic of Medusa**.

Dion

ⓖ PHILIPPI / Φιλίπποι / Philíppi

17 km north-west of Kavala, this archaeological site has **two basilicas**, a **Roman forum**, and a 2nd c. AD **palaistra**. It also has a **Roman crypt-cistern** where St. Paul, who founded here the first Christian church on European soil, was imprisoned. Finally you will see the ruins of a **theatre** built by Philip II (and radically modified by the Romans), the **Byzantine walls** with an **acropolis** and a **Byzantine cistern**. It was the scene of the great battle between Octavian and Antony's rivals in 48 BC. The **museum** exhibits finds from the region.

PELION

WHY AMONG THE BEST

Because of its magical combination of mountain and sea, its wonderful villages that have kept so much of the local colour, its traditional architecture, the beauty of its scenery and its ski centre.

CONTINENTAL GREECE

BEST's OPINION

Ideal for excursions both winter and summer, since the Centaurs' mountain is beautiful in different ways in every season.

Pelion's villages have kept their character and tourism has not made much of a dent on their authenticity.

PELION

IN BRIEF

The distinctive Pelion architecture, which reflects influences from Epirus and the islands, and customs such as the Dionysian revels on May Day or the special wedding rites, show off the rich traditions of the region. The apple, pear and cherry orchards and olive groves on the lower slopes, the wild poplars, plane trees, beeches and chestnut trees higher up, together with the abundance of herbs, have given Pelion the name "healing mountain". A multitude of springs, a cool climate and superb views are other features of this idyllic spot, where the gods of Olympus spent their summer holidays.

MYTHS AND HISTORY

Memories of many mythical beings and personalities still linger in Pelion. It was the home of the Centaurs, half men-half horse, Asklepios, the famous healer, Jason, the leader of the Argonauts and husband of the sorceress Medea, and Homer's hero, Achilles.

ARCHITECTURE

In 1423, the most important of Pelion's villages were founded with the building of the first fortified mansions. Houses tended to be grouped around monasteries, whose monks were able to offer protection to the lay people outside their walls. The cores of what were to become Pelion's 24 villages were all in existence by the early 17th c. The typical Pelion house is a fortresslike three-storey building. The first and second floors have very few, small openings, while the third floor, which is the summer quarters, is a light construction with large windows, enclosed balconies and wooden beams that support the roof. The stained-glass and painted windows alongside the transparent ones give an unusual look to the overall building. Around the middle of the 19th c., neo-classical features began to be added.

BEST SIGHTS: STEP BY STEP

❶ ANAKASSIA
Ανακασιά / Anakassiá

The **Theophilos Museum** in the house of **Giannis Kondou** is worth a visit; it contains murals painted by the well-known folk artist in 1912.

❷ MAKRYNITSA
Μακρυνίτσα / Makrinítsa

Built like an amphitheatre along the mountainside, it has been called the "eagle's nest" and "balcony" of Pelion and its **restored listed mansions** are still impressive, despite the recent tourist boom. The village was founded between 1204 and 1215 and its residents' trading around the Balkans was based on their silk-worm production and tanneries. Have a coffee under the plane-trees in the big square, with its panoramic view of the Pagasitic Gulf and its sculptured **marble fountain**. Pop into the 18th c. **monastery of the Panagia tis Makrynitissas** and ask to see the famous "**secret school**" where children studied during the Ottoman occupation. **The Topalis mansion** housing the **Museum of Folk Art and History** is fitted out as it would have been in the past.

Makrynitsa

❸ PORTARIA
Πορταριά / Portariá

The "gateway to Pelion", as it is often called, has plenty of tourists and the facilities to accommodate

Portaria

409

them. Its wonderful restored mansions, the cobblestone paths and running brooks account for its popularity. Take a look at the **church of the Panagia tis Portareas**, built in 1273 and then have a drink at **Karavos** where mini waterfalls tumble out of the mountainside. You could also hike up to **Pliasidi** peak at an altitude of 1,548 m, a three-hour walk that will give you a stupendous view of Mt Olympus and the Aegean.

④ HANIA
Χάνια / Hánia

The old inns or khans gave this area its name. Situated at an altitude of 1,200 m, this is the highest village on this side of Pelion before the **Agriolefkes** ski centre.

⑤ ZAGORA
Ζαγορά / Zagorá

Zagora

Pelion's biggest village with 3,000 inhabitants, Zagora consists of four autonomous communities, **Agia Paraskevi** or **Perahora**, **Agia Kyriaki**, **Agios Georgios** and **Agia Sotira**, strung out over 5 km. This is where the Patriarch **Kallinikos IV** founded the so-called **Riga Fereos school**, now a folk art museum open in summer. Visit the square of Agios Georgios with its spreading plane trees and beautiful 18th c. basilica, its 15,000-volume library and the church of **Agia Paraskevi**.

⑥ KISSOS
Κισσός / Kissós

A picturesque village enveloped by greenery with a lovely flagstone square. Visit the 17th c. **church of Agia Marina** and be sure to look at the gilded icon screen known as ⑥ **the treasure of Pelion**.

Kissos

⑦ TSANGARADA
Τσαγκαράδα / Tsangaráda

Spread out down the mountainside as far as the sea, this village has 800 inhabitants, traditional architecture and many facilities for its numerous visitors. It is composed of four, virtually autonomous communities, **Agii Taxiarchi**, **Agia Paraskevi**, **Agios Stephanos** and **Agia Kyriaki**, which are linked by a network of roads and some 70 km of traditional cobbled paths (kalderimia). The **walk** between Agii Taxiarchi and Agia Paraskevi is interesting and quite easy. Both churches are impressive, the former built in 1746, the latter with its traditional fountain and thousand-year-old plane tree, whose trunk measures 14m. in circumference. If you can, go down to **Damouhari**, a seaside hamlet with an enclosed fishing port, a ruined Venetian fortress and a pebbly beach.

Tsangarada

⑧ MILIES
Μηλιές / Miliés

The cultural and literary centre of Pelion in the 18th c., with old mansions, olive groves, kalderimia (cobblestone paths) and streams galore. The old **school house** still functions as the local high school and the once celebrated library has a collection of old heirlooms and valuable manuscripts. The **church of Pammegiston Taxiarchon**, built in 1741, has a gilded icon screen and wonderful frescoes. The legendary **miniature train** that used to serve the area has been restored after a 25 year break and puffs its way to Ano Lehonia on the coast and back during the summer. It is definitely worth a ride.

Milies

⑨ VYZITSA
Βυζίτσα / Vizítsa

A listed traditional village with imposing tower-houses, marvellous examples of local architecture in tune with nature.

OTHER THINGS TO DO
🎮🎮 TRAIN RIDE

Old Train Station

On summer weekends the miniature coal-burning train starts at **Lehonia** and makes the 28 km trip to Milies in 90 min passing wooded slopes, ravines, mountain hamlets and old stone bridges.

SKI CENTRE
Information: Tel. (0421) 96416
Usually one can ski at **Agriolefkes** from November 20 to April 30, depending on the snowfall. The centre has a refuge, restaurant, snack bar, three parking lots, a first-aid station, two lifts and two tows, three main slopes, beginners' slopes and a network of cross-country trails through beeches, poplars, chestnut and fruit trees.

Vyzitsa

WALKS
By following the web of well-marked, old cobbled footpaths, you can explore the mountain to your heart's content and discover magical spots accessible only to hikers. Information: Greek Mountain-climbing Association, Volos, tel. (0421) 25696.

☂ BEST BEACHES

The beaches on the Aegean coast are better – cleaner, but exposed to the north wind – than those on the Pagasitic Gulf, which tend to be shallow, more crowded and less appealing.

ON THE AEGEAN SIDE
🏖🏖 MYLOPOTAMOS

Three continuous, enchantingly beautiful, sandy / pebbly beaches. Two of them are separated by a dramatic rock with a natural tunnel through it. Since there are always waves here, be careful if you're not a good swimmer. A couple of good tavernas overlook the beaches.

Mylopotamos

CONTINENTAL GREECE

🏖️🏖️ HOREFTO

A summer resort with a pretty, but crowded, beach and tavernas. **Analipsi** and **Vrios** to the north are accessible by jeep. The spring at Analipsi makes it popular with campers.

Analipsi

Horefto

🏖️🏖️ AI GIANNIS

Here too, there are three superb beaches to choose from, **Plaka**, **Papa-nero** and **Mouressi**. They all have sand, clear waters, and lots of people. There are also quite a few attractive, good tavernas.

🏖️🏖️ FAKISTRA

A lovely sandy beach surrounded by imposing cliffs. You can get here via a dirt road. Access is difficult, so it's a nature-lover's retreat.

🏖️ DAMOUHARI

Pebbly beach with crystal waters, reachable from Tsangarada by road or footpath.

🏖️ LAMBINOU - KALAMAKI

Wonderful, almost deserted beaches for those who want to get away from it all.

PLATANIA

Sand and pebbles near the village of the same name. Clear, clean waters.

Platania

ON THE PAGASITIC GULF SIDE
KALA NERA

Trees shade this sandy beach, which is next to the village of Kala Nera. Ideal for families with small children.

HORTO

Next to the village of Horto, this area is filled with little harbours and coves for pleasant swimming.

MILINA

Sandy beach next to the summer resort village.

BEST HOTELS AND ROOMS

BEST LOCATION

Ideally, you should divide your time between these three areas: Makrynitsa-Portaria, Tsangarada and Vyzitsa-Milies. That way you'll get to know Pelion well, without having to spend a lot of time driving. If you're a skier, the first area will be the most convenient for you.

PRICES

The hotel prices mentioned below are the official ones set by the National Tourist Organization for double rooms, at low and high season, with breakfast. Since owners are allowed to modify the prices, always try to negotiate them.

MAKRYNITSA-PORTARIA AREA

✓✓ XENONAS KARAMARLI
(B Class)

Makrynitsa
Tel. (0428) 99570, fax 99779
Open: All year round

Description: Mansion built in 1730 and restored with taste and flair. Each room represents a different historical period in terms of its decor and furnishings.
Rooms: 9 rooms with TV and telephone.
Special features: Garden, bar, restaurant.
Price: 26,000-39,000 drs.
Value for money: ✹✹
Credit cards: All

✓✓ DESPOTIKO (A Class)

Portaria
Tel. (0428) 99046, fax 99600
Open: All year round

Description: A converted 19th c. mansion with an interesting view and style.
Rooms: 21 rooms with TV, telephone and bath.
Special features: Garden, garage, lounge with fireplace, bar, seminar room, and dining-room serving simple meals.
Price: 27,000-38,000 drs.
Value for money: ✹✹
Credit cards: Diners

✓ PORTARIA HOTEL
(B Class)

Portaria
Tel. (0428) 99014, 99541, 99891-3, fax 99066
Open: All year round
Description: A modern building with traditional local features. Splendid view over the Pagasitic Gulf and village.
Rooms: 40 rooms and 5 suites with central heating, music, TV, telephone and bath or shower.
Special features: Two pools, one indoor and heated, restaurant with traditional and modern cuisine, 3 bars, lounge with fireplace, gym, sauna, hydromassage, games room and conference hall.
Price: 27,000-34,000 drs.
Value for money: ✹
Credit cards: All

TSANGARADA AREA

✓ THE LOST UNICORN (C Class)

Tsangarada
Tel. (0426) 49930, fax 49931
Open: All year round

Description: British-style pension.
Rooms: 10 rooms with TV, telephone, bath or shower.
Special features: Garden, bar, restaurant and parking.
Price: 40,000 drs.
Value for money: ✹
Credit cards: None

✓✓ THYMELI (B Class)

Ai Giorgis, Tsangarada
Tel. & fax (0426) 49595
Open: All year round

CONTINENTAL GREECE

Description: Traditional farmhouse of 1857, with garden and view, in an idyllic setting. Perhaps the most beautiful in Tsangarada.
Rooms: 5 rooms with bath or shower.
Price: 25,000 drs. without breakfast
Value for money: ✽✽✽
Credit cards: None

✓ KASTANIES (A Class)

Tsangarada
Tel. (0426) 49135, fax 49169
Open: All year round
Description: A pleasant hotel amid chestnut trees.
Rooms: 5 rooms equipped with kitchen, TV, telephone and bath.
Special features: Ample breakfast with 17 different jams.
Price: 30,000 drs. without breakfast
Value for money: ✽✽
Credit cards: Visa

VYZITSA-MILIES AREA

✓ ARCHONTIKO BLANA (A Class)

Vyzitsa
Tel. (0421) 86840, fax 43614
Open: All year round
Description: Traditional Pelion mansion with wonderful views, decorated with flair and taste.

Rooms: 4 rooms with TV, telephone and shower, 1 suite with hydromassage.
Special features: Garden, bar, restaurant.
Price: 24,000-30,000 drs. without breakfast
Value for money: ✽✽
Credit cards: None

✓ XENONAS THETIS (B Class)

Vyzitsa
Tel. (0423) 86111, (0421) 53122, 45842
Open: All year round

Description: Beautiful, spotlessly clean inn with traditional local architecture and furniture.
Rooms: 8 rooms with TV and telephone, some with bath.
Special features: Parking, bar, restaurant.
Price: 12,500 drs. with bath, 10,500 drs. without bath.
Value for money: ✽✽✽
Credit cards: None

ALTERNATIVES

PANDORA (A Class)

Makrynitsa, tel. (0428) 99404, 99744, fax 90113.
Price: 39,000 drs.

ARCHONTIKO KANTARTZI (A Class)

Portaria, tel. (0428) 99388, 99444.
Price: 18,000-20,000 drs.

PALIOS STATHMOS (A Class)

Milies, tel. (0423) 86425. **Price:** 19,000 drs.

DIOGENES (C Class)

Tsangarada, tel. (0426) 43519, 49611-2, fax 49612.
Price: 18,000-22,000 drs.

AGNANTI (C Class)

Horefto, tel. (0426) 23114, 23158, fax 22518.
Price: 18,900-19.900 drs.

HAGIATI (C Class)

Horefto, tel. & fax (0246) 22405.
Price: 16,500-18,400 drs.

PELION 33

ALOE (B Class)
Ai Giannis, tel. (0426) 31240, fax 31341.
Price: 16,000-21,000 drs.

DIMITRIOS (C Class)
Horefto, tel. (0426) 22444, 22803, fax 22804.
Price: 14,000-27,000 drs.

Diogenis

BEST RESTAURANTS & TAVERNAS

MAKRYNITSA
The **Galini, Pantheon and Drosia** tavernas offer local dishes and expertly-cooked meats.
Price: All €

PORTARIA

✓ DIAKOUMIS
Tel. (0428) 99898
For delicious local cuisine.
Price: €

ZAGORA

PETROS
Tel. (0426) 22666
For fantastic meat dishes.
Price: €

HOREFTO

✓ THE TWO GORGONES
Tel. (0426) 22504, 22113
Fish taverna.
Price: € €

AKROGIALI
Tel. (0426) 22892
At the water's edge, fresh fish.
Price: € €

TSANGARADA

✓✓ DEIPNOSOPHISTIS
Tel. (0426) 43295
Surrounded by trees, wonderful atmosphere and music.
Price: € € €

✓✓ ANGELIKA'S
Tel. (0426) 49588

On the beach at Mylopotamos, fresh fish and sea view.
Price: € €

✓ ALEKA
Tel. (0426) 43380
Genuine Pelion home-cooking.
Price: €

PARADISOS OR RIGAKIS
Tel. (0426) 43209
Home-cooked specialities and breakfast.
Price: €

Paradisos

MILIES

✓✓ PALIOS STATHMOS (THE OLD STATION)
Tel. (0423) 86425
Wonderful savoury pies.
Price: €

Palios Stathmos

415

BEST ENTERTAINMENT

In Makrynitsa, sipping tsipouro (raki/schnapps) in **Theophilos'** cafe with its **murals** painted by the naif folk artist in 1910. In Tsangarada, the **Kentauros**, the **Skala** bar, and the **Deipnosophistis** restaurant, where the evening often turns into a party. Having coffee in traditional kafenions under the shade of the plane trees in the village squares.

Theophilos, Makrynitsa

Deipnosophistis

TIPS AND INFORMATION

HOW TO GET THERE

- Local transport (buses) does exist but you'll enjoy your trip much more with a private car. You can get to Volos by intercity bus, KTEL, tel. (01) 8317186, or by rail, OSE, tel. (01) 5297777, and rent a car there.
- To join an organized excursion from Athens contact Trekking Hellas, tel. (01) 3310323, and Pafsanias, tel. (01) 3820535.

BEST TIPS

HOW TO GET AROUND: By private car or rented vehicle. It's the only way to enjoy Pelion at your own pace.

BEST SEASON: There is no best season, they're all wonderful. In winter the mountain is spectacular, covered with snow and shrouded in mist, and you can ski. In summer, it's cool, drenched in greenery, and you can swim. Spring and fall are equally delightful.

BEST BUYS: Fresh aromatic oregano (**rigani**) and various kinds of herbal teas. Local preserves (spoon sweets), jams, homemade noodles and **trahana**. Woven fabrics, embroideries with traditional patterns, wood carvings.

BEST LOCAL FOOD: Spetzofai, a dish made with Pelion sausages and hot peppers, bean soup with chili peppers, red wine and **tsipouro**.

USEFUL TELEPHONE NUMBERS

VOLOS ....(0421)	**ZAGORA** ....(0426)
Town Hall 70951-9	Town Hall 22520
Tourist Police 27094	Police 22529
Tourist Bureau 23500	
Port Authority 20115, 23779	**TSANGARADA** ....(0426)
Taxis 24911, 27686	Town Hall 49238
	Police 49222
MAKRYNITSA ....(0421)	Rural Clinic 49208
Community Office 99140	
Police 99505	**MILIES** ....(0423)
	Town Hall 86204
PORTARIA ....(0421)	Police 86222
Town Hall 99128	Taxis 86342
Police 99105	

DELPHI · ARAHOVA

Delphi Arahova
Ossios Loukas Galaxidi

WHY AMONG THE BEST

Because of the cultural and archaeological interest of the site of Delphi and because of Arahova, vivid and swinging. Also because of the magnificent nature of the Parnassos national park with its ski resort, which will delight skiing enthusiasts.

CONTINENTAL GREECE

BEST's OPINION

This trip is proposed to those who like the idea of combining the archaeological tour of Delphi with skiing at Greece's biggest mountain resort and also with amusing nights out in Arahova. There is a choice of traditional tavernas with excellent food, restaurant-bars with atmosphere and "in" nightclubs. In winter book ahead for weekends in Arahova.

BEST SIGHTS: STEP BY STEP

❶ DELPHI
Δελφοί / Delphí

Perched on the mountain-side at the foot of Parnassos, Delphi – population 2,500 – presents a breathtaking view over the olive groves of Amphissa against a background of the blue Corinthian Gulf and the mountains of the Peloponnese.

Despite the efforts of the Ministry of Culture, the invasion of cement construction and tourist boutiques in the modern village have wiped out all authentic identity. This is why anyone who knows the area prefers to stay in nearby Arahova. In any case, the only attraction for tourists here is the exceptionally interesting archaeological site of Delphi.

DELPHI - ARAHOVA

HISTORY

The area's history begins in 1400 BC and is directly connected to the Oracle of Delphi.

Kings, warriors, as well as a multitude of ordinary pilgrims came to Delphi to consult the oracle, the usually obscure pronouncements, with double meanings, of Pythia (the priestess). In exchange they offered up fabulous treasures, and a specific tax, the **pelanos**. In this way, between the 6th and 4th c. BC, the oracle became one of the wealthiest sanctuaries of the ancient world. A town of 10,000 inhabitants gradually sprang up around it. From the 6th c. a confederation with religious roots was constituted in a military and political association, the renowned **Amphictyonic League**, which in 582 BC reorganized the **Delphic Games**, which then took place every four years in honour of the god Apollo.

In the 1st c. BC, Delphi was plundered by Romans. After Christianity was established, Constantine the Great stripped the oracle of its precious treasures, while subsequently Theodossios completed its devastation.

After the Ottoman domination, German archaeologists, (from 1840) and the French School of Athens (from 1892) instituted extensive systematic excavations in the area, which brought the sacred site of Delphi back to light.

THE ORACLE

The name of Delphi came from the word "**Dirphys**" meaning "chasm in the earth".

Originally the fumes emitted from this chasm had caused a shepherd by the name of **Kouritas** to mumble unintelligible sentences which sounded prophetic. This is how the most ancient goddess **Ge** or **Gaia** (Earth) acquired her oracle and her son, the monster **Python**, became its guardian. According to a later myth, two eagles let loose by **Zeus**, one from the east and one from the west, met at Delphi and dropped a sacred stone at this spot, known as **Navel of the Earth**.

The sun god Apollo killed Python, for which he was called **Pythios** or **Pythoktonos** (Python Killer) and the oracle was dedicated to him.

Daphne the mountain nymph, or according to others **Sibyl**, was the first priestess to pronounce the oracles. Later the prophetess, invariably a woman, was called **Pythia** from the name of Python.

In the innermost shrine of the temple, the sacred tripod was placed over the legendary chasm. After having purified herself in the **Castalian spring**, the Pythia chewed laurel leaves and, dazed by the fumes, delivered the oracles which the temple's priests would then interpret.

ARCHAEOLOGICAL SITE AND MUSEUM

Tel. (0265) 82312

Summer 7 am-9 pm, weekends 8:30 am-3 pm, winter 9 am-3:30 pm, weekends 8:30 am-2:45 pm, closed on holidays*

ⓖⓖⓖ SANCTUARY OF APOLLO

This very impressive site stands between two cliffs, the **Phaedriades**, in ancient times called **Yambleia** and **Nauplia** in ancient times.

① ⓖⓖⓖ **The Sacred Way**: A stone-paved road leading to the temple of Apollo. Along both sides, there were votive offerings, statues and treasuries offered by the Greek cities.

The Sacred Way

② ⓖⓖ **Treasury of the Athenians**: A restored structure in Doric style dedicated to Apollo by the Athenians to commemorate their victory over the Persians at Marathon. It was built with the spoils of the battle.

③ ⓖⓖⓖ **Temple of Apollo**: Erected originally in the 6th c. BC and destroyed by an earthquake in 373 BC, the temple whose ruins we see today was rebuilt with a Doric colonnade all round and finished in 327 BC. The interior consisted of three divisions: the pronaos or first room, the back chamber or inner cell (sekos) and the **adyton**, the subterranean innermost shrine, where Pythia delivered her prophecies.

Treasury of the Athenians

CONTINENTAL GREECE

ARCHAEOLOGICAL SITE OF DELPHI

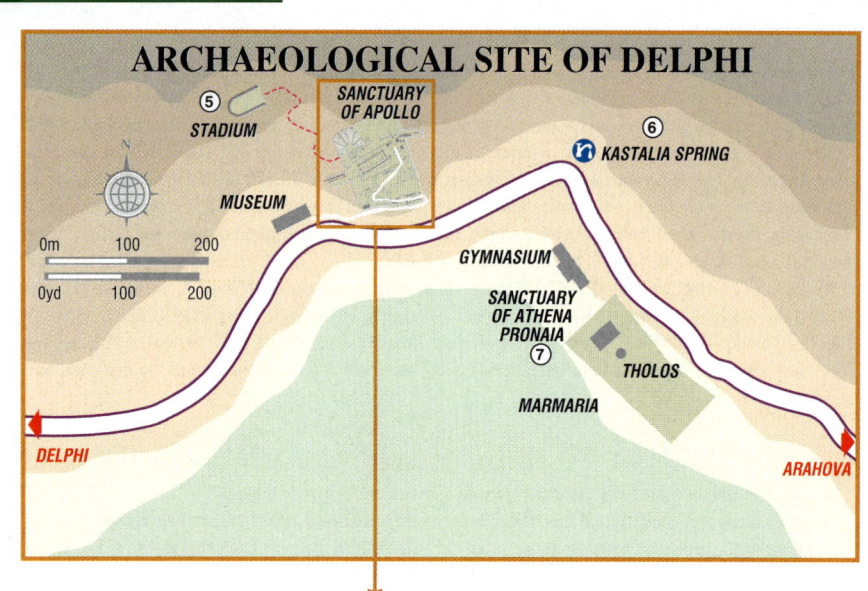

- (5) STADIUM
- SANCTUARY OF APOLLO
- MUSEUM
- (6) KASTALIA SPRING
- GYMNASIUM
- SANCTUARY OF ATHENA PRONAIA (7)
- THOLOS
- MARMARIA
- DELPHI
- ARAHOVA

SANCTUARY OF APOLLO

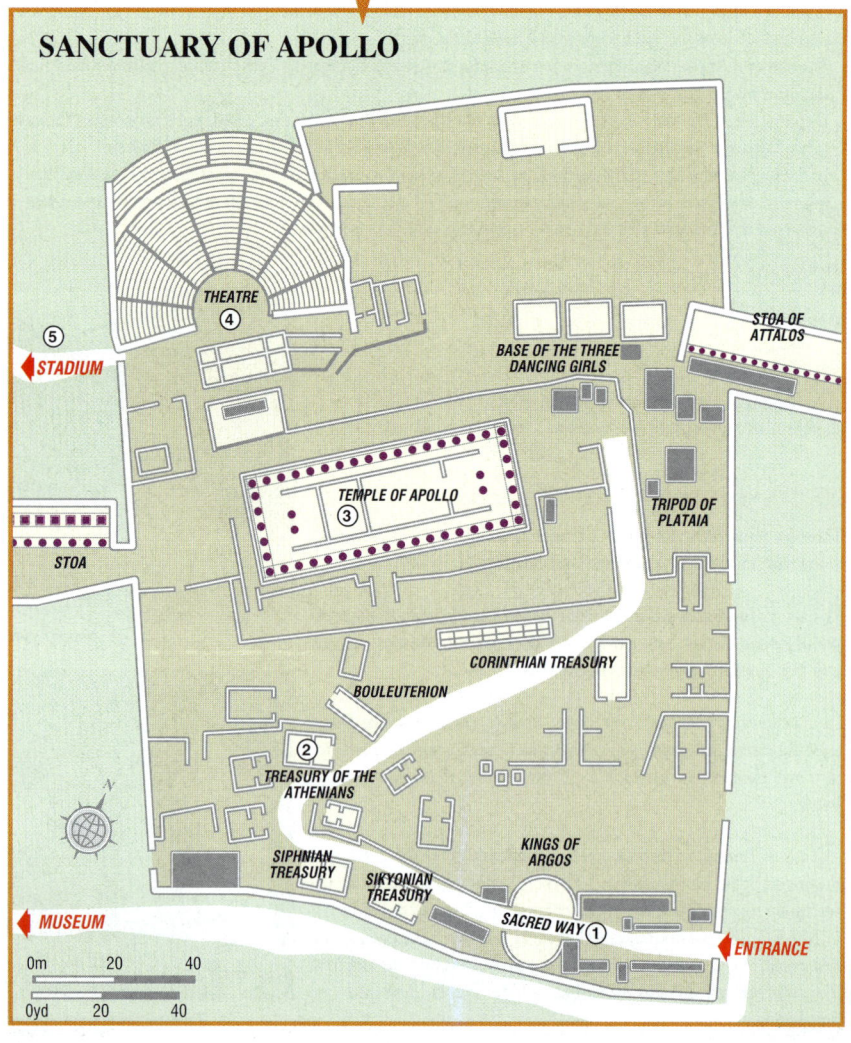

- THEATRE (4)
- (5) STADIUM
- BASE OF THE THREE DANCING GIRLS
- STOA OF ATTALOS
- TEMPLE OF APOLLO (3)
- TRIPOD OF PLATAIA
- STOA
- CORINTHIAN TREASURY
- BOULEUTERION
- TREASURY OF THE ATHENIANS (2)
- SIPHNIAN TREASURY
- SIKYONIAN TREASURY
- KINGS OF ARGOS
- SACRED WAY (1)
- MUSEUM
- ENTRANCE

420

DELPHI - ARAHOVA

④ The Theatre: At the NW corner of the sanctuary, it has a spectacular **view** of the site and the Delphic landscape. It was built in the 4th c. BC and repaired in 159 BC, with funds donated by King Eumenes of Pergamon. It is in good condition, seating 5,000 spectators.

⑤ Stadium: Almost 200 m long, but the track for the athletes – then in a straight line – was 178 m or 600 Roman feet. It was built initially in the 3rd c. BC and modified many times. What we see today dates to the end of the 2nd c. BC. It seated over 6,500 spectators for the Pythian Games which took place every four years.

⑥ The Castalian Spring: The water of the sacred source comes from a narrow fissure between the two Phaedriades rocks, flowing out just at their base and everybody who came to Delphi purified himself in it.

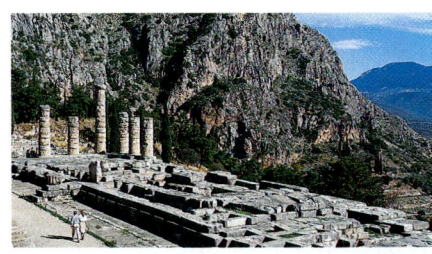

Temple of Apollo

The theatre

SANCTUARY OF ATHENA PRONAIA

Below the present road
It is locally called **Marmaria** and had five buildings: the **tholos**, the **Treasury of Massalia** – a fine 6th c. BC building – another **treasury**, Doric, of the 5th c. BC, of limestone and the two limestone **temples of Athena**, in Doric style also, one of the 6th c. BC, destroyed in the 4th c. BC and the other of later date.

Of greatest architectural interest is the **rotunda** "tholos" of the 4th c. BC with marble Doric columns. Restoration has conserved three of the twenty columns. Its purpose is still unknown.

MUSEUM

Although small, the museum of Delphi has 13 rooms with exhibits of major archaeological value.
In the entrance stands the Hellenistic copy of the **Navel Stone** from the temple of Apollo. Through the room with the Shields, on the right is the room of the **Siphnians**, dominated by the central **Sphinx of the Naxians** on an Ionic capital. On the walls, sculpture from the metopes of the **Siphnian Treasury**.
After this, through the rooms of the Kouroi and of the Bull we come back to the room of Shields and turn left into the room of the **Athenian Treasury** with fragments of the sculptured pediments and metopes from the monument, depicting deeds of Theseus and Herakles.
There are then five successive rooms with finds from the temple of Apollo and from the rotunda, until we come to the room of Agias where the imposing Ionic capital of an acanthus with the **Three Dancing Girls** (4th c. BC) is exhibited. In the next room there is the statue of the beautiful young favourite of the emperor Hadrian, **Antinous**.
The last room contains the most famous statue, of greatest archaeological worth, the **Charioteer**, an offering by Polyzalos for his victory at the Pythian games of 478 BC. The life-size bronze masterpiece is 1.80 m high and was discovered almost intact in the area of the theatre. Take particular note of the eyes, which are authentic, of magnesium and onyx, and of the perfection of the head and feet.

Sanctuary of Athena Pronaia

The Charioteer

CONTINENTAL GREECE

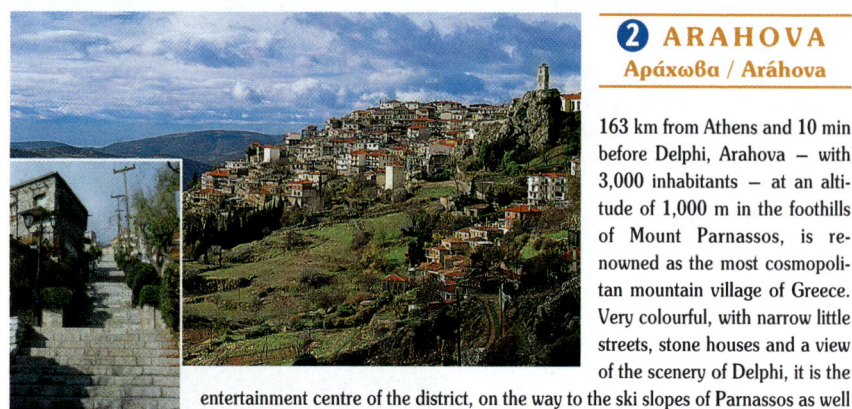

❷ ARAHOVA
Αράχωβα / Aráhova

163 km from Athens and 10 min before Delphi, Arahova – with 3,000 inhabitants – at an altitude of 1,000 m in the foothills of Mount Parnassos, is renowned as the most cosmopolitan mountain village of Greece. Very colourful, with narrow little streets, stone houses and a view of the scenery of Delphi, it is the entertainment centre of the district, on the way to the ski slopes of Parnassos as well as to Delphi.

❸ OSSIOS LOUKAS
Όσιος Λουκάς / Óssios Loukás

🕐 7 am-6 pm

The monastery of Ossios Loukas on the olive-planted slope of Mt Helicon gives the visitor a sense of serenity and contemplation.
Ossios (the Blessed) Loukas settled here in 946 AD at the age of 44, building his cell and a small church. The church of Ossios Loukas was built in the 11th c. and that of the Theotokos in the 10th or 11th c. Although they are joined together they are entirely different architecturally.
The monastery was severely damaged by earthquakes in the 16th and 17th c. and was restored in the 1960s. There is a small museum of sculpture in the precinct.
The ◉◉ **church of Ossios Loukas** is one of Greece's most beautiful of the Greek-cross-octagon design, with numerous openings and a wonderful dome that seems to float in the air. You must see the 11th c. ◉◉ **mosaics** of the main church and narthex, the **marble-paved** flooring and **marble revetments**, and the **sarcophagus of Ossios Loukas** with cruciform arched decoration.
Also see the ◉ **crypt** with splendid frescoes (the entrance is outside the church) and the ◉ **church of the Theotokos**, for comparison of its architecture with that of Ossios Loukas.

❹ GALAXIDI
Γαλαξίδι / Galaxídi

An old commercial port with grand listed neo-classical houses, evidence of its prosperity during the 18th and 19th c. On a fine day, it's a good choice for a meal in one of the fish-tavernas in the harbour.

DELPHI - ARAHOVA

OTHER THINGS TO DO

👁👁 PARNASSOS

Altitude 2,457 m. This is not only the mountain for skiing, it is also one of the most superb regions of Greece. Densely forested with firs, with rare varieties of wild flowers and shrubs, and featuring many picturesque villages amongst the greenery, it offers visitors the incomparable beauties of nature all year round.

Parnassos National Park

So designated in 1938, it covers 9000 acres. Its fauna include fox, badger, hare, squirrel as well as big birds such as eagles, hawks, buzzards and owls. There are numerous dirt tracks crisscrossing the forest, suitable for walking or mountain bikes.
Information: Greek Centre for Mountain Sports, Arahova, tel. (0267) 31846, (0932) 566206.
They organize rafting, hang gliding, skiing, climbing, kayaking, mountain biking, mountain and rock climbing, abseiling and canyoning.

👁👁 SKI RESORTS

20 km from Arahova, the Parnassos Ski Centre at the localities Fterolakka and Kellaria as well as the Athens Ski Club run Greece's most up-to-date skiing facilities for skiing enthusiasts.

Kellaria and Fterolakka (Kontokedro) locality
Altitude 1,750 m and 1,800 m
This has 12 runs: 2 for beginners (green), 1 intermediate (blue), 7 for the advanced (red) and 2 very difficult (black), There are also: 1 cable car, 6 chair-lifts and 7 T-bars, ski school, shops for equipment rental and purchase, chalet for meals.
Information: Ski Centre, tel. (0234) 22693-5, Greek National Tourist Office (EOT) Arahova, tel. (0267) 31630, 31692.

Gerontovrahos locality (Athens Ski Club)
Altitude 1,800 m
There are three runs, three ski-lifts – two of them Pomas, one for children – a ski school and a pretty chalet for meals. Non-members accepted.
Information: Athens Ski Club, tel. (01) 6433368, (094) 518302.

BEST HOTELS AND ROOMS

BEST LOCATION

Although at Delphi there are several comfortable hotels, the place has by now become so unsightly, smothered in concrete, that it no longer has any attraction. We therefore suggest that if you go there in the winter you should stay at one of the small hotels in Arahova where the charm of the village combines with good food in the tavernas and a lively nightlife. On the other hand, in the summer Arahova is rather dormant and we would propose instead that you choose the picturesque small town of Galaxidi.

PRICES

The hotel prices mentioned below are the official ones set by the National Tourist Organization for double rooms, at low and high season, with breakfast. Since owners are allowed to modify the prices, always try to negotiate them.

DELPHI

✓✓ AMALIA HOTEL (A Class)
1 Apollonos St.
Tel. (0265) 82101, fax 82290, tel. (01) 3237301, fax 3238792

Open: All year round
Description: A big hotel with a spacious lobby, the **Amalia** is considered the best of its kind in the area. You had better, however, avoid its noisy dining room and go to eat in Arahova.
Rooms: 188 rooms with balcony, telephone, bath

and A/C. Rooms No. 221-235 have recently been renovated and have wonderful views.
Special features: Pool, garden, gift boutique, parking, restaurant and 2 bars.
Price: 50,600 drs.
Value for money: ✶
Credit cards: All

ARAHOVA

✓✓✓ ELATOS RESORT (A Class)

Eptalofos Parnassou, 25 km north of Arahova
Tel. (0234) 61257, (01) 4598133, 854935,
fax 4282320
Open: All year round
Description: Isolated and peaceful, on the north side of Parnassos, a half hour from Arahova, situated in the forest, in total harmony with the natural surroundings. Ideal both for relaxation and for sports, it can be unreservedly recommended for a mountain holiday any time of year. The drive through the Parnassos forest is enchanting.
Rooms: There are 40 individual wooden cabins of the chalet type, dimensions 64 or 100 sq. m, with fireplace, kitchen and veranda.
Special features: Indoor pool, gym, sauna, Swedish massage, aerobic and scuba-diving lessons, ski school for beginners and children, archery, children's playroom, courtesy bus, games rooms, organized mountain hikes, restaurant, bar and conference room.
Price: 42,000-70,000 drs.
Value for money: ✶✶
Credit cards: None

✓ LYKOREIA (A Class)

Tel. (0267) 31180, 32132, 32590
Open: All year round except July and August
Description: If it's a cosy small hotel you're after, the Lykoreia, at the exit of Arahova toward Delphi, will delight you. It has a sublime view over the Delphic landscape. There is a pleasant reception area, with wall paintings and a fireplace, where the hotel's guests get together for breakfast or snacks, play backgammon, watch television or simply chat. From here you can also easily get around the village on foot, which solves the parking problem.

Rooms: 20 rooms with TV, telephone, bath and balcony. Rooms Nos. 41, 42 and 44-47 with view.
Special features: Restaurant, bar, parking.
Price: 15,200-65,000 drs.
Value for money: ✶✶✶
Credit cards: Visa, American Express

✓ GHENERALI GUEST HOUSE

Near the town clock Area, Arahova
Tel. (0267) 31529, fax 32287
Open: All year round except July and August
Description: Just the thing for those who prefer small traditional guest houses. You will feel more like a house guest than a hotel guest at Stamatis'. Unfortunately there are no parking facilities and there are steps.

Rooms: 6 rooms and one suite, each with a different decorative theme: "Companionship", "Helicopter", "Snow", "Winter", "Sunrise", "Clock", with fireplace, TV, Hi-Fi, telephone and bath. We recommend the rooms "Companionship" for its splendid veranda and "Helicopter" for its view.
Special features: Restaurant-bar where you can order ahead for home-cooked food of your choice.
Price: 18,000-31,000 drs.
Value for money: ✷✷✷
Credit cards: None

GALAXIDI
GANYMEDE (E Class)

Tel. (0265) 41328
Open: March-October
Description: The owner is Italian and serves a delicious breakfast with homemade jams. There is a view over a nice garden and a warm atmosphere.
Rooms: 13 rooms with bath.
Special features: Parking.
Price: 19,600 drs.
Value for money: ✷✷
Credit cards: None

ALTERNATIVES

XENIA (A Class) *Arahova, tel. (0267) 31230. A good choice.* **Price:** 58,000 drs.
ANEMOLIA (B Class) *Arahova, tel. (0267) 31640, fax 31642.* **Price:** 35,000-57,000 drs.
ARAHOVA INN (C Class) *Arahova, tel. (0267) 31353.* **Price:** 19,000-39,000 drs.
XENONAS MYLONA *Arahova, tel. (0267) 32111.* **Price:** 25,000 drs. without breakfast
VOUZAS (A Class) *Delphi, tel. (0265) 82232-4, fax 82033.* **Price:** 50,400 drs.
APOLLON (B Class) *Delphi, tel. (0265) 82580, fax 82455.* **Price:** 26,800 drs.
ARGO (C Class) *Galaxidi, tel. (0265) 41996.* **Price:** 27,000 drs.
VILLA OLYMPIA (Luxury Class) *Galaxidi, tel. (0265) 41810, fax 41746.* **Price:** 42,000-52,000 drs.

BEST RESTAURANTS & TAVERNAS

Arahova is well known for the good food at its tavernas. A number of restaurant-bars in good taste in charming traditional decors will satisfy your gourmet requirements, particularly in meat dishes. For fish, Galaxidi is preferable.

ARAHOVA

✓✓ FLOX

Tel. (0267) 31007

A pleasant stone-walled space with good, soft music, Greek and international. Rocket salad with parmesan, "dakos" (rusks with topping), variety of kebabs. The music gradually intensifies in volume and there is often revelry until the small hours. It has become the most "in" place for Athenians.
Price: €€€

✓✓ KAPLANIS (PLATANIA)

Tel. (0267) 31891
Open for lunch and dinner
A taverna with a fireplace, good traditional cooking and obliging service. Try the coq au vin, "gardoumba" (innards in a twist), and a variety of grills.
Price: €

✓ NEON

Tel. (0267) 31892, 31810
Open for lunch and dinner. Traditional decor. Try their very good appetizers.
Price: €

Neon

✓ KARAOULI

Tel. (0267) 31001
Open for lunch and dinner. A traditional taverna with a fabulous view, tasty hors d'oeuvre and grills.
Price: €

CONTINENTAL GREECE

✓ BABIS

On the plateau above Arahova
Tel. (0267) 32155

Open for lunch and dinner. On the way to the ski resort, a big place which gets very crowded because the food is excellent. Try the bean soup, lamb chops and wild mountain greens. **Price:** €

GALAXIDI - ITEA

When in Itea, for fish go to **Falkland**, tel. (0265) 34163, and in Galaxidi to the pretty taverna **To Barko tis Margaritas** which has good food. Tel. (0265) 41059.
Price: All € €

BEST ENTERTAINMENT

Emboriko

Arahova by night meets all tastes. From cafe-bars with soft music, for chatting — most of these on the main street — to advanced "in" nightclubs for wild nights till morning, just as good as in Athens. They say, quite rightly, that Arahova is the Mykonos of the mountains.

If what you prefer are much-frequented nightclubs with loud music, we propose **Snow-Me** (Cinema), **Banana Moon** and **Privilege** (Katafiyio/Refuge). For a cup of coffee or your first drink of the evening there are the cafe-bars **Dimarcheio**, **Retro**, **Bon Jour**, **Isidora**, and ☑ **Emboriko** – a charming traditional space with stonework and with gentle candlelight, delicious pastries and a few plats-du-jour.

TIPS AND INFORMATION

HOW TO GET THERE

- Your own car is certainly the best solution.
- To join an organized tour contact the travel agents Travelday, tel. (01) 3246701, Pausanias, tel. (01) 3820535 and Trekking Hellas, tel. (01) 3310323.
- By intercity bus, KTEL, 260 Liossion Ave, Athens, tel. (01) 8317173 (for Livadia, Arahova).

BEST TIPS

HOW TO GET AROUND: In your own car for flexibility and comfort. If you don't have one, there are taxis in Arahova.

BEST SEASON: To visit the archaeological site all seasons are suitable. If you are fans of skiing and après-ski, you will enjoy the winter season. The scenery is at its best in spring and autumn.

BEST BUYS: Dairy products, especially **formaela cheese**, a local speciality. Arahova is also known for its handwoven kilims and cloth.

USEFUL TELEPHONE NUMBERS

DELPHI .... (0265)	**ARAHOVA** .... (0267)	**GALAXIDI** .... (0265)
Town Hall 82310	Town Hall 31250	Town Hall 91226
Tourist Police 82220	Police 31333	Police 91222
Police 82222	Rural Clinic 31300	Rural Clinic 91255
Rural Clinic 82307	Pharmacy 31793	Port Authority 41390
Taxis 82000	Taxis 31566	Taxis 41272, 41243

Lake Plastira (Tavropou)

- Lake Plastira
- Agrafa

WHY AMONG THE BEST

Because of Lake Plastira, probably the most scenic in Greece. Because of the area's exquisite, virgin nature its mountain villages, untouched by time, and its fine monasteries and churches.

CONTINENTAL GREECE

BEST's OPINION

You can restrict your trip to the tour of Lake Plastira, where there are passable roads and adequate tourist facilities. However if you have hardy means of transport and are thrilled by adventure, it is worth wandering along the narrow, rough dirt-roads of Western Agrafa, where you'll come across very few other travellers and will forget the sound of automobiles. Petrol is obtainable in Karditsa and Mouzaki. Follow the green routes on the map, which are the most practicable, although there are other wonderful routes in the district.

BEST SIGHTS: STEP BY STEP

① CIRCUIT OF LAKE PLASTIRA (TAVROPOU)
Λίμνη Πλαστήρα (Ταυρωπού) / Límni Plastíra (Ταυροπού)

An artificial lake at an altitude of 1,000 m, with a maximum length of 14 km, width of 4 km and 60 m at its deepest. The dam is at the southernmost point of the lake, at **Kakavakia** in the community of Kastania. On the top is a narrow 200 m road, which is only for small vehicles. It was General Nikolaos Plastiras, a politician and military man, who, while looking at the Acheloos river dreamed that there could be a lake here and envisaged the idea of a dam on this spot. It was finally constructed in 1959, by the Public Power Corporation (DEI). Forests of fir and oak, gullies with plane-trees and lovely meadows surround the lake, creating an exceptionally beautiful setting. To circle it, set out from Karditsa or from **Mouzaki**, a pretty village draped in greenery. Approximately 3 km out of Mouzaki, at Balano, is a game-breeding farm, with partridges and pheasants, tel. (0445) 41653. The first village you'll come across close to the lake is **Kerassia**, with the

Kimissi tis Theotokou monastery, featuring frescoes dating to 1770. **Kryoneri** follows, at a height of 880 m, with a rich, green prairie extending to the lake shore, then **Pezoula**, in a gully with a forest of plane-trees. Next is **Neohori**, with a breathtaking view of the lake. Once the seat of the Fanariot Archbishopric, it was at its zenith in the 16th and 17th c. Today it has developed into the area's most important tourist centre, with hotels and tavernas. If you have time, make a detour of about 2 km, along a steep, but negotiable route, to visit the charming ⓖ **Panagia tis Pelekitis monastery**, hewn into the rocks, at a height of 1,400 m, built in 1529 by the holy martyr Damianos. On five levels, its interiors are impressive, with wooden and stone staircases, arched corridors, trap-doors, stone cells, the old still, a small oven chiselled out of the rock, the guest rooms and refectory. Returning to the main route, continue through ⓖ **Belokomyti**, where you'll be enchanted by the most stunning ⓖⓖ **view** of the lake. In **Kastania**, see the wood-carved **icon screen** in the **Kimissi tis Theotokou church**. Also visit the Mount Athos-style **Petras monastery**, dedicated to the Virgin Mary, with **frescoes** of 1625, 1672 and 1789. Completing the tour of the lake, you'll come across **Messenikolas**, famous for its wine, and **Morfovouni**, built amphitheatrically, with a view of the entire Thessalian plain. From Kerassia, you'll return to the starting point of Mouzaki.

Lake Plastira

Panagia Pelekiti

② TOURING THE VILLAGES OF AGRAFA
Άγραφα / Ágrafa

The rugged, mountainous region of Southern Pindos which links Thessaly with Roumeli. The people of Agrafa are traditionally fighters, hospitable and exceptionally proud. Successive mountain ranges, dense forests and deep ravines through which raging torrents race in winter, surround the 52 villages of Agrafa. Virtually untouched by time and plunged in deep greenery, they are ideal for mountain trekking. The route we suggest may take a whole day. Begin the excursion at Mouzaki again, because the road is passable, at least up to **Argithea**, which is crossed by the little river **Platania** and is built in a hollow amongst the fir-trees. If you have a suitable vehicle, you can continue driving along the bumpy roads to visit – with small detours – the villages **Messovouni**, **Anthiro**, where you can admire the single-arched ⓖ **Korako bridge**, **Karya**, altitude 1,000 m, and **Koumbouriana**. Shortly after, it is worth a detour to visit the renowned **monastery of Panagia tis Spilias**. Continuing, you can drive through the charming, tiny villages of **Leondito**, **Drosato** and **Vlasi**, before going through **Vrangiana** to reach **Belokomiti**.

OTHER THINGS TO DO
- **Mountain biking and canoeing:** Tavropos, at Kalivia, tel. (0441) 92552.
- **Riding Club:** At Kerassia, tel. (0441) 92855.
- **Activities at the lake and in the district:** Trekking Hellas, tel. (01) 3310323-6, Ef Zein, tel. (01) 9216285, 9230263.

BEST HOTELS AND ROOMS

BEST LOCATION
There is little choice here. The *Best* hotels we recommend are in the finest spots, with a lake view.

PRICES
The hotel prices mentioned below are the official ones, set by the National Tourist Organization for double rooms, at low and high season, with breakfast. Since owners are allowed to modify prices, always try to negotiate them.

NEOHORI

✓ ANATOLI (C Class)
Tel. (0441) 93063, fax 93150
Open: All year round
Description: Warm atmosphere, pleasant and tastefully designed interiors, spacious, comfortable rooms, superior to **Agnandi** hotel in everything but the view.
Rooms: 27 rooms with bath, telephone and heating.
Special features: Parking, restaurant and bar.
Price: 27,200 drs.
Value for money: ✷✷✷
Credit cards: None

AGNANDI (C Class)
Tel. (0441) 93190, fax 93150
Open: All year round
Description: A plain hotel, with a large veranda. Its main feature is a magnificent view of the lake.
Rooms: 12 rooms with bath, telephone and heating.
Special features: Parking, restaurant, lounge with a fireplace.
Price: 38,600 drs.
Value for money: ✷✷
Credit cards: None

ALTERNATIVES

MESSENIKOLAS PENSIONS (B Class)
Messenikolas, tel. (0441) 95419, fax 95228
Price: 10,000-12,000 drs.

PEZOULA PENSIONS (C Class)
Pezoula, tel. (0441) 92448, fax 92706
Price: 21,000 drs.

BEST RESTAURANTS & TAVERNAS

- At Pezoula, the **Pezoula** restaurant, tel. (0441) 92477, has tasty fish and appetizers, next to the lake where you can swim. For meat dishes, try **Zarnavalos** or **Klimataria**.
- At Neohori, **Kelepouris** serves traditional dishes and grilled meat. At the taverna in the **Agnandi** hotel, you can try grills, trout and salmon.
- On the Karvassara road, by the dam, **Evritos**, tel. (0441) 94881, serves fresh trout in a colourful spot by the brook.
- At Lambero, have a meal at the **Lambero** taverna, tel. (0441) 94114, next to the lake, with traditional cooking and very good meat dishes. Alternatively, at **Petrino**.
- At Tsardaki, above Moschato, the **Korombilias** taverna offers traditional dishes as well as grills.
Price: All €

TIPS AND INFORMATION

HOW TO GET THERE
Either by your own means of transport, or with organized groups. For an organized tour, contact Trekking Hellas, tel. (01) 3310323-6.

BEST TIPS
HOW TO GET AROUND: Ideally with a sturdy vehicle and map in hand.

USEFUL TELEPHONE NUMBERS

LAKE PLASTIRA VILLAGES .... (0441)	Neohori Community Office 93344
Pezoula Community Office 92298	Kastania Community Office 94240
Kerassia Community Office 92288	**AGRAFA VILLAGES** .... (0445)
Kryoneri Community Office 92466	Anthiros Community Office 31202

Meteora

WHY AMONG THE BEST

Because this unique geological phenomenon is one of the world's wonders and because the monasteries perched on these rocks are interesting in their own right.

CONTINENTAL GREECE

BEST's OPINION

This is one of the most extraordinary places in Greece. Go at your first opportunity! And combine your trip with other worthwhile *Best* excursions to neighbouring areas.

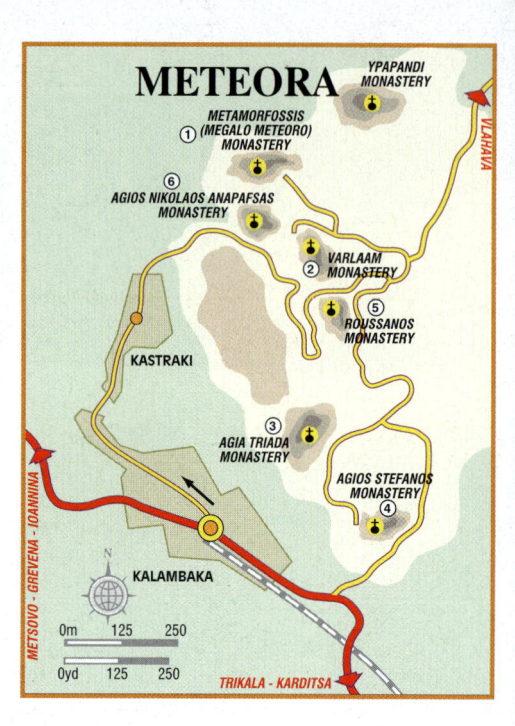

IN BRIEF

Meteora, these unusually sculpted rocks, crafted by nature for man to wonder at, seem to be suspended between the solid earth and the ethereal translucence of the heavens, as the Greek word implies. They are unquestionably among the most imposing and majestic Best sights in this country. Most probably, the rocks — which rise 100 to 150 m straight out of their flat surroundings — once formed part of the bed of a vast river that flowed from the Hassies mountains, flooding the plain of Thessaly.

Gradually over the millennia, its stones, sand and mud were compressed into a single cone-shaped mass and when the water in the lake finally drained into the Aegean, leaving the mound exposed, the erosive force of the wind, rain and earthquakes carved and moulded it into the shapes we see today.

Visitors to Meteora can find accommodation in nearby Kalambaka (6,000 inh.) on the banks of the Pinios river, an open town laid out on a grid, and flourishing on tourism, or the even closer village of **Kastraki** with its pretty square and good tavernas.

Hermitages (Skites)

HISTORY

Hermits shunning the material world started seeking refuge here around the 12th c. The first monasteries were founded some two centuries later, when the monks constructed inaccessible eagles' nests in the crannies of these rocks, out of reach of violence and looting. The oldest monastery was the **Panagia Doupiani**, whose abbots thereafter bore the title of **First among the Ascetics**; one of them, **Kyr Neilos**, founded another four monastic communities on rocks in the vicinity in 1367. Between 1356 and 1372, **Athanasios the Stylite** founded the **Great Meteora** with nine brothers, according to an extremely strict set of rules. In 1388, his disciple **Ioasaph**, son of the king of Serbia, expanded the monastery. The 16th c. saw the construction of most of the other monasteries and the renovation of the older ones. At that time, it is said that over twenty were inhabited, but disputes over ownership of their various estates eventually brought about their decline. Today only six monasteries are in operation.

METEORA

BEST SIGHTS: STEP BY STEP

TOUR OF METEORA

Time needed: at least 4 hours.

① ✪✪✪ Metamorphossis tou Sotira or Great Meteoron (Megalo Meteoron)
Tel. (0432) 22278
9 am-1 pm, 3 pm-6 pm, closed on Tuesdays and holidays*

Built on Platys Lithos, the tallest and largest rock in the district — it is 613 m high and covers an area of 50,000 sq. m — this is the most imposing of all the Meteora monasteries. One must climb 250 m from the parking lot to the front gate. It was founded by the monk **Athanassios Meteoretes**. Its church, a Greek cross-in-square with a 12-sided dome and side niches, is considered an architectural marvel. Its frescoes, dated 1552, are thought to be by the master of the art, **Theophanes of Crete**. The refectory, now a museum, has a fine collection of ecclesiastical objects, including a wooden cross which took a monk named **Daniel** 14 years to complete. There are three other churches dedicated to **St. John the Baptist**, **SS. Constantine** and **Helen** and **St. Athanassios**. The net and rope ladder were replaced in 1923 by a tunnel hollowed out of the rock and 146 steps.

② ✪✪ Varlaam or Agion Panton
Tel. (0432) 22277
9 am-1 pm, 3 pm-6 pm, closed on Fridays and holidays*

Perched on a pinnacle, this small monastery was initially accessible only by a succession of four rope ladders. Later, visitors used to ascend in a net hauled up with a pulley and it was not until 1923 that the 195 steps one climbs today were carved out of the rock. In 1350, the first monk to come here, **Varlaam**, founded the chapel dedicated to the **Three Hierarchs**, while the present monastery was founded in 1518 by two brothers who rebuilt the church and added two more, dedicated to **All the Saints** and **St. John the Baptist**. During the Nazi Occupation, it was looted and abandoned, and reopened in 1961. Make sure to see the **Treasury** with its collection of **manuscripts** and a **gospel** bearing the signature of the emperor **Constantine Porphyrogennitos**.
The katholikon is completely covered with **frescoes**, including a vivid rendering of the **Last Judgement**. The **chapel of the Three Hierarchs** also has frescoes, painted by one **Ioannis** of Kalambaka.

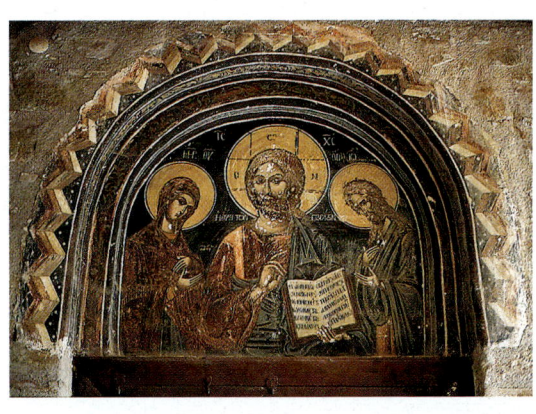

③ ✪✪ Agia Triada
Tel. (0432) 22220
9 am-1 pm, 3 pm-6 pm, closed on Thursdays and holidays*

This monastery, dedicated to the Holy Trinity, stands on a rock 65 to 100 m high, whose area at the summit is 6,000 sq. m Since 1925, one climbs 140 steps carved into the rock to gain access to it. It was founded in 1476 by the monk **Dometios**, but the narthex of the katholikon dates to 1692 and the frescoes were not painted until 1925. Looted during World War II, it was renovated in 1972 and 1997. Have a look, also, at the **chapel dedicated to St. John the Baptist**, erected in 1682.

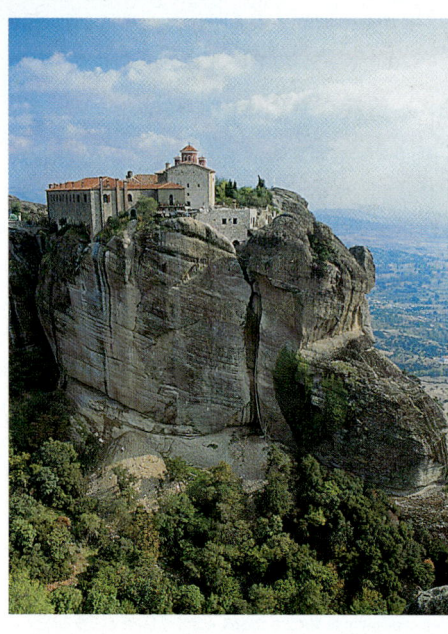

CONTINENTAL GREECE

④ Agios Stephanos
Tel. (0432) 22279

9 am-1 pm, 3 pm-6 pm, closed on Mondays and holidays*

Occupying the southernmost rock of the Meteora, this monastery was founded and reached its peak (no pun intended) in the 14th c. It is separated from the rest of the mountain by a ravine, straddled now by an 8 m long bridge. The hermit **Ieremias** was the first to retreat to this position around 1192, while in 1398, the abbot **Ioannis Vradislaos**, a Wallacho-Hungarian, expanded the monastery and donated the miraculous skull of **St. Haralambos**.

It acquired the epithet "royal" because the Byzantine emperor **Andronikos Paleologos** spent some time here. In 1545, it came under the jurisdiction of the Ecumenical Patriarch, which it is to this day. The monastery, now a convent, was badly damaged by bombs in World War II. But the recent frescoes in the rebuilt katholikon, dedicated to **St. Haralambos**, and the 14th c. church of **Agios Stephanos** with its original 16th c. frescoes by **Nikolaos** are both worth seeing. In the monastery museum there are rare manuscripts, precious icons and a gold embroidered «epitaphios» of 1857.

⑤ Roussanou or Agia Varvara
Tel. (0432) 22649

9 am-1 pm, 3 pm-6 pm, closed on Wednesdays and holidays*

The walls of this tiny, but impressive convent rise straight up from the sheer cliff overlooking the Kastraki-Meteora road. It seems to have been founded before 1545 by **Ioasaph** and **Maximos**. Its katholikon is dedicated to the **Transfiguration of Christ** and it contains some rather graphic **frescoes** depicting the trials of martyrdom executed in the style of the Cretan School in 1561. The bridges connecting it to the outside world were not installed until 1936. The convent's other church is dedicated to **St. Barbara**.

⑥ Agios Nikolaos Anapafsa
Closed, but visits can be arranged by talking to Father Polykarpos and making an appointment, tel. (0432) 22375. You can get there by taxi from Kalambaka or on foot, following the signs.

This small monastery is built on an 85 m high rock which seems like a rampart jutting out from the Great Meteora. Its church was built by the metropolitan of Larissa on the ruins of an earlier half-ruined church. It was rebuilt in 1961, and in 1972 its marvellous frescoes, painted by **Theophanes Strelitzas** of Crete in the 16th c., were restored. Make sure you see his naif rendition of **Adam naming the animals** with the **Kimissi tou Ephraim** painted over it. In addition to the main church, there is also a chapel dedicated to **St. John the Baptist**.

FREE TIME
Visit the Centre for Hang Gliding and Rock Climbing in a park covering 20,000 sq. m, with instructors and facilities for these exciting activities, plus playgrounds, a snack bar and picnic areas.

METEORA

BEST HOTELS AND ROOMS

BEST LOCATION

If you have a car, the small **Kynigi** hotel is an exception to the average Kalambaka tourist-oriented establishments. If however you insist on the comforts of a large luxurious hotel, any of the Best hotels we've selected should please you.

PRICES

The hotel prices mentioned below are the official ones set by the National Tourist Organization for double rooms, at low and high season, with breakfast. Since owners are allowed to modify the prices, always try to negotiate them.

KALAMBAKA

✓✓ DIVANIS (A Class)

Tel. (0432) 23330, fax 23638
Open: All year round
Description: Near Meteora, at the entrance to Kalambaka. A large hotel with all amenities. Ask for a room with a view of the rocks.

Rooms: 165 rooms with A/C, telephone, TV and bath.
Special features: Parking, restaurant, pool, conference room.
Price: 55,000 drs.
Value for money: ✱✱
Credit cards: All

✓✓ AMALIA (A Class)

Outside Kalambaka on the road from Trikkala
Tel. (0432) 72116, 72755, fax 72457
Open: All year round
Description: Large, comfortable hotel at the 5th km of the Kalambaka-Trikkala road. Its only disadvantage is its location outside town.
Rooms: 173 rooms with A/C, telephone, TV and bath.
Special features: Parking, restaurant, pool, and conference room.
Price: 50,800 drs.

Value for money: ✱✱
Credit cards: All

VITOUMAS

✓ KYNIGI (C Class)

7 km south-west of Kalambaka
Tel./fax (0431) 88354-55
Open: All year round
Description: In an idyllic setting surrounded by greenery, it used to be a hunters, lodge and now welcomes all visitors. Friendly, quiet atmosphere. Surely the best value, despite its distance from Meteora.

Rooms: 10 simple but attractive and comfortable rooms, with fireplace and bath.
Special features: Parking, bar, restaurant, special quarters for hunting dogs.
Price: 15,000-20,000 drs.
Value for money: ✹ ✹ ✹
Credit cards: None

ALTERNATIVES
EDELWEISS (B Class) *3 Venizelou St., Kalambaka, tel. (0432) 23966.* **Price:** *16,500-20,000 drs. without breakfast*

FAMISI (B Class) *103 Trikkalon St., Kalambaka, tel. (0432) 25090.* **Price:** *24,000 drs.*

AIOLIKOS ASTIR (C Class) *4 Athanassios Diakos St., Kalambaka, tel. (0432) 22325.* **Price:** *11,000-13,000 drs.*

BEST RESTAURANTS & TAVERNAS

The tavernas in Kalambaka are known for their good meat. The most famous is **Kipos**, tel. (0432) 23218, with its casseroles, roasts, local specialities and good service. Kastraki has several reputable tavernas, such as **Stavrodromi**, tel. (0432) 24574, with grills and local wine, and **Harama**, tel. (0432) 23976, with its traditional atmosphere and delicious souvlakia (shish kebab). Another excellent taverna is the **Tzaki**, tel. (0432) 22677, on the main road between Kalambaka and Ioannina, with its friendly waiters. The meat is grilled in the fireplace before your eyes and accompanied by good local wine.
Price: All €

BEST ENTERTAINMENT

In Kalambaka, on Trikkalon Street between Dimoula or Riga Ferreou Squares, have a drink or a coffee in one of the many bars and cafes, while gazing at the spot-lit rocks.

TIPS AND INFORMATION

HOW TO GET THERE

- Ideally with your own transport or with an organized tour run by one of the following travel agencies:
  Trekking Hellas, tel. (01) 3310323
  Manos, tel. (01) 3628077, 3627802
  Pyramis, tel. (01) 3254975, 3223886
  Travel Plan, tel. (01) 3238801-4, 3240224
- By intercity bus (KTEL) from Athens, 260 Liossion St., Athens, tel. (01) 8311434.
  By intercity bus (KTEL) from Thessaloniki to Trikkala, tel. (031) 545302.
  By intercity bus (KTEL) from Trikkala to Kalambaka and Meteora, tel. (0431) 73131.

BEST TIPS

HOW TO GET AROUND: Do as much walking as you can from monastery to monastery; that way you'll get the most out of the extraordinary landscape and discover magical places for picnics.

BEST SEASON: Not at its best when mist or fog conceal the awe-inspiring sight.

USEFUL TELEPHONE NUMBERS

KALAMBAKA	(0432)	Police	22109
Town Hall	22346	Taxis	22310

METSOVO

WHY AMONG THE BEST

Because in Metsovo you'll find a revival of tradition, beautifully restored buildings, a ski centre and superlative scenery. It was no accident that this was the first village in the interior of Greece to develop in the post-war era, while most of the others wasted away or were abandoned.

CONTINENTAL GREECE

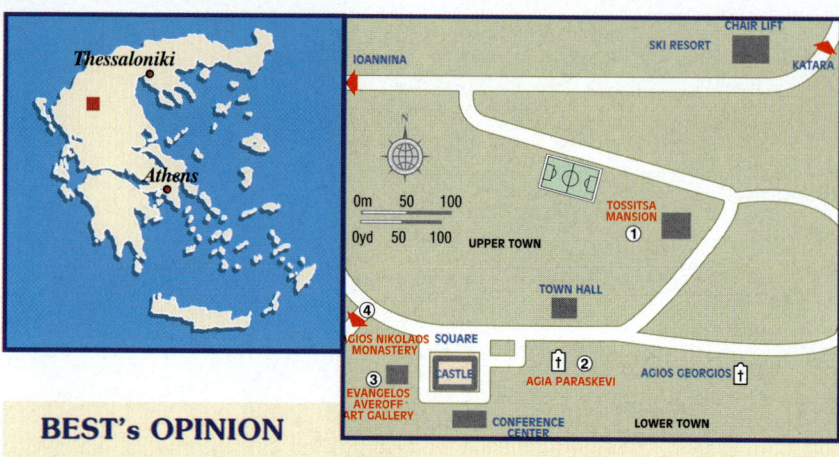

BEST's OPINION

Metsovo is interesting enough to merit a few days' stay, but it is also a good stop-over on the way to other worthwhile excursions in the region.

BEST SIGHTS: STEP BY STEP

① METSOVO
Μέτσοβο / Métsovo

Perched in the Pindos mountains at an altitude of 1,160 m, surrounded by forests of beech, fir and pine, Metsovo with its 4,000 inhabitants, is the birthplace of the Tossitsa family, noted for their philanthropic works locally and nationally. Occupying the only viable route between Epirus and Thessaly, it was most probably founded by the Romans to control the pass. In 1659, the Sultan Ahmet IV awarded the town exceptional privileges, which enabled it to become the centre of trade and culture in the area, with schools, churches and other institutions. In 1854 the Turks burnt it, while in 1912, guerrillas operating with the Greek Army liberated it from the Ottomans for good. The town contains some fine examples of Macedonian mountain architecture — ground floor of thick stone walls, upper floor with wooden-frame, glassed-in projecting balconies. The newer buildings are in the same style as the traditional prototypes.

WHAT TO SEE

THE TOSSITSA MANSION
Tel. (0656) 41084, 41205

Summer 9 am-1:30 pm and 4-6 pm, winter 9 am-1:30 pm and 3-5 pm, closed on Thursdays

A magnificent 18th c. building. The folklore museum housed within contains weapons, weavings, looms, agricultural and household tools and utensils and local costumes, among other exhibits.

The Tossitsa Mansion

AGIA PARASKEVI

The town's main church with its beautiful carved icon screen and the only example in Greece of a wall mosaic from Ravenna.

EVANGELOS AVEROFF ART GALLERY
Tel. (0656) 41684, 41210

Summer 10 am-7 pm, winter 10 am-4:30 pm, closed on Tuesdays

Agia Paraskevi

Paintings by well-known Greek artists of the 19th and 20th c.

AGIOS NIKOLAOS MONASTERY
Outside town. See the frescoes painted in 1700 by a certain Efstathios.

METSOVO

FREE TIME

The Ski Centre
Located in the Pindos, north-west of Metsovo, at Karakoli at 2 km and at Politses-Prophitis Ilias at 5 km. Tel. (0625) 41345

Cheese Dairy
Worth a visit to see how cheese is made.

Walks - Hikes
In the village lanes and the environs. Information: ECO Experience, tel. (0656) 41770.

BEST HOTELS AND ROOMS

BEST LOCATION
The hotels proposed are all in town. As you'll be seeing it on foot, their location doesn't make much difference.

PRICES
The hotel prices mentioned below are the official ones set by the National Tourist Organization for double rooms, at low and high season, with breakfast. Since owners are allowed to modify the prices, always try to negotiate them.

✓ APOLLON (C Class)
Tel. (0656) 41844, fax 42410

Open: All year round
Description: Traditional architecture, spacious, comfortable public areas, clean, tidy rooms, friendly atmosphere.
Rooms: 40 rooms with A/C, TV, telephone and bath.
Special features: Parking, restaurant and garden. Pets upon request.
Price: 21,000-30,000 drs.
Value for money: ✱
Credit cards: All

✓ ASTERI METSOVOU (C Class)
Tel. (0656) 42222, fax 41267
Open: All year round
Description: New, traditional style hotel with a view over the town and the mountains, with tasteful, comfortable rooms and public areas.
Rooms: 33 rooms, with A/C, TV, telephone and bath.
Special features: Parking, restaurant, garden and fireplace. Wheelchair accessible. Pets upon request.
Price: 15,000-22,000 drs.
Value for money: ✱ ✱ ✱
Credit cards: Visa, Mastercard

✓ GALAXIAS (C Class)
Tel. (0656) 41203, fax 41124
Open: All year round
Description: Stone-built guest house in traditional architecture with a view of the main square. Offers comfort and agreeable atmosphere.
Rooms: 10 rooms with heating, TV, telephone and bath.
Special features: Parking and restaurant.
Price: 18,400-22,900 drs.
Value for money: ✱ ✱
Credit cards: Visa, Mastercard, American Express

CONTINENTAL GREECE

✓ VIKTORIA (B Class)
Tel. (0656) 41771, 41761, 41898 fax 41454
Open: All year round
Description: Situated at Goura with a marvellous view of the mountains. Well-maintained public areas and rooms with traditional decor and furniture.
Rooms: 37 rooms with heating, TV, telephone and bath.
Special features: Parking, restaurant.
Price: 16,200-22,200 drs.
Value for money: ✱✱
Credit cards: None

ALTERNATIVES
GODEVANOS (A Class) Tel. (0656) 41166 fax 41945. **Price:** 13,000-15,000 drs

EGNATIA (C Class) Tel. (0656) 41900, 41263, fax 41485. **Price:** 20,000 drs.

KASSAROS (C Class) Tel. (0656) 41662, fax 41262. **Price:** 20,000 drs.

ADONIS (C Class) Tel. (0656) 42300, fax 42298. **Price:** 21,000-22,000 drs.

FLOKAS (C Class) Tel. (0656) 41309. **Price:** 13,000-17,500 drs.

BEST RESTAURANTS & TAVERNAS

✓ GALAXIAS
Tel. (0656) 41123

Classical Metsovo delicacies and beautifully cooked meat in the main square, under the shade of the plane trees. Good service. **Price:** €

KAFENIO TO PARADOSIAKO
Tel. (0656) 42776
A great variety of local specialities in this attractive, traditional "kafenion".
Price: €

ARHONTIKO
Tel. (0656) 42511
Exceptional local cuisine, view of the mountains and Anilio. Tables in the courtyard and on the balcony. Traditional decor and good service.
Price: €

Other tavernas where you'll eat good traditional cooking are **Marina**, tel. (0656) 42002, **Kryfi Folia**, tel. (0656) 41628, **Katoi**, tel. (0656) 42040, **Platanakia**, tel. (0656) 42435, **Metsovitiko Saloni**, tel. (0656) 42142, and **Athenai**, tel. (0656) 41725. At **Prophitis Ilias**, tel. (0656) 41095, next to the ski centre, with a fantastic view winter and summer, try the local dishes and baked desserts. **Price:** All €

TIPS AND INFORMATION

HOW TO GET THERE
- By air from Athens, west airport, with Olympic Airways (from 15,000 drs.), tel. (01) 9363363, to Ioannina, where you can rent a car.
- By intercity bus (KTEL), 100 Kifissou Ave., Athens, tel. (01) 5129363 to Ioannina, where you can get the bus to Metsovo, KTEL Ioannina, tel. (0651) 26404.

BEST TIPS

HOW TO GET AROUND: In town, on foot because of the parking problem.

BEST SEASON: Any time of year.

BEST BUYS: Traditional embroideries and weavings, wood carvings and wooden utensils.

BEST LOCAL FOOD: The Tositsa Foundation produces delicious cheeses. Other good things include the meat and **kokoretsi** (skewered innards), home-baked bread, savoury pies with home-made phyllo pastry, mountain honey and the excellent local wine.

USEFUL TELEPHONE NUMBERS

METSOVO	(0656)	Rural Clinic	41071
Town Hall	41207	OTE	42199
Police	41233	Taxis	41393

ZAGOROHORIA

Zagorohoria · Ioannina
Perama Cave · Bourazani

WHY AMONG THE BEST

Because the whole region between Ioannina and the Albanian border is one of the most beautiful places in Greece to explore winter and summer: from Lake Ioannina and its historic island to the fascinating Perama Cave, the exquisite traditional Zagoria villages and the Vikos gorge.

CONTINENTAL GREECE

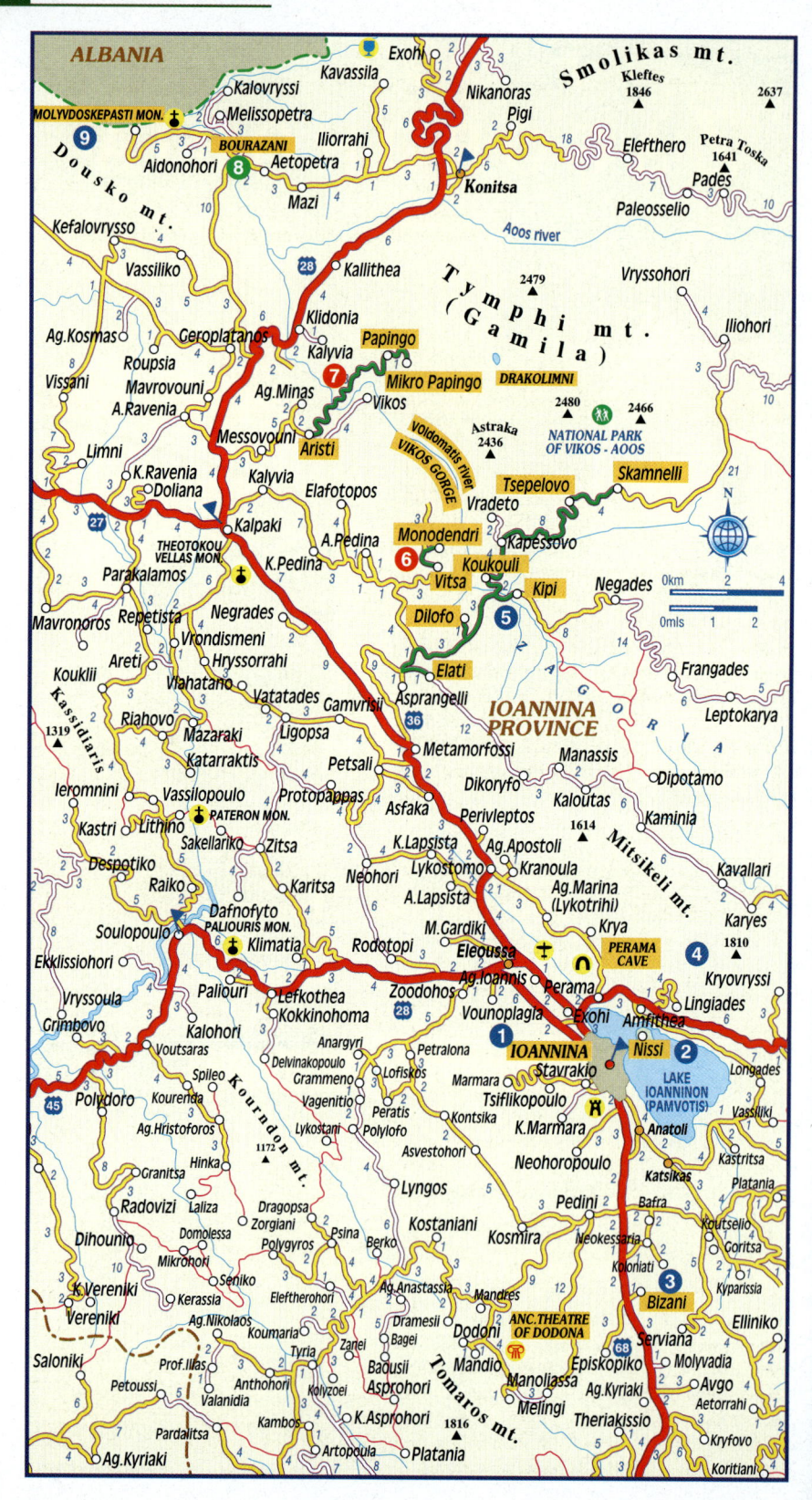

ZAGOROHORIA

BEST's OPINION

If nature, tradition and history are among your passions, then you'll be delighted with this trip. In order to do it justice, you will need at least four days, but a week would be even better in order to leave time for some of the walks we suggest. Make sure to reserve your hotel room before you set out, since there are only a few good hotels and they are all small.

BEST SIGHTS: STEP BY STEP

❶ IOANNINA TOWN
Πόλη Ιωαννίνων / Póli Ioannínon

A modern town for the most part, Ioannina is nonetheless rich in historic memories. It is built on a plateau 500 m above sea level, between the slopes of Mt Mitsikelli and the banks of Lake Pamvotis. It has 100,000 inhabitants, many lovely traditional buildings, and a university; it is also the most important business and cultural centre in the region of Epirus.

The city's name appears for the first time in historical sources in 1020. The Norman knight Bohemond conquered Ioannina in 1081 and fortified it with moats and forts. In 1204, it became the seat of the Despot of Epirus, Michael Komninos, and in 1430, surrendered to the Ottoman Turks. It was liberated by the Greek army in 1913.

WHAT TO SEE

THE KASTRO

Very interesting architecturally, the old fortress of the Despots would be a much more compelling attraction if the authorities were more interested in restoring it and keeping it clean.

The Kastro

Byzantine Museum
Tel. (0651) 25989, 39692, 39580
🕐 *8 am-2:30 pm, closed on Mondays and holidays**

Housed in a building in the large citadel (Its Kale) within the fortress, it consists of seven rooms with sculpture, coins and ceramics from the Early Christian to Post-Byzantine period. Next to it is a **Treasury** with a fine collection of silver and gold objects.

Municipal Museum
Tel. (0651) 26356
🕐 *8 am-8 pm, Sundays 8 am-2:30 pm, closed on holidays**

The **mosque of Aslan Pasha** contains exhibits from the town's three communities — Greek, Jewish, Turkish — while under the Ottoman Empire. See the **Turkish barracks** to the left of the museum, the **baths** and the renovated **library**. The **traditional buildings** with their characteristic Epirot features can be seen inside and outside of the fortress. Their grey colour comes from the region's stone, the dominant material used in their construction.

Mosque of Aslan Pasha

CONTINENTAL GREECE

The Clock

ARCHAEOLOGICAL MUSEUM
6, 25th Martiou Sq., tel. (0651) 25490

🕐 8 am-6 pm, Mondays 12:00-6 pm, Saturdays and Sundays 8:30 am-3 pm, closed on holidays*

Exhibits from the Classical period from Dodona, Monodendri, Kastritsa, Vitsa and from the Necromandion of Ephyra, an oracle of the dead. An art gallery with works by modern Greek painters shares the space.

THE CLOCK (ROLOI)
A work of Periklis Melirrhytos, this clock tower dominates the main square. The building was constructed in 1905 under Osman Pasha.

❷ IOANNINA ISLAND
Νησί Ιωαννίνων / Nissí Ioannínon

Connected daily with the city by little boats that make the 10 min trip every half hour from early morning till midnight. You can walk around the island in about two hours. Located in the northern sector of Lake Pamvotis, the island covers 350,000 sq. m and is home to some 120 families. Its charming traditional village, with its flower-filled courtyards and cobbled lanes, is surrounded by a small pine wood. The monasteries are open from 9 am until 1 pm.

Ioannina Island

ⓖ MONASTERY OF AGIOS PANTELEIMONAS
In the NE of the village; its 16th c. cells have been converted into a **Museum of the Prerevolutionary Period** with weapons, documents, uniforms, objects of every day use, jewellery, weavings, lithographs and engravings.

ⓖ PHILANTHROPINON MONASTERY
Built in 1292, it is full of wonderful late and post-Byzantine frescoes, including depictions of seven ancient philosophers, Plato, Aristotle, Apollonios, Solon, Plutarch, Thucydides and Chilon, in the narthex.

Museum of the Prerevolutionary Period

MONASTERY OF AGIOS NIKOLAOS
There are more fine frescoes here.

MONASTERY OF AGIOS NIKOLAOS (GOUMATON)
Its 15th c. icon of the Virgin Eleoussa is said to be able to work miracles.

MONASTERY OF AGIOS IOANNIS PRODROMOS
With interesting 18th c. frescoes.

Monastery of Agios Panteleimonas

ZAGOROHORIA

ALI PASHA

The Turko-Albanian **Ali Pasha** was a legendary figure in Epirus and one of the enigmas of early 19th c. history. Tough, revengeful, but also just, he set up his headquarters in Ioannina. Aware that he was on a collision course with the Sultan, the brilliant vizir strengthened the fortifications around his capital. In 1820, the Turkish forces of the Sublime Porte led by Hursit Pasha besieged Ioannina. Two years later, **Ali Pasha**, betrayed by all his men, retreated to the island with his beloved Greek wife, **Vassiliki**, and was defeated after a fierce battle. He was beheaded in one of the cells of the Agios Panteleimonas monastery and his head was shipped to Constantinople.

❸ PAVLOS VRELLIS MUSEUM OF GREEK HISTORY
Μουσείο Ελληνικής Ιστορίας Παύλου Βρέλλη / Moussío Ellinikís Istorías Pávlou Vrélli

13 km from Ioannina
Bizani, Tel. (0651) 92128

⊙ Summer 9:30 am-5 pm, winter 10 am-4 pm, closed on holidays*

The museum of the sculptor Pavlos Vrellis is housed in an 18th c. Epirot urban fortified dwelling. Founded in 1938 and completed in 1994, it is Ioannina's answer to Madame Tussaud's. Pavlos Vrellis has made life-sized sculptures in wax of scenes and personalities famous for their revolutionary activities before, during and after Greece's War of Independence. All the costumes, expressions and objects are completely accurate. A museum for both young and old.

Vrellis Museum of Greek History

❹ THE PERAMA CAVE
Σπήλαιο Περάματος / Spíleo Péramatos

Tel. (0651) 81521

⊙ 8 am-7 pm, closed on holidays*

An astonishing cave, one of the country's largest and richest in terms of amazingly shaped stalactites and stalagmites (19 types, including a unique cross-shaped stalagmite). The visitors' path covers only 1,100 m, while the entire cave system has a total area of 14,800 sq. m. Dedicated to Pluto and Persephone, it was discovered by chance in 1940. It consists of many corridors and chambers, extraordinary formations and lakes. Teeth and bones of prehistoric bears were found here.

The Perama Cave

⊚⊚⊚ ZAGOROHORIA (ZAGORIA)
Ζαγοροχώρια (Ζαγόρια) / Zagorohória (Zagória)

A chain of 46 traditional villages in the mountains north of Ioannina, whose natural boundaries are Mts Mitsikelli and Gamila and the Aoos river. Thick pine and fir forests, crystalline streams and stunning scenery – this district never fails to awe the visitor with its majestic virgin natural beauty, impregnable to modern encroachments. The human element, in complete harmony with the environment, is expressed through superb arched stone bridges, imposing mansions built in the austere local style, and lovely old churches. The villages, as far as we know, seem to have been founded around 912. But the area really developed during the Ottoman occupation, because of the privileges awarded to its inhabitants by the conquerors. In 1430, after an agreement with a representative of the Sultan, it was annexed to the Ottoman Empire, but retained certain self-governing powers. Influential merchants and craftsmen, the men of Zagori became even more prosperous and well educated when they emigrated around 1600 to Romania and Russia. Some of those who stayed behind, the so-called Vikos physicians, also made their mark by utilizing the herbs and therapeutic plants of the Vikos Gorge to cure illnesses. The region has given birth to a good number of Greek philanthropists.

Plakida bridge

Tsepelovo

Agia Paraskevi

❺ FROM ELATI TO SKAMNELLI
Ελάτη - Σκαμνέλι / Eláti - Skamnélli

If your time is limited, stop this excursion at Kipi, so as to leave room for the next two extraordinary drives.

⊚ ELATI
Take a moment to enjoy the panoramic ⊚ **view** of the whole Zagori district.

⊚ DILOFO
A traditional hamlet with picturesque stone lanes and impressive, well-preserved mansions; a perfect place for a walk. As you leave Dilofo, take a look at the **Kokkori bridge**.

⊚⊚ KIPI
One of the prettiest villages in the area, it has remained totally untouched. It has a **folk art museum**, with exhibits of local traditions from Agapios Tolis' collection. Nearby you'll see the unusual triple-arched **bridge of Plakida** and the eight old stone bridges over the Voidomatis river.

KOUKOULI
Stop here and taste the delicious Epirot cheese pies and see Kostas Lazaridis' rare collection of plants from the Vikos Gorge.

⊚ TSEPELOVO
The largest village in central Zagori, the birthplace of the actress Marika Kotopouli. Visit the famous **Rongovou monastery**, built in 1050, and its interesting frescoes.

SKAMNELLI

A delightful little village with chapels and traditional houses, many of which contain naif paintings of the 18th and 19th c.

❻ FROM VITSA TO MONODENDRI
Βίτσα - Μονοδένδρι / Vítsa-Monodéndri

◎◎ VITSA

One of the most important villages in central Zagori, it has a wonderful view, many old mansions, a lovely kiosk and churches whose architecture is typical of the 17th and 18th c.

◎◎ MONODENDRI

A beautiful traditional village in central Zagori, with superb stone mansions and picturesque stone paths, Monodendri overlooks the Vikos gorge. Visit the ◎ **monastery of Agia Paraskevi**, built in 1412, on the rim of the gorge. The

Vitsa

fabulous ◎◎◎ **view** from the top of the steep precipice to the floor of the gorge, 600 m below, will literally take your breath away. The daring can follow the narrow path along the cliffside to Megali Spilia, a large cave used as a hideout by many Greeks during the Ottoman years.
For an even more spectacular view, visit the natural ◎ **"balcony"-observation post** at Oxia, 7 km north-west of Monodendri, where there is a succession of enormous rocks protruding from parallel layers of stone, some thousand metres above the Vikos gorge.

❼ FROM ARISTI TO MIKRO PAPINGO
Αρίστη - Μικρό Πάπιγκο / Arísti-Mikró Pápingo

ARISTI

A delightful village above the Voidomatis river, with a fertile valley that squeezes through the Vikos gorge and extends into neighbouring Albania.

◎◎◎ MEGALO PAPINGO

Perhaps the most beautiful village of all the Zagorohoria, with traditional stone houses, flagstone lanes and charming churches with wonderful belltowers. It has several tavernas, places to stay, bars and cafes, since it attracts so many of the district's visitors.

Aristi

◎◎ MIKRO PAPINGO

This picturesque little village sits in the foothills of Astraka, in the shadow of some stunning high rocks from which anusual grey "towers" project. The clear waters of a small river flow next to it, forming a pool, but only for members of the "polar bear club".

Mikro Papingo

HIKING AND SPORTS IN VIKOS

The ✪✪✪ **Vikos-Aoos national park**, founded in 1973, has an area of 126,000 sq. km

The park lends itself to walks, hiking, rock climbing and mountain climbing, while the rivers are ideal for the exciting sports of **kayaking** and **rafting**. **Hang gliding** and **gliding** can be done from two take-off points in the mountains of Konitsa. The best months for such adventures are between July and October. Mountain climbers from the area's clubs organize treks with guides, which ensure safe passage over the dangerous and often unmarked trails in the mountains and gorges. These sports require special training and equipment. We propose simple solutions to help you start exploring this wonderful region and ideas for more daring excursions.

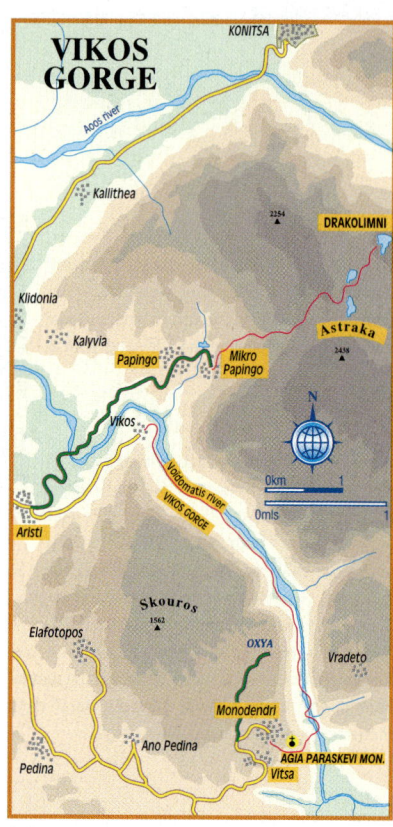

- The magnificent ✪✪✪ **Vikos gorge** is impressive with its unspoilt natural beauty, its precipitous cliffsides, the thick vegetation on its river banks and its towering wind-sculpted rocks, not to mention the variety of rare plants and animals that live in and around it. Many species that have disappeared from other parts of Greece have found refuge here, such as bears, wild goat, roebuck and jackals. It takes about seven hours to walk the gorge from **Monodendri**. The well-maintained but almost vertical path down to the gorge starts on the outskirts of the village to the right (south) and within about 30 min descent, you will reach the path that runs parallel to the Vikos riverbed. Another three and a half hours will bring you to the shrine of Agia Triada and a well. Two more hours and you'll reach the source of the Voidomatis river. From there, a path to the north-east winds back up the precipice, bringing you to Mikro Papingo in about two hours, while if you take the path to the west, you'll be in the village of Vikos within one hour.

- If you want to drive down from Aristi to Papingo, we suggest you leave your car beyond the bridge, on the open space to the right of the road, and once you've admired the lovely little pond formed by the river

Aoos river, Bourazani

⑧ BOURAZANI
Μπουραζάνι / Bourazáni

A historic spot, this is a private park covering some 120,000 sq. m, traversed by the **Aoos river**, with lush vegetation and shady plane trees and a **hotel**, also called Bourazani. Wild animals, such as deer, wild boar and bears, roam here freely. A photographic safari and guided tour through the park in a van takes about two and a half hours.

Molyvdoskepasti

⑨ MOLYVDOSKEPASTI MONASTERY
Μονή Μολυβδοσκέπαστης / Moní Molyvdosképastis

This famous monastery, perched on the Albanian border, took its name from the lead sheets that cover the roofs of its buildings. It has exceptional **frescoes**, some dating from as early as the 5th c., and 16th c. icons on the icon screen.

beside the bridge, follow the path along the ⓖⓖⓖ **banks of the Voidomatis**. You can walk as far as you like to the south, on an easy path and there are some delightful **picnic spots** along the way.

- Visit ⓖ **Drakolimni** (Dragon Lake) on Mt Gamila, at an altitude of 1,200 m. It's a round lake, 112 m in diameter and 12 m is its greatest depth. Starting out from Mikro Papingo, you will need to walk about 4 hrs to reach it, 5 hrs from Vradeto and 6 hrs from Tsepelovo and Skamnelli. For a more challenging ascent, take the path from Vryssohori, and you'll be there in 6 hrs. Among the denizens of the lake are two species of salamanders, black and grey with yellow spots.

- ⓖ **Astraka** is the place to go for rock climbing. There you'll find a refuge at an altitude of 1,950 m, some 3 hr walk from the peak of Gamila. Make sure you call the refuge from Megalo Papingo to secure a bed for the night.

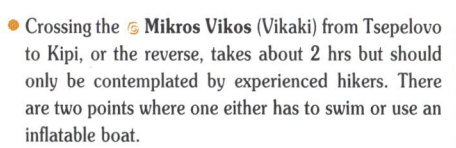

- Crossing the ⓖ **Mikros Vikos** (Vikaki) from Tsepelovo to Kipi, or the reverse, takes about 2 hrs but should only be contemplated by experienced hikers. There are two points where one either has to swim or use an inflatable boat.

- Going down the ⓖⓖⓖ **Voidomatis** in a kayak or rubber raft is fun, once you've gotten over your qualms.

- Kayaking and rafting are offered on the ⓖ **Aoos river**, too. Its swift current arouses all sorts of sensations in those who dare to try them.

Vikos gorge

Voidomatis

Information:
Trekking Hellas, tel. (01) 3310323-6
ECO Experience, Walking in Epirus, tel. (0656) 41770
Greek Mountain Climbing Association of Ioannina, tel. (0651) 22138
Greek Mountain Climbing and Skiing Association of Papingo, tel. (0653) 41138, 41115
Directorate of Forests, Ioannina, tel. (0651) 24594, 24391, 26482
Ioannina Forestry Service, tel. (0651) 27593, 36737

BEYOND THIS EXCURSION

ⓖ DODONA / Δωδώνη / Dodóni
Tel. (0651) 82287

🕐 *Mondays-Fridays, 8 am-7 pm,
Saturdays and Sundays, 8:30 am-3 pm, closed on holidays**

Visit the ruins of the Oracle of Zeus at Dodona, 22 km south-west of Ioannina. This was the oldest oracle in Greece; the priestesses used to utter their prophecies based on the rustling of a sacred oak tree. There are weekend performances of music and drama in the ancient ⓖ **theatre** from 10 June to 10 September.

Theatre

ⓖ LIAS / Λιας / Liás

This colourful village of stone houses is worth a visit. Situated at the foothills of Mourgana, 68 km NW of Ioannina, it became known from the book *Eleni* by **Nicholas Gage**. See the historic ⓖ **Gouras spring** where Kosmas Aetolos taught, **the church of Agia Paraskevi** with three icons by the folk artist **Theophilos** and the ruins of the **ancient acropolis** built in the 3rd c. BC by **Pyrrhos**, king of Epirus. You can stay overnight at the traditional **hostel of Lia**, tel. (0644) 41602, 41573.

CONTINENTAL GREECE

BEST HOTELS AND ROOMS

BEST LOCATION

We recommend that you spend one night in Ioannina, one night in Bourazani and the rest in one or more of the Zagori villages. On a long holiday weekend or during Easter, Christmas and August, make your reservations a few months ahead, especially for hotels in the Zagorohoria.

PRICES

The hotel prices mentioned below are the official ones set by the National Tourist Organization for double rooms, at low and high season, with breakfast. Since owners are allowed to modify the prices, always try to negotiate them.

IOANNINA

✓✓ HOTEL DU LAC (A Class)

Akti Miaouli & Ikkou St.
Tel. (0651) 22666, 59100, fax 59200

Open: All year round
Description: On the shores of the lake, an exceptional new (1998) complex built in traditional style. All the amenities, impeccable unobtrusive furnishings and decor. Our top choice in Ioannina.
Rooms: 130 rooms with heating, A/C, TV, telephone, hair dryer, mini bar, music and veranda.
Special features: Parking, restaurant, gardens, pool, bar, cafeteria, grill room, pool bar, lobby bar, reception room, boutiques, mini market, recreation rooms, playground, fitness centre and three-storey congress hall, equipped with the latest technology.
Price: 35,000-38,000 drs.
Value for money: ✻✻
Credit cards: All

✓ XENIA (B Class)

33 Dodonis St.
Tel. (0651) 47301, fax 47189

Open: All year round
Description: Situated in the middle of glorious gardens, in the centre of town, with many conveniences and good service. Recently renovated.
Rooms: 60 rooms with A/C, TV, telephone and bath.
Special features: Parking and restaurant.
Pets upon request.
Price: 29,400 drs.
Value for money: ✻
Credit cards: All

KAMARES (B Class)

74 Zalokosta St.
Tel. (0651) 79348

Open: All year round
Description: An old mansion with arches (kamares), heavy iron gates, an impressive inner courtyard and a romantic atmosphere. The spacious rooms overlook the court.
Rooms: 9 rooms with A/C, TV, telephone and bath.
Special features: Parking and garden.
Price: 19,200-21,000 drs.
Value for money: ✻✻
Credit cards: None

ZAGOROHORIA

KIPI

✓ XENONAS TOU ARTEMI
(A Class)
Tel. (0653) 51262, (0651) 23880
Open: All year round

Description: Mansion built in 1863, with simple traditional interiors and a sitting room with atmosphere, dominated by a mural of Napoleon and Josephine.
Rooms: 5 rooms with bath, heating and fireplace.
Special features: Kitchen open to guests, breakfast room. Pets upon request.
Price: 11,500-12,500 drs. without breakfast
Value for money: ✽✽✽
Credit cards: None

TSEPELOVO

✓ TO ARHONTIKO (B Class)
Tel. (0653) 81216, 81336
Open: All year round
Description: Built in 1787, this old mansion has arches, atmosphere and a pretty courtyard.
Rooms: 6 rooms, with bath.
Special features: Dining room where you can have breakfast, lunch or dinner. You can also prepare your own meals in the hotel kitchen.
Price: 12,000-16,000 drs.
Value for money: ✽✽
Credit cards: None

ZAGOROHORIA
MEGALO PAPINGO

✓✓ TA SPITIA TOU SAXONI
(B Class)
11 Daska St.
Tel. (0653) 41615, 41890, fax 41891
Open: All year round
Description: Perhaps the best in the area. Three independent buildings dating from 1900, 1750 and 1840 respectively, restored with great care. Comfortable without betraying their traditional style. In summer, breakfast is served in the lush garden. 
Rooms: 8 rooms with bath, 5 of them have a fireplace, too.
Special features: Comfortable living room with fireplace, breakfast room, garden, household pets upon request.
Price: 27,000-30,500 drs.
Value for money: ✽✽
Credit cards: None

✓✓ PAPAEVANGELOU IOANNIS
(A Class)
Tel. (0653) 41135, fax 41988

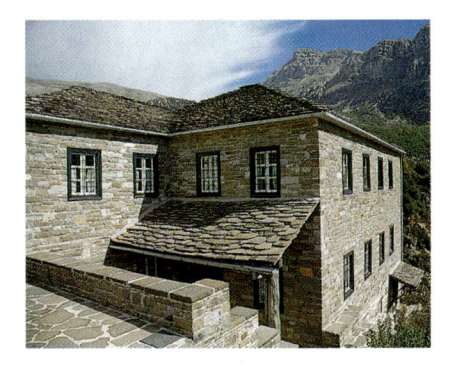

Open: All year round
Description: Traditional Zagori architecture with a splendid view of Mt Gamila and hospitable owners.
Rooms: 10 rooms with bath, heating, and an independent entrance; 5 of them have a fireplace.
Special features: Parking, garden and breakfast room with fireplace. Wonderful breakfasts with homemade jams.
Price: 26,000-29,000 drs.
Value for money: ✽✽
Credit cards: None

MIKRO PAPINGO

✓ DIAS (A Class)
Tel. (0653) 41257, 41892
Open: All year round

Description: A stone building with arched windows and tasteful interior decoration. Breakfast, drinks and local specialities served in the courtyard of a separate building, or in summer under the shade of the pergola.
Rooms: 5 rooms with bath.
Special features: Living room, garden restaurant. Ask the owner about the excursions he organizes.
Price: 17,800 drs.
Value for money: ✹✹✹
Credit cards: Visa

ANO PEDINA

✓✓ TO SPITI TOU ORESTI (A Class)
Tel./fax (0653) 71202, (0651) 32686
Open: All year round
Description: Two-storey stone mansion of the 19th c., beautifully restored. Decorated with genuine traditional furniture and bric a brac.
Rooms: 9 rooms with heating, 5 have en-suite bath and fireplace.
Special features: The restaurant serves breakfast with homemade jams and a variety of delectable local dishes at other hours.
Price: 25,500 drs.
Value for money: ✹✹
Credit cards: All

BOURAZANI

✓ HOTEL BOURAZANI (B Class)
60 km north of Ioannina
Tel. (0655) 61283, 61320, fax 61321
Open: All year round
Description: Secluded within the Bourazani park, through which the Aoos river flows. Built with attention to detail, discreet decor and furnishings.
Rooms: 20 rooms with TV, telephone and music.

Special features: Splendid restaurant, where game is a speciality. Private park, ideal for photo safaris.
Price: 18,000-28,000 drs.
Value for money: ✹✹
Credit cards: Visa, Mastercard

ALTERNATIVES

KRIKONIS SUITES-HOTEL APARTMENTS (A Class)
4 Panepistimiou St., Ioannina, tel. (0651) 44633, fax 45437. **Price:** 21,800 drs.

PALLADION (B Class)
1 Noti Botsari St., Ioannina, tel. (0651) 25856, fax 74034. **Price:** 18,400-26,130 drs.

BYZANTIO (C Class)
Voimoundou St., Ioannina, tel. (0651) 40453, fax 45980. **Price:** 21,600 drs.

GALAXIAS (C Class)
Pyrrhou Square, Ioannina, tel. (0651) 30724, fax 25432. **Price:** 21,600-22,600 drs.

OLYMPIC (C Class)
2 Melanidi St., Ioannina, tel. (0651) 25147, 25888, fax 22041. **Price:** 26,000-32,000 drs.

ZISIS (C Class)
Aristi, tel. (0653) 41147, 41088 & fax.
Price: 18,000 drs.

ASTRAKA (B Class)
Megalo Papingo, tel. (0653) 41693, 35801, fax 41693
Price: 17,500 drs.

RODI (B Class)
Megalo Papingo, tel. (0653) 41954, 41876.
Price: 17,000-20,000 drs. without breakfast

KALLIOPI (C Class)
Megalo Papingo, tel. (0653) 41081.
Price: 14,000 drs.

BEST RESTAURANTS & TAVERNAS

IOANNINA
✓✓ INORYCHIO
45 Averoff St., tel. (0651) 26477

Bar-restaurant. A jewel of a place in terms of space, furniture and original decor. High quality European cuisine, excellent wine cellar.
Price: €€€

✓ GASTRA
16A Kostaki St., Eleousa
Tel. (0651) 61530, 61797
One of the town's fashionable spots. The garden has a "gastra", a hearth with a traditional cast-iron cone used to cook meat until it melts in your mouth. Try their lamb and pork cooked in this way.
Price: €€

TOURIST PAVILION
(Touristiko Periptero)
Agia Triada Hill
Tel. (0651) 25495
For coffee and snacks, on a hill with a wonderful view. Large room decorated in traditional style.
Price: €

IOANNINA ISLAND
Tourist-oriented tavernas on the lake, with local specialities and fresh fish that you can choose yourself from tanks.
O Thomas, tel. (0651) 81819, **Kyra-Vasiliki**, tel. (0651) 81253 and **Pamvotis**, tel. (0651) 81081
Price: All €

ZAGOROHORIA
✓ TO SPITI TOU ORESTI
Ano Pedina, tel. (0653) 71202
Outstanding traditional Greek and international cuisine. In spring and summer, dinner is served in the delightful courtyard.
Price: €

✓ GIORGIOU IOANNIDI
Megalo Papingo, tel. (0653) 41124

Bar-restaurant, in a traditional stone building. Tables outside with a lovely view. Grills and ready-cooked dishes. Try their beef soup.
Price: €

✓ LITHOS
Dilofo, tel. (0653) 61362

One of the most attractive restaurants in the region, constructed in wood and stone. Specialities include wild boar, lamb in the "gastra" and traditional pies.
Price: €

KALLIOPI
Megalo Papingo, tel. (0653) 41081
Taverna in the hotel of the same name. Warm traditional atmosphere, courtyard shaded by vines. Renowned for its succulent Zagori pies made by Kyra Kalliopi herself. **Price:** €

RODI
Megalo Papingo, tel. (0653) 41954
Attractive restaurant in the hotel Rodi.
Price: €

O MICHALIS
Kipi, tel. (0653) 51240
Taverna serving skilfully cooked traditional dishes. Hospitable, with good service.
Price: €

CONTINENTAL GREECE

BEST ENTERTAINMENT

Nightlife in the area is confined to Ioannina. The presence of Ioannina University students livens up the town, creating interesting hang-outs, especially near the lake shore. On the lake-shore road, we've singled out **Naftakia**, an attractive cafe decorated in bright blue, with a swinging atmosphere and "young" music, **Monopolio**, **Apothiki** for serious folk music, and **Premiera** for belly dancing until dawn. You also have the nightclubs: **Agora** on Anexartisias Street, **Skala** on Ethnikis Antistaseos Street, and **Au Bar** on Dodonis Street.

Naftakia

TIPS AND INFORMATION

HOW TO GET THERE

- There's no question that you'll enjoy this excursion more if you have your own car or motorcycle. But if you don't want to drive all the way, you can always fly to Ioannina and rent a car when you get there.
- By air from Athens, west airport, with Olympic Airways (from 15,000 drs.), tel. (01) 9363363. From Thessaloniki's Makedonia airport with Olympic Airways (from 8,700 drs.), tel. (031) 260121.
- By intercity bus (KTEL), 100 Kifissou Ave., Athens, tel. (01) 5129363. By intercity bus (KTEL) from Thessaloniki, tel. (031) 512444.
- Contact Trekking Hellas for organized treks and adventure excursions, tel. (01) 3310323.

BEST TIPS

HOW TO GET AROUND: You'll have to have your own or rented transport. Make sure you have the right footgear.

BEST SEASON: Spring or autumn, but you won't be disappointed at other times of year.

BEST LOCAL FOOD: In Ioannina the city's best tastes are its cheese pies (**tiropittes**) and custard pies (**bougatses**). While visiting the island (Nissi), try the fried frogs legs and baked eel.
In the Zagori villages, almost everything is good, but especially the local meat, bean soup, charcoal grilled cheese, grilled trout, meat soup, home-baked bread, pies made with wild greens or cheese, baked sweets. Drinks include the local **tsipouro** (a kind of grape-based schnapps) and white and sparkling wines from Zitsa.

USEFUL TELEPHONE NUMBERS

IOANNINA	(0651)	Police	41294
Town Hall	79921	**VITSA**	(0653)
Tourist Police	25673	Community Office	61333
Police	26301	**KIPI**	(0653)
Hospital	33461	Police	51206
Regional Hospital	99111	**MONODENDRI**	(0653)
Taxis	46777	OTE	71340
MEGALO PAPINGO,		**TSEPELOVO**	(0653)
MIKRO PAPINGO, ARISTI	(0653)	Town Hall	81203
Municipality	41142	Police	81201

KASTORIA

⁶⁶Kastoria
⁶⁶Nymphaio ⁶⁶Prespes

WHY AMONG THE BEST

For the Byzantine churches, the lake of Kastoria with its swans and forested shores and the wetlands of Prespes. For the colourful Nymphaio and its horses, for "Arcturus" the bear-protection centre for a species nearing extinction and for the hotel "La Moara".

CONTINENTAL GREECE

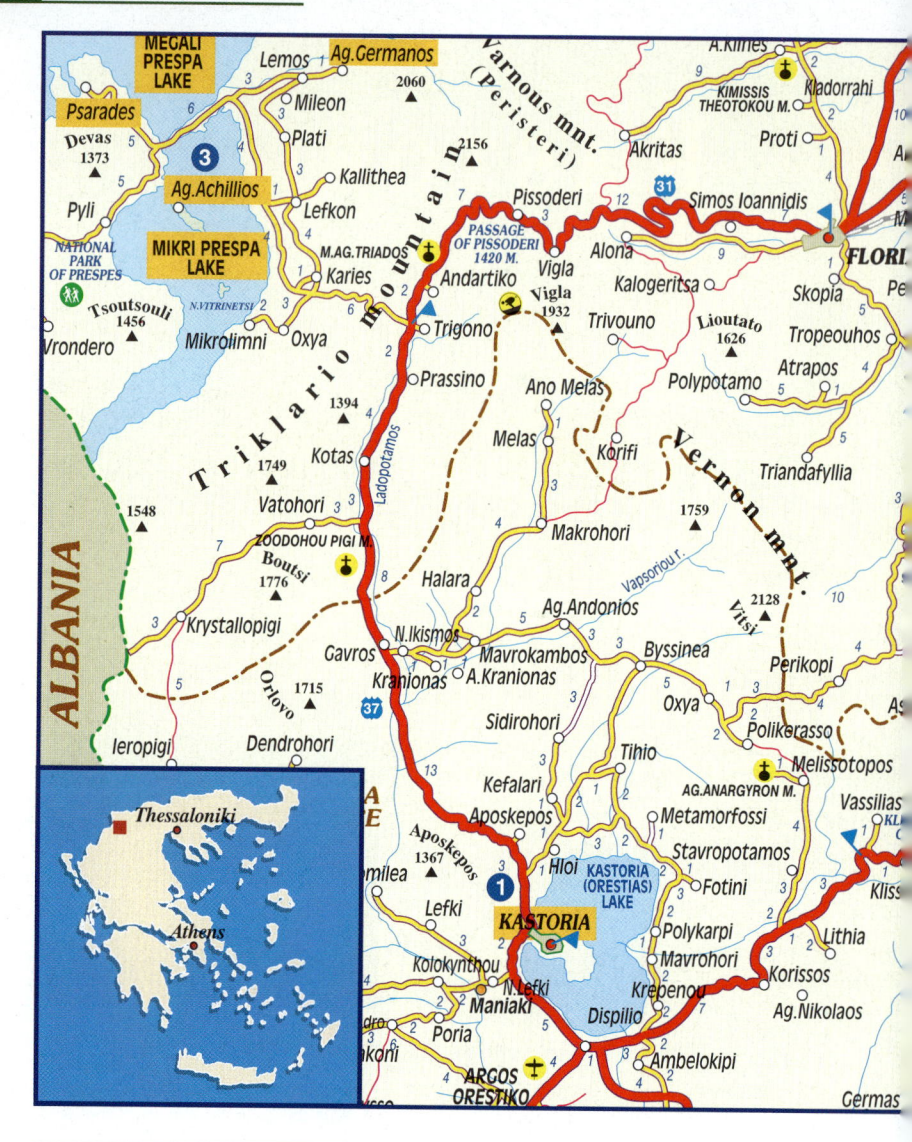

BEST's OPINION

A pleasant excursion for those interested in year-round explorations of little-known areas unspoiled by tourism. You will enjoy the routes leading you to the various sights and will experience precious moments of peace far from the crowds and the crush.

HISTORY AND ARCHITECTURE OF THE REGION

Inhabited from prehistoric times, this area where the small Macedonian state of Orestias once flourished has been the target of many invasions. Today, one can see mansions impressive for the high aesthetic standard of their architecture, influenced by that of Macedonia and Northern Europe. The lower floors are of masonry, with narrow openings, and the ground floor is of stone reinforced by horizontal half-timbering. The top floor is of wood, in the lath and plaster technique, with a projecting roofed loggia and overhanging enclosed gallery with wide glass panes to allow maximum light. The steeply sloping roofs successfully deal with heavy falls of snow. The interior is richly decorated with wall-paintings, carved wood-panelling on the ceilings, skylights with coloured glass panes, and the rooms in general are cosily arranged for comfort. The mansions are usually three-storeyed and most of those in Kastoria were built in the 18th and 19th c.

KASTORIA · NYMPHAIO · PRESPES   39

BEST SIGHTS: STEP BY STEP
❶ KASTORIA
Καστοριά / Kastoriá

The town is known for its fur workshops which have constituted its principal source of wealth and also for its Byzantine churches. It has 15,000 inhabitants and is surrounded by glorious mountain scenery. The town stands at the neck of a small peninsula on the west bank of the lake.

It used to be renowned for its mansions' unmatched architectural style and although nowadays concrete constructions have spoiled its unique aspect, the area's natural beauties still draw many appreciative visitors.

Also renowned are the more than seventy Byzantine and Post-Byzantine churches, dating from the 9th to 19th c., nearly all basilicas. The more noteworthy of these have splendid frescoes of great historical and artistic worth.

Kastoria is first mentioned in the 6th c. in the time of Justinian and may derive its medieval name from the beavers ("kastoras" in Greek) inhabiting the lake. In another version, the name comes from Kastoras, son of Zeus and mythical hero of Macedonia. In the course of its history, the region was overrun by a series of invaders, the Ottomans being the last, from whom it was liberated in 1912. Workshops for the production of fur garments developed in the town from the 17th c. on, as did also the arts of devotional painting, gold embroidery and weaving. Furs from Kastoria were exported to Vienna, Budapest, Paris and Moscow. The town thrived intellectually in the economic boom and generated famous schools with eminent teachers.

WHAT TO SEE

◎◎ BYZANTINE CHURCHES

*To visit the churches, ask for the keys at the Byzantine Museum, tel. (0467) 26781, on Dexamenis Square, next to the hotel **Xenia**.*

◎ Agios Stephanos

A triple-aisled basilica. The older **frescoes**, of the early 10th c., are in the narthex and side apses, the later ones in the medallions of the central nave and the more recent on the upper part of the same.

◎ Panagia Koumbelidiki

A cruciform church with a round dome and three apses. The interior of the main church and the older narthex are adorned with 13th c. **frescoes**, while those of its exterior were painted in 1946.

Panagia Koumbelidiki

457

CONTINENTAL GREECE

🌀🌀 Agii Anargyri

Basilica with three aisles. It has striking 11th and 12th c. **frescoes**.

🌀 Taxiarchis tis Metropolis

Triple-aisled, the burial place of the hero of the Macedonian struggle, Pavlos Melas. Take particular note of the 13th c. fresco of the **Virgin and Child** above the entrance and the external 15th c. wall-paintings of men, women and children buried in the church.

Agii Anargyri

🌀 Agios Nikolaos tou Kaznitzi

Single-chambered, with a wooden roof and a narthex. It was donated by the high official Nikiforos Kaznitzis who is depicted, with his wife Anna, on the west wall.

🌀🌀 FURS EXHIBITION
Έκθεση Γουναρικών / ΄Ekthessi Gounarikón
Chloe area
Tel. (0467) 27771
🕐 *9 am-5 pm, closed on Sundays and holidays**

This is a permanent exhibit, one of the world's biggest, where you can see and buy furs all year round. In May an international fair takes place which attracts buyers from all over the world.

🌀🌀 CIRCUIT OF THE PENINSULA (KASTORIA LAKE SHORE ROAD)
Γύρος Χερσονήσου (Παραλίμνιος δρόμος Καστοριάς) /
Gýros Hersoníssou (Paralímnios drómos Kastoriás)

Do not fail to take this enchanting route through scenery of lush greenery by the lake. There are ducks and geese there, while on Sundays you will encounter many people fishing. Make a stop at the monastery of 🌀 **Panagia Mavriotissa** (open from sunrise to sunset). The nave has remarkable 12th c. frescoes. Next to it is the little church of Agios Ioannis o Theologos with frescoes of 1552, combining local traditional and Cretan School techniques.

🌀 LAKE KASTORIA
Λίμνη Καστοριάς /
Límni Kastoriás

Lake Kastoria (or Orestias) is a remnant of the bay which once penetrated into Macedonia and separated it from Thessaly. It has a depth of 10 m, altitude 620 m and its perimeter is 20 km. The water is drinkable and there are all sorts of lake-fish as well as eels in it. If you have time, it is well worthwhile making its 🌀 **circuit**.

🌀 FOLK ART MUSEUM
Archontiko Nerantzi Aivazi
Doltso Quarter
Tel. (0467) 28603
🕐 *10:30 am-12 noon and 4-7 pm, closed on holidays**

As it is not always open, ask at the tourist office, tel. (0467) 26777
The exhibits include objects of daily use, implements for the dressing of fur, reproductions of interiors of old dwellings of Kastoria and local traditional costumes.

KASTORIA · NYMPHAIO · PRESPES   **39**

🅖 APOZARI AND DOLTSO QUARTERS
Συνοικίες Αποζάρι και Ντόλτσο /
Synikíes Apozári ke Dóltso

These are joined together by the lakeside, untouched by the intervention of decades of indiscriminate concrete-jungle building. The family mansions of the 🅖 **Tsiatsapas**, 🅖 **Mantzouras**, 🅖 **Sapountzis**, 🅖 **Broumidis**, 🅖 **Emmanouil**, 🅖 **Pouliopoulos**, 🅖 **Scoutaris**, 🅖 **Papaterpou** and others are significant examples of Kastoria's architecture.

Doltso

🅖 BYZANTINE MUSEUM
Βυζαντινό Μουσείο / Vyzantinó Moussío
Dexameni Sq. next to the Hotel Xenia
Tel. (0467)26781, 26649

🕒 *Summer 8:30 am-6 pm, winter 8:30 am-3 pm, closed on Mondays and holidays**

There is an interesting exhibition of 12th to 17th c. 🅖 **Byzantine and Post-Byzantine icons**, exceptional specimens of local devotional-painting.

Scoutari Mansion

TOWN WALLS
Τα τείχη της πόλης / Ta Tíhi tis Pólis

Only some ruins of the Justinian wall remain to the west as well as some, probably of the 11th c., to the east of town.

FREE TIME

SKIING
Visit the Kastoria Skiing Association's (Syllogos Hionodromias Kastorias) ski resort on Mt Vitsi, at an altitude of 1800 m. Information: Tel. (0467) 24884, (0932) 823222

CRUISE ON THE LAKE
The tourist boat conducts daily cruises. Information: Tel. (0467) 26777, (094)791439.

VISIT TO THE PETRIFIED FOREST
Over 15 million years old, situated near the village Nostimo, tel. (0467) 84591.

SAIL AND WATER SKI ON THE LAKE
Information from the Kastoria Yacht Club (Naftikos Omilos Kastorias), tel. (0467) 28956, 29400.

LAKE FISHING
From the local boats called "plaves" specially built to navigate amid ice in winter.

FESTIVITIES AND LOCAL EVENTS
- **The Ragoutsaria** is a local carnival which begins on 6 January and ends on 8 January.
- On the last Sunday of Carnival there is the **Boubounes** with games over bonfires.
- The **Furs Fair** is in May.
- Cultural events take place in July at the **Christopoulia** and **Kastorian Emigrants' Week** (Evdomada Apodimon Kastorianon).
- On **15 August** there is a representation of a local traditional wedding.

❷ NYMPHAIO
Νυμφαίο / Nymphéo

This beautiful village of 250 inhabitants, at an altitude of 1350 m on the slopes of Mt Vitsi, is a very special sight, with its charming cobbled lanes, stone mansions, beech forest, serene alpine scenery and meadows with

CONTINENTAL GREECE

horses. It has become better known since 1990 when the vintner Giannis Boutaris opened an exceptional hotel there, which is a wonderful spot for relaxation and contemplation. The village was the headquarters of the Macedonian struggle and, among other eminent protagonists, Pavlos Melas also came here. The prosperity of the area is due to tobacco and cotton cultivation, as well as gold and silver work.

WHAT TO SEE

ⓖ ARCTURUS BEAR SANCTUARY

Κέντρο Προστασίας Αρκούδας «Αρκτούρος» /
Kéntro Prostassías Arkoúdas "Arctoúros"
Tel. (0386) 41500

Here you can see for yourself indigenous brown bears living under the care and protection of the personnel of the **Arcturus** centre. These friends of the splendid beasts have set up an extensive fenced forest station in a ravine, in which bears rescued from capture and maltreatment live in restricted freedom in good conditions, under the constant attention of the wardens. You can also visit their veterinarian surgery in the nearby village of Fanos where sick and wounded bears are cared for.

ⓖ MISSIOS AND TSIRLIS MANSIONS

Αρχοντικά Μίσσιου και Τσίρλι /
Arhontiká Míssiou ke Tsírli

The first, belonging to a wealthy tobacco merchant, is on two floors and the rooms are decorated with flower, bird and patterned border motifs, while the other, Mihail Tsirlis', was, from 1904 to 1908, the headquarters of the Macedonian struggle.

The impressive mansions of the Mertzos, Papadopoulos, Boutaris and Sossidis families lend to the village a timeless grandeur, blending in harmony with the scenery and offering the visitor sights of exceptional charm.

Nikios School

ⓖ NIKIOS SCHOOL

Νίκειος Σχολή / Níkios Scholí

Founded by Ioannis Nikos, a fine two-storeyed building and example of a master stone-mason's work, with a Swiss clock.

FREE TIME

If you like riding, organize a trip to the forest or to Letoussia, Lakos, Profitis Ilias and Kosta. Phone the Riding Centre (Kendro Ipassias) first for an appointment, tel. (0386) 31132.

---

❸ PRESPES
Πρέσπες / Préspes

Wetlands of north-western Macedonia designated a national park, with twin lakes, ⓖⓖ **Megali Prespa** and ⓖⓖ **Mikri Prespa** / Greater and Lesser Prespa or Brigiis as was the ancient name. Greater Prespa, the Balkans' biggest lake, is bordered by Greece, Albania and the former Yugoslavia which meet at a tri-national point on the lake. Its altitude is 853 m and depth 50 m, its extent 288 sq. km, of which 37 belong to Greece. A narrow neck of land 200 m wide and 1000 m long divides the two lakes, whose waters communicate underground. Lesser Prespa's size is 44 sq. km, of which a small part belongs to Albania. It has an islet in the mid-

KASTORIA · NYMPHAIO · PRESPES

dle, Vitrinetsi, and another at the northern end, Agios Achillios. The shores of both lakes are steeply sheer and rocky in places and at others gently sloping with abundant vegetation. They teem with fish and on the banks of Lesser Prespa in reed thickets there are many rare species of water-fowl, attracting researchers, bird experts and institutes.

WHAT TO SEE
AGIOS ACHILLIOS
Άγιος Αχίλλειος / Ágios Achíllios

The islet in Lesser Prespa, with the ruins of an ancient settlement and Byzantine churches. Visit the ruined 11th c. **three-aisled basilica** of the same name, as well as the church of the **Panagia Porfyra** with 15th, 16th and 17th c. frescoes. The village will take you back fifty years with its picturesque shacks and mud lanes, where barefoot children and their pets play without the threat of traffic.

Lesser Prespa

AGIOS GERMANOS
Άγιος Γερμανός / Ágios Germanós

Here you will find a domed cruciform church of the 11th c. with inscriptions. Also take a look at the church of Agios Athanassios, dated 1816.

Agios Achillios

PSARADES
Ψαράδες / Psarádes

A striking traditional fishing village of 125 inhabitants on a peninsula of Greater Prespa. You can stay in the little pensions and have lake-fish in the tavernas.

HERMITAGES AND CHURCHES OF GREATER PRESPA
Ασκηταριά και Ναοί Μεγάλης Πρέσπας / Askitariá ke naoí tis Megális Préspas

Agios Germanos

At the southern end of the lake, you will find the 12th c. church of the **Metamorphosis** and in a cave, the chapel of the **Panagia tis Eleoussas** with **frescoes** of 1410. It is worth visiting the hermitages (called skates) with **rock paintings**: images of saints painted on the rocks by monks in the 14th and 15th c. The lakeside caves are remarkable, with beautiful blue-green reflections of light in the waters, stalactites and ceilings as if carved with reliefs. You can get there by boat from Psarades.

Rock painting

BEST HOTELS AND ROOMS

BEST LOCATION
As the distances are not great, if you can afford it, you should stay at the La Moara hotel in Nymphaio. Otherwise anywhere you choose to stay among the *Best* hotels we have to propose will adequately meet your basic needs.

PRICES
The hotel prices mentioned below are the official ones set by the National Tourist Organization for double rooms, at low and high season, with breakfast. Since owners are allowed to modify the prices, always try to negotiate them.

KASTORIA

✓ TSAMIS (B Class)

Dispilio (at the 30th km on the Kastoria-Athens road)
Tel. (0467) 85334, fax 85777
Open: All year round

Description: An unpretentious modern construction with traditional elements, a number of conveniences and in discreet good taste, with lake-view. Probably the best choice in town.
Rooms: 80 rooms with A/C, telephone and TV.
Special Features: Parking, restaurant.
Price: 21,400-28,000 drs.
Value for money: ✱
Credit cards: Visa, American Express, Diners

NYMPHAIO

✓✓ LA MOARA (Luxury Class)

Tel. (031) 287626, 287401, fax 287401
Open: All year round except Monday, Tuesday and July.
Description: In the Vlach dialect, the name means "water mill" and this is a most attractive traditional guest house with a mountain view, a flower garden with a well, and a paddock for horses. The interior is simply but tastefully decorated with simplicity and respect for heritage.
Rooms: There are 8 rooms with en suite bath, central heating, TV and a telephone exchange.

Special features: Dining room where breakfast and dinner are served. There is a basement wine-cellar with **130** different wines, a library, and billiards, television and video rooms.
Price: 46,000-58,000 drs. Breakfast and dinner included
Value for money: ✱
Credit cards: Visa, Diners, American Express

✓ TA LINOURIA (A Class)

Tel. (0386) 31133, (031) 287626, 287401
Open: All year round
Description: A stone building with a view to the mountain slope, comfortable and tasteful interior and friendly hosts.

Kastoria - Nymphaio - Prespes

Rooms: There are two 8-bed rooms, one twin-bed and three 4-bed rooms, all with en suite bath and central heating.
Special features: The inn's cafeteria serves breakfast, full meals, appetizers to accompany a drink, country pies and home-cooked desserts. There's a bookshop where you can buy books, mainly for children, and souvenirs of the village.
Price: 19,500 drs. without breakfast
Value for money: ✽✽✽
Credit cards: None

✓ ENTERNE (A Class)

Tel. (0386) 31230, 23406
Open: Only Fridays until Sunday evening
Description: On two floors, built in Nymphaio's characteristic architecture. An atmosphere of hospitality, well furnished, and it has a paved inner patio.
Rooms: 7 rooms with bath, 3 of them with kitchen and TV.
Special features: On the ground floor there is a breakfast room and a cafe-bar with a fireplace. Pets upon request.

Price: 15,000 drs.
Value for money: ✽✽
Credit cards: None

PRESPES

✓ AGIOS ACHILLIOS GUEST HOUSE (XENONAS AGIOU ACHILLIOU)

Agios Achillios (Lesser Prespa's island)
Tel. (0385) 46601, fax 46112
Open: All year round

Description: A modern well designed construction, with lofts, a large hall with two fireplaces, an imaginative decor and particular attention to furnishings. View of the lake, friendly atmosphere.
Rooms: 7 rooms with bath and heating, all with lake view.
Special features: Restaurant and a sitting room where you can have breakfast.
Price: 14,000 drs.
Value for money: ✽✽
Credit cards: None

ALTERNATIVES

WOMENS RURAL TOURISM ASSOCIATION (Agrotouristikos Syndesmos Gynekon)
Agios Germanos, Prespes, tel. (0385) 51320. **Price:** 11,000 drs.

I SYNTROFIA (B Class)
Psarades Prespon, tel. (0385) 46107. **Price:** 7,000-11,000 drs.

ORESTION (C Class)
1 Davaki Sq., Kastoria, tel. & fax (0467) 22257. **Price:** 16,500-18,000 drs.

ANESSIS (C Class)
10 Grammou St., Kastoria, tel. (0467) 83908, fax 83768. **Price:** 17,000 drs.

EUROPA (C Class)
12 Agiou Athanassiou St., Kastoria, tel. (0467) 23826.
Price: 17,500-18,500 drs.

Typical door

BEST RESTAURANTS & TAVERNAS

KASTORIA
For your meals, we chose the tavernas **Omonia**, Omonia Sq., tel. (0467) 25151, **Tzaki**, Ambelokipi, tel. (0467) 85198 and the particularly neat **Hagiati**, Ambelokipi, tel. (0467) 85249.
Price: All €

NYMPHAIO
To try the local specialities, tasty pies, wild mountain greens as well as well-cooked meat courses, go to the traditional **Arhondiko**, tel. (0386) 31107, or the hospitable **Neveska**, tel. (0386) 31442, in the village centre.
Price: All €

PRESPES
The tavernas we propose are **Lefteris**, tel. (0385) 51418 (Agios Germanos), **Akrolimnia**, tel. (0385) 46260, 46107, and **Paradossi**, tel. (0385) 46013 (Psarades), with a lake view. Price: All €

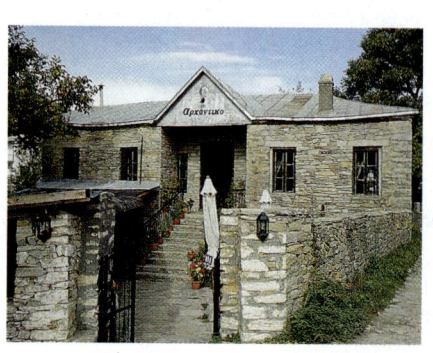

Taverna Arhondiko

TIPS AND INFORMATION

HOW TO GET THERE
- Ideally by your own car for mobility on this trip.
- By air from Athens, west airport, to Kastoria by Olympic Airways (15,800 drs.), tel. (01) 9363363. From there by hired car.
- For organized tours from Athens contact the travel agencies Trekking Hellas, tel. (01) 3310323-6, Marathon Tours, tel. (01) 3835136 and Pausanias, tel. (01) 3820535.

BEST TIPS

HOW TO GET AROUND: As the sights on this trip are scattered about, your best bet is to travel by car or motorbike.

BEST SEASON: All year round.

BEST BUYS: Kastoria is famous the world over for its excellent furs. You can pick the coat or jacket of your dreams at a good price in the shops or the permanent exhibit.

BEST LOCAL FOOD: The Prespes area is known for its beans and its delicious lake fish, either grilled or in fish soup or little sun-dried salt herrings.
In Kastoria try the very good fresh lake-fish and the speciality called **sarma** (leaves stuffed with meat, rice, vegetables and seasonings), as well as the local yoghurt.

USEFUL TELEPHONE NUMBERS

KASTORIA .... (0467)	Community Office 31382
Town Hall 22312, 28914	Police 31361
Tourist Bureau 26777	Rural Clinic 31360
Police 22100	**PRESPES** .... (0385)
Hospital 28341	Information Centre 51452
Taxis 82100	Agios Germanos Community Office 51419
Tourist Office of the Municipality 24484	Agios Germanos Police 51202
NYMPHAIO .... (0386)	Prespes Protection Institute 51211

VERGINA

°Lefkadia °Pella

WHY AMONG THE BEST

Because of the extremely important archaeological site of Vergina, with the renowned Macedonian tombs, which will fascinate not only lovers of archaeology, but any visitor.

CONTINENTAL GREECE

ANCIENT VERGINA

- ① ARCHAEOLOGICAL SITE AND MUSEUM (GREAT TUMULUS)
- ② ROMAIOS TOMB / EURIDICE TOMB
- ③ ANCIENT TOWN OF AIGAI / PALACE / THEATRE
- ④ PALATITSA TOMBS

BEST's OPINION

Apart from the archaeological sites, the area is not particularly interesting. So organize a brief excursion, just to satisfy the historian in you. When you leave, you'll be wiser for having discovered some aspects of the dynasty which produced Alexander the Great – one of the world's greatest army commanders of all time.

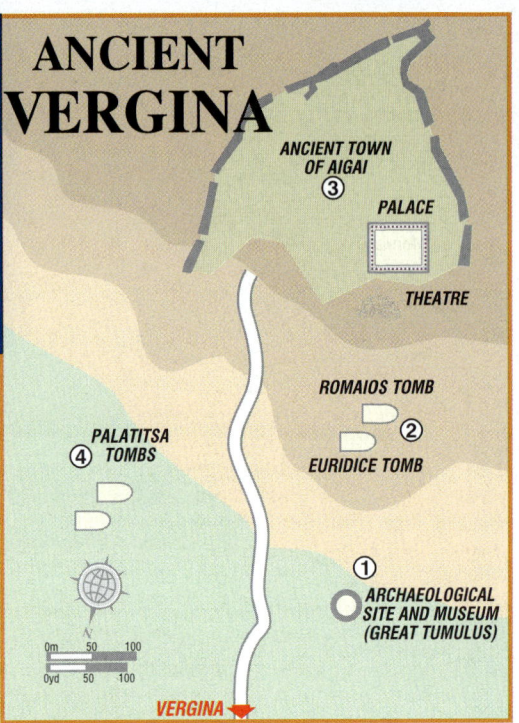

IN BRIEF

No one would have been interested in this hamlet of 1,500 inhabitants, if the 1977-78 excavations by the prominent Greek archaeologist, Professor **Manolis Andronikos**, had not uncovered finds of the utmost significance: They were tombs, in an enormous burial mound (Megali Toumba), 13 m in height and 110 m in diameter, at the western edge of the Tumulus Cemetery. On some heights south of Vergina, the remains of an ancient Macedonian city, **Aigai**, were also found.

HISTORY

The legendary king of the Macedonians, **Karanos**, once followed a flock of goats ("aiges" in Greek), in order to find the site on which he would build the privileged city of **Aigai**. The **Pieria mountains** protected its rear, while the fertile Imathia plain spread out before it, ensuring security and prosperity. Until approximately 400 BC, it was the capital of the state of Macedonia. When the capital was transferred to **Pella**, its sanctuaries and tombs remained here. In the second half of the 4th c. BC, the palace and the theatre were constructed, and the sanctuary of Eukleia was laid out. In the early 3rd c. BC, it was dominated by the king of Epirus, **Pyrros**, and in the mid-2nd c. BC, it was destroyed by fire, probably linked to a Roman invasion.

During the Byzantine Empire, there was only one hamlet in the area, known as **Palatitsa**, probably due to its proximity to the palace "palati".

Vergina, the place that once humbly concealed all that remained of the glory, the wealth and the power of the great Macedonians, now holds in its embrace only tombs and ruins.

ALEXANDER THE GREAT

The son of Olympias and Philip II, he was born in 356 BC. While still a child, he managed to tame the wild horse, Bucephalus. At the age of 20, in 336 BC, he was enthroned as king, following the assassination of his father.

His campaign in Asia Minor, the victorious battles of Granicos, Issos and Gavgamela, and the Indian campaign, led the Macedonians deep into the East. The great conqueror, with his fiery personality and unrestrained ambition, died on June 13, 323 BC, at the age of only 33, leaving behind "to the mightiest" the huge empire which he had created.

VERGINA 40

BEST SIGHTS: STEP BY STEP

① ◎◎◎ MUSEUM AND ARCHAEOLOGICAL SITE (THE GREAT TUMULUS)
Αρχαιολογικός και Μουσειακός Χώρος (Μεγάλη Τούμπα) / Archeologikós ke Mouseiakós Hóros (Megáli Toúmba)

Tel. (0331) 92347
☺ *Summer 8 am-7 pm, winter 8 am-2:30 pm, closed on Mondays and holidays**
Thessaloniki Tour Guides Association, tel. (031) 546037

A subterranean burial ground, similar to a crypt, it houses the four most important **Macedonian tombs**, decorated with their impressive, rich ◎◎◎ **finds**, which were transferred here from the Thessaloniki Archaeological Museum in 1998 and give a complete picture of the magnificence and wealth of the tombs. You'll see the ◎ **gold reliquaries** of Philip and his daughter, Cleopatra, the ◎ **silver urn** and the ◎◎ **wreath** of the prince, **Philip's** ◎◎◎ **gold wreath** of oak leaves, the **two pieces of cloth** that were Cleopatra's funeral shroud, interesting **funeral gifts**, **decorations of ivory** and **funerary stelae**.

Also on display are the remains of Philip's **funeral pyre** and an edifice which was probably a **monument** in his honour. From a distance, only a bushy mound can be seen – a picture similar to the ancient site. Entering from the anteroom, through a double gate, you'll find yourself in a hexagonal hall. As you look from right to left, you'll first notice the tomb of the prince, then, opposite, the royal tomb. To its left, is the monument and the tomb called 'of Persephone' and finally, the tomb "of the free-standing columns". The **tomb** – unlooted – of the ◎◎ **Prince** was thus named because the bones found inside were those of a youth, aged 13-16. A double chamber, with an interesting depiction of a chariot race in the anteroom, contained exquisitely fashioned silver objects, as well as a silver urn with a gold wreath. The ◎◎◎ **Royal tomb (or tomb of Philip II)** was

Gold wreath

Group of ivory figures

Gold casket

467

thus named, because it is believed to be the great Macedonian king's, father of Alexander the Great. It was constructed of local limestone, apart from the marble doors, with two chambers and a vaulted roof, 10 m in length and approximately 6 m wide. The Doric facade is decorated by two half-columns and two pilasters at the sides. Over the entablature, a large frieze depicts the hunt of lions, bears, antelopes, and wild boar in a semi-forested landscape.

In the main chamber, an ossuary was found, with a ⓖⓖⓖ **gold casket** containing bones wrapped in purple cloth and a priceless ⓖⓖⓖ **gold wreath**. Rich funeral gifts had been placed on the floor.

The looted ⓖ **tomb of Persephone** was found abutting the Great Tumulus, beside the foundations of the monument. A four-sided, oblong structure of limestone, with rich, striking decoration, it got its name from its fine wall paintings on three of the walls, probably by **Nikomachos**, the only intact painting of the period extant, depicting the myth of the "Abduction of Persephone by Hades", which is impressive for its vitality and the subtle use of a limited range of colours.

To the north, a fourth tomb – known as the **tomb of the free-standing columns** – was discovered, which owes its name to the free-standing colonnade on its facade. However, this tomb was almost totally destroyed. The museum's superb state-of-the-art technology makes the tour a unique experience. The finds, displayed in virtually invisible showcases, are lit by fibre optics.

② ⓖ THE ROMAIOS AND EURYDICE TOMBS
Τάφοι Ρωμαίου και Ευρυδίκης / Táphi Romaíou ke Evridíkis

Located on a hill, 500 m north of the village

The ⓖ **Romaios tomb** bears the name of the archaeologist, Professor K. Romaios. Its entrance has four **Ionic half-columns**, two on each side of the double marble doors.

A **peristyle**, **decorated frieze** and plain **triangular pediment** complete the facade. The main focus of interest is a splendidly designed ⓖ **marble throne**. It is 1.98 m high, with a footstool, carved white sphinxes on the arms and a painted back depicting griffins lacerating a deer.

The **tomb of Eurydice** was probably the final resting place of Philip's mother and Alexander's grandmother. It is located four metres east of the Romaios tomb and is one of the most singular tomb structures of its kind. It has two **vaulted chambers**, the main chamber and the anteroom. The narrow side of the far end of the chamber, fashioned as a pseudo-facade, constitutes the tomb's special feature, with a false door flanked by four Ionic half-columns and two false windows.

The columns flank the **Ionic peristyle** and the **blue frieze** with the **white anthemia**. A significant find is the richly decorated ⓖ **marble throne**, depicting a quadriga bearing the kings of the Underworld, sphinxes carved in the round and karyatids, in clever combinations. Painted strips depicting griffins, winged lions and a lacerated deer complete the throne's elaborate decoration.

③ THE ANCIENT CITY OF AIGAI
Η Πόλη των Αιγών / I Póli ton Aigón

Parking area 300 m south of the Romaios tomb

Aigai must have been built, according to archaeologists, on the site where Vergina is now located. Unfortunately, today one can see only the foundations of the Hellenistic houses and part of the wall, where there was the southern entrance to the fortress, called **Palioporta**.

The Theatre

It is part of the architectural complex of the palace, with an orchestra 28.5 m in diameter that had the stone base of the altar in its centre. Philip II was murdered here in 336 BC, as he celebrated the marriage of his daughter, **Cleopatra**, to the king of Epirus, **Alexander**.

Next to the theatre is the sanctuary of the great mother-goddess, Cybele. Here, an edifice has been excavated with two areas, probably containing central hearths that may have been used for initiation rites. Terracotta votive offerings and artefacts of worship were found, which date the temple at about mid-2nd c. BC.

The Palace

VERGINA 40

The Palace
The imposing ruins of the 4th c. BC palace, under the acropolis on the Agia Triada plateau, are all of limestone, except for the marble thresholds. Its crowning glory was a two-storey building, 104.5 m long and 88.5 m wide. Around the central square courtyard, the private apartments were laid out in a regular arrangement. The courtyard is bordered on its four sides by four Doric colonnades.

Next to the propylaia, a **votive inscription** was found, a dedication to Herakles, progenitor of the royal house of Macedonia, and the base of a throne. The five rooms on the south side, which had mosaic floors, were connected with the courtyard colonnade, through their two exterior chambers.

Today, you can admire the **mosaic**, which is still in place and preserved in good condition. It depicts a complex plant arrangement, which in its four corners is transformed into four female figures reminiscent of flowers. The slightly raised edging of red plaster was probably used for guests to sit on at symposiums.

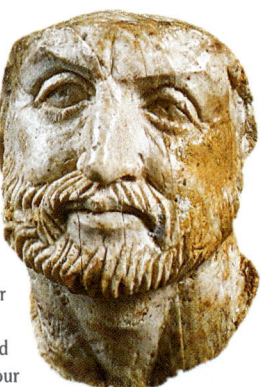

Philip II

Acropolis and Walls
The city of Aigai was surrounded by a triangular wall, constructed of limestone, with one side facing the plain. South-west, on a higher level, was the acropolis.

④ THE PALATITSA TOMBS
Οι Τάφοι της Παλατίτσας / I Táphi tis Palatítsas
Three groups of tombs have been excavated west of the village of Palatitsa.

The **L. Heuzey tomb** was named after the archaeologist, who excavated it in 1861, but who unfortunately made off with its two marble doors, taking them to the Louvre. The monument has two chambers and was built of rectangular limestone blocks.

Tomb I, the largest in the region, features a 7.8 m constructed road, which leads to the facade. Four Doric half-columns flank its door, two on each side. It has a simple peristyle, triglyphs and metopes, as well as a pediment with an unusually high cornice. In the chamber, there is a marble sarcophagus with carved and painted decoration.

Tomb II is a little older, but smaller in size. It has no anteroom and only a marble door. Depicted above the entrance is a dead warrior, flanked by a female figure offering him a wreath, and a seated warrior. In this tomb, a marble throne with a footstool was also found. **Tomb III** is much smaller and its only decoration is a pediment on the facade.

Silver strainer

BEYOND THIS EXCURSION
LEFKADIA
About 30 km NW of Vergina. Here were found a **late-Classical** and **Hellenistic cemetery**, ruins of **Hellenistic buildings** and the **Macedonian tombs** of **Krisi**, twin-chambered with two-storey facade; of the **Anthemia** (Flowers), also with two chambers and a facade representing

Pella

469

CONTINENTAL GREECE

an Ionic temple; the "Kinch" Tomb, also double-chambered, and the single-chamber **Lyson Kallikles** family tomb.

PELLA

About 55 km north of Vergina, between the villages Palia and Nea (Old & New) Pella there are the ruins of the greatest capital the Macedonian state, of 413-168 BC. See the **cemetery** with the pit graves, the **palace**, the **market place**, ruins of houses, the **late-Classical and Hellenistic cemetery**, the **baths** and the **basilica Apostolon Petrou ke Pavlou**. Visit the Archaeological Museum, tel. (0382) 31160, with **clay figurines**, **statuettes**, considerable **mosaics** and the **marble head of Alexander the Great**.

BEST HOTELS AND ROOMS

BEST LOCATION

There are no particularly good hotels in the area. But this trip has been recommended only for the visit to Vergina. We suggest that you combine it with Excursion 41 (Thessaloniki). If you definitely want to stay overnight here, choose one of the following hotels.

PRICES

The hotel prices mentioned below are the official ones, set by the National Tourist Organization for double rooms, at low and high season, with breakfast. Since owners are allowed to modify prices, always try to negotiate them.

HATZIAGAPIDOU (A Class) *Taphi, tel. (0331) 92510.* **Price:** 14,000 drs.

MAKEDONIA (B Class) *Veria, tel. & fax (0331) 66902.* **Price:** 22,350 drs.

TIPS AND INFORMATION

HOW TO GET THERE

From Athens to Thessaloniki
- By air from Athens to Thessaloniki with Olympic Airways, west airport, tel. (01) 9363363, (from 18,600 drs.). With Air Greece, east airport, tel. (01) 3255011. With Cronus Airlines, east airport, tel. (01) 9956400. With Air Manos, tel. (01) 3233562-4
- By train (OSE) from Athens, regular carriage (from 4,100 drs.), or Intercity (from 8,250 drs.), tel. (01) 5297777.
- By intercity bus, KTEL (from 7,700 drs.), 100 Kifissou Ave., tel. (01) 5148856, 260 Liossion St., tel. (01) 8317059, 18 Mavromataion St. & Alexandras Ave., Pedio tou Areos, tel. (01) 8225148.

From Thessaloniki to Vergina
- By rented car, or with organized tours run by travel agents, the price of which includes a guide. For information you can contact Zorbidis, tel. (031) 244400 or Doukas, tel. (031) 224100.

USEFUL TELEPHONE NUMBERS

VERGINA	(0331)	Rural Clinic	92336
Town Hall	92337	OTE	92333

THESSALONIKI

WHY AMONG THE BEST

Because Thessaloniki has been a centre for culture through the ages and was the European Cultural Capital in 1997. Because the people are friendly and cosmopolitan and because of the endless opportunities for quality entertainment and gourmet dining.

THESSALONIKI

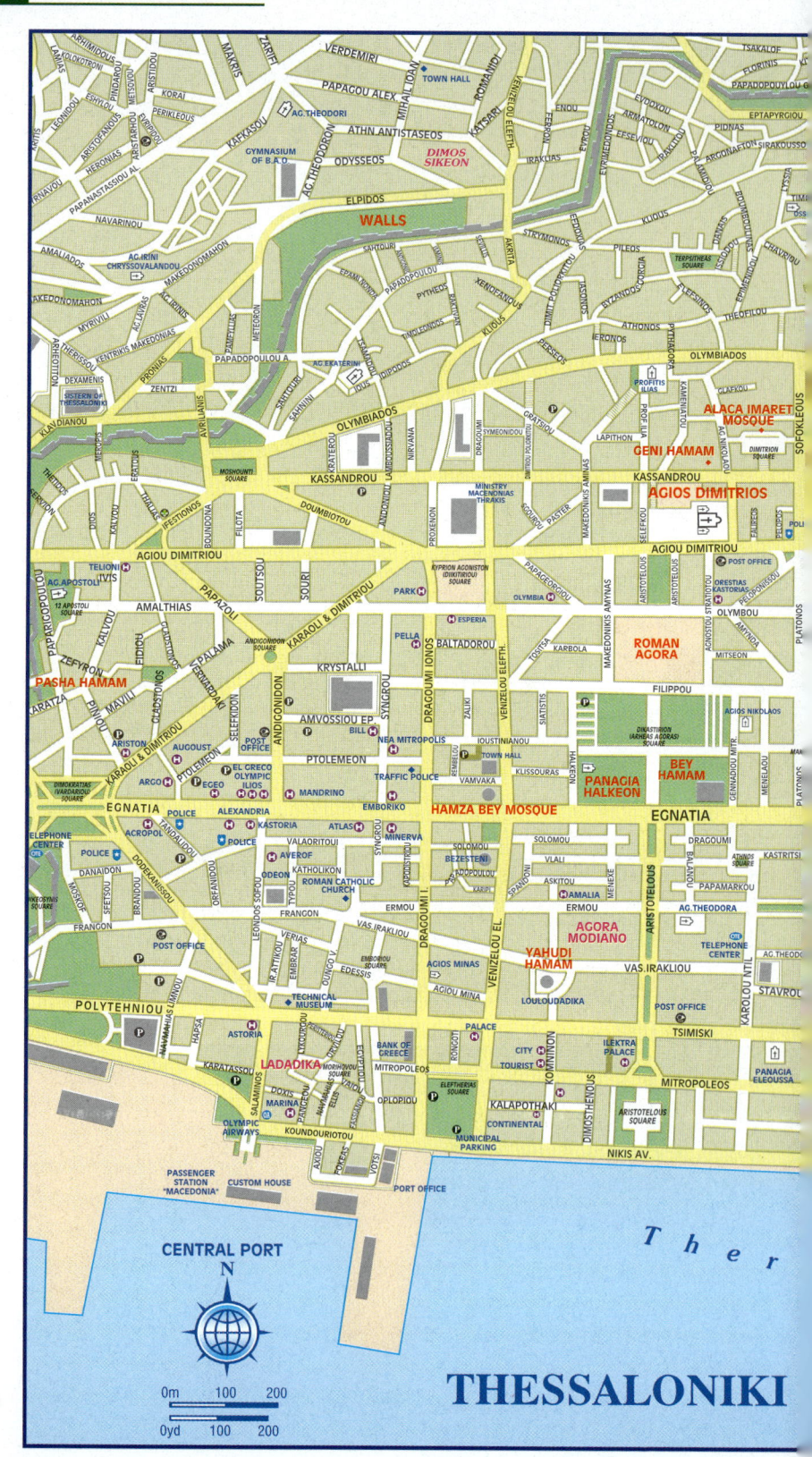

THESSALONIKI 41

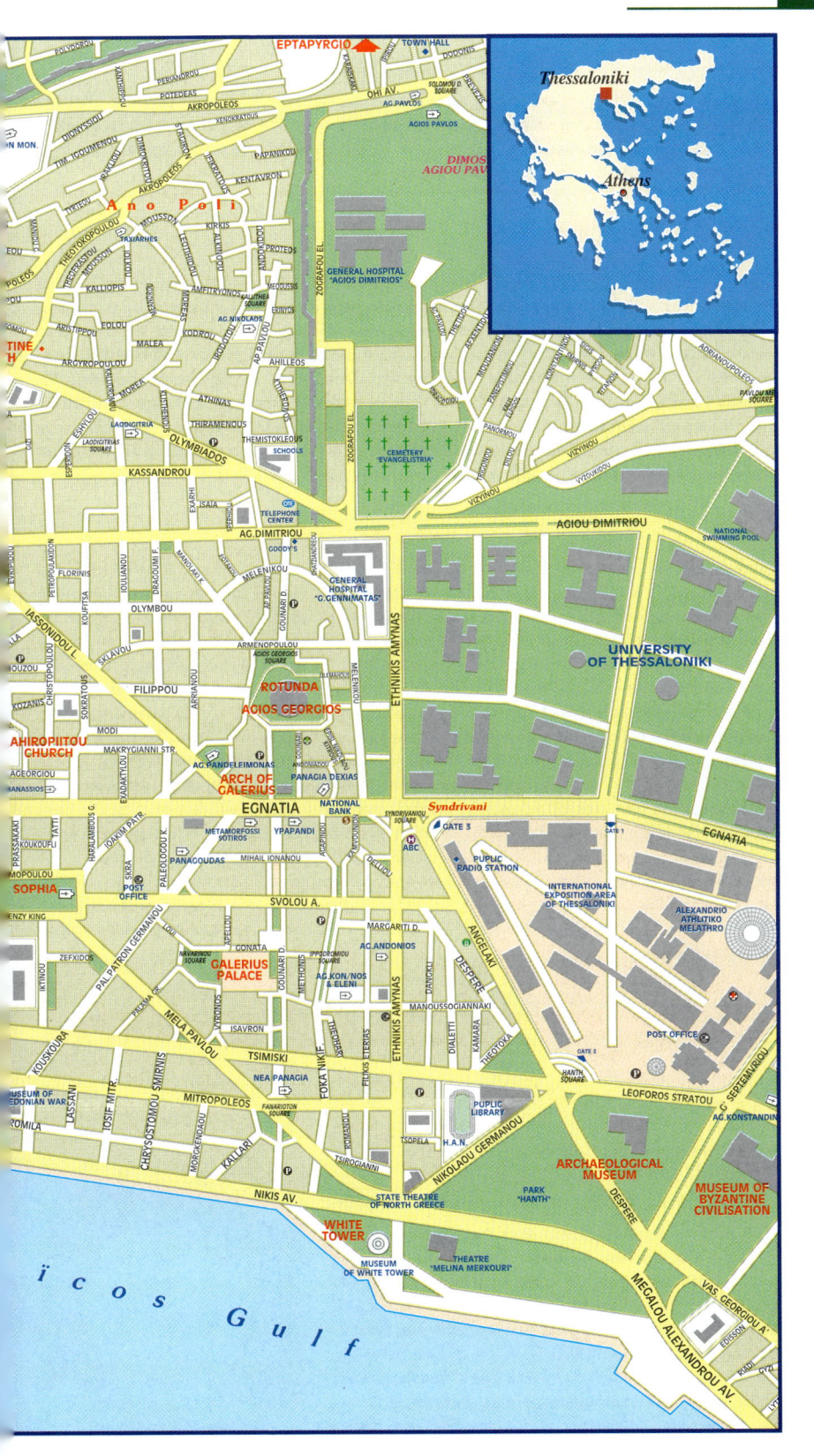

CONTINENTAL GREECE

BEST's OPINION

You need some time to adapt and become acclimatized to the life of the city, because of its size. The city sights will initially attract your attention and you can explore the centre on foot or by taxi. Tour the Upper Town, enjoy yourself at the Ladadika, visit the Agora, have a cup of coffee on the sea front and then follow *Best's* suggestions for an unforgettable night out.

IN BRIEF

Greece's second largest city with a population of some 1,000,000 and vital cultural, industrial and commercial activity, lies on the Thermaicos Gulf. It has an air of mystery, enchantment and vigour and is brimming with historical memories. The centre of Northern Greece, seat of a ministry and a university, it acts as a communication link between Greece, Turkey and the Balkans. It is situated on the slopes of Mt Hortiatis, reaching to the sea and is in effect divided in two by the White Tower Park. The Aristoteleian University, the National Theatre of Northern Greece, the Cinema Club, every kind of cultural and educational association, fringe theatre and art galleries, are some of the elements constituting the intellectual and cultural life of the city. Visitors from all over Greece and the world flock here every year to see its sights, to promote business affairs, expand their collaboration and participate in the cultural activities.

HISTORY

The region was first inhabited about 5,000 years ago and the most ancient city, built here in the 7th c. BC, was called **Thermai**. In 315 BC, the king of Macedonia, Kassandros, conjoined 25 scattered communities with Thermai and thus founded the city to which he gave the name of his wife Thessaloniki, sister of Alexander the Great. It was built according to the Hippodamian code (a sort of chess-board town-plan) and surrounded by ramparts. In 380 AD Theodosios made it Macedonia's administrative centre. The Byzantine fortifications were completed at this time or in the course of the 5th c. AD, when the city enjoyed a period of great prosperity as the seat of the eparch or prefect of Eastern Illyria. Its decline began from the 6th c. when it was weakened by repeated invasions of Avars and Slavs as well as a catastrophic earthquake. In the 9th c., the Byzantines developed an interest in Thessaloniki. In this period it was renovated and Agia Sophia adorned with mosaics. The city surrendered to the Venetians in 1423, while maintaining its privileges until 1430 when it was captured by the Ottomans, who plundered and massacred, converted churches into mosques and devastated the city. From the 15th c. the Jewish community became the custodians of the city's economic and cultural recovery. It was liberated on 26 October 1912, feast day of its patron saint Agios Dimitrios. In 1917, it was destroyed by fire and rebuilt in accordance with modern requirements, which unfortunately did away with some of its charming aspects. Nonetheless, the traces of its lengthy history and past upheavals are visibly preserved in its monuments and above all in the memories and customs of its inhabitants, which neither time nor stormy winds of change are able to erase.

BEST SIGHTS: STEP BY STEP

ⓖⓖⓖ ARCHAEOLOGICAL MUSEUM
Αρχαιολογικό Μουσείο / Archeologikó Moussío
6 Manoli Andronikou St., Hanth Sq.
Tel. (031) 831037, 830538
8 am-2:30 pm, Mondays 10:30 am-5 pm, closed on holidays*

Finds from prehistoric Macedonia, from the cemetery of Sindos, such as ⓖ **gold jewellery, figurines,** ⓖ **gold masks,** Corinthian and Attic vases, the famous ⓖⓖ **crater** (bowl for mixing wine with water) **of Derveni** and objects dating to the 4th c. There is also sculpture from the Archaic and Classical periods such as the ⓖⓖ **funerary stele** from Nea Kallikratia, as well as from Hellenistic and Roman times: portraits and remarkable ⓖ **funerary stelae,** ⓖ **the bronze head of Alexander Severus,** the headless ⓖ **statue of Aphrodite** and coloured glass vases. See the ⓖ **Roman**

Gold wreath from Derveni

mosaic floors with depictions of Dionysos and Ariadne, as well as of mythical sea monsters and the **Roman sarcophagi**, showing battles with the Amazons and representations of Dionysiac theatricals. Do not miss the marvellous exhibits of the **gold of the Macedonians**.

AGIOS DIMITRIOS
Άγιος Δημήτριος / Áyios Dimítrios

The first church was built in 313. Leontios made it into a triple-aisled basilica. It burned down in about 620 and was restored by the eparch Leo. Bishop Ioannis founded the five-aisled basilica which became a mosque in 1493. In 1917 it burned down again. It was rebuilt and opened again in 1948. Take note of the **marble revetments** and the **capitals** from the older church, the 5th to 12th c. **mosaics** and the 8th c. **fresco**. Visit the **crypt**, an underground maze-like area under the transept leading by a corridor to a pillared space with a niche, from which flowed the holy oil to fill the basins, as well as the **chapel of Agios Efthimios** with 13th c. frescoes.

Agios Dimitrios, crypt

LADADIKA
Τα Λαδάδικα / Ta Ladádika

The only quarter to survive the **1917** fire. It was once a storage and trading-place for olive oil ("ladi" in Greek) which developed into a red-light district for the entertainment of the merchants. Today, its buildings have been restored and is again a focal point with numerous tavernas and bars.

Ladadika

MUSEUM OF BYZANTINE CIVILIZATION
Μουσείο Βυζαντινού Πολιτισμού / Moussío Vizantinoú Politismoú

2 Stratou Ave., tel. (031) 868570-4

🕐 8 am-5 pm, Mondays 10:30 am-5 pm, closed on holidays*

The foundations of this museum, planned by the architect Kiriakos Krokos, were laid in 1989. The finds exhibited in it are arranged in groups according to subject matter.

AGIA SOPHIA
Αγία Σοφία / Ayía Sophía

Built in the 8th c. on the site of the five-aisled basilica of Agios Markos, it has 9th c. **mosaics** such as the **depiction of the Ascension** in the dome and **frescoes** of the early 11th c. The central drum is surrounded by pendentives and three apses. The columns have survived, with **early Christian capitals**.

THE WHITE TOWER
Λευκός Πύργος / Lefkós Pírgos

It was built either during the Venetian domination, or by Venetians in the first years of Ottoman domination. It is 30 m high and the diameter is 10 m. The Ottomans used it as a place for the execution of janissaries, which is why it was then known as "**Kanli-Koule**", the "**tower of blood**". It later became known as the White Tower because of its colour. It houses the **Museum of History and Art of Thessaloniki**, which presents by visual means the history of the city from the years AD 300 to 1430. There are also vases, tombstones, inscriptions, coins and icons.

The White Tower

CONTINENTAL GREECE

City Walls

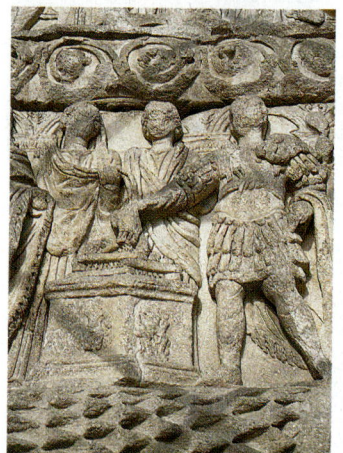

Arch of Galerius, relief

ⓢ WALLS AND EPTAPYRGIO
Τείχη και Επταπύργιο / Tíhi ke Eptapýrgio

The ancient walls were built by Kassandros at the end of the 4th c. BC and consisted of towers connected by curtain walls. The Byzantine fortifications were based on these, adding the acropolis and using the old Roman ramparts as foundations. On the flat spaces, triangular bulwarks were built, whereas on the safer inaccessible spots they are square.

ⓢ THE GALERIAN BUILDINGS
Το Γαλεριανό Συγκρότημα / To Galerianó Singrótima

ⓢ Rotunda (Agios Georgios)

This was part of a complex built in about AD 300. In the time of Theodosios the Great, it became the church of the Asomaton or Archangelon and in 1590 a mosque. Today it is a museum with antiquities of the Christian era.

ⓢ Arch of Galerius

It originally had four spans and its reliefs depict Galerius' victory in Asia in 298 AD.

Palace of Galerius

Built in the 4th c. AD, it consisted of a square **courtyard** surrounded by rooms. To the west, a luxurious **octagonal structure** has been discovered. To the east was the race course, the **Hippodrome**, over 400 m long, with the imperial box.

ⓢ THE TURKISH BATHS
Τα Χαμάμ / Ta Hamám

Bey Hamam, on Egnatias and Aristotelous Sts., was built in 1444. It is the biggest Turkish bath in Greece. **Pasha Hamami**, by the church of Agion Apostolon, built in 1520-30. **Yahudi Hamami** on Comnenon St. was built in about 1500-1550. **Geni Hamam** in Kassandrou St. dates to 1575-1600.

The Turkish Baths

ⓢ ROMAN AGORA
Ρωμαϊκή Αγορά / Romaikí Agorá

The forum, centre of public life under the Roman Empire. See the **crypt** and the **portico** where exhibitions are held, the paved **square**, the **odeon** where performances take place, the hot **baths** and the **brothel** next to them. The sculptures ornamenting the double portico on the ground floor were removed by the Frenchman Miller with a permit from the Turks and taken to the Louvre where they are on view today.

ⓢ FOLK ART-ETHNOLOGICAL MUSEUM OF MACEDONIA
Λαογραφικό και Εθνολογικό Μουσείο Μακεδονίας / Laografikó ke Ethnologikó Moussío Makedonías

Presently undergoing renovation, phone for information
68 Vassilisis Olgas St., tel. (031) 830591

In a three-storeyed building by architect Eli Modiano, under preservation, it was inaugurated in 1970. It contains exhibits of the cultural folk-art heritage and tradition of Northern Greece, such as traditional objects, costumes, handwoven cloth, embroideries.

THESSALONIKI

CHURCH OF THE ACHEIROPOIETOU
Ναός της Αχειροποίητου / Naós tis Ahiropíitou

A triple-aisled basilica with a wooden roof. In the middle of the southern wall there is a commemorative portal. It was built in 447 and is decorated with **sculptures**, **mosaics** and **paintings**. The **frescoes** are dated 1225-1250.

PANAGIA HALKEON
Παναγία Χαλκέων / Panayía Halkéon

Built in 1028 in a cross-in-square design with a dome, narthex and upper floor. Under Ottoman domination it became a mosque named **Kazantzilar tzami** meaning "of the coppersmith" (Greek "halkos" = copper). The wall paintings date back to the 11th, 12th and 14th c.

MOSQUES
Τα τζαμιά / Ta tzamiá

Hamza Bey, on the corner of Egnatias and Venizelou Sts, and **Alaca Imaret** (Isak Pasha) on the corner of Kassandrou and Sophokleous streets, built in **1484**.

MODIANO MARKET
Αγορά Μοδιάνο / Agorá Modiáno

Built by Eli Modiano in 1922, it is situated between Aristotelous, Ermou, B. Irakliou and Komnenon streets. It is oblong in shape with a pedimented facade and glass roof sheltering meat –and various kind of food– stalls. You'll discover friendly little watering-holes for ouzo and tsipouro, the local spirits, with traditional titbits and the atmosphere of Asia Minor to the sound of clarinets, drums and tabors inducing visitors and locals to lunchtime revelries.

Modiano Market

FREE TIME

The **International Fair** lasts for 9 days from the second Friday in September and promotes a wide range of industrial, artisanal, agricultural and animal-husbandry products. It is the biggest fair of the Balkans.
The **International Film Festival** in November attracts participants from the world over. The **Greek Song Festival** every September and the **Demetria** in October present artistic events. The **casino** is the country's largest, for those who enjoy gambling in a sophisticated cosmopolitan atmosphere.

BEST BEACHES

There are no good beaches near the city. Locals and young people tend to go to **Kassandra** in the Halkidiki Peninsula, an hour away. We recommend **Sithonia** (see **Excursion 42**), which is a little farther on the middle prong of the peninsula, as it has not been overly affected by tourism and has a number of exceptional beaches. Closer is **Agia Triada**, 22 km east of Thessaloniki, to which you can easily go and come back in a day.

BEST HOTELS

BEST LOCATION

Since the sights, most of the restaurants, cafes and bars are in the town centre, this is where you should stay. Thessaloniki's few better hotels are expensive and many are in poor condition externally, even when the interior has been renovated. If you have a car, arrange for parking space, which could be a problem in Thessaloniki.

PRICES

The hotel prices mentioned below are the official ones set by the National Tourist Organization for double rooms, at low and high season, with breakfast. Since owners are allowed to modify prices, always try to negotiate them.

CONTINENTAL GREECE

CENTRAL

✓✓✓ ELECTRA PALACE
(A Class)

9 Aristotelous Sq.
Tel. (031) 232221, 235947, fax 235947
Open: All year round

Description: Cosmopolitan atmosphere, comfortable, luxurious, and rooms with a view.
Rooms: 131 rooms with A/C, telephone, TV and bath.
Special features: Parking, restaurant, courteous service and lavish breakfasts.
Price: 35,800-49,400 drs.
Value for money: ✹✹✹
Credit cards: All

✓✓✓ MEDITERRANEAN PALACE
(Luxury Class)

3 Salaminos & Karatassou Sts.
Tel. (031) 552554, 551752, fax 552622
Open: All year round

Description: Luxury and comfort in the neo-classical style, perhaps occasionally excessive in the decoration but the service is excellent, with modern conveniences, a good view and high standards.
Rooms: 118 rooms with A/C, TV, telephone, room service, a safe and bath.
Special features: Parking, restaurant, bar, facilities for businessmen.
Price: 60,500 drs.
Value for money: ✹✹
Credit cards: Visa, American Express, Mastercard, Diners

✓✓ CAPSIS HOTELS (A Class)

18 Monastiriou St.
Tel. (031) 521321, 521421, fax 510555
Open: All year round

Description: Modernized and well equipped, with efficient services, conference and entertainment areas.
Rooms: 428 rooms with A/C, telephone, TV, room service.
Special features: Garage, restaurant, bar, pool and public spaces.
Price: 38,900-48,900 drs.
Value for money: ✹✹
Credit cards: All

✓ ABC (B Class)

41 Angelaki St.
Tel. (031) 265421, fax 276542
Open: All year round
Description: It has no view but is comfortable, impeccably clean and has good service. Modernized in stages since 1998. The best location for the International Fair. Simple, but good value.
Rooms: 99 rooms with A/C, TV, telephone and room service.
Special Features: Restaurant and bar. Pets upon request.
Price: 28,900-39,000 drs.
Value for money: ✹✹
Credit cards: All

LESS CENTRAL

✓✓✓ MAKEDONIA PALACE
(Luxury Class)

2 Megalou Alexandrou Ave.
Tel. (031) 861400, 861052, 860364, fax 868942
Open: All year round

THESSALONIKI 41

Description: The interior underwent general renovation in 1995, and in 1998 the suites and 8th floor were modernized. It is the best in town, with the **Porfira** restaurant, a fantastic view of the town and the sea, faultless service, a sophisticated air and luxurious, beautifully decorated interior.
Rooms: 287 rooms with A/C, TV, telephone, bath.
Special features: Parking, restaurant, pool, gym, facilities for businessmen, functions and conference room.
Price: 55,500-80,500 drs.
Value for money: ✹✹
Credit cards: Visa, American Express, Mastercard, Diners

✓✓ PANORAMA (A Class)

26 Analipseos St., Panorama
Tel. (031) 341123, fax 341266
Open: All year round

Description: A 1970 construction, with excellent interior renovation in 1996, a splendid view, friendly service. Don't be put off by the facade.
Rooms: 50 rooms with A/C, telephone, bath.
Special features: Parking, restaurant, bar.
Price: 54,400-63,700 drs.
Value for money: ✹
Credit cards: All

OUT OF TOWN

✓✓✓ HYATT (Luxury Class)

Hyatt Regency Thessaloniki
13th km, Thessaloniki - Peraia road
Tel. (031) 491234, fax 491257
Open: All year round
Description: Inaugurated in 1999. Surrounded by 90,000 sq m of grounds, this hotel represents the height of luxury and is one of the best in the Balkans.
Rooms: 152 rooms and suites, with A/C, minibar, satellite TV, radio, safe and telephone with automatic answering machine modem. Most rooms have access to the garden or balcony.
Special features: Parking, gym, 1 squash and 2 tennis courts, outdoor, indoor and children's pools, jacuzzi, children's supervision, reception room, Ambrosia restaurant, lobby lounge, Oceania grill bar, facilities for conferences and functions. The hotel organizes recreational activities such as mountain climbing, mountain biking, excursions. It also boasts an ultra-modern fitness centre and the Regency Casino, among the largest in Europe.
Price: 94,000 drs.
Value for money: ✹✹
Credit cards: All

✓✓ SUN BEACH (A Class)

Agia Triada, 24 km east of Thessaloniki
Tel. (0392) 51221, fax (0392) 51245
Open: All year round
Description: Next to the beach, with an excellent taverna by a swimming pool.
Rooms: 123 rooms with A/C, TV, telephone, room service.
Special features: Parking, restaurant, bar, pool, conference room, pets upon request.
Price: 29,500 drs.
Value for money: ✹✹
Credit cards: Visa, American Express, Mastercard

ALTERNATIVES

CAPITOL (A Class)
8 Monastiriou St., tel. (031) 516221, fax 517453. **Price:** 32,000-44,000 drs.

ASTORIA (B Class)
Tsimiski & 9 Salaminos Sts., tel. (031) 554902, fax 531564. **Price:** 40,000-48,000 drs.

HOTEL PHILIPPION (B Class)
7, Komvos, Thessaloniki ring road (Periferiaki Odos), tel. (031) 248500, fax 218528.
Price: 34,900 drs.

… CONTINENTAL GREECE

BEST RESTAURANTS & TAVERNAS

The city's appeal to the taste-buds is stimulating. Make your selection from the wide variety we have to propose according to your tastes and inclination.

✓✓ PORFIRA

2 Megalou Alexandrou St., Hotel Makedonia Palace, tel. (031) 861400

Probably the best restaurant in Thesssaloniki. The colours white and red predominate and add distinction to the decor. Dishes of impeccable appearance with the air of French cuisine, first-rate ingredients and imaginative combinations. View on the Thermaicos Gulf, irreproachable service.
Price: €€€

✓✓ LIVING ROOM

61, Twenty-Eight October St., tel. (031) 540607

The winter quarters of the **Moomba**, the "in" club-restaurant with good cuisine, luxurious and comfortable interior, attention to detail, customers of all ages and pleasing music.

Price: €€€

✓ CANTELLA'S

100 Themistokli Sophouli St., tel. (031) 420600

One of Thessaloniki's most "in" bar-restaurants, it suits all ages. Good music, good food and a view of the city and the Thermaicos Gulf.
Price: €€€

✓ ZYTHOS

21 Katouni St., Ladadika, tel. (031) 540284

The best and one of the oldest in Ladadika. A lively, friendly atmosphere, 50 different brands of beer, very good service, interesting combinations of dishes. Try the vegetable fritters, cypriot seftalia (grilled meat balls) and tagliatelle with vegetables.
Price: €

✓ MOOMBA

11th km on the Thessaloniki-Mihaniona road, tel. (031) 472160
A club-restaurant in the colonial style, for summer only.
Price: €€€

✓ OUZERI ARISTOTELOUS

Aristotelous Sq., tel. (031) 233195

One of the outstanding ouzeri (a traditional institution for drinking ouzo, accompanied by appetizers) in an arcade among old houses. Delicious mussels pilaf stuffed squid and charcoal-baked potatoes.
Price: €

THESSALONIKI

✓ ERMIS

4 Rongoti St., tel. (031) 224962, 270783

An "ouzeri" in a general store with the ambiance of the old days in an old building. Delicious hors d'oeuvres.
Price: €

✓ TASTE OF CHINA

64 Analipseos St., Panorama, tel. (031) 343880
Probably the best Chinese restaurant in Greece, specializing in lobsters.
Price: €€€

✓ ARCHIPELAGOS

1 Kanari St., Nea Krini, tel. (031) 435800, 444325
One of the best fish-tavernas with a varied choice and impressive aquarium. Marine decor, attentive service and pleasant atmosphere. Parking.
Price: €€

✓ AZZURO

86 Themistokles Sophoulis St., tel. (031) 419294
With a veranda by the sea, unusual flavours, a good wine list and relaxed ambiance.
Price: €€

✓ SHARK

2 Argonafton & Sofoulis Sts., tel. (031) 416855
A modernized club-restaurant on the seashore with top-notch food. The filet of beef is outstanding.
Price: €€

✓ NOVE CENTO

21 Andreou Georgiou St., Vilka,
Tel. (031) 528137
Superb authentic Italian cuisine, tasteful interior, satisfactory service and interesting wine list.
Price: €€

✓ PAO-PAO

21 Twenty-Six October St., Vilka,
Tel. (031) 556313-4
Hot spicy Mexican dishes in a decor filled with bright colours and Latin sounds. Try the tapas with vegetables, sea food or meat. Agreeable service, lively atmosphere.
Price: €€

✓ REMVI

2 Kanari St., Nea Krini, tel. (031) 447986
The old **Remvi** done over. Greek and international food.
Price: €€

✓ MAÏAMI

18 Thetidos St., Nea Krini, tel. (031) 447996
The place for fresh fish. First-class service.
Price: €€

✓ KRIKELAS

32 Ethnikis Antistasseos St., tel. (031) 351690
A taverna renowned since 1940, basks in its glory from the past, with a variety of hors d'oeuvre, tasty venison, desserts a speciality and well-stocked wine cellar. Time-tested quality and professional service.
Price: €

BEST ENTERTAINMENT

Those of you who like a night out in the town will find here that the "Bride of the Thermaicos Gulf" is the city of your dreams. Throngs of young people complement their university studies every night in the many bars, cafes and nightclubs, mingling with the visitors to the various fairs and events, as well as with the local inhabitants who have an age-old tradition in revelry and merry-making. Start with a cup of coffee on the boulevard along the waterfront or on Proxenou Koromila Street, at the "in hangouts" **Balkan** and **Ethnic** with mosaics and ethnic decor. In Ladadika, try the delicacies served in the typically Greek equivalents of a pub, frequented mostly by the young for drinks and snacks, while listening to the popular "rebetika" music. The **Bel Air** in Vogatsikou St. is the meeting place for the smart set any time of day. At the **Bulsit**, its owners, television stars, give a show to the bar's best advantage. Don't miss the airport area where among others, fans of the silver screen at **Mousses** provide good fun. At the **Ex-pose** in Angelaki St. you'll find pretty faces and a choice of advanced musical experiences. **Greco** in Pavlou Mela St. is on four levels, rock music and restaurant in the basement. To make the best acquaintances, with Greeks and lots of others, **Ipnovates** is the place. In the **Sfagia** area, you can choose among **Milos**, **Vilka** and **Fix** where the most demanding tastes will be satisfied.

Continental Greece

MILOS, tel. (031) 516945. On the premises of the old Hadjigianaki flour mill, at this time-proven domain of Thessaloniki's culture and recreation, famous personalities of the international arts, theatre and music world can be seen. In the **Kipos ton Pringipon**, the cafe, bars and clubs as well as the exhibition space are collected in these most attractive old stone constructions which have been aesthetically restored and simply, very elegantly decorated to combine past memories with operational efficiency and modern design. You can enjoy good films at the open air cinema.

VILKA, 21 Andreou Georgiou Street. A cultural and amusement centre, with a theatre since 1996, in what used to be a factory for burlap, canvas and sacks. Shops, cafes, restaurants, bars and art galleries for all tastes in a multi-purpose quality centre. The **Cinema** is for a coffee in the square with young people and film fans.

i TIPS AND INFORMATION

HOW TO GET THERE

- By air from Athens, west airport, by Olympic Airways (18,600 drs.), tel. (01) 9363363. By Air Greece, east airport, tel. (01) 3255011. By Cronus Airlines, east airport, tel. (01) 9956400.
- By rail, Athens OSE, ordinary ticket price from 4,100 drs. Intercity ticket price from 8,250 drs., tel. (01) 5297777.
- By intercity bus, Athens KTEL, 100 Kifissou Ave., tel. (01) 5148856, 260 Liossion Ave., tel. (01) 8317059, Attikis (18 Mavromateon St. & Alexandras Ave., Pedio tou Areos), tel. (01) 8225148, ticket price from 7,700 drs.

CONNECTIONS

- By air from Thessaloniki by Olympic Airways, tel. (031) 260121, to Rhodes, Corfu, Ioannina, Heraklio, Chania, Limnos, Mytilini, Samos, Chios. In summer there are flights to Mykonos and Santorini. There are also direct flights from Thessaloniki to London, Paris, Munich, Stuttgart, Frankfurt, Copenhagen, Belgrade, Istanbul, Milan, Brussels, Amsterdam, Berlin, Dusseldorf, Bucharest, Tirana, Larnaka, tel. (031) 230240. By Air Greece to Iraklio and Araxo Achaias. By Cronus Airlines, tel. (031) 870555, to Iraklio.
- By Minoan Flying Dolphins hydrofoil from Thessaloniki to Moudania Halkidiki, Alonissos, Skopelos, Skiathos, Skyros, Kymi, Ai-Gianni (Pelion), summer only. Thessaloniki office, tel. (031) 547407.
- By ferry from Thessaloniki to Limnos, Mytilini, Chios, Rhodes, Kos, Samos, Naxos, Volos, Mykonos, Paros, Santorini, Syros, Tinos, Skiathos, Heraklio. Only in summer to Alonissos, Skopelos, Skiathos. Thessaloniki Port Authority, tel. (031) 531505.
- By intercity bus, for destinations in Northern Greece, Thessaly, Epirus, Central Greece, Peloponnese, KTEL, tel. (031) 510835.

BEST TIPS

HOW TO GET AROUND: Since parking is such a problem, better go by taxi, or walk, for your trips around town. For sightseeing consult your hotel, they could book you on a coach tour.

BEST SEASON: Contrary to other parts of Greece, Thessaloniki is at its liveliest from September to November. In our opinion, any time of year is favourable for a visit, except high summer when the humidity and the heat can be unpleasant.

BEST LOCAL FOOD: Kondosouvli (skewered meat cubes), **soutzoukakia** (meat balls in tomato sauce), **tzigerosarmas** (stuffed lamb's caul), **gardoumba** (innards in a twist), **splina gemisti** (stuffed intestines), **ameletita** (lamb's fries), **loukaniko horiatiko** (country sausage), **kebab**, **kolokithokeftedes** (courgette fritters), **spedzofai** (sausage with hot peppers and tomato) and in the seafood line: mussels pan-fried or plain fried, mussel pilaf, grilled sardines, stuffed squid. There are also oriental syrupy sweetmeats such as **malebi** and **touloumbes** and especially the traditional cream-filled pastries called **bougatsa**, baked in a wood-burning oven.

USEFUL TELEPHONE NUMBERS

THESSALONIKI	(031)	Police	416787
Town Hall	238321	Tourist Guides	546037
Tourist Police	554871	Taxis	214841, 214900, 214780, 214964

SITHONIA

WHY AMONG THE BEST

Because Sithonia's scenery is of exceptional natural beauty — pine forests, superb sandy beaches in isolated bays and deserted coves, deep fjords, with steep cliffsides, sharply indenting the rugged coast which is ideal for spear-fishing. Because prices are reasonable and you can combine your trip with a visit to Mount Athos.

CONTINENTAL GREECE

SITHONIA

BEST's OPINION

Sithonia is perfect for quiet, inexpensive holidays far from urban stress. Young people may prefer neighbouring Kassandra, which offers more entertainment choices.
Sithonia numerous forests make it suitable for camping in many of its beautiful locations. More social activities can be found at the Porto Carras hotels.

IN BRIEF

Sithonia is the middle peninsula of Halkidiki, fertile, and lush, it boasts isolated coves and pretty beaches. It has a cool climate, with abundant rainfall in spring and autumn. Its villages are built in the traditional Macedonian style and the inhabitants are employed in tourism, farming and fishing.

HISTORY

Sithonia got its name from the Sithones, a Thracian tribe who settled there in the 5th c. BC. The Chalcidians established ancient Greek cities (Galipsos, Parthenopolis, Sartis, etc.), which later were subjected to the Persians. In 384 BC, they came under the sovereignty of Philip of Macedon and later, of his son Alexander the Great. They were conquered by the Romans in 168 BC.
During Byzantine times, most of Sithonia was a dependency of the Mount Athos monasteries, which suffered several barbarian invasions. In the 15th c. the region was under the Turkish yoke. Though it participated in the Greek revolution in 1821 it did not become part of the Greek state in 1912.

BEST SIGHTS: STEP BY STEP

❶ NEOS MARMARAS
Νέος Μαρμαράς / Néos Marmarás

Founded in 1922 by refugees from Asia Minor, it was once a dependency of the Mount Athos monastery of Agios Grigorios. Today, it is a large tourist village, with many small hotels and tavernas and most of Sithonia's entertainment locales. There is an interesting local event every September, the **tuna-fishing** festival.

❷ PARTHENONAS
Παρθενώνας / Parthenónas

A largely abandoned settlement, with traditional-style houses and traces of a Byzantine fortress and walls. In the village, you can have a meal or coffee at the **Parthenon** taverna, which offers a spectacular view of the sea and all of Kassandra.

❸ PORTO CARRAS
Πόρτο Καρράς / Pórto Karrás

(see **Best Hotels and Rooms**)
Even if you don't stay here, it's certainly worth a visit.

Parthenonas

CONTINENTAL GREECE

❹ FROM PORTO CARRAS TO ORMOS PANAGIAS

The excursion we propose is a circuit starting at Porto Carras, continuing to Porto Koufo and Vourvourou and reaching Panagia Bay. After Porto Carras take the road to the right going south between the main road and the sea. It is more scenic. You must definitely make this trip on which you'll be treated to magnificent landscapes, with verdant hills and plains, bays and promontories, coves and beaches with turquoise waters. Your first stop will be **Ormos Toronis**, a small promontory, with a wide, sandy beach. On the southern side, are the traces of an ancient fort, as well as the ruins of Early Christian basilicas. Continue towards **Porto Koufo**, Thucydides' Kofos Limenas, in a protected bay surrounded by forested hills and full of fishing caiques which bring in the fresh fish served in the small tavernas. Between Porto Koufo and Kalamitsi, you can sidetrack to **Akrotiri Drepano**, a rocky cape, with numerous creeks forming small fjords.

Porto Carras

Returning to the main road, you will reach **Sykia** and **Skala Sykias**, with its lovely **beach**, and cross **Sarti**, a small cultivated coastal plain with a number of quiet beaches. You can stop at any one of these for a quick dip, but don't forget that just a few kilometres down the road is the enchanting **Armenistis** beach, while a little further, just before **Vourvourou**, you can swim at **Karydi** beach. Vourvourou is a holiday village nestled in dense greenery, with attractive promontories, villas, hotels and restaurants, and in the background, the island of **Diasporos**. At the end of the excursion, you can relax in a picturesque village set in a rocky bay, **Ormos Panagias**. From here, boats leave every morning for Mount Athos.

Porto Koufo

BEYOND THIS EXCURSION

MOUNT ATHOS *(See Excursion 43)*
Visit Mount Athos by boat from Ormos Panagias.

PETRALONA CAVE - MUSEUM
In the village of Petralona or Kokkines Petres
Tel. (0373) 31300
Summer 9 am-6:30 pm, winter 9 am-4:30 pm, closed on holidays*.

In the cave, apart from a primeval Neanderthal-man skull, bones of animals were found, extinct for thousands of years (mammoth, rhinoceros, cave bear and lions). See the **Cemetery of Giants** hall, the spectacular stalactites and stalagmites in the passages which extend for 2 km and don't miss the finds on display at the adjacent museum.

KASSANDRA PENINSULA

An interesting one-day excursion to the most cosmopolitan of Halkidiki's prongs. Kassandra has a more developed tourist infrastructure but is less beautiful than Sithonia. It is the Thessalonikans' summer resort and many have built holiday homes there. Worth visiting are the coastal villages of **Polychronos**, **Hanioti** and **Pefkohori**, with their pretty beaches, and **Agia Paraskevi** with its mineral springs.

SITHONIA

🏖 BEST BEACHES

There are many beautiful beaches. And if you search, you'll find more.

⛱⛱⛱ KAVOUROTRYPES

One of Greece's most stunning beaches. The clear, blue waters, reminiscent of the Caribbean, and the rocks, which seem to have been sculpted by an artist, make it quite unique.

⛱⛱⛱ ARMENISTIS

An exquisite sandy beach with turquoise waters. Unfortunately, a camping site has fenced off some of the shore.

⛱⛱ KALOGRIA

A large beach with coarse-grained, but excellent quality, sand. Beach umbrellas and reclining beach chairs can be rented, but the environment remains unspoilt and beautiful. The pine-trees and poplars grow all the way down to the sand.

⛱⛱ LAGOMANDRA

Coarse sand beach with opportunity for water sports and tall pines for shade as well as unintrusive umbrellas, but nowhere in the neighbourhood to have a meal.

⛱⛱ KALAMITSI

A bay protected by rocks, with a marvellous sandy beach and an islet. The few hotels, tavernas and bars don't ruin the setting. To eat, go to Giorgakis.

⛱⛱ SKALA SYKIAS

At the signpost for Linaraki, turn into the narrow asphalt road. After a short, pleasant detour, you'll reach a series of lovely small beaches. For meals, the tavernas **5 Vimata Stin Ammo** or **Akrogiali** are best.

⛱⛱ PLATANITSI

A large beach with white sand, in a community camping site, which also allows non-campers to swim. A lot of shady trees and sheep to keep you company.

⛱⛱ KARYDI (VOURVOUROU)

South of Vourvourou. White sand, turquoise water, pine trees and striking rock formations. An excellent beach bar, **Lotos**, is located here.

🛏 BEST HOTELS AND ROOMS

BEST LOCATION

The best hotels as well as the nightlife are concentrated in the Porto Carras and Neos Marmaras areas. However, if you'd like to stay at Halkidiki's finest hotel complex, then choose **Sani Beach Hotel**, despite the fact that it's in Kassandra. In terms of luxury, it's on a par with Porto Carras, but a newer building. From there, you can visit Sithonia on one-day excursions. The prices in Sithonia are much more reasonable.

PRICES

The hotel prices mentioned below are the official ones, set by the National Tourist Organization for double rooms, at low and high season, with breakfast. Since owners are allowed to modify prices, always try to negotiate them.

✓✓ PORTO CARRAS HOTEL COMPLEX

Coastal resort on a private 4,500 acre estate, shipowner John Carras' life's work, completed in the early 1970s. The concept and the buildings were unique at that time and it was considered one of the finest and most luxurious resorts in Europe. The complex comprises two magnificent hotels, the **Meliton** and the **Sithonia**, as well as a coastal village with a marina, the **Village Inn**. Guests can choose from a broad range of activities such as water sports, tennis, etc.

One of the main features of the complex is the quiet, well-designed **casino**, with all games including 'one-armed bandits'. The golf course — rather neglected lately — is considered one of the finest, in terms of landscape architecture. The club has six beautiful horses for riding enthusiasts.

Near the hotels is John Carras' GG **model farm**, with olive, orange and lemon trees, plus vineyards producing top-quality wines. Don't miss the marvellous **walk** along the coastal road going south through the estate. Around you is the forest, the sea on your right and the estate's 33 coves are at your disposal.

After Carras's death, the hotels have been experiencing the problems of change of ownership. However, they are still an excellent choice.

✓✓ GRECOTEL MELITON HOTEL (Luxury Class)

Tel. *(0375) 71501, fax 71502*
Open: April-October
Description: A striking modern building, with numerous comforts and facilities, part of Porto Carras.
Rooms: 447 rooms with A/C, telephone, etc.
Special features: Superb view of the organized beach, a restaurant, bar and many other features.
Price: 36,400-56,300 drs.
Value for money: ✱✱
Credit cards: All

✓✓ SITHONIA CASINO BEACH HOTEL (A Class)

Tel: *(0375) 72500, 71381, 71121, fax 72504*
Open: All year round

Description: Modern building, hosting the casino. Part of Porto Carras.
Rooms: 453 rooms with A/C, telephone and sea view.
Special features: Comfortable, with a spectacular view and good service. Also features the outstanding ✓✓ **Orangerie** restaurant. Musical events are organized.
Price: 27,000-46,300 drs. (Reduction if you use the casino)
Value for money: ✱✱
Credit cards: All

✓✓ ATHENA PALLAS HOTEL (A Class)

Elia beach
Tel. *(0375) 81410, fax 81418*
Open: All year round
Description: Built in 1996 at Elia beach. Luxury, with outstanding architecture. Probably the best hotel after Porto Carras.
Rooms: 90 rooms and 3 suites, with A/C, TV, telephone and mini-bar.
Special features: Narrow private beach, swimming pool, small folk museum with traditional fabrics and looms, excellent taverna, children's playground, tennis court, bar and restaurant.
Price: 20,000-45,500 drs. half board
Value for money: ✱
Credit cards: Visa, American Express, Mastercard

✓ PARTHENONAS

Parthenonas
Tel. *(094) 382384*
Open: All year round
Description: Traditional-style building with a beautiful garden in peaceful surroundings.
Rooms: 12 rooms with bath.
Special features: Restaurant, lounge for breakfast, prepared by the hotel's owner, including homemade pies.

SITHONIA 42

Price: 13,000-15,000 drs.
Value for money: ✱✱
Credit cards: None

✓ ANTHEMUS SEA HOTEL-VILLAGE (C Class)

Nikiti
Tel. (0375) 7200, fax 72202
Open: April-October
Description: Built in 1993 in traditional style.
Rooms: 79 rooms with a view, A/C, TV, telephone.
Special features: Well-designed public areas. Swimming pool, plus a mediocre sandy beach with beach umbrellas and reclining beach chairs. Good service, bar, and taverna serving fresh fish.
Price: 23,300-41,000 drs.
Value for money: ✱
Credit cards: None

BEYOND THIS EXCURSION

✓✓✓ PORTO SANI VILLAGE (A Class)

Sani peninsula, Kassandra
Tel. (0374) 31570-3, fax 31574
Open: April-October
Description: A large complex, next to the peninsula. With a village, villas and a marina, in a luxuriant green environment. One of Northern Greece's best hotels.
Rooms: 489 deluxe rooms with A/C, TV, telephone, balcony.
Special features: Parking, swimming pools, gardens, verandas, restaurants, bars and water sports.
Price: 46,000-109,000 drs.
Value for money: ✱✱
Credit cards: All

ALTERNATIVES

KELYFOS HOTEL

Tastefully designed with garden and pool, above Porto Carras, tel. (0375) 72833.
Price: 24,000-34,000 drs.

ROOMS
MAGDA'S ANAGNOSTOUDI

Lagomandra, tel. (0375) 81397, 71056.
Price: 12,000 without breakfast

MARMARAS (C Class)

Neos Marmaras, tel. (0375) 72185, fax 72315.
Price: 13,000-16,000 drs.

LIKYTHOS VILLAGE (B Class)

11 km south of Neos Marmaras in the Koutsoupia area, tel. (0375) 72547-8, fax 72636
Price: 19,000-24,000 drs.

BEST RESTAURANTS & TAVERNAS

NEOS MARMARAS

✓ HARIS

Tel. (0375) 71465
Excellent, but expensive, serves fresh fish and appetizers.
Price: €€€

✓ TA KYMATA

Tel. (0375) 71371
On the sand, next to the sea. Fresh charcoal-grilled fish from the owner's own fishing boat.
Price: €€

CHRISTOS

Tel. (0375) 71974
Open all day. On a rock, next to the sea. Fish, as well as ready-cooked dishes. Food, service, surroundings and view are all outstanding.
Price: €€

ZOE'S LITTLE CHINA

Tel. (0375) 72064
Tasteful premises with well made Chinese specialities. A hospitable environment, with good service, view of the main square and the port.
Price: €€

Continental Greece

MYTHOS

Tel. (0375) 71441
Restaurant-beach bar. At Marmaras beach, in a pleasant setting. Open for lunch and dinner.
Price: €

PARADISSOS

Tel. (0375) 71376
At Paradissos beach, under a vine arbour, with a sea view. Ready-cooked, meat dishes and appetizers.
Price: €

PORTO CARRAS
✓✓ **ORANGERIE**

Sithonia Hotel, tel. (0375) 71221
International cuisine, for the most demanding palates. Superb decor, outstanding service and a view of the garden with orange trees. **Price:** € € €

Organgerie

VOURVOUROU
GORGONA (OR PULLMAN)

Tel. (0375) 91461
At the beach. The best fish taverna in Vourvourou.
Price: €

BEST ENTERTAINMENT

Sithonia's nightlife is concentrated along the Neos Marmaras coast road, featuring a variety of attractive cafes, bars and night clubs.
In Marmaras, we recommend the **Molos** – a particularly elegant bar with good music – and then **Vareladiko**, on the ring-road, for Greek music.
A very good choice is the **Ethnik** beach-bar, on the Tristinika beach, which combines swimming and entertainment all day.

TIPS AND INFORMATION

HOW TO GET THERE

- The best solution is to go by car so that you can explore Halkidiki.
- By air, from Athens to Thessaloniki, with Olympic Airways, west airport, tel. (01) 9363363. With Air Greece, east airport, tel. (01) 3255011. With Cronus Airlines, east airport, tel. (01) 9956400.
- By rail (OSE) to Thessaloniki, from Larissa station, Athens, ordinary service (from 4,100 drs.), or Intercity (from 8,250 drs.), tel. (01) 5297777.
- From Thessaloniki, you can hire a car to go to Sithonia.
- By intercity bus (KTEL) from Athens to Thessaloniki, (from 7,700 drs.), 100 Kifissou Ave., tel. (01) 5148856, 260 Liossion St., tel. (01) 8317059, Attiki (18 Mavromateion St. and Alexandras Ave., Pedio tou Areos), tel. (01) 8225148. From Thessaloniki by intercity bus (KTEL) to Sithonia, tel. (031) 924444.

BEST TIPS

HOW TO GET AROUND: An automobile or motorcycle is necessary to travel around Sithonia, as taxis and buses are few.

BEST SEASON: June or September, when the sea is warm, but even in July or August if you find accommodation, as the district is extensive and people are scattered among numerous beaches.

USEFUL TELEPHONE NUMBERS

NEOS MARMARAS	(0375)	Police	71111
Community Office	71242	Taxis	71500

MOUNT ATHOS (THE HOLY MOUNTAIN)

WHY AMONG THE BEST

Because Mount Athos, the Virgin's Garden, is a unique phenomenon in history, a purely Orthodox Christian monastic state. Nature has been virtually untouched by modern development. The monasteries with their Byzantine icons and frescoes, architecture, miniatures, manuscripts and rituals introduce the visitor (male) to a spiritual, intellectual and physical experience of the highest order.

CONTINENTAL GREECE

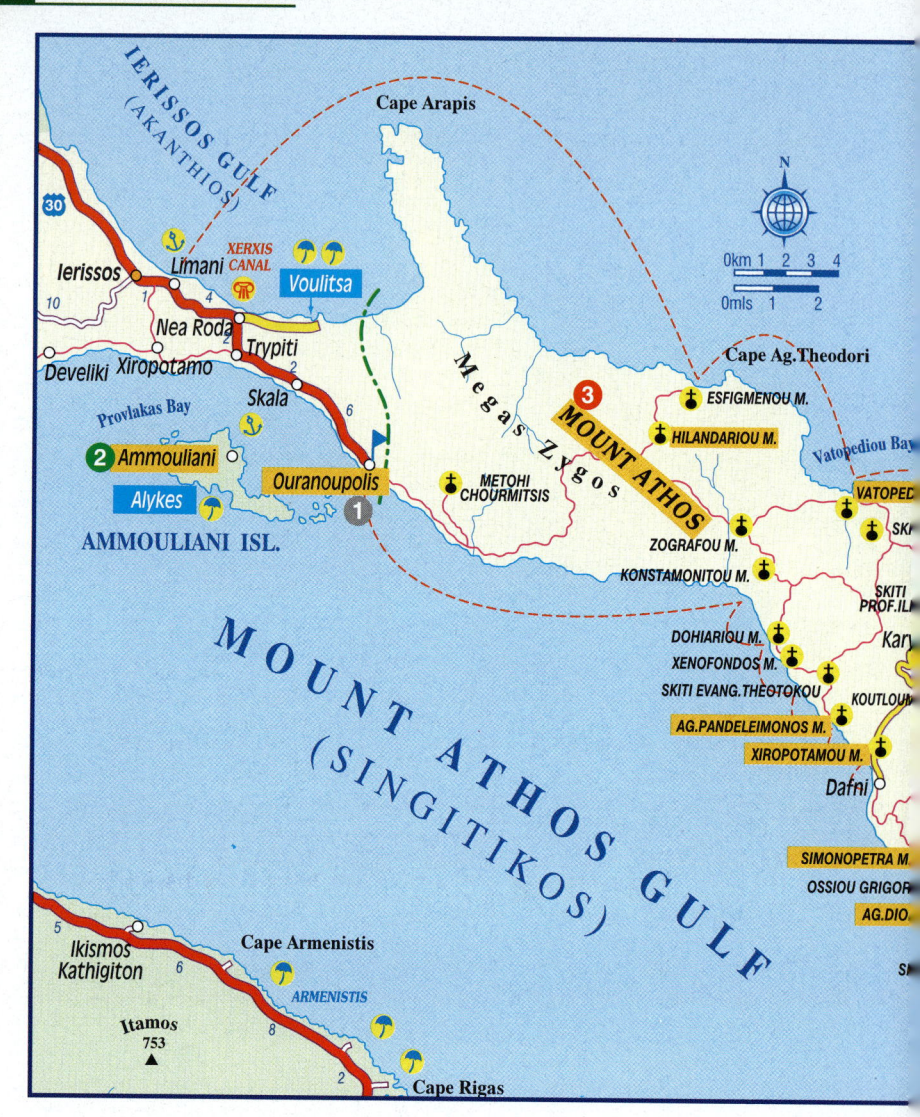

BEST's OPINION

This excursion is totally unlike any of the others in this guide, so before you decide to embark on it, study these pages carefully. Only men are permitted on the Holy Mountain itself, but women may get a taste, from a distance, of the beauty of the peninsula and the monasteries by taking a boat trip from nearby Ouranoupoli or from Cape Panagia on Sithonia.

Despite the encroachment of civilization and the sometimes bizarre behaviour of certain monks and lay people employed in the "worldly business" of the monastic state, Mount Athos remains a singular repository of inestimable religious, architectural and archaeological value.

Unfortunately you will see the most valuable treasures only in the illustrated books you may buy. Access to the heirlooms and libraries is prohibited without a special permit which is issued rarely and solely for scholarly purposes. What is left to the visitor is an unparalleled opportunity to live among pious people, to walk in magnificent scenery, and wander through medieval lanes and extraordinary buildings made by men who have renounced the material world and devoted their lives to the service of God.

MOUNT ATHOS

WHAT TO KNOW BEFORE YOU SET OFF

Access to the Holy Mountain is only possible by boat. Visitors depart from the port of Dafni or the harbour annexe at Iviron monastery. No other approach is possible without a special permit.

Greeks

a) Must address their request for a priority number to the Visitors' Office in Thessaloniki, tel. (031) **943181**, or in Ouranoupolis, tel. (0377) **71421**. You can give your particulars over the phone and will be added to the waiting list for an entry permit. The authorities allow entrance to 100 Orthodox and 10 non-Orthodox per day. The length of stay permitted is **4 days** (nights to be spent at 4 different monasteries). An extension (of **1** or **2** days) may be obtained by applying to the Holy Superintendency (Iera Epistasia) or you can also wait for a new stay permit *(diamonitirion)* and pay to be readmitted.

b) When you get to Ouranoupoli, you will need to present your ID and 4,000 drs. for the issuance of the stay permit. There is no charge for the hospitality offered at the monasteries (a bed and 2 meals).

Non-Greek Orthodox

Follow the same procedure as Greeks.

Non-Orthodox foreigners

a) Should first get a letter of recommendation from their embassy or consulate in Athens or Thessaloniki. Contact, tel. (031) **861611** for information.

b) Then apply for a permit from the Ministry of Foreign Affairs, the Ministry for Northern Greece or the Thessaloniki Aliens Bureau.

c) You will then be added to the waiting list of 10 people per day. It is advisable to apply well in advance, especially if you wish to visit in summer.

Additional notes

On Mount Athos the **avaton** is in force. This ban on women and all female animals was promulgated by the Byzantine emperor in 1060. Ships carrying women must remain at least 500 m from the coast of the peninsula. All visitors must observe the daily routine of the monasteries. Dress and behaviour must be in accordance with the sanctity of the place. Anyone creating a disturbance will be removed by the police. Groups and organized tours must be no larger than 15 people per day and need a written document from the Iera Epistasia and the monasteries.

Private yachts

Owners of pleasure craft and captains of ships that offer cruises around the peninsula are forbidden to come within 500 m of the Athos coast if women are on board. The use of loudspeakers and any other noises that might disturb the monks are also prohibited. Severe penalties are imposed on people who violate these rules and on women who attempt to slip through the avaton.

IN BRIEF

Mount Athos, the Holy Mountain, is the easternmost finger of the three-pronged Halkidiki peninsula. Its climate is humid and rainy and the landscape mountainous (Athos, the highest mountain is 2,033 m above sea level), with low, thickly wooded hills, rushing streams and dozens of rocky coves, where the trees often reach the water's edge. It is the home of more than a thousand monks and some 400 novices and hermits. Seventeen of the 20 monasteries are Greek, one is Russian (Agios Pandeleimon), one is Bulgarian (Zografou) and one Serbian

CONTINENTAL GREECE

(Hiliandari). There are also 12 sketes and at least 700 kellia and hermitages. The monasteries have divided up the peninsula and share its resources (logging in the forests, for example). They may be either **cenobitic**, whereby everything is owned in common or **idiorrhythmic**, where the monks work and eat individually. They are maintained with the revenues from the sale of timber and agricultural products, state subsidies and rents from their real estate in other parts of Greece. **Sketes**: Smaller establishments, either cenobitic or idiorrhythmic, which belong to some monastery. **Kellia**: Possessing a church and other buildings. The governing monastery awards them for life to three monks at a time. **Kalyves**: Isolated residences, also given for life to three monks by a monastery. **Kathismata**: Kalyves awarded for life to one monk each. **Hermitages**: Small caves or huts on the rocks where the hermit lives on whatever is brought to him, raising it up with a rope or pulley.

HISTORY

In the 8th c. BC colonists from the Euboean city-states of Eretria and Halkis settled on the peninsula and since then it has been known as Halkidiki. In Herodotos' day, 5th c. BC, the name Athos was used for the whole peninsula. Petros the Athonite was the first monk to arrive (7th c.). In 963, St. Athanasios the Athonite, together with a group of monks and with Nikephoros Phokas as benefactor, built the first and largest monastery, the Great Lavra, and drew up the **Proto Typiko**, which established the rules governing the monastic state.

The hermits were converted – not without resistance – to a communal way of life and began to cultivate the earth. In the 10th c. Vatopedi and Iviron were founded and in the 11th c. the emperor Alexios I Komninos passed decrees guaranteeing the autonomy of the Holy Mountain and prohibiting access to any female mammals. (Only hens and cats are permitted.)

The 12th c. ushered in a period of destruction and looting by Frankish Crusaders, the emperor Michail Palaiologos and the Catalan mercenaries of the emperor Andronikos Palaiologos (reducing the number of monks from 300 to 25). Under the Ottoman occupation the monastic state retained its independence and, until the 16th c., its prosperity. However, piracy and heavy taxation eventually caused the decline of the monasteries. In 1748 Mount Athos again became a spiritual centre with the founding of the **Athonite Academy**. In 1821 the monks took an active part in the Greek War of Independence, provoking the Turks to burn and loot the monasteries the following year.

Since 1926 Mount Athos has been a self-governing theocracy included within the Greek state. It is answerable to the Patriarchate in spiritual matters and to the local representative (prefectural governor) from the ministry of Foreign Affairs for secular matters. It is administered from Karyes by the **Holy Council** or **Iera Synaxis**, where each monastery has an equal number of deputies and which has authority over judicial matters. The **Iera Epistasia** consisting of four rotating members is the executive authority.

ARCHITECTURE, ART, MANUSCRIPTS

The oldest building on Mount Athos is the Protaton in Karyes, followed by the churches of Iviron and Vatopedi (10th c.). Externally the monasteries resemble for-

Devotional painting by Panselinos

MOUNT ATHOS

tresses, with high walls, towers, ramparts, bastions and platforms above the gates for pouring boiling oil onto assailants. In the centre of the courtyard stands the church, the **katholikon**, with marble floors, columns crowned with capitals, and frescoes. Surrounding the church are the cloisters with the monks' cells. The refectory (**trapeza**), where the monks take their meals, is a one-storey building across from the church. The **phiale** or font stands between the refectory and the katholikon.

The manuscripts of the Byzantine and Post-Byzantine era are superb works of art with their illuminations and calligraphy and bejeweled bindings. About 45,000 such manuscripts are known to exist, of which 25,000 are in Greece proper and 12,000 on Mount Athos. They contain the works of ancient Greek writers (600), texts by Church Fathers, Gospels and Byzantine writings. Hundreds of them are on parchment (6th-9th c.), written in capital letters. The oldest (6th c.) and most important parchment consists of four sheets from the Epistles of St. Paul. In the 18th c., miniature painting flourished on the Holy Mountain, especially at the studio of Anthimos at Grigoriou.

A DAY ON MOUNT ATHOS

When you arrive at a monastery around noon, you will be greeted by the **portaris** at the **Portariki** (gate house) who will escort you to the **Archontariki** or guest quarters. The **archondaris** or guestmaster will inform you as to the hours of mass and meals and will take you to your dormitory. There are clean toilets, basins and sinks for washing clothes. At 5 pm the gong will strike for vespers and at about 6:30 dinner will be served in the refectory (**trapeza**). During meals, a monk reads from a religious text until the word *Amen* is heard. At the end everyone rises for the next prayer, said by the abbot. He then leads the way out followed by the monks in order of seniority. Another service follows the evening meal (the **apodeipno** or compline) and afterwards the monks take relics of the saints from the Reliquary and invite the visitors to pay their respects. After this, you are free until 9 or 10 pm, when everyone retires to bed. Around 3 or 4 am you will be awakened for another prayer service, the **mesonyktiko** (literally midnight), followed by **matins**, **hours** and the **Divine Liturgy**, which last until 6-6:30 am. Breakfast is served immediately afterwards and luckily consists of a real meal (not just bread and coffee), because you won't be served anything else until the evening.

BEST SIGHTS: STEP BY STEP

❶ OURANOUPOLI
Ουρανούπολη / Ouranoupoli

Founded in 315 BC by Aristarchos, this is a quiet, clean village of about a thousand inhabitants, most of whom are engaged in tourism. It has some attractive restaurants, bars and fish tavernas.

WHAT TO SEE

The **tower** on the quai. Built in 1344 by monks when the area was a dependency of Vatopedi monastery.

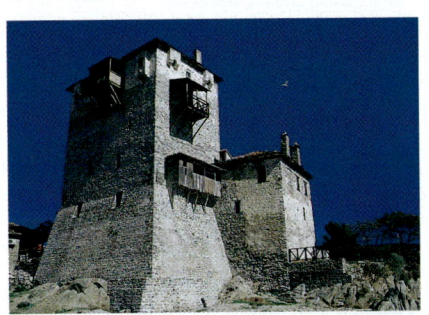

The Ouranoupoli tower

❷ AMMOULIANI
Αμμουλιανή / Ammoulianí

The verdant island of Ammouliani lies opposite Trypiti and can be reached from there by boat. Here you'll find unspoilt surroundings, deserted beaches and relative quiet. Once the island was a dependency of Vatopedi monastery. Take a look at the **Tarsanas** in the little harbour, where the monks used to keep their boats.

Nowadays many people come to its hidden coves with their boats to enjoy the wonderful **swimming** and eat fresh fish in one of its simple tavernas.

Ammouliani

CONTINENTAL GREECE

Skete of Agios Andreas

Karyes

Agiou Panteleimonos monastery

Xiropotamou monastery

Iviron monastery

❸ MOUNT ATHOS
Άγιον Όρος / Ágion Óros
(The Holy Mountain)

KARYES / Καρυές / Karyés

The capital of Mount Athos. It must be the only town in the world with no women's WCs. It does have a simple hotel (2,500 drs. a bed), a few restaurants and rudimentary shops for essentials. The **Protaton** is the town's cathedral. A cruciform basilica with three aisles, it was built in the 10th c. and has wonderful 14th c. **frescoes** by the famous painter Manuel Panselinos. Also worth seeing are the **Molyvoklissia** (lead church), the Athonias Theological Seminary and the **skete of Agios Andreas**.

🜨🜨 AGIOU PANTELEIMONOS MONASTERY / Μονή Αγίου Παντελεήμονος / Moní Agíou Panteleímonos

Tel. (0733) 23252

The original old monastery, which was built on a hillside, was founded in the late 10th c., but it was eventually abandoned and its monks erected a new monastery amidst the trees on the coast in 1765. A huge, barrack-like monastery, it once held 1,500 Russian monks but has a rather desolate air now owing to a fire in 1968. Numerous onion domes, a library full of Slavic manuscripts and Russian books and an enormous bell in the refectory are its proudest assets. The monastery honours its saint on July 27th.

🜨🜨 XIROPOTAMOU MONASTERY
Μονή Ξηροποτάμου / Moní Xiropotámou

Tel. (0733) 23251

Founded by the holy monk Pavlos Xiropotaminos, most of its buildings date from the 18th c. It was once especially wealthy and still has a good many treasures, including the largest known piece of the **Holy Cross**. It celebrates on March 9th, a day dedicated to the Forty Holy Martyrs.

🜨🜨🜨 SIMONOPETRA MONASTERY
Μονή Σίμωνος Πέτρας / Moní Símonos Pétras

Tel. (0733) 23254

Founded in the 13th c. by St. Simon. An impressive monastery with exceptional architecture, it consists of seven storeys built upon a high rock connected to the cliff by a single bridge. It contains 15 chapels, and it also counts a piece of the **Holy Cross** among its prize relics, as well as the hand of **Mary Magdelene**, and remains from other saints. It observes the Nativity of Christ (Dec. 25) as its feast day. It has been seriously damaged by fire on several occasions.

🜨🜨🜨 MEGISTIS LAVRAS MONASTERY (GRAND LAVRA) / Μονή Μεγίστης Λαύρας / Moní Megístis Lávras

Tel. (0733) 22586

The oldest and most impressive complex on Mount Athos was founded in the mid 10th c. by the monk Athanasios the Athonite. It is four-

MOUNT ATHOS

sided with 35 chapels and three sketes with the tower donated by the benefactor, emperor Tsimiskis, dominating the buildings from afar. This monastery has the richest collection of manuscripts, parchments and old books as well as exceptional frescoes by the great Cretan painter Theophanes in the refectory and katholikon, and the crown and vestments of Nikephoros Phokas in the sacristy. It celebrates the Annunciation of the Virgin on March 25th.

ⓖⓖⓖ IVIRON MONASTERY
Μονή Ιβήρων / Moní Ivíron

Tel. (0733) 23248

Founded in the 10th c. by Ioannis the Iberian (Georgian). This imposing monastery with its high walls contains the skete of **Timiou Prodromou** and 16 chapels, the most magnificent being the **Panagia tis Portaritissas** with its icon of the Virgin Guarding the Gate decorated with **precious stones**. It also boasts an important library and amongst its treasures is a piece of **Christ's robe** and **vestments belonging to the emperor Tsimiskis**. The Assumption of the Virgin on August 15th is the monastery's feast day.

ⓖⓖⓖ VATOPEDIOU MONASTERY
Μονή Βατοπεδίου / Moní Vatopedíou

Tel. (0733) 23219

Founded by three monks from Adrianople (Eastern Thrace). This commanding monastery has massive walls, towers and belfries, 18 chapels and 2 sketes. It possesses a rich library, mosaic portable icons of the 10th c. and many historic treasures, such as the **rod that supported the vinegar-soaked sponge from which Christ sipped while on the Cross** and the **Sacred Girdle of the Virgin Mary**. It celebrates the Annunciation (March 25th).

ⓖⓖ HILIANDARIOU MONASTERY
(SERBIAN) / Μονή Χιλιανδαρίου
/ Moní Hiliandaríou

Tel. (0733) 23797

Founded in the 12th c. by the Serbian prince Stefan Nemanja and his son Sava, who both became monks. Surrounded by thick vegetation, the fortified monastery was the spiritual centre of the Serbs for centuries. It has 13 chapels and its library contains Greek and Serbian codices and thousands of printed volumes. Among its prize relics is a piece of **Christ's shroud**, the **goblet** of the Serbian abbot **Stefan Dusan** and **five precious stones with the image of Christ**. The monastery celebrates the Presentation of the Virgin Mary on November 21st. The other **12 monasteries**, equally worth seeing and containing important art and relics, are: **Koutloumousiou**, **Zographou** (Bulgarian), **Docheiariou** and **Karakalou** (built like a fortress with a splendid tower on a thickly wooded slope), **Philotheou**, **Agiou Pavlou** and **Stavronikita** (with an aqueduct and Cretan School frescoes by Ioannis and his son Symeon), **Xenophontos**, **Grigoriou**, **Esphigmenou**, **Pantokratoros** and, finally, **Konstamonitou**, in a green gorge. Its library contains manuscripts, 3,500 printed books and a Gospel bound in gold and silver, which was a gift from the wife of Ali Pasha, the 19th c. "governor" of Epirus.

Vatopediou monastery

Koutloumousiou monastery

Stavronikita monastery

Docheiariou monastery

CONTINENTAL GREECE

BEST BEACHES

⛱⛱ AMMOULIANI
On this islet there are several lovely beaches with fine sand. Among them are **Alykes**, **Agios Georgios** and **Megali Ammoudara**.

⛱⛱ VOULITSA (NEA RODA)
A small bay with a beautiful sandy beach, clear waters and a bar with a pergola and flowers.

Alykes

BEST HOTELS AND ROOMS

BEST LOCATION
There are no hotels on Mount Athos, but visitors may stay as guests of the monasteries free of charge. Any women wishing to visit the area, as well as men before or after their stay on Mount Athos, will find accommodation in Ouranoupoli.

PRICES
The hotel prices mentioned below are the official ones set by the National Tourist Organization for double rooms, at low and high season, with breakfast. Since owners are allowed to modify the prices, always try to negotiate them.

OURANOUPOLI

✓✓ EAGLES PALACE (A Class)
4 km from Ouranoupoli
Tel. (0377) 31047, 33048 fax 31383
Open: April-October

Description: Built above the beach in a lush area opposite the Holy Mountain. This is one of the best hotels in the whole Halkidiki peninsula.
Rooms: 150 rooms, 16 bungalows and 10 suites with all the amenities.
Special features: Gym, tennis and volleyball courts, water sports, restaurants, pools, bar, parking, conference hall, etc.
Price: 49,000-69,000 drs.
Value for money: ✹✹
Credit cards: All

✓ XENIA OURANOUPOLIS (A Class)
Tel. (0377) 71412, fax 71362
Open: April-October
Description: Renovated in 1996, surrounded by luxuriant vegetation, on a good beach with a view of the islet of Ammouliani.

Rooms: 40 rooms with A/C, telephone and satellite TV.
Special features: Restaurant, pool, snack bar, sports facilities.
Price: 19,000-41,000 drs., half board obligatory
Value for money: ✹✹
Credit cards: All except Diners

MOUNT ATHOS

✓ AKRATHOS HOTEL (B Class)
Tel. (0377) 71100, fax 71164
Open: May-October
Description: New, built on a hillside with a view of Mount Athos, 90 m from the sea. Pleasant with nicely landscaped outdoor areas.
Rooms: 53 simple but comfortable rooms with fridge, TV, A/C and telephone.
Special features: Restaurant, pool, snack bar, sports facilities.
Price: 11,800-27,000 drs.
Value for money: ✸
Credit cards: Visa, Mastercard

Agionissi Resort

AMMOULIANI
✓ AGIONISSI RESORT (A Class)
Tel. (0377) 51102, (031) 254902, fax (0377) 51180
Open: April-October
Description: Surrounded by greenery, 50 m from the sea, with a view of Mount Athos.
Rooms: 40 rooms with A/C, telephone and satellite TV, mini bar and safe.
Special features: Good restaurant, pool, bar, parking, sports facilities and fitness programme.
Price: 19,000-41,000 drs.
Value for money: ✸✸
Credit cards: All

ALTERNATIVES
ARISTOTELES (B Class)
Ouranoupoli, tel. (0377) 71012, fax 24000
Price: 23,000-36,000 drs.

THEOXENIA (A Class)
Ouranoupoli, tel. (0377) 71060, fax 71079.
Price: 32,500-47,500 drs.

BEST RESTAURANTS & TAVERNAS

There are several restaurants and tavernas in Ouranoupoli, fish tavernas on Ammouliani and a few simple restaurants at Karyes. In the monasteries you will eat in the refectory with the monks at **no charge**. The meals consist mainly of pulses (bean and lentil soups, etc.), vegetables, olives, bread and fruit. Meat is never eaten. On Mondays, Wednesdays and Fridays – fast days – dishes are cooked with tomato sauce rather than olive oil but are surprisingly good. On Tuesdays, Thursdays and Saturdays, olive oil is used and feta cheese is served. Every now and then the monks treat themselves to fish.

TIPS AND INFORMATION

HOW TO GET THERE
From Athens to Thessaloniki
- By air with Olympic Airlines, west airport, (from 18,600 drs.), tel. (01) 9363363. With Air Greece, east airport, tel. (01) 3255011, and with Cronus Airlines, east airport, tel. (01) 9956400.
- By train, with the regular service in 9 hrs (from 4,100 drs.) or with the Intercity Express in 5 hrs 30 min (from 8,250 drs.), Stathmos Larissis tel. (01) 5297777.
- By intercity bus, KTEL, 100 Kifissou Ave., (from 7,700 drs.), tel. (01) 5148856. KTEL Attikis, 8 Mavromataion St. & Alexandras Ave., tel. (01) 8225148.

From Thessaloniki to Ouranoupoli and Ierissos
- If you have your own car, remember that you'll have to leave it for four days and nights in Ouranoupoli.
- By intercity bus, KTEL Thessalonikis, tel. (031) 924444.

CONTINENTAL GREECE

Docheiariou monastery

HOW TO GET AROUND

IF YOU'RE A MALE: You set off by boat at 9:45 am from Ouranoupoli harbour, tel. (0377) 71248, for Dafni on Mount Athos. On this route there are intermediary stops at the monasteries of Konstamonitou, Docheiariou, Xenophondos, Agiou Panteleimonos and Xiropotamou, where you can disembark if you wish. There is bus service from Dafni to Karyes. From Karyes you'll have to continue by foot, mule or private taxi (driven by monks). Mount Athos is full of paths that take you from one monastery to another. Take time in Karyes to plot your itinerary based on which monasteries you want to visit. From Ierissos harbour, tel: (0377) 22576, the boat leaves at 8:45 am for Iviron monastery with stops along the way for Esphigmenou, Vatopedi, Pantokratoros, Stavronikita and Koutloumousiou.

IF YOU'RE A FEMALE: There are small boats that run regularly in summer and in winter on demand to take women who wish to catch a glimpse of the Holy Mountain, even if from a distance of 500 m around the peninsula. These boats leave from both Ouranoupoli and Ierissos.

LENGTH OF STAY: As long as permitted. If you'd like more days on Mount Athos, you can go through the process again and get a stay permit for another four days.

BEST SEASON: Spring. Easter on Mount Athos is a unique experience, if you're up to the austerity of the ritual.

USEFUL TELEPHONE NUMBERS

OURANOUPOLI .... (0377)	Municipal Department 51208
Community Office 71216	**KARYES** .... (0377)
Port Authority 71248	Holy Council 23221
Information office for Mount Athos 71421	Police 23212
AMMOULIANI .... (0377)	Post Office 23214

Practical Information Guide

PRACTICAL INFORMATION

Location : 39^0 N, 22^0 E
Area : 131,900 sq. km including 25,050 sq. km of about 2,000 islands.
Population : 10.4 million
Capital : Athens, 4 million
Language : Greek
Literacy : 93%
Religion : 97% Greek Orthodox Christians
Currency : Drachma (approx. 300 drs. per US Dollar, 490 drs. per pound Sterling and 330 drs. per EURO)
Electricity : 220V, AC 50 Hz
Weights and measures : Metric system
Time zone : 2 hours ahead of GMT
Shop hours : Monday, Wednesday, Saturday: 8 am to 2:30 pm
Tuesday, Thursday, Friday: 8 am to 1:30 pm and from: 5:30 pm to 8:30 pm
International dialing code : 30, Athens (01), Thessaloniki (031)
Emergency numbers :

Ambulance	166
Police	100
Tourist police	171
Port police	108
Fire service	199
Road Assistance	104
Doctors SOS	(01) 3220015, 3220024
Poison treatment centre	(01) 7793777

VISA REQUIREMENTS

Nationals of the European Union, the USA, Canada, Australia and New Zealand, possessing a valid passport, may enter Greece and remain for three months without a visa. EU nationals may remain indefinitely. Visitors from all other nations must obtain a visa from the Greek embassy or consulate in their country of residence.
To extend their stay for more than three months, visitors must obtain permission from the Aliens Bureau in Athens, tel. (01) 770 5711 or from the local police departments outside Athens.

CUSTOMS

On entering Greece, you may bring in duty-free up to 200 cigarettes or 100 cigarillos or 50 cigars or 250 g tobacco, 1 litre of spirits or 2 litres of wine or liqueur, 50 g of perfume and 250 ml of eau de cologne. EU nationals arriving from the EU do not pass customs.
Taking antiquities out of the country without a permit is considered a serious offense and will be punished accordingly.

GREEK NATIONAL TOURIST ORGANIZATION

For any information regarding your visit to Greece, contact the National Tourist Organization (GNTO).
Its Athens headquarters are located at 2 Amerikis St., tel. (01) 327 1300-1. Local offices exist in many of the country's cities and resort areas.
The National Tourist Organization also has information offices in many countries round the world:

Australia and New Zealand: 51 - 57 Pitt St., Sydney, NSW 2000, tel. (02) 2411663

Canada: 1300 Bay St., Toronto, Ontario MSR 3K8, tel. (416) 968-2220

UK: 4, Conduit St., London W1R 0DJ, tel. (0171) 7345997

USA: Olympic Tower, 645 Fifth Ave., New York, NY 10022, tel. (212) 4215777

France: 3, Ave. de l'Opera, Paris 75001, tel. (01) 42606475

Italy: Via L. Bissolati 78-80, Roma 00187, tel. (06) 4744249

GREEK EMBASSIES

Following is a selection of Greek diplomatic missions abroad :
Australia: 9 Turrana St., Yarralumla, Canberra ACT 2600, tel. (0061-2) 62733883

Canada: 76 - 80 Maclaren St., Ottawa, Ontario K2P OK6, tel. (613) 2386271
Cyprus: Byron Boulevard 8 - 10, Nicosia, tel. (02) 441880
Denmark: Borgergade 16, 1300 Copenhagen, tel. (01) 114533
France: 17, rue Auguste, Vacquerie, 75116 Paris, tel. (01) 47237228
Germany: Koblenzer St. 103, 5300 Bonn 2, tel. (22) 883010
Ireland: 1 Upper Pembroke St., Dublin 2, tel. (01) 767254
Italy: Via S. Mercadante 36, Rome 00198, tel. (06) 8549630
Japan: 16-30 Nishi Azabu 3-chome Minato-ku, Tokyo 106, tel. (03) 4030871/2
New Zealand: 235-237 Willis St., 8th Floor, Wellington, tel. (04) 847556
Netherlands: Koninginnegracht 37, The Hague, tel. (070) 3638700
Spain: Avenida Doctor Arce 24, Madrid 28002, tel. (01) 5644653
Sweden: Riddargatan 60, 11457 Stockholm, tel. (08) 6637577
Switzerland: Jungfraustrasse 3, 3005 Bern, tel. (31) 441637
Turkey: Ziya-ul-Rahman Sokak 9-11, Gazi Osman Pasa, Ankara, tel. (04) 1368860
UK: 1A Holland Park, London W11 3TP, tel. (071) 728040
USA: 2221 Massachusetts Ave. NW, Washington DC 20008, tel. (202) 6673169

FOREIGN EMBASSIES IN GREECE

They are usually open from Monday to Friday from 8 am to 2 pm.
Australia: Dimitriou Soutsou 37, Athens 15452, tel. (01) 6450404
Canada: Genadiou 4, Athens 11521, tel. (01) 7273400
Cyprus: Herodotou 16, Athens 10675, tel. (01) 7232727
France: Leoforos Vasilissis Sofias 7 and Akadimias 2, Athens 10671, tel. (01) 3391000
Germany: Karaoli and Dimitriou 3, Athens 15124, tel. (01) 3694111
Ireland: Leoforos Vasileos Konstantinou 7, Athens 10674, tel. (01) 7285511
Italy: Sekeri 12, Athens 10674, tel. (01) 3617260
Japan: Leoforos Messogion 2, Athens 11527, tel. (01) 7758101
Netherlands: Vasileos Konstantinou 5-7, Athens 10674, tel. (01) 7239701
New Zealand: Semitelou 9, Athens 11521, tel. (01) 7770686
Turkey: Vassilios Georgiou B 8, Athens 10674, tel. (01) 7245915
UK: Ploutarchou 1, Athens 10675, tel. (01) 7236211
USA: Leoforos Vasilissis Sophias 91, Athens 11521, tel. (01) 7212951

GREECE AND THE GREEKS

People either come to Greece for a glimpse at archaeology and historical culture or because they like the beaches, the museums, the climate, the monasteries or the beautiful mountains that the Greeks themselves have only recently begun to appreciate.

Others come for the nightlife, the casinos, the modern summer resorts or for a cruise in the Aegean.

Many of the ten million or so tourists who arrive in Greece each year feel as though they have "returned home".

All these modern "conquerors" will come into contact and will become easily acquainted with the Greek people who have felt the influence of all the other real conquerors who have passed through this land: the Romans, Arabs, Franks, Italians, Turks. They will hear Greeks declare proudly that they are the descendants of the Ancient Greeks and of Alexander the Great. They will see them gesticulating with gusto as they describe this greatness of the past, hands carving the air to make their point.

Because of its strategic position at the crossroads of three continents, Greece was always a target of the successive waves of tribes and nations that dominated the region. The impact of these conquerors, some from the East, others from the West, contributed to the formation of a remarkable culture.

The modern Greek state was created in 1830, after 400 years of Ottoman occupation. It was extended to its present northern borders after the Balkan Wars of 1912-1913 and acquired the Dodecanese only in 1947, after Italy surrendered them to the Allies after World War II.

The Greeks today continue to ask themselves whether they belong more to the West or to the East. Economically, at any rate, there was a definite turn to the West in 1981 when Greece became a full member of the European Union. Since then its economic indicators have been gradually approaching those of the other member-states. A similar change in lifestyle concomitant with this shift is already taking place all over the country.

Nevertheless, despite the sweeping development of tourism since the 1960s and the transition from an agricultural economy to an increasingly globalized marketplace, many aspects of Greek society have remained traditional.

The institution of the family continues to be strong and is blessed by the powerful Orthodox Church. Friendships made in childhood and in school persist throughout a Greek's life, exemplifying this traditional bond.

If you venture off the beaten track to some mountain village untouched by tourism, you will have the chance to test the Greeks' reputation for hospitality. To see whether indeed they are high-spirited, inventive, humorous. If they really do go out strolling with their families in the evening and stop to chat with all the acquaintances they meet. These are traditions that are still very much alive in the countryside.

RELIGION

Ninety-seven percent of all Greeks belong to the Greek Christian Orthodox Church.

The role of religion in the life of the average Greek is still extremely important, even today, though certainly more so for older people and those living in rural areas than for Athenians and residents of the other large cities.

Although civil marriage has been legal in Greece since 1983, most couples prefer to be married in church. They also tend to celebrate their name-day rather than their birthday.

When passing a church, many Greeks will drop in to light a candle for a loved one or to say a prayer. And as you will see, they never have to go out of their way since throughout Greece, and particularly on the islands, apart from the large parish churches in every neighbourhood, there are hundreds of little chapels sprinkled all over the countryside. Many of these have been built over the centuries by private individuals, who have chosen this way to thank their patron saint for his/her assistance.

If you'd like to visit a church, especially a famous church or a monastery, you should ensure that you are respectably dressed: this means skirts below the knees for women and trousers, not shorts, for men.

POLITICS

According to the constitution of 1975, Greece from a kingdom became a republic. The official head of state is the president, who has a ceremonial function rather than any real authority.

The parliament consists of 300 deputies who serve a four-year term; of these 288 are elected by the people and 12 are appointed according to the parties' relative strength.

After the second world war and the civil war that continued until 1950, Greece was governed alternately by the centre and then by the right, with Constantine Karamanlis as the leading personality from the mid 50s until 1981, with an interruption of seven years (1967-1974) of military dictatorship. The last king Constantine, left the country in 1967 and the monarchy was officially dissolved by plebiscite in 1974. Since that time the former king has returned only for two brief visits.

In 1981, the first socialist government was elected, led by another prominent personality, Andreas Papandreou. His party, the Panhellenic Socialist Party (PASOK), has ruled the country ever since, except for three years (1990-1993), when the conservatives were returned to power, largely as a result of financial scandals in which Papandreou himself was implicated.

THE ECONOMY

A traditionally agricultural country until the 1970s, Greece's primary sources of income now are tourism, followed by industry and shipping.

The balance of payments and public debt remain its two main economic problems.

It receives considerable assistance from the European Union, which it joined in 1981, becoming a full member in 1993.

The austerity measures taken to bring the Greek economy into line with that of the other members, already seem to be producing the desired result. Inflation had dropped from the 15-20 percent levels of the 1980s to around 3 percent by the end of 1998. The drachma seems to have stabilized against the hard currencies and has set its sights on entering the second round of the European Monetary Union in 2001. Interest rates are also showing a downward trend and differ only slightly from those in Western Europe.

Unemployment, according to official statistics, hovers around 8 to 10 percent. One reason for this relatively low rate is the Greek's desire to be his own boss. Two-thirds of the active population is self-employed.

The recent changes in the Balkans had positive as well as negative consequences for the Greek economy. On the one hand, Greece has become, for the first time in its modern history, a country to which needy people immigrate — the Greeks themselves have been emigrating for centuries — while, on the other, it has taken advantage of its location to invest and do business with the emerging Balkan economies.

GEOGRAPHY

Greece is situated in the southernmost part of the Balkan peninsula. It covers an area of 131,900 sq. km (50,961 sq. mi), including about 2,000 islands. It is divided into nine regions : Thrace, Macedonia, Epirus, Thessaly, Sterea Ellada (Central Greece), the Aegean Islands, Ionian Islands, Peloponnese, Crete and Greater Athens.

It consists of 51 prefectures (nomi) and the self-governing Mount Athos. Since the municipal elections of 1998, which revised the distribution of local authority, the country is divided into 900 municipalities and 133 smaller units called kinotites (communities).

Only one-third of continental Greece is cultivable. This explains in part the large waves of emigration to Northern Europe, the Americas, Australia and South Africa which began as early as the last c., increased in the early 1950s and slowed to a trickle only in the past two decades. It is also one reason for the abandonment of the countryside for the cities, which is a global phenomenon. Half the Greek population of about 10 million live in the two largest cities, Greater Athens-Piraeus, which accounts for some 4 million people, and Thessaloniki with 1 million inhabitants.

The Pindus mountain range, which runs from north to south, is known as the backbone of Greece. Most of the country's main rivers have their source in these mountains. Greece's highest mountain is the legendary Olympus, at

2,917 m (9,570 ft).

After some four thousand years of deforestation, initially caused by ship-building and felling trees for firewood but compounded by infinite generations of ravenous goats and devastating summer forest fires in recent years, a large part of the land is not suitable for crops. Nevertheless, until recently, one-third of the population were farmers.

FLORA

Greek flora is among the richest in Europe. From early March until mid-June some 6,000 species of wild flowers make their appearance, including daisies, irises, poppies, tulips, marigolds and about 100 types of orchids.

Olive Trees

The tree that dominates the Greek landscape is the olive, which was held sacred in antiquity. Olive oil is the primary source of fat in the Greek diet, and certain types of olives grown here are known throughout the world. The pruned branches are used for firewood, larger pieces are carved into attractive utensils, bowls and small sculptures.

There are ten national parks in Greece with beautifully landscaped recreation areas and signed paths: Ainos in Kefalonia, Vikos-Aoos and Valia Kalda in Epirus, Prespes in Macedonia, Olympus in Thessaly, Iti and Parnassos in Central Greece, Samaria in Crete, and Parnitha and Sounion in Attica, near Athens.

FAUNA

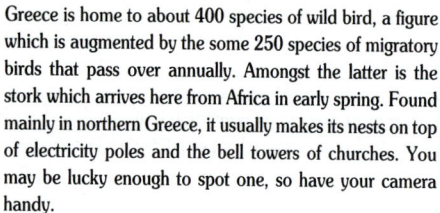

Greece is home to about 400 species of wild bird, a figure which is augmented by the some 250 species of migratory birds that pass over annually. Amongst the latter is the stork which arrives here from Africa in early spring. Found mainly in northern Greece, it usually makes its nests on top of electricity poles and the bell towers of churches. You may be lucky enough to spot one, so have your camera handy.

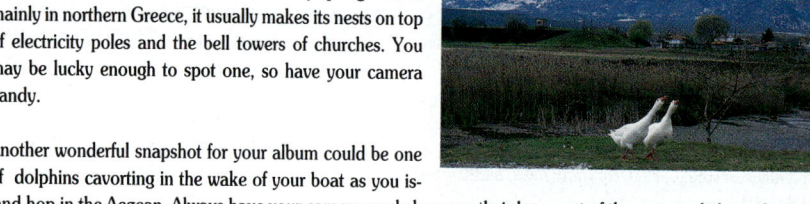

Another wonderful snapshot for your album could be one of dolphins cavorting in the wake of your boat as you island hop in the Aegean. Always have your camera ready because their leaps out of the water only last a few seconds.

The monk seal is one of the rarest mammals in the world. There are only 300 or so left in Europe and most of these live in the Aegean, in a protected zone in the Northern Sporades Islands where Greece's only marine park is located.

The beaches of the Ionian island of Zakynthos attract not only thousands of tourists but many endangered sea turtles, caretta caretta, which have been going there for millennia to lay their eggs. Very few of the hatchlings ever make it back to the sea because of the many threats along the way, not the least of which are those posed by us humans and our beach-side development projects.

The most common animals in Greece are the ubiquitous goats and sheep which graze freely in both mountain and valley. Plus, of course, the uncountable cats. A small population of large and small mammals live in the mountain forests of northern Greece, like the bear (Urcus Arctos), the wolf (Canis Lupus), the wildcat (Felis Silvestris) and the wild boar (Sus Scrofa). The fox (Vulpes Vulpes) and the golden jackal live in most regions of Greece, with relatively large populations in the Peloponnese. The bear, wolf and jackal are protected species.

Hunting birds, in season, include partiges, pheasants, quails ducks and wood pigeons.

THE CLIMATE

It's fair to say that most of Greece enjoys a typically Mediterranean climate, although there are considerable differences between north and south, islands and mainland. The summers are hot and dry, the winters cool and rainy or snowy in the mountains.

In July and August, when the mercury reaches its highest, strong northerly winds known as meltemia offer considerable relief, particularly in the Aegean.

	JAN.		MARCH		MAY		JULY		SEPT.		NOV.	
	F° Min max	C° Min Max	F° Min max	C° Min Max	F° Min max	C° Min Max	F° Min max	C° Min max	F° Min Max	C° Min Max	F° Min max	C° Min Max
Athens	43 - 54	6 - 13	46 - 61	8 - 16	61 - 77	16 - 25	73 - 91	23 - 33	66 - 84	19 - 29	54 - 66	12 - 19
Corfu	44 - 56	5 - 13	46 - 62	7 - 16	58 - 74	13 - 24	70 - 88	18 - 31	64 - 81	16 - 28	51 - 65	10 - 18
Iraklion-Crete	48 - 61	9 - 16	50 - 63	10 - 17	59 - 73	15 - 23	67 - 80	19 - 26	65 - 80	19 - 26	56 - 70	14 - 21
Thessaloniki	35 - 50	2 - 9	44 - 59	5 - 14	58 - 76	12 - 23	70 - 89	18 - 30	64 - 82	15 - 26	47 - 60	9 - 15
Rainfall mm/ month	53		32		18		4		16		65	
Sunshine hours/ day	6		8		11		13		9		5	

WHEN TO GO

One should not forget that Greece, a country with a population of 10 million, receives almost the same number of visitors in the course of every year.

In the high season (late June-early September and particularly 20 July - 20 August) you should be aware that you will probably have difficulty finding a room, that you'll meet many of your compatriots in the museums, you may have to wait for a table in a restaurant, and you could find a host of people already "parked" on that deserted beach you'd chosen.

In winter (December-late March), most tourist facilities, especially on the islands, are closed. But if you decide to come then, you should be compensated by cloudless skies. November, January and even February have a high percentage of sunny, relatively warm days, and you will be able to carry out many of the excursions we propose in this book.

Spring in Greece is a festival of nature that lasts about three months — from April to mid June. The big wave of tourists abandoning their grey Northern lands has not yet arrived and the Greeks manage to get to their own favorite holiday spots only on weekends. Then, the countryside is not burnt to a crisp by the sun, but is incredibly green and abloom with wild flowers. You can even swim from May on and return back home with a tan before the thermometre hits the high thirties in July.

The fall is the second best season after spring. The weather is mild, the sea is warm and the masses of tourists have departed.

WHAT TO TAKE WITH YOU

If you are absolutely set on bringing with you everything you need — even items easy to find in Greece — and are planning a summer visit, then do not forget a good pair of sunglasses, suntan lotion with a high protection factor and a light hat.

As for what to wear, avoid clothes made of synthetics. The best choice is light-coloured cotton fabrics which you can wear all day, although you should bring a shawl or cotton jumper/sweater for the evenings, which can be much cooler than you would imagine.

If you haven't planned on arduous hikes for which you'll need special boots, then pack your most comfortable walking shoes for exploring and buy a pair of leather sandals in Greece at a very reasonable price. You will not need a coat and tie even if you belong to the jet set.

If you're bringing electrical appliances — shavers/hair dryers — you should know that in Greece, as in the rest of Europe, the current is 220 volts/50 Hz AC and that wall sockets have two round holes or three for appliances that need grounding. Be sure to bring along an adaptor if need be.

WHAT TO BUY

Although Greece is not as cheap as it used to be up until the early 80s, you can still buy some goods and objects which will be well worth the expense particularly in places where there is little tourism.

For example, you can find good value, genuine leather sandals, bags and jackets. Even better value may be the furs. Kastoria in northern Greece is the centre of the fur industry and Greece one of the world's largest producers. Jewelry, especially gold, is on sale in all resorts and towns; look for designs based on ancient models as well as striking modern ones. Icons are still painted here in the age-old way using traditional media (oil, gold, egg, etc.) mainly on wood panels. They definitely make an original gift. Another good buy, if a bit cumbersome, is ceramics, both for household use or for decoration.

In mountain towns and villages, you can often find rugs and kilims in traditional patterns, and flokatis. Flokatis are shaggy wool rugs made by hand; they can also be used as bed covers.

If nothing of the above suits you, then perhaps you'd like a reproduction of an ancient work of art. Copies of gold and silver jewellery, statuettes in plaster or marble, vases, games etc. are available at many of the country's museums.

WHAT TO EAT

After a series of studies comparing the eating patterns of various nations round the world, it has been proven that the traditional Mediterranean diet offers its followers good health and longevity.

Greek cuisine is perhaps the most characteristic example of the Mediterranean diet. Without aiming to impress with fancy touches, it is based on olive oil, a limited amount of red meat, fish and seafood when available, hardly any butter and milk, but plenty of sheep's and goat's cheese and yogurt, an abundance of fresh vegetables and fruit, plus nuts of various kinds and honey-sweetened desserts.

Greek salad

So if you haven't come to Greece to dine in the Western fast-food chains — Macdonalds, Wendy's, KFC — their Greek lookalike Goody's, or the pizzerias that have popped up virtually everywhere nowadays, just sit yourself down in a Greek seaside taverna under the stars and prepare to enjoy yourself.

As an aperitif, try a glass of **ouzo** (a clear anise-flavoured drink made from distilled grape lees) with **mezedes** (appetizers). Some of the best known are **taramosalata** (a dip made from fish roe), **tzatziki** (yogurt mixed with garlic and cucumber), **dolmades** (vineleaves stuffed with rice), **gigantes** (giant beans baked with tomato sauce) and **feta cheese** (made from sheep's milk) with pungent large **black olives**.

For your main dish, most tavernas and restaurants will let you have a look at

Tzatziki

Moussakas

what's simmering on their stove or what's chilled in their display case cum refrigerator. This is customary and the owner will often explain, most probably in broken English, what dish is which, while telling you what a good cook his wife is.

Frequently there is quite a large choice. Some of the most common offerings are: **moussaka** (a layered baked dish of fried sliced aubergines, potatoes and minced beef, topped with bechamel sauce), **pastitsio** (baked macaroni and mince with bechamel), **lachanodolmades** (stuffed cabbage leaves with egg-lemon sauce), tomatoes and peppers stuffed with rice and herbs, and **briam**, the Greek version of ratatouille. A heavier dish, more often found in winter, is **stifado**, stewed beef or rabbit with sweet caramelized onions in a winey tomato sauce. **Cheese** and **spinach pies** are usually delicious, **kalamarakia** (fried squid) a universal favourite, and salads of all kinds are often on the menu, including the famous "Greek Salad".

To accompany your rich meal (Greeks usually order much more than they can actually eat), there are some delicious red and white **wines** to choose from. Some of the bigger wine producers include Boutaris, Cambas, Hadjimichalis, Tsantalis and Porto Carras. Gone are the days when retsina was the only wine on hand; in fact it is getting increasingly hard to find, especially in summer. But many tavernas do have their own barrel wine, resinated or not, and try it, because it is inevitably cheaper than the bottled variety.

Baklavas

At a taverna, the end to the meal is usually **fresh fruit**, **halva** (semolina pudding sprinkled with cinnamon) or more rarely (thick creamy Greek) **yogurt** and **honey**. If you crave one of those anatolian delicacies — **baklava** and **kataifi** (strudel leaves or "shredded wheat" laced with walnuts and honey), you'll usually have to go to a zacharoplasteio (sweet or pastry shop); there is usually one close by.

The service charge is always included in the bill. Greeks habitually leave another 10 to 15% as tip for the busboy.

Bread

TRAVELLING TO GREECE

By air
There are 18 international airports in Greece (Athens, Chania, Heraklion, Karpathos, Rhodes, Kos, Santorini, Mykonos, Samos, Lesvos, Kavalla, Thessaloniki, Skiathos, Corfu, Preveza, Cephallonia, Zakynthos, Kalamata) and 17 local airports (Kastoria, Ioannina, Kozani, Skyros, Limnos, Chios, Syros, Paros, Naxos, Ikaria, Leros, Astypalaia, Milos, Kassos, Siteia, Kastellorizo and Kythera).

Olympic Airways, the state carrier beset by many financial problems, still manages to perform satisfactorily most of the time. In summer it schedules additional flights to all domestic airports (Information in Athens, tel. (01) 966 6666). In recent years private companies, such as Cronus Air (tel. (01) 331 5515) and Air Greece (tel. (01) 325 5011-4) are trying to benefit from the public's frustration with the delays and cancellations that can upset travelling with Olympic Airways.

In summer, reservations should be made several days ahead, particularly for such popular destinations as Rhodes, Santorini, Corfu, Mykonos, Heraklion and Chania in Crete, for weekends and throughout August one should also check in at the airport one hour before takeoff.

By bus
The long-distance bus service is run by KTEL (Greek acronym). It is comprehensive, well organized and offers frequent service. Most buses are comfortable but few have air-conditioning and none have toilets or refreshments, although they do stop along the way on long trips.
The fares vary according to the distance and average 1,000 drs. per 100 km (7,000 drs. for Thessaloniki, 3,000 drs. for Patras, etc.).

By rail

Greece's railway network, the state-owned OSE, lags behind those of the rest of Europe in terms of speed and comfort. Nevertheless, some people prefer it because a regular ticket is cheaper than the bus and because the train passes through beautiful regions such as Diakofto-Kalavryta in the northern Peloponnese, the Nestos river valley in northern Greece and Mt Pelion in central Greece.

Athens is the starting point for two railway lines. The first, to the Peloponnesian town of Kalamata in the south: one via Corinth, Patras and Pyrgos, the other via Corinth, Argos and Tripolis. The second, from Athens to Alexandroupolis in the north on the border between Turkey and Greece, and from there to Istanbul, passes through Lamia, Larissa, Katerini, Thessaloniki, Serres, Drama, Xanthi and Komotini. From Thessaloniki other lines go to Skopje (Former Yugoslav Republic of Macedonia) via Verria, Edessa and Florina; Belgrade, Yugoslavia; and Sofia, Bulgaria via Kilkis and Sidirokastro.

The Intercity express trains also run between Athens and the major cities – Larissa, Thessaloniki, Patras, and Kalamata; they are the quickest way of travelling on the Greek mainland.

By sea

The more than 10 million tourists who arrive in Greece every year visit at least one island. To serve them (and the islanders themselves), a well-organized privately operated fleet of large, modern ships, hydrofoils, and catamarans has been set up, making the most far-flung island accessible. The inter-island ferries have special air-conditioned lounges for a more comfortable journey. Make sure you buy your ticket at least one week before your departure and be at the harbour an hour in advance.

Hydrofoils

Piraeus, the country's largest port, 14 km from Athens, is where the ships depart for the islands of the Argosaronic Gulf, most of the Cyclades, the Dodecanese and Crete, tel. (01)4226000. The hydrofoils for the Argosaronic leave from there and from the nearby yacht harbour of Zea, as do those for the Cyclades, tel. (01) 4280001, 3220351. Many ships and hydrofoils also leave from Rafina (50 km east of Athens) for the Cyclades, tel. (0294) 28888 and a few more distant islands.

Ships bound for the Ionian islands leave from Patras, tel. (061) 341 002, while the Epirot port of Igoumenitsa also serves Corfu. For the Northern Sporades islands, the ferries and hydrofoils leave from Agios Konstantinos, tel. (0235) 31759 and Volos.

By road

The road network in Greece is not of the same standard as in Western Europe. The accident rate is higher, particularly on weekends. Drive with caution and get a good map before setting off, since the road signs sometimes leave a bit to be desired. Particular care should be observed on the islands if you decide to rent a motorbike and by all means request a helmet.

In order to drive in Greece you will need your licence, the car's registration papers (if you bring your own) and the green card (International Certificate of Insurance). Wearing seatbelts is obligatory and children under the age of 10 must use the back seat. General information regarding driving in Greece and road conditions can be obtained from the Tourist Police, tel. 177 and ELPA (Automobile and Touring Club of Greece), tel. (01) 7791615.

If you wish to hire a car, you will find all the well known agencies at your disposal in Athens and the large towns and resorts.

AVIS, tel. (01) 3224951
HERTZ, tel. (01) 9968185
BUDGET, tel. (01) 9222442

AUTORENT, tel. (01) 9238438
EUROCAR, tel. (01) 9248810
THRIFTY, tel. (01) 9221211

EURODOLLAR, tel. (01) 9230548
EUROPEAN, tel. (01) 9246777
COSMOS, tel. (01) 9234697

COMMUNICATIONS

Public telephones are to be found in the most remote corner of the country. The property of the state-owned Hellenic Telecommunications Organization (OTE), they function with cards that may be purchased easily from kiosks and other shops. You may send faxes from local OTE offices, which exist in all major towns and islands, and from some post offices.

Post offices are open in Greece from Monday through Friday from 7:30 am to 2 pm. But you can also buy stamps at most kiosks, which charge a 10% commission. If you plan to stay anywhere for a few weeks, you can arrange to have mail sent Poste Restante and just claim it with your passport as identification.

Radio frequencies are as saturated in Greece as they are elsewhere in Europe. But with a little effort and a middle or short wave radio, you can pick up the BBC World Service. Antenna radio station broadcasts the news in English.

The television scene in Greece is similar, with new channels, especially local ones being added all the time. Between the state-owned channels – ET1, NET, ET3 – and the larger private channels (Mega, Antenna, Sky and Star) there are dozens of English language films and documentaries shown every week. Among the foreign satellite channels, you can usually see CNN, the French TV5, the Italian RAI, and the Spanish TVE.

NEWSPAPERS AND MAGAZINES

In most mainland cities and all the islands, you'll be able to find most European newspapers, almost all the international weekly and monthly magazines and many other periodicals.

A good source of information on what's going on locally and around the world is the Athenian English-language daily, Athens News. In addition, it contains a full directory of telephone numbers and events that tourists will find very useful.

For more complete political and financial analysis, the International Herald Tribune is published daily except Mondays in tandem with an abridged English edition of Athens' most prestigious morning paper, Kathimerini.

Other sources of information are Greece's Weekly, a kind of "what's on", and Hellenic Times, both published on Fridays in English.

In each of these publications you will find all the entertainment news: TV and radio programmes, cinema showings (foreign films are always shown in the orginal language with Greek subtitles), and programmes of the major summer festivals round the country.

HEALTH

There are hospitals in almost all mainland cities and the larger islands. The mainland villages and smaller islands have at least one doctor. All tourists are entitled to free medical care in an emergency and if involved in an accident. This includes helicopter transport to a metropolitan hospital if required.

Residents of the European Union have the right to free medical and pharmaceutical coverage in state hospitals with the sole condition that they complete form E111.

Visitors from other countries would do better to take out some form of personal travel insurance as a precaution. In this case, make sure that your insurance also covers activities that are considered risky, such as driving a motorcycle or scuba diving.

In Greece, when temperatures can get uncomfortably hot in summer, do treat the sun with some respect. Wear a hat, good quality sun glasses and high protection factor sun lotion.

As on any other trip, don't forget to bring along any prescriptions for drugs you may need during your holiday. But be aware that it is forbidden to import codeine into the country.

ENTERTAINMENT

With its 110 winter **cinemas**, some 90 open-air ones that show films in the summer months — a great Greek feature — 85 theatres, the world class **Athens Concert Hall**, numerous **clubs** and **discos**, **ellinadika** (nightclubs specializing in traditional and contemporary Greek music), and **rebetadika** (the Greek version of the blues, the lyrics usually focus on love, social criticism, hashish, life in prison, and so on.), Athens is a paradise for night owls (see pages 71-74).

In all tourist areas there are clubs and bars and usually at least one summer cinema (you'll see the posters about town). We recommend the latter as a fine pastime on a starlit evening, since all films are in their original language, usually English.

You can see traditional folk dance performances in Athens and Rhodes in special theatres, and at many tourist-oriented restaurants and large hotels. Otherwise, you are almost sure to see some dancing at a local taverna where there is Greek music and singing.

There is no dearth of more serious art forms, either, for virtually every town and island has its summer festival, whether of classical drama in a nearby ancient theatre or music. Attending one of these performances can be a truly memorable experience.

MAJOR CULTURAL EVENTS AND FESTIVALS

Sound and light performances
- in Athens at Pnyx, opposite the Acropolis, April - October, tel. (01) 3227944, 9226210.
- in Rhodes at the Municipal Garden, Grand Master's Palace, April - October, tel. (0241) 21922.
- in Corfu at the Old Fortress, 15 May - 30 September, tel. (0661) 37520.

Folk Dances
- in Athens at Dora Stratou's theatre - Philoppapou Hill, 20 May - 30 September, tel. (01) 3244395.
- in Rhodes at Greek Folk Dances Theatre in the Old Town, May - October, tel. (0241) 20157.

Drama and Music Festivals
- Athens Festival (ancient drama, opera, music and ballet) in the Herod Atticus Odeon theatre, at the foot of the Acropolis, 1 June - 30 October, tel. (01) 3221459, 3232771.
- Epidavros Festival (ancient drama) in the ancient theatre, tel. (01) 3221459, (0753) 22066
- Dimitria Festival (music theatre, opera)

in Thessaloniki, October - November, tel. (031) 281068.
- Renaissance Festival (music, theatre) in Rethymnon Crete, August - September, tel. (0831) 50800.
- Philippi Festival in the ancient theatre of Philippi - Kavala, tel. (051) 223504, 227820.
- Nafplion Festival (classical music, theatre) in Nafplion - Peloponnese, tel. (0752) 28607.
- Patras Festival (classical music, traditional music, theatre) in Patras - Peloponnese, tel. (061) 275272.

Wine Festivals
- Patras - Peloponnese, 28 August - 13 September, tel. (061) 279866.
- Rethymno - Crete, 11-26 July, tel. (0831) 22522.

SPORTS

Until the late 80s, the most popular sport in Greece was football (soccer). Since then, thanks to some outstanding triumphs, basketball has nudged it out of first place in the hearts of many fans. Both the national team and the professional teams of Athens and Thessaloniki are among Europe's most successful.

Skiing is a sport which has taken off in the past few decades. Though it was virtually unknown in the 60s, Greece now has 17 ski centres. For information, call the Greek Skiing Federation, tel. (01) 323 0182.

There are four golf courses in Greece: at Glyfada near Athens, tel. (01) 8946820, in Halkidiki near Thessaloniki, tel. (0375) 71221, in Corfu, tel. (0661) 94220-1 and in Rhodes, tel. (0241) 51257. Several others are in the plans.

BARGAINING

Bargaining in Greece is no longer expected as it is in Arab countries, but nor is it as rare as in Western Europe. Most shops do have set prices, but you can always try to bargain in tourist shops, at open-air markets and in hotels and rented rooms during the off-season.

PUBLIC HOLIDAYS

1 January	New Year's Day
6 January	Epiphany
Moveable	Ash Monday
25 March	Greek Indipendence Day Annunciation
1 May	Labour Day
Moveable	Good Friday (Friday before Orthodox Easter)
Moveable	Orthodox Easter Sunday and Monday
15 August	Assumption of Virgin Mary
28 October	National Holiday
25 December	Christmas Day
26 December	Boxing Day

Roasting the Easter lamb

SAFETY

Up until a few years ago, before the arrival in Greece of refugees from poorer nations in search of a better life, Greece was considered one of the safest countries in Europe. This wave of immigration has been accompanied by a spectacular increase in crime, particularly robberies, in the cities and in remote mountainous areas. Even today, however, in places where there are lots of people, you run little risk of being assaulted or robbed. Nevertheless, take the usual precautions you would on a visit to any other European country.

ORGANIZATIONS OF INTEREST TO TRAVELLERS

Greek Alpine Club, Plateia Kapnikareas 2, Athens, tel. (01) 3234555

Hellenic Federation of Mountaineering Clubs, 7 Karagiorgi Servias St., Athens 11563, tel. (01) 3234555

Hellenic Ornithological Society, 53 Benaki St., Athens 106 81, tel. (01) 3811271

Greek Automobile Club, 2-4 Messogion Ave., Athens 105 63, tel. (01) 7791615

Hellenic Skiing Federation, 7 Karagiorgi Servias St., Athens 11563, tel. (01) 3230182

Hellenic Yachting Federation, 55 Possidonos St., Piraeus, tel. (01) 9304825

Greek Camping Association, 76 Solonos St., Athens 106 80. tel: (01) 3621560

Trekking Hellas, 7 Filellinon St., Athens tel. (01) 3234548

International Student and Youth Travel Service, 11 Nikis St., Athens 105 57, tel. (01) 3233767

Greek National Tourist Organisation,
2 Amerikis St., Athens 10564,
tel. (01) 3271300-1

Hellenic Speleological Society, 32 Sina St.,
tel. (01) 3617824

Golfing in Greece
- Athens: Glyfada Golf Course, tel. (01) 8946820
- Halkidiki - Thessaloniki : tel. (0375) 71221
- Corfu : tel. (0661) 94220
- Rhodes : tel. (0241) 51257

HOTELS AND RENTED ROOMS

The Greek National Tourist Organization (EOT) has designated six categories of hotel :

Luxury, A and B class all have en suite bathrooms, Luxury class establishments also have at least one bar and restaurant and offer a large breakfast with a large menu. A and B class hotels offer buffet breakfasts in a special room. Most C class hotels also have en suite bathrooms but D and E class hotels only have showers and they may not always be private.

Rented rooms used to be specially arranged areas of private houses aimed at accommodating visitors wishing to pay less than at a hotel. Now, however, they are more often small purpose-built apartments which offer nothing except the essential furniture — sometimes equipped with kitchen, fridge and cooker — hot water and cleanliness. They are divided into three categories, A, B and C. They must be registered with the EOT and have their licence and rates prominently displayed.

The EOT has also fixed the prices to be charged by each category. Room prices must be displayed in each room on a special card, usually hung behind the door, where breakfast charges (if applicable) are also printed. However, due to EU regulations, the hotel owners are allowed to charge prices other than those specified, usually lower. You should therefore always negotiate them.

CURRENCY

The Greek monetary unit is the drachma (dr). Coins circulate in denominations of 5, 10, 20, 50 and 100 drachmas, bills in 100, 200, 500, 1,000, 5,000 and 10,000 drachmas.

There is no limit to the amount of money you can bring into the country in either cash or traveller's cheques. But you must declare any funds worth more than 600,000 drachmas in any currency, if you wish to export them on your departure.

You can change money at all banks, in many post offices, and exchange bureaus, at your hotel and at certain travel agencies.

You can use your credit card almost anywhere in Greece, to pay most hotel and restaurant bills or to get cash from the automatic teller at banks round the country. However, for remote, off-the-beaten-track excursions, you will need cash.

WEIGHTS AND MEASURES

In Greece as in the rest of continental Europe, the metric system is used, with only two exceptions: distances at sea, which are measured in nautical miles (n mi.) and plots of land, which are measured in stremmata (1 stremma=1,000 sq. m, or 4 acres).

FILMS AND PHOTOGRAPHS

Most well known brands of film are readily available in Greece. But they are relatively expensive, particularly in places that attract lots of tourists. Ultra rapid development service is also apt to be pricey. Developing slides takes several days outside of Athens, where they are sent for development from all over Greece.

You may take photos in museums as long as you don't use a flash or a tripod. To use a video camera or a professional camera, you usually have to pay a fee. In archaeological sites and in monasteries and churches, it is always better to ask whether you may take photos. Do the same when people are involved, although most Greeks would probably have no objection. Taking still or video pictures is forbidden near military installations.

FURTHER READING

Homer's *Iliad* and *Odyssey*, written in the 8th c. BC, were the first epics in the History of Western civilization, and perhaps your trip to Greece would be enhanced by reading or rereading them.

If you want a History of ancient Greece and of Greek civilization, A.R. Burns' *The Penguin History of Greece* is considered a classic of its kind.

To get a taste of ancient Greek philosophy, take a look at Plato's *Republic* and *Symposium*.

For a brief History of Hellenism from Byzantium to the start of the 1980s, C.M. Woodhouse, *Modern Greece: A Short History* (Faber & Faber) is an excellent introduction.

If you like poetry, try to find an anthology of the two most important Greek poets of the 20th c., George Seferis and Odysseas Elytis, both of whom won the Nobel Prize for Literature in 1963 and 1979, respectively.

Nikos Kazantzakis may not have won the Nobel but he remains equally prominent in the minds of his Greek and foreign readers. The film, *Zorba the Greek*, based on his book by the same name, made him famous all over the world. Other popular books include *The Last Temptation Christ Recrucified* and *Report to Greco* (Faber & Faber). Kazantzakis' very personal description of the Greece of yesterday will help you understand a good deal about the Greece of today.

Of the books written about Greece and the Greeks by foreign writers, the following stand out: Lawrence Durrell's *Prospero's Cell* and *Reflections on a Marine Venus* about Corfu and Rhodes (Faber & Faber), Nicholas Gage's *Eleni* (Collins Harvill/Ballantine), Patrick Leigh Fermor's *Mani* and *Roumeli* (Penguin), Henry Miller's *The Colossus of Maroussi* (Minerva), and the recent best seller *Captain Corelli's Mandolin* (Minerva) by Louis de Bernieres.

THE GREEK ALPHABET

Α, α	alpha	a
Β, β	vita	v
Γ, γ	ghama	gh, y
Δ, δ	dhelta	dh
Ε, ε	epsilon	e
Ζ, z	zita	z
Η, n	ita	i
Θ, θ	thita	th
Ι, ι	iota	i
Κ, κ	kapa	k
Λ, λ	lamdha	l
Μ, μ	mi	m
Ν, ν	ni	n
Ξ, ξ	ksi	x
Ο, ο	omikron	o
Π, π	pi	p
Ρ, ρ	ro	r
Σ, σ	sighma	s
Τ, τ	taf	t
Υ, υ	ipsilon	i, y
Φ, φ	fi	f
Χ, χ	khi	ch
Ψ, ψ	psi	ps
Ω, ω	omega	o

NUMBERS

1.	éna	11.	éndeka	30.	triánda
2.	dío	12.	dódeka	40.	saránda
3.	tría	13.	déka - tría	50.	penínda
4.	téssera	14.	déka - téssera	60.	eksínda
5.	pénde	15.	déka - pénde	70.	evdhomínda
6.	éksi	16.	déka - éksi	80.	ogdónda
7.	eptá	17.	déka - eptá	90.	enenínda
8.	októ	18.	déka - októ	100.	ekató
9.	enéa	19.	déka - enéa	1000.	hília
10.	déka	20.	íkosi	10.000.	déka hiliádes

USEFUL WORDS & PHRASES

Yes	né	In the evening	to vrádi
No	óhi	Good	kaló
Please	parakaló	Bad	kakó
Thank you	efharistó	Cheap	ftinó
Excuse me	signómi	Expensive	akrivó
Do you speak English ?	miláte angliká ?	with	mazí
Today	símera	Where?	pou ?
Tomorrow	ávrio	How?	pos ?
Now	tóra	Why?	yatí ?
Open	aniktó	How much?	póso káni ?
Closed	klistó	Good morning	kalí méra
In the morning	to proí	Good night	kalí níkta
In the afternoon	to apógevma	Good bye	yásu

Index

Ancient Thera	245
Ancient Tyrins	84
Andimachia	321
Andipaxi (Ionian islands)	377
Andriomonastiro (Peloponnese)	129
Andritsena	114
Andronikos, Manolis	466
Andros	195
Angelokastro (Corfu)	374
Angistri (Argosaronic)	166
Animal life	506
Ano Boularii	143
Ano Korakiana (Corfu)	373
Ano Mera (Mykonos)	203
Ano Meria (Folegandros)	237
Ano Prinos (Thassos)	392
Ano Syros (Syros)	195
Anogia (Crete)	283
Anthiro (Karditsa)	429
Antiparos	194, 218
Antipaxi	360, 361, 377
Aoos, river	449
Apiranthos (Naxos)	197
Apocalypse tou Ioanni	348
Paleopolis	370
Palia Perithia	373
Panagia Kremasti	368
Paxi	377

INDEX

A

Academy (Athens)..40
Achilleio (Corfu)..376
Acrocorinth..88
Acropolis...27-29
Acropolis Museum...29
Aigina (Argosaronic)..166
Agamemnon..85
Agia Eleni, beach (Skiathos)..............................397
Agia Kyriaki (Samos)..392
Agia Marina (Leros)..322
Agia Marina (Kasos)...321
Agia Marina, beach (Symi)................................342
Agia Paraskevi (Metsovo)..................................438
Agia Pelagia (Kythera).......................................171
Agia Sophia, church (Mystras)..........................152
Agia Sophia, cave (Kythera)..............................170
Agia Sophia, church (Monemvassia)................158
Agia Triada, church (Paros)..............................218
Agia Sophia (Thessaloniki)................................475
Agia Varvara, village (Peloponnese).................100
Agii Anargiri, church (Kastoria).........................458
Agii Theodori, church (Mystras)........................152
Agii Theodori, church (Athens)...........................40
Agios Achillios...461
Agios Dimitrios..475
Agios Dimitrios (Corfu).....................................376
Agios Dionysios, church (Zakynthos)................362
Agios Eleftherios, Panagia Gorgoepikoos (Athens).....34
Agios Emilianos, beach (Peloponnese).............181
Agios Georgios, beach (Corfu).........................379
Agios Gerassimos Monastery (Cephalonia)......361
Agios Germanos..461
Agios Giannis, beach (Milos)............................196
Agios Gordis, beach (Corfu).............................379
Agios Ioannis Theologos...................................347
Agios Ioannis Theologos, beach (Kos).............321
Agios Kyrikos (Ikaria)..391
Agios Markos (Corfu)..372
Agios Mattheos (Corfu).....................................375
Agios Nikitas (Lefkada).....................................362
Agios Nikolaos (Crete)......................................307
Agios Nikolaos, beach (Kythera)......................172
Agios Nikolaos, church (Peloponnese).............142
Agios Panteleimonas, beach (Crete)................308
Agios Pavlos, beach (Crete).............................263
Agios Sostis, beach (Mykonos)........................206
Agios Spyridon, church (Corfu)........................368
Agios Spyridonas, church (Peloponnese)........141
Agios Stephanos (Corfu)..................................372
Agios Stephanos, church (Kastoria).................457
Agni (Corfu)...372
Agora, ancient (Athens).....................................30
Agrafa (Karditsa)..429
Agrari, beach (Mykonos)..................................206
Agriolivado, beach (Patmos)............................349
Ai Giannis, beach (Pelion)................................412
Edipsos (Evvia)...388
Aigai..466
Akamatra (Ikaria)..391
Akronafplia (Nafplio)..82
Akrotiri (Santorini)..245
Akrotiri Drastis (Corfu).....................................373
Alexander the Great...466
Ali Pasha..445
Alinda (Leros)...322
Almyrida (Crete)...271
Aloizianika (Kythera)..171
Alonissos (Sporades).......................................389
Alykes, beach (Ammouliani).............................498
Ambelakia...378
Ammouliani...495
Amorgos (Cyclades)...197

Anafi (Cyclades)..198
Anafiotika (Athens)...32
Anakassia...409
Ancient Agora (Kos)...321
Ancient Bassae, Temple of Apollo Epikourios....114
Ancient Corinth (Peloponnese)....................86-87
Ancient Epidaurus (Peloponnese).....................89
Ancient Gortyna (Crete)...................................292
Ancient Gortyna (Peloponnese).......................112
Ancient Ialyssos (Rhodes)...............................332
Ancient Kamiros (Rhodes)...............................331
Ancient Lappa (Crete)......................................272
Ancient Messene, Ancient Ithomi (Peloponnese)....126
Ancient Mycenae (Peloponnese).......................85
Ancient Nemea (Peloponnese)..........................86
Ancient Olympia (Peloponnese)......................118
Ancient Thera..245
Ancient Tiryns (Peloponnese)...........................84
Antimacheia (Kos)...321
Antipaxi (Ionian islands)..................................377
Andriomonastiro (Peloponnese).....................129
Andritsena (Peloponnese)..............................114
Andronikos, Manolis.......................................466
Andros (Cyclades)..195
Angelokastro (Corfu)......................................374
Angistri (Argosaronic).....................................166
Ano Boularii (Peloponnese)............................143
Ano Korakiana (Corfu)....................................373
Ano Mera (Mykonos).......................................203
Ano Meria (Folegandros)................................237
Ano Prinos (Thassos).....................................392
Ano Syros (Syros)...195
Anogia (Crete)...283
Anthiro (Karditsa)..429
Antiparos (Cyclades)...............................194, 218
Antipaxi (Ionian islands)....................360, 361, 377
Aoos, river..449
Apiranthos (Naxos)...197
Apocalypse tou Ioanni....................................348
Apokoronas (Crete)..271
Apollonia (Sifnos)...227
Apozari quarter (Kastoria)..............................459
Aptera (Crete)..271-272
Arahova...422
Arcadian Highlands (excursion 5)..........109-116
Archaeological Museums
  Ancient Corinth...87
  Athens..38-39
  Chania..259
  Corfu...369
  Delos..205
  Delphi...421
  Fira...244
  Heraklio..299-300
  Ioannina...444
  Kos...321
  Nafplio..83
  Paros..217
  Rethymno...280
  Rhodes...327
  Sifnos...228
  Sparta...150
  Thessaloniki...474
  Vravrona..48

Archaeological Sites
  Akrotiri..245
  Delos..204
  Delphi...420
  Dodona...448
  Knossos...296-298
  Lindos...330
  Pella..469
  Vergina...467

INDEX

Archaic period 14
Archilochos 217
Arcturus 460
Areopolis 142
Argos 84
Argosaronic, gulf 166
Argyroupoli (Crete) 272
Ariadne 296
Aroniadika (Kythera) 171
Aristi 446
Arkadi, monastery (Crete) 281
Arkii (Dodecanese) 320, 355
Arkos, beach (Skiathos) 398
Armata 180
Arnas (Andros) 195
Artemonas (Sifnos) 227
Arvanitohori (Kassos) 321
Asklepeion (Kos) 321
Aspronissia, beach (Dodecanese) 356
Aspros Potamos (Crete) 316
Assos (Cephalonia) 361
Astraka 449
Astypalaia (Dodecanese) 322
Ateni (Andros) 195
Athens
   Academy 40
   Acropolis 27-29
   Acropolis Museum 29
   Agii Theodori, church 40
   Agios Eleftherios, Panagia Gorgoepikoos 34
   Agora, ancient 30
   Anafiotika 32
   Archaeological Museum of Athens 38-39
   Archaeological Museum of Vravrona 48
   Athens Environs 45-50
   Beaches 50
   Benaki Museum 41
   Byzantine Museum 42
   Cave Koutouki 49
   Concert Hall 44
   Contemporary Athens 35-43
   Cycladic Art Museum 41-42
   Dafni Monastery 47
   Dionysos, theatre 29
   Entertainment 71-73
   Erechtheion 28
   Festivals 43-44
   Giousouroum, Flea Market 33
   Glyfada, beach 50
   Glyfada Golf Club 50
   Grande Bretagne 40
   Hadrians Arch 32
   Herod Atticus Theatre 29, 43
   Historical Athens 25-34
   Hotels 52-60
   Iliou Melathron 40
   Information 74
   Kanellopoulos Museum 33
   Kapnikarea, church 34
   Kerameikos 31
   Kerameikos Museum 31
   Kaisariani Monastery 47
   Kifissia 49
   Kolonaki 41
   Koutouki, cave 49
   Lake Marathon 49
   Library 40
   Lykabettus hill 43
   Lykabettus theatre 44, 43
   Lyssicratis, monument 32
   Marathon 49
   Metamorphosis, church 33
   Monastiraki 33
   National Art Gallery 43

   National Gardens 41
   Ophthalmiatreio (Eye Hospital) 40
   Parliament 41
   Parnis, mountain 48
   Parthenon 28
   Petra, theatre 44
   Philopappos, hill 30
   Pireas, Piraeus 47
   Plaka 32-33
   Plakentias castle, festival 44
   Pnyx 30
   Propylaia 28
   Psyrri 34
   Restaurants 61-70
   Russian church 34
   Schinias, beach 50
   Sound and Light 44
   Sounio 48
   Stoa of Attalos 31
   Stoa of Eumenes 28
   Syntagma square, Constitution square 40
   Temple of Apteros Nike 28
   Temple of Hephaistos 31
   Temple of Olympian Zeus 31-32
   Temple of Poseidon (Sounio) 48
   Thission 30-31
   Tower of the Winds 33
   University 40
   Varkiza, beach 50
   Voula, beach 50
   Vouliagmeni 48
   Vouliagmeni, beach 50
   Vravrona 48
   War Museum 43
   Zappeion 41
Athens and Environs 24-50
Athens Environs 45-50
Athos, Holy Mountain 496-497
Athos (excursion 43) 491-500
Atreus 85
Averoff, Evangelos Art Gallery (Metsovo) 438
Avgonyma (Chios) 391
Avlemonas (Kythera) 171

B

Banana, beach (Skiathos) 397
Banknote Museum (Corfu) 369
Barbati, beach (Corfu) 379
Bargaining 513
Bassae, Temple of Apollo Epikourios (Peloponnese) 114
Batsi (Andros) 195
Battle of Navarino 133
Bella Vista (Corfu) 374
Belokomitis (Karditsa) 429
Benaki Museum (Athens) 41
Benitses (Corfu) 376
Bouboulina, Laskarina 179
Bourazani 448
Bourtzi (Nafplio) 82
Bourtzi (Skiathos) 395
Bronze Age 12
Byzantine Museums
   Athens 42
   Corfu 368
   Ioannina 443
   Kastoria 459
   Rhodes 328
   Thessaloniki 475
Byzantium 17

C

Campiello (Corfu) 368

519

INDEX

Canal d' amour (Corfu) 373
Carnival (Patras) 76
Capodistrias, Ioannis 80, 369
Casino
   Corfu 371
   Loutraki 90
   Rhodes 329
   Sithonia 488
   Thessaloniki 479
Castello (Corfu) 372
Cathedral (Mystra) 152
Caves
   Agia Sophia (Kythera) 170
   Cave of the Apocalypse (Patmos) 348
   Diros (Peloponnese) 143
   Drogarati (Cephalonia) 361
   Koutouki (Attica) 49
   Melissani (Cephalonia) 361
   Perama 445
   Petralona 486
   Sfendoni (Crete) 283
Cephalonia 361
Chania 258-260
Chania (Pelion) 410
Chios 390-391
Chios, town 390-391
Christos Elkomenos, church (Monemvassia) 157
Chromonastiri (Crete) 281
Chryssi Akti, beach (Paros) 220
Chryssopigi (Sifnos) 229
Classical period 14
Climate 507
Clytemnestra 85
Cog wheeled railway (Peloponnese) 105
Communications 511
Concert Hall (Athens) 44
Contemporary Athens 35-43
Contemporary Greece 20
Contents 4-5
Continental Greece 377-380
Corfu 360
Corfu (excursion 31) 363-386
Corfu
   Achilleio 376
   Agios Dimitrios 376
   Agios Georgios, beach 379
   Agios Gordis, beach 379
   Agios Markos 372
   Agios Mattheos 375
   Agios Spyridonas, church 368
   Agios Stephanos 372
   Agni 372
   Antipaxi 377
   Angelokastro 374
   Ano Korakiana 373
   Archaeological Museum 369
   Banknote Museum 369
   Barbati, beach 379
   Bella Vista 374
   Benitses 376
   Byzantine Museum 368
   Campiello 368
   Canal d' amour 373
   Casino 371
   Castello 372
   Drastis, cape 373
   Erikoussa 377
   Ermones 374
   Gardiki, fort 375
   Gialiskari, beach 378
   Glyfada, beach 378
   Golf 376
   Gouvia 371
   Halikouna, beach 379
   Chlomos (Corfu) 375
   Ionian Academy 369
   Kalami 372
   Kanoni 370
   Kassiopi 373
   Kerassia, beach 379
   Kommeno 371
   Kondogialos, beach 378
   Kondokali 371
   Kouloura 372
   Lake Korission 375
   Liston 367
   Mathraki 377
   Messonghi 376
   Mon Repos 370
   Mt Pantokrator 372
   Myrtiotissa, beach 378
   Nymphes 373
   Old Town 366-69
   Othoni 377
   Palace 368
   Palaiokastritsa 374
   Palaiopolis 370
   Palia Perithia 373
   Panagia Kremasti 368
   Panagia Myrtidiotissa, monastery 378
   Panagia Palaiokastritsa, monastery 374
   Paxi 377
   Pelekas 375
   Peroulades 373
   Petriti 376
   Pontikonissi 370
   Prassoudi, beach 378
   Reading Society 369
   Sidari 373
   Sinarades 375
   Skripero 373
   Spartilas 372
   Spianada 367
   Vido island 370
   Monastery Vlahernas 370
Corinth Canal, Isthmus 88
Corinth, ancient 86,7
Crete 253-254
Crete
   Archaeological Museum of Heraklio 299-300
   Aspros Potamos 316
   Chania 258-260
   Elounda 306
   Frangokastello 273
   Gorge Samaria 261
   Heraklio 298-300
   Hora Sfakion 272-3
   Knossos 296-298
   Matala 290
   Phaestos 291
   Rethymno 277
   Vai 315
   Vamos 271
Cultural events 512-513
Currency 514-515
Customs 502
Cyclades 193-198
Cycladic Art Museum (Athens) 41-42
Cycladic civilization 12

D

Dadia forest 380
Daedalus 296
Dafni (Ikaria) 391
Dafni monastery (Attica) 47
Damnoni, beach (Crete) 283
Damouhari, beach (Pelion) 412

INDEX

Dellagratsia (Syros) 195
Delos (Cyclades) 194, 203
Delphi 418-419
Delphi-Arahova (excursion 34) 417-426
Despots palace (Mystra) 152
Diaskari, beach (Crete) 316
Dilofo 446
Dimitsana (Peloponnese) 111
Dion 380
Dionysos, theatre (Acropolis) 29
Diros, cave (Peloponnese) 143
Dodecanese 319-22
Dodona 449
Dokos (Argosaronic) 166
Doltso quarter (Kastoria) 459
Domnista 405
Donoussa (Cyclades) 198
Dorians 13
Douliana (Crete) 271
Doxis, artificial lake (Peloponnese) 97
Drakaious (Samos) 391-392
Drakolimni 449
Drepano, cape 486
Drogarati, cave (Cephalonia) 361
Drosato (Karditsa) 429
Dryopis, cave (Kythnos) 196
Duchy of the Aegean 217

E

Eastern Crete (excursion 26) 313-318
Economy 505
Ekatontapyliani, church (Paros) 217
Elafonissi, beach (Crete) 263
Elafonissos, island 166, 172
Elati 446
Eleutherna (Crete) 281
Elia, beach (Mykonos) 206
Elounda (Crete) 306
Elounda (excursion 25) 305-312
Embassies 502-503
Emborio, Nimborio (Santorini) 245
Emborios, Nimborio (Symi) 341
Entertainment 511
Epidaurus, old 89
Epidaurus, theatre 89
Eptanissa, Ionian islands 359-362
Erechtheion (Acropolis) 28
Erikoussa (Ionian islands) 361, 377
Ermones (Corfu) 374
Ermoupoli (Syros) 195
Etia (Crete) 315
Evangelistria, church (Tinos) 195
Evans, Arthur 296
Evdilos (Ikaria) 391
Evritania 379
Evros delta 379
Evvia 388-389

F

Fakistra, beach (Pelion) 412
Falassarna, beach (Crete) 263
Farangas, beach (Paros) 220
Faros (Sifnos) 228
Fassolou, beach (Sifnos) 230
Fauna 506
Festivals 512-513
Films 515
Finika (Syros) 195
Finikounda 134
Fira (Santorini) 244
Firostefani (Santorini) 244
Fiskardo (Cephalonia) 361

Flora 506
Folegandros (Cyclades) 195
Folegandros (excursion 18) 235-240
Folk Art Museum (Nafplio) 82
Fonias, gorge (Samothraki) 392
Fourni, islet (Ikaria) 391
Frangia, beach (Mykonos) 207
Frangista 379
Frangokastello, beach (Crete) 274
Frangokastello, castle (Crete) 273
Franks 18
Frikes (Ithaki) 362
Frilingianika, (Kythera) 171
Fyri Ammos, beach (Kythera) 172

G

Galaxidi 422
Galazies Spilies (Zakynthos) 362
Gardiki, fortress (Corfu) 375
Gavalohori (Crete) 271
Geography 505
Geometric period 13
Gerakari (Kythera) 171
Gerakas, beach (Zakynthos) 362
Geraki (Peloponnese) 159
Gerolimenas (Peloponnese) 143
Gialiskari, beach (Corfu) 378
Gialos (Symi) 340
Giousouroum, Flea Market 33
Glossary 516
Glyfada, beach (Attica) 50
Glyfada, beach (Corfu) 378
Golf
  Corfu 376
  Glyfada (Attica) 50
  Rhodes 332
  Sithonia 488
Gorges
  Gorge of the Dead (Crete) 315
  Imbros (Crete) 272
  Kourtaliotiko (Crete) 282
  Loussios (Peloponnese) 112-3
  Samaria (Crete) 261
  Therissos (Crete) 261-262
  Vikos (Continental Greece) 448-449
  Virou (Peloponnese) 142
  Vouraikos (Peloponnese) 105
Gorgianades 379
Gortyna, ancient (Crete) 292
Gortyna, ancient (Peloponnese) 112
Goura (Peloponnese) 97
Gouves (Evvia) 388-389
Gouvia (Corfu) 371
Gramvoussa, beach (Crete) 263
Granitsa 379
Great Tumulus 467
Greece 503
Greek Islands 163-164
Greeks 503
Gregolimano (Evvia) 388
Grikos (Patmos) 348
Grotto of the Nymphs (Ithaki) 362
Gytheion (Peloponnese) 144

H

Hadrian's Arch (Athens) 32
Halikouna, beach (Corfu) 376
Halki (Dodecanese) 322
Halkida (Evvia) 388-389
Halkidiki 485, 493
Halkos, beach (Kythera) 173
Handras (Crete) 315-316

521

INDEX

Health 511
Hellenistic era 16
Helmos, mountain (Peloponnese) 104
Heraklio (Crete) 298-300
Hermes by Praxiteles 122, 217
Herod Atticus Theatre (Athens) 29, 43
Herronissos (Sifnos) 227
Hippocrates 321
Historical Athens 25-34
History and Culture 11-22
Holidays 513
Hora (Samothraki) 392
Hora (Alonissos) 389
Hora (Amorgos) 197
Hora (Anafi) 198
Hora (Andros) 195
Hora (Astypalaia) 322
Hora (Ios) 197
Hora (Kythera) 169
Hora (Mykonos) 201
Hora (Patmos) 347
Hora (Serifos) 196
Hora (Sikinos) 198
Hora (Skopelos) 389
Hora (Skyros) 389-390
Hora (Kimolos) 197
Hora Sfakion (Crete) 272-273
Hora Triffilias 133
Hora, Ioulis (Kea) 196
Horefto, beach (Pelion) 412
Horio (Kalymnos) 321
Horio, (Symi) 341
Hotels 514
How to use Best 6-7
Hydra (Argosaronic) 166
Hydra (excursion 14) 185-192
Hydraulic Power Museum (Peloponnese) 111

I

Ia (Santorini) 243
Ikaria (North-east Aegean) 391
Iktinos 114
Iliou Melathron (Athens) 40
Imbros, gorge (Crete) 272
Imerovigli (Santorini) 244
Independence War 19
Ioannina 443
Ioannina island 444
Ionian Academy 369
Ionian islands 359-386
Ios 197
Ioulis, Hora (Kea) 196
Iraklia (Cyclades) 198
Isthmia (Peloponnese) 88
Istron (Crete) 308
Ithaki (Ionian islands) 362
Ithome, Ancient Messene 126

K

Kaiadas (Peloponnese) 152
Kaiafas (Peloponnese) 123
Kaladi, beach (Kythera) 172
Kalafatis, beach (Mykonos) 207
Kalamaki, beach (Pelion) 412
Kalambaka 432
Kalami (Corfu) 372
Kalamitsi, beach (Halkidiki) 487
Kalavryta (Peloponnese) 103
Kalavryta (excursion 4) 103-108
Kaliani (Peloponnese) 96
Kallithea (Samos) 392

Kalo Nero (Peloponnese) 129
Kalogria, beach (Mani) 76
Kalogria, beach (Halkidiki) 487
Kalymnos (Dodecanese) 321
Kamares (Lipsi) 356
Kamares (Sifnos) 227
Kamares, beach (Sifnos) 230
Kamari, beach (Kos) 321
Kambos, beach (Patmos) 349
Kanellopoulos Museum (Athens) 33
Kanoni (Corfu) 370
Kapnikarea, church (Athens) 34
Kapsali (Kythera) 170
Karathonas, beach (Peloponnese) 90
Karavas (Kythera) 171
Karavostassi (Folegandros) 237
Kardamyli (Peloponnese) 141
Karditsa 428
Karlovassi (Samos) 391-392
Karpathos (Dodecanese) 321
Karpenissi 379
Karya (Karditsa) 429
Karydi (Crete) 271
Karydi, beach (Halkidiki) 487
Karyes 496
Karystos (Evvia) 389
Karytena (Peloponnese) 113
Kassos (Dodecanese) 321
Kassandra Peninsula 486
Kassiopi (Corfu) 373
Kastania (excursion 2) 95-98
Kastania (Karditsa) 429
Kastania (Peloponnese) 97
Kastellorizo, Megisti 322
Kastoria 457
Kastoria (excursion 39) 455-464
Kastoria, lake 458
Kastro (Sifnos) 228
Kastro (Skiathos) 396
Katakilo (Andros) 195
Katarrakti 405
Katergo, beach (Folegandros) 236
Kato Korakiana (Corfu) 372
Kato Koufonissi (Cyclades) 198
Kato Livadi (Kythera) 170
Kato Potamia (Naxos) 197
Kato Zakros (Crete) 315
Kavourotrypes, beach (Halkidiki) 487
Kea, Tzia (Cyclades) 196
Kefalas (Crete) 271
Kefalos (Kos) 321
Kechries, beach (Skiathos) 397
Kerameikos (Athens) 31
Kerameikos Museum (Athens) 31
Kerassia (Karditsa) 428
Kerassia, beach (Corfu) 379
Kerkini, lake 379
Kaisariani Monastery (Attica) 47
Kifissia (Attica) 49
Kimolos (Cyclades) 197
Kioni (Ithaki) 362
Kipi 446
Kissos 410
Kita (Peloponnese) 143
Kleftiko, beach (Milos) 196
Knights of St. John 321
Knossos (Crete) 296-298
Knossos-Heraklio (excursion 24) 295-304
Kokkari (Samos) 391-392
Kokkini Ammos, beach (Santorini) 247
Kolokotronis, Theodoros 81
Kolokytha, beach (Crete) 308
Kolonaki (Athens) 41
Koloumbos, cape (Santorini) 247

INDEX

Kolymbithres, beach (Paros) 219
Kombonada, beach (Kythera) 173
Kommeno (Corfu) 371
Kommos, beach (Crete) 293
Kondogialos, beach (Corfu) 378
Kondokali (Corfu) 371
Koraka, beach (Crete) 274
Korakia, beach (Peloponnese) 181
Korakou bridge (Karditsa) 429
Korfos (Peloponnese) 89
Korission, lake (Corfu) 375
Koroni (Peloponnese) 135
Koryschades 379
Kos (Dodecanese) 321
Kosiki (Ikaria) 391
Kostoula, beach (Peloponnese) 181
Koufonissi, (Crete) 316
Koukouli 446
Koule, fortress (Crete) 300
Kouloura (Corfu) 372
Koumbouriana (Karditsa) 429
Koundouriotis, Georgios 187
Koundouros (Kea) 196
Kouremenos, beach (Crete) 316
Kourna, lake (Crete) 272
Kourtaliotiko, gorge (Crete) 282
Koutouki, cave (Attica) 49
Krini (Peloponnese) 106
Kritsa (Crete) 307
Kymi (Evvia) 389
Kyparissi (Peloponnese) 159
Kyparissia (Peloponnese) 129
Kyriakoulou, beach (Kythera) 172
Kythera (excursion 12) 167-176, 166, 360
Kythera, central 172
Kythera, northern 171
Kythera, southern 169
Kythnos (Cyclades) 196
Koundouriotis, Pavlos 187

L

Labyrinth 296
Ladadika 475
Ladiko, beach (Rhodes) 332
Lafka (Peloponnese) 96
Lagia (Peloponnese) 144
Lagomandra, beach (Halkidiki) 487
Lake Plastira (excursion 35) 427-430
Lakes
   Doxis (Peloponnese) 97
   Kastoria, Orestias 458
   Korission (Corfu) 375
   Kremaston 379
   Marathon (Attica) 49
   Megali Prespa 460
   Mikri Prespa 460
   Orestias, Kastoria lake 458
   Plastira 428-429
   Stymphalia (Peloponnese) 96
   Tsivlou (Peloponnese) 100-101
Lakki (Leros) 322
Lalaria, beach (Skiathos) 397
Lambes, beach (Peloponnese) 135
Lambinou, beach (Pelion) 412
Lamyra (Andros) 195
Langeri, beach (Paros) 220
Lassithi plateau (Crete) 308
Lato (Crete) 307
Lefkada (Ionian islands) 362
Lefkes (Paros) 218
Lefki Ammos, beach (Santorini) 247
Leondito (Karditsa) 429
Leros (Dodecanese) 322

Lesvos, Mytilini 390
Lia, beach (Mykonos) 206
Lias 449
Library (Athens) 40
Limenas Geraka 158
Limeni (Peloponnese) 142
Limnionas, beach (Kythera) 170
Limnon, cave (Peloponnese) 106
Limnos (North-east Aegean) 392
Lindos (Rhodes) 329
Lindos, beach (Rhodes) 333
Lipsi (Dodecanese) 320, 355
Liston (Corfu) 367
Little Venice (Mykonos) 202
Livadi (Kythera) 170
Logothetianika (Kythera) 171
Loussios, gorge 112-113
Loutraki casino 90
Loutro (Crete) 273
Lower Loussi 106
Lykabettus, hill (Athens) 43
Lykabettus, theatre (Athens) 44, 43
Lyssikratis, monument (Athens) 32

M

Madouri, islet (Lefkada) 362
Magazines 511
Makria Ammos, beach (Peloponnese) 135
Makrygialo (Crete) 316
Makrynitsa 409
Mandraki (Hydra) 188
Mandraki (Nisyros) 322
Mandraki, beach (Skiathos) 397
Manganari, beach (Ios) 197
Mani (excursion 9) 139-148
Marathi (Dodecanese) 320, 355
Marathi (excursion 30) 353-358
Marathon (Attica) 49
Margarites (Crete) 282
Marmara, beach (Crete) 274
Marmari, beach (Peloponnese) 144
Mastic villages (Chios) 391
Matala (Crete) 290-291
Matala, beach (Crete) 293
Mathraki (Ionian islands) 361, 377
Mavromati (Peloponnese) 126
Mavromichali family tower 142
Mavrovouni, beach (Peloponnese) 144
Megali Ammoudara, beach 498
Megali Prespa, lake 460
Megalo Horio 379
Megalo Horio (Tilos) 322
Megalo Meteoro, (Monastery Metamorphosi Sotira) ... 433
Megalo Papingo 447
Meganissi, islet (Lefkada) 362
Megisti, Kastellorizo 322
Melidoni, beach (Kythera) 172
Melissani, cave (Cephalonia) 361
Mesi Potamia (Naxos) 197
Messene, ancient (excursion 6) 125-130
Messenikolas (Karditsa) 429
Messonghi (Corfu) 376
Mesovouni (Karditsa) 429
Mesta (Chios) 391
Metamorphosis, church (Athens) 33
Meteora 431
Meteora (excursion 36) 431-436
Methana (Argosaronic) 166
Methoni (Peloponnese) 134
Methoni, castle (Peloponnese) 134
Metsovo 438
Metsovo (excursion 37) 437-440
Mikri Prespa, lake 460

523

INDEX

Mikro Horio (Tilos) 322
Mikro Papingo 447
Milies 410-411
Milos (Cyclades) 196
Minoan civilization 12, 296-298
Minos 296
Minotaur 296
Mirabello, gulf (Crete) 307
Mitata (Kythera) 171
Mithymna, Molyvos (Lesvos) 390
Modern times 22
Mochlos (Crete) 308
Molyvos, Mithymna (Lesvos) 390
Mon Repos (Corfu) 370
Monasteries
  Agia Elessa (Kythera) *170*
  Agia Lavra (Peloponnese) *105*
  Agia Paraskevi (Zagoria) *447*
  Agia Triada Tsangarolon (Crete) *262*
  Agia Triada (Meteora) *433*
  Agia Varvara, Roussanou (Meteora) *434*
  Agion Panton, Varlaam (Meteora) *433*
  Agios Ioannis (Crete) *262*
  Agios Nektarios (Aegina) *166*
  Agiou Georgiou Feneou (Peloponnese) *97*
  Agiou Ioannou Prodromou (Peloponnese) *112*
  Agiou Nikolaou Anapafsa (Meteora) *434*
  Agiou Panteleimonos (Mount Athos) *496*
  Agiou Pavlou (Mount Athos) *497*
  Agiou Stephanou (Meteora) *434*
  Agnoundos (Peloponnese) *89*
  Arkadi (Crete) *281*
  Docheiariou (Mount Athos) *497*
  Aimyalon (Peloponnese) *113*
  Esphigmenou (Mount Athos) *497*
  Evangelistrias (Skiathos) *395*
  Gouvernetou (Crete) *262*
  Hiliandariou (Mount Athos) *497*
  Hozoviotissa (Amorgos) *197*
  Iviron (Mount Athos) *497*
  Karakalou (Mount Athos) *497*
  Kimisseos Theotokou (Peloponnese) *86*
  Konstamonitou (Mount Athos) *497*
  Koutloumousiou (Mount Athos) *497*
  Longovardas (Paros) *219*
  Makellarias (Peloponnese) *106*
  Mega Spileon (Peloponnese) *105*
  Megisti Lavra (Mount Athos) *496*
  Metamorphosi Sotira, Megalo Meteoron (Meteora) *433*
  Molyvdoskepasti (Continental Greece) *448*
  Myrtidion (Kythera) *170*
  New Philosophou (Peloponnese) *112-113*
  New Voulkano (Peloponnese) *128*
  Old Philosophou (Peloponnese) *112*
  Old Voulkano (Peloponnese) *128*
  Osios Loukas *422*
  Panagia Chryssopigi (Sifnos) *229*
  Panagia Kalamiotissa (Anafi) *198*
  Panagia Kera (Crete) *308*
  Panagia Kounistra (Skiathos) *396*
  Panagia Myrtidiotissa (Corfu) *378*
  Panagia Palaiokastritsa (Corfu) *374*
  Panagia Peleketis (Karditsa) *429*
  Panagia Prousiotissa *405*
  Panagia Spilianis (Nisyros) *322*
  Panagia Spilias (Karditsa) *429*
  Panagia Vrondiani (Samos) *389-390*
  Pantanassa (Mystra) *152*
  Panormitis (Symi) *341*
  Pantokratoros (Mount Athos) *497*
  Perivleptos (Mystras) *152*
  Petra (Karditsa) *429*
  Philanthropinon, monastery *444*
  Philotheou (Mount Athos) *497*
  Preveli (Crete) *282*
  Roussanou, Agia Varvara (Meteora) *434*
  Simonos Petra (Mount Athos) *496*
  St. John the Divine (Patmos) *347*
  Stavronikita (Mount Athos) *497*
  Toplou (Crete) *315*
  Valsamonero (Crete) *292*
  Varlaam, Agion Panton (Meteora) *433*
  Vatopedi (Mount Athos) *497*
  Vlahernas (Corfu) *370*
  Vrondissiou (Crete) *292*
  Xenofontos (Mount Athos) *497*
  Xiropotamou (Mount Athos) *496*
  Zographou (Mount Athos) *497*
  Zoodochos Pigi (Patmos) *348*
Monastiraki (Athens) 33
Monastiri, beach (Paros) 219
Monemvassia (Peloponnese) 156
Monemvassia (excursion 11) **155-162**
Moni (Argosaronic) 166
Monodendri 447
Morfovouni (Karditsa) 429
Morosini, fountain Crete 300
Mount Athos, Holy Mountain (excursion 43) **491-500**
Mouzaki (Karditsa) 428
Museum of Greek History, Pavlos Vrellis 445
Museum of Modern Art (Andros) 195
Mycenae (Peloponnese) 85
Mycenaean civilization 13
Mykonos (Cyclades) 195, 201
Mykonos (excursion 15) **199-214**
Myli (Crete) 281
Mylopotamos (Kythera) 170
Mylopotamos, beach (Pelion) 411
Mylopotas, beach (Ios) 197
Myrina (Limnos) 392
Myrtiotissa, beach (Corfu) 378
Mystra (Peloponnese) 151
Mystra (excursion 10) **149-154**
Mytilini, Lesvos 390

N

Nafpaktia Highlands 379
Nafpaktos 406
Nafplio (Peloponnese) 80
Nafplio (excursion 1) **77-94**
Nanou, beach (Symi) 342
Naoussa (Paros) 217-8
National Art Gallery (Athens) 43
National Gardens (Athens) 41
National Sporades Sea Park 389
National Tourist Organization 502
Navagio, beach (Zakynthos) 362
Naxos (Cyclades) 197
Nea Kameni, islet (Santorini) 246
Nea Moni (Chios) 391
Necromanteio 380
Necropolis 380
Nemea (Peloponnese) 86
Neohori (Peloponnese) 106
Neohori (Karditsa) 429
Neolithic era 12
Neos Marmaras 485
Nestor's Palace 133
Newspapers 511
Nike of Samothraki 392
Nimborio (Halki) 322
Nimborio, Emborios (Symi) 341
Niokastro (Peloponnese) 134
Nisyros (Dodecanese) 322
North-east Aegean Islands 390-392

524

INDEX

Nydri (Lefkada) 362
Nymphaio 459
Nymphes (Corfu) 373

O

Odysseus 362
Old Town, Nafplio 80-84
Old Town, Rethymno 279
Old Town, Chania 258-260
Old Town, Corfu 366-69
Old Town, Rhodes 326
Old Epidavros (Peloponnese) 89
Olymbi (Chios) 391
Olymbos, Elimbos (Karpathos) 321
Olympia, ancient 118
Olympic games 118
Olympus, mountain 378
Ophthalmiatreio, Eye Hospital (Athens) 40
Orestias, lake (Kastoria) 458
Osios Loukas, monastery 422
Othoni (Ionian islands) 361, 377
Otto, king 80
Ottoman domination 18
Ouranoupoli 495

P

Pahia Ammos, beach (Crete) 308
Palace of SS Michael & George (Corfu) 368
Palace of the Grand Master (Rhodes) 326
Palaio Pyli (Kos) 321
Palamidi (Nafplio) 81
Palatitsa 469
Palaiohora (Kythera) 171
Palaiokastritsa (Corfu) 374
Palaiopoli (Kythera) 171
Palaiopoli, beach (Kythera) 172,3
Palaiopolis (Corfu) 370
Palaiopolis (Samothraki) 392
Palia Kameni, islet (Santorini) 246
Palia Perithia (Corfu) 373
Paliokastro (Peloponnese) 134
Panagia Gorgoepikoos, Agios Eleftherios (Athens) 34
Panagia Koumbelidiki (Kastoria) 457
Panagia Kounistra (Skiathos) 396
Panagia Kremasti (Corfu) 368
Panagia Mavriotissa (Kastoria) 458
Panagia Odigitria (Mystras) 152
Panagia Ouranofora (Sifnos) 227
Panagia Paraportiani (Mykonos) 202
Panagias, bay 486
Pandeli (Leros) 322
Pano Koufonissi (Cyclades) 198
Pano Potamia (Naxos) 197
Panormos (Crete) 282
Panormos (Tinos) 195
Panormos, beach (Mykonos) 207
Pantokrator, mountain (Corfu) 372
Papadiamantis, Alexandros 395
Papafranga, cave (Milos) 196
Paradise, beach (Mykonos) 207
Paradissos, beach (Kos) 321
Paranga, beach (Mykonos) 207
Parasporos, beach (Paros) 220
Parga 380
Parikia (Paros) 217
Parliament (Athens) 41
Parnassos, mountain 423
Parnis, mountain (Attica) 48
Paros (Cyclades) 194, 215
Paros (excursion 16) 215-224
Parthenon (Athens) 28

Parthenonas 485
Pasiphae 296
Patitiri (Alonissos) 389
Patmos (excursion 29) 345-352
Patmos (Dodecanese) 320
Patras 76
Paxi (Ionian islands) 360, 361, 377
Pelekas (Corfu) 375
Pelion (excursion 33) 407-416
Peloponnese 75-76
Pera Kastro (Kalymnos) 321
Perama, cave 445
Perissa, beach (Santorini) 247
Perivolos, beach (Santorini) 247
Peroulades (Corfu) 373
Petalidi (Peloponnese) 135
Petra, theatre (Athens) 44
Petralona 486
Petralona (Kokkines Petres) 486
Petrified forest (Lesvos) 390
Petriti (Corfu) 376
Petropouli (Ikaria) 391
Petrouni, (Kythera) 171
Pezoula (Karditsa) 429
Phaestos (Crete)) 291
Phaestos-Matala (excursion 23) 289-294
Feneos (Peloponnese) 97
Philip II 467
Philippi, ancient 380
Philopappos, hill (Athens) 30
Photographs 514
Phrases 516
Fri (Kassos) 321
Pireas, Piraeus (Attica) 47
Pyrgos Dirou 142
Pisso Livadi, beach (Paros) 220
Plaka (Athens) 32-33
Plaka (Milos) 196
Plaka, beach (Naxos) 197
Plakentias castle, festival (Attica) 44
Plastira lake, Tavropou lake 428
Platanias, beach (Crete) 263
Platanitsi (Halkidiki) 487
Platanos (Leros) 322
Platys Gialos (Sifnos) 228
Platys Gialos, beach (Sifnos) 230
Plomari (Lesvos) 390
Plytra, beach (Peloponnese) 159
Pnyx (Athens) 30
Politics 504
Politika (Evvia) 388
Pontikonissi (Corfu) 370
Poros (Argosaronic) 166
Portara (Naxos) 197
Portaria 409
Porto Carras 485
Porto Heli (Peloponnese) 180
Porto Kagio (Peloponnese) 143
Porto Katsiki (Lefkada) 362
Porto Katsiki, beach (Lefkada) 362
Porto Koufo 486
Post-war period 21
Potamia (Thassos) 392
Pothia (Kalymnos) 321
Pounta, beach (Paros) 220
Practical information 501-516
Prassoudi, beach (Corfu) 378
Prespes 460
Preveli, beach (Crete) 283
Preveli, monastery (Crete) 282
Preveza 380
Proastio (Peloponnese) 142
Prophitis Ilias (Santorini) 246

525

INDEX

Propylaia (Acropolis) 28
Psarades 461
Psari (Peloponnese) 96
Psarou, beach (Mykonos) 207
Psathi, beach (Ios) 197
Psili Ammos, beach (Patmos) 349
Psyrri (Athens) 34
Pyli (Kos) 321
Pylos (Peloponnese) 133
Pylos (excursion 8) **131-138**
Pyrgi (Chios) 391
Pyrgos (Santorini) 246
Pythagorio (Samos) 391

R

Reading 515
Reading Society (Corfu) 369
Religion 504
Rethymno (Crete) 278-279
Rethymno (excursion 22) **277-288**
Revelation 348
Rho (Dodecanese) 322
Rhodes (excursion 27) **320, 323-338**
Rhodes
    Ancient Ialyssos *332*
    Ancient Kameiros *331*
    Archaeological Museum *327*
    Asklepeio *330*
    Byzantine Museum *328*
    Casino *329*
    Castle Walls *327*
    Colossus of Rhodes *328*
    Epta Piges *329*
    Filerimos *331*
    Fourni *330*
    Fourni, beach *333*
    Glystra, beach *333*
    Golf *332*
    Hot Springs of Kallithea *329*
    Ladiko, beach *332*
    Lindos *329*
    Lindos, beach *333*
    Monolithos *330*
    Murat Reis Mosque *328*
    Old Town *326*
    Palace of the Grand Master *326*
    Plimmiri, beach *333*
    Prassonissi, beach *333*
    Roloi, clock *328*
    Street of the Knights *327*
    Suleimans Mosque *328*
    Tharri, monastery *330*
    Turkish Baths *328*
    Turkish Library *328*
    Valley of the butterflies *331*
Rhenia, beach (Mykonos) 207
Roman domination 17
Rooms 514
Russian church (Athens) 34

S

Safety 513
Saladi, beach (Peloponnese) 90
Salamina (Argosaronic) 166
Samos (Northeastern Aegean) 391-392
Samothraki 392
Sanctuary of Asklepios 90
Santorini (Cyclades) 194
Santorini, Thera (excursion 19) **241-252**

Sarti 486
Schinias, beach (Attica) 50
Schinoussa (Cyclades) 198
Schliemann, Heinrich 85
Schwarz 378
Select your excursion 8-9
Seralia (Sifnos) 228
Serifos (Cyclades) 196
Sfaktiria, beach (Peloponnese) 135
Shopping 507
Sidari (Corfu) 373
Sifnos (Cyclades) 194
Sifnos (excursion 17) **225-234**
Sigri (Lesvos) 392
Sikinos (Cyclades) 198
Simos, beach (Elafonissos) 172
Sinarades (Corfu) 375
Sithonia (excursion 42) **483-490**
Skala (Patmos) 348
Skala Eressou (Lesvos) 390
Skala Sykias (Halkidiki) 486
Skala Sykias, beach (Halkidiki) 487
Skamneli 447
Skandia (Kythera) 171
Skaros (Santorini) 244
Ski Resorts
    Kalavryta *106-7*
    Karpenissi *379*
    Metsovo *439*
    Parnassos *423*
    Pelion *411*
Skiathos (excursion 32) **393-402**
Skiathos town 395
Skopelos (Sporades) 389
Skorpios, islet (Lefkada) 362
Skoutari, beach (Peloponnese) 144
Skripero (Corfu) 373
Skyros (Sporades) 389-390
Sotira (Thasos) 392
Souda, beach (Crete) 284
Sougia, beach (Crete) 263
Sound and Light (Athens) 44
Sounio, cape (Attica) 48
Source of the Styx 101
Spa of Kaiafas 123
Sparagario beach (Kythera) 172
Sparta (Peloponnese) 150
Spartilas (Corfu) 372
Spathi (Kea) 196
Spetses (Argosaronic) 166, 179
Spetses (excursion 13) **177-184**
Spianada (Corfu) 367
Spili (Crete) 282
Spinalonga (Crete) 307
Sporades 389-390
Sports 513
Stavri (Peloponnese) 143
Stavros, beach (Crete) 263
Steli (Ikaria) 391
Stemnitsa (Peloponnese) 111
Stoa of Attalos (Athens) 31
Stoa of Eumenes (Acropolis) 28
Stoupa, beach (Peloponnese) 145
Street of the Knights 327
Strofylia, forest 76
Strongyli (Dodecanese) 322
Stymphalia, lake (Peloponnese) 96
Super Paradise, beach (Mykonos) 207
Sykaminia (Lesvos) 390
Sykia 486
Symi (excursion 28) **320, 339-344**
Syntagma square, Constitution square (Athens) 40
Syros (Cyclades) 195

526

INDEX

T

Taxiarchis tis Metropolis 458
Taygetos, mountain (Peloponnese) 152
Tempe 404
Temple of Apollo Epikourios, Ancient Bassae (Peloponnese) 114
Temple of Apteros Nike (Acropolis) 28
Temple of Artemis (Leros) 322
Temple of Athena Aphaia (Aigina) 166
Temple of Hephaistos (Acropolis) 31
Temple of Olympian Zeus (Athens) 31-32
Temple of Poseidon (Sounio) 48
Thasos (North-east Aegean) 392
Theologos (Thasos) 392
Theotokos (Peloponnese) 152
Thera, Santorini (Cyclades) 245
Thermaicos, gulf 474
Thermi (Lesvos) 390
Theseus 296
Thessaloniki (excursion 41) **471-482**
Thessaloniki
   Agia Sophia 475
   Agios Dimitrios 475
   Alaca Imaret 477
   Arch of Galerius 476
   Archaeological Museum 474
   Bey Hamam 476
   Byzantine Museum 475
   Casino 479
   Church of the Acheiropoietou 477
   Eptapyrgio 476
   Film Festival 477
   Folk Art and Ethnological Museum 476
   Geni Hamam 476
   Hamza Bey mosque 477
   International Fair 477
   Ladadika 475
   Modiano, market 477
   Panagia Halkeon 477
   Pasha Hamam 476
   Roman agora 476
   Thermaicos, gulf 474
   White Tower 475
   Yahudi Hamam 476
Thirassia, islet (Santorini) 246
Thission (Athens) 30-31
Tiganakia, beach (Arkii) 356
Tilos (Dodecanese) 322
Tinos (Cyclades) 195
Tiryns, ancient (Peloponnese) 84
Toronis, bay 486
Tositsa Mansion 438
Tower of the Winds (Athens) 33
Travelling 509-510
Triopetra, beach (Crete) 284
Trojan war 13
Tsangarada 410
Tsepelovo 446
Tsivlou, lake (Peloponnese) 100-101
Tsougria, islet (Skiathos) 398
Tzia, Kea (Cyclades) 196
Tzoumerka, Athamanika Mountains 379

U

University (Athens) 40
Upper Loussi (Peloponnese) 106

V

Vagia (Anafi) 197
Vai, beach (Crete) 315
Valley of the Butterflies (Paros) 219
Vamos (Crete) 271
Vamos (excursion 21) **269-276**
Vaporia (Syros) 195
Varkiza, beach (Attica) 50
Vatera (Lesvos) 390
Vathia (Peloponnese) 143
Vathy, beach (Sifnos) 230
Vathy (Kalymnos) 321
Vathy (Samos) 391-392
Vathy (Sifnos) 228
Velouchi 18
Venetians 217
Venus de Milo 465
Vergina 465
Vergina (excursion 40) **465-470**
Vido island (Corfu) 370
Vikos, gorge 448-449
Villages of Messaria (Ikaria) 391
Visa 502
Vitsa 447
Vlassi (Karditsa) 429
Vlyhada, beach (Santorini) 247
Voidokilia, beach (Peloponnese) 135
Voidomatis 449
Voila (Crete) 315
Volcano (Nissyros) 322
Voriza (Crete) 292
Votomos (Crete) 292
Voula, beach (Attica) 50
Vouliagmeni (Attica) 48
Vouliagmeni, beach (Attica) 50
Voulisma, beach (Crete) 308
Voulitsa, beach 498
Vouraikos, gorge (Peloponnese) 105
Vourgarelli 379
Vourkari (Kea) 196
Vourvourou 486,7
Vrangiana (Karditsa) 429
Vravrona (Attica) 48
Vrellis, Pavlos 445
Vromolimnos, beach (Skiathos) 397
Vytina (Peloponnese) 110-111
Vyzitsa 411

W

War Museum (Athens) 43
Western Crete (excursion 20) **255-268**
White Tower 475

X

Xerokambos, beach (Crete) 316
Xerxes bay, beach (Skiathos) 397

Z

Zaglanikianika (Kythera) 171
Zagora 410
Zagoria,Zagorohoria 446-447
Zagorohoria (excursion 38) **441-454**
Zagorohoria, Zagoria 446-447
Zakros (Crete) 315
Zakynthos (Ionian islands) 361
Zappeion (Athens) 41
Zaros, lake (Crete) 292
Zarouchla (Peloponnese) 100
Zarouchla (excursion 3) **99-101**
Zoniana (Crete) 283

your house in Mykonos!

Mykonos.
The living legend of the international jet-set, the dreamland for millions of people all over the world, the island that became the symbol of irresistible beauty, now, surrenders its glamour to you. Because, today, you have the opportunity to acquire your own land, build or let us build for you your own house or even buy one of the already existing houses with the most favorable terms and simplest procedures!

In the center of the best part of Mykonos, just a few minutes drive from the town or the airport, Agrari Village, with its wonderful pool, its two tennis courts and the spectacular view over the vast blue of the Aegean sea, is a modern housing proposition of the highest standards that combines all that seem incompatible: Night life and serenity, exceptional scenery and immediate access to the town! And even more, while you enjoy a unique summer house, you do not have to worry about its maintenance; we will take care of it for you! Today, the quest for the myth comes to an end, for it is just a matter of decision!

AXON CONSTRUCTION S.A. 52, AIGIALIAS STR., 151 25 MAROUSI, GREECE · TEL. (01) 6856 093 · FAX: (01) 6856 095 · e-mail: axon@hol.gr

ROAD EDITIONS

Discover Greece, using the best maps available

MAINLAND GREECE — 1:250 000

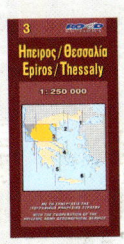

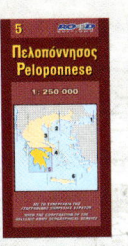

1	Θράκη / Thrace
2	Μακεδονία / Macedonia
3	Ήπειρος / Θεσσαλία / Epiros / Thessaly
4	Στερεά Ελλάδα / Central Greece
5	Πελοπόννησος / Peloponnese
6	Κρήτη / Crete

GREEK MOUNTAINS — 1:50 000

41	Πάρνηθα / Parnitha
33	Πήλιο / Pilion
43	Οίτη / Iti
52	Πάρνωνας / Parnonas
51	Ταΰγετος / Taygetos
31	Όλυμπος / Olympos
42	Παρνασσός / Parnassos
21	Άθως / Athos

Coming soon:
- Northern Pindos
- Southern Pindos

GREEK ISLANDS — 1:20 000 - 1:100 000

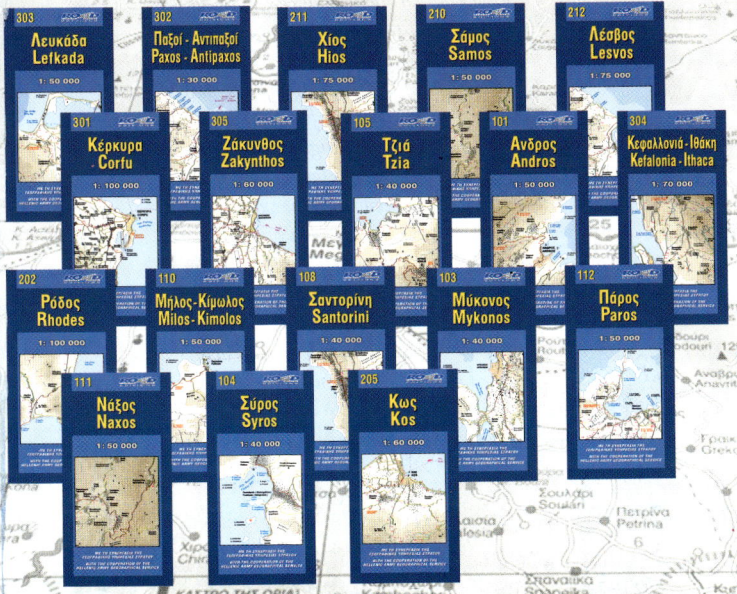

#	Title	Scale
303	Λευκάδα / Lefkada	1:50 000
302	Παξοί - Αντίπαξοι / Paxos - Antipaxos	1:30 000
211	Χίος / Hios	1:75 000
210	Σάμος / Samos	1:50 000
212	Λέσβος / Lesvos	1:75 000
301	Κέρκυρα / Corfu	1:100 000
305	Ζάκυνθος / Zakynthos	1:60 000
105	Τζιά / Tzia	1:40 000
101	Άνδρος / Andros	1:50 000
304	Κεφαλλονιά - Ιθάκη / Kefalonia - Ithaca	1:70 000
202	Ρόδος / Rhodes	1:100 000
110	Μήλος - Κίμωλος / Milos - Kimolos	1:50 000
108	Σαντορίνη / Santorini	1:40 000
103	Μύκονος / Mykonos	1:40 000
112	Πάρος / Paros	1:50 000
111	Νάξος / Naxos	1:50 000
104	Σύρος / Syros	1:40 000
205	Κως / Kos	1:60 000

Coming soon:
- Limnos
- Karpathos
- Skiathos
- Skopelos
- Alonissos
- Amorgos
- Tinos

U.K. Distributor: Portfolio tel.:20 8997 9000 fax:20 8997 9097

1230

Call your TELESTET Personal Mobile Guide and learn "how to go around Greece" from your mobile!

TELESTET has created your first **TELESTET Personal Mobile Guide**. An exclusive service to learn how to go around Greece but also to have a direct access to a group of useful information, wherever and whenever you need them, 24 hours per day.

The service is available in 4 languages: Greek, English, Italian and German. Just dial **1230** from your mobile, while the indication "GR TELESTET" is on your display. If you do not see this indication take the following steps: • Enter the menu of your terminal • Select "Manual Network Selection" • Choose "GR TELESTET".

TELESTET wishes you a pleasant stay in Greece!

TELESTET Personal Mobile Guide provides you useful information on:

- More than 40 important monuments, archeological sites and museums of Greece, such as: Acropolis, Ancient Delos, Ancient Theater of Epidavros, Ancient Thera (Santorini), Ancient Olympia, Vergina, Delfi, National Archeological Museum, Knossos, Mycenae, Sounio.
- Direct access to all Emergency Calls.
- Ships & Flying Dolphins timetable and Airplanes scheduled flights.
- Cultural Events and entertainment.
- Car Rental.
- Phone Catalogue and direct connection with the number of your choice.
- Radio Taxi Service.
- Direct connection to the TELESTET Exclusive.

(Calls to the TELESTET Personal Mobile Guide are charged at national call rate when roaming.)